The Globalization of World Politics

AN INTRODUCTION TO INTERNATIONAL RELATIONS

EDITED BY

John Baylis and **Steve Smith**

OXFORD

UNIVERSITY PRESS

OXFORD

UNIVERSITY PRESS

Great Clarendon Street, Oxford OX2 6DP

Oxford University Press is a department of the University of Oxford.
It furthers the University's objective of excellence in research, scholarship,
and education by publishing worldwide in

Oxford New York

Athens Auckland Bangkok Bogotá Buenos Aires Calcutta
Cape Town Chennai Dar es Salaam Delhi Florence Hong Kong Istanbul
Karachi Kuala Lumpur Madrid Melbourne Mexico City Mumbai
Nairobi Paris São Paulo Singapore Taipei Tokyo Toronto Warsaw

with associated companies in Berlin Ibadan

Oxford is a registered trade mark of Oxford University Press
in the UK and in certain other countries

Published in the United States
by Oxford University Press Inc., New York

Editorial arrangement © John Baylis and Steve Smith 1997
The individual chapters © the several contributors 1997

The moral rights of the author have been asserted
Database right Oxford University Press (maker)

First published 1997
Reprinted as paperback 1997, 1998 (twice), 1999

British Library Cataloguing in Publication Data
Data available

Library of Congress Cataloging in Publication Data
The globalization of world politics : an introduction to international
relations / edited by John Baylis and Steve Smith.
Includes bibliographical references
1. International relations.   I. Baylis, John.   II. Smith, Steve.   1952–
JX1395.G585   1997   32.1'01—dc21   96–24110
ISBN 0–19–878108–3
ISBN 0–19–878109–1 (pbk)

10 9 8 7 6 5

Typeset in Stone Serif
Printed in China

THE GLOBALIZ

TO PROFESSOR JACK SPENCE

for his contribution to the study of
International Politics

Editor's Preface

Considerable debate has occurred amongst scholars of international politics during the 1990s about the significance of changes which are taking place in the world. Much of this debate centres on the concept of Globalization which forms a coherent organizing theme for this exciting introductory textbook. The book brings together a wide range of experts who have differing views about globalization. For some globalization is transforming the traditional state system while for others international politics remains largely unchanged.

The purpose of this book is not to provide a single perspective but to give students a comprehensive understanding of contemporary international politics by considering different approaches to the subject, within an overall unifying theme.

Key Features of the Book

1. The book is divided into four main sections which deal with the Historical Context, different Theoretical Approaches to the subject, Structure and Process in International Politics, and important Contemporary Issues.

2. Each of the chapters is designed to be accessible and easy to read with a number of novel learning aids including:

Reader's Guide. A brief summary of the main points is provided at the beginning of each chapter.

Boxed Sections. Key concepts, important quotations, case studies, and historical chronologies are contained in boxes.

Bullet Points. Key sections of each chapter end with a series of bullet points to highlight the most important points of the section.

Diagrams and Maps. These provide useful information to supplement the text.

End of Chapter Questions. Each chapter ends with a series of questions which can be used for discussion or essay-writing purposes.

Further Reading. Each chapter also provides a brief guide to further reading on the subject covered.

Consolidated Bibliography. At the end of the book a detailed list of sources is provided.

Acknowledgements

The editors would like to thank Tim Barton of Oxford University Press for his enthusiasm, advice and continuous support during the writing and production of the book. Thanks are also due to Elaine Lowe for helping to produce the final manuscript of the book. The book is dedicated to Professor Jack Spence, who has provided enormous support to both editors over the past twenty-five years.

Contents

Contents

x

Contents

Missing

6. International history since 1989

9. Contemporary mainstream approaches: neo-realism + neo-liberalism

10. Marxist theories of IR

11. Reflectivist + constructivist approaches to international theory.

21. Culture in world affairs

23. European + regional integration

25. The communications + internet revolution

29. Globalization + the transformation of political community

30. Globalization and the post-cold war order.

Detailed Contents

List of Figures

List of Boxes

List of Tables

About the Contributors

John Baylis is a Professor in the Department of International Politics, University of Wales, Aberystwyth. His latest publications include: *Dilemmas of World Politics*, ed. with N. J. Rengger (Oxford University Press, 1992), *The Diplomacy of Pragmatism: Britain and the Formation of NATO* (Macmillan, 1993), and *Ambiguity and Deterrence: British Nuclear Strategy 1945–1964* (Oxford University Press, 1995).

Chris Brown is Professor of Politics at the University of Southampton. He is author of *International Relations Theory: New Normative Approaches* (Harvester Wheatsheaf, 1992), editor of *Political Restructuring in Europe* (Routledge, 1994), and has written numerous articles on international political theory. His next book *Understanding International Relations* is to be published by Macmillan in 1997.

Fiona Butler is Jean Monnet Lecturer in European Integration in the Department of International Politics, University of Wales, Aberystwyth. Her latest publications include: with Clive Archer *The European Union: Structure and Process* (Pinter, 2nd edn., 1996), 'Political Community in Integration Theories: A Blind Alley?' in *Politics* 16(1) 1996, and 'The EC's Common Agricultural Policy', in Juliet Lodge (ed.), *The EC and the Challenge of the Future* (Pinter, 2nd edn., 1993).

Susan L. Carruthers is a Lecturer in the Department of International Politics, University of Wales, Aberystwyth. She is an international historian who specializes in the media, and who is the author of *Winning Hearts and Minds: British Governments and Colonial Counterinsurgency, 1944–60* (Leicester University Press, 1995), and co-editor of *War, Culture and the Media* (Flick Books, 1996). She is currently writing a volume entitled *The Media at War*.

Richard Crockatt is Senior Lecturer in American History at the University of East Anglia where he also teaches international relations. He is author of *The Fifty Years War: The United States and the Soviet Union in World Politics, 1941–1991* (Routledge, 1995), and editor of *British Documents on Foreign Affairs, 1940–1945* (University Publications of America, forthcoming).

Timothy Dunne is a Lecturer in International Politics at the University of Wales, Aberystwyth. He has published a number of articles on international society, including 'The Social Construction of International Society', *The European Journal of International Relations* 1(3) 1995: 367–89. His forthcoming book, to be published by Macmillan, is *Inventing International Society: A History of the English School* (London: St Antony's/Macmillan, forthcoming 1998).

Owen Greene is Senior Lecturer in International Relations and Security Studies at the Department of Peace Studies, Bradford University. He trained in mathematics and physics, and researched in theoretical physics for several years before turning to international relations. He is author or co-author of nine books and over 100 other research works on international environmental issues and international security problems. His recent work has focused on the development, implementation, and effectiveness of international regimes, particularly in the areas of climate change, ozone depletion, regional sea pollution, and the significance of monitoring, transparency, and review processes.

Fred Halliday is Professor of International Relations at the London School of Economics. His books include *Rethinking International Relations* (Macmillan, 1994) and *Islam and the Myth of Confrontation* (I. B. Tauris, 1996).

Steve Hobden is a Lecturer in the Department of International Politics, University of Wales, Aberystwyth. He has just completed a research project looking at the relationships between historical sociology and international relations. He teaches in the areas of international political theory, the United Nations, and Latin America.

Darryl Howlett is a Lecturer in International Relations in the Department of Politics at the University of Southampton. His most recent works include: 'The 1995 NPT Review and Extension conference: Assessment and Implications', in Vicente Garrido, Antonio Marquina, and Harald Muller (eds.), *The Implication of 1995 NPT Review and Extension conference: A Spanish point of view* (Complutense University, 1996), and CD-ROM 'The Cold War Years: 1945–1996' (forthcoming).

Robert H. Jackson is a Professor at the University of British Columbia. He studies normative issues in world politics. His publications include *Quasi-States* (Cambridge University Press, 1990) and *States in a Changing World*, ed. with A. James (Clarendon Press, 1993). He is completing a book entitled *The Global Covenant: Power and Responsibility in World Politics*.

Richard Wyn Jones is a Lecturer in International Politics at the University of Wales, Aberystwyth where he has special responsibility for teaching through the medium of the Welsh language. He has published a number of articles on Critical Security Studies and on various aspects of radical political thought.

Richard Little is Professor in the Department of International Politics, at the University of Bristol. He is currently working with Barry Buzan on a book which will establish a framework for examining historical transformations in the international systems. His most recent book, jointly authored, is *The Logic of Anarchy: Neorealism to Structural Realism* (Columbia University Press, 1993).

Simon Murden is a Lecturer in the Department of International Politics, University of Wales, Aberystwyth. He specializes in the Middle East, with particular regard to issues of political economy and of strategy. He is the author of *Emergent Regional Powers and International Relations in the Gulf, 1988–1991* (Ithaca Press, 1995) and is currently doing research on Iraq since the Gulf War, and the cultural impact of market economics in the Middle East.

Jan Jindy Pettman is Reader, and Director of the Centre for Women's Studies at the Australian National University. She writes especially on gender issues, globalization and the politics of identity. Her most recent book is *Worlding Women: A Feminist International Politics* (Routledge,1996).

Jan Aart Scholte is a Senior Lecturer in International Relations at the University of Sussex. His chief publications include *International Relations of Social Change* (Open University Press, 1993) and *Globalisation: A Critical Introduction* (Macmillan, forthcoming). His current research explores the role of transborder social movements in global economic governance.

Len Scott is a Lecturer in the Department of International Politics, University of Wales, Aberystwyth. He works in the fields of international history and security studies, and is author of *Conscription and the Attlee Governments: The Politics and Policy of National Service 1945–51* (Oxford University Press, 1993). He is currently completing two books, on *Britain and the Cuban Missile Crisis 1962* and (with Stephen Twigge) *The Command and Control of British Nuclear Weapons 1945–1964*.

Steve Smith is Professor in the Department of International Politics, University of Wales, Aberystwyth. He specializes in international political theory. His latest publications include *International Relations Theory Today*, edited with Ken Booth (Polity Press, 1995) and *International Theory: Positivism and Beyond*, ed. with Ken Booth and Marysia Zalewski (Cambridge University Press, 1996).

Paul Taylor is Professor of International Relations at the London School of Economics, where he specializes in international organization, particularly the economic and social arrangements of the United Nations and the politics of the institutions of the European Union. Most recently he has published *International Organization in the Modern World* (Pinter, 1993) and *The European Union in the 1990s* (Oxford University Press, 1996). He has edited and contributed to a number of books on international organization with A. J. R. Groom, and since June 1994 has been editor of *the Review of International Studies*.

Caroline Thomas is a Reader in Politics at the University of Southampton. She has a special interest in the South in International Relations. Her latest publications include (with P. Wilkin) *Globalisation and the South* (Macmillan, 1997), and (ed.) *Rio: Unravelling the Consequences* (Frank Cass, 1994).

Roger Tooze is a Reader in the Department of International Politics, University of Wales, Aberystwyth. His latest publications include *Technology, Culture and Competitiveness* (Routledge, 1997) and he is currently working on a book exploring the theorization of international political economy.

Nicholas J. Wheeler is a Lecturer in the Department of International Politics at the University of Wales, Aberystwyth. He is the author of 'Guardian Angel or Global Gangster: a Review of the Ethical Claims of International Society', *Political Studies*, 44 (1) (March 1996) and 'Agency, Humanitarianism and Intervention', in B. Parekh (ed.), *Humanitarian Intervention* (special issue of the *International Political Science Review,* January 1997).

Brian White is Professor of International Relations and Head of the Department of International Relations and Politics at Staffordshire University. He is the author of *Britain, Detente and Changing East-West Relations* (Routledge, 1992). He also co-edited and contributed to *British Foreign Policy: Tradition, Change and Transformation* (Unwin Hyman, 1988), *Understanding Foreign Policy: The Foreign Policy Systems Approach* (Elgar, 1989), and *Issues in World Politics* (Macmillan, 1997).

Peter Willetts is Reader in International Relations at City University. He has written extensively on international organizations, including editing two books on NGOs, *Pressure Groups in the Global System* (Pinter, 1982) and *'The Conscience of the World': The Influence of Non-Governmental Organizations in the UN System* (Hurst, 1996).

Introduction

Steve Smith and John Baylis

The aim of this book is to provide the reader with an overview of contemporary world politics. The title of the book is not accidental; first, we want to introduce you to world politics, as distinct from international politics or international relations; second, many think that the contemporary, post-cold war world is distinctly different from previous periods because of globalization. We think that it is especially difficult to explain world politics in such an era because globalization is a particularly controversial term. It is controversial because there is considerable dispute over just what it means to talk of this being an era of globalization, and whether that means that the main features of world politics are any different to those of previous eras. In this Introduction we want to explain how we propose to deal with the concept of globalization and offer you some arguments in favour of seeing it as an important new development in world politics and also some arguments against such a view.

Before turning to look at globalization in order to set the scene for the chapters that follow, we want to do two things. We will first say something about the various terms used to describe global politics, and then we will spend some time looking at the main ways in which global politics has been explained up to the late 1990s. We need to do both of these things because our aim in this Introduction is not to put forward one view of how to think about globalization, agreed by all the contributors to this volume; rather we want to give the reader a context within which to read the chapters that follow and that means giving a variety of views on globalization and how to think about it. Our central concern is to point out that the main theoretical accounts of world politics all see globalization differently; some treat it as nothing more than a temporary phase in human history, and one which does not mean that we need to rethink how we understand world politics; others see it as but the latest manifestation of the growth of Western capitalism and modernization; and others see it as representing a fundamental transformation of world politics, one that requires new ways of understanding. The contributors to this book hold no one agreed view, and in fact there are representatives of all the responses just mentioned. From what we have said so far you should note that there are three main aims of this book:

- To offer an overview of world politics in an era of globalization.
- To summarize the main theoretical approaches available to explain contemporary world politics.
- To provide the material necessary to answer the question of whether globalization marks a fundamental transformation in world politics.

From International Politics to World Politics

Why does the main title of this book refer to world politics rather than international politics or international relations? These are the traditional names used to describe the kinds of interactions and processes that are the concern of this book. Indeed, you could look at the table of contents of many other introductory books and find a similar listing of main topics dealt with, yet often these books would have either international relations or international politics as their main title. Furthermore, the discipline that studies these issues is nearly always called International Politics or International Relations. Our reason for choosing the phrase 'world politics' is that we think it is more inclusive than either of the alternative terms. It is meant to denote the fact that our interest is in the **politics** and **political patterns** in the world, and not only those between nation-states (as the term international politics implies). Thus, we are interested in relations between organizations that may or may not be states (such as, for example, multi-national companies or terrorist groups; these are known as non-governmental organizations (NGOs)). Similarly, the term 'international relations' seems too exclusive; of course, it does represent a widening of our concern from simply the political relations between nation-states, but it still restricts our focus to *inter-national* relations, whereas we think that relations between, say, cities and other governments or international organizations can be equally important to what states do. So we prefer to characterize the relations we are interested in as those of world politics, with the important proviso that we do not want the reader to define politics too narrowly. You will see this issue arising time and time again in the chapters that follow, since many contributors want to define politics very widely. One obvious example concerns the relationship between politics and economics; there is clearly an overlap, and a lot of bargaining power goes to him or her that can persuade others that the existing distribution of resources is 'simply' economic rather than a political issue. So, we want you to think about politics very loosely for the time being, and several of the chapters will describe as political, features of the contemporary world that you may not have previously thought of as such. Our focus, then, is with the patterns of political relations, defined broadly, that characterize the contemporary world. Many will be between states, but many, perhaps most, will not.

Theories of World Politics

The basic problem facing anyone trying to understand contemporary world politics is that there is so much material to look at that it is difficult to know which things matter and which do not. Where on earth would you start if you wanted to explain the most important political processes? Whenever individuals are faced with such a problem they have to resort to **theories**, whether they are aware of them or not. A theory is not simply some grand formal model with hypotheses and assumptions; rather **a theory is some kind of simplifying device that allows you to decide which facts matter and which do not**. A good analogy is with sunglasses with different coloured lenses; put on the red pair and the world looks red, put on the yellow pair and it looks yellow. The world is not any different, it just looks different. Well, so it is with theories. Shortly we are going to summarize the three main theoretical views that have dominated the study of world politics, so you will get an idea of which 'colours' they paint world politics. But before we do so, please note that we do not think that theory is an option. It is not as if you can say that you do not want to bother with a theory, all you want to do is to look at the 'facts'. We believe that this is simply impossible, since the only way in which you can decide which of the millions of possible facts to look at is by adhering to some simplifying device which tells you which ones matter the most. We think of theory as such a simplifying device. Note also that you may well not be aware of your theory, it may just be the view of the world that you have inherited from family, peer group, or the media. It may just seem common sense to you and not at all anything complicated like a theory. But we fervently believe that all that is happening in such a case is that your theoretical assumptions are implicit rather than explicit, and we prefer to try and be as explicit as possible when it comes to thinking about world politics; otherwise we may be looking at the world through the equivalent of red sunglasses without even being aware that we are wearing them.

People have tried to make sense of world politics for centuries, and especially so since the separate academic discipline of International Politics was formed in 1919 when the Department of International Politics was set up at Aberystwyth. Interestingly, the man who set up that Department, a Welsh industrialist called David Davies, saw its purpose as being to help prevent war. By studying international politics scientifically, academics could find the causes of the world's main political problems and put forward solutions to help politicians solve them. For the next twenty years, the discipline was marked by such a commitment to change the world. This is known as a **normative** position, with the task of academic study being one of making the world a better place. Its opponents characterized it as **Idealism**, in that it had a view of how the world *ought to be* and tried to assist events to turn out that way. In its place its opponents preferred an approach they called **Realism**, which, rather unsurprisingly stressed seeing the world *as it really is* rather than how we would like it to be. And, the world as it really is is not seen by Realists as a very pleasant place; human beings are at best selfish and probably much worse. Notions such as the perfectibility of human beings and the possibility of an improvement of world politics seem far-fetched. This debate between Idealism and Realism has continued to the present day, but it is fair to say that Realism has tended to have the upper hand. This is mainly because it appears to accord more with common sense than does Idealism, especially when the daily media bombards us with images of how awful humans can be to one another. Having said which we would like you to think about whether such a Realist view is as neutral as it is common-sensical? After all, if we teach world politics to generations of students and tell them that people are selfish, then doesn't that become common-sense and don't they, when they go off into the media or to work for government departments or the military or even when they talk to their kids over the dinner table, simply repeat what they have been taught and, if in positions of power, act accordingly? We will leave you to think about this as you read the rest of this book; for now we would like to keep the issue open and simply point out that we are not convinced that Realism is as objective or non-normative as it is portrayed as being.

What is certainly true is that Realism has been the dominant way of explaining world politics in the last one hundred years. What we are now going to do is to summarize the main assumptions underlying Realism and then do the same for its two main rivals as theories of world politics, **Liberalism** and **World-System Theory**. These three theories will be discussed in much more detail in Part Two of this book, along with a chapter dealing with the most recent approaches that seek to explain contemporary world politics. They will also be reflected in the other three parts that comprise the book. In Part One we look at the **historical** background to the contemporary world. In Part Three we will look at the main **structures and processes** of contemporary world politics. In Part Four we will deal with some of the main **issues** in the globalized world. So although we will not go into much depth now about these theories, we do need to give you a flavour of their main themes since we want, after summarizing them, to say something about how each might think about globalization.

Realism and World Politics

For Realists the main actors on the world stage are **states**, which are legally sovereign actors. **Sovereignty** means that there is no actor above the state that can compel it to act in specific ways. Other actors such as multinational corporations or international organizations all have to work within the framework of inter-state relations. As for what pro-

pels states to act as they do, Realists see human nature as centrally important. For Realists, human nature is fixed and crucially it is selfish. To think otherwise is to make a mistake, and it was such a mistake that the Realists accused the Idealists of making. As a result, world politics (or more accurately for Realists international politics) represents a struggle for **power** between states each trying to maximize their national interests. Such order as exists in world politics is the result of the workings of a mechanism known as the **balance of power**, whereby states act so as to prevent any one state dominating. Thus world politics is all about bargaining and alliances, with diplomacy a key mechanism for balancing various national interests, but finally the most important tool available for implementing states' foreign policies is military force. Ultimately, since there is no sovereign body above the states that make up the international political system, world politics is a **self-help system** in which states must rely on their own military resources to achieve their ends. Often these ends can be achieved through co-operation, but the potential for conflict is ever-present. In recent years, an important variant of Realism, known as Neo-Realism, has developed. This view stresses the importance of the **structure** of the international political system in affecting the behaviour of all states; thus during the cold war there were two main powers dominating the international system and this led to certain rules of behaviour; now that the cold war has ended the structure of world politics is said to be moving towards multipolarity, which for Neo-Realists will involve very different rules of the game.

Liberalism and World Politics

Liberals have a different view of world politics, and like Realists, have a long tradition. Earlier we mentioned Idealism, and this was really one rather extreme version of Liberalism. There are many variants of Liberalism (or, as it is often known, **Pluralism**) as you will see when you read the chapter on it in Part Two, but the main themes that run through Liberal thought are that human beings are perfectible, that democracy is necessary for that perfectibility to develop, and that ideas matter. Behind all this lies a belief in **progress**. Accordingly, Liberals reject the Realist notion that war is the natural condition of world politics. They also question the idea that the state is the main actor on the world political stage, although they do not deny that it is important. But they do see multinational corporations, transnational actors such as terrorist groups, and international organizations as central actors in some issue-areas of world politics. In those issue-areas in which the state acts, they tend to think of the state not as a unitary or united actor but as a set of bureaucracies each with its own interests. Therefore there can be no such thing as a **national** interest, since it merely represents the result of whatever bureaucratic organizations dominate the domestic decision-making process. In relations between states, Liberals stress the possibilities for **co-operation**, and the key issue becomes devising international settings in which co-operation can be best achieved. The picture of world politics that results from the Liberal view is of a complex system of bargaining between many different types of actors. Military force is still important but the Liberal agenda is not as restricted as is the Realist one. Liberals see national interests in much more than military terms, and stress the importance of economic, environmental, and technological issues. Order in world politics emerges not from a balance of power but from the interactions between many layers of governing arrangements, comprising laws, agreed norms, international **regimes** and institutional rules. Fundamentally, Liberals do not think that sovereignty is as important in practice as Realists think it is in theory. States may be legally sovereign, but in practice they have to negotiate with all sorts of other actors, with the result that their freedom to act as they might wish is seriously curtailed. **Interdependence** between states is a critically important feature of world politics.

World-System Theory and World Politics

The third main theoretical position we want to mention, **World-System Theory** is also known as **Structuralism** or **Neo-Marxism**, which immediately gives you clues as to its main assumptions. We want to point out that World-System Theory has been historically the least influential of the three theories we are discussing, and it has less in common with either Realism or Liberalism than they do with each other. For World-System Theory, the most important feature of world politics is that they take place within a world capitalist economy. In this world economy the most important actors are not states but **classes**, and the behaviour of all other actors is ultimately explicable by class forces. Thus states, multinational corporations, and even international organizations represent the dominant class interest in the world economic system. World-System Theorists differ over how much leeway actors such as states have, but all agree that the world economy severely constrains the freedom of manœuvre of states. Rather than world politics being an arena of conflict between national interests or an arena with many different issue-areas, World-System Theorists conceive of world politics as the setting in which **class conflicts** are played out. As for order in world politics, World-System Theorists think of it primarily in economic rather than in military terms. The key feature of the international economy is the division of the world into core, semi-periphery, and periphery areas. Within the semi-periphery and the periphery there exist cores which are tied into the capitalist world economy, whilst within even the core area there are peripheral economic areas. In all of this what matters is the dominance of the power not of states but of **international capitalism**, and it is these forces that ultimately determine the main political patterns in world politics. Sovereignty is not anything like as important for World-System Theorists as it is for Realists since it refers to political and legal matters, whereas the most important feature of world politics is the degree of economic autonomy, and here World-System Theorists see all states as having to play by the rules of the international capitalist economy.

The Three Theories and Globalization

These three theoretical perspectives together have tended to be the main theories that have been used to understand world politics. In the 1980s it became common to talk of there being an **inter-paradigm** debate; that is to say that the three theories (known as paradigms after the influential philosopher of natural science, Thomas Kuhn) were in competition, and that the 'truth' about world politics lay in the debate between them. At first sight each seems to be particularly good at explaining some aspects of world politics better than the others, and an obvious temptation would be to try and combine them into some overall account. But we need to warn you that this is not the easy option it may seem. This is because the three theories are not so much different views of the same world, but are instead **three views of different worlds**. Let us explain this briefly: whilst it is clear that each of the three focuses on different aspects of world politics (Realism on the power relations between states, Liberalism on a much wider set of interactions between states and non-state actors, and World-System Theory on the patterns of the world economy) each is saying more than this. Each view is claiming that it is picking out **the most important features** of world politics and that it offers a **better account** than do the rival theories. Thus, the three approaches are really in competition with one another; and, whilst you can certainly choose between them it is not so easy to add bits from one to the others. For example, if you are a World-System Theorist, you think that state behaviour is ultimately determined by class forces; forces that the Realist does not think affect state behaviour. In other words these three theories are really versions of what world politics is like rather than partial pictures of it. They do not agree on what the 'it' is!

We now need to be clear that we do not think that any one of these theories has all the answers when it comes to explaining world politics in an era of globalization. In fact each sees globalization differently. We do not want to tell you which theory seems best, since the purpose of this book is to give you a variety of conceptual lenses through which you might want to look at globalization. All we will do is to say a few words about how each theory might respond to globalization. We will then go on to say something about the rise of globalization and offer some ideas on its strengths and weaknesses as a description of contemporary world politics.

1. For Realists, globalization does not alter the most significant feature of world politics, namely the territorial division of the world into nation-states. Whilst the increased interconnectedness between economies and societies might make them more dependent on one another, the same cannot be said about the states-system. Here, states retain sovereignty, and globalization does not render obsolete the struggle for political power between states. Nor does it undermine the importance of the threat of the use of force, or the importance of the balance of power. Globalization, then, may affect our social, economic and cultural lives, but it does not transcend the international political system of states.

2. For Liberals, the picture looks very different. They tend to see globalization as the end product of a long-running transformation of world politics. For them, globalization fundamentally undermines Realist accounts of world politics since it shows that states are no longer as central actors as they once were. In their place are a myriad of actors, of differing importance according to the issue-area concerned. Liberals are particularly interested in the revolution in technology and communications represented by globalization. This economically and technologically led increased interconnectedness between societies results in a very different pattern of world political relations from that which has gone before. States are no longer sealed units, if ever they were, and as a result the world looks more like a **cobweb** of relations than like the state model of Realism or the class model of World-System Theory.

3. For World-System Theorists, globalization is a bit of a sham. It is nothing particularly new, and is really only the latest stage in the development of international capitalism. It does not mark a qualitative shift in world politics, and nor does it render all our existing theories and concepts redundant. Above all it is a Western-led phenomenon which basically simply furthers the

development of international capitalism. Rather than make the world more alike, it further deepens the existing divide between the core, semi-periphery and the periphery.

By the end of the book we hope you will work out which of these theories (if any) best explains globalization. We spend a lot of time in Part Two outlining these theories in more detail so as to give you much more of an idea of the main ideas involved.

But the central point we want to make here is to reinforce our comment earlier that theories do not portray 'the' truth. In other words, the theories we have mentioned will see globalization differently because they have a **prior** view of what is most important in world politics. Therefore the option is not available of simply answering the tempting question of which theory has the 'truest' or 'correct' view of globalization.

Globalization and its Precursors

The focus of this book is globalization, and as we have already said our concern is with offering you an overview of world politics in a globalized era. **By globalization we simply mean the process of increasing interconnectedness between societies such that events in one part of the world more and more have effects on peoples and societies far away.** A globalized world is one in which political, economic, cultural, and social events become more and more interconnected, and also one in which they have more impact. In other words, societies are affected more and more extensively and more and more deeply by events of other societies. These events can conveniently be divided into three types, **social**, **economic**, and **political**. In each case, the world seems to be 'shrinking', and people are increasingly aware of this. The World Wide Web is but the most graphic example of this, since it allows you to sit at home and have instant communication with web sites around the world. Electronic mail has also transformed communications in a way that the two editors of this book would not have envisaged even five years ago. But these are only the most obvious examples. Others would include: worldwide television communications, global newspapers, international social movements such as Amnesty or Greenpeace, global franchises such as McDonalds, Coca Cola, and Pizza Hut, the global economy (go and look in your nearest supermarket and work out the number of countries' products represented there), and global risks such as pollution, AIDS, etc. There are, of course, many other examples, but we are sure that you get the picture. It is this pattern of events that seems to have changed the nature of world politics from what it was just a few years ago. The important point to stress is that it is not just that the world has changed but that the changes are qual-

itative and not merely quantitative; a strong case can be made that a 'new' world political system has emerged as a result of globalization.

Having said which, we want to point out that globalization is not some entirely new phenomenon in world history; indeed, as we will note later on, many argue that it is merely a new name for a long-term feature. Whilst we want to leave it to you to judge whether in its current manifestation it represents a new phase in world history or merely a continuation of processes that have been around for a long time, we do want to note that there have been several precursors to globalization. In other words, globalization bears a marked similarity to at least nine features of world politics discussed by writers before the contemporary period. We will now note these briefly.

First, globalization has many features in common with the **theory of modernization** (see Modelski 1972 and Morse 1976). According to these writers, industrialization brings into existence a whole new set of contacts between societies, and changes the political, economic, and social processes that characterized the pre-modernized world. Crucially, industrialization alters the nature of the state, both widening its responsibilities and weakening its control over outcomes. The result is that the old power-politics model of international relations becomes outmoded. Force becomes less usable, states have to negotiate with other actors to achieve their goals, and the very identity of the state as an actor is called into question. In many respects it seems that modernization is part of the globalization process, differing only in that it applied more to the developed world and involved nothing like as extensive a set of transactions.

Second, there are clear similarities with the arguments of influential writers such as Walt Rostow (1960) who argued that **economic growth** followed a pattern in all economies as they went through industrialization. Their economies developed in the shadow of more 'developed' economies until they reached the stage where they were capable of self-sustained economic growth. What this has in common with globalization is that Rostow saw a clear pattern to economic development, one marked by stages which all economies would follow as they adopted capitalist policies. There was an automaticity to history that globalization theory tends also to rely on.

Third, there was the important literature emerging out of the Liberal paradigm discussed above. Specifically there were very influential works on the nature of **economic interdependence** (Cooper 1968), the role of transnational actors (Keohane and Nye 1971) and the resulting cobweb model of world politics (Mansbach, Ferguson, and Lampert 1976). Much of this literature anticipates the main theoretical themes of globalization, although again it tends to be applied much more to the developed world than is the case with globalization.

Fourth, there are notable similarities between the picture of the world painted by globalization and that portrayed in Marshall McLuhan's influential work on the **'global village'** (1964). According to McLuhan, advances in electronic communications resulted in a world where we could see in real time events that were occurring in distant parts of the world. For McLuhan, the main effects of this development were that time and space become compressed to such an extent that everything loses its traditional identity. As a result, the old groupings of political, economic, and social organization simply do not work any more. Without doubt, McLuhan's work significantly anticipates some of the main themes of globalization, although it should be noted that he was talking primarily about the communications revolution, whereas the globalization literature tends to be much more extensive.

Fifth, there are significant overlaps between some of the main themes of globalization and the work of writers such as John Burton (1972), who spoke of the emergence of a **'world society'**. According to Burton, the old states-system was becoming outmoded, as increasingly significant interactions took place between non-state actors. It was Burton who coined the phrase of the 'cobweb'

model of world politics. The central message here was that the most important patterns in world politics were those created by trade, communications, language, ideology, etc., along with the more traditional focus on the political relations between states.

Sixth, in the 1960s, 1970s, and 1980s, there was the visionary work of those associated with the **World Order Models Project** (WOMP), which was an organization set up in 1968 to promote the development of alternatives to the inter-state system which would result in the elimination of war. What is most interesting about their many studies (see, for example, Mendlovitz (1975), and Falk (1975; 1995b)), is that they focused on the questions of global government that today are central to much work going on under the name of globalization. For WOMPers (as they were known), the unit of analysis is the individual, and the level of analysis is the global. Interestingly by the mid-1990s WOMP had become much wider in its focus, concentrating on the world's most vulnerable people and the environment.

Seventh, there are important parallels between some of the ideas of globalization and the thoughts of those who argued for the existence of an **international society**. Prominent amongst these was Hedley Bull (1977), who pointed to the development over the centuries of a set of agreed norms and common understandings between state leaders, such that they effectively formed a society rather than merely an international system. However, although Bull was perturbed by the emergence of what he called the 'new medievalism', in which a series of sub-national and inter-national organizations vied with the state for authority, he did not feel that the nation state was about to be replaced by the development of a world society.

Eighth, globalization theory has several points in common with the infamous argument of Francis Fukuyama (1992) about the **'end of history'**. Fukuyama's main claim is that the power of the economic market is resulting in liberal democracy replacing all other types of government. Though he recognizes that there are other types of political regimes to challenge liberal democracy, he does not think that any of the alternatives such as communism, fascism, or Islam will be able to deliver the economic goods in the way that liberal democracy can. In this sense there is a direction to history and that direction is towards the expansion of the economic market throughout the world.

Finally, there are very marked similarities between some of the political aspects of globalization and long-standing ideas of liberal progress. These have most recently been expressed in the **'liberal peace' theory** of writers such as Bruce Russett (1993) and Michael Doyle (1983*a* and 1983*b*), although they go back centuries to writers such as Immanuel Kant. The main idea is that liberal democracies do not fight one another, and although of course there can be dispute as to what is a liberal democracy, adherents to this view claim quite plausibly that there is no case where two democracies have ever gone to war. The reason they claim this is that public accountability is so central in democratic systems that publics will not allow leaders easily to engage in wars with other democratic nations. Again the main link with globalization is the assumption that there is progress to history, and that this is making it far more difficult to start wars.

Globalization: Myth or Reality?

Our final task in this Introduction is to offer you a summary of the main arguments **for** and **against** globalization. We do not expect you to decide where you stand on the issue at this stage, but we think that we have to give you some of the main arguments so that you can keep them in mind as you read the rest of this book. Because the arguments for globalization being an important new phase of world politics have been rehearsed above, and also because they are most effectively summarized in the chapter that follows, we will spend a little more time on the criticisms. The main arguments in favour of globalization comprising a new era of world politics are:

1. The pace of **economic transformation** is so great that it has created a new world politics. States are no longer closed units and they cannot control their economies. The world economy is more interdependent than ever, with trade and finances ever expanding.

2. **Communications** have fundamentally revolutionized the way we deal with the rest of the world. We now live in a world where events in one location can be immediately observed on the other side of the world. Electronic communications alter our notions of the social groups we work and live in.

3. There is now, more than ever before, a **global culture**, so that most urban areas resemble one another. The world shares a common culture, much of it emanating from Hollywood.

4. The world is becoming more **homogeneous**. Differences between peoples are diminishing.

5. **Time and space seem to be collapsing**. Our old ideas of geographical space and of chronological time are undermined by the speed of modern communications and media.

6. There is emerging a **global polity**, with transnational social and political movements and the beginnings of a transfer of allegiance from the state to sub-state, transnational, and international bodies.

7. A **cosmopolitan culture** is developing. People are beginning to 'think globally and act locally'.

8. A **risk culture** is emerging with people realizing both that the main risks that face them are global (pollution and AIDS) and that states are unable to deal with the problems.

However, just as there are powerful reasons for seeing globalization as a new stage in world politics, often allied to the view that globalization is progressive, that is to say that it improves the lives of people, there are also arguments that suggest the opposite. Some of the main ones are given below.

1. One obvious objection to the globalization thesis is that it is merely a buzz-word to denote the latest phase of capitalism. In a very powerful critique of the globalization theory, Hirst and Thompson (1996) argue that one effect of the globalization thesis is that it makes it appear as if national governments are powerless in the face of global trends. This ends up paralysing governmental attempts to subject global economic forces to control and regulation. Believing that most globalization theory lacks historical depth they point out that it paints the current situation as **more unique than it is** and also as more firmly entrenched than it might in fact be.

Current trends may well be reversible. They conclude that the more extreme versions of globalization are 'a myth', and they support this claim with five main conclusions from their study of the contemporary world economy (2–3): **First**, the present internationalized economy is not unique in history. In some respects they say it is less open than the international economy was between 1870 and 1914. **Second**, they find that 'genuinely' transnational companies are relatively rare, most are national companies trading internationally. There is no trend towards the development of international companies. **Third**, there is no shift of finance and capital from the developed to the underdeveloped worlds. Direct investment is highly concentrated amongst the countries of the developed world. **Fourth**, the world economy is not global, rather trade, investment, and financial flows are concentrated in and between three blocks—Europe, North America, and Japan. **Finally**, they argue that this group of three blocks could, if they co-ordinated policies, regulate global economic markets and forces. Note that Hirst and Thompson are only looking at *economic* theories of globalization, and many of the main accounts deal with factors such as communications and culture more than economics; nonetheless, theirs is a very powerful critique of one of the main planks of the more extreme globalization thesis, with their central criticism being that seeing the global economy as something beyond our control both misleads us and prevents us from developing policies to control the national economy. All too often we are told that our economy must obey 'the global market', but Hirst and Thompson believe that this is a myth.

2. Another obvious objection is that globalization is very **uneven in its effects**. At times it sounds very much like a Western theory applicable only to a small part of humankind. To pretend that even a small minority of the world's population can connect to the World Wide Web is clearly an exaggeration when in reality most people on the planet have probably never made a telephone call in their lives. In other words, globalization only applies to the developed world. In the rest of the world, there is nothing like the degree of globalization. We are in danger of overestimating the extent and the depth of globalization.

3. A related objection is that globalization may well be simply **the latest stage of Western imperialism**. It is the old modernization theory discussed above in new guise. The forces that are being globalized are conveniently those found in the Western world. What about non-Western values? Where do they fit into this emerging global world? The worry is that they do not fit in at all, and what is being celebrated in globalization is the triumph of a Western world view, at the expense of the world views of other cultures.

4. Critics have also noted that there are very considerable **losers** as the world becomes more globalized. This is because it represents the success of liberal capitalism in an economically divided world. Perhaps one outcome is that globalization allows the more efficient exploitation of less well-off nations, and all in the name of openness. The technologies accompanying globalization are technologies that automatically benefit the richest economies in the world, and allow their interests to override local ones. So, not only is globalization imperialist it is also exploitative.

5. We also need to make the straightforward point that not all globalized forces are necessarily **'good' ones**. Globalization makes it easier for drug cartels and terrorists to operate, and the World Wide Web's anarchy raises crucial questions of censorship and preventing access to certain kinds of material.

6. Turning to the so-called **global governance** aspects of globalization, the main worry here is who are the transnational social movements responsible and democratically accountable to? If IBM or Shell becomes more and more powerful in the world, does this not raise the issue of how accountable are they to democratic control? David Held has made a strong case for the development of what he calls 'cosmopolitan democracy' (1995), but this has clearly defined legal and democratic features. The worry is that most of the emerging powerful actors in a globalized world precisely are NOT accountable. This argument also applies to seemingly 'good' global actors such as Amnesty International and Greenpeace.

7. Finally, there seems to us to be **a paradox** at the heart of the globalization thesis. On the one hand it is usually portrayed as the triumph of Western, market-led values, but how do we then explain the tremendous economic success that some national economies have had in the glob-

alized world? We are thinking here in the main of the so-called 'Tigers' of Asia, countries such as Singapore, Taiwan, Malaysia, and Korea, which have enjoyed some of the highest growth rates in the international economy, but subscribe to very different 'Asian' values. These nations emphatically reject Western values, and yet they have had enormous economic success. The paradox then is whether these countries can continue to modernize so successfully without adopting Western values. If they can, then what does this do to one of the main themes of globalization, namely the argument that globalization represents the spreading across the globe of a set of values? If these countries do continue to follow their own roads towards economic and social modernization, then we must anticipate future disputes between 'Western' and 'Asian' values over issues like human rights, gender, and religion.

We hope that these arguments for and against globalization will cause you to think deeply about the utility of the concept of globalization in explaining contemporary world politics. The chapters that follow do not take a common stance for or against globalization. We will end by posing some

questions that we would like you to keep in mind as you read the remaining chapters:

- Is globalization a new phenomenon in world politics?
- Which theory discussed above best explains globalization?
- Is globalization a positive or a negative development?
- Is globalization merely the latest stage of capitalist development?
- Does globalization make the state obsolete?
- Does globalization make the world more or less democratic?
- Is globalization merely Western imperialism in a new guise?
- Does globalization make war less likely?

We hope that this introduction and the chapters that follow help you to answer these questions, and that this book as a whole provides you with a good overview of the politics of the contemporary world. Whether or not you conclude that globalization is a new phase in world politics, and whether you think it is a positive or a negative development we will now leave you to decide.

GUIDE TO FURTHER READING

There are several good introductory guides to globalization. M. Waters, *Globalization* (London: Routledge, 1995) is a clear overview, written by a sociologist. J. A. Scholte, *International Relations of Social Change* (Buckingham: Open University Press, 1993) is an extremely clear and comprehensive introduction to the social relations aspects of globalization. A. McGrew and P. Lewis, *Global Politics* (Cambridge: Polity Press, 1992) is a good collection of essays about global politics and contains some very relevant chapters on the relationship between the three theories discussed above and globalization. R. Robertson, *Globalization: Social Theory and Global Culture* (London: Sage, 1992) is a very widely cited survey of the relations between globalization and global culture. P. Hirst and G. Thompson, *Globalization in Question* (Cambridge: Polity Press, 1996) is a powerful critique of the economic version of the globalization thesis. J. N. Rosenau and E.-D. Czempiel, *Governance without Government* (Cambridge: Cambridge University Press, 1992) is a good collection of essays dealing with the political aspects of globalization. J. N. Rosenau, *Turbulence in World Politics* (Princeton: Princeton University Press, 1990) and J. A. Camilleri and J. Falk, *The End of Sovereignty* (Aldershot: Edward Elgar, 1992) are both very good at looking at the main trends in world politics at the beginning of the 1990s.

1 The Globalization of World Politics

Jan Aart Scholte

READER'S GUIDE

This opening chapter considers the implications of globalization for the states-system and for the nature of world politics more generally. Its first section elaborates a general definition of globalization. The second section describes how globalization has been shifting world politics away from the Westphalian system and its central premise of sovereign statehood. The third section reviews four emergent patterns of global governance: (*a*) the growth of transborder links between substate authorities; (*b*) the expansion of global law; (*c*) increased private-sector involvement in global regulation; and (*d*) the spread of global social movements. The chapter ends by arguing that current trends in world governance under conditions of globalization have worrying implications for democracy.

Introduction: A Globalizing World

When a new word becomes popular, it is often because it captures an important change that is taking place in the world. A new idea is needed to describe a new condition. For example, when the philosopher Jeremy Bentham coined the term 'international' in the 1780s, it caught hold because it highlighted a deepening reality of his day, namely, the rise of nation-states and of cross-border transactions between them. People had not spoken of 'international relations' before this time, since humanity had not previously been organized into national communities governed by territorial states.

Two hundred years later, in the 1980s, talk of 'globalization' became rife. The term quickly entered standard vocabulary—not only in academic circles, but also amongst journalists, politicians, bankers, advertisers, and entertainers. Broadly equivalent notions have emerged roughly simultaneously across many languages. 'Globalization' in English has been paralleled by *Quan Qui Hua* in Chinese, *globalizzazione* in Italian, *глобалйзацйя* in Russian, *jatyanthareekaranaya* in Sinhalese, etc. It has become common to speak of global markets, global communications, global conferences, global threats, and so on. During the 1980s students of International Relations and other disciplines began to examine questions of **global** (as distinct from international) governance, **global** environmental change, **global** gender relations, **global** political economy, and more. The word 'globalization' has also found its way onto the cover of the present book.

It is true that ideas of globality were circulating well before 1980. English-speakers began to use the adjective 'global' to designate 'the whole world' at the end of the nineteenth century. Previously the word had only meant 'spherical'. The terms 'globalize' and 'globalism' were introduced in a little-read book published in 1944, while the noun 'globalization' entered a dictionary for the first time in 1961 (Reiser and Davies 1944: 212, 219; Webster 1961). Nevertheless, although global-speak had this long gestation period, it did not become part of the vocabulary of everyday life until the last quarter of the twentieth century. For example, hardly any titles of books and articles published before 1975 include references to global-ness, whereas today, on the threshold of the twenty-first century, the concept has become pervasive.

Globalization: A Definition

Should we conclude that, as was the case with the word 'international' two centuries ago, the recent proliferation of references to globalization signals that a far-reaching change is taking place in world affairs? If so, what is the nature of this change more precisely? Critics have rightly objected that the term 'globalization' is often used vaguely and inconsistently. (See Box 1.1 for samples of different conceptions.) In particular, many authors fail to specify how 'global' relations differ from 'international' relations. Indeed, people frequently employ the notions 'globalization' and 'internationalization' interchangeably. Yet if the concepts refer to the same conditions, then talk of globalization is redundant. Current debates about globalization would in this case merely rehash the same arguments that realists, liberalists, and Marxists rehearsed twenty, sixty, and even a hundred and more years ago. The survey of theories in Part Two of this book would then include nothing that might not equally have been written in an International Relations textbook of the 1930s or the 1970s.

However, a significant change *has* been unfolding in the world during roughly the last four decades of the twentieth century, and the term 'globalization' characterizes it well. As the word is used here, globalization refers to **processes whereby social relations acquire relatively distanceless and borderless qualities,** so that human lives are increasingly played out in **the world as a single place.** Social relations—that is, the countless and complex ways that people interact with and affect each other—are more and more being conducted and organized on the basis of a planetary unit. By the same token country locations, and in

---

Box 1.1. Globalization: A Collection of Definitions

'Globalization refers to all those processes by which the peoples of the world are incorporated into a single world society, global society.'

(Martin Albrow 1990)

'Globalization can . . . be defined as the intensification of worldwide social relations which link distant localities in such a way that local happenings are shaped by events occurring many miles away and vice versa.'

(Anthony Giddens 1990)

'*Die Globalisierung* . . . global networking that has welded together previously disparate and isolated communities on this planet into mutual dependence and unity of "one world".'

(Emanuel Richter, translated from German)

'The characteristics of the globalization trend include the internationalizing of production, the new international division of labor, new migratory movements from South

to North, the new competitive environment that accelerates these processes, and the internationalizing of the state . . . making states into agencies of the globalizing world.'

(Robert Cox 1994)

'The world is becoming a global shopping mall in which ideas and products are available everywhere at the same time.'

(Rosabeth Moss Kanter 1995)

'Globalization does not simply refer to the objectiveness of increasing interconnectedness. It also refers to cultural and subjective matters [namely, the scope and depth of consciousness of the world as a single place].'

(Roland Robertson 1992)

'Globalization is what we in the Third World have for several centuries called colonization.'

(Martin Khor 1995)

---

particular the boundaries between territorial states, are in some important senses becoming less central to our lives, although they do remain significant. Globalization is thus an ongoing trend whereby the world has—in many respects and at a generally accelerating rate—become one relatively borderless social sphere.

Globalization needs in this light to be distinguished from internationalization. As the construction of that term indicates, 'internationalization' refers to a process of **intensifying connections between national domains**. As a result of internationalization, countries may come to have wide-ranging and deep effects on each other, but they remain distinct and separate places. In international relations, countries are divided from each other by clearly marked frontiers as well as by the substantial time that is generally required to cover the distance between their respective territories. To put the difference in a nutshell, the international realm is a patchwork of bordered countries, while the global sphere is a web of transborder networks. Whereas international links (for example, trade in cocoa) require people to cross considerable distances in comparatively long time intervals, global connections (for example, satellite newscasts) are effectively distanceless and instantaneous. Global phenomena can extend across the world at the same time and can move between places in no time;

they are in this sense **supraterritorial**. While the patterns of 'international' interdependence are strongly influenced by national-state divisions, the lines of 'global' interconnections often have little correspondence to territorial boundaries. International and global relations can coexist, of course, and indeed the contemporary world is at the same time both internationalized and globalizing.

Aspects of Globalization

The distinctiveness of global relations will perhaps become more clear if we take a quick survey of some of their main manifestations. In terms of **communications**, for example, globalization has been occurring through computer networks, telephony, electronic mass media, and the like. Such technologies permit persons to have nearly immediate contact with each other, irrespective of their location on earth and regardless of the state borders that might lie between them. Hence a fax will reach a destination across the ocean almost as quickly as a receiver next door.

In respect of **organizations**, globalization has been transpiring through the proliferation and growth of companies, associations, and regulatory agencies that operate as transborder networks.

Bodies such as Nissan Corporation, Amnesty International, and the World Intellectual Property Organization treat the whole planet as their field of activity and regard humanity at large as their actual or potential clients.

Ecologically, globalization has been taking place through such phenomena as planetary climate change (or 'global warming'), stratospheric ozone depletion, the pending worldwide exhaustion of certain natural resources, and a decline in Earth's biodiversity. None of these environmental developments can be isolated in one or the other country; they have arisen in, and affect, the world as a single place.

In respect of **production**, so-called 'global factories' have expanded in sectors like motor cars and micro-electronics. Here the various stages of manufacture (e.g. research and development, processing of materials, preparation of components, assembly of parts, finishing, and quality control) are not confined within a national economy, but link up across several countries in a single production line. Concurrently, globalization has been unfolding in respect of money and finance, with the emergence of round-the-clock round-the-world stock markets, the spread of globally recognized credit cards, the increasing use of currencies like the yen and the Mark all over the world, and so on.

Meanwhile the **military** sphere has seen the advent of global weaponry. Intercontinental ballistic missiles, spy satellites, and the like have in certain respects turned the world as a whole into a single strategic realm. Although the Gulf War of 1990–1 was fought on the ground in Iraq and Kuwait, it equally involved satellite remote sensing, supersonic bombing raids, electronic transborder payments to fund the operations, a propaganda struggle in the global mass media, and a worldwide coalition against Baghdad legitimated through a global governance agency, the United Nations.

Globalization has also encompassed many **norms** that govern our lives, including thousands of technical standards and (purportedly) universal human rights. These and an ever-increasing number of other rules have acquired a supraterritorial rather than a country-specific character.

Finally, globalization has been evident in **everyday thinking**. People living at the end of the twentieth century are aware of the world as a single place to an extent that earlier generations were not. Perhaps the greatest spur to this shift in consciousness came in 1966, with the production of the first photographs taken from outer space showing planet Earth as one location.

Taking the preceding observations in sum, we see that globalization has had a very wide-ranging scope. Indeed, the process has in some way touched every aspect of social relations. The radio brings reports from Buenos Aires and Beijing straight to our breakfast tables. Swings on the global financial markets make and break our fortunes, sometimes from one day to the next. We drink Coca-Cola, munch a Big Mac, wear jeans, listen to the latest hit singles, and watch the newest video releases simultaneously with millions upon millions of other people all over the globe. Our car adds to the greenhouse effect together with the bus in Bombay. Via the Internet, the worldwide network of computer networks, our office can be in immediate contact with Warsaw or Washington. The European Union is determining our food prices, while soldiers from our national army are joining troops from a dozen other states in a single UN peacekeeping operation. Our contributions to Oxfam translate overnight into relief work in Rwanda. These sorts of circumstances did not exist when our parents were children, and there is at present every indication that our children will experience globality even more intensely than we currently do. Today we live not only in a country; in very direct and immediate senses we also live in the world as a single place.

Historical Origins

It is hard to determine a specific moment when globalization started. Periodization is always imprecise and contentious, largely because change and continuity are invariably intertwined. History shows no obvious and exact watersheds on which everyone will agree. Researchers have variously dated the onset of globalization from the dawn of human civilization (e.g. Gamble 1994), or from the start of the modern era (e.g. Modelski 1988), or from the middle of the nineteenth century (e.g. Robertson 1992), or from the late 1950s (e.g. Rosenau 1990), or from the 1970s (e.g. Harvey 1989). However, if we conceive of globalization as the rise of supraterritoriality, then its chronology lies in a combination of the Robertson and Rosenau positions. (See Box 1.2 for a chronology of some major events in the development of globalization.)

Box 1.2. Some Key Events in the History of Globalization

1866	first permanent transoceanic telegraph cable comes into service		1963	issuance of the first eurobond (by a borrower in Italy, in US dollars, on the London market)*
1865	creation of the first global regulatory agency (the International Telegraph Union)		1966	first photographs of planet Earth from outer space
1884	introduction of worldwide co-ordination of clocks (in relation to Greenwich Mean Time)		1969	construction of the first wide-body passenger jet (the Boeing 747)
1891	first transborder telephone calls (between London and Paris)		1969	creation of the first large-scale computer network
1919	initiation of the first scheduled transborder airline services		1971	establishment of the first wholly electronic stock exchange (the US-based NASDAQ system)
1929	institution of the first offshore finance arrangements (in Luxembourg)*		1972	first global issue conference (the United Nations Conference on the Human Environment)
1930	first global radio broadcast (the speech of George V opening the London Naval Conference, relayed simultaneously to 242 stations across six continents)		1974	US Government eliminates foreign exchange controls (other states follow in later years)
1946	construction of the first digital computer		1976	launch of the first direct broadcast satellite (i.e. transmitting to rooftop dishes)
1949	introduction of package holidays sets the stage for large-scale global tourism		1977	first commercial use of fibre-optic cables, vastly increasing capacities of telecommunications
1954	establishment of the first export processing zone (in Ireland)		1977	creation of the SWIFT system for electronic interbank fund transfers worldwide
1954	launch of the 'Marlboro cowboy'		1987	appearance of a near-complete 'ozone hole' over Antarctica raises global ecological awareness
1955	first McDonald's restaurant			
1956	first transoceanic telephone cable link			
1957	advent of intercontinental ballistic missiles		1987	stock-market crash on Wall Street spreads world-wide overnight
1957	issuance of the first eurocurrency loan (by a Soviet bank, in US dollars, on the London market)*		1991	introduction of the World Wide Web
			1997	completion of a continuous round-the-world fibre-optic cable link
1960	Marshall McLuhan coins the phrase 'global village'			
1962	launch of the first communications satellite		*	The terms 'offshore', 'eurocurrencies', and 'eurobonds' are further clarified in Chapter 22 on Global Trade and Finance
1963	introduction of direct dialling of transborder telephone calls			

Robertson is right that early signs of globalization appeared scores of years ago, although to a much smaller extent and at a far slower pace. For example, telegraphic communication commenced in the 1840s. Several global social movements (e.g. feminism) and regulatory bodies (e.g. the Universal Postal Union) emerged later in the nineteenth century. Intercontinental short-wave radio programmes multiplied in the 1920s. Intergovernmental meetings on transboundary pollution were held as early as the 1930s.

On the other hand, globalization did not figure continually, comprehensively, intensely, and with rapidly increasing frequency in the lives of a large proportion of humanity until around the 1960s. Indeed, almost all of the illustrations of globalization given earlier relate only to the second half of the twentieth century, and not before. Worldwide direct dialling was not available before the 1980s, for example. It is only since the 1960s that the world has acquired most of the 1990s figures of 830 million television receivers, 40,000 transnational corporations, several thousand operational satellites, 15,000 transborder citizens associations, US$1,230 billion in foreign exchange transactions *every day*, over a billion commercial airline passengers per year, various global ecological problems, and metaphors of a global village. Fully-fledged globalization—a process with such weight that it requires us to make fundamental adjustments to our understanding of world politics—is a fairly new development.

Qualifications

Having established that globalization is a major and on the whole relatively recent turn in world history, we need to sober our judgements by expressing a number of reservations concerning its extent, depth, causes, and consequences. Unfortunately, many discussions of globalization suffer from over-simplifications, exaggerations, and wishful thinking. As a result of such intellectual sloppiness, certain sceptics have gone to an opposite extreme and dismissed notions of globalization as mythology (e.g. Hirst and Thompson 1996). The following five qualifications respond to some of the critics' main objections and point towards a more measured and sophisticated understanding of the process.

First, globalization has not been experienced everywhere to the same extent. On the whole, the decreased importance of distance and territorial borders has gone markedly further in North America, the Pacific Rim, and Europe than in Sub-Saharan Africa and Central Asia. Phenomena like global companies and electronic mail have been mainly concentrated in the so-called North of the world. In addition, globalization has generally affected city dwellers, professional people, and younger generations relatively more than other groups, although the process has left no one completely untouched. The point about globalization is not that certain conditions come to exist in all places and for all people to the same degree. Rather, it means that many things happen in the contemporary world largely irrespective of territorial distances and borders.

Second, globalization is not the straightforward process of homogenization that some accounts would have us believe. True, the transcendence of territorial geography by electronic mass media and the like has helped to give worldwide currency to a host of objects, ideas, standards, and habits. However, globalization has by no means brought an end to cultural diversity. For instance, different audiences interpret a global film differently, and a global product may be used differently in different places in accordance with specific local needs and customs. Moreover, the experience of having the whole world converge on one's home turf has prompted many people defensively to reassert their distinctiveness, in some cases even more insistently than ever. In this way globalization has contributed to a proliferation of national, ethnic, and religious revivalist movements since the 1960s (Scholte 1996). So globalization involves a complex mix of concurrent tendencies towards cultural convergence on the one hand and increased inter-group differentiation on the other.

Third, globalization has not eliminated the significance of place, distance, and territorial borders in world politics. Yes, the process has introduced additional dimensions of geography to social relations, with the arrival of cyberspace, communication via electromagnetic waves, and so on. However, this does not mean that the old geography of latitudes, longitudes, and altitudes no longer matters at the end of the twentieth century. For example, place obviously remains important in respect of the location of natural resources, feelings of national identity, and much more. Distance retains significant restraining and buffering effects when it comes to things like terrestrial travel and merchandise trade. Meanwhile state frontiers continue to inhibit migration and smuggling even if border guards can do nothing to stop missile attacks or electronic money transfers. Hence globalization has not brought 'the end of geography', but rather has created a new supraterritorial space alongside, and interrelated with, the old territorial geography. The 'map' of world affairs has consequently become more complicated than ever.

Fourth, globalization cannot be understood in terms of a single driving force. For instance, the process is not reducible to an American or Western plot. Nor is it simply the inevitable outcome of capitalism, or the preordained end-result of the Industrial Revolution, or the consequence of a modern secular quest for universal truth. There is probably something to all of these arguments and others, too, but each thesis by itself offers at best only a partial insight. A fuller explanation of globalization needs to consider a complex and fluctuating mix of interlinked political, economic, cultural, ecological, and psychological forces, some of which are mutually reinforcing and some of which are contradictory.

Fifth, and perhaps most importantly, globalization is not a panacea. Some liberalist accounts have heralded the coming of a 'borderless world' as the dawn of universal equality, prosperity, peace, and freedom (e.g. Ohmae 1990). Regrettably, evidence of the past several decades sooner points to contrary outcomes. For one thing, people have—depending on their sex, class, race, nationality, religion, and other social categories—generally had unequal access to, unequal voices in, and unequal benefits from globalization. Poverty is still rampant in the contemporary globalizing world. Ecological degradation has never been worse. Although a third world war has thus far been avoided, thirty-five major armed conflicts (i.e. those involving over 1,000 deaths per year) were underway as of 1993 (Weiss *et al.* 1994: 18). Nor has globalization proved to be a formula for democracy (as will be detailed later) or an answer to problems of alienation. Clearly there is no automatic link between globalization and emancipation.

Nevertheless, to acknowledge the above limitations to change is not to say that nothing has changed in world politics as a result of globalization. Although some commentators are prone to exaggerate its extent, a substantial, wide-ranging and deeply penetrating shift in the spatial character of world politics has been unfolding in recent decades. In this light globalization most definitely warrants the mass of attention that it has attracted of late.

Key Points

- Globalization refers to a process—still ongoing—through which the world has in many respects been becoming a single place.

- Globalization has in one way or another encompassed every sphere of social life.

- Although considerable groundwork for globalization was laid from the middle of the nineteenth century onwards, the fully fledged trend dates from around 1960.

- Many accounts of globalization suffer from oversimplifications, exaggerations, and wishful thinking.

Globalization and the States-System

Discussions of globalization often involve explorations of far-reaching historical change. Researchers are asking whether, as the world becomes a single place, it also becomes a fundamentally different kind of place. For example, might the declining importance of distance and territorial boundaries trigger significant changes in prevailing modes of production? Might globalization shift the way that people construct their senses of identity and community, so that, for instance, they become less (or perhaps more) nationalistic? Might the process alter relationships between human beings and the natural environment? Might globalization change the way people formulate knowledge of the world, for example, encouraging a resurgence of religious belief? Might globalization transform structures of governance, that is, the ways rules are made and authority exercised in the world?

In response to such questions, commentators have variously linked globalization to the rise of the **information society**, the onset of **late capitalism**, the advent of **post-modernity**, the demise of communism, and even **the end of history** (see Box 1.3). In these accounts globalization is depicted as a transition phase between epochs of history. The present chapter is not the place to evaluate these larger claims and draw overall conclusions about the implications of globalization for social change. I attempt this broader analysis elsewhere (Scholte 1997). The rest of this chapter only offers some general reflections on the implications of globalization for the states-system and wider patterns of governance.

The Westphalian Order

Before the onset of intensified globalization several decades ago, world politics was chiefly organized on the basis of the so-called Westphalian system. The name is derived from the Peace of Westphalia (1648), which contains an early official statement of the core principles that came to dominate world affairs during the subsequent three hundred years. The Westphalian system was a states-system. In the nineteenth and twentieth centuries, as states increasingly took the form of nation-states, people came to refer to 'international' as well as interstate relations and frequently described the Westphalian order as 'the international system'.

Box 1.3. Key Concepts of Contemporary Social Change that are Often Associated with Globalization

---

Information Society

A number of social theorists have argued since the early 1970s that contemporary society is experiencing a major shift in the focus of production. Whereas previously economic activity revolved around agriculture and manufacturing, in the newly emerging circumstances—including in particular those of globalization—information and knowledge are said to constitute the principal sources of wealth. Computers, mass media, telecommunications, and the like are allegedly becoming the most important assets in the economy, taking precedence over land, labour, industrial plant, and money. Instead of referring to an 'information society', some commentators advance similar arguments in terms of 'the information age', 'post-industrial society', 'the services economy', or 'the knowledge society'.

Late Capitalism

Both Marxists and others have invoked this phrase to suggest that contemporary history has brought changes in the institutions and processes of capitalism. Like theorists of information society, some authors highlight a shift in the focus of surplus accumulation away from older industries to economies of data, signs, and images. Others emphasize the rise of global companies, or moves towards decentralized corporate management, or the emergence of a neo-imperialism vis-à-vis the so-called 'Third World', and so on. Some writers have made points of this kind while speaking of 'the end of organized capitalism' or even 'post-capitalist society' rather than 'late capitalism'.

Post-modernity

Along with globalization, 'post-modernity' and 'post-modernism' rank amongst the prominent buzzwords of contemporary social theory. Like globalization, their meaning can be quite elusive. Notions of the post-modern usually suggest some kind of crisis in, or depar-

ture from, the circumstances of modernity. For example, many commentators associate post-modernity with a demise of foundational knowledge. From this perspective, the post-modern condition involves the loss of the modern, rationalist, positivist conviction that we can, via science, establish fixed and universal truths and meanings. Ideas of post-modernity often also refer to intensified preoccupations in contemporary society with questions of identity. The post-modern individual has a 'fractured self' with multiple and fluctuating senses of being and belonging (e.g. in terms of nationality, gender, race, sexuality, and so on). Many authors furthermore discuss post-modernity with reference to experiences of rapid change and ephemerality in a world dominated by mass media, consumerism, and the like. Post-modernists in International Relations in addition frequently highlight an end to the certainties of territoriality and sovereign statehood that once dominated the theory and practice of world politics. In each of these and other ways, post-modernity introduces increased uncertainty, insecurity, and disorder into social life. Note, however, that other commentators question such claims and suggest that recent historical developments involve an extension rather than a transcendence of modernity. They prefer to describe present-day circumstances in terms of 'high modernity', 'late modernity', or 'hyper-modernity'.

The End of History

This controversial thesis gained widespread attention in the early 1990s through the pen of Francis Fukuyama, a former official of the US Department of State. Fukuyama (1992) argued that the demise of communist regimes heralded a worldwide triumph of liberal democracy over all rival forms of governance. Since, in his view, liberal democracy was free of fundamental internal contradictions and answered the deepest human longings, its triumph marked the end of social evolution.

The Westphalian system was a framework of governance. That is, it provided a general way to formulate, implement, monitor and enforce social rules. At the core of this mode of governance stood the principles of statehood and sovereignty. Statehood meant that the world was divided into territorial parcels, each of which was ruled by a separate government. This modern state was a centralized, formally organized public authority apparatus that enjoyed a legal (and mostly effective) monopoly over the means of armed violence in the area of its jurisdiction. The Westphalian state was more-

over sovereign, that is, it exercised comprehensive, supreme, unqualified, and exclusive control over its designated territorial domain. **Comprehensive** rule meant that, in principle, the sovereign state had jurisdiction over all affairs in the country. **Supreme** rule meant that, recognizing no superior authority, the sovereign state had the final say in respect of its territory. **Unqualified** rule meant that, although Westphalian times witnessed occasional debates about possible duties of humanitarian intervention, on the whole the state's right of total jurisdiction was treated as sacrosanct by other states. Finally, **exclusive** rule meant that sovereign states did not share competences in regard to their respective domestic jurisdictions. There was no 'joint sovereignty' amongst states; 'pooled sovereignty' was a contradiction in terms.

It must be stressed that the Westphalian order was a historical phenomenon. In other words, the system of sovereign states was a particular framework of governance that arose at a specific time owing to the peculiar circumstances of a certain period. Sovereign statehood is not a timeless, natural condition. Politics operated without this organizing principle prior to the seventeenth century, and there is no reason why world history could not once again carry on without a system of sovereign states.

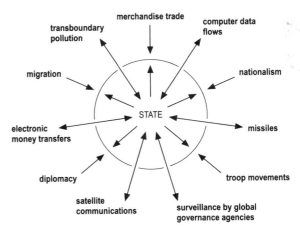

Fig. 1.1. **The state in a globalizing world**

The End of Sovereignty

In fact, it can be argued that, largely owing to globalization, the Westphalian system is already past history. The state apparatus survives, and indeed is in some respects larger, stronger, and more intrusive in social life than ever before. However, the core Westphalian norm of sovereignty is no longer operative; nor can it be retrieved in the present globalizing world. The concept of sovereignty continues to be important in political rhetoric, especially for people who seek to slow and reverse progressive reductions of national self-determination in the face of globalization. However, both juridically and practically, state regulatory capacities have ceased to meet the criteria of sovereignty as it was traditionally conceived.

State sovereignty was premised on a territorial world. In order for governments to exercise total and exclusive authority over a specified domain, events had to occur at fixed locations, and jurisdictions had to be separated by clearly demarcated boundaries which officials could keep under strict surveillance. Yet when, with globalization, social relations acquire a host of nonterritorial qualities, and borders are dissolved in a deluge of electronic and other flows, crucial preconditions for effective sovereignty are removed. (See Fig. 1.1.)

On the one hand, a number of material developments have undercut state sovereignty. The contemporary state is quite unable by itself to control phenomena like global companies, satellite remote sensing, global ecological problems, and global

stock and bond trading. None of these things can be grounded in a territorial space over which a state might endeavour to exercise exclusive jurisdiction. Computer data transmissions, nuclear fallout, and telephone calls do not halt at frontier checkpoints. Global mass media have detracted from the state's dominion over language and education. In the face of huge offshore bank deposits and massive worldwide electronic money transfers, states have also lost sole ownership of another former hallmark of sovereignty, the national currency.

Alongside these material changes, globalization has also loosened some important cultural and psychological underpinnings of sovereignty. For example, as a result of the growth of transborder networks, many people have acquired loyalties that supplement and perhaps even override feelings of national solidarity that previously lent legitimacy to state sovereignty. With the help of global conferences, global telecommunications, and so on, significant supraterritorial bonds have been cemented in women's movements, amongst a transnational managerial class, in lesbian and gay circles, amongst disabled persons, and in thousands of computer-mediated communities formed through newsgroups on the Internet. At the same time, globalization has also, as already mentioned, often reinvigorated more localized loyalties, for example, amongst indigenous peoples and other substate ethnic groups. In addition, many people in the contemporary globalizing world have become increasingly ready to give values such as economic growth, human rights, and ecological sustainability a higher priority than state sovereignty and the associated norm of national self-determination.

States have affected the manner and rate at which they have lost sovereignty in the face of globalization, but they have not had the option to retain it. Even the Chinese government, which has been particularly insistent on perpetuating a sovereignty-centred world order, put 'global interdependence' at the heart of its Ten-Year Economic Blueprint for the 1990s. Of course there were violations of sovereignty under the Westphalian system, too, but at that time the norm was at least hypothetically realizable. A state could, by strengthening its institutions and instruments, graduate from mere legal sovereignty to effective sovereignty. In contrast, under conditions of contemporary globalization, governance in terms of supreme and exclusive territorial state authority has become utterly impracticable. No amount of institution building and unilateral legislation will allow a state to achieve absolute control of its realm. Indeed, many new post-colonial states—established during the recent time of globalization—have never been sovereign.

The Persistence of the State

Yet although globalization has brought an end to sovereignty, it has not so far augured the demise of the state. On the contrary, with the exception of a few implosions of government (e.g. in Somalia and Afghanistan), the state has proved to be highly robust in recent times. Even the turbulence attending the collapse of communist rule yielded only certain changes to state borders. As a structure of governance the state has remained intact in the territories of Eastern Europe and the former Soviet Union.

Indeed, most governments have during the time of globalization actually enlarged their payroll, budget, scope of activities, and surveillance capacities. For the moment there is little sign that globalization is leading either to a centralized, sovereign world government, as liberal universalists have long predicted and advocated, or to world-scale anarchical governance through local communities, as promoted by some radical ecologists. Hence globalists forecast the demise of the territorial state

at their peril. Neither they nor the state-centric realists have it right. Globalization is not dissolving the state, but it has not left it untouched either. The challenge for students of politics is to determine how the growth of supraterritorial social space is altering the activities and role of the state in contemporary history. Two possible general shifts can be briefly mentioned here.

First, it could well be that, under the influence of globalization, the constituency of the state is changing. The sovereign state normally promoted domestic interests and acted as a protective barrier against external intrusions. In contrast, the post-sovereign state often advances global as well as national causes. For example, the Iranian state during the 1980s gave extensive support to worldwide Islamicism. More generally, contemporary states frequently serve the interests of global capital in addition to (and sometimes to the detriment of) national capital.

Second, it may be that globalization is reducing the chances of major interstate war. It is striking that most contemporary warfare takes the form of internal insurrection against a national government rather than armed conflict between states. Although it is too early to draw definitive conclusions on this point, the expansion of global interests would seem to be substantially reducing incentives for states to embark on territorial conquest. Interstate warfare generally advances little purpose for—and sooner positively harms—global capitalism, global environmental management, global tourism, and so on.

Key Points

- Globalization is connected to a number of potentially far-reaching changes in world order.
- Globalization has presented a fundamental challenge to the Westphalian states-system and its central principle of state sovereignty.
- Although globalization has brought the demise of sovereignty, it is by no means dissolving the state.
- The post-sovereign state may well behave differently from its Westphalian predecessor.

Post-Sovereign Governance

If world politics is no longer based on the core principle of sovereign statehood, how is governance being conducted in the contemporary globalizing world? Preceding paragraphs have stressed that the state is still very much in the picture, although its capacities, orientations, and activities have changed with the decline of sovereignty. At the same time, however, other parties besides the state have also acquired important roles in the process of world governance. Their efforts to shape rules and norms sometimes complement the actions of states, but on other occasions they may compete with and possibly override the initiatives of national governments. In any case, world governance is today far from reducible to the states-system.

Substate Global Governance

One striking development in present times of globalization has been the growth of direct trans-boundary links between substate authorities, who have consequently taken a substantial number of policy initiatives that bypass central governments. For example, various Canadian and Chinese provinces and most of the US federal states now have their own 'diplomatic' missions abroad that operate relatively independently from their respective national embassies. In Europe some fifty regional governments in seventeen countries now maintain direct contacts through the Assembly of European Regions, the European Union's Committee of the Regions, and several other such bodies created since the 1970s.

At a municipal level, too, numerous 'trans-sovereign' policies have been developed by local authorities concerning matters such as pollution control, crime prevention, disarmament, and development co-operation. This trend is hardly surprising, particularly in regard to metropolitan centres. Global capital flows, air corridors, and telecommunications webs often connect world cities like Singapore and Frankfurt more to each other than to their respective national hinterlands.

Suprastate Global Governance

At the same time that some initiative in world policy-making has shifted 'downwards' to provincial and municipal governments, numerous other competences have moved 'upwards' to suprastate authorities. Intergovernmental regulatory frameworks are by no means new to the second half of the twentieth century, but their number, scope, and impact has greatly expanded with globalization.

For one thing, regional governance arrangements have proliferated and grown (albeit to differing degrees) in every part of the world from the Caribbean to South-East Asia. In total over a hundred such agreements have been concluded since 1945, twenty-nine of them in 1992–5 alone. The furthest developed regional organization, the European Union, has issued some 20,000 regulatory measures.

At the same time new and pre-existing worldwide bodies like the United Nations have also seen their tasks enlarged. Indeed, in the light of their increased initiative and influence, what used to be called 'international organizations' might now suitably be renamed, say, 'global governance agencies'. In other words, far more now occurs in these quarters than the 'intergovernmental' consultation and co-ordination for which the older institutions were originally established.

The growth of suprastate regulation covers a very wide spectrum, only part of which can be mentioned here. In the field of **macroeconomic policy**, for example, the Organization for Economic Co-operation and Development (OECD) has since the 1960s issued influential guidelines on a whole host of matters, including new information technologies, retrenchment of the welfare state, jobs creation, and a code of conduct for transnational corporations. Since 1979 the International Monetary Fund and the World Bank have supplemented their already significant liquidity and development functions with far-reaching stabilization policies and structural adjustment programmes in almost 100 countries. In a number of these cases IMF and World Bank officials have been dispatched to occupy and supervise national finance ministries. The World Trade Organization (WTO), established in 1995, covers a much wider range of activities with substantially greater powers than its forerunner, the General Agreement on Tariffs and Trade. Meanwhile the Bank for International Settlements has since the mid-1970s undertaken some oversight of global financial markets. In the area of **conflict management**, suprastate agencies like the United Nations, the Organization of African Unity, and the Organization for Security and Co-operation in Europe have acquired much-increased prominence. Suprastate governance has also greatly expanded in the field of **human rights**, including an unprecedented number of multinational humanitarian interventions during the 1990s. Although the idea of human rights goes back centuries, most formalized global law on the subject has emerged since 1960. Beginning with the UN Conference on the Human Environment in 1972, a proliferation of global meetings, legal instruments, and institutions have addressed **ecological degradation** throughout the world. In regard to **electronic media**, the handbook of technical standards established by the International Telecommunication Union now runs to some 10,000 pages. As these examples indicate, rulers and citizens alike have increasingly recognized that the territorial governance offered by states cannot by itself provide adequate management of supraterritorial phenomena linked to contemporary information, communications and weapons technologies, global ecological changes, global markets, and so on.

Of course significant limitations to suprastate governance remain. Official global regulation is still considerably underdeveloped in various fields, including competition policy, labour standards, and arms control, for example. In addition, most global governance institutions are inadequately staffed and chronically underfinanced. Poor co-ordination between agencies and the frequent absence of effective enforcement mechanisms have further undermined the reputation of global law. Nevertheless, suprastate regulation has become sufficiently widespread and effective that it forms a major part of governance in today's globalizing world.

Marketized Global Governance

This review of contemporary world governance would be incomplete if it only covered **official**

agencies at substate, state, and suprastate levels. Not all rules in the globalizing world of the late twentieth century emanate from the public sector. Markets, too, have played an important role in global regulation, often stepping in where states and global governance agencies have left gaps.

The construction and implementation of **rules** by private-sector bodies has perhaps gone furthest in respect of the global financial markets, where very little effective official governance has been developed. With regard to global stock markets, for example, codes of conduct have emanated mainly from the International Federation of Stock Exchanges (founded in 1961), the International Securities Market Association (1969), and the semi-official International Organization of Securities Commissions (1984). Meanwhile debt security rating agencies such as Moody's Investors Service and Standard & Poor's have effectively filled a regulatory role in the global credit markets (Sinclair 1994). In addition, commercial banks have taken considerable initiative alongside official agencies like the IMF in managing (some would say mismanaging) the recurrent financial crises of debt-ridden countries since 1982.

Global policy initiatives by the private sector have ranged well beyond the financial markets, too. For example, the World Economic Forum, founded in 1971, now unites some 900 major companies under the motto of 'entrepreneurship in the global public interest'. Amongst its many initiatives, the Forum has undertaken conciliation attempts in several major interstate conflicts, including the Arab–Israeli dispute. The WEF was also instrumental in launching the Uruguay Round of world trade negotiations that resulted in the creation of the WTO. Scores of private endowments have also become active in global policy-making. Two prominent examples are the Ford Foundation (which has been especially influential in the field of development aid since the 1960s) and the Soros Foundations (which have been major promoters of liberalization in the former Soviet bloc). Set up in 1991, a World Business Council for Sustainable Development has injected a corporate input into global environmental management. There have even been proposals to create a permanent 'chamber of companies' in the United Nations alongside the General Assembly of states. Even if this suggestion were not adopted—as seems likely—it is clear that global governance is not an affair of the public sector alone.

Global Social Movements

Market institutions are not the only actors outside the public sector that contribute to governance in the contemporary globalizing world. Much initiative also emanates from a non-official, non-profit 'third sector' of global social movements. Here popular concern and protest are mobilized in campaigns to reshape policies and the deeper structures of social relations (like militarism or capitalism, for example) that those policies reflect. The associations are global both insofar as they address whole-world problems and in the sense that they pursue their causes by exploiting the circumstances of globalization (air travel, computer networks, global laws, and so on). As noted earlier, precursors of today's transborder social movements date back to the nineteenth century; however, contemporary activities involve far larger numbers of people, greater institutional resources, and bigger impacts.

Global social movements show enormous diversity. For one thing, they address an extremely wide spectrum of issues, from aboriginal rights to HIV/AIDS. They also hold extremely divergent visions of the transformed world that they wish to create, drawing inspiration variously from anarchism, neo-fascism, a host of traditional and new religions, and much else. Some of the movements are global in the sense that they work through world-wide networks, like Development Alternatives with Women for a New Era (DAWN). In contrast, others 'think globally and act locally', that is, they hold a global orientation while operating at a grassroots level. Some groups campaign in isolation, while others pursue their aims through large coalitions. Illustrating the latter approach, the Pesticides Action Network encompasses some 350 groups in over fifty countries. Social movement activity includes both sporadic amateur improvisations (such as many student protests) and long-term professionalized and institutionalized programmes (of the kind sustained by Greenpeace and Christian Aid). Finally, global social movements embrace a variety of strategies. Some activists see fit to work with governments, global governance agencies, and business associations, while others regard any collaboration with 'the establishment' as an unacceptable compromise of their principles.

Although global social movements often suffer from shortages of resources and divisive internal disputes, they can exert considerable influence in contemporary world governance. Amongst other things, these forces have contributed substantially to policy innovation in areas such as ecological sustainability, human rights protection, disaster relief, welfare provision, and community improvement. By 1990 most of the major global governance agencies had set up offices for liaison with what they generally call non-governmental organizations, or 'NGOs' (see Ch. 15). Many social-movement associations have played important roles both in advising the official institutions and in helping to implement their policies. Indeed, bodies like the World Bank and the Office of the United Nations High Commissioner for Refugees have sometimes become quite dependent on NGO assistance.

Box 1.4. HIV/AIDS: A Case Study in Global Governance

Acquired immunodeficiency sydrome (AIDS) was first identified in 1981. In a globalizing era, when several hundred million passengers take transborder flights each year, the number of recorded cases of AIDS grew to 150,000 worldwide in 1988 and over 400,000 by the end of 1991. Over the same period a further 8–10 million people contracted HIV, the virus believed to cause the disease, so that, in the absence of curative therapies, millions more AIDS cases are in prospect.

HIV/AIDS has attracted global attention as no previous transborder epidemic. The plight quickly became the focus of global panic, global conferences, global support groups, global policies, and global commemoration with an annual World AIDS Day on 1 December. It was soon recognized that, in the words of a former Prime Minister of France, 'AIDS will be conquered everywhere or it will not be conquered at all'.

The global campaign against AIDS has involved a very wide range of governance agencies. For their part, states have activated their public health systems, both individually and through regular intergovernmental consultations. At the same time, suprastate bodies have taken initiatives such as the AIDS Task Force of the European Union and the Global Programme on AIDS of the World Health Organization. Some global companies like Benetton have sponsored public service advertising to combat the spread of the disease. The International Red Cross and other nonprofit associations involved in patient care have maintained regular transboundary communication and co-ordination. At the grassroots, afflicted individuals have formed a Global Network of People Living with HIV and AIDS. No such multifaceted attempt at extensive global regulation met, say, the worldwide influenza epidemic of 1918–19, let alone the intercontinental bubonic plague of the fourteenth century.

Thousands of civic groups have attended the various UN-sponsored global issue conferences held since the 1970s, where they have lobbied officials and influenced the resultant programmes of action. Such scenarios provide an illustration of a new politics that has been emerging in the last decades of the twentieth century, whereby social movements channel many of their efforts to reshape national and local government policies through suprastate regulatory agencies.

In this and other ways, many activists in global social movements have aimed—and to some extent succeeded—not only to change policies, but also to reconstruct the very nature of politics. Their initiatives have frequently challenged prevailing concepts, procedures, and tactics of political action. For example, a number of these associations have adopted nonhierarchical modes of decision-taking, and in general they have included women to a greater extent than is found in official and commercial channels. As a result of global social movements, popular participation in world politics has become far more direct and extensive than in Westphalian days, when citizen involvement tended to mean no more than a vote in national elections to determine which political party would conduct the state's foreign policy.

Key Points

- Globalization has encouraged increased direct transborder collaboration between provincial and municipal governments.

- Globalization has brought a major expansion of suprastate regulation by global governance agencies.

- The private sector takes an active role in contemporary global governance, e.g. through supervisory agencies, think-tanks, foundations, and advisory councils.

- With great diversity of organizational form, issue-focus, and tactics, global social movements inject much dynamism and innovation into contemporary world politics.

The Challenge of Global Democracy

We have now seen that globalization has encouraged a shift in governance of the world away from a single focus on the states-system to a multi-layered complex of rule-making and order creation where no location is sovereign. Politics now lacks a clear centre of command and control of the kind previously provided by the Westphalian state. In addition, considerable initiative in the construction of norms is now found outside public-sector bodies, namely, in market agents and social movements. What do these developments imply for democracy?

Democracy—rule by the people—is widely regarded to be the central legitimating ethic of modern governance. Although definitions of democracy and mechanisms to achieve it have shown considerable diversity from one country and time period to the next, there is a broad and fairly solid consensus in today's world that good governance means democratic governance. Hence before closing this chapter it is appropriate to ask a critical normative question, namely, what is happening to democracy in the contemporary globalizing world?

At first glance globalization might seem to offer possibilities for enhancing democracy. As we saw earlier, globalization has been unravelling state sovereignty, and there has always been a fundamental tension between sovereignty and democracy. Sovereignty implies comprehensive, supreme, unqualified, and exclusive power, whereas democracy is generally presumed to rest on limited, dispersed, conditional, and collective power. Even where governments are popularly elected, there remains a potentially dangerous concentration of power in the state. To this extent the removal of sovereignty ought, in principle, to present opportunities for increasing democracy.

Regrettably, however, globalization has thus far as often as not made things worse. Contemporary post-sovereign governance is strewn with democratic deficits. The state, global governance agencies, the market, and global social movements all suffer from shortfalls in respect of popular participation and access, consultation and debate, inclusion and representativeness, constitutionality and accountability.

Globalization and the Democratic State

Some enthusiasts have assumed that globalization and democratization would be two sides of the same coin. Adopting this perspective, liberalists have celebrated a worldwide wind of democratic change in the late twentieth century with the collapse of apartheid, communism, and other one-party systems. However, multiparty competition has not by itself provided a guarantee for greater popular participation in and control of the state. Countless governments continue habitually to violate human rights in the current time of globalization. Meanwhile even those states who receive top ratings from Amnesty International rarely consult their populations specifically on global policies. For example, citizens rarely have any significant say in a state's decision whether or not to adopt an IMF structural adjustment programme. Moreover, even were the state fully to involve its residents in these matters, national governments often, as we have seen, have limited control over global flows. To this extent the state does not offer the means to secure the popular will in relation to global capital, global ecological problems, and so on. Democratically run government has to be supplemented, perhaps even replaced, by other instruments and institutions.

Global Governance Agencies and Democracy

Unfortunately, global governance agencies do not at the moment provide the necessary further guarantees of democracy. To begin with, there is very little direct popular involvement in these institutions. Most meetings of the World Bank Board of Governors, the European Council of Ministers, the UN Security Council, and other such decision-taking bodies are held behind closed doors. Moreover, most of the world's citizens are completely ignorant of the day-to-day workings of these bodies. The organizations are largely realms of 'technopolitics', where economists, accountants, managers, engineers, chemists, lawyers, and other 'experts' are largely exempted from democratic scrutiny. When their policies have unhappy consequences—as in the case of the detrimental welfare effects of many structural adjustment policies, for instance—the agencies concerned are not held formally and publicly accountable.

Some people would argue that global governance agencies are indirectly representative, insofar as state delegations are in attendance to speak for the various national populations of the world. However, most states have pretty dubious democratic credentials. Moreover, the rule of one-state-one-vote that prevails in many global organs means that, formally at least, Andorra and India have an equal say. Elsewhere, the reservation of permanent membership and veto powers in the Security Council to five states is democratically unjustifiable. So, too, are quota-based votes in the IMF and World Bank, where one-quarter of the member states control three-quarters of the votes.

The undemocratic character of global governance agencies is being increasingly acknowledged. In the case of the European Union, some (limited) steps have been taken since the late 1970s to increase popular access and direct participation in suprastate governance. Most of these organizations have also moved towards greater public disclosure of information concerning their operations. However, such reforms are few in number and half-measures at best. Proposals for more far-reaching democratization have so far gone nowhere.

Global Market Democracy?

Other worrying reductions of democracy have resulted from the previously described marketization of governance. True, champions of *laissez faire* claim that the market enlarges the scope for popular participation and control. From their perspective, global democracy is achieved when consumers and capitalists (rather than citizens) vote with their pocketbooks (rather than their ballots) for the best value for money (rather than the maximization of human potential) in a global market (rather than a territorial state).

However, this vision presumes that money and materialism are the be-all and end-all of politics. Traditional democratic concerns with human dignity and equal opportunity are subordinated to obsessions with managerial efficiency and product quality. In market democracy accountability means the boardroom's responsibility to shareholders and the company's responsibility to the customer. Yet in practice shareholders rarely affect corporate policies and consumers are often captives of oligopoly. Most disturbingly, of course, access and participation in market governance are determined primarily by wealth and income. Very few people receive invitations to attend meetings of the World Economic Forum and like bodies.

Global Social Movements and Democracy

In contrast to the marketeers, other commentators have looked to global social movements as the way to secure democracy in the contemporary globalizing world. It is certainly the case that **global civic activism** has shown impressive growth in recent decades. In particular, globalization has provided opportunities for women, disabled persons, lesbians and gay men, and indigenous peoples to mobilize to a degree that was generally unavailable to them in Westphalian territorial politics.

However, these gains for democracy need to be kept in perspective and set against other profoundly undemocratic features of contemporary global social movements. For one thing, only a very small proportion of the world's people has been directly involved in these initiatives. The vast dispossessed majority of humanity lacks the funds, the language skills (or translation facilities), access to the Internet, and other resources on which the influence of global social movements depends. As a result, this activism has for the most part remained

the preserve of a narrow, mainly white, and overwhelmingly middle-class population residing chiefly in North America, Western Europe, and Japan. In spite of recent increases, fewer than 15 per cent of the NGOs with consultative status at the UN are based in the so-called South. Moreover, in the South as well as the North, members of global social movements are generally self-elected and follow no formal procedures to ensure transparency of their operations and accountability towards those whom they claim to serve.

In sum, then, democracy is in a precarious position across all areas of contemporary governance. In the present-day globalizing world, the construction and implementation of rules occurs mainly through élite competition rather than through representative, let alone participatory, democracy. At the moment it is unclear whether and how democracy can be realized in the emergent globalized future. Hence imaginative rethinking of democracy is arguably the prime task facing political theory today.

Key Points

- Globalization makes it impossible to achieve democracy solely through the state.
- Global governance agencies suffer from severe democratic deficits.
- Global governance by the market implies deep inequalities and the rule of efficiency over democracy.
- Global social movements, too, generally have shaky democratic credentials.

Conclusion

This opening chapter has, like the rest of the book to follow, indicated that globalization has changed, and continues to change, the nature of world politics. The character and extent of those changes are much debated. Analysts are deeply divided when it comes to definitions, measurements, explanations, prognoses, and moral assessments of globalization. Indeed, many of my colleagues in the field of International Relations will disagree with parts or

the whole of the argument put forward in this chapter. However, it is clear that we today face some different issues and dynamics of world affairs. It will not do to study 'international relations' in the way of earlier generations of students.

To recapitulate, I have suggested that contemporary history is witnessing a significant shift in the spatial character of world politics. In addition to the old geography of places, distances, and borders, we now have an extensive global dimension in which certain circumstances are effectively placeless (i.e. they can occur anywhere on earth), distanceless (i.e. they can cross the planet in no time), and borderless (i.e. they can move between countries unhindered by state frontiers). The accelerated spread of global phenomena since the middle of the twentieth century has had a number of important implications for patterns of governance. On the one hand, globalization has rendered the old core principle of sovereignty unworkable, although the state nevertheless continues to play a key role in the regulation of social life. On the other hand, globalization has encouraged the growth of a number of other aspects of authority and rule in world politics, including transborder substate relations, suprastate laws, regulatory initiatives by market institutions, and the campaigns of global social movements.

Thus students of International Relations today need to explore the workings of world governance as a whole. We cannot, following the traditional pattern, automatically take the state and the states-system as the starting point of investigation. Nor can we assume, complacently, that old models of sovereignty and democracy will provide our salvation in a globalizing world. Assuring democracy in post-sovereign governance is one of the key challenges in the construction of global security for the twenty-first century.

QUESTIONS

1. How is globalization distinct from internationalization?

2. How new is the phenomenon of globalization?

3. Specify some of the misconceptions that are commonly associated with the idea of globalization.

4. What are some of the driving forces behind globalization?

5. What is meant by state sovereignty?

6. How has globalization eroded sovereign statehood?

7. Why does the state persist in the contemporary era of globalization?

8. Assess the relationship between globalization and war.

9. Discuss recent advances in, and continuing limitations of, suprastate law.

10. Illustrate how the private sector contributes to global governance.

11. What are global social movements, and how do they participate in world politics?

12. How does globalization pose challenges to democracy?

GUIDE TO FURTHER READING

Bull, H., *The Anarchical Society: A Study of Order in World Politics* (London: Macmillan, 1977). This classic study of international theory explores the emergence, subsequent evolution, and future prospects of the states-system.

Carlsson, I. *et al.*, *Our Global Neighbourhood* (Oxford: Oxford University Press, 1995). This report of the Commission on Global Governance (a group of academics, activists, and statespersons from around the world) surveys the development of world-scale regulation, especially through the

United Nations system. It highlights various shortcomings in present arrangements and makes a number of suggestions for institutional reform.

Featherstone, M. (ed.), *Global Culture: Nationalism, Globalization and Modernity* (London: Sage, 1990). This volume brings together selections from a number of sociologists and anthropologists with interests in globalization, especially its implications for the ways that we experience world politics.

Hirst, P., and Thompson, G., *Globalization in Question: The International Economy and the Possibilities of Governance* (Cambridge: Polity Press, 1996). This book presents an argument against 'globalist' presumptions that globalization is new, irreversible, and wholly beyond state control.

Kofman, E., and Youngs, G., (eds.), *Globalization: Theory and Practice* (London: Pinter, 1996). The essays in this book develop insights about globalization that are gained from a cross-disciplinary dialogue between International Relations and Geography. Insofar as globalization involves a transformation of the spatial aspects of social life, it is a subject on which geographers have much of interest to say.

Peterson, V. S., and Runyan, A. S., *Global Gender Issues* (Boulder, Col.: Westview Press, 1993). This textbook highlights a number of important but often neglected ways that gender relations (i.e. social constructions of femininity and masculinity) are involved in globalization.

Rosenau, J. N., and Czempiel, E.-O., (eds.), *Governance without Government: Order and Change in World Politics* (Cambridge: Cambridge University Press, 1992). This collection of essays by North American theorists of international relations explores issues of statehood, sovereignty, global governance, and democracy in world politics of the late twentieth century

Sakamoto, Y. (ed.), *Global Transformation: Challenges to the State System* (Tokyo: United Nations University Press, 1994). In this volume published by the United Nations University, academics from different parts of the world give their perspectives on changing contours of contemporary world politics.

Scholte, J. A., *Globalisation: A Critical Introduction* (London: Macmillan, 1997). This text takes a historical–sociological perspective on globalization, assessing the trend in respect not only of patterns of governance (as in the above chapter), but also structures of production, identity, ecology, and knowledge.

Sklair, L., *Sociology of the Global System* (Hemel Hempstead: Harvester Wheatsheaf, 1991). This investigation of the political economy of globalization focuses on the role of transnational corporations and a global culture of consumerism.

Waters, M., *Globalization* (London: Routledge, 1995). This introductory sociology text offers a concise survey of theories of globalization and also reviews the economic, political, and cultural repercussions of the process.

Part One
The Historical Context

In this part of the book, we want to provide you with a historical context within which to make sense of globalization. We have two main aims: **first**, we want to introduce you to the main aspects of international history and we will do this by giving you an increasingly more chronologically concentrated set of chapters. We start with an overview of international society from its origins in Ancient Greece through to the twentieth century. We think that you need to have some basic understanding of the main developments in the history of world politics, as well as some kind of context for thinking about the contemporary period of world history. This is followed by two chapters that look at the main themes of twentieth-century history, one dealing with the period before the Second World War, the other dealing with the period after it. Our final chapter is more specifically concerned with the period since the late 1980s, and concentrates on the most significant historical development of that period, namely the end of the cold war. We want these chapters to give you a lot of historical information which will be of interest in its own right, but our **second** aim is to draw to your attention the main themes of international history so that you can develop a deeper understanding of the issues, both theoretical and empirical that are dealt with in the remaining three sections of this book. As such we think that an overview of international history gives you a context within which to begin thinking about globalization: is it a new phenomenon that fundamentally changes the main patterns of international history or are there precedents for it that make it seem less revolutionary?

2

The Evolution of International Society

Robert H. Jackson

READER'S GUIDE

This chapter discusses the idea of international society and some of its historical manifestations. The starting point is human beings organized into geographically separate political communities and the horizontal relations of conflict and co-operation that ensue from their joint political existences. International society should be understood as a distinctive institutional response to accommodate that reality of political coexistence. It has assumed different forms from ancient times to the present era but it also discloses common features the most important being a relationship of independence between political communities, usually conceived as states.

I would like to acknowledge Kal Holsti and Ron Deibert for their helpful criticisms of an earlier draft.

Origins and Definitions

In order to understand the contemporary world and the significance of globalization we need to consider the evolution of international society. The historical origin of international relations can only be a matter of speculation. But, speaking conceptually, it was a time when people began to settle down on the land and form themselves into separate territory-based political communities. Each group faced the inescapable problem of co-existing with neighbouring groups whom they could not ignore or avoid because they were right there next door. Each group also had to deal with groups that were farther away but still capable of affecting them. Their geographical contiguity must have come to be regarded as a zone of political proximity if not a frontier or border of some kind. (The institution of formally demarcated international boundaries is of course a much later invention of the modern European society of states.) Where contact occurred it must have involved activities such as competition, disputes, threats, intimidation, intervention, invasion, conquest and other belligerent interactions. But it also must have involved dialogue, collaboration, exchange, communication, recognition, and similar non-belligerent relations.

That social reality of group relations on a horizontal plane could be considered, figuratively speaking, as the core problem of international relations, which is built on a fundamental distinction between our collective selves and other collective selves in a territorial world of many such collective selves in contact with each other. If there were no horizontal lines of territorial division between 'we' and 'they' there could still be human societies: perhaps isolated political communities, perhaps roaming or marauding groups, perhaps a vertical society such as an empire, possibly even a cosmopolitan world society of all humankind devoid of fundamental group differentiation, or some other social formation or arrangement. But there could not be international relations in the usual meaning of the term. In short, international relations as historically and conventionally understood are relations of territorially based and delimited political groups.

We now begin to arrive at a definition of 'international society'. As already indicated, it stands for relations between politically organized human groupings which occupy distinctive territories and enjoy and exercise a measure of independence from each other. International society can thus be con-

---

Box 2.1. **Key Concepts**

coexistence: the doctrine of live and let live between political communities, or states.

territory: a portion of the earth's surface appropriated by a political community, or state.

state sovereignty: a state's characteristic being politically independent of all other states.

suzerain state: a state which dominates and subordinates neighbouring states, without taking them over.

empire: a state which possesses both a home territory and foreign territories: an imperial state.

theocracy: a state based on religion.

hegemony: power and control exercised by a leading state over other states.

reason of state: the practical application of the doctrine of realism and virtually synonymous with it.

balance of power: a doctrine and an arrangement whereby the power of one state (or group of states) is checked by the countervailing power of other states.

national security: a fundamental value in the foreign policy of states.

society of states: an association of sovereign states based on their common interests, values, and norms.

international law: the formal rules of conduct that states acknowledge or contract between themselves.

international order: a shared value and condition of stability and predictability in the relations of states.

non-discrimination: a doctrine of equal treatment between states.

self-determination: the right of a political community or state to become a sovereign state.

right of self-defence: a state's right to wage war in its own defence.

world society: the society produced by globalization.

global covenant: the rules, values, and norms which govern the global society of states.

> ## Box 2.2. **The Earliest Records of 'International Society'**
>
> There are recorded formal agreements among ancient city-states which date as far back as 2400 BC, alliances dating to 1390 BC, and envoys as early as 653 BC (Barber 1979: 8–9).

ceived as a society of political communities which are not under any higher political authority. In the language of international relations such detached communities are referred to as states which are usually conceptualized as consisting of (1) a permanent population (2) occupying a defined territory (3) under a central government (4) which is independent of all other governments of a similar kind (Brownlie 1979). That condition of constitutional or political independence is ordinarily spoken of as state sovereignty (James 1986: 25). Hedley Bull (1977: 8) sums up the foundation of the subject: 'The starting point of international relations is the existence of states, or independent political communities, each of which possesses a government and asserts sovereignty in relation to a particular portion of the earth's surface and a particular segment of the human population.'

Hedley Bull (1977: 13) offers the following definition of international society: 'A society of states (or international society) exists when a group of states, conscious of certain common interests and common values, form a society in the sense that they conceive themselves to be bound by a common set of rules in their relations with one another, and share in the working of common institutions.' International society is basically a pluralistic or 'liberal' political arrangement. The core value is the political opportunity of people to enjoy a geographically separate group existence free from unsolicited interference from neighbouring groups and other outsiders. Independence is the core value in a cluster of important international values, including self-determination, non-intervention, right of self-defence, and the like. The basic institutional arrangement which embodies and expresses those values is state sovereignty.

One of the most noteworthy and characteristic arrangements between sovereign states is diplomacy which obviously is intended primarily to facilitate and smooth their relations. Of course diplomatic arrangements have been expressed differently from one time or place to the next: diplomacy in ancient Greece was not the same as diplomacy in Renaissance Italy which was different again from the classical diplomacy of the eighteenth century or the global diplomacy of the twentieth century (Nicolson 1954). Another arrangement is international law, which is a more recent innovation dating back only as far as the sixteenth and seventeenth centuries when the first recognizable international legal texts were written that sought to document the rather novel legal practices of what at that time were recently discerned entities known as sovereign states. Other such arrangements include recognition, reciprocity, the laws of war, international conferences, and much else. In the past century an increasingly important arrangement is the large and extensive complex of international organizations—universal, regional and functional—by means of which much of the business of international relations is nowadays conducted.

One point deserves particular emphasis so that the idea and expression of international society is understood in its proper historical context. Vertical or hierarchical relations between political groups are a historical commonplace throughout most of the world as far back as recorded history can take us. Political empire is the prevalent form of group relations. Horizontal relations between political groups is comparatively rare. The ancient Greeks constructed an international society which survived for several centuries in a surrounding political environment of various hegemonic empires, including Persia, Macedonia, and the Roman empire. At that time there were also great empires and suzerain-state systems beyond Europe and the Middle East, including the Chinese empire which was the greatest of them all and which lasted for millennia, albeit in different dynastic incarnations.

Empire was the prevalent mode of large-scale political group relations in Western Europe throughout the era of the Roman empire and that of its successor, medieval Christendom, which lasted until about the sixteenth century. In the late Middle Ages (1300–1500) the Renaissance Italians constructed and operated a small regional international society based on the city states of northern and central Italy. The first modern international society based on large-scale territorial states came into existence a little later in north-western Europe out of which the contemporary global international society has evolved (see chronology below). But empires continued to exist in Europe and many other parts of the world down to the twentieth century. Eastern Europe was dominated by empires until the end of the First World War. Although Europeans created a society of states among themselves which was the very definition of political modernity, at the very same time they constructed vast empires to rule non-European political communities in the rest of the world. International society is thus uncommon in history even though it has become globalized in the twentieth century and now prevails in every continent.

Key Points

- International society is an association of member states who not only interact across international borders but also share common purposes, organizations, and standards of conduct.

- There are different historical versions of international society the most important of which is the contemporary global international society.

- In understanding international society it is important to keep in mind contrasting group relations, such as empires, which are far more common historically.

- Political independence is the core value of international society.

Ancient Greece and Renaissance Italy

In an important survey Adam Watson (1992) identifies, among others, the independent city-states of Classical Greece, the states-system of Renaissance Italy, the anti-hegemonial Peace of Westphalia, the Concert of Europe, the globalization of the European states-system, the era of the two superpowers, and the contemporary international society. So we are dealing with a large historical subject of which only a few highlights can be examined in this chapter.

In this section I shall briefly discuss two incipient and important forerunners of the idea and institution of international society: ancient Greece and Renaissance Italy. The first historical manifestation of an international society is ancient Greece, then known as Hellas, which was a geographical area and a cultural unity but not a single political entity or state. Hellenic international society comprised a large number of city-states based geographically on the lower Balkan Peninsula and the many islands in the surrounding Aegean, Adriatic, and Mediterranean seas. The Hellenes thought of themselves as sharing a common ancestry, language, religion, and way of life, all of which distinguished them from neighbours whom they regarded as 'barbarians'—those who did not speak Greek—of whom the Persians were the defining case (Wight 1977: 46–7; 85). Athens was the most famous of the Greek city-states but there were also many others, such as Sparta and Corinth, which taken together formed the first international society in Western history. It is important to emphasize, then, that ancient Greece was not a state: the Greeks referred to themselves as Hellenes. Hellenic international society consisted of city-states which were more or less independent of each other but shared a common culture that was essential to their cohesion as an international society. Furthermore, as indicated, the ancient Greeks sharply distinguished Hellas from neighbouring non-Greek 'barbarians', such as the Persians, with whom they had political relations but no cultural affinities or political association.

There were extensive and elaborate relations between the city-states of Hellas. Their religion, customs, traditions, and politics were similar even though each city-state had its own identity, ceremonies, cults, oracles, and political arrangements.

Box 2.3.	**Approximate Chronology of International Society**
500–100 BC	Ancient Greek or Hellenic
1300–1500	Renaissance Italian
1500–1650	Early Modern European
1650–1950	European cum Western
1950–	Global

The Oracle at Delphi was consulted as a source of authority in disputes between city-states. The ancient Greeks evolved a special political vocabulary that included 'reconciliation', 'truce', 'convention', 'alliance', 'coalition', 'arbitration', 'treaty', 'peace', among other translated words. They had a concept of neutrality which was expressed by a word that translates 'to stay quiet' (Nicolson 1954: 3–14). They did not possess an institution of diplomacy based on resident ambassadors which was an invention of the Italian Renaissance. They nevertheless developed a comparable institution, known as proxeny, which served the same basic function and involved local residents from other Greek cities (Wight 1977: 53–6).

Whether there existed an international society as defined above by Hedley Bull, of which the Greek cities were self-consciously members, is less clear and more controversial. The ancient Greeks did not articulate a body of international law because they could not conceive of the *polis*—the city-state political communities in which they lived—as having rights and obligations in relation to other city-states on some basis of rough equality (Wight 1977: 51) The ancient Greek city-states were politically self-contained even though they were based on a common culture and religion; they were not part of a larger political association consisting, for example, of a common body of international law. Their international society, to the extent that it existed, was cultural–religious rather than legal–political.

Even though the ancient Greeks had no explicit conception of international law as such, they did nevertheless recognize that certain principles ordained by the gods or dictated by practical reality should govern the conduct of international affairs between the city-states of Hellas. Treaties were under the special custody of Zeus, the all-powerful ruler of gods and men, and it was considered an offence to break a treaty without a recognized justification, or to abandon an ally in the middle of a military campaign. According to Harold Nicolson (1954: 5), among the ancient Greeks 'there seems . . . to have existed a religious sanction, mitigating the unrestrained barbarities of war and analogous to our Geneva Convention'. That analogy might be misplaced because the Geneva Conventions are an elaborate and explicit body of international law. But narrow expediency and strict opportunism in both war and foreign policy were considered wrong: it was immoral to engage in a surprise military attack; atrocities were associated with the conduct expected of barbarians but not Greeks. Some states, such as Sparta, were censured for their diplomatic unreliability. And apart from the laws and customs which obtained among the cities of Hellas, according to Nicolson (p. 10) the Greeks did dimly recognize the existence of certain standards of conduct which applied to all mankind, civilized and barbarian alike.

These practices obviously come close to Hedley Bull's concept and so it is not surprising that ancient Greece is often seen as the first significant international society in the Western tradition. But it should again be emphasized that the Greeks did not operate with a concept of equal sovereignty. Some states clearly were more equal than others: there were a few major powers, such as Athens and Sparta, and many lesser powers who often became entangled in their rivalries, coalitions, and wars. Minor states were not the equals of major powers. That is made clear by Thucydides in his account of the Peloponnesian war (431–404 BC) between Athens and Sparta which polarized Greek international society. In a famous dialogue the people of Melos, a small city-state, appeal for justice from the powerful Athenians, who have presented them with an ultimatum. But the Athenians spurn this appeal with the response that justice between states depends on equality of power: 'the strong do what they have the power to do and the weak accept what they have to accept . . . This is the safe rule—to stand up to one's equals, to behave with deference towards one's superiors, and to treat one's inferiors with moderation'. (Thucydides, trans. Warner 1972: 402; 407). Here is the classic statement of the political ethics of Realism in the Western tradition (see Ch. 6).

Hellas was finally overwhelmed by imperial Macedonia, which was a continental state based on the Balkan peninsula. Even the greatest power in the ancient Greek world, Athens, lacked the power to withstand the Macedonian bid for supremacy over the Hellenes. That ushered in an age of hierarchy and empire in the relations of political communities in that part of the world. The Romans, who eventually displaced the Macedonians, developed an even greater empire in the course of conquering, occupying, and ruling most of Europe and a large part of the Middle East and North Africa. Although the Romans recognized a primitive law of nations (*jus gentium*) it was not an express law for independent or sovereign states. Rome was the only sovereign and its relations with all other political communities in its domain were imperial rather than international. Instead of dialogue and conciliation between independent states, under the Roman *imperium* there was only the alternative of obedience or revolt.

After a long period of decline the (Western) empire at Rome disintegrated in the fourth century AD under the impact of 'barbarian' assaults from the imperial peripheries. It was eventually succeeded by a theocracy—that is, a government based on organized religion, in this case Latin Christendom which was one of two successor empires to that of Rome. The (Eastern) empire at Constantinople— which also was a theocracy—was not overthrown but lived on for another thousand years in the incarnation of Greek—i.e. Orthodox—Christianity (Byzantium). It was finally destroyed in the mid-fifteenth century by the Ottoman Turks, a rising Muslim imperial state. In North Africa the Roman empire was eventually succeeded, after the passing of several centuries, by rising Islamic states; that same area came to be dominated much later by the Ottoman empire. The Middle Ages were thus an age of empire, and the relations and conflicts of different empires, and not an age of international society based on sovereign states.

Medieval Europe in the West, which lasted for about a thousand years from the year 500 until about 1500, has been called a *Respublica Christiana*: a universal society based on a joint structure of religious authority (*sacerdotium*) and political authority (*regnum*) which gave at least minimal unity and cohesion to Europeans whatever their language and wherever their homeland happened to be (Wight 1977: 47). That at least was the formal arrangement acknowledged in medieval political theory (Gierke 1987: 13) In practice, of course, medieval Europe was fragmented along feudal lines at both the regional and local level of society. Medieval Europeans had a customary political loyalty to their immediate feudal superiors in those numerous local communities in which the vast majority lived out their lives. Their loyalty to the king (or in other words the secular state) was weak. Medieval Europeans as a whole nevertheless did have a customary religious obedience to the (Western) Church which was an overarching hierarchy of bishops and priests headed by the Bishop of Rome, the Pope. The Pope could also assert, and occasionally he did assert, his vocation as judge in disputes between secular rulers. Even as late as the start of the early modern period (1500–1650) the Pope was still revered in many parts of Europe and periodically he performed the role of a mediator between sovereign rulers, as when Pope Innocent IV settled the division of the newly discovered American continent and surrounding oceans between Spain and Portugal.

In the course of time, however, the European kings beat down the feudal barons and challenged the Pope and in that way they became state defenders against internal disorder and external intervention or threat. This political transformation is perfectly summarized by Martin Wight (1986: 25): 'The common man's inner circle of loyalty expanded, his outer circle of loyalty shrank, and the two met and coincided in a doubly definite circle between, where loyalty before had been vague. Thus the modern state came into existence; a narrower and at the same time a stronger unit of loyalty than medieval Christendom.' The medieval ecclesiastical–political order began to unravel during the sixteenth century under the impact of the Protestant Reformation and the new political theology of Martin Luther which enhanced the authority of kings and the legitimacy of their kingdoms. By that time the papacy itself had long since become a state and indeed a significant power: one among several rival Italian powers (Burckhardt 1958: 120–42). The Renaissance papacy, infamous for nepotism and corruption, nevertheless went on to contribute innovations in diplomacy, such as resident ambassadors and rules for the diplomatic corps at Rome. It is one of the curious paradoxes of European history that the papacy acted not only to resist and undermine but also to foster the institution and expansion of early modern international society.

The second noteworthy historical experiment in the evolution of international society involved the small states of the Italian Renaissance which were the first to break free from the medieval empire and flourished in northern Italy between the fourteenth and the sixteenth centuries. The Renaissance was an enlightenment in the arts and sciences launched by the recovery of ancient learning, particularly that of Greece and Rome, which had been kept alive by Arabic scholars in the Muslim world during the Middle Ages. In inventing the Renaissance the Italians also invented the modern independent state, or *stato*, of which the most prominent examples were Venice, Florence, Milan, and the Papal states. They were usually based on a city and its environs—although they sometimes extended farther afield, as in the case of the Venetian republic which occupied extensive territories along the northern and eastern Adriatic Sea. By instituting their own free-standing political systems the new Italian men of the *stato* were of course defying and breaking free from medieval religious–political authority (Burckhardt 1958: 26–44). The republic of Venice, the predominant trading state of that era, brought many diplomatic practices and institutions of international society to Europe having acquired them from their political and trading relations with Byzantium. The Venetian republic set the standard for other Italian states, later for France and Spain, and eventually for Europe as a whole (Nicolson 1954: 24).

The conviction that the interests of the state and the conduct of statecraft must be guided by a separate political ethics was given a free rein by the Italians. That Realist kind of political thinking based on what we would term 'power politics' and the 'national interest' came to be known as reason of state and later as *realpolitik* in which the morality of the state and the ethics of statecraft is distinguished from universal religious ethics or common morality and is elevated above them (Vincent 1982: 74). The Italian city-states did nevertheless institute among themselves for about a century (1420–1527) a social order based on diplomatic dialogue. The Renaissance Italians also had an acute insight into the importance of the balance of power for maintaining international order among themselves. But the agreements they made were all too often based on expediency, which was an inadequate foundation for the development of a permanent international society among themselves. It also encouraged intervention by external powers in the support of one Italian state (or combination of states) against another, which eventually destroyed the society of Italian states and put in its place a system of foreign domination from across the Alps.

In the end the Italian city-states were too small, too weak, and too divided to defend themselves against the far larger territorial states which were being politically engineered by ambitious rulers in Western Europe. France or Spain by themselves were as large as all the Italian states put together. The Italian states were thus confronted by a new and altogether more dangerous external challenge to their independence than had ever come from among themselves. They might have resisted the new territorial states more effectively had they been able to unite politically and militarily into one large

---

Box 2.4. Renaissance Theories of Statecraft

Statecraft was theorized by Machiavelli (1469–1527), particularly in his classic study of *The Prince*, as an instrumental foreign policy outlook in which political virtue was equated with astuteness in the development and employment of state power, and political vice was a naïve (i.e. Christian) faith in justice. Honour, glory, fortune, necessity, and above all virtue—in the strictly secular sense of adroit statecraft—are central ideas for Machiavelli and other Renaissance political commentators (such as Francesco Guicciardini the political historian of Florence). These ideas form an important part of what has come to be known as the classical theory of realism (Angelo 1969: ch. 7).

---

territorial state of their own. Machiavelli (1965) called for a united Italy in the early years of the sixteenth century, and devoted much thought to how it might be brought about not only politically but also militarily in a book on the art of war. But Italian rulers were unable or unwilling to do that probably owing to the exceptionally well-entrenched rivalries between their various city-states and the extent of their personal or dynastic ambitions. In the sixteenth century they were overwhelmed by the Austro-Spanish Habsburgs and the French whose long hegemony over the Italian peninsula did not finally end until the mid-nineteenth century.

Key Points

- Two forerunner international societies were ancient Greece and Renaissance Italy.

- Two empires which contrasted with these international societies and also served as a historical bridge between them were the Roman empire and its direct Christian successor in the West, the medieval *Respublica Christiana*.

- Greek international society was based on the *polis* and Hellenic culture.

- Italian international society was based on the *stato* and the strong urban identities and rivalries of Renaissance Italians.

- These small international societies were eventually overwhelmed by neighbouring hegemonic powers.

Robert H. Jackson

European International Society

Medieval cathedrals took many years, sometimes centuries, to reach their final form: similarly, the classical European international society which began to be constructed as early as the sixteenth and seventeenth centuries was only completed in the eighteenth and nineteenth. The modern territorial state upon which it was based was a derivative of the Italian Renaissance and the Protestant Reformation. The rulers of the new European states took their cue from the Italians and, as a result, the arts and sciences of the Renaissance, including the art of statecraft, spread to all of Western Europe. The political theology of Martin Luther—with its 'impulse towards disengaging political elements from religious modes of thought' (Wolin 1960: 143)—also disengaged the political legitimacy of the state from the religious sanction of the medieval *Respublica Christiana*. Machiavelli and Luther are important architects of the modern society of states.

In the modern era secular politics, and particularly the politics of the state and the art of statecraft, was liberated from the moral inhibitions and religious constraints of the medieval Christian world. The sovereign state now shaped the relations of the main political groupings of Europe, and those relations were now recognizable international relations. Many European rulers were ambitious to expand their territories, while many others were anxious to defend their realms against external encroachments. As a result international rivalries developed which often resulted in wars and the enlargement of some countries at the expense of others. At various times France, Spain, Austria, England, Holland, Denmark, Sweden, Poland, Prussia, Russia, and other states of the new European international society were at war. Some wars were spawned by the Protestant Reformation which profoundly divided the European Christian population in the sixteenth and seventeenth centuries. But other wars (increasingly a majority) were provoked by the mere existence of independent states whose rulers resorted to war as a principal means of defending their interests, pursuing their ambitions, and, if possible, expanding their territorial holdings. War became an international institution for resolving conflicts between sovereign states.

The Catholic Habsburgs, who controlled a sprawling dynastic state which comprised extensive disjointed territories in Austria, Spain, the Netherlands, Italy, Bohemia, Hungary, and other parts of Western and Eastern Europe, tried—in the name of the *Respublica Christiana*—to impose their *imperium* on a Europe that was fracturing into religious-cum-political communities, some Catholic and some Protestant, under the impact of the Protestant Reformation and the Catholic Counter-Reformation. That bid for European supremacy led to the devastating Thirty Years War (1618–48) in which the Habsburgs were defeated and peace treaties were negotiated at Westphalia in 1648 (Wedgwood 1992). That was not the first gamble for political mastery in Europe and it would not be the last. But after 1648 the language of international justification would gradually change, away from Christian unity and religious orthodoxy and towards international diversity based on a secular society of sovereign states. The treaties of Westphalia and those of Utrecht (1713) still referred to the *Respublica Christiana*, but they were the last to do that. For what had come into historical existence in the meantime was a secular European society of states in which overarching political and religious authority was no longer in existence in any substantive sense.

The Reformation and Counter-Reformation conflicts made it clear by the mid-seventeenth century that Protestant states and Catholic states must coexist. The fundamental problem of their relations was thus recognized to be political and not religious. The war itself was not fought along religious lines: it was fought along political–territorial lines with some Catholic states—most notably France—aligned with Protestant states such as Sweden in an alliance against the Catholic Habsburgs. The anti-Habsburg alliance also demonstrated the doctrine of the balance of power: the organization of a coalition of states whose joint military power is intended to operate as a counterweight against bids for political hegemony and empire. The doctrine of reason of state took precedence over any residual obligation to support *Respublica Christiana* which was now seen in many quarters as merely the ideology of one side in the conflict. That secular move away from religious legitimacy has been a cornerstone of international society ever since. The treaties of Westphalia form-

Box 2.5. **Westphalian International Society**

Westphalian international society was based on three principles. The first principle was *rex est imperator in regno suo* (the king is emperor in his own realm). This norm specifies that sovereigns are not subject to any higher political authority. Every king is independent and equal to every other king. The second principle was *cujus regio, ejus religio* (the ruler determines the religion of his realm). This norm specifies that outsiders have no right to intervene in a sovereign jurisdiction on religious grounds. The third principle was the balance of power: that was intended to prevent any hegemon from arising and dominating everybody else.

Box 2.6. **Grotius and International Law**

The emerging idea of international law was spelled out by Hugo Grotius, a Dutch Protestant diplomat and philosopher, whose Laws of War and Peace (1625) provided an intellectual foundation for the subject that was enormously influential and is still regarded as a founding text. Grotius hoped to restrict war and expand peace by clarifying standards of conduct which were insulated against all religious doctrines and could therefore govern the relations of all independent states, Protestant and Catholic alike.

ally recognized the existence of separate sovereignties in one international society. Religion was no longer a legal ground for intervention or war among European states. The settlement thus created a new international covenant based on state sovereignty which displaced the medieval idea of *Respublica Christiana*. The seeds of state sovereignty and non-intervention that those seventeenth-century statespeople planted would eventually evolve into the Charter of the United Nations, the Geneva Conventions, and other contemporary bodies of international law.

The procedural starting point of modern European international society, speaking very generally, is thus usually identified with the Peace of Westphalia. That at least is the conventional view. Martin Wight (1977: 150–2) argues, somewhat to the contrary, that Westphalia is the coming of age but not the coming into existence of European international society, the beginnings of which he traces to the Council of Constance (1415) which, in effect, transformed the papacy into a quasi-secular political power with its own territory. F. H. Hinsley (1967: 153) argues, on the other side, that modern international society only fully emerged in the eighteenth century, because prior to that time the *Respublica Christiana* was still in existence. But however we choose to look at it, the multinational treaties of Westphalia, and those which came after, were conceived as the foundation of secular international law or what came to be known as the 'public law of Europe' (Hinsley 1967: 168).

Adam Watson (1992: ch. 17) captures the Westphalian moment very aptly: 'the charter of a Europe permanently organized on an anti-hegemonial principle.' That European society of states had

several prominent characteristics which can be summarized.

- First, it consisted of member states whose political independence and juridical equality was acknowledged by international law.

- Second, every member state was legitimate in the eyes of all other members.

- Third, the relations between sovereign states were managed, increasingly, by a professional corps of diplomats and conducted by means of an organized multilateral system of diplomatic communication.

- Fourth, the religion of international society was still Christian but that was increasingly indistinguishable from the culture which was European.

- Finally, a balance of power between member states was conceived which was intended to prevent any one state from making a bid for hegemony.

The anti-hegemonial notion of a countervailing alliance of major powers aimed at preserving the freedom of all member states and maintaining the pluralist European society of states as a whole was only worked out by trial and error and fully theorized much later. The greatest historical threat to the European balance of power before the twentieth century was posed by Napoleon's bid for continental hegemony (1795–1815). British and later American foreign policy can be read as historical lessons in attempting to preserve or restore the balance of power. In the eighteenth and nineteenth centuries Britain often played the role of the defender of the balance of power by adding military (especially naval) weight to the coalition which formed against the hegemon, most notably in the case of post-revolutionary Napoleonic France. The

United States played a similar role in the Second World War against Nazi Germany and Imperial Japan, and in the cold war against Communist Russia. Insofar as both Britain and the United States accepted and indeed defended the principles of international society against contrary revolutionary ideologies, they could not themselves be regarded as hegemons in the classical political meaning of the term.

In sum: the first fully articulated conception of the theory and practice of international society as an explicit covenant with a legal and political foundation is worked out in Europe among its sovereign states. Edmund Burke, with his eye on the alleged threat posed to monarchical and dynastic Europe by republican and revolutionary France, went so far as to refer to eighteenth-century Europe as 'virtually one great state having the same basis of general law, with some diversity of provincial customs and local establishments'. Burke saw European international society as based on two fundamental principles: a 'law of neighbourhood'—recognition of neighbouring states and respect for their independence—and 'rules of prudence'—the responsibility of statespeople not only to safeguard the national interest but also preserve international society (Raffety 1928: 156–61). Similar ideas were expressed by many European publicists of the day and there is little doubt that modern international society is rooted in the political culture and political thought of the European peoples.

Key Points

- The Peace of Westphalia was the first explicit expression of a European society of states which served as a precedent for all subsequent developments of international society.

- That international society displaced and succeeded the medieval *Respublica Christiana*.

- It was the external aspect of the development of modern secular states which had to find an orderly and legitimate way to conduct mutual relations without submitting to either superior authority or hegemonic domination from abroad.

- It was the first completely explicit international society with its own diplomatic institutions, formal body of law, and enunciated practices of prudential statecraft, including the balance of power.

The Globalization of International Society

The spread of European political control beyond Europe which began in the late fifteenth century and only came to an end in the early twentieth century proved to be an expansion not only of European imperialism but also, later, of international society (Bull and Watson). The history of modern Europe is—in very significant part—a history of political and economic rivalry and particularly war between sovereign states. European rivalries were conducted wherever European ambitions and power could be projected—i.e. eventually on a global scale. European states entered into competitions with each other to penetrate and control economically desirable and militarily useful areas in other parts of the world. Until the nineteenth century large-scale wars were fought by those states outside Europe. Non-European territories and populations came under the control of European governments by conquest or occupation, and were sometimes transferred from one European state to another as happened in the case of French Canada which the British annexed at the end of their successful Seven Years War with France (1756–63). However, a 'remarkable achievement' of the nineteenth-century Concert of Europe—a balance of power coalition originally formed by the great powers that defeated Napoleon (Britain, Austria, Prussia, and Russia)—was their avoidance of war in the course of their competitive expansion outside Europe—in marked contrast to 'the incessant acts of war against each other overseas in previous centuries' (Watson 1992: 272). International law, diplomacy, and the balance of power thus came to be applied around the world and not only in Europe or the West. By the late nineteenth century even isolated and previously inaccessible continents, like the interior of Africa, were under the jurisdiction and manipulation of European powers.

Not every non-Western country fell under the political control of a Western imperial state. But those countries which escaped were still obliged to accept international law and follow the diplomatic practices of international society. The Ottoman empire (Turkey), which geographically and ethnically was a partly European state, had for centuries been in close contact with European states but had never accepted the conduct requirements of international society. Instead, the Ottomans insisted on treating European states on their own Islamic terms. Although for several centuries the Ottoman empire regularly intervened in Europe with the aim, usually, of undercutting their Habsburg enemies, they held aloof from the conventions of Christian and later European international society with regard to which, as Moslems, they considered themselves superior. At the height of their power between the mid-fifteenth century and the turn of the seventeenth century the Ottomans were able to dictate terms to European states. By the mid-nineteenth century, however, they had long been in decline and were obliged by what were now clearly superior European powers to accept international law and other dictates of Western states. Japan elected to do the same a little later although without the same compulsion and humiliation. Japan successfully acquired the persona and substance of a modern power and by the early twentieth century had defeated the Russian empire in a major war and had become a colonial power herself. China was subjected to extensive territorial encroachments by European states, the United States, and Japan, and did not acquire full membership in international society until 1945 at which time China became a permanent member of the UN Security Council. Most other non-Western political systems were not able to resist Western imperialism and lost their independence as a result. That proved to be the case throughout South Asia, South-East Asia, most of the Middle East, and virtually all of Africa, the Caribbean, and the Pacific.

The second stage of the globalization of international society was via reactive nationalism and anticolonialism. In that reaction indigenous political leaders made claims for decolonization and independence based on European and American ideas of self-determination. That involved a further claim for subsequent equal membership of a universal international society open to all cultures and civilizations without discrimination (Jackson 1990). That 'revolt against the West', as Hedley Bull put it,

Box 2.7. The Right of Self-Determination

The principle of legitimacy that sanctioned decolonization was spelled out in the celebrated 1960 UN General Assembly Declaration on the Granting of Independence to Colonial Countries and Peoples (Resolution 1514) which declared not only that 'all peoples have the right to self-determination' and thus membership of international society but also that 'the further continuation of colonialism . . . is a crime which constitutes a violation of the Charter of the United Nations'.

was the main vehicle by which international society expanded after the Second World War. In a short period of some twenty years, beginning with the independence of India and Pakistan in 1947, most colonies in Asia and Africa became sovereign states and full members of the United Nations. European decolonization in the Third World more than tripled the membership of the society of states from about 50 to over 160.

The final act of European decolonization which completed the globalization of international society was the dissolution of the Soviet Union at the end of the cold war. Here self-determination was based not on overseas colonies but, rather, on the internal borders of the former Russian (Tsarist) empire which the communists took over and preserved after their revolution in 1917. Those old Russian imperial frontiers thus became new international boundaries. The dissolution of the Soviet Union together with the simultaneous breakup of Yugoslavia, Ethiopia, and Czechoslovakia expanded the membership of international society to well over 180. Today, for the first time in world history, there is one continuous international society of global extent—without any intervening gaps of isolated aboriginal government or imposed colonial jurisdiction and also without any external hegemons—based on local territorial sovereignty and a common set of rules the most important of which are embodied by the United Nations Charter.

Key Points

- Through their rivalries and wars European states developed the military organization and technology to project their power on a global scale and few non-European political systems could block their expansion.

- European international law, diplomacy, and the balance of power came to be applied around the world.

- Indigenous non-Western nationalists eventually went into revolt and claimed a right of self-

determination which led to decolonization and the expansion of international society.

- That was followed by a further expansion after the cold war brought about by the disintegration of the Soviet Union and several other communist states.

- Today, for the first time in history, there is one inclusive international society of global extent.

Problems of Global International Society

The core values and norms of the contemporary global society of states are international peace and security, state sovereignty, self-determination, non-intervention, non-discrimination and generally the sanctity, integrity, and inviolability of all existing states regardless of their level of development, form of government, political ideology, pattern of culture or any other domestic characteristic or condition. We can speak of these values and norms as embodying and expressing the global covenant of contemporary international society. This social framework exists fundamentally to validate and underwrite the sovereignty of the member states of global international society. State sovereignty, arguably the main pillar, is universally affirmed.

But this global construct also involves problems and predicaments some of which are unprecedented in the history of international society. Only the most important can be discussed briefly as a conclusion to this chapter.

First, there is a noteworthy absence of a common underlying culture to support global international society which cuts across all the major cultures and civilizations. There is no cultural support, comparable to Christianity or European civilization which helped to sustain European cum Western international society. Perhaps the norms and values of free markets, human rights, liberal democracy, and the rule of law can provide that support. They are avowed and generally observed by the vanguard developed states of the present day, such as the members of the OECD. But the fact remains that other important members of international society, such as many states of East Asia and many Islamic states, dispute some of these norms and values. Russia may yet revert to that position too.

Second, if the global covenant is going to be supported in the future, that support is likely to be widely forthcoming only if its core norms and values respond to the interests and concerns of the vast majority if not all the members of contemporary international society. That probably requires that they be divorced or at least distanced from the norms and values of any particular culture, including that of the West. All members still clearly and publicly avow the above-noted core norms and values of international society most of which are incorporated into regional international organizations, such as the Charter of the Organization for African Unity (Brownlie 1971: 2–8).

Third, the regional diversity of contemporary global international society is far more pronounced than that of European international society or any other previous society of states. That is conducive to international pluralism based on groupings of states, such as South-East Asia, Western Europe, Latin America, or Africa, which share a geographical region and may also have cultural affinities and an interconnected economic life. To accommodate successfully that regional–cultural pluralism the global covenant cannot be encumbered with intrusive norms and values of a particular culture, including those of the Western democracies.

Fourth, since 1945 there has been a definite freezing and sanctifying of international boundaries as the globe has been enclosed by local sovereign jurisdiction based on self-determination. That has evidently discouraged states from engaging in acts of aggression or armed intervention in other states with a view to territorial expansion which were not uncommon practices of historical European international society between the members of which recurrent wars were fought over territory and other issues. However, that has also created a barrier to the formation of new jurisdictions by effectively prohibiting a reshuffling of certain territorial jurisdictions of international society in response to changing socio-political identities and consequent demands for national self-determination, such as witnessed in Croatia and Bosnia-Herzegovina.

Fifth, the doctrine of non-intervention has created an inversion of the traditional security dilemma in many states, particularly post-colonial and post-communist states. In those states the security threat is more likely to come from within: the prevailing pattern of warfare is internal rather than international (Holsti 1996). In more than a few sub-Saharan African countries, for example, the main security threat comes from armed rebels or from the government, or both, which often hold citizens hostage in what are referred to as failed or collapsed states (Zartman 1995). The doctrine of non-intervention makes it difficult if not impossible for international society to address the problem. It is also difficult to institute some kind of international trusteeship for obviously failed states, such as Somalia, owing to the fact that the institution and law of trusteeship which currently exists is designed for colonies and not for independent countries. International society currently has no generally accepted procedures for dealing with the problem of failed states.

Sixth, the current global international society, although based on formally equal state sovereignty, in fact contains huge substantive inequalities between member states, particularly between the rich OECD states and the poorest Asian and African Third World States. That socio-economic disparity has led to an unprecedented theory and practice of international aid in which rich states are called upon to help ameliorate poverty in poor states. That has changed the ethos of international society: the traditional ethos was national self-reliance and reciprocity; the new ethos when it comes to poor states is international benevolence and non-reciprocity. International material assistance is still largely voluntary, but poor states and their advocates have endeavoured to make it obligatory for rich states to devote a certain share of their GNP to international aid. Global international society contains a normative asymmetry of non-reciprocal rights and responsibilities which previous international societies of more or less equally developed states did not contain.

> **Box 2.8. UN Charter of Economic Rights and Duties of States**
>
> 'Every State has the right to benefit from the advances and developments in science and technology . . . Every State has the duty to co-operate in promoting . . . the welfare and living standards of all peoples, in particular those of developing countries . . . International co-operation for development is the shared goal and common duty of all States . . . developed countries should grant generalised preferential, non-reciprocal and non-discriminatory treatment to developing countries . . .' (Charter of the Economic Rights and Duties of States, UN General Assembly, 1974).

Seventh, global international society is perhaps evolving into a world society, both organizationally and normatively, which differs significantly in several important respects from previous international societies. It involves cosmopolitan norms, such as human rights, which sanctify and indemnify human beings regardless of their citizenship. It involves global norms, such as environmental protection, which place new responsibilities, legal as well as moral, on sovereign states, particularly those states with the greatest capacity to cause pollution. It involves the rebirth of minorities, the awakening of aboriginal groups, and the rise of gender in world politics. And it involves a rapidly expanding role for non-governmental organizations (NGOs), such as Greenpeace or Amnesty International, which are assuming growing importance in world politics. NGOs have always existed, of course, but they are more prominent today than they have been since the sovereign state gained ascendancy over all other political and social groups in the seventeenth century.

Finally, this tendency for international society to evolve into a world society raises important questions about the continuing primacy of state sovereignty. Many of these issues are raised in other chapters in this book and cannot be dealt with at length here. Suffice it to say, by way of conclusion, that state sovereignty has been a defining characteristic of international politics for 350 years. However, state sovereignty is not a static institution. On the contrary, it is a dynamic institution and it continues to evolve. For example, at one time dynastic families held state sovereignty, but today it is the collective entitlement of entire national populations. At one time sovereign states had a right to initiate aggressive war in pursuit of their self-defined interests, but that right has been denied and extinguished in the twentieth century. At one time sovereign states could control foreign populated territory as colonial dependencies. That right has also been extinguished. Many other examples of state sovereignty as a dynamic, evolving institution could also be given. But perhaps these examples are sufficient to make us sceptical about claims that world politics is moving beyond state sovereignty. It is far more likely that state sovereignty is evolving yet again.

However, it must be emphasized that historical change is ongoing, the dust is swirling all about, and it will be some time before anyone can get a clear view of this fundamentally important issue. But if I had to bet on the shape of world politics at the end of the twenty-first century my money would be on the prognosis that our great grandchildren will be living in a world which is still defined fundamentally by state sovereignty and probably even by existing states on the map. But I would not bet that sovereign states then will be the same institutions that they are today. History will see to that.

Key Points

- Today international society is a global social framework of shared norms and values based on state sovereignty.
- An important manifestation of that social framework is the UN Charter.
- But those shared norms and values have provoked unprecedented problems and predicaments of contemporary world politics.
- There is a current debate about the future of state sovereignty and thus also about the future of the contemporary global international society.

QUESTIONS

1. What does international society tell us about the political values and inclinations of human beings around the world?

2. What is the core value of international society?

3. Briefly discuss and evaluate Hedley Bull's concept of international society.

4. Compare the international society of ancient Greece with that of Renaissance Italy.

5. Discuss the Peace of Westphalia as a new stage in the evolution of international society.

6. Why has an originally European society of states been generally accepted around the world?

7. Can a global international society which contains both extremely rich members and extremely poor members be viable over the longer term?

8. Is global international society part of the solution or part of the problem when it comes to the issue of failed states?

9. Does international society based on state sovereignty have any future?

GUIDE TO FURTHER READING

Watson, Adam, *The Evolution of International Society* (London: Routledge, 1992). The definitive study of the history of various international societies and rival or related empires.

Bull, Hedley, and Watson, Adam (eds.), *The Expansion of International Society* (Oxford: Clarendon Press, 1984). The only elaborate account of the historical expansion of European society to the rest of the world.

Armstrong, David, *Revolution and World Order* (Oxford: Clarendon, 1993). An important study of revolutionary states in international society.

Hamilton, K., and Langhorne, R., *The Practice of Diplomacy* (London: Routledge, 1995). An excellent history of the evolution of the idea and institution of diplomacy.

Stern, Geoffrey, *The Structure of International Society* (London: Pinter, 1995). An outstanding recent textbook on international society.

Lyons, Gene M., and Mastanduno, Michael (eds.), *Beyond Westphalia?* (Baltimore and London: Johns Hopkins University Press, 1995). A recent exploration of the question whether international society is evolving beyond a society of sovereign states.

3 International History 1900–1945

Susan L. Carruthers

READER'S GUIDE

This chapter seeks to identify and suggest explanations for the key transformations in international relations between 1900 and 1945. These years were marked by massive upheaval. Within 45 years, the world experienced two Total Wars, a global economic slump, and the ending of four major empires, with Tsarist Russia being overthrown by a Bolshevik Revolution. This chapter identifies turmoil within Europe, and its eclipse as the arbiter of international affairs, as the most significant feature of the first half of the twentieth century. By 1945, Europe was shattered by its long crisis. The Continent was divided between two newly emergent superpowers—the United States and the USSR, both of which had primarily concentrated on their own internal development in the inter-war years. How do we account for the decline of Europe? The chapter looks both at developments within the continent and further afield: what role did the US and the USSR play between the wars, and how did Japan rise to prominence in the Far East? The chapter concludes with an examination of the historical controversy surrounding the origins of the Second World War, which dramatically brought about Europe's collapse.

Introduction

The year 1900 forms a convenient, but not necessarily the most helpful, starting point for an analysis of **modern** international history. Eric Hobsbawm has suggested that the twentieth century really only began in 1914, with a cataclysmic war which swept away the nineteenth century status quo, whereby a handful of European states dominated the affairs of the world (Hobsbawm 1994: 3). Before the First World War, Europe had not experienced a major war involving most of its dominant states for a century. The world had **never** experienced a war which dragged in so many different countries and peoples. Not only was this war truly a 'world war', but it was also the century's first '**Total War**', during which the major protagonists mobilized virtually their whole populations—whether as soldiers at the front line or as workers on the 'Home Front'.

The consequences of the First World War were enormous. After over four years of war, the diplomats and political leaders who gathered at Versailles in 1919 to forge a peace settlement were adamant that their endeavours must not just resolve the immediate post-war issues (what to do with the vanquished countries, especially Germany, and with the Austro-Hungarian and Ottoman empires which had collapsed during the war) but also make war impossible in the future. 'Never again' was the overwhelming popular sentiment. And yet only twenty years after the **Treaty of Versailles**, another world war was under way—this one even more global in its reach than the first. The years 1900–45 thus mark the most destructive period in human history. Not only did human beings kill one another in greater numbers than in any other span of four decades, but they also found more barbaric methods of doing so: from the Nazi genocide of six million Jews carried out in the concentration camps, to America's dropping of atomic bombs on the Japanese cities of Hiroshima and Nagasaki in August 1945.

The world of 1945 was almost unrecognizable from that of 1900 (as Boxes 3.1 and 3.2 suggest). The story of these years is, overwhelmingly, one of disintegration. A series of empires collapsed in Austro-Hungary, Turkey, and Russia in the course of World War I. Imperial China, long subject to foreign incursions, also slid into prolonged civil war. The international economy collapsed after the **Wall Street Crash** of 1929. And, partly as a result of the ensuing Depression, democracies crumbled in the 1930s, while extreme right-wing dictatorships flourished in Germany, Italy, Spain, Japan, and many countries of Latin America. The culmination of these turbulent years, which with hindsight we call the 'inter-war period', was another Total War which left few of the world's citizens entirely untouched.

The most globally significant transformation during the first half of the twentieth century was the effective collapse of Europe as the world's dominant continent. A world dominated in 1900 by a

---

Box 3.1. Key Features of the World in 1900

- European states dominate the global pattern of international relations

  1 in 4 of world's population lives in Europe (approximately 400m. of a 1600m. total)

  the European 'great powers' (Britain, France, Italy, Germany, Austria-Hungary, and Russia) have a concentration of military power, as well as dominating world trade

- Colonial empires of European states (especially Britain and France, but also Belgium, the Netherlands, and Portugal) cover much of the world

  approximately 500m. people live under European colonial rule

  search for colonies continues; especially Germany in Africa, and Tsarist Russia in Asia

- Several territorial empires in a protracted state of collapse

  the Habsburg empire (covering Austro-Hungary and much of central Europe and the Balkans)

  the Ottoman empire (centred on Turkey, and encompassing much of the Middle East and the Balkans)

  Tsarist Russia

  Imperial China

- Global capitalist economy

  in 1900 centred primarily on the UK, as the world's largest imperial and trading power, but increasingly under threat

  rapid industrial expansion in North America

  Japan modernizing and industrializing

Box 3.2. **Key Features of the World in 1945**

- prominence of the US and USSR

  US first nuclear superpower, after explosion of atomic bombs on Hiroshima and Nagasaki, August 1945

  US emerges from World War II as major creditor nation, and centre of the international economy

  USSR in economic ruin after war, but Red Army occupies all Eastern and much of Central Europe, to Berlin and beyond

- collapse of Europe

  rapidly divided between East and West; Germany split until 1989

  national economies in ruin; large debts owing to US

  European colonial empires undermined by war; by Japanese overrunning of colonies in South-East Asia

- growing nationalism in the colonial empires

  wartime 'Atlantic Charter' makes commitment to national self-determination

  India seeking independence (achieved in 1947)

  Ho Chi Minh declares Vietnam an independent republic in 1945

- civil war in China

  ended with victory of Mao and establishment of the People's Republic of China in 1949

  together with the population of the USSR, one third of the world now lives under communist rule

---

small group of economically prosperous and populous European states, whose rule stretched over much of the globe, by 1945 had been replaced by one in which the major arbiters of international affairs were the two new 'superpowers'—the United States of America and the Soviet Union. Europe, at least temporarily, was in a state of ruin, and indebtedness, with Eastern and Central Europe lying under Soviet occupation. The Second World War finally brought about Europe's disintegration. But in fact that war only underlined a process which had been going on for several decades. Many historians would argue that the Second World War was essentially a continuation of the First, and that Europe was not so much suffering a '**Twenty Year Crisis**' (E. H. Carr's description of the period 1919–39 (Carr 1939)), as undergoing a '**Thirty Year War**', whose roots stretched back to the 1870s.

The Origins of World War One

Why did Europe lose its predominant place in the world in the years between 1900 and 1945? The answer lies partly in Europe itself and partly beyond. European states fought viciously with one another. However, the continent which had given birth to the Industrial Revolution, and had formed the hub of global financial activity, also faced economic challenges from rapidly industrializing states—most obviously the United States. Similarly, in the Far East, Japan underwent rapid expansion in the early twentieth century, posing a significant economic and military challenge to the European powers' trading and colonial interests in East Asia.

We will consider global economic developments in due course, but first we will examine the **internal roots** of Europe's instability. These are frequently dated back to the 1870s, when the continent's relative tranquillity following the Napoleonic Wars was disturbed by the creation of a single, unified German nation-state.

Germany's Bid for World Power Status

The unified Germany's territorial ambitions rapidly became apparent. Although Bismarck himself had cautioned against further German expansionism, his successors were less circumspect, and sought to assert German parity with the other great powers by acquiring the most important badge of great power status—an overseas empire. **Imperial disputes**

Box 3.3. The 'German Problem'

Germany before Unification

- Until 1871, 'Germany' did not exist in anything like the shape we know it today.
- 'Germany' was a collection of twenty-five states, ranging in size from small principalities to the economically and militarily assertive Prussia with a population of some 30m. (Bavaria, the second largest, contained 5.5m.)
- Some ethnic Germans lived under the sovereignty of other states; as in Alsace-Lorraine, which was part of France, and Schleswig-Holstein, ruled by Denmark.

Unification

- The bringing together of these states, and the annexation of 'foreign' lands containing ethnic Germans, was the work of the Prussian Chancellor Otto von Bismarck.
- Three wars were fought to secure German unification, and to ensure that Prussia predominated to Austria's exclusion: against Denmark (1864) over Schleswig-Holstein; Austria-Hungary (1866); and France (1870) over Alsace-Lorraine.

Germany After Unification

- For the first time in modern history, the centre of Europe was dominated by a single, vast state.
- Germany's population of nearly 67m. (by 1913) was second in size only to the Russian empire.
- Germany underwent rapid industrialization. Germany's coal, iron, and steel production (in the 1870s well below the UK's) outstripped Britain's by 1914
- From 1871 to 1914, the value of Germany's agricultural output doubled; industrial production quadrupled and overseas trade more than tripled.
- With such great reserves of territory, population, military, and industrial strength, Germany had the capacity—and the inclination, many believed—for outward expansion. The birth of a unified Germany thus constituted the birth of 'the German problem'.

---

years of the twentieth century thus saw a hitherto unlikely alliance of Britain, France, and Tsarist Russia merging in an attempt to halt Germany's determined search for territory and markets. The Germans, however, saw themselves not as the aggressors but rather as the victims of an imperial system which operated entirely to their disadvantage: Britain and France dominated Africa, Asia, and the Middle East; Russia, Japan, and Britain competed in China, while the US held sway in Latin America. Between them, these powers appeared to have carved up the international market to their satisfaction. Gaining colonies was thus not solely a matter of prestige or status, but was regarded as an economic imperative for Germany. The main areas of contention were **North Africa**, where clashes occurred with France and Britain over Morocco in 1906 and in 1911, and the **Middle East**, as Germany sought to build a railway from Berlin to Baghdad.

But the European colonial powers had come into conflict over imperial issues before, and these disputes alone are insufficient to explain the war which broke out in July 1914. Historians have fiercely debated the war's origins. Some concur with, others dispute, the verdict of the war's victors—that 'war guilt' belonged to Germany alone. The most famous explication of this view was Fritz Fischer's *Griff nach der Weltmacht* (*Bid for World Power*), published in 1961, which emphasized the extent of Germany's annexationist aims in the war, arguing that the German government deliberately went to war in their pursuit. Other historians have argued that a general war came about more by accident than design, partly due to the way in which military plans had been drawn up. German strategy, drawn up by Count Alfred von Schlieffen, was devised to counter the prospect of Germany fighting a war on two fronts against France and Russia. His plan therefore envisaged a decisive blow against France, before German troops turned to the tardily mobilized Russians. Thus the **'Schlieffen plan'** served to widen the war rapidly, once the opening shots had been fired. Those opening shots were fired, not by Germany, but in Sarajevo at Archduke Franz Ferdinand (the heir to the throne of the Austro-Hungarian empire) by a Serb nationalist. This assassination should alert us to other deep-seated origins of Europe's crisis, and ultimately the war.

were thus an important contributory factor to the outbreak of war in 1914. Certainly, Britain was not keen to see its own position as the world's most powerful trading nation overshadowed by Germany, with whom it was now engaged in fierce naval rivalry. France had equally compelling reasons to fear German expansion. The opening

The 'Eastern Question'

Besides the 'German problem' the other main source of instability in late nineteenth- and early twentieth-century Europe was the so-called **'Eastern Question'**, which arose from the slow collapse of the Ottoman empire. The European great powers each took considerable interest in how the power vacuum that was spreading from the Balkans to the Middle East would be filled. But the peoples over whom the Ottoman dynasty had ruled were also keen to assert, in the age of nationalism, their right to rule themselves. In the Balkans, rival national groups clashed in a series of wars, with the backing of various European great powers. Consequently, the Tsarist Russian empire (although itself in a state of terminal collapse) refused to watch impassively while Austro-Hungary threatened Russia's fellow Slavs in Serbia after the assassination of Franz Ferdinand in June 1914. What might have been a localized incident quickly sparked a general war, as the complicated alliance system built up over the two decades preceding 1914 soon ensured that Austria-Hungary and Germany, on the one side, confronted Britain, France, and Russia on the other. The war was to last for over four years. Much of it was marked by a military stalemate—most vividly, and horrifically, epitomized by the trench-warfare which decimated a generation of young French, British, and German men.

Key Points

- Europe's long-term instability can be traced back to the creation of a unified Germany in the 1870s, which disrupted the balance of power.
- The European powers clashed over imperial issues in the late nineteenth and early twentieth centuries, as Germany sought colonies and markets.
- A number of European dynasties were in a state of collapse, and nationalism was growing, particularly in the Balkans and Central Europe.
- A combination of these tensions ultimately resulted in the First World War.

Peace-Making, 1919: The Versailles Settlement

Post-War Problems

When the war finally ended, the peacemakers who gathered at Versailles in 1919 confronted a daunting set of problems. The war left millions of individual casualties, either through death, injury or the loss of homes and livelihoods. The teetering Austro-Hungarian and Ottoman empires were also victims of the war, while a Bolshevik revolution had overthrown the Tsarist regime in Russia. Had anyone really **won** the war? Certainly the victors' economies, no less than those of the vanquished, were depleted by the strain of four years of Total War. On all sides, the combatants had sought to pursue this war until their enemies were utterly defeated. Total War demanded Total Victory, but the cost of totally defeating an enemy was near ruination of one's own state. The domestic ruin facing France in particular, on whose soil much of the fighting had occurred, added a punitive dimension to the peacemakers' agenda: how could reparations (money, goods, or raw materials) be extracted from Germany to finance domestic reconstruction? How, most critically, could the peacemakers ensure that Germany did not seek to dominate Europe ever again?

It should come as no surprise, given both the intractability of Europe's problems and the diversity of the victorious coalition, that the peacemakers failed to agree amongst themselves on the shape of the post-war order. The principal European victors, Britain and France, concurred over German responsibility for the war, which justified a harsh settlement, but they differed over its terms. However, the guiding force at Versailles was not one (or more) of the European powers, but the President of the United States.

Susan L. Carruthers

President Wilson's 'Fourteen Points'

America had joined the war in its latter stages, and its President provided an idealistic set of principals which he intended should shape the subsequent peace. How was war to be avoided? Woodrow Wilson's 'Fourteen Points' called for a new approach to international diplomacy: 'open covenants, openly arrived at', would replace the old-style secret diplomacy which produced various private inter-state deals over who would gain what territory after the First World War. Wilson also believed that the avoidance of war could be furthered by creating an international organization, based on the principle of **'collective security'** (see Ch. 10). His scheme for a **League of Nations** was premised on the 'peace-loving' member states regarding any threat to the international peace—any violation of the sovereignty of one member by another state—as an act of aggression which ultimately threatened them all, and therefore had to be responded to collectively. Ideally, however, the very existence of the League would serve to ensure that aggressive states desisted from expansionist actions. The League was thus one of the distinctive features of the post-1919 world: the first formalized attempt to create an international body designed to mediate disputes with permanent structures and a codified Charter. Despite its ignominious failure to take assertive action against Japanese, Italian, and German aggression in the 1930s, the League provided a model for the United Nations Organization in 1945.

Self-Determination: The Creation of New States

Just as significant as Wilson's insistence on an international collective security body was his commitment to the principal of **'national self-determination'**. Wilson was an opponent of imperialism, and believed passionately in the right of distinct national groups to govern themselves by being accorded sovereignty over their own territory. To each nation a state: this was Wilson's ideal. However, in practice, the nationalities of those parts of Europe where empires had recently crumbled—especially the Balkans, and Central and Eastern Europe—were not neatly territorially separate from one another. The peacemakers therefore faced a difficult task of drawing the boundaries of the new states of Europe, some of which had never existed before. Often the boundaries reflected uneasy compromises: for example, Czecho-

---

Box 3.4. Wilson's 'Fourteen Points': A Summary

1. Open covenants of peace, openly arrived at; international diplomacy to be carried on publicly.

2. Absolute freedom of navigation on the seas.

3. The removal, as far as possible, of all economic barriers.

4. Disarmament undertaken, and guaranteed, by states to the lowest point consistent with domestic safety

5. A free, open-minded, and impartial adjustment of all colonial claims, based on the principle that the interests of the population concerned must have equal weight with the equitable claims of the government whose title is to be determined.

6. The evacuation of all Russian territory and settlement of questions affecting Russia.

7. Belgium must be evacuated and restored.

8. French territory to be evacuated and restored, and Alsace-Lorraine to be returned to French rule.

9. Italian frontiers to be adjusted along clearly recognizable lines of nationality.

10. The peoples of Austria-Hungary to be given the opportunity for autonomous development.

11. Romania, Serbia, and Montenegro to be evacuated; Serbia to be given access to the sea; and international guarantees of the independence and territorial integrity of the Balkan states to be made.

12. The Turkish portions of the Ottoman empire to be assured a secure sovereignty; other nationalities to be allowed to develop autonomously; the Dardanelles to be permanently open to shipping.

13. An independent Polish state to be established, with free and secure access to the sea.

14. A general association of nations to be formed to afford mutual guarantees of political independence and territorial integrity to all states.

slovakia, a state for the first time in 1919, was composed of some many national groups that Mussolini scornfully referred to it as 'Czecho-Germano-Polono-Magyaro-Rutheno-Romano-Slovakia'.

The result of Wilson's **idealism** was the creation of a series of relatively weak states in Southern, Eastern, and Central Europe—Hungary, Yugoslavia, Rumania, Bulgaria, Czechoslovakia, Poland. These new states suffered not only from ethnic cleavages but also from weak economies and political institutions—as one might expect in states which had only just come into existence, or been reconstituted. Why, given the problems of boundary-drawing, and the weakness of the resulting states, which resulted in Germany being surrounded by relatively defenceless neighbours, did the peacemakers demur to Wilson's insistence on self-determination? The answer lies in the West European powers' preoccupation with a new threat. At Versailles, the peacemakers certainly feared a possible future resurgence of Germany, but perhaps equally vividly they were haunted by the spectre of Bolshevism spreading from Lenin's newly created Union of Soviet Socialist Republics (USSR) into Western Europe. Lenin, after all, explicitly stated that the Soviet revolution was but the start of a world revolution—an historical inevitability which the Moscow-led Communist International (**Comintern**) was dedicated to hastening. Moreover, the war seemed to have provided the ideal breeding ground for communist parties in Western Europe, which the Soviets could infiltrate and use as vehicles of world revolution.

Fear of Bolshevism thus explains British and French politicians' enthusiasm for self-determination. After all, these new states were virtually bound to be anti-Soviet since they were largely created from land formerly belonging to Russia: Finland, the Baltic Republics, Poland, and Rumania. They were the ideal 'quarantine belt' for the USSR. But they did **not** address the threat which Germany posed to European security: thus the interwar era saw another period of alliance-building and treaty-signing, as France and Britain (and Italy, by the Locarno treaty of 1925) extended guarantees to various Eastern and Central European states to take action if their boundaries were violated by an aggressor.

The Future of Germany

In many ways the territorial settlement which Versailles established stored up problems for the future, not least in its reshaping of Germany. When the peacemakers came to determine Germany's fate, they did not apply the principal of self-determination rigidly. Largely at French insistence, France regained the lost province of Alsace-Lorraine and occupied the Saar—the key industrial area on Germany's western flank—in order to extract coal, steel, and iron. French troops also occupied the Rhineland, to ensure that Germany remained demilitarized, as the treaty insisted. Additionally, German politicians (and much of the population) resented the inclusion of Germans in the reconstituted Poland. Poland had not existed as an independent state since the eighteenth century, but now it divided the vast bulk of Germany from East Prussia. This anomalous situation resulted from the peacemakers' determination that Poland should have an outlet to the sea at the port of Danzig (or Gdansk). Where was Danzig's right to self-determination, Germans demanded?

The territorial arrangements of 1919, under which Germany lost 13 per cent of her land and nearly seven million people, angered many Germans, providing a potent grievance for Hitler's National Socialists to manipulate in the 1930s. But what perhaps hurt even more was the inscription of German 'war guilt' into the treaty.

'War Guilt' and Reparations

The victors included the 'war guilt' clause largely in order to justify the extraction of swingeing reparations from Germany. Popular pressure in Britain and France encouraged the peacemakers to 'squeeze the German lemon until the pips squeak', a line most vigorously pursued by the French premier, Georges Clemenceau. The British Prime Minister, Lloyd George, also agreed that reparations should be exacted from Germany, though not at such a punitive level as France sought. The issue of exactly **how much** Germany should pay in reparations was in fact never settled at Versailles. Unable to agree, the allies left the matter to a Reparations Commission (and ultimately, the sum was scaled ever downwards).

Fig. 3.1. **Europe after the First World War**
Map reproduced from Keylor (1992: 93)

While it is easy to understand why the economic dismemberment of Germany appealed to these leaders—punishing Germany was electorally popular, and also seemed to guarantee future German inability to launch all-out wars—the wisdom of such a move was questionable. It was indeed called into question almost before the ink had dried on the treaty. In 1919, the eminent British economist, John Maynard Keynes (an adviser to the British delegation at Versailles) produced an influential indictment of the treaty entitled *The Economic Consequences of the Peace*. Keynes advanced a compelling argument that economic ruination of Germany—the result of punitive reparations—would prevent the economic recovery of Europe as a whole. Germany was the motor of the European economic engine: in punishing Germany, the Allies were effectively prolonging their own wartime privations.

To sum up, then, as the French general Foch acutely predicted after the signing of the treaty, Versailles would not bring peace, only an armistice for twenty years. It had solved none of Europe's fundamental problems. In economic terms, it was (if one followed Keynes's reasoning) too hard on Germany, and consequently on Europe as a whole. The interwar years thus saw Europe's economic position decline further relative to that of the United States, which emerged from the war as the net beneficiary, being owed huge sums by Britain and France, which Wilson insisted they repay. In its territorial arrangements, and the selective application of Wilsonian principles, the peace was also arguably too severe on Germany—this was certainly the argument many Germans advanced, most vehemently under Hitler's regime. Moreover, a growing number of non-Germans had some sympathy with the view that Versailles had given Germany legitimate grievances: this in part explains the policy of **appeasement** pursued by

British governments in the 1930s. But, according to another line of reasoning (advanced by, amongst others, the historian A. J. P. Taylor), the real problem with Versailles was that it was **not hard enough**. The 'German problem' was unresolved, insofar as Germany still remained the largest unitary state in the heart of Europe, and Germany's potential to wage war again had not been absolutely destroyed. However viewed—whether as too punitive or not sufficiently so—the Treaty of Versailles was almost bound to fail, not least in the absence of any major power absolutely committed to upholding it.

Key Points

- Many of the terms of the peace treaties concluded following World War I (referred to as the Versailles Settlement) were shaped by the idealistic 'Fourteen Points' supplied by American President, Woodrow Wilson.

- Future wars were to be deterred by the League of Nations, which would take collective action against aggressor states.

- A series of new states was created in the Balkans and Eastern and Central Europe, where the Ottoman and Austro-Hungarian empires had collapsed.

- Germany was found 'guilty' of having begun the war: Germany lost land to Poland; Alsace-Lorraine was returned to France; Germany was to be disarmed, with France occupying the Rhineland as a security zone; and reparations were to be repaid to the victorious powers.

- Many critics found fault with the settlement, either because it was too hard, or not sufficiently severe, on Germany.

The Global Economic Slump, 1929–1933

In the 1920s America came to assume the pivotal position in the global economy that Britain had occupied prior to 1914. By 1929, the US produced 42 per cent of the world's industrial output, with Germany, Britain, and France together accounting for only 28 per cent (Hobsbawm 1994: 97). Initially,

the vibrancy of the US economy provided the illusion that the world economy had survived the rigours of World War I relatively intact, albeit with the US replacing Britain as the new key financier. The survival of the pre-1914 system transpired to be an illusion, as the war had irreparably damaged the

Susan L. Carruthers

Box 3.5. **The US and the USSR between the Wars**

One reason why the 1919 peace settlement did not last, it is often argued, was the failure of any major power, particularly the US, to sponsor it. After the Second World War, the US and the USSR emerged as 'superpowers', and their mutual hostility—the cold war—dominated the world for forty years. Why were both relatively inactive on the international scene in the twenty years after the First World War?

The USSR

Nov. 1917	The **Bolshevik Revolution** brought a Marxist-Leninist regime to power in the former Tsarist empire.
Mar. 1918	Lenin concluded a **separate peace treaty** with Germany (in which one-fourth of Russian territory and a third of its population were surrendered), in order to concentrate on consolidating the revolution.
1918–20	Before consolidation could occur, **Civil War** broke out. Trotsky's Red Army quelled the counter-revolutionary forces of the White Russians, who were aided by interventions from France, Britain, Japan, and the US.
1924	Josef Stalin came to power, following Lenin's death, and concentrated on building **'socialism in one country'**.
1929	The first **Five-Year Plan** for the Soviet economy was introduced, and Stalin stepped up the pace of state planning of industry, together with the collectivization of agriculture.
1936–8	Stalin undertook the **Great Purge** of the enemies of his dictatorship.
Aug. 1939	Stalin signed a **non-aggression pact with Nazi Germany**. This suggests how small a role ideology now played in Soviet foreign policy (although Stalin did not altogether abandon the USSR's support for communist parties around the world). Instead Soviet security concerns were uppermost, and the Pact promised the USSR land in the Baltic, in return for Soviet acquiescence towards Hilter's march into Poland.

The US

Mar. 1920	The US **Senate refused to ratify the Treaty of Versailles**, concluding a separate peace with Germany in 1921 which did not include the 'war guilt' clause, or the terms of the League of Nations. The US had thus embarked upon an essentially isolationist foreign policy, which it pursued until the Japanese attack on Pearl Harbour. However, the US government did remain concerned with, and involved in, a number of international issues, particularly those relating to disarmament and security—not least in the Pacific, a traditional area of US concern, where Japan was in the ascendant.
1921–2	The **Washington Disarmament Conference** was notable for the manner in which it dealt with Japan's growing power in the Pacific. The relative strength of the navies of the US, UK, Japan, France, and Italy was fixed in a ratio of 5 : 5 : 3 : 1.75 : 1.75. The sovereignty of **China** was also affirmed, and an 'Open Door' policy of trade with China maintained.
1931	The US government's concern with Japanese aggression against China was evident in its response to the **Manchurian crisis**, beginning in 1931, when Japanese forces occupied an ever greater part of the North Chinese province of Manchuria. Although not a member of the League of Nations, the US did offer to assist its efforts to establish the origins of the crisis. However, the US stopped far short of actually using—or encouraging the League to use—force to reverse Japan's aggression.

Throughout the inter-war years, America's primary influence on the world lay not so much in the diplomatic sphere, as in the realm of economics, where the US economy was emerging as the world's strongest. US capital helped rebuild Germany, with loans enabling Germany to make reparations to Britain and France, who could then repay their own debts to the US.

---

globalized world economy evolving since the time of the Industrial Revolution. The **Wall Street stock-market crash** of 29 October 1929, and its aftermath, starkly revealed the illusory nature of post-war economic regeneration. Soon no one could be in doubt that the world financial system was in convulsion.

The underlying causes of 'the largest global earthquake ever to be measured on the economic historians' Richter Scale—the Great Inter-War

Table 3.1. **Major wartime and post-war foreign loans of US government** (in millions of dollars)

Recipient nation	Pre-Armistice (cash)	Post-Armistice (cash & supplies)	Total indebtedness
Great Britain	3696.0	581.0	4277.0
France	1970.0	1434.8	3404.8
Italy	1031.0	617.0	1648.0
Russia	187.7	4.9	192.6
Belgium	171.8	207.3	379.1

Source: Harold Moulton and Leo Pasvolsky, *War Debts and World Prosperity* (1932: 426), and Thomas A. Bailey, *A Diplomatic History of the American People* (1974: 657).

Depression' (Hobsbawm 1994: 86) continue to be disputed, and cannot be rehearsed at any length here. Beyond dispute, however, is the truly global impact of the Depression. The impact of the stock-market crash around the world illustrates the degree to which states in the interwar years were not entirely independent entities, determining their own fates. Rather they were at the mercy of profound economic forces over which national governments had little or no control.

The results of **the Depression** in America and Europe are familiar enough to Western readers. Western Europe depended on American loans in various forms, so when they dried up America's Depression was duplicated in Europe. Its symptoms included spiralling inflation and a collapse of consumer demand in the leading industrial countries which led to a decline in manufacturing industry. This in turn meant massive unemployment. In the era before social welfare provision was seen as part of the state's duty to its citizens (an era ushered in by World War II in most parts of Western Europe and America), unemployment meant utter destitution and grinding poverty for millions. Even for those who remained employed, hyper-inflation—and in some countries the complete collapse of currencies—led to the overnight elimination of savings, and to paper money becoming virtually worthless, as in Weimar Germany.

Perhaps less well known in Europe or America are the results of the Depression elsewhere in the world. Every country that participated in international trade was affected—whether they were independent states (as in Latin America) or colonial territories under the rule of Western European powers. The precipitous drop in the western world's demand for goods and crops did not just mean unemployment for workers in factories in the West. It also spelt ruin for the producers of raw materials from which consumer goods were manufactured. To take but one example, Japanese silk farmers suddenly found their livelihoods ruined as Americans ceased to buy silk stockings in the Depression of the early 1930s. Similarly growers of crops farmed in what we now know as the Developing World (or Third World), which were sold to the developed world, found that the prices they received for their commodities plummeted. Brazil's coffee growers attempted to prevent the coffee price from collapsing by selling it to Brazilian railway companies as an alternative fuel to coal.

In economic terms, the result of the Depression was that the globalization of the world economy halted and went into reverse. Rather than a global free trade system continuing to develop (as it had from the Industrial Revolution up to 1914), the major capitalist states now sought to isolate their national economies as far as possible from the vagaries of the international market. Free trade was abandoned in favour of protectionist policies, whereby states attempted to make their economies as self-sufficient as possible. High tariff barriers were erected to dissuade domestic manufacturers from importing foreign goods. As a result the volume of international trade fell sharply. America led the way in protectionism, being in the fortunate position of needing other countries' products less than, for example, did Britain and many other industrialized states.

The economic crisis of the 1930s was accompanied by profound political upheavals. We might question whether, without the Depression, Hitler would have found such fertile soil for Nazism in Germany. It may be simplistic to argue that the

Depression alone accounts for Hitler's accession to power in 1933: Nazism can be seen as the culmination of long-standing trends in German development, and the Depression itself did not **cause** Nazism. However, the broad point remains that the Depression—and its human costs—made extremist political solutions appear attractive during the 1930s. In Europe, extremist experiments of the Right were most in evidence. Having secured power in Germany, Hitler proceeded to encourage Nazi movements on Germany's borders, especially in Austria and Czechoslovakia. Meanwhile, Mussolini completed the construction of the 'Fascist State' in Italy in the 1930s, and in Spain Franco ultimately defeated the Popular Front ranged against him. But the emergence of more extreme forms of politics was not simply a European phenomenon. Several Latin American regimes toppled during the 1930s, to be replaced with new ones of either a pronounced left- or right-wing complexion. In the colonized world, nationalist movements were also given a powerful impetus by the Depression. In India, for example, Gandhi mobilized a mass campaign of civil disobedience against British rule, while in French Indo-China, Ho Chi Minh's communist nationalists embarked on the long road to independence which would ultimately entail protracted wars with both France and America after 1945.

Key Points

- Since the Industrial Revolution, a global capitalist economy had been developing, with an expanding level of world trade.

- The First World War disrupted this development, with a profound negative impact on the international economic system, which was initially masked by the vibrancy of the US economy in the 1920s.

- In 1929, the Wall Street Stock-Market Crash introduced a world depression, illustrating the degree to which national economies were affected by international economic forces.

- Depressions in many countries around the world resulted in extremist political movements gaining strength, many of which were of an extreme right-wing nature.

The Origins of World War Two in Asia and the Pacific

Up to this point, we have devoted little attention to developments in the Far East. However, if we are to understand the outbreak of World War II, or indeed Japan's international prominence thereafter, then we must clearly examine interwar developments in Asia, particularly in Japan and China.

In some respects Japan's position in Asia during the first decades of the twentieth century was akin to Germany's in Europe. After unification, Germany underwent rapid modernization and industrialization. It had sought an enlarged empire, challenging those of France and Britain in the years prior to 1914. Germany emerged from the First World War aggrieved at the treatment meted out by the victors and determined to reverse key aspects of the Versailles Settlement—a 'revisionism' heightened by the catastrophic consequences of the Depression. Under an extreme right-wing regime, Germany sought a solution to its problems through outward expansion, and found its path eased by the weakness of the states geographically closest to it. Much of this could also be said of Japan.

Japan and the 'Meiji Restoration'

During the period from 1868 to 1912, the reign of the Emperor Meiji, Japan experienced rapid industrialization, following a model borrowed from the industrialized Western economies. This was accompanied by a modernization of Japanese society and political life: the feudal agricultural system was abolished; the army was reorganized and conscription introduced, heralding the disintegration of the Samurai caste; education and foreign travel were encouraged; and a new parliamentary system was implemented. Like Germany, Japan in the late nineteenth century developed imperialistic inclinations. Unlike Germany, Japan did not naturally possess within its own frontiers an abundance of the raw materials for industrialization. Both, however, shared a belief that their population was growing so rapidly that the populace would soon outstrip the state's geographical and financial capacity to support it. Thus Hitler sought 'Lebensraum' for the German people in Central and Eastern Europe, while Japan looked towards China as the most suitable sphere for expansion.

Japanese Expansion in China

Just as Germany profited from the decline of its imperial neighbours (in Austria-Hungary, Turkey, and Russia), Japan's expansionism was likewise eased by the state of near-extinction in which China languished. China, once a great dynastic empire, by the late nineteenth century had almost ceased to function as a state. The last emperor was toppled in 1911, and China slid into a protracted state of civil war. As provincial warlords fought one another, the Nationalist Guomindang movement under Sun Yat Sen (and latterly Chiang Kai Shek) clashed with Mao Zedong's Chinese Communist Party, which ultimately triumphed in 1949. Such internal chaos, and the absence of strong central government, provided fresh opportunities for foreign 'profiteers'. China had long been infiltrated by outside powers, anxious for a share of its 'exotic' goods—tea, spices, opium, silk—and to trade with the world's most populous state. Britain in the nineteenth and early twentieth century had the most extensive China trade, but Tsarist Russia was also heavily involved in railway-building in northern China. Japan took particular interest in the region of Manchuria, and clashed with Russia during 1904–5 in a war which marked the first major defeat in modern times of a European power by an Asian state. Japan's position in China was strengthened still further as a result of the First World War, during which Japan fought against Germany, using the opportunity to secure Germany's Chinese possessions.

Although Japan had opposed Germany, both felt dissatisfied by the terms of the Versailles settlement. Japan had tried, and failed, to have the principle of racial equality written into the terms of the treaties. That the Western powers were indeed racially prejudiced against the Japanese seemed to be confirmed by America's 1924 immigration legislation, which virtually prevented further Japanese immigration into the US. Japan also felt that she had not received sufficient territory in recognition for her part in the war. Moreover, as the 1920s progressed Japan came to resent the way in which America and Britain sought, through the **Washington treaties**, to limit her naval construction and to prevent China falling more effectively under Japanese domination.

Some Japanese policy-makers remained committed to an internationalist policy during the 1920s. In particular they believed that Japan should behave as a responsible member of the international community, and take an active role in the League of Nations. But increasingly the army gained prominence in Japanese political life, and the officer class (especially that part of it stationed in northern China following Japan's victory in the 1904–5 war with Russia) pressed ever more forcibly for Japanese expansion in China. Japan's experience of social upheaval strengthened the appeal of militarism. In the late 1920s, Japan suffered from two destabilizing tremors, one literal, the other metaphorical. The Great Kanto Earthquake of 1923 resulted in nearly 100,000 deaths and the destruction of about 2,000,000 homes. The volcanic eruption seemed to symbolize the volatility of Japanese society during a period of rapid modernization. The second, metaphorical, great tremor to hit Japanese society was the Depression. As in Europe, the socio-economic conditions of Japan's depression were a fertile soil for right-wing extremism. Outward expansionism looked even more attractive, and Japanese political and military leaders increasingly talked of establishing a 'co-prosperity sphere' in Asia. This phrase was a euphemism for Japanese economic hegemony (if not outright rule) over various neighbouring states. Such imperialistic aspirations were fuelled by rising Japanese nationalism, the ideological foundation of which was **Shintoism**: a belief in the divinity and infallibility of the emperor, to whom each citizen owed personal allegiance.

The Manchurian Crisis and After

Japan's foreign policy thus became increasingly assertive. The 'Manchurian crisis' of 1931 demonstrated this, and is sometimes regarded as the opening shot of the Second World War. Japan used a minor skirmish between Japanese soldiers and Chinese 'bandits' as a pretext to occupy a greater portion of Manchuria. Despite Chinese protests to the League of Nations, Japan was unrepentant, and by 1932 had established a puppet state in the whole of Manchuria, called **Manchuguo**. The League's response to the first blatant act of aggression by one of its member states against another was insipid: a Commission under the British Earl Lytton was dispatched to investigate the initial Sino-Japanese incident which had sparked the crisis. Its Report was a year in the making, and even then recommended moderation—urging both non-recognition of Manchuguo and international mediation of Japan and China's differences, but not any forcible action against Japan for its violation of international law.

Would Hitler's aggression in Europe and Mussolini's in East Africa (where he tried to capture Abyssinia, the last independent African state) have been deterred had the League acted decisively over Manchuria? The answer seems almost certainly not. Neither dictator had much regard for the niceties of international law, and most historians agree that both had long-term territorial ambitions which would scarcely have been deflected by a firmer League response to the Manchurian crisis. However, the League's abject failure to check Japanese aggression did perhaps help create a permissive atmosphere, which emboldened the European dictators to disrespect international law in the expectation that they would not incur international sanctions. Certainly, in the Far East, the Japanese were not deterred from further aggression by the upshot of the Manchurian crisis. The puppet state of Manchuguo continued to exist until the end of the Second World War, and the fact that most states chose not to recognize its existence made little odds to the Japanese, and doubtless was of small comfort to the Manchurians themselves.

By 1937, Japan was involved in full-scale war with China, and this too lasted until 1945. But Japan's mounting incursions into neighbours' territory—the so-called **'New Order'** in East Asia—were not altogether ignored by the Western powers. In 1939, the US government cancelled its 1911 trade agreement with Japan, thus restricting the latter's ability to import raw materials necessary to its war machine. Not surprisingly, relations between the two states deteriorated rapidly and dramatically, culminating in Japan's bombing of the US navy at Pearl Harbour in December 1941. As a result, Britain

---

Box 3.6. The Origins of the War in the Pacific: A Chronology

18 Sept. 1930	Mukden incident in Manchuria between Japanese troops and Chinese 'bandits'. Marks the start of Japan's conquest of Manchuria.
24 Feb. 1933	League of Nations adopts the Lytton Report, which recommends international mediation in the dispute between Japan and China, and urges League members not to recognize the Japanese puppet state in Manchuria (Manchuguo), but does not seek to impose sanctions on Japan.
27 March 1933	Japan announces her withdrawal from the League.
29 Dec. 1934	Japan denounces the 1922 Washington naval treaty.
15 Jan. 1936	Japan withdraws from London naval conference.
25 Nov. 1936	Germany and Japan sign the Anti-Comintern Pact.
7 July 1937	Outbreak of war between Japan and China.
6 Nov. 1937	Italy joins the Anti-Comintern Pact.
14 June 1939	Japan begins a blockade of the Chinese city of Tientsin.
26 July 1939	America retracts 1911 trade treaty with Japan.
30 Aug. 1940	Japan occupies northern Indo-China.
13 April 1941	Japan signs neutrality pact with USSR.
21 July 1941	Vichy France permits Japan to occupy the whole of Indo-China.
26 July 1941	America freezes Japanese assets.
7 Dec. 1941	Japan attacks the US Navy at Pearl Harbour.
8 Dec. 1941	Britain and America declare war on Japan.
11 Dec. 1941	Germany and Italy declare war on the US.

---

and the US declared war on Japan on 8 December, while Germany and Italy reciprocated with a declaration of war on the USA three days later. The Second World War was now unquestionably global in scope. However, for many months there had been no doubt as to where the main lines of division lay in Asia, nor that an axis was emerging between Japan, Germany, and Italy. A Three-Power Pact was concluded in 1940, which was transformed into a military alliance in 1942. Thus while the German army overran huge swathes of continental Europe, the Japanese occupied large parts of Asia hitherto colonized by European states. The Dutch East Indies and French Indo-China fell to Japan, just as Holland and France lay under Nazi rule. And although Britain itself avoided German invasion, the same was not true of its South-East Asian colonies, Burma, Ceylon, and Malaya.

Key Points

- From 1868 onwards, Japan underwent a rapid period of industrialization and modernization,

with profound social, economic, and political consequences.

- To find new markets, raw materials, and land for Japan's growing population, Japan began to expand into northern China, whilst China was in a protracted state of civil war.

- Japan, although it fought against Germany during World War I, emerged from that war similarly dissatisfied with the post-war settlement.

- Between 1931 and 1933, Japan consolidated its hold over Manchuria, establishing a puppet state, 'Manchuguo': the League of Nation's response to the most blatant act of aggression it had thus far faced was minimal.

- By 1937, Japan was at war with China, which caused worsening relations with the US—ultimately leading to Japan's attack on Pearl Harbour.

The Path to War in Europe

As the crisis in the Far East deepened during the 1930s, Europe lurched from one crisis to the next: Italy's invasion of Abyssinia (Ethiopia); Germany's remilitarization of the Rhineland; civil war in Spain; Germany's expansion into Austria, then Czechoslovakia, followed by Poland, at which point Britain and France declared war on Germany in September 1939.

The Controversy over the Origins of the Second World War

It was suggested earlier in this chapter that in many ways the Second World War was a continuation of the First: another manifestation of Europe's deep-rooted instability, and a reflection of the imbalance of power which had existed on the continent ever since the unification of Germany. However, many historians would argue that besides the profound structural forces which were at work undermining the stability of Europe, human agency also played a role in bringing about the Second World War. Indeed, to tell the story of the origins of that war without reference to Hitler, would be akin to telling

the story of Adam and Eve without the serpent. To many (historians or otherwise), the Second World War was, quite simply, 'Hitler's war', which he planned, and which was the conscious result of his determination to achieve world mastery. This was also the verdict of the post-war Nuremberg trials of Nazi war criminals.

However, the origins of the Second World War have been—perhaps surprisingly—a matter of considerable historiographical dispute. While most historians agree that responsibility for the war rests with Hitler and Nazi Germany, they have differed over whether Hitler actually **planned** the war, and what the extent of his territorial ambitions was—mastery of Europe, or German hegemony of the world? Did Hitler have a timetable for the expansionist ambitions he had set out in his autobiography-cum-manifesto *Mein Kampf*? Had he decided, by 1937, to take Czechoslovakia and then Poland, before turning to Western Europe, as a document (entitled the Hossbach Memorandum) used in the Nuremberg tribunal seemed to suggest? Did he think he could expand German power in Europe **without** causing a major war? Or did he believe that a Total War was inevitable, but did not foresee this coming about until the 1940s, when the German economy would be fully mobilized for such a war? All these questions have been posed by historians, and divergent answers given (Robertson 1971; Martel 1986).

The most controversial treatment of the war's origins by a serious historian remains A. J. P. Taylor's *The Origins of the Second World War*, first published in 1961 to a barrage of criticism. The cause of the furore was Taylor's suggestion that Hitler essentially resembled any other European statesman. Nazi ideology—though responsible for the 'evil of the gas chambers'—did not suffice to explain the war. Hitler, like his Weimar predecessors, had merely sought to enhance Germany's position after the Versailles settlement, and to reverse its unfavourable, and unfair, aspects. Far from having a timetable for expansion, and general war, Hitler was an opportunist, who capitalized on the blunders of others, and the opportunities afforded him by the appeasers in Britain and France. War in September 1939 caught Hitler essentially by surprise. Although Taylor later claimed in his autobiography that his view of Hitler as blunderer and opportunist had become the new orthodoxy, this is something of an exaggeration (Taylor 1983: 299). It is probably truer to say that most historians believe that Hitler had a long-term fixity of purpose—expansion in Europe, if not further afield—coupled with a short-term flexibility in his tactics and timing. Certainly, most reject Taylor's contention that Nazi ideology had nothing whatever to do with the Second World War.

The Rise of Fascism and Nazism in Europe

A. J. P. Taylor aside, most academic historians regard Nazi and fascist ideology as essential to understanding the origins of the war. Fuelled by popular dissatisfaction with the 1919 settlement, extreme right-wing movements arose in the 1920s and 1930s. These fed on the social, economic, and political instabilities engendered by World War I. Italy had never really achieved stable central government despite unification in the nineteenth century. Although fascist mythology claimed that Mussolini seized power with his **'March on Rome'**, in reality he was invited to form a parliament by the king and conservative politicians in 1922, because the traditional right-wing parties had failed to form a stable government. Far from marching on Rome, he was

brought to the capital by special train. Once Prime Minister, Mussolini set about conducting a 'fascist revolution' in Italian life, which no doubt horrified at least some of those responsible for bringing him to power.

As many historians and political philosophers have pointed out, 'fascism' is an elusive doctrine to pin down. In fact, arguably it is so incoherent as not to even merit the term 'doctrine'. As practised in Italy, its essential features were the establishment of a type of **totalitarian state**, in which the state intervened in almost all aspects of its citizens' lives. In the sphere of employment, trade unions were abolished and 'corporations' of employers and employees established, overseen by fascist bureaucrats, which ensured that the interests of big business prevailed over those of the labour movement. In politics, opposition parties were eliminated, and a personality cult was built around the figure of Mussolini, *'Il Duce'*. Social life was also imbued with fascist ideology—from women's institutes, to football clubs and youth leagues.

Fascism also had an impact on foreign policy, although there was some continuity of purpose between Mussolini and his predecessors. Fascist thought glorified violence and struggle, within society and between states, as both natural and heroic. War was the ultimate test not only of individual 'manhood' but of a state's maturity and position in the international hierarchy. Mussolini was thus committed not only to reversing that part of the Versailles settlement which had subtracted territory from Italy in the Adriatic but also to expanding the 'New Roman Empire' into North Africa, by war if necessary. The obvious target was Abyssinia—the last remaining independent state in Africa—and in 1935, Italian troops moved to seize control of the country from Haile Selassie. This became a more protracted campaign than Mussolini had probably envisaged. Its most obvious beneficiary was not *Il Duce* himself, but Adolf Hitler, who used the cover of Mussolini's North African adventure to proceed with his own plans for dismantling the 1919 settlement in Europe.

Hitler came to power in Germany over a decade after Mussolini's accession in Italy. After years of street-fighting and rabble-rousing in beer cellars, Hitler's National Socialist party achieved success at the German polls in 1933. Once in power as Reich Chancellor, Hitler—like Mussolini—moved to consolidate the grip of his party over both the organs of the state, and the German people as a whole. Nazis assumed power in central and local government; the state directed industry, and controlled the German mass media. Opposition parties were abolished, and dissent stifled, either by physical punishment or the fear of it. Hitler's particular targets of detestation—the Jews, gypsies, and homosexuals—were sent in ever increasing numbers to concentration camps. No aspect of German life was left untouched by the Nazi party and ideology. The latter resembled Italian fascism in many respects but had distinct, and more virulent, strains, especially in its genocidal anti-semitism. At the heart of Hitler's world view was his racist belief in the superiority of the pure German people—the Aryan race. Not only did he believe that Germany had been unfairly robbed of land and people in 1919, but his territorial aims went far beyond mere rectification of the wrongs of Versailles. In pursuit of more *lebensraum* (living space), the Aryans could legitimately expand eastwards (the *drang nach osten*), at the expense of the slavonic *untermenschen* ('subhumans') who inhabited Eastern Europe, and the Soviet Union in particular. Hitler's world view thus rested on a debased Social Darwinism, in which the 'fittest' race was destined to expand at the expense of its genetically inferior neighbours.

From Appeasement to War

The Nazis made no secret of their territorial ambitions; *Mein Kampf* spelt out Hitler's racial views and expansionist plans quite explicitly. Why, therefore, did the governments of Britain and France not do more to prevent Hitler from realizing these plans? Why was Hitler allowed to remilitarize the Rhineland, annex Austria, and invade Czechoslovakia before the Allies confronted him over his incursion into Poland in September 1939? Why, in short, was Hitler appeased for so long?

The policy of appeasement pursued by the Western powers throughout much of the 1930s has received considerable scholarly attention, and remains a potent source of historical analogies for politicians. The first generation of post-war historians was extremely (if understandably) harsh in its verdict on the appeasers: Chamberlain and his French counterparts were the **'Guilty Men of Munich'**. By cravenly appeasing Hitler, the leaders of France and Britain simply fed his appetite, and emboldened the Führer to believe that he could suc-

cessfully carry off ever more audacious violations of the Treaty of Versailles.

A number of subsequent historians have been somewhat kinder to the 'appeasers'. Certainly we should not underestimate the magnitude of the domestic and international crises confronting West European policy-makers and diplomats in the 1930s. Japan's violations of Chinese sovereignty were a source of concern in the Far East. Events in Asia thus provided a convenient cover for Hitler to leave the Geneva disarmament conference and the League in 1933, and to begin the process of German rearmament. Germany also profited from Italy's invasion of Abyssinia, and was a far from reliable ally to Mussolini during the ensuing war there. Although Mussolini announced the formation of a **'Rome–Berlin Axis'** between Germany and Italy in November 1936, in fact, Hitler had sent some arms to Haile Selassie's beleagured forces in Abyssinia—precisely to protract the war, and thus enable Germany to tear more gaping holes in the fabric of the Versailles settlement, while British and French attention was still focused on north-east Africa. And while the League was still grappling with the issue of whether or not to apply sanctions to Italy over Abyssinia, civil war broke out in Spain, which highlighted starkly the ideological fissures in Europe.

British and French politicians thus faced the daunting scenario of war on three fronts: in the Pacific (against Japan); the Mediterranean (against Italy), and central Europe (against Germany). Neither Britain nor France was prepared militarily for such an eventuality. Nor, for much of the 1930s, did public opinion appear to favour going to war to prevent or reverse acts of aggression. There were after all pressing domestic issues to be attended to: the Depression had created chronic unemployment and poverty. Moreover, the memory of World War I was still vivid, and this made politicians, mindful of the publics they served, cautious about embarking on military solutions to international problems. Appeasement, some historians would thus argue, was in certain respects a justifiable attempt to 'buy time'. It enabled British and French rearmament to proceed, and public opinion to be mobilized, so that if Germany **did** have to be challenged militarily, and Hitler's pose as a 'man of peace' was proved a sham, then at least a serious military effort could be mounted against him.

However, this more charitable interpretation of appeasement might be criticized on the grounds that it credits the appeasers with considerable fore-sight—with seeking a breathing-space which would enable them, ultimately, to wage more effective war against Hitler, whereas in fact they tended to believe that by giving in to his demands, the Führer would cease to make them. Chamberlain not only accepted that Germany did have some legitimate grievances but additionally regarded Hitler in the same light as other statesmen, assuming that differences between European statesmen could be ironed out through negotiation and compromise, as all essentially wanted peace. This misperception of Nazi intentions consequently enabled Hitler to launch a spectacular series of assaults on the Versailles settlement with impunity. He reoccupied the Rhineland in 1936, with surprisingly little response from France. He encouraged Nazi movements in Austria, and pressurized the Austrian chancellor Schuschnigg to include Nazis in his government. Then in March 1938 he dispatched German troops over the border to secure the 'unification' of Austria with Germany (*Anschluss*). Czechoslovakia was next. Here, Hitler again played on the argument that Germany had been wronged in 1919, when three and a half million Germans of the Sudetenland had been incorporated within the new Czech state. German troop movements against Czechoslovakia began in May 1938. While British and French leaders were clearly alarmed by this development, they nevertheless continued to appease Hitler, and indeed the high-point of the policy was the now notorious **Munich conference** of September 1938. At Munich, the British and French premiers agreed to German occupation of the Sudetenland, but offered a guarantee (with Italy and Germany) of the borders of the remaining Czech state. Hitler also promised Chamberlain that their two countries would 'never go to war with one another again'—the famous piece of paper which Chamberlain claimed would secure **'peace for our time'**.

As we know, it did not. In March 1939, Germany invaded the remainder of Czechoslovakia, and Britain and France ignored their pledges made at Munich, with Chamberlain having decided some

months earlier that Czechoslovakia was indefensible. However, in the wake of Germany's effective occupation of all Central Europe, the Western powers showered guarantees on the remaining free states of Eastern Europe and the Balkans. Why this sudden diplomatic revolution? The answer seems to be that appeasement was no longer morally defensible once Hitler's ambitions had clearly outstripped the revision of German grievances with the 1919 settlement. By sending German troops into Prague, Hitler had revealed that his territorial greed was not just for 'Germanic' lands, and there was no reason to believe that he would be satisfied with Czechoslovakia. Poland, the Low Countries, and France all now appeared in imminent danger of German expansionism. Fearing for their own territorial integrity, the leaders of Britain and France thus determined to go to war with Hitler over Poland in September 1939. The Czechs might have been sacrificed on the altar of appeasement, but the Poles would not suffer the same fate without a fight.

Key Points

- The origins of the Second World War have been the subject of particular historiographical controversy, with historians disputing how far Hitler actually **planned** the war.

- Fascism and Nazism, as practised in Italy and Germany, led to a complete reordering of those societies along totalitarian lines, while in foreign policy terms, ambitious territorial plans were mapped which went far beyond the revision of aspects of the Treaty of Versailles.

- Confronted with numerous international crises—in China, Abyssinia, and Europe—policymakers in Britain and France adopted a policy of appeasing Hitler.

- Once Germany invaded Prague in March 1939, appeasement was abandoned, and Britain and France declared war on Germany once it invaded Poland in September 1939.

Box 3.7. The Origins of World War Two in Europe: A Chronology

30 Oct. 1922	Mussolini becomes Prime Minister of Italy.	22 Sept. 1938	Chamberlain and Hitler meet at Godesburg.
30 Jan. 1933	Hitler becomes Chancellor of Germany.	29/30 Sept. 1938	Munich Conference.
14 Oct. 1933	Germany leaves the Geneva disarmament conference and walks out of the League of Nations.	28 March 1939	End of Spanish Civil War.
		31 March 1939	Britain and France extend a guarantee to Poland that they will defend Poland's territorial integrity from German attack, after Germany occupies the remainder of Czechoslovakia.
14/15 June 1934	Hitler and Mussolini meet in Venice.		
25 July 1934	Murder of Austrian Chancellor, Dollfuss, by Austrian Nazis.	17 April 1939	USSR proposes alliance to Britain and France.
16 March 1935	Germany reintroduces conscription.	22 May 1939	Pact of Steel signed between Italy and Germany.
3 Oct. 1935	Italy invades Abyssinia/Ethiopia.	12 Aug. 1939	Britain and France begin military talks with USSR.
11 Oct. 1935	League decides to impose sanctions against Italy.	23 Aug. 1939	Stalin signs Nazi–Soviet Pact.
7 March 1936	Germany reoccupies the Rhineland (which the Treaty of Versailles had established as a demilitarized zone).	25 Aug. 1939	Britain signs treaty with Poland.
		1 Sept. 1939	Germany invades Poland; Italy remains neutral.
9 May 1936	Italy annexes Abyssinia.	3 Sept. 1939	Britain and France declare war on Germany.
17 July 1936	Civil war breaks out in Spain between Franco's fascist forces and the communist/socialist/syndicalist Popular Front.	17 Sept. 1939	USSR invades Poland.
		30 Nov. 1939	USSR invades Finland.
		9 April 1940	Germany invades Denmark and Norway.
1 Nov. 1936	Mussolini announces the existence of the Rome–Berlin Axis.	10 June 1940	Italy enters the war.
11 Dec. 1937	Italy leaves the League of Nations.	22 June 1940	France signs armistice with Germany.
13 March 1938	Austria united with Germany (*Anschluss*).		
20 May 1938	Rumours of German troop movements against Czechoslovakia.	22 June 1941	Germany invades USSR.
15 Sept. 1938	British PM Chamberlain meets Hitler at Berchtesgaden.	8 Dec. 1941	US enters the war.

Conclusion

This chapter has emphasized the protracted crisis which existed in Europe since the late nineteenth century, and which was manifest in the two Total Wars which engulfed Europe and the wider world in the first half of the twentieth century. The First World War left many European states economically ruined, and with political structures weakened. Indeed, a number of empires based in Europe collapsed during the war—those of Austro-Hungary, Turkey, and Tsarist Russia. The war also profoundly disrupted the growth of an effectively functioning international capitalist economy. Although this consequence of the war was initially masked by the buoyancy of the American economy, when the latter collapsed in October 1929, a general Depression soon spread thereafter to all parts of the world which had been engaged in international trade. The Depression thus reveals not only the economic interconnectedness of the interwar world, but the degree to which the formerly predominant European economies (particularly Britain's) had been eclipsed by America.

But the threat to the primacy of the European democracies did not come from American economic growth alone. Japan was an emergent force in East Asia, which had undergone rapid industrialization, and, by the 1930s, was embarking on a search for territory in China, and beyond. And within Europe, post-war conditions and popular dissatisfaction with the Treaty of Versailles encouraged extremist political movements, most notably fascism in Italy (and Spain) and Nazism in Germany. Both Mussolini and Hitler set out to enlarge the boundaries of their states, and even if Hitler did not plan the type of war which ultimately broke out in September 1939, there is no doubt that he was prepared to risk war in order to achieve his ambitions.

The Second World War, as the next chapter explores, had profound **global** consequences. It saw an unlikely alliance of Britain, America, and the USSR come together to fight the Axis powers of Japan, Italy, and Germany. But this alliance was not to survive the onset of peace, and had shown signs of severe strain even as the war progressed. Indeed one might argue that the cold war was emerging while the World War was still being fought. Thus some revisionist historians, most notably the American Gar Alperovitz, suggest that America's dropping of the atomic bombs on Hiroshima and Nagasaki was actually the first shot of the cold war—the bombs being aimed less at persuading Japan to surrender (which it was about to do in any case) than at intimidating the Soviet Union with a show of American might. Whatever the merits of this argument, certainly the two superpowers, having emerged from their interwar isolationism, found it impossible to agree on the shape of the post-war world. America wanted a world based on free markets and liberalization. The Soviets wanted if not the spread of communism worldwide, as many Americans feared, then at least a 'security zone' of satellite states in Eastern Europe. The post-war stalemate resulted in the division of Europe into two camps for the next forty-five years, and the temporary solution of the 'German problem' with the division of Germany into two separate states.

The war profoundly affected the map of Europe. It also radically reshaped Europe's position in the world. The two superpowers were now predominant, as was evident from the degree of physical and economic influence they exercised over their respective European 'satellites'. Moreover, the war had dramatically undercut the power and prestige of the European imperial powers in their colonies. In Asia, the British, French, and Dutch found many of their territories overrun by the Japanese, and the colonial powers' attempts to regain control after the war were largely short-lived. In a world dominated by two superpowers who professed to be anti-colonial, and following a war which had encouraged nationalist movements, imperialism increasingly appeared anachronistic. The era of European domination of the world was over.

QUESTIONS

1. In what ways did Europe dominate international politics at the start of the twentieth century?

2. Why was Germany regarded as a 'problem' after its unification in 1871?

3. What factors resulted in the outbreak of World War I in 1914?

4. What were the main weaknesses with the post-war peace settlement?

5. Was Germany treated unfairly by the Treaty of Versailles?

6. Why were the US and the USSR not more active in international politics between the First and Second World Wars?

7. Why did the Wall Street Stock-Market Crash of October 1929 have such profound inter-national consequences?

8. In what ways was Japan a 'threat' to the European great powers during the first half of the twentieth century?

9. Is it fair to regard the Second World War as 'Hitler's War'?

10. What were the weaknesses with the policy of appeasement?

11. How far was the Second World War responsible for Western Europe's eclipse by other powers?

GUIDE TO FURTHER READING

General

Hobsbawm, E., *Age of Extremes: The Short Twentieth Century 1914–91* (London: Michael Joseph, 1994). This is an extremely readable and thought-provoking look at the century which Hobsbawm regards as beginning in 1914.

Keylor, W., *The Twentieth Century World: An International History* (New York: Oxford University Press, 1992). This book provides an excellent overview of the entire century, with lengthy sections of the period up to 1945. Economic factors are dealt with particularly well.

Ross, G., *The Great Powers and the Decline of the European States System, 1914–45* (London: Longmans, 1983). A short, but detailed, diplomatic history, outlining the collapse of the 'states system' comprised by the European Great Powers, and containing useful chronologies.

World War I and After

Henig, R., *Versailles and After, 1919–33* (London: Methuen, 1984). A pamphlet setting out the main terms of the post-war peace settlement.

Joll, J., *The Origins of the First World War* (London: Longmans, 1984). A useful synthesis of the debate on the origins of the war.

World War II

Iriye, A., *The Origins of the Second World War in Asia and the Pacific* (London: Longmans, 1987). In the same series as Joll's book, this volume examines the growth of Japanese imperialism and the onset of the war.

Martel, G. (ed.), *The Origins of the Second World War Reconsidered: The A. J. P. Taylor Debate after Twenty-Five Years* (London: Allen & Unwin, 1986). Contains more recent scholarship on the war's origins.

Robertson, E. M. (ed.), *The Origins of the Second World War: Historical Interpretations* (London: Macmillan, 1971). A useful collection of articles illustrating the extent of the row over Taylor's thesis; including a vicious exchange between Taylor and his chief opponent, Hugh Trevor-Roper.

Taylor, A. J. P., *The Origins of the Second World War* (Harmondsworth: Penguin, 1961). This book sparked a huge controversy on account of Taylor's claim that Hitler—an ordinary European states-man—blundered into the war. Taylor also has much to say about Versailles and appeasement.

4 International History 1945–1990

Len Scott

READER'S GUIDE

This chapter examines some of the principal developments in international politics from 1945 to 1990. Fundamental changes in politics, technology, and ideology took place in this period, with enormous consequences for world affairs. The onset of the cold war, the creation of nuclear weapons, and the end of European imperialism are the principal developments explored in the chapter. Since 1945 world politics has been greatly influenced by the conflict between the United States and the Soviet Union, each of which emerged as 'superpowers'. The ideological, political, and military interests of these two states and their allies extended around the globe. How far, and in what ways, conflict in Europe, Asia, and elsewhere was promoted or prevented by the cold war are central questions. Similarly, how the process of decolonization became intermingled with cold war conflicts is a central issue in understanding many wars and conflicts in the 'Third World'. Finally, how dangerous was the nuclear confrontation between East and West ? Did nuclear weapons keep the peace between the superpowers or did they provoke conflict and risk global catastrophe? The chapter raises these questions, and explores the relationship between nuclear weapons development and phases in East–West relations, first with *détente*, and then with the deterioration of Soviet–American relations in the 1980s.

Introduction

As Chapter 3 has shown the Second World War was **global** in scope and **total** in nature. It helped bring about fundamental changes in world politics after 1945. Before 1939 Europe had been the arbiter of world affairs, and both the Soviet Union and the United States remained, for different reasons, preoccupied with internal development at the expense of any significant global role. The war brought the Soviets and the Americans militarily and politically deep into Europe, and helped transform their relations with each other. This transformation was soon reflected in their relations outside Europe where various confrontations developed. Like the Second World War, the cold war had its origins in Europe but quickly spread with enormous consequences for countries and peoples around the world.

After 1945 European power was increasingly in eclipse, although this was not always apparent to those who held power or to their supporters. The economic plight of the wartime belligerents, including those Western European countries who had emerged as victors, was nevertheless increasingly and transparently obvious, as was the growing realization of the military and economic potential of the United States and the Soviet Union. Both countries emerged as **'superpowers'**, combining global political objectives with military capabilities that included weapons of mass destruction and the means to deliver them over intercontinental distances. In Europe the military involvement of the superpowers soon took the form of enduring political commitments, notwithstanding early American intentions to withdraw and demobilize their troops after 1945. European political, economic, and military weakness contrasted with the appearance of Soviet strength and the growing Western perception of malign Soviet intent. The onset of the cold war in Europe marked the collapse of the wartime alliance between the UK, the USSR, and the USA. How far this alliance had been a marriage of convenience, and how far its breakdown was inevitable after 1945 remain crucial and contentious issues. What is beyond doubt is that the legacies of the Second World War provided a heavy burden for succeeding generations. Arguably the most notable, and certainly the most dramatic, legacy was the atomic bomb, built at enormous cost and driven by fear that Nazi Germany might win this first nuclear arms race, with terrifying consequences. After 1945 nuclear weapons presented unprecedented challenges to world politics and to the leaders responsible for conducting post-war diplomacy. The cold war provided context and pretext for the growth of nuclear arsenals which threatened the very existence of humankind, and which remain (and have continued to spread) beyond the end of the cold war and the East–West confrontation.

Since 1945 world politics has been transformed in a variety of ways. These changes reflected political, technological, and ideological developments, of which three are examined in this chapter: (1) The End of Empire: the withdrawal of European countries from their empires in Africa and Asia; (2) The cold war: the political and military confrontation between the United States and the Soviet Union; (3) The Bomb: the development of the atomic bomb and the hydrogen bomb, and the means of their delivery. There have of course been other important changes, and indeed equally important continuities, some of which are explored in other chapters. The transformation of the international political economy and the creation of the United Nations are among several key developments. Nevertheless, the three principal changes outlined above provide a framework for exploring events and trends which have shaped the post-war world.

End of Empire

The collapse of imperialism in the twentieth century was a fundamental change in world politics. It reflected and contributed to the decreasing importance of Europe as the arbiter of world affairs. The belief that national self-determination should be a guiding principle in international politics marked a transformation of attitudes and values. During the age of imperialism political status had accrued to imperial powers. After 1945 imperialism was viewed with growing international hostility.

Table 4.1. **Principal acts of European decolonization 1945–1980**

Country	Colonial state	Year of Independence
India	Britain	1947
Pakistan	Britain	1947
Burma	Britain	1948
Indonesia	Holland	1949
Ghana	Britain	1957
Malaya	Britain	1957
French African colonies		1960
Algeria	France	1962
Guinea-Bissau	Portugal	1974
Mozambique	Portugal	1975
Cape Verde	Portugal	1975
Sao Tome	Portugal	1975
Angola	Portugal	1975
Zimbabwe	Britain	1980

Colonialism and the United Nations Charter were increasingly recognized as incompatible, though independence was often slow and sometimes marked by prolonged conflict and war. The cold war often complicated and hindered the transition to independence. Various factors influenced the process of decolonization: the attitude of the colonial power; the ideology and strategy of the anti-imperialist forces; and the role of external powers. Political, economic, and military factors played various roles in shaping the timing and nature of the transfer of power. Different imperial powers and newly emerging independent states had different experiences of withdrawal from empire. Three of the principal European experiences of withdrawal from empire are discussed below.

Britain

In 1945 the British empire extended across the globe. Between 1947 and 1980 forty-nine territories were granted their independence. There was debate within Britain over Britain's imperial role, which can be traced back to the nineteenth century, but after 1945 growing recognition of the justice of **self-determination** combined with realization of the strength of nationalism brought about a reappraisal of policy. Withdrawal from India, the 'Jewel in the Crown' of the empire, in 1947 was the most dramatic, and in (most) British eyes, successful, act of decolonization, and one which paved the way for

the creation of the world's largest democracy. How far the ensuing hostility between India and Pakistan was avoidable, and how far it reflected previous British efforts to divide and rule, remains a matter for debate. What is clear is that India was something of an exception in the early post-war years, and that successive British governments were reluctant to rush toward decolonization. The key period for the British empire in Africa, came toward the end of the 1950s and early 1960s, symbolized by Prime Minister Harold Macmillan's speech in South Africa in 1960 when he warned his hosts of the **'wind of change'** blowing through their continent.

The transition from empire was on the whole peaceful, and led to the creation of democratic and stable states. There were some conflicts with indigenous revolutionary elements, notably in Kenya (1952–6) and Malaya (1948–60), but these were of limited scale and in Malaya, an effective counter-insurgency policy was pursued. From the European perspective, the British experience was more successful than the French. In Rhodesia/Zimbabwe, however, the transition to 'one person one vote' and black majority rule, was prevented by a white minority prepared to disregard both the British government and world opinion. This minority was aided and abetted by the South African government. Under **apartheid**, after 1948, the South Africans engaged in what many saw as the racial equivalent of imperialism. South Africa also practised a more traditional form of imperialism in its occupation of Namibia, and exercised a key influ-

Box 4.1. **Key Concepts**

Superpower: term used to describe the United States and the Soviet Union after 1945, denoting their global political involvements and military capabilities, including in particular their nuclear arsenals.

'Wind of Change': reference by British Prime Minister Harold Macmillan in a speech in South Africa in 1960 to the political changes taking place across Africa heralding the end of European imperialism.

Apartheid: system of racial segregation introduced in South Africa in 1948, designed to ensure white minority domination.

Hegemony: political (and/or economic) domination of a region, usually by a superpower.

Truman doctrine: statement made by President Harry Truman in March 1947 that it 'must be the policy of the United States to support free people who are resisting attempted subjugation by armed minorities or by outside pressures'. Intended to persuade Congress to support limited aid to Turkey and Greece the doctrine came to underpin the policy of containment and American economic and political support for its allies.

Containment: American political strategy for resisting perceived Soviet expansion, first publicly espoused by an American diplomat, George Kennan, in 1947. Containment became a powerful factor in American policy toward the Soviet Union for the next forty years.

North Atlantic Treaty Organization (NATO): organization established by treaty in April 1949 comprising 12 (later 16) countries from Western Europe and North America. The most important aspect of the NATO alliance was the American commitment to the defence of Western Europe.

Détente: relaxation of tension between East and West; Soviet–American *détente* lasted from the late 1960s to the late 1970s, and was characterized by negotiations and nuclear arms control agreements.

Rapprochement: re-establishment of more friendly relations between the People's Republic of China and the United States in the early 1970s.

Ostpolitik: The West German government's 'Eastern Policy' of the mid to late 1960s, designed to develop relations between West Germany and members of the Warsaw Pact.

Glasnost: policy of greater openness pursued by Soviet President Mikhail Gorbachev from 1985, involving greater toleration of internal dissent and criticism.

Perestroika: policy of restructuring, pursued by Gorbachev in tandem with *Glasnost*, and intended to modernize the Soviet political and economic system.

Sinatra Doctrine: statement by the Soviet foreign ministry in October 1989 that countries of Eastern Europe were 'doing it their way' (a reference to Frank Sinatra's song 'I did it my way') and which marked the end of the Brezhnev doctrine and Soviet hegemony in Eastern Europe.

Brezhnev Doctrine: declaration by Soviet premier Leonid Brezhnev in November 1968 that members of the Warsaw pact would enjoy only 'Limited Sovereignty' in their political development

Mutually Assured Destruction (MAD): condition in which both superpowers possessed the capacity to destroy their adversary even after being attacked first with nuclear weapons.

---

ence in post-colonial/cold war struggles in Angola and Mozambique. Britain, like France, sought to ensure that independence was granted on terms advantageous to the colonial power, even where the decision to leave often reflected the judgement that the cost of fighting the nationalists was too great. Britain and France sought to maximize their interests by economic and political frameworks designed to serve their advantage. The British Commonwealth and the French Union in Africa were the main instruments of this, though the British Commonwealth developed its own identity, and frequently voiced views and concerns at variance with those of the British government. In the 1980s for example the Commonwealth played a major part in the campaigns against apartheid South Africa, bringing it into conflict with the Thatcher government in Britain.

France

The British experience of decolonization stood in contrast to that of the French. France had been defeated during the Second World War, and successive governments sought to preserve French prestige in international affairs by maintaining her imperial status. In Indo-China after 1945 the French attempted to preserve their colonial role, only withdrawing after prolonged guerrilla war and military defeat at the hands of the Vietnamese revolutionary forces, the Viet Minh, led by Ho Chi Minh. In Africa, the picture was different. The wind of change also blew through French Africa, and under President Charles de Gaulle, France withdrew from empire, while attempting to preserve its influence by means of the French Union and later the French Community. In Algeria, however, the

French refused to leave. Algeria was regarded by many French people to be part of France itself. The resulting war, from 1954 to 1962, led to up to 45,000 deaths, and France itself was brought to the edge of civil war.

Portugal

The last European empire in Africa was that of Portugal, and when the military dictatorship was overthrown in Lisbon, withdrawal from empire followed swiftly. The transition to independence occurred with relative ease in Guinea-Bissau, Cape Verde and Sao Tome, but in Mozambique and Angola the anti-colonial struggle was already giving way to conflict among the different anti-colonial groups. These organizations received support from various external powers (America, the Soviet Union, Cuba, and South Africa) which helped arm and finance them. The pattern of resulting conflict reflected a complex of anti-colonial, tribal and ideological allegiances. The consequences were continuing civil war and, eventually, in the case of Mozambique, famine and mass starvation. How far political and ideological divisions, and how far tribal factors were responsible for conflict is a question, and one that was to be asked of many newly emergent African states. Indeed, in general, how far tribal divisions were created or made worse by the imperial powers is an important question in examining the political stability of the newly independent states. Equally important is how capable the new political leaderships in these societies were in tackling their political and economic problems.

Legacies and Consequences: Nationalism or Communism?

The pattern of decolonization in Africa was thus diverse, reflecting the attitudes of the colonial powers, the nature of the local nationalist or revolutionary movements, and in some cases the involvement of external states, including the main cold war protagonists. In Asia, the relationship between nationalism and revolutionary Marxism was a potent force. In Malaya the British defeated an insurgent communist movement (1948–60). In Indo-China the French failed to do likewise

(1946–54). For the Vietnamese, centuries of foreign oppression—Chinese, Japanese, French—soon focused on a new 'imperialist' adversary, the United States. For the Americans, early reluctance to support European imperialism gave way to incremental and covert involvement, and from 1965, increasing and open commitment to the newly created state of South Vietnam. The American aim of containing communism was soon applied to the conflicts of Indo-China. Chinese and Soviet support for North Vietnam and the Viet Cong (the communist guerrillas) were part of the cold war context of the war. The United States, however, failed to devise limited war objectives with a political strategy for defeating these forces. North Vietnamese success in revolutionary warfare eventually led Washington to search for 'peace with honour' once political objectives could not be achieved, and 'victory' was no longer possible. The Viet Cong's Tet (Vietnamese New Year) offensive in 1968 marked a decisive event in the war, though it was not until 1973 that American forces were finally withdrawn, two years before South Vietnam was defeated.

The global trend toward decolonization has been a key development since 1945, but one frequently offset by local circumstances. Some countries have lost their independence since 1945, such as Tibet, invaded by China in 1950, and East Timor, invaded by Indonesia in 1975. Yet, while imperialism has generally withered, other forms of domination or **hegemony** have arisen. The notion of hegemony has been used as criticism of the behaviour of the superpowers, most notably with Soviet hegemony in Eastern Europe, and American hegemony in Central America.

Key Points

- Different European powers had different attitudes to decolonization after 1945: some, such as the British, decided to leave while others wished to preserve their empires, in part (the French) or whole (the Portuguese).

- European powers adopted different attitudes to different regions/countries; e.g. British withdrawal from Asia came much more quickly after 1945 than from Africa.

- The process of decolonization was relatively peaceful in many cases; it led to revolutionary wars in others (e.g. Algeria, Malaya, and Angola), depending on the attitudes of the colonial power and the nationalist movements.

- The struggle for independence/national liberation became involved in cold war conflicts when the superpowers and/or their allies became involved, e.g. Vietnam.

- Whether decolonization was judged successful depends, in part, on whose view you adopt—the European power or the independence movement.

The Cold War

The rise of the United States as a world power after 1945 was of paramount importance in international politics. Its conflict with the Soviet Union provided one of the crucial dynamics in world affairs, and one which affected—directly or indirectly—every part of the globe. In the West, historians have debated, with vigour and acrimony, who was responsible for the collapse of the wartime relationship between the United States and the Soviet Union. The rise of the Soviet Union as a global power after 1945 is equally crucial in understanding international affairs in this period. Relations between the Union of Soviet Socialist Republics (USSR) and its Eastern European 'allies', with the People's Republic of China (PRC), and with various revolutionary movements and governments in the 'Third World', have been vital issues in world politics, as well as key factors in Soviet–American affairs.

Discerning phases in East–West relations casts light on key characteristics of the cold war. How such phases are defined is a matter of debate. The issue of when the cold war began, for example, is closely bound up with the question of who (if anyone) was responsible. Some historians date the origins of the cold war back to the 'Russian revolution' of 1917, while most focus on various dates between 1945 and 1950. Whether the cold war was inevitable, whether it was the consequence of mistakes and misperceptions by political leaders, or whether it was the response of courageous Western leaders to malign and aggressive Soviet intent, are central issues in debates about the origins of the cold war, and its subsequent development. Hitherto, these debates have drawn from Western archives and sources, and are often focused on Western actions and reactions. With the end of the cold war greater evidence is appearing about Soviet actions, and how Moscow perceived the issues. The following sets out various key phases of the cold war (with which not all historians would agree), but which helps understand key features and changes in East–West relations after 1945.

1945–1953: Onset of the Cold War

The onset of the cold war in Europe reflected failure to implement the principles agreed at the wartime conferences of Yalta and Potsdam. The future of Germany, and of various Central and Eastern European countries, notably Poland, were issues of growing tension between the former wartime allies. Reconciling the principles of national self-determination with perceptions of national security was a formidable task. In the West there was a growing feeling that Soviet policy toward Eastern Europe was guided not by historic concern with security but by ideological expansion. In March 1947 the Truman administration sought to justify limited aid to Turkey and Greece with a rhetoric designed to arouse awareness of Soviet aims, and a declaration that America would support those threatened by Soviet subversion or expansion. **The Truman Doctrine** and the associated policy of **Containment** expressed the self-image of the United States as inherently defensive, and was underpinned by the Marshall Plan for European economic recovery, proclaimed in June 1947, which was essential to the economic rebuilding of Western Europe. In Eastern Europe democratic socialist and other anti-communist forces were systematically undermined and eliminated as Marxist-Leninist regimes loyal to Moscow were installed. The only exception was in Yugoslavia, where the Marxist leader, Marshal Tito, consolidated his position while maintaining independence from Moscow. Subsequently Tito's Yugoslavia was to play an important role in the 'Third World's' Non-Aligned Movement.

The first major confrontation of the cold war took

place over Berlin in 1948. The former German capital had been left deep in the heart of the Soviet zone of occupation, and in June 1948 Stalin sought to resolve its status by severing road and rail communications. The city's population and its political autonomy were kept alive by a massive airlift. Stalin ended the blockade in May 1949. The crisis also saw the deployment of American long-range bombers in Britain, officially described as 'atomic-capable', though none were actually armed with nuclear weapons. The American military deployment was followed by the political commitment enshrined in the **North Atlantic Treaty Organization (NATO)** treaty signed in April 1949. The key principle of the treaty was that an attack on one member would be treated as an attack on all. In practice the cornerstone of the alliance was the commitment of the United States to defend Western Europe. In reality, this meant the willingness of the United States to use nuclear weapons to deter Soviet 'aggression'. For the Soviet Union 'political encirclement' soon entailed a growing military, and specifically nuclear, threat.

While the origins of the cold war were in Europe, events and conflicts in Asia and elsewhere, also played a key part. In 1949 the thirty-year long Chinese civil war ended in victory for the communists under Mao Zedong. This had a major impact on Asian affairs and on perceptions in both Moscow and Washington. In 1950 the North Korean attack on South Korea was interpreted as part of a general communist offensive, and a test case for American resolve and the will of the United Nations to withstand aggression. The resulting American and UN commitment, followed in October 1950 by Chinese involvement, led to a war lasting three years and in which over three million people died before prewar borders were restored. North and South Korea themselves remained locked in seemingly perpetual hostility, even after the end of the cold war.

1953–1969: Conflict, Confrontation, and Compromise

One consequence of the Korean war was the build-up of American conventional forces in Western Europe, in case communist aggression in Asia was a feint to detract from the real intent in Europe. The idea that communism was a monolithic political entity controlled from Moscow became an enduring American fixation, not shared in London and

elsewhere. Western Europeans nevertheless depended on the United States for military security and this dependence deepened as the cold war confrontation in Europe was consolidated. The rearmament of the Federal Republic of Germany in 1954 precipitated the creation of the Warsaw Pact in 1955. The build-up of military forces continued apace, with unprecedented concentrations of conventional and moreover nuclear forces. By the 1960s there were some 7,000 nuclear weapons in Western Europe alone. NATO deployed these nuclear weapons to offset Soviet conventional superiority, while Soviet 'theatre nuclear' forces were to compensate for overall American nuclear superiority. Toward the end of the 1950s the United States also deployed nuclear missiles Europe.

The death of Stalin in 1953 was an important event and had significant consequences for the USSR at home and abroad. Stalin's eventual successor, Nikita Khrushchev, strove to modernize Soviet society, but helped unleash reformist tendencies in Eastern Europe. While Polish reformism was controlled, the position in Hungary threatened Soviet hegemony, and in 1956 Soviet intervention brought bloodshed to the streets of Budapest, and international condemnation on Moscow. This condemnation might well have been greater had not two western democracies, Britain and France, then been involved in attacking Egypt over the Suez canal, much to the consternation of the United States. American economic sanctions effectively curtailed what was seen as the last spasm of British imperialism.

Khrushchev's policy toward the West was a mixture of seeking coexistence while pursuing confrontation. Soviet support for movements of national liberation aroused fears in the West of a global communist challenge and further strengthened American determination to support friends and subvert enemies in the 'Third World'. American commitments to liberal democracy and national self-determination were mediated by cold war perspectives, as well as by perceptions of American economic and political interest. Crises over Berlin in 1961 and Cuba in 1962 marked the most dangerous moments of the cold war. In both there was risk of direct military confrontation, and certainly in October 1962 the possibility of nuclear war. How close the world came to Armageddon in the Cuban missile crisis and exactly why peace was preserved remains a matter of great debate among historians and surviving officials.

Table 4.2. **Cold war crises**

1948–9	Berlin	USSR/US/UK/France
1954–55	Taiwan straits crisis	US/PRC
1961	Berlin	USSR/US/NATO
1962	Cuba	USSR/US/Cuba
1973	Arab/Israeli war	Egypt/Israel/Syria/US/USSR
1983	Exercise *Able Archer*	USSR/US/NATO

The events of 1962 were followed by a more stable period of coexistence and competition. Nuclear arsenals continued to grow and both superpowers continued to support friends and subvert enemies. At the same time as America's commitment in Vietnam was deepening, Soviet–Chinese relations were deteriorating. Indeed, by 1969 China and the USSR fought a minor border war over a territorial dispute. Despite these tensions, the foundations for what became known as *détente* were laid between the USSR and USA, and for what became known as *rapprochement* between China and the United States. *Détente* in Europe had its origins in the *ost-politik* of the German Socialist Chancellor, Willy Brandt, and resulted in agreements that recognized the peculiar status of Berlin, and the sovereignty of East Germany. Soviet–American *détente* had its roots in mutual recognition of the need to avoid nuclear crises, and in the economic and military incentives in avoiding an unconstrained arms race.

Both Washington and Moscow also looked toward Beijing in making their 'bilateral' calculations.

1969–1979: The Rise and Fall of *Detente*

The period known as *détente* represented an attempt by both superpowers to manage their relations with each other within a framework of negotiations and agreements. In the West *détente* was associated with the political leadership of President Richard Nixon and his adviser Henry Kissinger, who were also instrumental in Sino-American *rapprochement*. This new phase in Soviet–American relations did not mark an end to political conflict as each side sought to pursue various political goals, some of which were to prove increasingly incompatible with the aspirations of the other superpower. Both sides maintained support for friendly regimes and move-

Table 4.3. **Revolutionary upheavals in the 'Third World', 1974–1980**

Ethiopia	Overthrow of Haile Selassie	Sept. 1974
Cambodia	Khmer Rouge takes Phnom Penh	April 1975
Vietnam	North Vietnam/Viet Cong take Saigon	April 1975
Laos	Pathet Lao takes over state	May 1975
Guinea-Bissau	Independence from Portugal	Sept. 1974
Mozambique	Independence from Portugal	June 1975
Cape Verde	Independence from Portugal	July 1975
Sao Tome	Independence from Portugal	July 1975
Angola	Independence from Portugal	Nov. 1975
Afghanistan	Military coup in Afghanistan	April 1978
Iran	Ayatollah Khomeini installed in power	Feb. 1979
Grenada	New Jewel Movement takes power	March 1979
Nicaragua	Sandinistas take Managua	July 1979
Zimbabwe	Independence from Britain	April 1980

Source: Halliday (1986: 92).

ments, and this came at a time when various political upheavals were taking place in the 'Third World' (see Table 4.3). How far the superpowers were able to control their friends and how far they were entangled by their commitments was underlined in 1973 when the Arab–Israeli war embroiled both the US and the USSR in what became a potentially dangerous confrontation.

In Washington, Soviet support for revolutionary movements in the 'Third World' was seen as evidence of duplicity. Some Americans claim that Moscow's support for revolutionary forces in Ethiopia in 1975 killed *détente*. Others cite the Soviet role in Angola in 1978. Furthermore, the perception that the USSR was using arms control agreements to gain military advantage was linked to Soviet behaviour in the 'Third World'. Growing Soviet military superiority was reflected in growing Soviet influence, it was argued. The view from Moscow was different, reflecting different assumptions about the scope and purpose of *détente*. Other events were also seen to weaken American influence. The overthrow of the Shah of Iran in 1979 resulted in the loss of an important western ally in the region, though the militant Islamic government was as hostile to the USSR as to the USA.

December 1979 marked a point of transition in East–West affairs. NATO agreed to deploy land-based Cruise and Pershing II missiles in Europe if negotiations with the Soviets did not reduce what NATO saw as a serious imbalance. Later in the month, Soviet armed forces intervened in Afghanistan to support their revolutionary allies. The USSR was bitterly condemned in the West and in the 'Third World' for its actions, and soon became committed to a protracted and bloody struggle which many compared to the American war in Vietnam. In the United States the impact on the Carter administration was to change the President's view of the Soviet Union. In 1980 Ronald Reagan was elected President, aided by criticisms of *détente* and arms control, and committed to a more confrontational approach with the Soviets.

1979–86: 'The Second Cold War'

The resulting period of tension and confrontation between the superpowers has been described as the '**Second Cold War**' and compared to the early period of confrontation and tension between 1946 and 1953. In Western Europe and the Soviet Union there was real fear of nuclear war. Much of this was a reaction to the rhetoric and policies of the Reagan administration. American statements on nuclear weapons (see below) and military intervention in Grenada in 1983 and against Libya in 1986 were seen as evidence of a new belligerence. Reagan's policy toward Central America, and support for the rebel *Contras* in Nicaragua, was a source of controversy within the United States and internationally. In 1986 the International Court of Justice found the United States guilty of violating international law for the CIA's covert attacks on Nicaraguan harbours.

The Reagan administration's use of military power was none the less limited, and some operations ended in humiliating failure, notably in the Lebanon in 1983. The rhetoric and the perception, however, were at variance with the reality. Nevertheless, there is evidence that the Soviet leadership took very seriously the words (and deeds) of the Reagan administration and believed that the US leadership was planning a nuclear first strike. In 1983 Soviet air defences shot down a South Korean civilian airliner in Soviet airspace. The American reaction and the imminent deployment of US nuclear missiles in Europe created a climate of great tension in East–West relations. And in November 1983 Soviet intelligence misinterpreted a NATO training exercise (codenamed *Able Archer*) and led the Soviet leadership to believe that NATO was preparing to attack them. How close the world came to a serious nuclear confrontation in 1983 is not yet clear.

Throughout the early 1980s the Soviets were handicapped by a succession of ageing political leaders (Brezhnev, Andropov, and Chernenko) whose ill-health further inhibited Soviet responses to the American challenge and the American threat. This changed dramatically after Mikhail Gorbachev became President in 1985. Gorbachev's 'new thinking' in foreign policy and his domestic reforms created a revolution both in the USSR's foreign relations and within Soviet society. At home the policies of **glasnost** (or openness) and **perestroika** (or restructuring) unleashed nationalist and other forces which, to Gorbachev's dismay, were to destroy the Union of Soviet Socialist Republics.

Gorbachev's aim in foreign policy was to transform relations with the United States and Western Europe. His domestic reforms were also a catalyst for change in Eastern Europe, though, unlike Khrushchev, Gorbachev was not prepared to respond with force or coercion. When confronted with revolt in Eastern Europe, Gorbachev's foreign ministry declared that countries of Eastern Europe were 'doing it their way' and invoked Frank Sinatra's song 'I did it my way' to mark the end of the **Brezhnev doctrine** which had limited Eastern European sovereignty and political development. The **Sinatra doctrine** meant that Eastern Europeans were now allowed to 'do it their way'. Throughout Eastern Europe Moscow-aligned regimes gave way to democracies, in what for the most part was a peaceful as well as speedy transition (see Chapter 5). Most dramatically, Germany became united and East Germany (the German Democratic Republic) disappeared.

Gorbachev's policy toward the West used agreements on nuclear weapons as a means of building trust, and demonstrating the serious and radical nature of his purpose. Despite similar radical agreements on conventional forces in Europe, culminating in the Paris agreement of 1990, the end of the cold war, however, marked success in nuclear arms control but not the beginning of nuclear disarma-ment. The histories of the cold war and of the bomb are very closely connected, but while the cold war is now over, nuclear weapons are still very much in existence.

Key Points

- There are disagreements about when the cold war started, why, and who was responsible.

- The cold war began in Europe with the failure to implement the agreements reached at Potsdam and Yalta.

- Distinct phases can be seen in East–West relations during which tension and the risk of direct confrontation grew and receded.

- Some civil and regional wars were intensified and prolonged by superpower involvement; others may have been prevented or shortened.

- The end of the cold war has not resulted in the abolition of nuclear weapons.

The Bomb

Using the Bomb in 1945

Nuclear weapons preceded and post-dated the cold war. The Western allies developed the atomic bomb in the war against Nazi Germany and Imperial Japan, and intended to use the weapon in much the same way as they had used strategic bombing against German and Japanese cities. The destruction of the Japanese cities of Hiroshima and Nagasaki was of great significance in post-war affairs, but, as Table 4.4 shows, the scale of the casualties and the extent of the devastation were not exceptional. The precise importance of Hiroshima and Nagasaki in post-war affairs remains a matter of continuing controversy. Aside from the moral issues involved in attacking civilian populations, the destruction of the two cities has generated fierce debate, particularly among American historians, about why the bomb was dropped. Gar Alperovitz in his celebrated book *Atomic Diplomacy*, first published in 1965, claimed that as President Truman knew that Japan was defeated his real reason for dropping the bomb was to coerce the Soviet Union in post-war affairs to serve American interests in Europe and Asia. Such claims generated angry and dismissive responses from other historians. Ensuing debates have benefited from more histori-cal evidence, though this has only partially resolved the controversies. Inasmuch as a consen-sus exists now among historians it is that Truman's decision reflected various considerations. Debate remains about how far Truman dropped the bomb simply to end the war and how far other factors, including the coercion of the Soviet Union in post-war affairs, entered his calculations.

Whether Hiroshima and Nagasaki should have been destroyed nevertheless remains a matter for debate. So too is the question of what were the effects of their destruction. Whether the use of nuclear weapons demonstrated the awesome power of such weapons to post-war decision-mak-ers and thereby inhibited their use or whether by accelerating the development of the Soviet atomic bomb Hiroshima speeded up or even started the nuclear arms race are questions to consider.

Table 4.4. **Second World War estimated casualties**

Hiroshima (6 August 1945): 70–80,000 'prompt'; 140,000 by end 1945; 200,000 by 1950

Nagasaki: (9 August 1945): 30–40,000 'prompt'; 70,000 by end 1945; 140,000 by 1950

Tokyo (9 March 1945): 100,000 +

Dresden (13–15 February 1945): 60–135,000

Coventry (14 November 1940): 568

Leningrad (siege 1941–4): 900,000 +

Sources: Rhodes, R., *The Making of the Atomic Bomb* (New York: Simon & Schuster, 1986); Committee for the Compilation of Materials, *Damage Caused by the Atomic Bombs in Hiroshima and Nagasaki, Hiroshima and Nagasaki: The Physical, Medical, and Social Effects of the Atomic Bombings* (New York: Basic Books, 1981); Gilbert, M., *Churchill: A Life* (London: Heinemann, 1991).

Toward the Global Battlefield

The bomb that was dropped on Hiroshima was equivalent in destructive power to 12,500 tons of TNT. In 1952 the United States exploded a thermo-nuclear or hydrogen bomb, equivalent to 10,400,000 tons of TNT. Subsequent nuclear weapons were measured in this new megaton range, each capable of destroying the largest of cities in a single explosion. Equally significant was the development of the means to deliver them. In 1945 the American bomber that destroyed Hiroshima took some six hours to cross the Pacific and reach its target. Initially the United States did not possess bombers that had the range to reach the USSR from the USA, and used British and other bases to hold at risk Soviet targets. Both super-powers developed long-range bombers, and then ballistic missiles that could target the other super-power from their own territory. In 1957 the USSR tested an Intercontinental Ballistic Missile (ICBM) and later that year launched a satellite, *Sputnik*, into space using such a missile. In 1960 the United States began deploying ballistic missiles on submarines. (For details of the technological arms race see Table 4.5.)

By then the world was potentially a global bat-tlefield in which both superpowers could fire nuclear weapons at each other's territory from their own, and in no more than the 30–40 minutes it took a ballistic missile to travel from one continent to the other. The global dimension was increased by

Table 4.5. **The nuclear technology race**

Weapon	Date of Testing or Deployment	
	USA	USSR
Atomic bomb	1945	1949
Intercontinental bomber	1948	1955
Jet bomber	1951	1954
Hydrogen bomb	1952	1953
Intercontinental Ballistic Missile	1958	1957
Submarine Launched Ballistic Missile	1960	1964
Anti-Ballistic Missile	1974	1966
Multiple Independently targetable Re-entry Vehicle	1970	1975

Source: McNamara, R., *Blundering into Disaster* (New York: Pantheon, 1987: 60).

Len Scott

Table 4.6. **The Arms Race: American and Soviet nuclear bombs and warheads 1945–1990**

	1945	1950	1955	1960	1965	1970	1975	1980	1985	1990
USA	2	450	4,750	6,068	5,550	4,000	8,500	10,100	11,200	9,680
USSR	0	0	20	300	600	1,800	2,800	6,000	9,900	10,999

Sources: McNamara, R., *Blundering into Disaster* (New York: Pantheon, 1987: 154–5); International Institute for Strategic Studies, *The Military Balance 1990–1991* (London: IISS, 1991). Soviet figures given here are based on Western estimates.

the emergence of other nuclear weapon states—Britain in 1952, France in 1960 and People's Republic of China in 1964. In the 1950s there was growing concern at the spread or **proliferation** of nuclear weapons and in the 1960s a nuclear Non-Proliferation Treaty (NPT) was negotiated in which those states which had nuclear weapons committed themselves to halt the arms race, while those states who did not have nuclear weapons promised not to develop them. Despite the apparent success of the NPT agreement several states are known to have developed nuclear weapons (Israel, India, and apartheid South Africa) and others have invested considerable effort in doing so (Iraq, North Korea, and Pakistan).

Both the Soviet Union and United States also made some attempt to develop missiles that could shoot down incoming ballistic missiles and thereby provide defence against nuclear attack. These anti-ballistic missiles (ABMs) were technologically ineffective and both sides continued to rely on offensive nuclear weapons for their security. In 1972 an agreement was concluded which limited ABM defences to a token level. However in 1983 President Reagan cast doubt on the principles of this agreement by launching the Strategic Defense Initiative (SDI) (see below).

The growth in Soviet and American arsenals is often characterized as an arms race, though how far perception of the adversary and how far internal political and bureaucratic pressures caused the growth of nuclear arsenals is a matter for debate. For the United States, commitments to its NATO allies also provided pressures and opportunities to develop and deploy shorter range ('tactical' and 'theatre') nuclear weapons. At the strategic (or long-range) level qualitative change was as significant as quantitative change. In particular, the fear that one side would have sufficient weapons of sufficient accuracy to destroy the other side's nuclear arsenal became a mutual fear. Robert Oppenheimer, one of

the scientists who created the American atomic bomb, characterized the atomic age as like two scorpions trapped in a glass jar. The scorpions have no means of escape and no alternative but to threaten that which it would be suicidal to carry out. Yet the logic of what became known in the West as **Mutually Assured Destruction (MAD)** depended upon each side being able to destroy its adversary after being attacked. For much of the cold war both sides feared that the other was moving, or believed it was moving, to a position of meaningful superiority. What is clear is that ideas of MAD were of only limited relevance to the military force structures and strategies adopted by the superpowers.

The situation was further complicated by the differences in the attitude of the two superpowers. The Soviet Union was confronted first by a situation of American monopoly, and then by enduring US superiority. This was coupled with political encirclement and growing antagonism with a nuclear armed China. From the American side misperception of Soviet nuclear strength in 1950s was allied with concern about Soviet political ambitions. This was further complicated by US military and political commitments, especially to NATO, and its determination to use nuclear weapons against, and thereby to deter, Soviet aggression toward Western Europe. Even if a nuclear war could never be won, the policies and strategies of both superpowers, and of NATO, can be seen to be ambiguous on these critical issues.

Rise and Fall of *Détente*: Fall and Rise of Arms Control

How far the arms race was the result of mutual misperceptions, how far the unavoidable outcome of irreconcilable political differences are central questions. Some influential Americans believed that the

Table 4.7. **Principal arms control and disarmament agreements**

Treaty/agreement	Weapon/delivery system	Signed	Parties
Geneva protocol	Chemical weapons: bans use	1925	100+
Limited Test Ban Treaty	Bans atmospheric, underwater, outer-space nuclear tests.	1963	100+
Nuclear Non-Proliferation Treaty	Limits spread of nuclear weapons	1968	100+
Biological Weapons Convention	Bans production/use	1972	80+
SALT 1	Limits strategic arms*	1972	US/USSR
ABM Treaty	Limits Anti-Ballistic Missiles	1972	US/USSR
SALT II	Limits strategic arms*	1979	US/USSR
Intermediate Nuclear Forces Treaty	Bans two categories of land-based missiles	1987	US/USSR
START 1	Reduces strategic arms*	1990	US/USSR

* Strategic arms are long range weapons.

Source: adapted from Harvard Nuclear Study Group, 'Arms Control and Disarmament: What Can and Can't be Done', in Holroyd, F. (ed.), *Thinking About Nuclear Weapons* (London: Croom Helm, 1985: 96).

Soviets were bent on world domination, which the communist rhetoric of world revolution certainly encouraged. What is clear is that nuclear weapons provided the context and pretext for their more dangerous confrontations, most notably when the Soviet Union deployed nuclear missiles in Cuba in 1962. It is also clear that when political confrontation gave way to Soviet–American *détente*, agreements on nuclear weapons became the most tangible achievement of *détente*. Yet, just as *détente* was a way of managing East–West conflict, and did not resolve the basis of disagreement, so too, arms control was a means of regulating the growth of nuclear arsenals, not eliminating them (see Table 4.6). On the other hand, critics argued, arms control served to legitimize the existence and growth of nuclear arsenals. Disarmament meant getting rid of weapons. While arms control was sometimes presented as a first step to disarmament it was more generally recognized as a means of managing nuclear weapons.

Yet just as *détente* collapsed in the 1970s, the achievements of the SALT (Strategic Arms Limitation Talks) process gave way to renewed conflict and debate over nuclear weapons. In the West, critics of *détente* and arms control argued that the Soviets were acquiring nuclear superiority. Some of these critics also urged that the United States should now pursue policies and strategies based on the idea that victory in nuclear war was possible. The election of Ronald Reagan to the American Presidency in 1980 was a watershed in Soviet–American relations. The period of the 'Second Cold War' marked a new phase in the political and nuclear relationship between East and West. One issue which Reagan inherited, and which loomed large in the breakdown of relations between East and West, was nuclear missiles in Europe. NATO's decision to deploy land-based missiles capable of striking Soviet territory precipitated a period of great tension in relations between NATO and the USSR, and political friction within NATO. Reagan's own incautious public remarks reinforced perceptions that he was as ill-informed as he was dangerous in matters nuclear, though some of his arms policies were consistent with those of his predecessor, Jimmy Carter. On arms control Reagan was disinterested in arms agreements that would freeze the status quo for the sake of getting an agreement, and the Soviet and American negotiators proved unable to make progress in talks on long-range and intermediate range weapons. One particular initiative had significant consequences for arms control and for the USA's relations both with the Soviets and its allies. The **Strategic Defense Initiative** (SDI), quickly dubbed 'Star Wars', was a research programme designed to explore the feasibility of space-based defences against ballistic missiles. The Soviets appear to have taken SDI very seriously, and claimed that President Reagan's real purpose was to regain the nuclear monopoly of the 1950s. The technological advances claimed by SDI proponents did not materialize, however, and the programme was reduced and then terminated by Reagan's successors.

The advent of Mikhail Gorbachev paved the way for agreements on nuclear and conventional forces, which helped ease the tensions that had characterized the early 1980s. In 1987 Gorbachev travelled to America to sign the Intermediate Nuclear Forces (INF) Treaty banning intermediate range nuclear missiles, including Cruise and Pershing II. This agreement was heralded as a triumph for the Soviet President, but NATO leaders, including Thatcher and Reagan argued that it was vindication of the policies pursued by NATO since 1979. The INF treaty was concluded more quickly than a new agreement on cutting strategic nuclear weapons, in part because of Soviet views on SDI. And it was Reagan's successor, George Bush, who concluded a Strategic Arms Reductions Treaty (START) agreement, which reduced long-range nuclear weapons (though only back to the level they had been in the early 1980s). By the time that a follow-on START–2 agreement was reached in 1992, the USSR had disintegrated. The collapse of the USSR meant that four nuclear weapons states were now created (Russia, Kazakhstan, Belarus, and Ukraine). Nevertheless, all the new states made clear their commitments to the treaty and to the new cordial relations with the West, which marked the end of the cold war. On the other hand, the disintegration of the Soviet Union has raised fears about the spread of nuclear technologies and nuclear technologists.

Moreover, the continuing proliferation of nuclear weapons raises the prospect of regional arms races and crises, such as when India and Pakistan are believed to have come close to nuclear confrontation in 1990. The end of the cold war may have reduced some nuclear problems—it may well have increased others. It has certainly not solved the problem of nuclear weapons.

Key Points

- There remains a debate about the use of the bomb in 1945, and the effect that this had on the cold war.
- Nuclear weapons have been an important factor in the cold war. How far the arms race has had a momentum of its own is a matter of debate.
- Agreements on limiting and controlling the growth of nuclear arsenals have played an important role in Soviet–American (and East–West) relations.
- States with nuclear weapons have agreed on the desirability of preventing the spread of nuclear weapons to other states.
- Various international crises have occurred in which there has been the risk of nuclear war. Judging how close we came to nuclear war at these times remains a matter of debate.

Conclusion

The changes that have taken place in world politics since 1945 have been enormous. Assessing their significance raises many complex issues about the nature of international history and international relations. The question of who won the cold war, and how, and with what implications, are matters on which fierce controversy has been generated. Several points are emphasized in this conclusion concerning the relationship between the three trends explored in the chapter (End of Empire, Cold War, and The Bomb). The period of history since 1945 has witnessed the end of European empires constructed before, and in the early part of, the twentieth century, and has also witnessed the rise

and fall of the cold war. The end of the cold war has also been followed by the demise of one of the two principal protagonists in that conflict, the Union of Soviet Socialist Republics (see Ch. 5). The relationship between end of empire and cold war conflicts in the 'Third World' is a close though problematic one. In some cases cold war involvement of the superpowers helped bring about change. In others, where the superpowers became directly involved it resulted in the escalation and prolongation of the conflict. Marxist ideology in various forms provided inspiration to many 'Third World' liberation movements, but provocation to the United States and others. The example of Vietnam is most obvious in these respects, but in a range of anti-colonial struggles the cold war played a major part. Precisely how the cold war influenced decolonization is best assessed on a case by case basis. One key issue is how far the values and objectives of revolutionary leaders and their movements were nationalist rather than Marxist. It is claimed that both Ho Chi Minh in Vietnam and Fidel Castro in Cuba were primarily nationalists who could have been won over to the West, but turned to Moscow and to communism in the face of American and Western hostility. The divisions between the USSR and the People's Republic of China also demonstrate the diverging trends within Marxism. In several instances conflict between communists became as bitter as conflict between communists and capitalists.

Similarly, the relationship between the cold war and the history of nuclear weapons is a close though problematic one. Some historians contend that the use of atomic weapons by the United States played a decisive part in the origins of the cold war. Others would see the paranoia created by the threat of total annihilation to be central to understanding Soviet defence and foreign policy: the unprecedented threat of devastation provides the key to understanding the mutual hostility and fear of both sets of leaders in the nuclear age. It is also argued that without nuclear weapons direct Soviet–American conflict would have been much more likely, and that had nuclear weapons not acted as a deterrent then war in Europe would have been much more likely. On the other hand there are those who contend that nuclear weapons have played a relatively limited role in East–West relations, and that in political terms their importance is exaggerated.

Nuclear weapons have been a focus for political agreement, and during *détente* nuclear arms agreements acted as the currency of international politics. How far and why nuclear weapons have helped keep the peace (if indeed they have) raises very important questions not only for assessing the cold war but for contemplating the proliferation of nuclear and other weapons of mass destruction into the next century. How close we came to nuclear war in 1961 (Berlin) or 1962 (Cuba) or 1973 (Arab–Israeli war) or 1983 (Exercise 'Able Archer') and what lessons might be learned from these events are crucial questions for historians and policy-makers alike. One central issue is how far cold war perspectives and the involvement of the nuclear armed superpowers imposed stability in regions where previous instability had led to war and conflict. The cold war may have led to unprecedented concentrations of military and nuclear forces in Europe, but this was a period characterized by both stability and great economic prosperity, certainly in the West. How far this stability was bought at the risk of an ever present danger of nuclear confrontation is a question historians are still exploring and debating.

Both the cold war and the age of empire are over, though across the globe their legacies, good and bad, seen and unseen, persist. The age of 'the bomb', and of other weapons of mass destruction (chemical and biological) continues. How far the clash of communist and liberal/capitalist ideologies helped facilitate and/or retard the process of globalization is a matter for debate. Despite the limitations of the human imagination the global consequences of nuclear war remain all too real. The accident at the Soviet nuclear reactor at Chernobyl in 1986 showed that radioactivity knows no boundaries. In the 1980s some scientists suggested that only a fraction of the world's nuclear weapons, exploded over a fraction of the world's cities, could bring an end to life itself in the northern hemisphere. While the threat of strategic nuclear war has receded the global problem of nuclear weapons remains a common and urgent concern as humanity approaches the millennium.

QUESTIONS

1. Was Harry Truman to blame for the collapse of the wartime alliance after 1945 and the onset of the cold war?

2. Why did the United States become involved in wars in Asia after 1945? Illustrate your answer by reference to either the Korean or Vietnam wars.

3. Did *détente* succeed?

4. Should Ronald Reagan or Mikhail Gorbachev claim the greater credit for the ending of the cold war?

5. Why did France try to remain an imperial power in Indo-China and Algeria?

6. What were the consequences of the collapse of the Portuguese empire in Africa?

7. Were the British successful at decolonization after 1945?

8. Compare and contrast the end of empire in Africa with that in Asia after 1945.

9. Why were atomic bombs dropped on Hiroshima and Nagasaki?

10. Did nuclear weapons help prevent war in Europe after 1945?

11. How close did we come to nuclear war during either the Berlin crisis (1961) or the Cuban missile crisis (1962)?

12. What role did nuclear weapons play in Soviet–American relations during the 1980s?

GUIDE TO FURTHER READING

General

Vadney, T. E., *The World since 1945* (Harmondsworth: Penguin, 1987). Provides an account of the major developments in world politics from 1945 to 1986, and explores the relationship between the superpower confrontation and the 'Third World'.

Dunbabin, J. P. D., *International Relations since 1945*, i. *The Cold War: the Great Powers and their Allies*, and ii. *The Post-Imperial Age : The Great Powers and the Wider World* (London: Longmans, 1994) This 2-volume work provides a fairly detailed analytical account of the principal events and developments in international politics since 1945. Vol. 1 focuses on the superpower conflict and the role of Europe in the cold war; Vol. 2 covers decolonization, regional issues, and the new challenges facing the international system in later decades.

The Cold War

Gaddis, J., *Russia, The Soviet Union and the United States: An Interpretative History* (New York: McGraw Hill, 1990). Provides an overview of relations between Russia, then the Soviet Union and the United States, and examines the different phases of the relationship, including the origins, dynamics, and end of the cold war.

Halliday, F., *The Making of the Second Cold War* (London: Verso, 2nd edn. 1986). Explores the phase in the cold war of Soviet–American antagonism, 1979–85, and places this in a broader thematic and historical analysis of the cold war.

The Bomb

Lebow, R. N., and Stein, J. G., *We All Lost the Cold War* (Princeton: Princeton University Press, 1994). Provides a revisionist interpretation of the cold war and reassesses the role and risks of nuclear deterrence by detailed examination of two case studies: the Cuban missile crisis and the Arab–Israeli war of 1973.

Newhouse, J., *The Nuclear Age* (London: Michael Joseph, 1989). Provides a history of nuclear weapons which examines the technological and political dimensions of the arms race, from the use of the bomb at Hiroshima to the debates and issues of the 1980s.

Alperovitz, G., *The Decision to Use the Atomic Bomb* (London: Harper Collins, 1995). This is a detailed study of the American decision to use the atomic bomb on Japan, which assesses the debate about the use of the bomb and the origins of the cold war.

Decolonization

Low, D. A., *Eclipse of Empire* (Cambridge: Cambridge University Press, 1993). This provides a detailed analysis of the British withdrawal from empire, and draws comparisons with other experiences such as the French in Africa and the Dutch in Indonesia.

5 The End of the Cold War

Richard Crockatt

READER'S GUIDE

The end of the cold war represented a turning point in the structures of international politics, in the roles and functions of nation-states and in international organizations. The chief cause of the end of the cold war was the collapse of communism in the Soviet Union and Eastern Europe. This had deep internal roots in the history of Soviet bloc societies but a full explanation of the end of the cold war must include examination of external pressures, particularly the policies of the United States, and growing relative economic disadvantage experienced by the Soviet bloc over the post-war period. Ultimately the Soviet bloc was unable to compete because it failed to keep step with the globalization of capitalism. Since the end of the cold war the most obvious characteristic of international politics is the absence of any clear principle of order or structure.

Introduction

Historical events do not come with labels upon them, telling us precisely how important they are. Only the passage of time can do that, and it may take years. Communist Chinese Prime Minister Chou En Lai is reported to have said, in reply to a question about the significance of the French Revolution, that 'it's too soon to tell'. Nevertheless, some events are sufficiently momentous in their immediate effects for us to be able to say with confidence that something important has happened, even if full explanations are as yet unattainable.

The events of 1989–1991, from the collapse of the Iron Curtain to the dismantling of the Soviet Union in December 1991, represent a turning point in three respects. **First**, they marked the end of the broadly bipolar structure, based on US–Soviet rivalry, which the international system had assumed since the late 1940s.

A **second** set of important changes took place at the level of the nation-state. Former communist states experienced serious problems of transition, ranging from economic collapse, which affected them all, to (in the case of the Soviet Union, Czechoslovakia, and most explosively Yugoslavia), the disintegration of the nation itself. Even those nations which maintained communist systems, such as China, North Korea, and Cuba, faced enormous challenges, since they had to accommodate themselves to positions of increased marginality. Yet those states not in the throes of post-communist transition were also forced to redefine their national interests and roles in the light of the radical change in the international balance of power. This applied as much to large states such as the United States, whose policies had been premissed on the Soviet threat, as to small states in the Third World which had been to a greater or lesser degree 'client' states of the superpowers. The general point is that the end of the cold war enforced a redefinition of national interests on all states and in some cases a reshaping of the nations themselves.

The **third** important indicator of change in the end of the cold war lay in new or modified roles for international organizations. Most obviously the ending of the virtually automatic split in the United Nations (UN) Security Council along cold war lines, which had found the United States and the Soviet Union routinely using the veto against each other's proposals, released the potential for the UN to work as a genuinely collective body. The novel possibility of consensus on major issues in the Security Council did not ensure that the UN would act decisively or with authority—it was still a creature of the nations which composed it and they continued to guard their national sovereignties—but it did remove one obstacle to collective decision-making and one which had crippled the UN during the cold war (see Ch. 14).

The end of the cold war also had an impact on various multilateral treaty organizations. The Warsaw Pact (or Warsaw Treaty Organization) was disbanded, while the North Atlantic Treaty Organization (NATO) struggled to reconceive itself in a context in which European security as a whole was being redefined. Questions too were raised about possible roles for other existing European security organizations such as the Western European Union (WEU) and the Conference on Security and Co-operation in Europe (CSCE). The European Union (EU) debated expansion of its membership to include nations from Eastern Europe. However tenative these gestures, however unrealized the ambition to create a new European and a new international order, the end of the cold war forced such questions on to the agenda (see Ch. 21).

In short, the end of the cold war saw radical change at the system level, at the level of the nation state, and in international organizations.

Before examining the causes and consequences of these transformations, two preliminary points must be made. The first has to do with what is meant by the term 'cold war'. It has been used in *two* distinct senses:

1. First, in a narrow sense to refer to the years between the Truman Doctrine (1947) and the Khrushchev thaw of the mid–1950s, during which virtually unrelieved antagonism existed between the superpowers. To the extent that the open antagonisms of these years were reproduced later in, for example, the Kennedy years and the first Reagan administration, then the term cold war is also applied to these instances. The term refers to a certain kind of **behaviour**, characterized by open ideological confrontation. Such periods of cold war alternated with periods of *détente* (1953–60, 1969–75, 1985–9),

during which negotiations and tension reduction were firmly on the agenda.

2. The second meaning of 'cold war', and the one which is adopted here, has to do with the **structure** rather than the *behaviour* of East–West relations. To the extent that key elements of that structure remained continuous throughout the post-war period, then cold war refers to the whole period from the late 1940s to the late 1980s. Viewed from this perspective, *détente* was part of the cold war rather than a departure from it, in that while there was behavioural change in periods of *détente*, the fundamental structure of US–Soviet relations remained constant. When we talk of the end of the cold war we therefore mean the end of that structural condition which was defined by political and military rivalry between the United States and the Soviet Union, ideological antagonism between capitalism and communism, the division of Europe, and the extension of conflict at the centre to the periphery of the international system.

A second preliminary point involves the relationship between the collapse of communism and the end of the cold war. On the face of it, they are one and the same thing. The **great game** of US–Soviet conflict ended when one of the competitors gave up the fight. However, while it is true that communism's demise was the proximate cause of the end of the cold war, it is wrong to suggest that it is to be wholly explained in these terms. In what follows we shall analyse the end of the cold war with

reference to three sets of factors: (1) internal developments in the Soviet bloc; (2) external forces in the form of Western policies towards the Soviet bloc; and (3) the changing relative position of the Soviet bloc with respect to the West. This will be followed by a discussion of the immediate global consequences of the end of the cold war. The chapter will end with some inevitably tenative ideas about possible futures.

Key Points

- The end of the cold war was a major historical turning point as measured by changes in the international system, the nation-state, and international organizations.

- The term 'cold war' can refer both to the behavioural characteristics of US–Soviet relations, which fluctuated over the period 1945–89, or to the basic structure of their relations, which remained constant.

- The key structural elements of the cold war are political and military (above all nuclear) rivalry between the United States and the Soviet Union, ideological conflict between capitalism and communism, the division of Europe, and the extension of superpower conflict to the Third World.

- The collapse of communism was the proximate cause of the end of the cold war but does not explain all aspects of the transformation of international politics since 1989.

Internal Factors: The Collapse of Communism in the Soviet Union

Structural Problems in the Soviet System

Among the most striking features of communism's collapse was its suddenness, a surprise as much to most Western experts on the Soviet Union and Eastern Europe as to political leaders and the public. One Western Soviet expert, whose views are fairly representative, wrote in a study published in 1986, that 'it is unlikely that the [Soviet] state is now, or will be in the late 1980s, in danger of social or political disintegration. Thus we must study the

factors which made the regime stable in the post-Stalin era and are still at work at the present' (Bialer 1986: 19). It is true that revolutionary change by its nature contains a large element of the incalculable. Institutional inertia, social customs, and psychological habit ensure that systems can maintain their outer shapes long after they have begun to decay internally. Perhaps the most useful general observation on the causes of revolution remains that of the French political philosopher Alexis de Tocqueville: that revolutions happen not when dictatorial regimes are at their most repressive but when they are seeking to reform themselves. In seeking to institute and legitimize their reforms, the old regimes make political concessions to their opponents and in doing so chip away at the foundations of their own power. This model, generalized as it is, is a useful starting point for an understanding of Mikhail Gorbachev's revolutionary period in power.

Gorbachev's accession to power in March 1985 was itself an event of considerable significance. He was the first General Secretary of the Soviet Communist Party to have reached maturity after the Second World War. He had little adult experience of the Stalinist period and was less beholden to the Stalinist legacy than his predecessors. He had been appointed to the ruling Politburo as recently as 1978 towards the end of the **era of stagnation** under Brezhnev. In projecting a new dynamism as a representative of the rising class of educated professionals, he presented a striking contrast to the ageing and intellectually stultified leaders of the Brezhnev period. His path to leadership was not immediate on Brezhnev's death. Following the latter's death in 1982 an interregnum ensued during which first Yuri Andropov and then Konstantin Chernenko were appointed and died in each case within little more than a year in office. The passing of the old guard, combined with Gorbachev's power base among advocates of change, which enabled him to make key changes in personnel, conveyed the sense that Gorbachev was inaugurating a new era in Soviet history.

Crucially, however, it was evidently not his intention to dismantle the Soviet Union. His widely read political credo, *Perestroika* (1988), was firmly anti-Stalinist but not anti-socialist. 'Through *perestroika* and *glasnost*,' he wrote, 'the ideals of socialism will gain fresh impetus'; and they would do so through a return to the ideals of Lenin, who 'lives on in the minds and hearts of millions of people' (Gorbachev 1988: 131; 25). Indeed the sense of renewal which Gorbachev projected did not seem to presage the end of the cold war. On the contrary, it was felt by many on the Right in the United States that a reinvigorated Soviet Union would present a more severe challenge to the West than the old sclerotic leadership.

How, then are we to explain the transformation of the next few years? We can usefully distinguish between **long-term** and **short-term** causes. The chief long-term problem was **economic**, though

---

Box 5.1. Change in the Soviet Union

1985 March	On death of Konstantin Chernenko, Mikhail Gorbachev becomes General Secretary of the Soviet Communist Party.
1987	Publication of Gorbachev's book *Perestroika*.
1988 April	The Soviet Union undertakes to withdraw troops from Afghanistan by February 1989; October Gorbachev becomes President of the USSR, replacing Andrei Gromyko.
1989 March	Elections held for the Congress of People's Deputies.
1990 March	Congress of People's Deputies abolishes the leading role of the Communist Party; Lithuania declares independence from the USSR.
1991 Aug.	Coup against Gorbachev.
Dec.	USSR ceases to exist and CIS (Commonwealth of Independent States) comes into being.

---

arguably it had political roots, in that economic policies and practices were dictated by political ideology. Structural weaknesses were built into the system of the command economy which relied on inflexible central planning, rewarded gross output of goods rather than productivity, and offered disincentives to innovation in management and production techniques. In place of a market relation between consumer demand and supply, from the late 1920s the centre dictated what kinds of goods should be produced and at what prices, according pre-eminence to heavy industrial production with a view to forced-marching the Soviet economy into the twentieth century. Arguably, this approach succeeded up to a point; the Soviet Union's ability to withstand Germany's onslaught in 1941 and ultimately to defeat the Third Reich owed a good deal to the brutal pace at which Stalin pushed the Soviet economy and the Soviet people in the 1930s. Such success came at enormous human cost and at the cost of entrenching the primacy of heavy industry in Soviet economic thinking far beyond the point of utility. That point was reached somewhere in the 1970s when the computer and automation revolution overtook the West but virtually bypassed the Soviet Union except in the military sector. Even there the Soviet Union found it hard to keep pace with the West (Dibb 1988: 266). Furthermore, agriculture was a notoriously weak sector of the Soviet economy. In agriculture, as in industry, central planning stifled productivity and promoted inflexible practices.

These problems were **systemic** and of long standing. If so, why was the Soviet Union able to survive so long and why did these problems become critical in the 1980s? The answers to both questions have political as well as economic components. Survival was possible economically because, as mentioned above, the Soviet economy performed well in certain fields such as the production of heavy industrial goods and military equipment. It also had large reserves of oil which could be sold for hard currency. Politically, the legacy of discipline and repression supplied by the Communist Party served to stifle dissent and more positively to promote an ethos of collective sacrifice such as is undertaken by governments in wartime. Indeed the Soviet system could be described as essentially a war economy. As for the question of why conditions became critical in the 1980s, economically, as we have seen, the failure to modernize in line with the West was of paramount importance. Furthermore, a serious decline in harvests in the late 1970s and a slowdown in production in some key industries suggested a general climate of economic stagnation. Commentary also began to appear in the West during the early 1980s on a decline in general health in the Soviet Union, rising death rates and infant mortality rates (Hobsbawm 1994: 472).

The Effects of Gorbachev's Reforms: Glasnost and Political Restructuring

However, even these problems might not have been critical, given the capacity of the Soviet system to sustain itself despite handicaps. It took specific initiatives by Gorbachev to turn these systemic problems into a systemic crisis. The first of these initiatives was the decision to permit dissemination of knowledge about the realities of Soviet life (*glasnost* or 'openness'), the second and third were political and economic restructuring (*perestroika*). Elements of these programmes had been present in previous reform efforts in the Soviet Union, for example during the Khrushchev period. If there was one element which differentiated Gorbachev's approach from that of his predecessors it was his conviction that consent rather than coercion should, as far as possible, guide implementation of these changes.

> ### Box 5.2. Internal Causes of the Collapse of Soviet Communism
>
> **Long-term causes**
> - structural weaknesses in the economy, including:
> - inflexible central planning system
> - inability to modernize
> - inefficiency and absence of incentives in agricultural production
>
> **Short-term causes**
> - economic stagnation in the 1970s and 1980s
> - poor harvests in the late 1970s and early 1980s
> - Gorbachev's political and economic reforms

Glasnost was in one sense the old communist tradition of self-criticism writ large. The difference was that *glasnost* was less purely ritualistic, less hedged around with restrictions, and more open-ended than the usual forms of self-criticism which took place in the pages of *Pravda* and similar publications. Designed to purify and cleanse rather than destroy, to serve as a means of gaining public support for Gorbachev's reforms rather than a vehicle for attacks on the system itself, **glasnost** quickly exceeded the bounds set for it. Once controls on the press, radio, television, and the film industry were loosened, control of public opinion began to slip from Gorbachev's grasp. (Indeed only now could one begin to speak of public opinion in the Soviet Union.) Freedom of expression gave a voice to those who opposed Gorbachev as well as to those who wanted to go farther and faster than he did. While *glasnost* did not of itself create opposition parties, the logic of *glasnost* was ultimately to undermine the fundamental principle of the Party's leading role. Although the Party's privileged position, guaranteed by Article 6 of the Soviet Constitution, was not abolished until 1990, a sequence of reforms, culminating in major changes proposed at the 19th Party Congress in June 1988, effected a fundamental shift in the balance of political forces within the Soviet state. Perhaps it would be truer to say that in these reforms Gorbachev was acknowledging the existence of a newly emerging **civil society** distinct from the interest of the Communist Party and the government.

Gorbachev's major proposal was for a new legislature, only one-third of whose delegates would be reserved for the Communist Party and its affiliated organizations. The other delegates to the Congress of People's Deputies, as the new body was known, would be directly elected on the basis of popular choice. At a stroke, following the elections of 1989, the political system was transformed by the entry into public life of a mass of new participants, a large proportion of whom were not beholden to the Communist Party. Indeed huge numbers of Communist candidates were defeated. The first meeting of the Congress in May 1989 has been described as 'the most momentous event in the Soviet Union since the 1917 Revolution'. There took place 'a whirlwind of free debate that scattered every known communist taboo' (Roxburgh 1991: 135).

The other major element of political restructuring was the creation of an executive presidency, a post for which Gorbachev insisted he be allowed to stand unopposed. His aim was to maintain a grip on the direction of change, but it was inevitable that his critics, and even some of his supporters, should note the irony of a leader who preached democracy but claimed the right to stand above it himself. Arguably, however, Gorbachev's pursuit of reform from the top down, self-serving though it was, was both very much in the Russian/Soviet tradition and understandable in a country which was subject to growing splits. The erosion of the integrative force of the Communist Party transformed the dynamics of the political institutions at the centre but also threatened the structure of the Soviet Union itself.

Box 5.3. Essentials of *Glasnost* and *Perestroika*

Essentials of *Glasnost* (Openness)
- promotion of principle of freedom to criticize
- loosening of controls on media and publishing
- freedom of worship

Essentials of *Perestoika* (Restructuring)
- new legislature, two-thirds of which was to be elected on the basis of popular choice (i.e. allowing non-communists to be elected)
- creation of an executive presidency
- ending of the 'leading role' of the Communist Party
- Enterprise Law, allowing state enterprises to sell part of their product on the open market
- Joint Ventures Law, allowing foreign companies to own Soviet enterprises

---

The Collapse of the Soviet Empire

A multi-ethnic, multilingual entity, composed of fifteen 'autonomous' republics and numerous sub-units within them, the Soviet Union was in all but name an empire, held together by powerful central institutions, pressure for ideological conformity, and the threat of force. The Communist Party played a key role in each of these areas and the erosion of the Party's power released aspirations for freedom which had been suppressed but not destroyed by seventy years of Soviet rule. Demands for independence came in particular from the Baltic republics, Estonia, Latvia, and Lithuania, and from Georgia, but the power of example supplied by these movements affected virtually all the Soviet republics. A more tangled and bloody conflict arose in Azerbaijan, resulting from the desire of Armenians in Ngorny Karabakh (an Armenian region administered by Azerbaijan) for incorporation into the Soviet Republic of Armenia.

For the purposes of understanding the collapse of Soviet rule **two** points are important about these events:

1. The 'nationalities question' was evidently a blind spot of Mikhail Gorbachev's. He was noticeably unsympathetic to their demands and, though keen to maintain his credibility as a liberal by claiming that the more violent attempts to suppress nationalism in the republics had been undertaken without his orders, he insisted that Moscow could not countenance secession.

2. However, when faced with the reality of secessionist actions (above all in the Baltic republics), he was unwilling in practice to use the full force of Soviet military power to suppress them. The result was that Gorbachev succeeded in alienating both **liberals**, who argued that Russia should not stand in the way of independence movements, and **conservatives**, who saw in Gorbachev's concessions to nationalism a betrayal of the integrity of the Soviet Union.

During 1990 and 1991 Gorbachev oscillated between trying to satisfy conservatives and liberals. To the former he promised suppression of nationalism by force. Swinging to the latter in the early months of 1991, he announced a proposal for a new 'Union treaty' which would devolve power substantially to the Soviet republics. It was this move which provoked conservatives to mount the coup of August 1991, during which Gorbachev was held for several days in the Crimea, while Boris Yeltsin defied the coup plotters in Moscow and thus laid the basis for his subsequent career as President of Russia. The coup's failure did not, contrary to Gorbachev's hopes and expectations, restore his position and status in the eyes of the Soviet people, not least because it was felt that Gorbachev's indulgence of the Right had helped to make the coup attempt possible. Furthermore, Gorbachev seemed unaware of how far public opinion had moved under the stimulus of the movement he had set in motion. In a press conference on his return to Moscow after the coup, he continued to defend the Communist Party. He seemed clearly yesterday's man. Within a few months the logic of *perestroika* and nationalism was followed through with the dismantling of the Soviet Union and its replacement by a loose Confederation of Independent States (CIS).

Economic Restructuring

Economic restructuring in a sense cannot be separated from politics, since, as was suggested above, under the Soviet system economics like all areas of social life was subject to a political and ideologically derived rationale. Nevertheless, economic initiatives were important in their own right under Gorbachev, in that their goal was precisely to effect a separation of the economic from the political, or at least to go some way in that direction. Real changes began in 1987 with the legalization (within clearly specified limits) of private farming and business co-operatives. A year later the Enterprise Law granted limited freedom to managers of state enterprises to sell a proportion of their products on the open market rather than, as had been the practice, having to sell all of it to the government (Goldman 1992: 111–17).

In all these measures there was a partial move towards a free market or, more precisely, an attempt to straddle the gap between the stifling command economy and an incentive-led market system. In the sphere of foreign economic policy a new law on Joint Ventures allowed foreign companies ownership of enterprises in the Soviet Union (initially 49 per cent and then, following amendment in 1990, 100 per cent). This was a huge innovation for an economy which had generally sought to insulate itself from capitalism. Such trade as had taken place

with the West had been tightly controlled by the Ministry of Foreign Trade. Now individual companies could make their own arrangements (Hough 1988: 66–72).

The effect of these economic changes was catastrophic. The reforms managed to cut the ground from under the old system without putting in its place viable new economic mechanisms. State planning was in abeyance but there was no fully operating market mechanism in its place; price levels were inconsistent, some reflecting the input of government subsidies and some reflecting what consumers would pay. Inflation, shortages, and declining production were the harvest of five years of *perestroika* and *glasnost*. To these could be added rising crime rates, a sense of social disarray, and a general feeling of uncertainty about the future. By the time Gorbachev left office in 1991 much of the exhilaration which had attended the liberation from communist oppression had been expended. De-structuring perhaps inevitably proved easier than re-structuring.

Key Points

- The suddenness of the collapse of communism defied the predictions of experts.

- Gorbachev's accession to power represented the advent of a new generation in the Soviet leadership, though Gorbachev gave little indication early on that he would break the mould of Soviet politics.

- The Soviet Union suffered from systemic economic problems which were compounded in the 1980s by poor harvests and a failure to meet the challenge of the computer revolution.

- *Glasnost* began with relaxation of censorship which Gorbachev hoped to be able to control, but the process soon eluded his grasp as something approaching a genuine public opinion emerged.

- A combination of *glasnost* and political restructuring undermined the role of the Communist Party and ultimately the Soviet Union itself which by the end of 1991 had dissolved into separate republics.

- Economic restructuring had the effect of destroying the rationale of the old system without putting viable new mechanisms in its place.

The Collapse of Communism in Eastern Europe

The collapse of communism in Eastern Europe, marked most graphically by the destruction of the Berlin Wall in November 1989, was intimately related to events in the Soviet Union but also had roots of its own. The nations of Eastern Europe had experienced only forty years of communist rule as opposed to the seventy of the Soviet Union and in all cases except Yugoslavia had had communism imposed on them rather than choosing it themselves. The suddenness of communist collapse in Eastern Europe, the relative ease with which citizens shed the habits of forty years, suggests that those habits were to a considerable extent a matter of form. One important force which had held them in place since the late 1940s was the threat of Soviet intervention to reimpose orthodoxy should Eastern Europeans stray from the path set down for them. **Two** things therefore need explaining:

1. The sources of opposition in Eastern Europe to commmunist rule.
2. The Soviet Union's decision not to intervene to check the uprisings which took place in the summer and autumn of 1989.

The Legacy of Protest in Eastern Europe

After Stalin's draconian imposition of Soviet rule between 1947 and 1953 Khrushchev had acknowledged the principle of **separate paths to socialism**, though within strict limits. In practice this meant that where socialism and the integrity of the bloc itself seemed at risk, as in the popular uprisings in Hungary in 1956 and Czechoslovakia in 1968, Moscow would act uncompromisingly. The crushing of the Czechoslovak revolt in August 1968 was justified on the principle of 'limited sovereignty' for Eastern bloc nations (also known as the **Brezhnev Doctrine**). Where, as in Poland in 1956 and 1980–1, indigenous leaders could be found to enforce Moscow's will, direct intervention could be avoided. Where, however, as in Romania and Albania, communism developed distinctively national forms but within the framework of rigid dictatorships, Moscow was prepared to tolerate, or at least grudgingly accept, a greater or lesser degree of detachment from Moscow. In the case of Albania,

a small nation with no border with the Soviet Union, this went as far as alignment with China in the growing split between the Soviet Union and China. Romania under Ceausescu maintained a somewhat ambiguous relationship with Moscow and the Warsaw Pact, not unlike France's with NATO: political and military independence within the framework of broad bloc alignment. In short, the Eastern bloc was more diverse and potentially more fragile than the the word 'bloc' would suggest.

In accounting for the events of 1989 it would be hard to overestimate the importance of the rise of **Solidarity** in Poland in 1980. Poland had always been critical to Moscow both because of its strategic position on the Soviet border and because of the legacy of hatred between the Poles and the Russians. Formed in the shipyards of Gdansk as a union of workers, **Solidarity** quickly assumed the

---

Box 5.4. Revolutions in Eastern Europe

1988

May   Janos Kadar replaced as General Secretary of the Czechoslovak Communist Party.

1989

Jan.   Hungarian parliament permits independent parties.

April   Ban on Solidarity in Poland repealed.

June   Elections in Poland won overwhelmingly by Solidarity candidates.

July   Solidarity invited by General Jaruselski to form coalition government.

Sept.   Hungary allows East German refugees to cross into Austria.

Oct.   Hungary adopts new constitution which guarantees multiparty democracy. East German leader Erich Honecker resigns and is replaced by Egon Krenz.

Nov.   3rd: Czechoslovakia opens border for East seeking to go to the West. 10th: Berlin Wall dismantled; General Secretary of the Bulgarian Communist Party, Zhivkov, resigns. 24th: Czechoslovak leadership resigns.

Dec.   6th: East German government resigns. 22nd: Ceausescu overthrown in Romania and executed (on the 25th).

status of a quasi-political body independent of the Communist Party, its membership comprising one-third of the Polish people. It called for a referendum on Polish membership of the WTO and on the principle of one-party rule. With alarm bells ringing furiously in Moscow, Soviet military intervention was forestalled only by the insertion of a new Polish leader, General Jaruselski, who was willing to do Moscow's bidding by declaring martial law and banning Solidarity. However, the difference from earlier instances of suppression of opposition was that Solidarity continued a thriving underground existence during the 1980s, while the Catholic Church carried on public opposition along lines laid down by Solidarity. Dissidence thus achieved momentum and extended beyond small groups of intellectuals.

Beyond Poland, though events were less dramatic, dissidence also had a history and gained some new stimulus from the development of organizations designed to monitor compliance of Eastern bloc governments with the human rights provisions of the Helsinki Conference on Security and Co-operation in Europe (1975). Particularly important was **Charter 77** in Czechoslovakia. A similar group existed in Moscow itself. Though these organizations were hounded by the authorities, their members imprisoned and in some cases deported, they attracted enormous attention in the West and exerted some leverage over Soviet bloc governments. They were after all simply demanding that their governments make good the promises they had made on human rights in signing the Helsinki Accords. In this way the *détente* agreements proved to have important subterranean effects in the Soviet bloc.

Flowing directly from this point, and of crucial significance in accounting for the timing of the collapse of communism in Eastern Europe, was the demonstration effect of *glasnost* and *perestroika* in the Soviet Union. After 1985, above all in Poland and Hungary, while dissidents demanded the same—indeed more—from their governments as Gorbachev was giving to the Soviet people, the Eastern European leaderships were bereft of the instrument they had always been able to rely on in the past—the threat of Soviet intervention. By the middle of 1988 the opposition in Hungary had forced the removal of the Communist Party leader, Janos Kadar. In January 1989 General Jaruselski was forced to repeal the ban on Solidarity and hold elections. In the elections, which were won decisively

by Solidarity, Jaruselski found himself being urged by Gorbachev to accede to a Solidarity-led government (Gati 1990: 167; Dawisha 1990: 155).

Gorbachev and the End of the Brezhnev Doctrine

Why did Gorbachev abandon the **Brezhnev Doctrine**? Doubtless there were many reasons, but the chief one was probably the recognition that suppression of change in Eastern Europe would have been totally inconsistent with his domestic reforms in the Soviet Union. His credibility at home, which was fragile enough once the economy began to fail, required that he endorse similar policies in the Soviet Union's 'internal empire', though it is doubtful that he foresaw the radically destabilizing effect which such changes would have on the governments of Eastern Europe. If reform in the Soviet Union was led from the top, at least initially, in Eastern Europe it had a popular base which immediately threatened the communist leaderships and created a revolutionary situation.

A further reason for Gorbachev's reluctance to enforce the **Brezhnev Doctrine** was that he had made much in his speeches and writings of his vision of a **common European home** which would bring to an end the division of Europe. Again one wonders whether he foresaw that this would entail the end of communism; it is more likely that he envisaged a reformed and reinvigorated communist system pursuing moderate policies of genuinely peaceful coexistence with the West, expanded trade, and greatly increased contacts across the board. In any event, the logic of his non-interventionist position was to preclude direct Soviet control over the processes of change in Eastern Europe.

There were foreign policy considerations too in the policy of **laissez-faire** towards Eastern Europe. Retrenchment, in the form of withdrawal from the costly, increasingly unpopular, and futile intervention in Afghanistan (1979), was the order of the day rather than new ventures. Revision of military policy in line with **new thinking** in foreign policy generally (treated below in greater detail) ruled out the kind of aggressive and interventionist policies which had characterized the later Brezhnev years. Finally, Gorbachev could hardly expect to maintain good relations with the West, achieve arms agreements and improved trade terms if he was seen to be engaging in the suppression of freedom in Eastern Europe.

It was in these circumstances that governmental authority decayed in Poland and Hungary during the early months of 1989 and finally collapsed in all of Eastern Europe by the end of the year. Collapse was initiated by the removal of the security fence between Austria and Hungary, allowing thousands of East Germans to pass over the border and through to West Germany during September. Suddenly, with Hungary's connivance in this flight from East to West, the illusion of communism, which had been sustained by the Iron Curtain, evaporated. Efforts to check the process of collapse in East Germany, then Czechoslovakia and Bulgaria by bringing in new leaders proved futile. Changes of personnel only delayed the inevitable briefly. The Berlin Wall was breached by demonstrators in November, opening up the possibility, which had been unthinkable for close to a generation, of German unification. In Czechoslovakia, in the face of massive popular protest, the government fell in November and Vaclav Havel, playwright and dissident, was elected President. Only in Romania did violence take place, as President Ceausescu's security police undertook a savage and short-lived attempt to defend his rule and destroy the popular opposition. By the end of December Ceausescu and his wife had been captured and executed. Only in Albania did communism linger on, but there too during 1990 the old leadership fell to the inexorable logic of events.

The manner of communist collapse in Eastern Europe suggested that their systems were both rigid and brittle and that they had relied on the ultimate threat of Soviet force to maintain their shapes. With that threat removed, the stimulus to change which had always been present was able to express itself.

Key Points

- The end of communism in Eastern Europe was sudden but protest against communist rule was nothing new.

- The Soviet Union had always been forced to acknowledge the existence of national differences and desires for autonomy among Eastern European nations and had tried to maintain a balance between maintaining the integrity of the Soviet bloc and allowing some diversity.

- The Polish union Solidarity illustrated the deep currents of dissent, whose momentum was maintained even after the banning of the organization in 1981.

- A catalyst for the revolutionary process was Gorbachev's abandonment of the **Brezhnev Doctrine** of limited sovereignty.

- Failure of the attempts by Eastern European leaders to stem the tide of revolution in 1989 by installing new personnel illustrated the degree to which the crisis of communism was systemic.

External Factors: Relations with the United States

Debate About US Policy and the End of the Cold War

Debate about who or what was responsible for ending the cold war began as soon as it had happened and quickly generated a large literature (see Hogan 1992). It became an issue in the US presidential election of 1992 (Kennan 1992; Pipes 1992). The Republican Party's claim, stripped to essentials, was that President Reagan's tough stance towards the Soviet Union, especially his refusal to compromise on the development of the Strategic Defense Initiative (SDI), had been decisive in forcing the

Soviet Union to the negotiating table and subsequently bringing about the fall of communism itself. The United States had proved that it was prepared to outspend the Soviet Union, particularly in nuclear arms, thereby forcing the Soviet Union either to match the West and bankrupt itself or come to terms and negotiate real reductions in nuclear arms. Gorbachev chose the latter course, signalled by his signing of the Intermediate Nuclear Forces (INF) Treaty in December 1987, by his unilateral reduction in conventional forces announced at the UN in 1988, and by progress towards the Strategic Arms Reduction Treaty (START) I, signed in 1991. Without these agreements, Gorbachev

Box 5.5. **US–Soviet Summitry 1985–1991**		
1985	Nov.	Geneva Summit (Gorbachev–Reagan)
1986	Oct.	Reykjavik Summit (Gorbachev–Reagan)
1987	Dec.	Washington Summit (Gorbachev–Reagan) at which INF (Intermediate Nuclear Forces) Treaty is signed
1988	May–June	Moscow Summit (Gorbachev–Reagan)
1989	Dec.	Malta Summit (Gorbachev–Bush)
1990	May	Washington Summit (Gorbachev–Bush)
1991	July	START (Strategic Arms Reduction) Treaty signed in Moscow (Gorbachev–Bush)

could not hope to fund his domestic renewal plans. Ultimately, it was argued, Reagan's policies, which built on the legacy of Truman's containment, brought Gorbachev and the Soviet Union to its knees.

There were **two** responses to this argument:

The **first** was to say, as did Raymond Garthoff, author of the most substantial analysis of the end of the cold war, *The Great Transition*, that the West did not, as was widely believed, win the cold war through geopolitical containment and military deterrence. Still less was the cold war won by the Reagan military buildup. Instead ' "victory" came when a new generation of Soviet leaders realized how badly their system at home and their policies abroad had failed. What containment did do was to successfully preclude any temptation by Moscow to advance Soviet hegemony by military means' (Garthoff 1994: 753).

The **second** response to the Western triumphalist argument is the claim that Reagan's policies not only did not end the cold war but actually delayed its end. 'The Carter–Reagan buildup did not defeat the Soviet Union,' write Richard Ned Lebow and Janet Gross Stein; 'on the contrary it prolonged the cold war. Gorbachev's determination to reform an economy crippled in part by defense spending urged by special interests, but far more by structural rigidities, fueled his persistent search for an accommodation with the West. That persistence, not SDI, ended the Cold War' (Lebow and Stein 1994: 37).

These two responses have in common a conviction that **internal factors** were primarily responsible for the end of the cold war. Neither discounts external pressures, but they interpret them quite differently.

Was Reaganism of no account in the collapse of communism, as Garthoff claims, or was it an active hindrance, as Lebow and Stein argue? We can evaluate the significance of external pressures by looking at the record of diplomacy between 1985 and 1991.

Soviet–American Diplomacy 1985–1991

It must be emphasized at the outset that Soviet–American relations did not change overnight on the accession of Gorbachev. On the American side deep scepticism prevailed towards Gorbachev until as late as Autumn 1989. Despite the signature of the INF Treaty in December 1987, which was the first arms reduction as opposed to arms control treaty of the cold war period, progress was slow in other areas. Reagan was evidently inclined to reach arms agreements but not at the cost of what he considered to be essential elements of security. Bush took no initiatives towards the Soviet Union during the first nine months of his presidency (January–September 1989). Bush's Secretary of Defense, Richard Cheyney, remarked in May 1989 that he felt Gorbachev could easily fail with *perestroika* and be overthrown by hardliners. It was therefore dangerous to put much trust in Gorbachev (*Guardian* 3 May 1989: 26). Bush indicated that he did not share these views but they were evidently common in some government circles. It was only with the collapse of communism in Eastern Europe that the entire structure of East–West relations can be said to have changed.

Nevertheless, there was a qualitative difference in US–Soviet relations in the period between 1985 and 1989 as compared with the years which preceded it. As recently as 1983 Reagan had labelled the Soviet Union an **evil empire**. (Nor, incidentally, did he abandon this view, however much he moderated his public rhetoric later.) Furthermore, among his chief foreign policy priorities during his first term as President were a massive nuclear and conventional arms buildup and support for groups in the Third World—most notably the Contras in Nicaragua and the Mujaheddin in Afghanistan—

which were opposing Soviet power or governments of what were taken to be Soviet client states. The Soviet Union for its part was heavily embroiled in Afghanistan and was assuming an intransigent stand on the issue of intermediate and theatre nuclear forces in Europe. The latter years of the Carter administration and Reagan's first term indeed represented what has been called the **second cold war** (Halliday 1983).

One important stimulus for change was the new philosophy of foreign affairs which Gorbachev brought to bear on US–Soviet relations. **New Thinking** in foreign policy meant in the first place acknowledging that in an age of weapons of mass destruction, against which there was no reliable defence, security could not be achieved by amassing more and more weapons. Achieving security was a political rather than a military task and could be undertaken only in cooperation between the contending parties. Recognition of **common security** interests, of interdependence, and of common global challenges replaced the traditional Soviet assumption of the inevitability of conflict between capitalism and communism. Associated with this revision of Soviet orthodoxy was the military doctrine of **reasonable sufficiency** which involved an explicit renunciation of aggressive motives and enabled the Soviet leadership for the first time to contemplate asymmetrical cuts in troops and weaponry. Without this change in philosophy the INF Treaty could not have been signed, since it involved the abandonment of principles—such as the insistence that the British and French nuclear deterrents be considered in conjunction with American weapons—which had been integral to the Soviet negotiating position since the 1960s.

In other areas of foreign policy too concession seemed the order of the day. In August 1989 it was announced that Soviet troops would be withdrawn from Afghanistan. During the following year in a speech to the United Nations Gorbachev restated his new foreign policy doctrines and added a commitment to nuclear disarmament by the year 2000 and a unilateral reduction of Soviet armed forces by 500,000 (White 1990: 159–61; Oberdorfer 1992: 316–19). There can be little doubt, **first**, that Gorbachev had indeed abandoned principles and practices which had been integral to Soviet policy until the 1980s and, **second**, that these concessions were responsible in large part for the sea-change in US–Soviet relations during these years.

It seems clear also that Reagan's refusal to move on SDI and other issues faced Gorbachev with the choice of either failing to reach any agreement or making concessions in order to reach agreements. Even if, as some claim, Reagan's intransigence initially delayed agreements, Gorbachev seems to have calculated that the further forward he went with domestic *perestroika* the less flexibility he had in foreign policy. To that extent, Reagan's maintenance of a hard line on key issues did have the effect of forcing concessions from the Soviet Union.

That is not the whole story, however. Movement was not all one way; nor did all the advantage in these agreements lie with the United States. On the critical question, for example, of Gorbachev's decision not to make Soviet agreement to the INF Treaty conditional on the abandonment of SDI, Gorbachev evidently recognized that SDI was a politically contentious issue in the United States and that he had more to gain by moderating his position. This proved to be the case, since following signature of the INF Treaty the American Congress moved to limit funds for SDI. Furthermore, the issue of verification of the Treaty was as problematic for the American military as for the Soviet military, both of whom harboured deep suspicions of intrusive verification regimes. Most significant, however, was the character of Ronald Reagan, whose stance on nuclear weapons was more complex and contradictory than his most aggressive public statements would suggest.

We have to reckon with a Reagan who came close at the Reykjavik summit of 1986 to agreeing with Gorbachev to the establishment of a nuclear-free world, who regarded SDI, with evident sincerity, as a wholly peaceful (because **defensive**) initiative which would render offensive weapons redundant once both sides were supplied with it, and who above all, again with evident sincerity, had a visceral hatred of nuclear weapons and an equally strong desire to be rid of them. Reagan had never really subscribed to the theory of nuclear deterrence and its associated concept of Mutually Assured Destruction (MAD). On a visit to the US nuclear command centre in 1980 he had been shocked to discover that the centre could be destroyed by a direct hit from a Soviet missile. Hence his determination to promote the development of SDI. In short, like many on the left, but for quite different reasons, Reagan had emancipated himself to a degree from inherited nuclear doctrines. He was not prepared to give ground unilaterally or put American security at risk. Indeed he had shown during his first term that he was willing to commit vast new sums of money to American defence. However, he was in many respects bolder in seeking arms agreements (or more foolhardy, as some of his critics suggested) than many of his advisers who had been schooled in the orthodoxy of nuclear deterrence. Besides, it was easier for a known conservative to reach agreements with the Soviet Union than for a liberal. Richard Nixon's promotion of *détente* was another example. Since there could be no doubt about their Americanism and commitment to anti-communism, they had a freedom to reach accommodations with the Soviet Union which would have been the object of deep suspicion if they had been made by liberals.

The conclusion must be that, while the main story is of Soviet concessions to the United States, there was some movement on the American side too. Reagan's signature of the INF Treaty was not without political risks. The Treaty encountered considerable opposition from conservatives in the United States and from some European leaders too who felt that it represented a reduced American commitment to the nuclear defence of Europe. The departure from the Reagan administration during his second term of well-known foreign policy 'hawks'—among them Defense Secretary Weinberger and Assistant Secretary of Defense Richard Perle—demonstrates a mellowing of policy towards the Soviet Union as compared with the years 1981–5. There was thus an element of interaction between the Reagan administration and the new leadership in the Soviet Union, which casts doubt on those explanations of the end of the cold war which see it as a simple either–or: either Reagan's policies were the catalyst or Gorbachev's policies were wholly responsible.

Key Points

- Opinion about the American role in ending the cold war has tended to polarize: either the Reagan hard line forced the Soviet Union to its knees or Reagan's policies were immaterial or actually served to prolong the cold war.

- Soviet–American relations did not change overnight with the advent of Gorbachev. The United States responded cautiously to his initiatives.

- Gorbachev's **new thinking** in foreign policy overthrew the conventional wisdom of Soviet foreign policy.

- Gorbachev's concessions, which helped to produce the INF Treaty and generally improve the climate of Soviet–American relations, were promoted initially in a controlled fashion but tended to become more unilateral and sweeping as the pace of domestic reform quickened.

- The story is not simply one of Soviet concessions. The United States made some significant movement too, indicating that a polarized interpretation of the end of the cold war is too simple and schematic.

The Interaction between Internal and External Environments

Isolation of the Communist System from the Global Capitalist System

The end of the cold war is not to be explained only in terms of specific decisions or policies of the superpowers. There are some factors which are given in the underlying conditions of the relationship between East and West. The most important of these was the isolation of the Soviet Union and the communist bloc from the modernizing current of capitalism. Initially, communist doctrine had held that the success of the Bolshevik Revolution could only be guaranteed by the spread of revolution, preferably throughout the world but in any event to the developed nations of Europe. When this did not happen in the years immediately following 1917 Stalin invented the doctrine of **socialism in one country** to justify the restriction of the Revolution to Russia. The subsequent extension of communism to Eastern Europe, China, North Korea, and Cuba after the Second World War was in theory a stepping-stone to world revolution but in practice the advance of communism coincided with the expansion of world capitalism in what Eric Hobsbawm has called 'the golden years' (Hobsbawm 1994). The clash of these two processes, of course, gave the cold war its global character during and after the 1950s (see Ch. 4).

For our purposes the most important feature of these developments was the continued separation of the communist and capitalist blocs, a symbol of which was the Soviet Union's refusal to participate in the US Marshall Plan for post-war reconstruction (1948–52). The Soviet Union believed, with justification, that the conditions for participation demanded by the United States, which involved opening the Soviet bloc to Western investment and hence to Western economic and political leverage, would undermine the autonomy of the Soviet system and leave it at a disadvantage with respect to the West. Nor did the decision to undertake separate development initially seem to harm the Soviet bloc. During the 1950s Soviet growth rates actually exceeded those of all the capitalist nations except West Germany and Japan (Munting 1982: 132, 137; Van der Wee 1987: 50). Clearly this was from a low starting point and barely hid structural weaknesses in industrial production and agriculture. Nevertheless, the gross figures were impressive, and the launch of Sputnik in 1957 ahead of the US space satellite programme appeared to suggest considerable dynamism in the Soviet economy, sufficient at least to offer a real military threat to the West. Khrushchev announced in 1960 that he expected the Soviet economy to out-produce the United States within 10 years and there were many in the West across the political spectrum who believed him.

From the perspective of the end of the cold war, the West's anxiety in the 1950s and early 1960s looks misplaced. We know that Soviet growth rates slowed in the 1960s and fell sharply in the 1970s and 1980s, and that the Soviet leadership's motive for *détente* with the West in the 1970s was in part to gain imports of 'high tech' goods in recognition of the Soviet Union's increasing backwardness. The key conclusion to be drawn is that the Soviet bloc suffered not merely from low levels of growth and productivity in absolute terms but from increasing **relative** disadvantage with respect to the West. The world was changing around the Soviet bloc, bearing out Trotsky's prediction (considered heretical by

Stalin in the late 1920s) that a Soviet island of communism could not survive in a capitalist sea.

Crucially too, Soviet bloc efforts to develop fuller trade links, greater travel opportunities and cultural exchanges with the West exposed the vulnerability of communism to Western economic and cultural influence rather than strengthening it. Economically this was manifested in the debts owed by such nations as Poland and Hungary to Western banks. Culturally, citizens of Eastern Europe were increasingly able to make comparisons between their own lives and those lived in the West. West German TV, for example, was widely viewed in East Germany and Czechoslovakia; Radio Free Europe and similar stations beamed their programmes to the Eastern bloc. One must also take account of the growth of the trans-European peace movement in the 1970s, which linked anti-nuclear and pro-democracy forces on both sides of the Iron Curtain. While there is dispute about how far such pressures influenced government policies in the West, it is plausible to assume that they helped to generate the ferment in Eastern Europe (Thompson 1990; Kaldor 1995). In short, isolationism and economic autarky (separate development in isolation from world trade), which had arguably fostered growth and ideological cohesion in the Eastern bloc in the early post-war period, later became a liability and was ultimately impossible to sustain.

It is helpful to view the cold war as having been composed of **two** distinct but overlapping systems:

1. A **cold war system** which was defined by US–Soviet antagonism, the nuclear stand-off, and the extension of these central conflicts to the periphery of the international system.
2. The **global capitalist system** which was defined by the expansion of production and trade and growing economic interdependence.

The Soviet Union's existence was defined and limited by the cold war, while the United States was a full, indeed the chief, participant in the growth of world capitalism. However great the United States' economic problems from the 1970s onwards—and they were considerable—they were not such as to produce the disabling crisis of political legitimacy experienced by the Soviet Union. One way of putting this is to say that the United States was never wholly consumed by the cold war, politically or economically. By contrast, the Soviet Union, limited as it was by ideology and history to a debilitating isolationism, was unable to meet the challenge posed by the **globalization** of the capitalist political economy (Crockatt 1995: 370–1).

Key Points

- The causes of the end of the cold war are to be found not only in internal and external condi-
- tions considered separately but in the interaction between the two.
- The separation of the communist bloc from capitalism, though not apparently disadvantageous to communism until the 1970s, left it at an increasing **relative** disadvantage to the capitalist West.
- Growing consciousness of relative disadvantage was a factor in the collapse of communism.

Conclusion: Consequences and Implications

It is too early to come to definitive conclusions about the end of the cold war but we can point to some immediate consequences and offer some inevitably speculative thoughts about the future. The end of the cold war removed more or less at a stroke the **structural** and **ideological** conditions which underlay superpower conflict over the previous forty years. This in itself seemed to promise a general relaxation of tension and a reduction in the threat of major, especially nuclear, war. To the extent that superpower conflict lay behind regional conflicts in various parts of the world, then the end of the cold war held out the possibility of resolution of these conflicts. On the most optimistic reading, conditions were now present for a **new world order** in which American power, in concert with other members of the UN Security Council, would serve as a global stabilizer. One writer, expressing the triumphalism which characterized early American reactions to the end of the cold war, talked of a 'unipolar moment' (Krauthammer 1990–1). The Gulf War of 1991 was taken by some to be the model for a new type of collective international action in which the UN, with strong US backing, would act as its founders had intended as a genuine collective security organization. Beyond this, the end of the cold war would bring a 'peace dividend' both financial and political. Nations could now afford to expend fewer resources on military and foreign policy, and devote it to domestic growth.

At the opposite extreme was the view that the cold war had served to stabilize international politics, that indeed it had fostered the **long peace** of the post-war years, defined as the absence of war between the major powers (Gaddis 1986). From this perspective the end of the cold war was therefore a destabilizing event, however much one might wel-

come the collapse of communism. The most pessimistic predictions were of chaos and violence in the successor states of the Soviet Union and Eastern Europe, as long-suppressed national and ethnic forces achieved expression, and a general rise in global instability (Mearsheimer 1993).

Within months of the collapse of communism discussion along both the above lines (and along others too) had generated an extensive literature. Both camps could call on evidence to prove their own contentions since, not surprisingly, the post-cold war world displayed varied and conflicting tendencies. The **pessimists** could point to the violent disintegration of Bosnia and other successor states of the former Yugoslavia into competing ethnic groups and the eruption of comparable ethnic and national impulses in other parts of the world. **Optimists** could point to the agreement of Ukraine, Belarus, and Kazakhstan to submit their nuclear weapons to Russian control and the joint Russian and American decision to cease targeting each other with nuclear weapons. Many nuclear dangers remained, but these agreements represented steps on the road to defusing the nuclear tensions which had existed for over forty years (see Ch. 17). There is little point, however, in drawing up a simple balance sheet, since each new development contained potentially positive and negative tendencies. It is more appropriate to ask how the end of the cold war affected the environment in which international conflict took place.

Instability itself was surely nothing new in international politics. It was endemic during the cold war in many parts of the world. It is doubtful whether there was a single year during the post-war period which was free of war, whether civil or national. For many, especially in the Third World, there was no **long peace** (Brecher and Wilkenfeld 1991). Nevertheless, there was some novelty in the absence of any obvious structure in the post-cold war international system. Great as American power was, there seemed little likelihood of a **pax Americana** emerging, not least because Americans themselves could not agree about what kind of international role the United States should play in the absence of the familiar threat of Soviet power. While **internationalism** remained a powerful force in the United States, **isolationism** was a factor which any American president was forced to reckon with (see M. Cox 1995).

Nor did a new structure of collective security, based on the United Nations, appear, though that body was notably active in supervision of elections and peace-keeping operations after 1989, and in several cases, including the Gulf War and the former Yugoslavia, endorsed the use of extensive military force by other bodies for nominally UN purposes. But the UN remained a creature of the nations which composed it and lacked a will of its own. The possibility of radical change in the UN's remit could not be ruled out but did not look likely in the short or medium term.

A third possible structure, that of a 'concert of powers' such as emerged after the Napoleonic wars, also seemed unlikely, though perhaps the G7 (or advanced industrial nations) had the potential to become such a body. That they did not and are unlikely to was perhaps a reflection of the reluctance of other powers, however small and powerless, to be dictated to. Whatever the actual power differentials in the international system, a democratic ethos existed which resisted granting legitimacy to the kind of 'Great Power' rule which characterized nineteenth-century diplomacy. Furthermore, in a world in which economic and military power did not always go together and in which the currency of power itself was unstable, who exactly were the Great Powers? In short, in the post-cold war world, institutions and principles of order derived from the past did not have obvious or direct application, which left theorists and practitioners of international relations alike with much to do.

Key Points

- The end of the cold war offered grounds for both pessimistic and optimistic speculation.

Box 5.6. **Key Concepts**

Brezhnev Doctrine: the idea of 'limited sovereignty' for Soviet bloc nations, which was used to justify the crushing of the reform movement in Czechoslovakia in 1968.

Civil Society: the network of social institutions and practices (economic relationships, family and kinship groups, religious and other social affiliations) which underlie strictly political institutions. For democratic theorists the voluntary character of the above associations is taken to be essential to the workings of democratic politics.

Common European Home: Gorbachev's concept (associated with his **New Thinking** in foreign policy) of the essential unity of Europe and of the need to overcome the 'artificiality and temporariness of the bloc-to-bloc confrontation and the archaic nature of the "iron curtain".'

Evil Empire: Reagan's term, used in a speech of 1983, to describe the Soviet Union.

New Thinking: the general label given by Gorbachev to his reforms in domestic and foreign policy.

Pax Americana: Latin phrase (literally American peace, adapted from *Pax Romana*) implying a global peace dictated by American power.

Reasonable Sufficiency: Gorbachev's term (associated with his **New Thinking** in foreign policy) for a defence policy which relied on the minimum necessary level of weaponry consistent with national security, and designed to overcome the spiralling dynamics of the nuclear arms race.

Separate Paths to Socialism: Khrushchev's acknowledgement of the existence of diversity in the Soviet bloc and of the validity (within strict limits) of separate routes to the common socialist goal.

Socialism in One Country: Stalin's term used to justify the Soviet Union's departure from the orthodox Marxist view that socialism in the Soviet Union could succeed only in conjunction with socialist revolutions in advanced industrial nations.

- Both the above approaches could find evidence for their contentions in the varied and conflicting tendencies in post-cold war international developments.

- The novelty of the post-cold war international system lay not in the existence of instability and conflict but in the environment in which conflict took place.

- Concepts of international order drawn from the past do not provide clear guides to the present or the future.

QUESTIONS

1. Does an examination of the end of the cold war help in understanding how systemic change occurs in world politics?

2. What do you think Gorbachev hoped to achieve through *glasnost* and *perestroika*?

3. What are the connections between change in the Soviet Union and the revolutions in Eastern Europe?

4. Why did changes of leadership in Eastern Europe in the summer and autumn of 1989 fail to stem the collapse of communism?

5. Can you find ways, other than those presented in this chapter, of conceptualizing the relationship between external and internal causes of the collapse of communism in the Soviet Union?

6. Did the West 'win' the cold war?

7. What role, if any, did the Reagan administration play in bringing about the end of the cold war?

8. Why did experts by and large fail to anticipate the collapse of communism?

9. Is the post-cold war international system more unstable than the cold war international system?

10. What ordering principles, if any, operate in post-cold war international politics?

11. Can communism be regarded as a victim of the 'globalization of world politics'?

GUIDE TO FURTHER READING

The fullest international history of the end of the cold war is R. Garthoff, *The Great Transition: American–Soviet Relations and the End of the Cold War* (Washington, DC: Brookings Institution, 1994) but D. Oberdorfer, *The Turn: From the Cold War to a New Era* (New York: Touchstone Books, 1992) is a highly intelligent, readable, and comprehensive journalistic account. Michael Beschloss and Strobe Talbott, *At the Highest Levels: The Inside Story of the End of the Cold War* (Boston: Little Brown, 1993) gives a blow by blow account of the high politics of the years 1989–91. A range of viewpoints is contained in M. Hogan (ed.), *The End of the Cold War: Its Meaning and Implications* (Cambridge: Cambridge University Press, 1992). Long perspectives can be gained from E. Hobsbawm, *Age of Extremes: The Short Twentieth Century, 1914–1991* (London: Michael Joseph, 1994) who presents the end of the cold war in the light of the twentieth century as a whole, and R. Crockatt, *The Fifty Years War: The United States and the Soviet Union in World Politics, 1941–1991* (London: Routledge, 1995) who covers US–Soviet relations from 1941–1991.

On the collapse of communism in the Soviet Union a good place to start is with two books by journalists: A. Roxburgh, *The Second Russian Revolution* (London: BBC Publications, 1991) and David Remnick, *Lenin's Tomb: The Last Days of the Soviet Empire* (London: Viking, 1993). M. Goldman, *What Went Wrong With Perestroika* (1992) is good on economic issues. Eastern European developments are well covered in C. Gati, *The Bloc that Failed: Soviet-East European Relations in Transition*

Richard Crockatt

(Bloomington: Indiana University Press, 1990), K. Dawisha, *Eastern Europe, Gorbachev and Reform: The Great Challenge* (Cambridge: Cambridge University Press, 1990). On the American side see John L. Gaddis, *The United States and the End of the Cold War: Implications, Reconsiderations, Provocations* (New York: Oxford University Press, 1992).

Part Two

Theories of World Politics

In this part of the book we introduce you to the main theories that try to explain world politics. We have two main aims: **first**, we want you to be able to grasp the main themes of the theories that have been most influential in explaining world politics. To this end, we have included in this section chapters on the three main theoretical perspectives on world politics: Realism, World-System Theory, and Liberalism. Of these, Realism has been by far the most influential theory but, as we mentioned in the Introduction, it has also attracted fierce criticism for being an ideology masquerading as an objective theory. Most of the history of international relations theory has seen a dispute between Realism and its two main rivals, with the debate between Realism and Liberalism being the most long-standing and well-developed debate. We then want to introduce you to the most recent theoretical work in world politics, thereby giving you an up-to-date survey of the theoretical literature. So, by the end of this section we hope that you will be able to understand the main themes of the various theories and be able to assess their comparative strengths and weaknesses. Our **second** aim is to give you the overview of theory that you need to be able to assess the significance of globalization for our understanding of world politics. After reading these chapters on theory we hope that you will be in a better position to see how these theories of world politics might interpret globalization in different ways. We feel that you should then be able both to decide for yourself which interpretation you find most convincing and what kind of evidence you might find in the remaining sections of the book to enable you to be able to work out just how much globalization marks a new, distinct stage in world politics, requiring new theories, or whether it is simply a fad or fashion which might alter the surface of world politics but not its main underlying features.

6 Realism

Timothy Dunne

READER'S GUIDE

Realism is the dominant theory of International Relations. Why? Because it provides the most powerful explanation for the state of war which is the regular condition of life in the international system. This is the bold claim made by realists in defence of their tradition, a claim which will be critically examined in this chapter. The second section will ask whether there is one Realism or a variety of Realisms? The argument presented below suggests that despite important differences, particularly between historical realism and structural realism, it is possible to identify a shared core which all realists subscribe to. Section three outlines these common elements: Self-help, Statism, and Survival. In the final section, we will return to the question how far Realism is relevant for explaining or understanding *our* world? Although it leaves many areas of the globalization of world politics uncharted, Realism's emphasis upon material forces such as state power remains an important dimension of international relations after the cold war.

Introduction: The Timeless Wisdom of Realism

Metaphorically speaking, the book of academic International Relations opens after the Great War (1914–18). Chapter one tells the story of the inter-war idealists, with their passionate belief in the capacity of humankind to overcome the scourge of war. In chapter two, we read about the realist destroyers of **Idealism**. Both on the battlefields of Europe, and in the relative safety of Whitehall, theorists and practitioners were once again, in a *Don Quixote* like posture, tilting at the windmill of power politics. The rest of the International Relations story, is in many respects, a footnote to Realism.[1]

From 1939 to the present, leading theorists and policy-makers have continued to view the world through realist lenses (see Ch. 10). The prescriptions it offered were particularly well suited to America's rise to become the global **hegemon** (or leader). Realism taught American leaders to focus on interests rather than ideology, and to realize that great powers can coexist even if they have antithetical values and beliefs. The fact that Realism offers something of a 'manual' for maximizing the interests of the state in a hostile environment explains in part why it remains 'the central tradition in the study of world politics' (Keohane 1989a: 36). The core elements of Realism are: the state is the key actor and **statism** is the term given to the idea of the state as the legitimate representative of the collective will; the first priority for state leaders is to ensure the **survival** of their state; **self-help** is the principal of action in an anarchical system where there is no global government. These 'three Ss' constitute the corners of the realist triangle.

Before engaging with realist thought in detail, let us return to the metaphor of academic International Relations as a single book. It is important for the student to remember that the story of the discipline, like all texts, is open to multiple readings. Moreover, the final chapters have yet to be written. An interesting thought experiment is to ask whether Realism will have the last word. When 'the end of the world as we know it' is upon us, and the conclusion to the 'book' of International Relations is being hastily drafted, will it be written by a realist? Many contemporary theorists would argue that the discipline's centre of gravity is already shifting away from Realism towards a new kind of Liberalism, a theory more appropriate for the post-cold war era perhaps. Other more radical voices argue that what is needed is nothing less than a transformation in our political imagination, in terms of widening our sense of community beyond the confines of the sovereign state which realists (and some Liberal thinkers) take for granted. Although the chapter does not have the space to do justice to these critical arguments, the 'headlines' are presented in Box 6.3 in the hope that the reader will consult them in their original form.

By way of a response to the critics, it is worth reminding them that the death-knell of Realism has been sounded a number of times already, by the scientific approach in the 1960s and transnationalism in the 1970s, only to see the resurgence of a more robust form of Realism in the late 1970s and 1980s. In this respect Realism shares with Conservatism (its ideological godfather) the recognition that a theory without the means to change is without the means of its own preservation. The question of Realism's resilience touches upon one of its central claims, namely, that it is the embodiment of laws of international politics which remain true across time (history) and space (geopolitics). This argument is articulately made by a leading contemporary realist, Robert Gilpin, who cast doubt on 'whether or not twentieth-century students of international relations know anything that Thucydides and his fifth-century BC compatriots did not know about the behaviour of states' (1981: 227–8). Thucydides was the historian of the Peloponnesian War, a conflict between two great powers in the ancient Greek world, Athens and Sparta. One minor episode in this historic struggle, known as the 'Melian dialogue', represents a fascinating illustration of a number of key realist principles. Case Study 1 (Box 6.1) reconstructs the dialogue between the realist Athenian leaders who arrived on the island of Melos to assert their right of conquest over the islanders, and the idealist response this provoked.

In short, what the Athenians are asserting over the Melians is the logic of power politics. Because of their vastly superior military force, they are able to present a *fait accompli* to the Melians: either submit peacefully or be exterminated. The Melians for their part try and 'buck' the logic of power politics, appealing in turn with arguments grounded in justice, God, and their allies the Spartans. As the dia-

---

Box 6.1. Case Study 1: The Melian Dialogue—Realism and the Preparation for War[2]

ATHENIANS. Then we on our side will use no fine phrases saying, for example, that we have a right to our empire because we defeated the Persians . . . And we ask you on your side not to imagine that you will influence us by saying that you, though a colony of Sparta, have not joined Sparta in the war, or that you have never done us any harm . . . you know as well as we do that, when these matters are discussed by practical people, **the standard of justice depends on the equality of power to compel** and that in fact **the strong do what they have the power to do and the weak accept what they have to accept.**

MELIANS. Then in our view (since you force us to leave just-ice out of account and to confine ourselves to self-interest) . . . you should not destroy a principle that is to the general good of all men—namely, that in the case of all who fall into danger there should be such a thing as fair play and just dealing.

ATHENIANS. We do not want any trouble in bringing you into our empire, and we want you to be spared for the good both of yourselves and of ourselves.

MELIANS. And how could it be just as good for us to be the slaves as for you to be the masters?

ATHENIANS. You, by giving in, would save yourselves from disaster; we by not destroying you, would be able to profit from you.

MELIANS. So you do not agree to our being neutral, friends instead of enemies, but allies of neither side?

ATHENIANS. No . . . if we were on friendly terms with you, our subjects would regard that as a sign of weakness in us, whereas your hatred is evidence of our power. . . . So that **by conquering you we shall increase not only the size but the security of our empire**.

MELIANS. But do you think there is no security for you in what we suggest? For here again, since you will not let us mention justice, but tell us to give in to your inter-ests, we, too, must tell you what our interests are and, if yours and ours happen to coincide, we must try to persuade you of the fact. Is it not certain that you will make enemies of all states who are at present neutral, when they see what is happening here and naturally conclude that in course of time you will attack them too? . . . Yet we know that in war, fortune sometimes makes the odds more level.

ATHENIANS. Hope, that comforter in danger!

MELIANS. We trust that the gods will give us fortune as good as yours, because we are standing for what is right against what is wrong; and as for what we lack in power, we trust that it will be made up for by our alliance with the Spartans, who are bound, if for no other reason, then for honour's sake, and because we are their kinsman, to come to our help.

ATHENIANS. So far as the favour of the gods is concerned, we think we have as much right to that as you have. . . . Our opinion of the gods and our knowledge of men lead us to conclude that **it is a general and necessary law of nature to rule whatever one can**. This is not a law that we made ourselves, nor were we the first to act upon it when it was made. We found it already in exist-ence, and we shall leave it to exist forever among those who come after us. We are merely acting in accordance with it, and we know that you or anybody else with the same power as ours would be acting in precisely the same way. And therefore, so far as the gods are con-cerned, we see no good reason why we should fear to be at a disadvantage. But with regard to your views about Sparta and your confidence that she, out of a sense of honour, will come to your aid, we must say that we congratulate you on your simplicity but do not envy you your folly . . . of all people we know the Spartans are most conspicuous for believing that what they like doing is honourable and what suits their inter-ests is just.

MELIANS. But this is the very point where we can feel most sure. Their own self-interest will make them refuse to betray their own colonists, the Melians.

ATHENIANS. You seem to forget that if one follows one's self-interest one wants to be safe, whereas **the path of justice and honour involves one in danger**. . . . Do not be led astray by a false sense of honour. . . . You, if you take the right view, will be careful to avoid this. And, when you are allowed to choose between war and safety, you will not be so insensitively arrogant as to make the wrong choice. You will see that there is nothing disgraceful in giving way to the greatest city in Hellas when she is offering you such reasonable terms—alliance on a tribute-paying basis and liberty to enjoy your own property. **This is the safe rule—to stand up to one's equals, to behave with deference to one's superiors, and to treat one's inferiors with moderation**.

MELIANS. Our decision, Athenians, is just the same as it was at first. We are not prepared to give up in a short moment the liberty which out city has enjoyed from its foundation for 700 years.

ATHENIANS. You seem to us . . . to see uncertainties as realities, simply because you would like them to be so.

---

logue makes clear, the Melians were forced to submit to the realist iron law that 'the strong do what they have the power to do and the weak accept what they have to accept'. Later realists would concur with Thucydides' suggestion that the logic of power politics has universal applicability. Instead of Athens and Melos, we could just as easily substitute, for example, Nazi Germany and Czecho-slovakia in 1939, the Soviet Union and Hungary in 1956, or Indonesia and East Timor in 1975. In each case, the weaker state had to submit to the will of the stronger. Power trumps morality, and the threat or use of force triumphs over legal principles such as the right to independence (sovereignty).

The question whether Realism does embody 'timeless truths' about politics will be returned to in the conclusion of the chapter. Could a scholar who understood the history of international conflict in the fifth century BC *really* apply the same conceptual tools to global politics at the end of the second millennium? In the following section we will begin to unravel Realism in order to reveal the way in which the tradition has evolved over the last twenty-five centuries. After considering the main tributaries which flow into the Realist stream of thinking, the third section will attempt to disinter a 'core' of realist principles to which all realists could subscribe.

Key Points

- Realism has been the dominant theory of world politics since the beginning of academic International Relations in 1919.

- Outside of the academy, Realism has a much longer history. Scepticism about the capacity of human reason to deliver moral progress resonates through the work of classical political theorists such as Thucydides, Machiavelli, Hobbes, and Rousseau.

- In 'The Melian Dialogue', one of the episodes of *The Peloponnesian War*, Thucydides uses the words of the Athenians to highlight the realist view of a number of key concepts such as self-interest, alliances, balance of power, capabilities, and insecurity. The people of Melos respond in Idealist verse, appealing to justice, fairness, luck, the gods, and in the final instance, to common interests.

- At the end of the millennium, Realism continues to attract academicians and inform policy-makers, although the passing of the cold war has seen a revival in the fortunes of Liberalism, and a variety of more critical approaches grouped under the banner of Postpositivism.

One Realism, or Many?

The whole enterprise of articulating a unified theory of Realism has been criticized by writers sympathetic to the tradition (M. J. Smith 1986: 3) and those who are critical of it. In the words of a leading critic of Realism, 'there is no single tradition of political realism, but rather a knot of historically constituted tensions, contradictions and evasions' (Walker 1993: 106). Consistent with the argument that there is not *one* Realism, but many, is the attempt (below) to delineate different types of Realism. The most simple distinction is a form of periodization; classical realism (up to the twentieth century), modern realism (1939–79), and neo-realism (1979 onwards). These different periods do not, however, overcome the problem of diversity. For example, not all classical realists agree on the causes of war, or whether the balance of power is a natural state or one which must be created.

An alternative form of classification is thematic (a summary of the varieties of realism outlined below is contained in Table 6.1). One of the most convincing of these is R. B. J. Walker's distinction between historical realism and structural realism (1993: 108–22) which the following classification builds on.[3] Machiavelli is the leading classical exponent of **historical realism**, advocating a set of maxims which permit state leaders to bring the external environment under their control. E. H. Carr is the modern Machiavelli, advocating a foreign policy which recognizes the interplay of both power and morality, force and appeasement. The **structural realist** lineage begins with Thucydides, with his representation of power politics as a law of human behaviour. This reduction of realism to a condition of human nature is one which frequently reappears in the leading works of the realist canon, most famously in the work of the high priest of post-war realism, Hans J. Morgenthau. It can usefully be thought of as a 'structural' theory—**structural realism** I—because human nature is viewed by realists as *the* determining structure, one which stands outside of history and cannot be transcended. The more frequent use of the term 'structural' in the literature—**structural realism II**[4]—is to denote the form of realist argument which attributes the cause of conflict to the anarchic structure of the international system, which prevents sovereign princes (in the case of Rousseau) or states (in the case of Waltz) from entering into co-operative agreements to end the state of war. Thus, the structure of the system can drive states to war *even* if state leaders desired peace (Butterfield 1951: 21). But as a number of scholars have pointed out, those contemporary realists like Waltz and Mearsheimer who have tried to construct a realist theory without relying on an assumption about human nature often 'smuggle' into their idea of a 'system' behavioural assumptions about states as competitive and egoistic entities. Moreover, in the work of contemporary structural realists, these traits appear to be *prior* to the interactions of states as though they existed before the game of power politics began.

The fourth and final type of realism develops out of a reading of Thomas Hobbes. Although his great work *Leviathan* is often cited by realists for its graphically pessimistic portrayal of human nature, Hobbes can more usefully be deployed in support of **liberal realism**. His analogy between individu-

als in a state of nature and sovereigns in a state of war suggests a kind of permanent cold war where states are constantly living in fear of being attacked. But crucially, Hobbes believed that states are less vulnerable than individuals in the state of nature, and are therefore able to coexist with other sovereigns. As elementary rules of coexistence are formulated, such as the principles of sovereignty and non-intervention, the anarchical system becomes an **anarchical society**, and Realism metamorphoses into a form of liberal realism. This liberal wing of realism has appealed in particular to British international relations theorists, who have, as John Vincent put it, 'flattered Hobbes by imitating him' (1981: 96).[5]

Given the varieties of Realism on offer, it is hardly surprising that the overall coherence of Realism as a tradition of inquiry into international relations has been questioned (Forde 1992: 62). The answer to the question of 'coherence' is, of course, contingent upon how strict the criteria are for judging the continuities which underpin a particular theory. Here it is perhaps a mistake to understand traditions as a single stream of thought, handed down in a neatly wrapped package from one generation of realists to another. Instead it is preferable

Table 6.1. **A taxonomy of realisms**

Type of Realism	Key thinkers (classical and modern)	Key texts	'Big idea'
Structural Realism I (Human Nature)	Thucydides (c.430–400 BC)	*The Peloponnesian War*	International politics is driven by an endless struggle for power which has its roots in human nature. Justice, law, and society have either no place or are circumscribed.
	Morgenthau (1948)	*Politics Among Nations*	
Historical or Practical Realism	Machiavelli (1532)	*The Prince*	Political realism recognizes that principles are subordinated to policies; the ultimate skill of the state leader is to accept, and adapt to, the changing power political configurations in world politics.
	Carr (1939)	*The Twenty Years' Crisis 1919–1939*	
Structural Realism II (International System)	Rousseau (c.1750)	*The State of War*	It is not human nature, but the anarchical system which fosters fear, jealousy, suspicion and insecurity. Conflict can emerge even if the actors have benign intent towards each other.
	Waltz (1979)	*Theory of International Politics*	
Liberal Realism	Hobbes (1651)	*Leviathan*	The international anarchy can be cushioned by states who have the capability to deter other states from aggression, and who are able to construct elementary rules for their coexistence.
	Bull (1977)	*The Anarchical Society*	

to think of living traditions like Realism as the embodiment of both continuities and conflicts. For this reason it is important for students to read realists in their historical and political contexts, to try and understand the world they were speaking to and the forces they were reacting against.

Whilst recognizing the danger of imposing a 'mythology of coherence' (Skinner 1988: 39) on the various theorists and practitioners identified with Realism, there are good reasons for attempting to identify a shared core of propositions which all realists subscribe to (see section below, 'The Essential Realism'). In the first instance, there is virtue in simplicity; complex ideas can be filtered, leaving a residual substance which may not conform to any one of the ingredients but is nevertheless a virtual representation of all of them. A second reason for attempting to arrive at a composite Realism is that, despite the different strands running through the tradition, there is a sense in which all realists share a common core of propositions. These will be considered in the third section of this chapter.

Key Points

- There is a lack of consensus in the literature as to whether we can meaningfully speak about realism as a single coherent theory.

- There are good reasons for delineating different types of realism. The most important cleavage is between those who see realism as a licence to take any course of action necessary to ensure political survival (historical realists) and those who see realism as a permanent condition of conflict or the preparation for future conflicts (structural realists).

- Structural realism divides into two wings: those writers who emphasize human nature as the structure (structural realism I) and those who believe that anarchy is the structure which shapes and shoves the behaviour of states (structural realism II).

- At the margins of Realism we find a form of liberal realism which rejects the pessimistic picture of historical and structural realists, believing that the state of war can be mitigated by the management of power by the leading states in the system and the development of practices such as diplomacy and customary international law.

- The question whether it is legitimate to speak of a coherent tradition of political realism touches upon an important debate conducted by historians of ideas. Most classical realists did not consider themselves to be adherents of a particular tradition, for this reason Realism, like all other traditions, is something of an invention.

- Once we admit to a variety of realisms, we are in danger of exaggerating the particular characteristics of each thinker and the context within which they wrote, at a cost of gleaning a better understanding of Realism as a whole.

The Essential Realism

The previous paragraphs have argued that Realism is a theoretical broad church, embracing a variety of authors and texts. Despite the numerous denominations, all realists subscribe to the following 'three Ss': statism, survival, self-help.[6] Each of these elements is considered in the subsections below.

Statism

For realists, the meaning of the sovereign state is inextricably bound up with the use of force. In terms of its internal dimension, to illustrate this

relationship between violence and the state we need to look no further than Max Weber's famous definition of the state as 'the monopoly of the legitimate use of physical force within a given territory'.[7] Within this territorial space, **sovereignty** means that the state has supreme authority to make and enforce laws. This is the basis of the unwritten contract between individuals and the state. We trade our liberty in return for a guarantee of security. Once security has been established, civil society can begin. But in the absence of security, there can be no art, no culture, no society. All these finer aspects social life are secondary in importance. The first move, then, for the realist is to organize power domestically. In this respect, 'every state is fundamentally a *Machstaat*' or power state (Donelan 1990: 25). Only after power has been organized, can community begin.

Whilst the state is able to exercise authority (or legitimate power) internally, in its external relations, a sovereign state coexists with other states in an **anarchic system**, defined as the absence of a common power. In anarchy, states compete with other states for security, markets, influence, and so on. And the nature of the competition is zero-sum; in other words, more for one actor means less for another. This competitive logic of power politics prevents agreement on universal principles, apart from the principle of non-intervention in the internal affairs of other sovereign states. This international legal aspect of sovereignty functions as a 'no trespass sign' placed on the border between states. But even this principle, designed to facilitate coexistence, is suspended by realists who argue that in practice non-intervention does not apply in relations between great powers and their 'near abroad'.

Given that the first move of the state is to organize power domestically, and the second is to accumulate **power** internationally, it is self-evidently important to consider in more depth what realists mean by their ubiquitous fusion of politics with power. What *kind* of power are realists talking about? Traditionally, power has been defined narrowly in military strategic terms. It is the ability to get what you want either through the threat or use of force. Other actors in world politics may have influence, but they don't have *real* power. It is this sentiment which Stalin embodied in his rhetorical question 'how many divisions has the Pope'? One often quoted criticism of classical and modern Realism is its over-reliance on a one-dimensional view of power. There are two important exceptions to this tendency. First, the more liberal wing of Realism has long noted the importance of more subtle understanding of power *as* prestige; in other words, the ability to get what you want without either the threat or the use of force but through diplomatic influence or authority. Second, E. H. Carr grafted economic and ideological dimensions onto the traditional realist equation of power 'equals' military force. Despite these revisions, Realism has been purchased at a discount precisely because its currency, power, has remained undertheorized and inconsistently used. Simply by asserting that states seek power provides no answer to crucial questions. Why do states struggle for power? Why is the accumulation of power, as Morgenthau argued, 'always the immediate aim'? Surely power is a means to an end rather than an end in itself?

Contemporary structural realists have in recent years sought to bring more conceptual clarity to bear on the meaning of power in the realist discourse. Kenneth Waltz tries to overcome the problem by shifting the focus from power to **capabilities**. He suggests that capabilities can be ranked according to their strength in the following areas: 'size of population and territory, resource endowment, economic capability, military strength, political stability and competence' (1979: 131). The difficulty here is that resource strength does not always lead to military victory. For example, in the 1967 Six Day War between Israel and Egypt, Jordan, and Syria, the distribution of resources clearly favoured the Arab coalition and yet the supposedly weaker side annihilated its enemies' forces and seized their territory. The definition of power as capabilities is even less successful at explaining the relative economic success of Japan over China. A more sophisticated understanding of power would focus on the ability of a state to control or influence its environment in situations which are not necessarily conflictual.

An additional weakness with the realist treatment of power concerns its exclusive focus upon state power. For realists, states are the *only* actors which *really* 'count'. Transnational corporations, international organizations, and religious denominations, like all other ideologies, rise and fall but the state is the one permanent feature in the landscape of modern global politics. Moreover, it is not clear that these non-state actors are autonomous from state power, whether this be Italy in the case of the papacy or the US in the case of corporations like Microsoft. The extent to which non-state actors bear the imprint of a statist identity is further endorsed by the fact that these actors have to make their way in an international system whose rules are made by states. There is no better example of this than the importance of American hegemonic power 'underwriting' the Bretton Woods trading system which has set the framework for international economic relations in the post–1945 period. The motivation for this was not altruism on the part of the US but the rational calculation that it had more to gain from managing the international system than to lose by refusing to exercise leadership.

The final reason for the explicit realist focus on

states is an ethical argument, albeit one which is often implicit in their writings. States are not simply power containers, they are territorial bodies whose identity is framed by blood and belonging. As Case Study 2 (Box 6.4) highlights, the wars in the former Yugoslavia have demonstrated the consequences of the fateful realist triangle: ethnicity, territoriality, insecurity. Drawing on the work of Hegel and other German realists, a number of post-war realists, such as Morgenthau and Niebuhr, identified the state as the guardian of the political community. In order to fulfil this function the state must pursue the **national interest**.

Survival

The second principle which unites realists of all persuasions is the assertion that, in international politics, the pre-eminent goal is **survival**. Although there is an ambiguity in the works of the realists as to whether the accumulation of power is an end in itself, there is no dissenting from the argument that the ultimate concern of states is for security. Moreover, survival is a precondition for attaining all other goals, whether these involve conquest or merely independence. As Waltz puts it, 'beyond the survival motive, the aims of states may be endlessly varied'.

Niccolo Machiavelli tried to make a science out of his reflections on the art of survival. His short and engaging book, *The Prince*, was written with the explicit intention of codifying a set of maxims which will enable a leader to maintain his hold on power. Machiavelli derived these maxims from his experience as a diplomat and his studies of ancient history. For instance, he was full of admiration for the Roman empire which annexed all potential enemies through conquest and imperial domination. *Ergo*, the lesson that Princes or Sovereigns must be prepared to break their promises if it is in their interests, and to conquer neighbouring states before they (inevitably) attack you.

The need for survival requires state leaders to distance themselves from traditional morality which attached a positive value to caution, piety, and the greater good of humankind as a whole. Machiavelli argued that these principles were positively harmful if adhered to by state leaders. It was imperative that state leaders learned a different kind of morality which accorded not to traditional Christian

virtues but to political necessity. There are a number of ethical and practical difficulties associated with Machiavelli's recommendations, particularly when relating these to contemporary international politics. Indeed, it is the perceived moral bankruptcy of Realism which has provoked a number of the most influential criticisms of the theory, summarized in Box 6.3.

In important respects, we find two related Machiavellian themes recurring in the writings of modern realists, both derive from the idea that the realm of international politics requires different moral and political rules than those which applies in domestic politics. The task of understanding the *real* nature of international politics, and the need to protect the state at all costs (even if this may mean the sacrifice of one's own citizens) places a heavy burden on the shoulders of state leaders. In the words of Henry Kissinger, the academic realist who became Secretary of State during the Nixon Presidency, 'a nation's survival is its first and ultimate responsibility; it cannot be compromised or put to risk' (1977: 204). Their guide must be an **ethic of responsibility**: the careful weighing up of consequences; the realization that individual acts of an immoral kind might have to be taken for the greater good. By way of an example, think of the ways in which governments frequently suspend the legal and political rights of 'suspected terrorists' in view of the threat they pose to 'national security'. A realist would argue that letting a suspected terrorist out of prison because there is insufficient evidence for prosecution would be an irresponsible act which might jeopardize the lives of innocent civilians. An ethic of responsibility is frequently used as a justification for breaking the laws of war, as in the case of the United States decision to drop nuclear bombs on Hiroshima and Nagasaki in 1945. The principle difficulty with the realist formulation of an 'ethics of responsibility' is that, whilst instructing leaders to consider the consequences of their actions, it does not provide a guide to *how* state leaders should *weigh* the consequences (M. J. Smith 1986: 51).

Not only does Realism provide an alternative moral code for state leaders, it suggests a wider objection to the whole enterprise of bringing ethics into international politics. Starting from the assumption that each state has its own particular values and beliefs, realists argue that the state is the supreme good and there can be no community beyond borders. Without a common culture, and common institutions, the idea of an 'international community', so frequently articulated by journalists, is seriously premature. E. H. Carr turned scepticism about moral universals into a 'critical weapon' which he wielded in order to reveal how the supposedly universal principles adumbrated by the Great Powers (such as the virtue of free trade or self-determination) were really 'unconscious reflexions of national policy' (Carr 1946: 87). This **moral relativism** has generated a substantial body of criticism, particularly from liberal theorists: if all values are relative, how can we judge the actions of state-leaders? Are there not some policies which are wrong irrespective of which states commit them, such as torture or the denial of civil rights? Whilst the intuitive answer to these questions is 'yes', the argument gets more murky when other states with non-Western cultures argue that what we call 'torture' they call a 'rite of passage' (as in the case of genital mutilation in certain African states). Moreover, many developing states argue that civil rights undermine social cohesion by privileging the individual's rights over the collective good. A realist would therefore see the pursuit of human rights in foreign policy as the imposition of one state's moral principles on another (Morgenthau 1978: 4).

Self-Help

Kenneth Waltz's path-breaking work *The Theory of International Politics* brought to the realist tradition a deeper understanding of the **international system** within which states coexist. Unlike traditional realists, Waltz argued that international politics was not unique because of the regularity of war and conflict, since this was as familiar in domestic politics. The key difference between domestic and international orders lies in their **structure**. In the domestic polity, citizens do not have to defend themselves. In the international system, there is no higher authority to prevent and counter the use of force. Security can therefore only be realized through **self-help**. But in the course of providing for one's own security, the state in question will automatically be fuelling the insecurity of other states. The term given to this spiral of insecurity is the **security dilemma**.[8] According to Wheeler and Booth, security dilemmas exist 'when the military preparations of one state create an unresolvable uncertainty in the mind of another as to whether

those preparations are for "defensive" purposes only (to enhance its security in an uncertain world) or whether they are for offensive purposes (to change the status quo to its advantage)' (1992: 30).

Is there any escape from the security dilemma? There is a divergence in the realist camp between structural realists who believe the security dilemma to be a perennial condition of international politics, and historical realists who believe that, even in a self-help system, the dilemma can be mitigated. The principle mechanism by which it may be mitigated is through the operation of the **balance of power**. Throughout the history of the modern states system, the balance of power has been considered to be essential to preserving the liberty of states. Maintaining a balance of power therefore became a central objective in the foreign policies of the Great Powers; this idea of a contrived balance is well illustrated by the British foreign office memorandum quoted in Box 6.2.

In a self-help system, structural realists argue that the balance of power will emerge even in the absence of a conscious policy to maintain the balance (i.e. prudent statecraft). Waltz argues that balances of power result irrespective of the intentions of any particular state. A fortuitous balance will be established through the interactions of

---

Box 6.2. British Foreign Policy and the Balance of Power

History shows that the danger threatening the independence of this or that nation has generally arisen, at least in part, out of the momentary predominance of a neighbouring State at once militarily powerful, economically efficient, and ambitious to extend its frontiers or spread its influence . . .The only check on the abuse of political predominance derived from such a position has always consisted in the opposition of an equally formidable rival, or a combination of several countries forming leagues of defence. The equilibrium established by such a grouping of forces is technically known as the balance of power, and it has become almost an historical truism to identify England's secular policy with the maintenance of this balance by throwing her weight now in this scale and now in that, but ever on the side opposed to the political dictatorship of the strongest single State or group at a given time.

Memorandum by Sir Eyre Crowe on the Present State of British Relations with France and Germany, January 1, 1907 (Viotti and Kauppi 1993: 50)

states in the same way that an equilibrium is established between firms and consumers in a free economic market (according to classical liberal economic theory). Liberal realists are more likely to emphasize the crucial role state leaders and diplomats play in maintaining the balance of power. In other words, the balance of power is not natural or inevitable, it must be constructed.

All varieties of Realism are united in the view that the balance of power is not a stable condition. Whether it is the contrived balance of the Concert of Europe in the early nineteenth century, or the more fortuitous balance of the cold war, balances of power are broken—either through war or peaceful change—and new balances emerge. What the perennial collapsing of the balance of power demonstrates is that states are at best able to mitigate the worst consequences of the security dilemma but are not able to escape it. The reason for this terminal condition is the absence of trust in international relations.

Historically realists have illustrated this by reference to the the parable of the 'stag hunt'. In *Man, the State and War*, Kenneth Waltz revisits Rousseau's parable:

Assume that five men who have acquired a rudimentary ability to speak and to understand each other happen to come together at a time when all of them suffer from hunger. The hunger of each will be satisfied by the fifth part of stag, so they 'agree' to co-operate in a project to trap one. But also the hunger of any one of them will be satisfied by a hare, so, as a hare comes within reach, one of them grabs it. The defector obtains the means of satisfying his hunger but in doing so permits the stag to escape. His immediate interest prevails over consideration for his fellows (1959: 167–8)

Waltz argues that the metaphor of the stag hunt provides not only a justification for the establishment of government, but a basis for understanding the problem of co-ordinating the interests of the individual versus the interests of the common good, and the pay-off between short-term interests and long-term interests.

In the self-help system of international politics, the logic of self-interest mitigates against the provision of collective goods such as 'security' or 'free trade'. In the case of the latter, according to the theory of comparative advantage, all states would be wealthier in a world that allowed freedom of goods and services across borders. But individual states, or groups of states like the European Union, can increase their wealth by pursuing protectionist

policies providing other states do not respond in kind. Of course the logical outcome is for the remaining states to become protectionist, international trade collapses, and a world recession reduces the wealth of each state.

The contemporary liberal solution to this problem of collective action in self-help systems is through the construction of **regimes** (see Ch. 12). In other words, by establishing patterns of rules, norms and procedures, such as those embodied in the General Agreement on Tariffs and Trade (GATT), states are likely to be more confident that other states will comply with the rules and that defectors will be punished. Contemporary structural realists agree with liberals that regimes can facilitate co-operation under certain circumstances, although realists believe that in a self-help system co-operation is 'harder to achieve, more difficult to maintain, and more dependent on state power' (Grieco, in Baldwin 1993: 302).

A more thoroughgoing challenge to the way in which realists have set up the problem of collective action in a self-help system comes from constructivsm[9] (see Chs. 9 and 10). Although this is a complex argument, the key move in the critique is to argue that anarchy need not imply a self-help system. Historically, anarchy has accommodated varieties of inter-state practices. In the eighteenth century, philosophers and lawyers portrayed the European states system as a commonwealth, a family of nations, with common laws and customs. In the twentieth century, the decentralized international system has witnessed a diverse pattern of interactions, from a literal state of war to brief periods of collective security to examples of regional integration. Only the first of these three conditions could be described in terms of self-help. As Alexander Wendt puts it: 'Self-help presupposes self-interest; it does not explain it. Anarchy is what states make of it' (1994: 388).

Key Points

- **Statism** is the centrepiece of Realism. This involves two claims. First, for the theorist, the state is the pre-eminent actor and all other actors in world politics are of lesser significance. Second, state 'sovereignty' signifies the existence of an independent political community, one which has juridical authority over its territory.

- **Key Criticism:** Statism is flawed both on empirical (challenges to state power from 'above' and 'below') and normative grounds (the inability of sovereign states to respond to collective global problems such as famine, environmental degradation, and human rights abuses).

- **Survival:** The primary objective of all states is survival; this is the supreme national interest to which all political leaders must adhere. All other goals such as economic prosperity are secondary (or 'low politics'). In order to preserve the security of their state, leaders must adopt an ethical code which judges actions according to the outcome rather than in terms of a judgement about whether the individual act is right or wrong. If there are any moral universals for political realists, these can only be concretized in particular communities.

- **Key Criticism:** Are there no limits to what actions a state can take in the name of necessity?

- **Self-help:** No other state can be relied upon to guarantee your survival. In international politics, the structure of the system does not permit friendship, trust, and honour; only a perennial condition of uncertainty generated by the absence of a global government. Coexistence is achieved through the maintenance of the balance of power, and limited co-operation is possible in interactions where the realist state stands to gain more than other states.

- **Key Criticism:** Self-help is not an inevitable consequence of the absence of a world government; self help is the game which states have chosen to play. Moreover, there are historical and contemporary examples where states have preferred collective security systems, or forms of regional integration, in preference to self-help.

Conclusion: Realism and the Globalization of World Politics

The chapter opened by considering the often repeated realist claim that the pattern of international politics—wars interrupted for periods characterized by the preparation for future wars—have remained constant over the preceding twenty-five centuries. In the concluding paragraphs below, we will briefly evaluate whether Realism can speak to *our* world, or has become, as its critics suggest, an anachronistic theory.

It has often been argued that the end of the cold war dealt a fatal blow for Realism. Despite its supporters' faith in the capacity of Realism to predict changes in the international system, most contemporary structural realists predicted the continuity of a stable bipolar (or two superpowers) system well into the next century (Waltz 1979: 210). It seemed that the critics of structural realism were right in objecting to its inability to theorize changes in the international system. (Although, in fairness to Realism, none of the other paradigms of international politics managed to predict the disintegration of the cold war system with the clarity of many Central and East European intellectuals and dissidents.) The understandable Idealism which greeted

the end of the Soviet empire has become more muted in the last few years as the world has witnessed some of the most horrific conflicts of the twentieth century. In the former Yugoslavia we have seen war crimes committed by all of the protagonists, crimes that Europe thought had been banished by the defeat of Nazism. Whilst it would be too strong to claim that the Balkan war was a realist war (because of the multiplicity of complex causes) its origins in the fear engendered by the collapse of the Yugoslav state allied to the contagion of a form of nationalism defined by the fiction of a pure ethnic identity, bear a resemblance to an atavistic realism of blood and belonging. As Case Study 2 (Box 6.4) shows, the precarious peace treaty, signed in Dayton Ohio in November 1995, was unambiguously a realist peace.

There seems little doubt that realist ideas will be drawn upon in the future by state leaders who believe the use of force is the *only* instrument left to insure their survival. And just as in the example of the Daytona peace accord, it is likely that future regional conflicts will only be brought to a close when a new balance of power has emerged

Timothy Dunne

Box 6.3. **What the Critics Say**

R. ASHLEY: Structural realists portray the structure of the international system as though there is only *one* structure (that of power) and its existence is independent of states (rather than constructed *by* them). For this reason, contemporary structural realism is a static, conservative theory (1986).

C. BEITZ: The analogy between individuals in a state of nature and states in international anarchy is misplaced for four reasons. States are not the only actors; the power of states is massively unequal; states are not independent of each other; patterns of co-operation exist (even if motivated by self-interest) despite the absence of a global government capable of enforcing rule (1979).

K. BOOTH: Realism cannot speak to our world. Survival for the majority of individuals in global politics is threatened not by armies of 'foreign' states but more often by their own governments, or more broadly, structures of global capitalism which produce and reproduce the daily round of 'human wrongs' such as malnutrition, death from preventable diseases, slavery, prostitution, and exploitation (1995).

C. BROWN: The strongest argument against Realism's moral scepticism is that states employ a moral language of rights and duties in their relations with each other (1992).

J. BURTON: Interactions of states is only one of many levels of interaction in world society. Rather than an image of states as billiard balls impacting on each other at random, Burton argues we should think about international relations as a 'cobweb model' of interactions and linkages between multiple actors (firms, individuals, groups, etc.) (1990).

R. COX: Realism is problem-solving theory. It accepts the prevailing order, and seeks only to isolate aspects of the system in order to understand how it works. The idea of theory serving an emancipatory purpose—i.e. contemplating alternative world orders—is not in the structural realist's vocabulary (1986).

F. HALLIDAY: The realist conception of the state in international politics (where states are equal, they are in control of their territory, they coincide with nations, and represent their peoples) is very *unrealistic*. A more adequate interpretation of the state is provided by sociology, which makes an analytical distinction between the state and society, the state and government, and the state and nation (1994).

M. HOLLIS AND S. SMITH: Realism assumes that the methods of the natural sciences can be employed to explain the social world (of which international relations is part). Realism can therefore be equated with a form of positivism which seeks to uncover causal laws that can both explain and predict the occurrence of events in world politics (1990).

F. KRATOCHWIL: Contrary to the expectations of contemporary structural realism, the end of the cold war was not brought about by any radical shift in the distribution of power in the international system, and moreover, this shift occurred without a major war (1993).

A. LINKLATER: We must go beyond the structural realist emphasis upon constraints, and the liberal realist predilection for order, in order to develop an emancipatory form of theory which seeks to deepen the sense of solidarity, and widen the bonds of community in global politics (1990).

V. SPIKE PETERSON: The realist emphasis upon national security is contradictory for women, since it masks over 'women's systemic *insecurity*'. Taking feminism seriously requires a radical rethink of the way in which security is framed by a form of sovereignty which legitimizes violence against women and gendered divisions of resources and identities (1992).

J. ROSENBERG: Realism is a conservative ideology. Fundamental to this conservatism is the autonomy realists accord to the international realm. 'The borders and landscapes of this environment are set and policed by the twin concepts of sovereignty and anarchy' (1994: 30).

M. J. SMITH: Despite the argument that values should not impact objective policy formulation, Realism too often appears as nothing more than the (traditional) values and beliefs of the author in question, leaving the suspicion that it is conservative intuitionism masquerading as an international political theory (1986).

C. SYLVESTER: From Machiavelli to the late twentieth century, the qualities 'men' have ascribed to 'women'—such as irrationality, intuition, temptation—have been regarded as a danger to international affairs. For this reason, historical realists argue that statecraft should remain 'mancraft' (1994).

J. VASQUEZ: A statistical analysis of International Relations literature in the 1950s and 1960s underscores the dominance of the realist paradigm in terms of the overwhelming reliance on the core assumptions of Realism. However, although Realism dominated the field, it *failed* to adequately explain international politics. According to the findings, over 90% of the 7,000 realist hypotheses were falsified (1979).

and is underwritten by a Great Power with the economic and political capability to bribe, cajole, and blackmail the protagonists.

This is not to suggest that Realism is only useful as a guide to understanding the origins and settlement of wars. It will continue to serve as a critical weapon for revealing the interplay of national interests beneath the rhetoric of universalist sentiments. There is no more powerful example of this than Realism's potential to deconstruct a Marxist or

Box 6.4. Case Study 2: The Bosnian Dialogue—A Realist Peace?

June 1991 Tension between the republics of the former Yugoslavia ignites into a conflict. Croatian claim to independence resisted by local Serbs. Bitter civil war eventually contained by the imposition of 14,000 UN peacekeeping troops in Croatia.

April 1992 European Union recognizes Bosnia's independence. Bosnian Serbs fear for their security; war erupts between the Bosnian government and Bosnian Serbs.

February 1994 During the Serbian siege of Sarajevo, a shell lands in a market-place killing 68 civilians. NATO air power called upon to protect 'safe areas' and UN peacekeepers.

March 1994 The United States brokers an agreement between the Bosnian government and Croatia, representing a crucial shift in the **balance of power** which enables both to turn against the Bosnian Serbs.

July 1995 Bosnian Serbs take the UN declared 'safe area' of Srebrenica. Thousands of refugees remain unaccounted for. Growing recognition among Western state leaders that the strategy of peacekeeping must make way for a tougher peace enforcement policy.

August 1995 With the tacit support of the US, Croatia launches a massive attack against Croatian Serb-held Krajina. Rapidly followed by a Muslim–Croat offensive in north-western Bosnia resulting in tens of thousands of Serbian refugees. In neither case does President Milosevic of Serbia intervene in view of his calculation that Serbian interests are better served by courting international approval, thereby increasing the possibility of ending sanctions against Serbia.

28 August 1995 Another shell hits central Sarajevo, killing and maiming more civilians. NATO launches a massive air attack on Serb targets in Bosnia until the Serbs agree to move weapons away from Sarajevo.

5 October 1995 The US seizes the moment to broker a general cease-fire following the successive defeats of the Bosnian Serbs. All of the combatants are locked into peace talks in the US Air Force Base in Dayton Ohio.

21 November 1995 President Clinton announces a peace deal. America succeeds where the UN and the European Union failed. The 'peace' agreement is founded on a division of territory that recognizes the fact of territorial redistribution according to the principle of ethnic purity. Eastern Bosnia, where Serbian forces ruthlessly expelled Bosnian Muslims from April 1992 onwards, has been allocated to the Serb Republic. The Muslim–Croat federation remains in control of former Serb-held Kraijina, following the massive offensive against ethnic Serbs living in the region in August, 1995.

Eric Hobsbawm on the Peace Plan:

It is based on ruthless realism. Essentially the peace was made by scaring the Serbs (economic blackmail) and strengthening the Croats, without whose US-backed and trained military advances the Bosnians Serbs would not have given in. In spite of the rhetoric about arming the Bosnians, they will get least out of the settlement. They will be an appendix to the 'Croat–Muslim' federation, guaranteed at most against further genocide and ethnic expulsion and the formal survival of the Bosnian state frontiers. In most other respects the division of Bosnia between Croatia and Serbia, which Milosevic and Tudjiman planned, will be realized. (*Independent*, 22 November 1995)

---

a Liberal progressivist view of history which sees the gradual triumphing of European ideas and values throughout the world. A realist has no problem understanding aspects of the globalization of world politics—indeed structural realists could claim to have theorized more completely the nature of the international system than any other paradigm on offer. What is interesting about a realist theory of globalization is the *acceptance* of the militarization of the international system, and the patterns of political control and domination which extend beyond borders (such as hegemonic control or spheres of influence), but a concomitant *rejection* of the idea that globalization is accompanied by a deepening sense of community. From Rousseau to Waltz, realists have argued that interdependence brought about through intimate contact with modernity is as likely to breed 'mutual vulnerability' as peace and prosperity.

There are good reasons for thinking that the twenty-first century will be a realist century. The Western sense of immortality, fuelled by the Enlightenment discoveries of reason and democracy, was dealt a fatal blow by the Holocaust. Despite the efforts of federalists to rekindle the idealist flame, Europe continues to be divided by interests and not united by a common good. Outside of Europe and North America, many of the assumptions which underpinned the post-war international order, particularly those associated with human rights, are increasingly being seen as nothing more than a Western idea backed by economic dollars and military 'divisions'. As the axis of world politics shifts to the Asia-Pacific region, this model

Timothy Dunne

Box 6.5. Key Concepts in Realist Thought

anarchy	Does not imply chaos, but the absence of political authority.	**national interest**	Invoked by realists and state leaders to signify that which is most important to the state—survival being at the top of the list.
anarchic system	The 'ordering principle' of international politics, and that which defines its structure.	**power**	The ability to control outcomes e.g. state A is able to get state B to act in a way which maximizes the interests of A.
balance of power	Refers to an equilibrium between states; historical realists regard it as the product of diplomacy (contrived balance) whereas structural realists regard the system as having a tendency towards a natural equilibrium (fortuitous balance).	**self-help**	In an anarchical environment, states cannot assume other states will come to their defence even if they are allies.
		sovereignty	The state has supreme authority domestically and independence internationally.
capabilities	Population and size of territory, resources, economic strength, military capability, political stability, and competence (Waltz 1979: 131).	**state**	A legal territorial entity composed of a stable population and a government; it possesses a monopoly over the legitimate use of force; its sovereignty is recognized by other states in the international system.
ethic of responsibility	For historical realists, an ethic of responsibility is the limits of ethics in international politics; it involves the weighing up of consequences and the realization that positive outcomes may result from amoral actions.		
		statism	The ideology which supports the organization of humankind into particular communities; the values and beliefs of that community are protected and sustained by the state.
idealism	Holds that ideas have important causal effect on events in international politics, and that ideas can change. Referred to by realists as utopianism since it underestimates the logic of power politics and the constraints this imposes upon political action.		
		state of war	The condition (often described by classical realists) where there is no actual conflict, but a permanent cold war that could become a 'hot' war at any time.
interdependence	A condition where the actions of one state impact upon other states (can be strategic interdependence or economic). Realists equate interdependence with vulnerability.	**structure**	In the philosophy of the social sciences a structure is something which exists independently of the actor (e.g. social class) but is an important determinant in the nature of the action (e.g. revolution). For contemporary structural realists, the number of great powers in the international system constitutes the structure.
hegemony	The influence a great power is able to establish on other states in the system; extent of influence ranges from leadership to dominance.		
international system	A set of interrelated parts connected to form a whole. Systems have defining principles such as hierarchy (in domestic politics) and anarchy (in international politics).	**survival**	The first priority for state leaders, emphasized by historical realists such as Machiavelli, Meinecke, and Weber.

---

of democratic individualism which the liberal West has tried to export to the rest of the world is being revealed as culturally contingent and economically retarded. This comes as no surprise to realists who understand that words are weapons and that internationalist ideas are the continuation of statism by other means. Here we find an alliance between Realism and many non-Western states' leaders who recognize that values are shared *within* particular communities and not *between* them, that knowledge is contingent and not grounded in universal reason, that global cultures are fragmented and contested. Rather than transforming global politics in its own image, as liberalism has sought to do in *this* century, the West may need to become more realist in order to survive the next.

QUESTIONS

1. How does the Melian dialogue represent key concepts such as self-interest, the balance of power, alliances, capabilities, empires, justice, etc.?

2. Do you think there is one Real*ism*, or many?

3. Do you know more about international relations than an Athenian student during *The Peloponnesian War*?

4. Is the practice of international politics realist? How does Realism inform state practice? Through what channels or processes does it shape foreign policy?

5. Do realists confuse a *description* of war and conflict, for an *explanation* of why it occurs?

6. How can the security dilemma be escaped or mitigated?

7. Is Realism any more than the ideology of powerful, satisfied states?

8. How far do the critics of Realism overlook the extent to which the theory is grounded in an ethical defence of the state?

9. How would realists try to explain the origins of the wars in the former Yugoslavia? Do you find their arguments convincing?

10. Will the West have to learn to be more realist, and not less, if its civilization is to survive in the 21st century?

GUIDE TO FURTHER READING

The most comprehensive book on twentieth-century Realism is Michael Joseph Smith, *Realist Thought from Weber to Kissinger* (Baton Rouge: Louisiana State University Press, 1986). For an effective single chapter survey, particularly on structural realism, see Martin Hollis and Steve Smith *Explaining and Understanding International Relations* (Oxford: Clarendon, 1990), chapter 5. The Paul Viotti and Mark Kauppi *International Relations Theory: Realism, Pluralism, Globalism* (New York: Macmillan, 1993) textbook has an extensive treatment of Realism in chapter 2, including important excerpts from the classical precursors.

The best single work on historical realism is N. Machiavelli, *The Prince*, ed. Q. Skinner (Cambridge: Cambridge University Press, 1988). E. H. Carr, *The Twenty Years' Crisis 1919–1939: An Introduction to the Study of International Relations* (London: Macmillan, 1946) is a hugely important and thought-provoking work which brings historical realism into the twentieth century, see especially chapters 5 and 6. The bible for liberal realism is Hedley Bull, *The Anarchical Society: A Study of Order in World Politics* (London: Macmillan, 1977). Structural realism I, with its emphasis upon laws of human nature, is exemplified in Hans J. Morgenthau, *Politics among Nations: The Struggle for Power and Peace* (New York: Knopf, 1978), chapter 1. Kenneth Waltz, *Theory of International Politics* (Reading, Mass.: Addison-Wesley, 1979) is the exemplar for structural realism II, see in particular, chapters 1 and 6. Alongside this work, the student should consult Robert Keohane, *Neorealism and its Critics* (New York: Columbia University Press, 1986). This collection of essays includes key chapters by Waltz, an interesting defence of realism by Robert Gilpin, and powerful critiques by Richard Ashley, Robert Cox, and J. G. Ruggie. A more recent collection which takes the debate further is David A. Baldwin, *Neorealism and Neoliberalism: The Contemporary Debate* (New York: Columbia University Press,

1993). For the more penetrating constructivist challenge to Realism, see A. Wendt in *International Organization*, 46:2 (1992), 395–421; and *American Political Science Review*, 88:2 (1994), 384–96.

NOTES

1. Realism, *realpolitik*, and *raison d'état* are broadly interchangeable. In this chapter, Realism with an upper case 'R' will be used to signify the general tradition. When discussing particular realists, or types of realism (such as historical realism), lower case 'r' will be used.
2. This is an edited extract from Thucydides, *The Peloponnesian War*, trans. Rex Warner (London: Penguin Classics, 1954), 360–5.
3. The other 'critical' distinction is made by Richard Ashley who contrasts the 'practical realism' of Machiavelli and Carr with the 'technical realism' of Gilpin and Waltz (1981: 221).
4. What I have termed 'structural realism II' is often referred to in the literature as Neo-Realism. Robert Keohane argues that Neo-Realism differs from earlier forms of realism 'in that it does not rest on the presumed iniquity of the human race' (1989: 40). Although Keohane is right to note the shift in causation from human nature to anarchy, he is wrong to believe that this is anything other than a change from one kind of structure to another (hence the use in the chapter of 'structural realism I' and 'II').
5. The extent to which British liberal realism, found in the work of Martin Wight and Hedley Bull constitues a break from Realism, is a matter of some debate in the literature. For contrasting answers, compare Booth (1995) and Wheeler (1996).
6. There are a number of similar versions of this idea of a 'shared core' to Realism in the literature. Keohane distils the core into: state as actor, state as rational, state as power maximizer (Keohane 1989: 39) and (Gilpin 1986: 304–5) are two examples among many.
7. M. J. Smith, 23. Weber is rightly regarded by Smith as the theorist who has shaped twentieth-century realist thought, principally because of his fusion of politics with power.
8. It is important to note that not all conflict results from the security dilemma (since both parties have benign intent); historically, more conflicts have been caused through predator states.
9. Alex Wendt defines constructivism in the following terms: 'Constructivism is a structural theory of the international system which makes the following core claims (1) states are the principal units of analysis for international political theory; (2) the key structures in the states system are intersubjective, rather than material; and (3) state identities and interests are in important part constructed by these social structures, rather than given exogenously to the system by human nature or domestic politics' (1994: 385). Arguably, the liberal realist wing has a good deal in common with constructivism, and likewise, can be fashioned into a critique of structural realism (Dunne: 1995).

7 World-System Theory

Steve Hobden and Richard Wyn Jones

READER'S GUIDE

This chapter will introduce, outline, and assess the approach to the study of world politics known as world-system theory. This approach has its origins in Marxist thought and argues that world politics can only be correctly understood when viewed in the context of the structure of global capitalism. The chapter stresses that for world-system theorists, the features pointed to by proponents of the globalization thesis are hardly novel, indeed, they are merely the modern manifestations of centuries-old tendencies within the world-system.

Introduction

Compared to realism and pluralism, world-system theory presents a rather unfamiliar view of international relations. Whilst the former portray world politics in ways which resonate with those presented in the foreign news pages of our newspapers and magazines, world-system theory aims to expose a deeper, underlying—indeed hidden—truth. This is that the familiar events of world politics—wars, treaties, international aid operations, etc.—all occur within a structure which shapes, determines, and defines those events. That structure is that of a world-system organized according to the logic of global capitalism. Thus any attempt to understand world politics must be based on a broader understanding of the processes which operate within the world-system.

In addition to presenting a rather unfamiliar view of world politics, world-system theory is also discomforting, for it argues that the effect of the structure of the world system is to ensure that the powerful and wealthy continue to prosper at the expense of the powerless and the poor.

We are all aware that there is gross inequality in the world. Statistics concerning the human costs of poverty are truly numbing in their awfulness (see Box 7.1). Approximately a third of the world's population use up the vast bulk of the world's resources with the rest having to make-do as best they can. Indeed, according to the 1996 United Nations Human Development Report, the total wealth of the world's 358 billionaires is equal to the combined incomes of the poorest 45 per cent of the world's population.

World-system theorists argue that the relative prosperity of the few is *dependent* on the destitution of the many. To state the case emotively: their claim is that the majority in the so-called 'Third World' must suffer so that we in the 'West' can continue to enjoy our privileged existence. The structure of a world-system organized according to the logic of global capitalism is such that the 'good life' of the few is dependent on the misery of the many. Here world-system theorists are reiterating an argument made by Karl Marx who claimed that:

Accumulation of wealth at one pole is, therefore, at the same time accumulation of misery, agony of toil, slavery, ignorance, brutality at the opposite pole.

Box 7.1. **Indicators of World Inequality**

- One-fifth of the world's 5.6 billion population are living in extreme poverty.
- One-third of the world's children are undernourished.
- Half the world's population lacks regular access to the most essential drugs.
- 12.2 million children under five die every year, 95% from poverty-related illness.
- 130 million children—80% of them girls—are denied the chance to go to school.
- In 70 countries average incomes are less than they were in 1980, and in 43 less than in 1970.
- Per-capita water supply in developing countries has dropped by two-thirds since 1970.
- In 1960 the richest 20% of the world's population were 30 times better off than the poorest 20%. By 1996 this figure had increased to 61 times wealthier.
- The wealth of the world's 358 billionaires exceeds the combined incomes of countries with nearly half the world's population.
- World military spending is $US 778 billion each year.

Sources: World Health Organization, United Nations, World Bank

---

The fact that world-system theorists echo the ideas of Marx should come as no surprise given that Marx, and Marxism more generally, have been major influences on the development of world-system theory. It is to this that we now turn in order to trace the origins of world-system theory .

Key Points

- World-system theorists argue that world politics occurs within a world-system dominated by the logic of global capitalism.
- One of the key effects of the world-system is that the rich and powerful prosper at the expense of the poor and the weak.

The Origins of World-System Theory

In his inaugural address to the Working Men's International Association in London in 1864, Karl Marx told his audience that history had 'taught the working classes the duty to master (for) themselves the mysteries of international politics'. However, despite the fact that Marx himself wrote copiously about international affairs, most of this writing was journalistic in character. He did not incorporate the international dimension into his theoretical mapping of the contours of capitalism. Given the vast scope of Marx's work, this 'omission' should perhaps not surprise us. The sheer scale of the theoretical enterprise in which he was engaged, as well as the nature of his own methodology, inevitably meant that Marx's work would be contingent and unfinished. That said, since his death many of those who have taken inspiration from Marx's approach have attempted to apply his theoretical insights to international relations.

The first sustained attempt to utilize Marxian ideas to analyse the international sphere was the critique of imperialism advanced by such thinkers as Hobson, Luxemburg, Bukharin, Hilferding, and Lenin (see Brewer 1990) at around the turn of the twentieth century.

Without doubt, the most well-known and influential work to emerge from this debate about the nature of imperialism was a pamphlet written by Lenin, and published in 1917, called *Imperialism, the Highest Stage of Capitalism*. Lenin's ideas represented both a development on and a departure from those of Marx. A development *on* Marx in that Lenin accepted Marx's basic thesis that it is the economic mode of production that ultimately determines broader social and political relations: a relationship usually summarized *via* the famous base-superstructure model. Lenin also accepted Marx's contention that history can only be correctly understood in terms of class conflict. In capitalist society this means the conflict between the bourgeoisie and the proletariat.

However, Lenin argued that the nature of capitalism had changed somewhat since Marx published the first volume of his monumental work *Capital* in 1867. Capitalism had entered a new stage—indeed, its highest and final stage—with the development of *monopoly capitalism*. One of the effects of this transformation was that—analytically speaking—capitalism now had to be viewed in a broader, international context, rather than the predominantly domestic context scrutinized by Marx. This 'departure from' Marx's work had far-reaching implications in terms of Lenin's analysis.

Marx's conception of capitalism led him to posit a simple divergence of interests between the proletariat on the one hand, and the bourgeoisie on the other. This divergence was the same no matter what the geographical location of the worker or the capitalist. Thus, objectively speaking, there was no conflict of interests between the workers of different countries, and if they could break themselves free from the binds of dominant bourgeois ideologies they would recognize this. As Marx famously proclaimed: 'Workers of the world unite, you have nothing to lose but your chains.'

However, Lenin argued that imperialism had created a two-tier structure within the world-economy with a dominant *core* exploiting a less-developed *periphery*. Such a structure dramatically complicates Marx's view of a simple divergence of interests between the proletariat and bourgeoisie. With the development of a core and periphery, there was no longer an automatic harmony of interests between all workers. The bourgeoisie in the core countries could use profits derived from exploiting the periphery to improve the lot of their own proletariat. In other words, the capitalists of the core could pacify—or bluntly, buy off—their own working class through the further exploitation of the periphery. Thus, according to Lenin's analysis, the structural division between the core and periphery determines the nature of the relationship between the bourgeoisie and proletariat of each country.

Even this rather simplistic summary of Lenin's theory of imperialism should alert us to two important features of the world-system approach to the understanding of world politics. The first is that all politics, international and domestic, takes place within the framework of a capitalist world-economy. The second is the contention that states are not the only important actors in international relations, rather social classes are also very significant. Moreover, it is the location of these states and classes within the structure of the capitalist world-economy that constrains their behaviour and determines patterns of interaction and domination between them.

Marxist-influenced analyses of world politics remained widely influential at least until the early years of the cold war. In retrospect, it is easy to understand why this may have been so. The First World War seemed—and indeed, still seems—like a pointless and futile quarrel between rival imperialistic cliques in the capitalist core. That grotesquely bloody war was followed by a sustained period of economic crisis which led many to believe—and not only on the left of the political spectrum—that capitalism had entered its final death-throes. In this climate, it is not surprising that Marxist categories of analysis, and the critique of imperialism in particular, fell on fruitful ground. It is particularly significant in this respect that the book seen by many as heralding the genesis of modern Realism, E. H. Carr's *The Twenty Years' Crisis* (1939), is obviously heavily influenced by Marxist ideas.

However, after the Second World War, interest in Marxist-influenced conceptual tools as a means of understanding world politics waned quickly. The long post-war economic boom meant that capitalism appeared to have overcome the problems of the inter-war period. Furthermore, the decolonization process suggested that the core countries could survive and even prosper without having to exploit colonies in peripheral areas. In addition, in the post-Hiroshima age of mutually assured nuclear destruction the Marxists' preoccupation with economic issues may have seemed a rather frivolous distraction from the 'real issues' of world politics—the possibility of the annihilation of the human race.

Key Points

- World-system theory has its origins in Marxist thought, with the critique of imperialism being especially influential.

- Lenin's analysis of imperialism argued that the world economy was divided into a core and periphery, and that capitalists in the core used profits derived from the exploitation of the periphery to pacify their own workers.

- Lenin's theory of imperialism was especially influential in the 1917–39 period when the great Depression of the 1920s and 1930s appeared to confirm that capitalism was going through its final crisis.

- Theories of international relations derived from the Marxist critique of imperialism became much less influential in the West following the end of the Second World War.

Wallerstein and World-System Theory

There can be little doubt that it was developments in the real world of world politics that led to a resurgence of interest in Marxist-influenced analyses. The oil shocks and deep global recession of the 1970s, combined with the parallel process of *détente* between East and West, served to push economic issues centre-stage. What had previously been rather dismissively referred to as 'low politics', that is questions pertaining to global economic relations, were now at the centre of the political agenda. Analyses which stressed the indissoluble linkage between the economic and the political realms, appeared far better placed to make sense of 'really existing' world politics than the theoretical lenses worn by most scholars of international politics. In these circumstances, Marxist-influenced approaches received a huge fillip and were developed with renewed vigour.

Without doubt, the outstanding figure to emerge from this intellectual ferment is Immanuel Wallerstein. The rest of this chapter will concentrate on his work. But before proceeding any further, two caveats are in order. First, it must be stressed that Wallerstein's work is only one of many approaches which can loosely be described as Marxist-influenced. In Box 7.2 we briefly summarize a number of others, many of whom were key influences on Wallerstein. Secondly, Wallerstein's project is still evolving. He remains an impressively prolific author and thus in the following, we can do no more than offer a snapshot of what is still 'work in progress'.

Wallerstein's first works were studies of African states in the pre- and post-colonial era. As his work progressed, Wallerstein became increasingly dissatisfied with the kind of approach that only looked at

Box 7.2. Other Theorists of Global Capitalism

This chapter has concentrated on the work of Immanuel Wallerstein as a key example of someone who has developed a radical approach to understanding international relations. However this should not detract from the fact that numerous other writers have contributed to the development of a radical perspective on the nature of global capitalism.

The Dependency (or *dependencia*) School is the name given to a group of scholars who have studied the nature of economic relations between Latin America and the developed world. The key figures in this group include: Frank, Cardoso, and Prebisch.

Andre Gunder Frank is a key figure in the dependency school and is largely responsible for generating an interest in the approach in North America. Frank has been criticized from within the dependency school for providing a rather crude version of the theory. More recently Frank has become deeply involved in the world-system approach. Key Work: *Dependent Accumulation and Underdevelopment* (New York: Monthly Review Press, 1979).

Raúl Prebisch was the first Executive Director of the United Nations Economic Commission for Latin America. Together with a team of Latin American economists he was responsible for the development of concepts which became central for the Dependency school. These included developing Lenin's notion of centre–periphery relations, and the idea that countries in the developing world were on the losing side of the declining terms of trade: namely that year by year the earnings from the sale of primary products (the main export of developing countries) could purchase less in the way of manufactured goods (the main export of developed countries). Key Work: *Towards a New Trade Policy for Development* (New York: United Nations, 1964).

The Annales School is the name given to a group of scholars associated with the French journal *Annales d'histoire économique et sociale*. The *Annales* school comprised a marked change from traditional historical approaches. In contrast to conventional historical approaches which concentrate on the very detailed description of specific events, and life histories of individuals (usually kings, politicians, and soldiers), the *Annalistes* sought a rather different approach which focused on long-term social change. Key writers include Fernand Braudel, Marc Bloch, and Lucien Febvre.

Fernand Braudel is a key influence on Wallerstein, primarily due to his analysis of historical time. In his major works Braudel employs a three-way approach based on different conceptions of time. The 'long term' (or *la longue durée*) concerns how environmental factors, such as climate change, affect human development. The 'middle term' is concerned with tracing the effects of human structures such as capitalism, racism, and patriarchy. The 'short term' is the level of more con-

ventional history and relates events. Key work: *The Mediterranean and the Mediterranean World in the Age of Philip II* (London: Fontana, 1975).

Paul Baran developed Lenin's views on monopoly capitalism in the post-World War II period. Baran stressed the absolute (rather than relative) losses that were involved in trade between developed and underdeveloped countries. Essentially countries of the developing world became underdeveloped as a result of their trading relations with the rest of the world. Furthermore the extraction of wealth was not used for investment purposes in the developed world, but was instead squandered through advertising, and more importantly arms expenditure. Key Work: *The Political Economy of Growth* (New York: Monthly Review Press, 1957).

Christopher Chase-Dunn lays much more emphasis on the role of the inter-state system than does Wallerstein. He argues that the capitalist mode of production has a single logic in which both politico-military and exploitative economic relations play key roles. Key Work: *Global Formation: Structures of the World-Economy* (Oxford: Blackwell, 1989).

Janet Abu-Lughod has challenged Wallerstein's account of the emergence of the modern world-system in the sixteenth century. She argues that during the medieval period Europe comprised a peripheral area to a world-economy centred on the Middle East. Key Work: *Before European Hegemony: The World System AD 1250–1350* (Oxford: Oxford University Press, 1989).

Henrique Fernando Cardoso is now president of Brazil! He was also a contributor to, and critic of, the Dependency School. Most famous for his work with Enzo Faletto on Brazil. They argued that rather than there being one situation of dependency between core and periphery, situations of dependency would vary depending on the different relationships of domestic classes, transnational capital, and core state Governments. Key Work: with Enzo Faletto, *Dependency and Development in Latin America* (Berkeley: University of California Press, 1979).

Walter Rodney extended a structuralist approach to the study of Africa, concentrating on the impact of slavery and colonialism in undermining the dynamism of African societies. Key Work: *How Europe Underdeveloped Africa* (London: Bogle-L'Ouverture, 1972).

Johan Galtung stressed the importance of considering a wide range of factors in the analysis of imperialism. He argued that Lenin and Hobson had concentrated too much on an economic analysis. It was also necessary to consider other factors of dominance such as political, military, cultural, and communications. Galtung also emphasized the importance of examining the relationships and coinciding interests between élites in the core and in the centre (i.e. *comprador* class). Key work: 'A Structural Theory of Imperialism', *Journal of Peace Research*, 8: 1 (1971), 81–117.

one country at a time. There was much that could not be explained about the continued poverty of many African countries if they were only studied individually. Thus, in order to understand their development, or, more correctly, lack of development, it would be necessary to analyse specific countries within one social whole: an entity that he was to label the **modern world-system**.

The world-system is the central feature of Wallerstein's work. He contends that 'the appropriate "unit of analysis" for the study of social or societal behaviour is a "world-system".' (1991a: 267) One should note that this is a claim which, if true, has very far-reaching implications. For what Wallerstein is in effect arguing is that **all** social phenomena, from poverty in West African villages to ethnic conflict in the Balkans, and from international relations to the nature of family life, have to be understood in the context of this larger entity. To understand what he means by world-system, it is useful to unpack the term itself.

For Wallerstein, a **system** has two defining characteristics. First, all the elements within a system are **interlinked**. They exist in a dynamic relationship with each other and if one is to understand the attributes, the functions or the behaviour of one element, one must understand its position within the whole. Accordingly, Wallerstein argues that attempts to distinguish and differentiate between, for example, economic phenomena and political and socio-cultural phenomena are misleading. Nothing in the system can be understood in isolation: a holistic approach is the only valid one.

Second, life within the system is more or less **self-contained**. This means that if the system were cut off from all external influences the outcomes within that system would be identical. Thus anyone seeking to explain changes within the system must seek to focus upon those internal dynamics responsible for change rather than search for external (exogenous) factors.

When attached to the term world-system, the prefix **world** is not meant to imply that any particular system necessarily encompasses the whole globe. Rather 'world' is used here to refer to a discrete, self-contained realm. For example, Wallerstein would consider that the Roman empire was a world-system even though its boundaries did not incorporate the whole globe. Thus world-system refers to a particular geographical area governed by the logic of single system. That said, it should be noted that one of the novel features of

the world-system that we inhabit—the **modern world-system**—is that it has grown to incorporate the whole globe.

Wallerstein argues that history has witnessed two types of world-system: **world-empires**, and **world-economies**. The main distinction between a world-empire and a world-economy relates to how decisions about resource distribution—crudely, who gets what—are made. In a world-empire a centralized political system uses its power to redistribute resources from peripheral areas to the central core area. In the Roman empire this took the form of the payment of 'tributes' by the outlying provinces back to the Roman heartland. By contrast, in a world-economy there is no single centre of political authority, but rather we find multiple competing centres of power. Resources are therefore not distributed according to central political decree, but rather through the medium of a **market**. However, although the mechanism for resource distribution is different, as we shall see, the net effect in both a world-economy and a world-empire is similar, and that is the transfer of resources from the peripheral areas to the core.

The modern world-system is an example of a world-economy. According to Wallerstein this system emerged in Europe at around the turn of the sixteenth century. It subsequently expanded to bring about the current situation where there is no corner of the globe which is not thoroughly implicated within it. The driving force behind this seemingly relentless process of expansion and incorporation has been the 'ceaseless accumulation of capital': or, in a nutshell, **capitalism**. Thus the modern world-system is above all else a capitalist system—it is this which provides its central dynamic.

Wallerstein defines capitalism as 'a system of production for sale in a market for profit and appropriation of this profit on the basis of individual or collective ownership' (1979: 66). Note that this is a description of a **relationship** rather than a particular set of institutions. Indeed, Wallerstein is adamant that within the context of this broader relationship, institutions are continually being created and recreated. This state of flux not only extends to what are normally considered to be narrowly economic institutions such as particular companies or even industries. It is equally true for what are often thought to be permanent, even primordial institutions, such as the family unit, ethnic groups, and states. According to Wallerstein, none of these are timeless—none remain the same. To claim otherwise is to adopt an **ahistoric** attitude, that is, to fail to understand that the characteristics of social institutions are historically specific. For Wallerstein and his colleagues, all social institutions, large and small, are continually adapting and changing within the context of a dynamic world-system.

Furthermore, and crucially, it is not only the elements within the system which change. Wallerstein argues that the system itself is historically bounded. It had a beginning and, as we shall see, Wallerstein argues that it is nearing its end. To understand the nature of the system we shall now turn to the more formal description of its characteristics and attributes.

Key Points

- For exponents of world-system theory such as Immanuel Wallerstein, all social events have to be analysed within the context of a world-system.

- Systems have two main features: all features within a system are interrelated; and all developments within the system can be explained by internal factors.

- Historically there have been two types of world-system: world empires and world-economies. The modern world-system is an example of a world-economy.

- The world-economy is a capitalist system, which started to emerge in Europe in the sixteenth century.

The Modern World-System in Space and Time

The modern world-system has features which can be described in terms of space and time. The **spatial** dimension focuses on the differing economic roles played by different regions within the world-economy. As we have seen, Lenin's theory of imperialism posited a core–periphery division based on a geographical division of labour. According to this view, the core is home to those production processes which require the highest levels of skills and the greatest concentrations of capital, whilst the periphery acts as a source of raw materials and extensive surplus extraction. This model was subsequently taken up by other writers especially the dependency school (see Box 7.2). However, Wallerstein has (somewhat controversially) included another economic zone in his description of the world-economy, an intermediate **semi-periphery**.

According to Wallerstein, the semi-peripheral zone has an intermediate role within the world-system displaying certain features characteristic of the core and others characteristic of the periphery. For example, although penetrated by core economic interests, the semi-periphery has its own relatively vibrant indigenously owned industrial base (see also Fig. 7.1). Because of this hybrid nature, the

semi-periphery plays important economic and political roles within the modern world-system. In particular, it provides a source of labour that counteracts any upward pressure on wages in the core and also provides a new home for those industries that can no longer function profitably in the core (for example, car assembly and textiles). The semi-periphery also plays a vital role in stabilizing the political structure of the world-system—a point that will be elaborated upon in the next section.

According to world-system theorists, the three zones of the world-economy are linked together in an exploitative relationship in which wealth is drained away from the periphery to the centre (see Box 7.3). As a consequence, the relative positions of the zones become ever more deeply entrenched: the richer get richer whilst the poor become poorer.

Together, the core, semi-periphery, and periphery make up the spatial dimension of the world-economy. However, described in isolation they provide a rather static portrayal of the world-system. In order to understand the dynamics of their interaction over time we must turn our attention to the **temporal** dimensions of Wallerstein's description of the world-economy. It is these, when

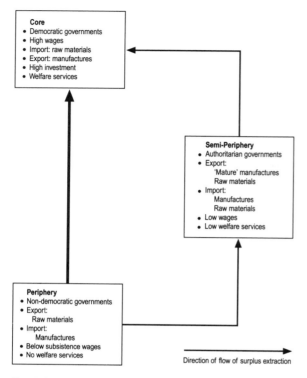

Fig. 7.1. **Interrelationships in the world-economy**

combined with the spatial dimensions, which determine the historical trajectory of the system.

Wallerstein has outlined four temporal processes at work in the modern world-system: cyclical rhythms, secular trends, contradictions, and crisis.

The first temporal dimension, **cyclical rhythms**, is concerned with the tendency of the capitalist world-economy to go through recurrent periods of

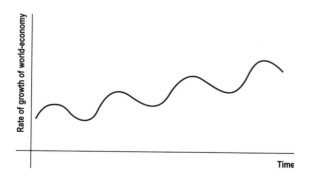

Fig. 7.2. **Cycles in the world-economy**

expansion and subsequent contraction, or more colloquially, boom and bust. Wallerstein has enthusiastically endorsed the work of the Russian economist Kondratieff who amassed an impressive set of data to demonstrate that these periods of expansion and contraction take place in regular 40–60 year cycles (Fig. 7.2). Although evidence to support the existence of these cycles—often called Kondratieff waves—is overwhelming, there is much controversy as to their cause. Nevertheless, they clearly form one of the central dynamics at work within the modern world-system.

Whatever the underlying processes responsible for these waves of growth and depression, it is important to note that each cycle does not simply return the system to the point from which it started. Rather, if we plot the end-point of each wave we discover the **secular trends** within the system (Fig. 7.3). Secular trends refers to the long-term growth or contraction of the world economy.

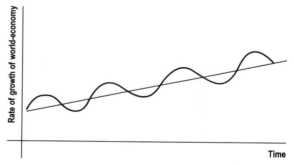

Fig. 7.3. **Mapping trends in the world-economy**

The third temporal feature of the world-system is **contradictions**. These arise because of 'constraints imposed by systemic structures that make one set of behaviour optimal for actors in the short run and a different, even opposite set of behaviour optimal for the same actors in the middle run' (1991a: 261). These constraints can best be explained and understood by examining what Wallerstein regards as one of the main contradictions confronting the capitalist system, the crisis of underconsumption.

In the short term it is in the interests of capitalists to maximize profits through driving down the wages of the producers, i.e. their workers. However, to realize their profits, capitalists need to sell the products that their workers produce to consumers

Box 7.3. Exploitation of Peripheral Areas

World-system theorists argue that the different zones of the world-economy are linked together in an exploitative relationship in which wealth is extracted from the peripheral areas by the core. As a result, their relative positions become more deeply entrenched as the rich prosper at the expense of the poor.

There is a great deal of empirical evidence to support this general line of argument. The UN Human Development Report published in 1996 shows that the gap between rich and poor is expanding. Between 1960 and 1991, the richest 20% of the world's population increased their share of the world's wealth from 70% to 85% whilst the poorest 20% saw their share fall from 2.3% to 1.4%. Throughout this period there was a massive net transfer of resources from the so-called developing world to the richer countries despite their much-heralded—but ultimately half-hearted—aid programmes.

However, whilst the empirical evidence does suggest that exploitation of the peripheral areas is taking place, describing the exact mechanisms through which this occurs has proven to be more difficult. Generally speaking, world-system theorists deploy a range of different arguments in order to try and show how wealth is drained from the periphery to the core. None of these is entirely satisfactory but two have been particularly influential.

Raul Prebisch (see Box 7.2) argued that countries in the periphery were suffering as a result of what he called **'the declining terms of trade'**. Put simply he suggested that the price of manufactured goods increased more rapidly than raw materials. So, for example, year by year it requires more tons of coffee to pay for a refrigerator. As a result of their reliance on primary goods, each year countries of the periphery are becoming poorer relative to the core.

Arghiri Emmanuel's theory of **'unequal exchange'** has also been very influential amongst world-system theorists. Emmanuel argues that an unequal relationship exists between the core and periphery because of unequal wage levels. His argument is that structural factors mean that wage rates in the core and periphery do not equalize over time in the way predicted by classical economic theory. These structural factors include institutionalized workers' rights and higher levels of technology in the core, and controls on labour mobility from the periphery to the core because of immigration controls. Because of these, the ability of workers in the periphery to increase their wage levels is dramatically curtailed. The upshot is that when comparing goods containing equal amounts of labour time, those produced in the core and purchased in the periphery are overpriced compared to those produced in the periphery and purchased in the core: an inherently unequal relationship in which the high-wage area benefits at the expense of the low-wage area.

Whatever the exact mechanisms through which the core exploits the more peripheral parts of the world economy, world-system theorists regard them as one of the central features of the modern world-system.

who are willing and able to buy them. The contradiction arises from the fact that the workers (the producers) are also the potential consumers, and the more that wage levels are driven down in the quest to maximize profits, the less purchasing-power the workers enjoy. Thus, capitalists end up with shelves full of things that they are unable to sell and no way of getting their hands on the profits. So, although in the short term it might be beneficial for capitalists to depress wage levels, in the longer term this might well lead to a fall in profits because wage earners would be able to purchase fewer goods: in other words, it would create a crisis of underconsumption. Thus, contradictions in the world-economy arise from the fact that the structure of the system can mean that apparently sensible actions by individuals can, in combination or over time, result in very different—and possibly unwelcome—outcomes from the ones originally intended.

In everyday language we tend to use the word crisis to dramatize even relatively minor problems. Our football teams, governments, and personal finances seem to be in perpetual states of crisis! However, in the context of the world-system, Wallerstein wishes to reserve the term to refer to a very specific temporal occurrence. For him, a crisis constitutes a unique set of circumstances that can only be manifested once in the lifetime of a world-system. It occurs when the contradictions, the secular trends and the cyclical rhythms at work within that system combine in such a way as to mean that the system cannot continue to reproduce itself. Thus, a crisis within a particular world-system heralds its end and replacement by another system.

Interestingly, Wallerstein argues that it is in a period of crisis that the actors within a world-system have most freedom of action. When a system is operating smoothly behaviour is very much determined by the nature of its structure. Indeed Wallerstein goes so far as to argue that 'within a functioning historical system there is no genuine free will. The structures constrain choice and even create choice' (1991a: 235). However, when the system enters a period of terminal decline—its period of crisis—the structures lose much of their power and individual or collective action becomes far more meaningful. In another section of this chapter we will discuss Wallerstein's contention that our own world-system has entered such a period.

Key Points

- The modern world-system has both spatial and temporal features.

- The spatial features describe the geographical division of the world-system into a core, semi-periphery, and periphery. Each of these plays a different economic role, and are linked together in an exploitative relationship in which the richer areas benefit at the expense of those which are poorer.

- The temporal features (cycles, trends, contradictions, and crisis) describe the periods of expansion and contraction in the world-economy and account for its eventual demise.

Politics in the Modern World-System: The Sources of Stability

The sketch of the modern world-system outlined thus far may well strike the reader as rather abstract. Where indeed is the politics in all of this? At one level we would suggest that such a response would be to miss the whole point of Wallerstein's position. For if the study of world politics really is about discovering who gets what, where, when, why, and how on a global scale (Booth 1995a: 329), then surely the structure of the world-economy has enormous political implications? Indeed, for all those who have in any way been influenced by Marxist thought, one of the main weaknesses of mainstream approaches to the study of world politics is that they tend to draw an utterly misleading distinction between politics and economics. By concentrating on politics in isolation from economics, such approaches generate a hopelessly skewed understanding of reality.

However, whilst this point is well taken, the danger is that they themselves succumb to the opposite fallacy by viewing everything through the lens of economics. It should be noted that Wallerstein and his colleagues have gone to great lengths to disassociate themselves from such **economic reductionism**, even if some critics remain unconvinced (see also Box 7.4). For Wallerstein, the economic and political realms are inextricably interlinked: they are **dialectically** related to each other. Neither can be reduced to the other, and without an under-

standing of their interaction we cannot hope to understand the historical development of the world-system as a whole.

In this section we will examine the role of some of the main political institutions and cultural practices which characterize the modern world-system. In particular, we will examine their crucial importance in maintaining the system's structural stability.

Stability is of course a relative concept and Wallerstein is well aware that the past 500 years of world history have been characterized by major upheaval. However, for him, what is noteworthy is that despite the upheaval of war, famine, industrialization, colonization and decolonization, the basic structure of the world system has remained relatively stable since its emergence in sixteenth-century Europe. Even if its boundaries have expanded, the world-economy is still divided into three distinct economic zones linked together in an exploitative relationship.

Whilst broadly economic factors, such as the existence of a semi-peripheral zone, are partly responsible for this stability, various political institutions, processes, and practices are also vitally important. Particularly important for the so-far successful reproduction of the modern world-system has been the fact that the sovereign state, organized within an inter-state system, has provided the basic political structure of that system.

Box 7.4. Criticisms of World-System Theory

Wallerstein's world-system theory has provoked a storm of controversy. Some critics have focused on the theory itself whilst others have questioned how well Wallerstein's interpretations match up to the historical record.

Critics of world-system theory *as theory* have concentrated on several central assumptions.

Is Wallerstein's definition of capitalism correct? Wallerstein locates his definition of capitalism in the sphere of exchange. He argues that the prime characteristic of capitalism is the appropriation of the profit from exchange by selling goods at a higher price than they were purchased.

However for Marxists, the production process is the locus of capitalism. For them, capitalism is a particular mode of production in which production is controlled by a class of owners and managers, and in which labour is brought and sold like any other commodity leading to class conflict between the capitalists and workers. According to this view, profit is generated through an exploitative relationship whereby the labourers do not receive the full value of the goods they produce.

Is this issue of definition important? Writers such as Brenner suggest that it is (1977). Brenner argues that production for exchange has been a feature of many societies that are generally regarded as pre-capitalist, which, by implication, makes a nonsense of Wallerstein's use of the term. Furthermore, for Marxists, it is the analysis of that production process which provides an understanding of the dynamism, the contradictions, and the crises of capitalism.

Is Wallerstein's analysis deterministic? Wallerstein's work is certainly open to the charge that his analysis is deterministic because of his view that the various elements within the world system—ethnic groups, classes, sovereign states, households, etc.—are a *product of* that system, and that their behaviour is determined by their *position within* it. He certainly suggests that actors have very little, if any, room for autonomous action. This position has come under strong attack, especially from those who argue that states can and do have a significant amount of autonomy whose importance should not be underestimated.

The charge of determinism may be correct in its essence, even if it does not do full justice to Wallerstein's position. For example, he accepts that state initiatives have permitted certain countries to move from one zone of the world-economy to another e.g. Japan. However, this is within very specific constraints and, as Wallerstein has pointed out, the same policies followed by another state may not lead to the same results. Additionally, during the transition between one system and another, Wallerstein is well aware that the structures weaken allowing much more room for autonomy. Even so, rather than attempt to defend Wallerstein against charges of determinism as if this were a major weakness, it may be more valuable for students of world politics to consider whether he is actually right. Do state leaders really have many real choices when it comes to policy-making? Aren't their options ultimately very constrained and isn't the source of these constraints the structure of the world-system? The example of the Arbenz government in Guatemala outlined in Box 7.5 graphically demonstrates what happens to those who try to exercise other options.

Is Wallerstein's work teleological? To accuse an analysis of teleology is to suggest that it imputes a particular *meaning* or *purpose* to events. In the case of Wallerstein, it is also to suggest that he projects back from the contemporary condition of the world-system, and interprets all past events solely in terms of their contribution to a historical process which he views as having had one possible outcome. The problems with this are twofold. The first is that it implies too much coherence to history; the second is that he succumbs to the fallacy that things could only have 'turned out' in a certain way thus ignoring a myriad other possibilities. Thus, according to one critic, 'Wallerstein's decisions about history were made before he began . . . on the basis of his theory' (Chirot 1982: 562).

This last point leads us to another set of criticisms which suggest that when viewed independently of the distorting lenses of Wallerstein's theory, the historical evidence actually undermines a number of his work's central propositions.

Has Wallerstein exaggerated the level of trade in his description of the early modern world-economy? P. O'Brien has argued that the levels of trade in the sixteenth century are much lower than implied by Wallerstein. He estimates that less than 1% of Europe's output was sold to Africa, Asia, Latin America, the Caribbean, and the slave states of America, and that only a very low proportion of consumption by Europeans comprised imports from these areas (1984: 53). This criticism raises the question of whether it is possible to talk about a world-economy in the sixteenth century. Without significant levels of trade there can be no division of labour between different zones, a central part of Wallerstein's theory.

Is the semi-periphery a useful concept? Wallerstein's views on the semi-periphery have led to considerable criticism. Contrary to his argument that the semi-periphery provides a zone of political stability between the core and the periphery, it has been argued that it represents a particularly unstable zone from where any threat to the stability of the world-system is likely to emanate. Witness, for example, the tensions in the Middle East.

It has also been suggested that there is little evidence that the semi-periphery provides a site for capital to escape from pressures for higher wages in the core. However, the behaviour of multinational companies make it difficult to sustain this view.

States and the Interstate System

For Wallerstein and his colleagues, the fact that a capitalist world-economy coexists with a political structure of competing sovereign states is no mere coincidence. Rather, both are vital to the existence of the other. Or to put it another way, the capitalist world-economy could not function without the inter-state system, and the inter-state system could not continue in its present form without the capitalist world-economy. They are interlinked with each part depending on the other. Why is this so?

States in general are vital to the successful operation of the capitalist world-economy in at least two ways. First, they provide a framework within which property rights can be upheld and enforced. In the absence of such a framework, capitalists do not have the relatively predictable environment necessary for investment, the extension of credit facilities, and other practices vital to the functioning of a capitalist economy. This is not to claim that all states must approximate to the Western ideal of the state as a law-based guardian of individual rights. What is important is predictability, and corrupt regimes can provide as predictable an environment as that provided by democratic governments. However, if state authority collapses and is replaced by disorder, then capitalist development is effectively stymied.

Second, states have a vitally important role to play in reducing the **contradictions** which are inevitably generated within the capitalist world-economy. As we have seen in the previous section, contradictions arise because the structure of the system can dictate that behaviour which is rational in the short run may be self-defeating in the longer term. Nowhere can this be seen more clearly than in the failure of capitalists to invest in the human and physical infrastructure necessary for their long-term prosperity. Organizing and funding programmes for basic general education and transportation links, for example, would be irrational for any individual capitalist enterprise. Yet both are essential to the success of the capitalist economy. States of all kinds help to resolve contradictions of this nature through legislation and public expenditure.

However, whilst the existence of states is vitally important to the reproduction of the capitalist world-economy, equally crucial is the fact that they are organized into an inter-state system in which no one state has complete dominance over the others.

The presence of competing centres of power means that governments are unlikely to impose overly restrictive controls on their own capitalists for fear of damaging their states' relative prosperity, and hence, standing. Of course, should a single world state come into existence—in Wallersteinian terms, such a state would be a world empire—then that entity would have the ability to erode the independence of capitalists without fearing that they might transfer their activities into areas beyond the state's jurisdiction. Thus a world empire would undermine the very basis of the capitalist world-economy.

But precisely because the world-system is organized into a competitive interstate structure, the development of a world government is highly unlikely. This is because competition between rival capitalist enterprises leads to regular fluctuations in the relative power of various countries and regions within the system. One effect of this is that since the development of the modern world-system, no one state has ever amassed enough power to control every other state within the system.

So we see that for Wallerstein and other world-system theorists, the capitalist world-economy and the interstate system reinforce each other. They are opposite sides of the same coin: inextricable parts of the same whole.

This stress on the linkage between the interstate system and the capitalist world-economy, and the insistence that they can only be understood when viewed as part of the same overarching system, distinguishes the world-system approach from that of the realists. Another important distinguishing feature is that unlike the realists, Wallerstein and his colleagues do not regard all states as functionally similar. It will be recalled that realists argue that all states pursue power and differ only in their relative capabilities. However, world-system theorists adopt a more nuanced view and argue that despite the broad similarities already outlined, states have fundamentally different functions depending on their position within the division of the modern world-system into three distinct economic zones.

Core States—Hegemonic Leadership and Military Force

Core states have two vital functions in the maintenance of the structure of the modern world-system. First, some core states have played a hegemonic leadership role within the interstate system. Second, and more generally, core states are invariably the dominant military powers within that system and use that power in order to discipline those who refuse to accept the 'rules of the game'.

According to Wallerstein, 'the cyclical rise and fall of hegemonic powers . . . has provided the crucial degree of equilibrium' necessary to allow 'process of capital accumulation to proceed without serious hindrance' (1996: 102). A hegemonic power is a state which, because of its productive efficiency, enjoys a position of economic and military superiority over all its rivals. According to Wallerstein, three states have attained hegemonic status within the life of the modern world-system, Holland in the mid-seventeenth century, followed by Britain in the mid-nineteenth, and the United States in the mid-twentieth centuries.

The importance of these periods arises from the fact that the hegemonic powers play a leadership role within the world-system. Their supremacy allows them to impose or underwrite certain practices or institutions which dominate **all** international transactions. Whilst these are doubtless intended to serve the ends of the hegemonic powers themselves, the net effect is to generate a relatively predictable environment in which capital accumulation can proceed successfully throughout the system. So, for example, the Bretton Woods system of global economic regulation established under American hegemony at the end of the Second World War, provided the underpinning for the long post-war boom.

Thus we see that the importance of what Wallerstein calls 'hegemonic cycles' lies in the fact that they establish a certain order throughout the world-system—an order which tends to survive even when the power of the hegemon begins to wane until it is eventually reshaped by another emerging hegemonic power. In a sense, an interstate system dominated by successive hegemonic powers provides a kind of half-way house avoiding the equally damaging extremes of a world empire which would, as we have seen, stifle capitalism, and a totally anarchical situation in which capitalism would not have the stability necessary to function effectively.

Military supremacy is an important element in the attainment of hegemonic status by a particular core state. Nevertheless, even if one state in the core has a preponderance of military force over the others, when viewed in terms of the world-system as a whole, it must be recognized that the core states more generally have far greater military capability than the states of the semi-periphery and periphery. These core states have proven more than willing to use their military might in order to uphold their dominant position within the world-economy. They have intervened repeatedly to ensure that they retain access to raw materials and to important markets. In addition, they have also utilized military force to undermine states in the periphery and semi-periphery which are regarded as threatening the stability of the capitalist world order.

Examples of such interventions are legion. The Gulf War of 1992 is a case in point. The coalition forces justified the launching of Operation Desert Storm in terms of reinstating Kuwaiti sovereignty and ensuring respect for the norms of behaviour essential for the functioning of international society. However, others would argue that it was Kuwait's, and in particular Saudi Arabia's, pivotal position in the global petroleum market which was the main factor in the calculations of American President Bush and his allies. Further examples of the use of military force by core states to defend the stability of the world-system can be found in the repeated American attempts to overthrow left-wing governments in Latin America; even when those governments were democratically elected, as in the case of Guatemala (1954), Chile (1973), Nicaragua (1979–90). See Box 7.5.

Semi-peripheral States—Making the World Safe for Capitalism

As we have already seen, the existence of a semi-periphery is a crucial stabilizing factor within the modern world-system. The nature of semi-peripheral states plays a vital part in the fulfilment of this role.

Compared to states in the periphery, semi-peripheral states are characterized by relatively coherent and efficient administrative structures. These structures are focused on the task of developing and implementing strategies of national development. In the language of world-system theory, they attempt to shift their countries' position within the world-economy from the semi-periphery to the core: an aim to which most aspire but very few achieve.

However, the relative efficacy of these states is only one of their characteristics; another, and related trait, is their authoritarianism. Even when

Steve Hobden and Richard Wyn Jones

Box 7.5. The United States, The United Fruit Company, and Guatemala

There are many examples of core states acting to protect the interests of their capitalists active in the periphery. On many occasions the United States government has intervened in the domestic affairs of Latin American countries at the request of US-based Transnational Corporations. Particularly notorious is the involvement of the US at the time of the Eisenhower presidency in the overthrow of a democratically elected government in Guatemala in 1954.

The government of Jacabo Arbenz gained 65% of the vote in 1950, in an election generally regarded to be open and free. Part of Arbenz's election campaign had been a promise of land reform. The distribution of land in Guatemala in the 1950s was particularly inequitable with 2% of the population owning 72% of the farm land. Much of this land lay idle whilst the rural population suffered from poverty and malnutrition. The large US multinational United Fruit owned 42% of Guatemala's farm land. In 1953 the Arbenz government announced that it intended to expropriate 234,000 acres (from a total of 3 million acres) of the land held by United Fruit as part of the land reform programme.

As a response to these moves United Fruit lobbied the United States government to take action against this expropriation of land. This lobbying effort was no doubt aided by the fact that several key members of the American foreign policy staff had close financial links to the company. Soon the US government launched a large operation to train a group of disaffected Guatemalan military personnel. At the same time the US launched a hemisphere-wide campaign denouncing communist involvement in the Arbenz government. In the final event the coup was relatively bloodless. A group of 150 rebels under the control of Castillo Armas crossed from Honduras into Guatemala on 18 June 1954. When the expected popular uprising against Arbenz failed to occur, Eisenhower ordered a small number of aircraft to take over Guatemala City. These frightened the population by dropping sticks of dynamite which created loud explosions. Fearing that this was the beginning of a much larger invasion Arbenz ordered the arming of a worker-peasant militia. The Guatemalan military refused to co-operate and defected from Arbenz to the rebels. Arbenz resigned the presidency and the US ambassador installed Armas.

In the aftermath of the intervention, the expropriated land was returned to United Fruit, the military regime summarily executed more people than had died during the coup, and a pattern of brutal military rule was established that persisted for forty years.

---

nominally democratic, semi-peripheral states are often run by small élites with the military waiting in the wings to 'restore order' should democracy threaten vested interests. One of the main functions of these states' coercive capacity is to control labour organizations. This helps ensure that wages and working conditions are lower in the semi-periphery than in the core, where relatively complex and costly welfare systems have been developed in order to ensure social stability.

In terms of the semi-peripheral states themselves, low labour costs allow them a competitive advantage *vis à vis* the core states in traditional industries, thus aiding the process of national development. In terms of the world-system as a whole, it is the fact that authoritarian semi-peripheral states control the labour force within their own countries that allows the semi-peripheral zone to play its crucial stabilizing role.

Peripheral States—At home with the Comprador Class

Another source of stability within the world-system is the existence of a dominant, so-called comprador class within the developing world. A number of more radical theorists have claimed that the ruling élites in most, if not all, peripheral, and even some semi-peripheral states, behave in ways which advance the interests of the core within their own societies rather than in ways which might improve the lot of their compatriots. Core states and MNCs actively encourage this state of affairs and will often intervene, directly or indirectly, in order to support client regimes or to overthrow governments who threaten the position of the comprador class. One classic example of such behaviour was the overthrow of the left-wing Allende government in semi-peripheral Chile in 1973.

Critics have suggested that a *de facto* understanding exists between the core and the élites in the 'Third World' along the following lines. If Western business and political interests are protected then 'Third World' regimes will not be seriously taken to task no matter how oppressive or brutal their behaviour towards their own population. This would certainly explain why Western countries have colluded with so many odious regimes in the developing world. The nature of this understanding is succinctly, if rather crudely, summed up in a description proffered by one American president of a particularly loathsome Central American dictator: 'he may be a mean son-of-a-bitch, but at least he's our son-of-a-bitch' (Booth and Walker 1993: 130).

The existence of a comprador class means that at least some of the tensions that would otherwise be generated by the inequalities of the modern world-system are neutralized, thus ensuring far greater stability in North–South relations than would otherwise be the case.

Geoculture

In his more recent writings Wallerstein has become increasingly preoccupied with 'geoculture'. Geoculture refers to the cultural framework of the modern world-system, with culture being viewed in the broadest terms to include values and thought processes. Wallerstein describes geoculture as that part of the system which is 'hidden from view and therefore more difficult to assess, but the part without which the rest would not be nourished.' (1991b: 11) What he suggests is that the particular patterns of thought and behaviour—even language— inscribed in geoculture, are not only essential to ensure that the modern world-system functions effectively, but also provide much of its underlying legitimation. Thus, geoculture, along with states and the interstate system, has been an essential stabilizing factor in ensuring the thus-far successful reproduction of the dominant world order.

Wallerstein's depiction of the operation of geoculture concentrates on two aspects in particular: the first is the role of liberalism as the dominant ideology in the system; the second is the dominant 'knowledge system' which is termed 'scientism'. We will briefly examine both in turn.

Ideologies are incredibly powerful: people live and die for them. The existence of an ideology which leads people to believe in the prevailing order is ultimately a far more powerful and effective means of upholding that order than simple coercion. Wallerstein argues that for the past two hundred years, the modern world-system has been sustained by a remarkably successful ideology which has convinced most people that the modern world-system provides the only rational, indeed, the only conceivable, way of organizing world society. That ideology is liberalism.

Liberalism has been the dominant ideology within the system to such an extent that other apparently 'competing' ideologies such as conservatism and socialism have accepted its central tenets and have become, in effect, variations on a theme—conservative liberalism and socialist liberalism. For example, Wallerstein points to the broad similarities between the liberalism of American President Woodrow Wilson and the version of Marxism propagated by Lenin. Following the Enlightenment tradition of the eighteenth century, both firmly believed that humanity, acting rationally, could construct a better society based on secular principles. Both believed that this better society could and would embrace the whole of humankind: their ambitions were universal. Finally, both believed that the state provided the key mechanism for bringing about this 'new world order'. This later point is crucial for, as Wallerstein argues, 'Liberalism is the only ideology that permits the long-term reinforcement of the state structures, the strategic underpinning of a functioning capitalist world-economy.' This is because 'Conservatism and socialism [when not harnessed to liberalism] appeal beyond the state to a "society" which finds expression in other institutions' (1991b: 10). Liberal ideology has thus been crucial in buttressing the organization of the modern world-system into competing states.

The second geocultural pillar of the modern world-system has been provided by scientism. This is the term used by Wallerstein to describe the knowledge system that evolved within that system as society became secularized and knowledge was increasingly validated in terms of the instrumental manipulation of the material world. The spectacular success of the natural sciences in discovering what appeared to be universal laws, applicable across time and space, had very significant implications for production processes, and hence capital accumulation. It also led to the scientific model of knowledge being posited as the correct approach for other disciplines including the social sciences.

The common thread between both these aspects of geoculture are provided by their universalizing impulses. Scientism is concerned with discovering universal laws and applying them for, ultimately, universal benefit. Liberalism attempts to apply universal principles to the organization and conduct of the state. The problem is that this universalist thrust implies within it a notion of equality which is in stark contrast to the massive inequalities inherent in the functioning of the world-system. This poses the dilemma of 'how to maintain/restore hierarchy without renouncing universalism, a necessary component of the geo-culture' (Wallerstein 1996: 97). The answer is provided by racism and sexism, both of which Wallerstein regards as vital elements of geoculture. Their value to the system is that they supply the justifications for the unequal outcomes which occur within the world-system despite the stress on universalism. Whilst universalism implies that all are equal, racism and sexism justify why some are more equal than others.

Key Points

- The modern world-system has remained remarkably stable since the sixteenth century. Its boundaries have extended, but a three-way spatial division between core, semi-periphery, and periphery has persisted.
- This stability is accounted for in two main ways: through the emergence of an interstate system, in which states in different zones of the world economy play different roles; and the existence of a geoculture generated by the modern world-system and dominated by the twin ideologies of liberalism and scientism.

Crisis in the Modern World-System

Between them, these various aspects of geoculture, when combined with the political organization of the modern world-system into competing sovereign states, account for much of its remarkable stability. However, as we have already mentioned, one of the interesting aspects of Wallerstein's work is his claim that this stability is currently being undermined, and that the modern world-system is entering its period of crisis. Why might this be so given the strong stabilizing pressures which have just been outlined? After all, given the collapse of the Soviet bloc and the more general crisis of confidence on the left of the political spectrum, is it not the case that most now accept that there is no alternative to free-market capitalism and liberal democracy? And in these circumstances, does it not seem more sensible to speak of the triumph of the prevailing order rather than herald its immanent demise?

Wallerstein's belief that the current world-system is in serious trouble stems from several sources. For the sake of clarity we will summarize the forces undermining the stability of the system as they affect the economic, the political, and the geocultural spheres. However, the reader should bear in mind that Wallerstein and other world-system theorists are adamant that these spheres are all intimately intertwined.

The Economic Sources of Crisis

The sources of economic crisis have their roots in the fundamental contradictions of capitalism already outlined in the fourth section of this chapter. Wallerstein argues that, historically speaking, one of the main routes through which the problem of recurrent depression has been overcome has been the **expansion** of the world-economy. Expansion has taken two main forms. The first is the geographical expansion of the world-economy to include more of the globe, thus opening up new markets and new sources of labour and raw materials. The second is the intensification of capitalist economic relations within those areas already incorporated into the world-economy. This later process takes many forms, the most prominent of which are urbanization and commodification. Urbanization has forced more and more of the world population to abandon rural areas—which are often characterized by a mixture of capitalist and pre-capitalist socio-economic relations—to live in the rapidly expanding, and wholly capitalistic, urban areas. Commodification refers to the process whereby more and more aspects of daily life are being drawn into the orbit of the market. Both phenomena serve to extend the scope of the capitalist world-economy.

However, Wallerstein contends that expanding the world-economy is becoming an increasingly less viable means of escaping its problems. Geographically, the world-economy has long since expanded to include the whole globe. In addition, the world has now been almost fully urbanized. Furthermore, there are now very few aspects of life which have not been thoroughly commodified. This escape route is, to all intents and purposes, closed.

Even more fundamentally, five centuries of relentless capital accumulation has led to the massive degradation of the global ecology. Such is the degree of degradation that many have foreseen an impending ecological catastrophe which would have disastrous implications for the world-system. However, the structure of the system militates against any serious effort to avoid such a possibility. Addressing ecological problems will be enormously costly and yet, as Wallerstein points out, no sector of the world-system is in any position to pay without undermining the balance of the system itself.

If it is the enterprises [that pay], it will vitiate the unending accumulation of capital. And if it is achieved by reducing popular welfare, this will be the last straw in the possibility of maintaining the social cohesion of the states. (1996: 105)

The Political Sources of Crisis

The inequalities and recurrent upheavals which characterize the world-system have always generated opposition from various groups; groups which world-systems theorists have termed **anti-systemic movements**. Such movements have played a somewhat schizophrenic role within the world-system in that they 'simultaneously undermine and reinforce' the dominant structure (Wallerstein 1991*a*: 268). This apparently contradictory situation becomes clearer when it is realized that successive waves of anti-systemic movements have been co-opted and incorporated into the system. Through this process, the interest groups which the movements represent have developed a stake in the continuation of the prevailing order and social cohesion has been maintained.

However the co-option of anti-systemic movements has costs which are becoming increasingly onerous. In particular, the pacification of labour movements in the core has been achieved through the development of increasingly elaborate, and expensive, state-based welfare provision. However, a combination of economic stagnation and demographic trends means that it will be increasingly dif-

ficult for governments to maintain present levels of welfare provision without undermining the process of capital accumulation. However, failure to protect welfare levels will inevitably seriously undermine the legitimacy of the dominant political and economic order amongst those who are currently protected from the worst effects of the world-economy. It will also make it almost impossible for these governments to incorporate marginalized groups within their own societies or proffer assistance to the marginalized majority in the rest of the world.

Therefore the intensifying problems of the world-economy will not only help create more anti-systemic forces, but it will also make it increasingly difficult to deal with them. All this is compounded by the growing sophistication of contemporary anti-systemic movements. Unlike their predecessors, they recognize that seizing state power solves very few problems. So rather than attempt to construct centralized and disciplined political parties, new social movements are characterized by decentralized forms of political organization allied together in diffuse, so-called 'rainbow coalitions'. These types of organization, because of their very nature, are very difficult to co-opt.

Further intensifying these problems is the fact that the global communications revolution has made it harder to conceal the glaring inequalities which characterize the modern world-system. Wallerstein speculates that this may well aid the development of a global political awareness which could, in turn, lead to the forging of global political mobilization (1994).

The Geocultural Sources of Crisis

Wallerstein also points to what amounts to a tectonic shift in geocultural underpinnings of the modern world-system. Specifically, he argues that the dominant position of liberalism has been fatally eroded, with the revolutionary turmoil of 1968 signifying as a major watershed. In 1968, radical students united with workers in a series of strikes and demonstrations which Wallerstein regards as having fundamentally undermined some of the main pillars of the world-system. For although the upheaval was largely centred on a few centres—with Prague, Paris, and Mexico City among the most prominent—its significance was much broader.

1968 was above all else an attack on the statism of the prevailing order. States—including both the welfare states of the West and the so-called socialist states of the East—were rejected as bureaucratic, paternalistic, and fundamentally inimicable to human freedom. Although the turmoil was short-lived, and in some cases repressed with great brutality, the statism so fundamental to liberalism was permanently tarnished. No longer are citizens willing to entrust themselves to the state—a development with far-reaching implications for the future stability of the world-system.

Furthermore, 1968 was also a fundamental challenge to the traditional anti-systemic movements. The protests took place outside the framework of such movements, and were as much a reaction to their quiescence as they were to the iniquities of the system itself. As a result, 1968 signalled the emergence of new forms of anti-systemic movement unwilling to accept traditional forms of politics and thus far less amenable to co-option by the political structures of the world-system.

In addition to the growing crisis of liberalism, Wallerstein also points to what he regards as the fundamental challenges currently undermining the whole system of knowledge which underlies the world-system, that is scientism. These challenges emanate in particular from the natural sciences, where scholars are increasingly calling into question the ideal of absolute truth so central to scientism, and stressing in its place such notions as contingency and uncertainty. The result is that another central plank of the dominant geoculture is inexorably being eroded.

The Crisis and the Future: Socialism or Barbarism?

As was discussed in the fourth section of this chapter, a crisis is a period in which a historical system breaks down because the 'contradictions of the system have come to the point that none of the mechanisms for restoring the normal functioning of the system can work effectively any longer' (Wallerstein 1994: 15). If we accept Wallerstein's diagnosis that the modern world-system has entered such a period, then there are two crucial questions which we must address. First, how long is the crisis likely to last? Second, what is likely replace the current world-system?

In answer to the former, Wallerstein argues that the crisis will probably persist for between twenty-five and fifty years. However, he believes that no one is in a position to answer the later question with any precision. The modern world-system will certainly be replaced by another system or systems. However, the nature of the replacement or replacements will depend on the outcome of political struggles in years ahead. Recall that Wallerstein argues that in a period of crisis the prevailing structures lose much of their power to determine outcomes within the system. Rather, individual and collective action can actually influence the course of events to a far greater extent than is the case when the system is functioning effectively.

There is no doubt that Wallerstein himself hopes that the struggles of future decades will result in some form of socialist world government. Indeed, he argues that one of the important tasks facing scholars like himself in coming years is to map-out plausible alternatives to the prevailing order. However, he also stresses that the establishment of a socialist order—even if desirable—is by no means inevitable. A crisis is a period of uncertainty and any number of outcomes are possible. Indeed, the present crisis might well result in an order which is even less palatable than the decaying modern world-system.

The point for Wallerstein is that we are in a position to make a difference. Humanity can either struggle to create a just and humane society, or it can allow another system to develop which intensifies the despair, destruction, and cruelty so characteristic of the contemporary world. To echo a long-standing slogan of the revolutionary left, humanity must choose between 'socialism or barbarism'.

Key Points

- Despite the apparent stability of the modern world-system, Wallerstein claims that it is now entering into a period of terminal crisis.

- This crisis can be accounted for through a combination of economic, political, and geocultural factors.

- Wallerstein claims that the form of the world-system which will replace the existing one is not inevitable. It is possible for individual action to influence the type of world-system that will emerge.

World-System Theory and Globalization

In this chapter, we have attempted to trace the origins of world-system theory, and in particular the version developed by Immanuel Wallerstein. In this concluding section we will discuss how world-system theorists view the phenomenon of globalization.

As was outlined in the first chapter of this book, globalization is the name given to the process whereby social transactions of all kinds increasingly take place without account for national or state boundaries, with the result that the world has become 'one relatively borderless social sphere'. The particular trends pointed to as typifying globalization include: the growing integration of national economies; a growing awareness of ecological interdependence; the proliferation of companies, social movements, and intergovernmental agencies operating on a global scale; and a communications revolution which has aided the development of a global consciousness.

World-system theorists would certainly not seek to deny that these developments are taking place, nor would they deny their importance, but they would reject any notion that they are somehow novel. Rather, in the words of Chase-Dunn, they are 'continuations of trends that have long accompanied the expansion of capitalism' (1994: 97).

According to world-system theorists like Wallerstein, the globe has long been dominated by a single integrated economic and political entity—the modern world-system—which has gradually incorporated all of humanity within its grasp. Within this system, all elements have always been interrelated and interdependent. 'National economies' have long been integrated to such an extent that their very nature has been dependent on their position within a capitalist world-economy. The only thing 'new' is an increased awareness of these linkages. Similarly, ecological processes have always ignored state-boundaries, even if it is only recently that growing environmental degradation has finally allowed this fact to permeate into public consciousness.

The growth of multinational corporations certainly does not signify any major change in the structure of the modern world-system. Rather, they form part of a long-term trend towards the further integration of the world-economy. Neither, is international contact between anti-systemic movements a new development. In fact, as even the most cursory examination of the historical record will amply attest, such movements, be they socialist, nationalist, or ecological in character, have always drawn inspiration from, and forged links with, similar groups in other countries. Finally, the much-vaunted communications revolution is the latest manifestation of a long-term trend in the world-system whereby space and time are becoming increasingly compressed.

Whilst the intensity of cross-border flows may be increasing, this does not necessarily signify the fundamental change in the nature of world politics proclaimed by so many of those who argue that we have entered an era of globalization. World-system theorists insist that the only way to discover how significant contemporary developments really are is to view them in the context of the deeper structural processes at work in the world-system. When this is done, we may well discover indications that important changes are afoot. Wallerstein, for example, regards the delegitimation of the sovereign-state as one manifestation of the crisis engulfing the modern world-system. However, the essential first step in generating any understanding of those trends regarded as evidence of globalization must be to map-out the contours of the modern world-system itself. If we fail to do so, we will inevitably fail to gauge the real significance of the changes which are occurring.

Another danger of adopting an ahistoric and uncritical attitude to globalization is that it can blind us to the way in which reference to globalization is increasingly becoming part of the ideological armoury of élites within the world-system. Globalization is now regularly cited as a reason to promote measures to reduce workers' rights and lessen other constraints on business. Many politicians and business leaders argue that unless businesses are allowed to function without constraints, they will not be able to compete in a globalizing economy.

Such ideological justifications for policies which favour the interests of business can only be countered through a broader understanding of the relationship between the political and the economic structures of the world-system. As we have seen, the understanding proffered by the world-system theorists suggests that there is nothing natural or inevitable about a world order based on a global market. The current world-system, like all other historical systems, will eventually come to an end. Therefore, rather than accept the inevitability of the present order, the task facing us is to lay the foundations for a new world-system—a global society which is more just and more humane than our own.

Key Points

- World-system theorists are rather sceptical about the emphasis currently being placed on the notion of globalization.

- Rather than being a recent phenomenon they see the recent manifestations of globalization as being part of long-term trends in the development of the world-economy, within which all features have been interconnected.

- Furthermore the notion of globalization is increasingly being used as an ideological tool to justify reductions in workers rights and welfare provision.

QUESTIONS

1. How did Lenin's approach to international relations differ from that of Marx?

2. To what extent is the affluence of people in the developed world dependent on the poverty of people in the less developed world?

3. How does a world-economy differ from a world-empire?

4. How useful is Wallerstein's notion of a semi-periphery?

5. What accounts for the stability of the modern world-system?

6. What is the role of a 'comprador' class?

7. Do you agree with Wallerstein's view that the modern world-system is now entering a period of crisis?

8. How do world-system theorists view the notion of 'globalization'?

9. What do you regard as the main contribution of world-system theory to our understanding of world politics?

A GUIDE TO FURTHER READING

The most complete account of the world-system approach to the study of international relations is to be found in the work of Immanuel Wallerstein. If you have the time and energy the three volumes of *The Modern World-System*, are well worth studying (San Diego: Academy Press, 1974, 1980, 1989). Wallerstein's many articles, which give an insight to his views on the cold war, and indicate the directions in which his work is heading, have been collected in a number of volumes (see Wallerstein 1979, 1984, 1991*a*, 1991*b*, 1995). Also worth looking at is an up-to-date account of his views on the relationship between the interstate system and the world economy, which also includes a discussion of hegemony and the likely direction of the world-economy: I. Wallerstein,

'The Inter-State Structure of the Modern World-System', in S. Smith *et al.*, *International Theory: Positivism and Beyond* (Cambridge: Cambridge University Press, 1996).

Of the many people that have worked closely with Wallerstein we particularly recommend the work of Christopher Chase-Dunn, esp. *Global Formation: Structures of the World-Economy* (Oxford: Blackwell, 1989). Chase-Dunn has in particular focused on theorizing the relationship between the world-economy and the system of states.

Of the other theorists of global capitalism we suggest looking in more depth at any of the writers discussed in Box 7.2. To see Dependency Theory in its most lively form see especially A. G. Frank, *Dependent Accumulation and Underdevelopment* (New York: Monthly Review Press, 1979), and for a particularly sophisticated account F. H. Cardoso and E. Faletto, *Dependency and Development in Latin America* (Berkeley: University of California Press, 1979).

The strength of the world-system approach is perhaps best reflected by the extent to which it has attracted criticism. As well as the critics discussed in Box 7.4, see also:

Skocpol. T., 'Wallerstein's *World Capitalist System*: A Theoretical and Historical Critique', American Journal of Sociology, 82: 5 (1977).

Worsley, P., 'One World or Three? A Critique of the World-System Theory of Immanuel Wallerstein', *Socialist Register* (London: Merlin Press, 1980).

Harvey, D., 'The World Systems Theory Trap', *Studies in Comparative Development*, 22: 1 (1987).

Washbrook, D., 'South Asia, The World System and World Capitalism', *Journal of Asian Studies*, 49: 3 (1990).

8 Liberalism

Timothy Dunne

READER'S GUIDE

The practice of international relations has not been accommodating to Liberalism. Whereas the domestic political realm in many states has witnessed an impressive degree of progress, with institutions providing for order *and* justice, the international realm in the era of the modern states system has been characterized by a precarious order and the *absence* of justice. In the introductory section, the chapter will address this dilemma of Liberalism's false promise as well as considering the moments in history when Liberalism has impacted significantly on the theory and practice of international relations. Like all grand theory, Liberalism is an aggregation of a number of different ideas. Section two seeks to uncover the most important variations on the Liberal theme, beginning with the visionary liberal internationalism of the Enlightenment, through to the liberal idealism of the inter-war period, and ending with the liberal institutionalism which became popular in the immediate post-war years. This discussion begs two important questions, dealt with in section three. What has become of these three historic elements in liberal thinking on international relations? And how have contemporary writers situated in these various strands sought to cope with globalization? The final section summarizes the arguments that have gone before, as well as reflecting more broadly on the fate of liberalism in international relations at the end of the millennium.

I would like to thank Nick Wheeler for casting his analytical eye over this chapter, tightening the argument considerably as a result. I would also like to thank Stephen Hobden for his careful reading and considered comments.

Introduction

Although Realism is regarded as the dominant theory of international relations, Liberalism[1] has a strong claim to being the historic alternative. Rather like political parties, Realism is the 'natural' party of government and Liberalism is the leader of the opposition, whose *raison d'être* is to hound the talking heads of power politics for their remorseless pessimism. And like historic parties of 'opposition', Liberalism has occasionally found itself in the ascendancy, when its ideas and values set the agenda for international relations. In the twentieth century, Liberal thinking influenced policy-making élites and public opinion in a number of Western states after the First World War, an era often referred to in academic International Relations as **Idealism.** There was a brief resurgence of liberal sentiment at the end of World War II, with the birth of the United Nations, although these flames of hope were soon extinguished by the return of cold war power politics. The end of the cold war has seen a resurgence of Liberalism as Western state leaders proclaimed a 'New World Order' and liberal intellectuals provided theoretical justifications for the inherent supremacy of Liberalism over all other competing ideologies.

One of the most respected contemporary theorists in the field, Stanley Hoffmann, once famously wrote that 'international affairs have been the nemesis of liberalism'. 'The essence of liberalism', Hoffmann continues, 'is self-restraint, moderation, compromise and peace' whereas 'the essence of international politics is exactly the opposite: troubled peace, at best, or the state of war' (Hoffmann 1987: 396). This explanation comes as no surprise to realists, who argue that there can be no progress, no law, and no justice, where there is no common power. The fact that historically international politics has not been hospitable to liberal ideas should not be interpreted as a surrender by liberals to the logic of power politics. Liberals argue that power politics itself is the product of ideas, and crucially, ideas can change. So, even if the world hasn't been accommodating to liberalism to date, this does not mean that it cannot be *made* into a liberal world order. Given this disposition, it is not surprising that Liberalism is described in the literature as the 'tradition of optimism' (Clark 1989: 49–66).

Once we move beyond generalizations about the Liberal 'mind' we soon discover that there is not one Liberalism, but many. As Box 8.1 demonstrates,

---

Box 8.1. Liberalism and the Causes of War, Determinants of Peace

One of the most useful analytical tools for thinking about differences between individual thinkers or particular variations on a broad theme such as Liberalism, is to differentiate between levels of analysis. For example, Kenneth Waltz's *Man, The State and War* examined the **causes** of conflict operating at the level of the individual, the state, and the international system itself. The table below turns Waltz on his head, as it were, in order to show how different liberal thinkers have provided competing explanations (across the three levels of analysis) for the causes of war and the determinants of peace.

'Images' of Liberalism	Public Figure / Period	Causes of Conflict	Determinants of Peace
First Image: (Human Nature)	Richard Cobden (mid-19th c.)	Interventions by governments domestically and internationally disturbing the natural order	Individual liberty, free trade, prosperity, interdependence
Second Image: (The State)	Woodrow Wilson (early 20th c.)	Undemocratic nature of international politics; especially foreign policy and the balance of power	National self-determination; open governments responsive to public opinion; **collective security**
Third Image: (The Structure of the system)	J. A. Hobson (early 20th c.)	The balance of power system	A **world government**, with powers to mediate and enforce decisions

liberals offer radically different answers to what they take to be the pre-eminent dilemma in international relations, namely, why wars occur: are they caused by imperialism, the balance of power, or undemocratic regimes? Furthermore, liberals diverge on whether peace is the goal of world politics, or order? And how should this be established, through collective security, commerce, or world government? Finally, liberals are divided on the issue of how liberal states should respond to non-liberal states (or civilizations), by conquest, conversion, or toleration?

Key Points

- From the seventeenth century onwards, Liberalism has continued to influence the practice of world politics.

- The high-water mark of Liberal thinking in international relations was reached in the interwar period in the work of Idealists who believed that warfare was an unnecessary and outmoded way of settling disputes between states.

- In view of the significant divergences within the liberal tradition—on issues such as human nature, the causes of wars, and the relative importance different kinds of liberals place on the individual, the state, and international institutions in delivering progress—it is perhaps more appropriate to think of not one Liberal*ism*, but contending liberal*isms*.

Varieties of Liberalism

Liberal thinking on international relations originated with the various plans for peace articulated by philosophers (and theologians) from the early sixteenth century onwards. Early liberals rejected the idea that conflict was a natural condition for relations between states, one which could only be tamed by the careful management of power through balance of power policies and the construction of alliances against the state which threatened international order. In 1517 Erasmus first iterated a familiar liberal theme; war is unprofitable. To overcome it, the kings and princes of Europe must desire peace, and perform kind gestures in relations with fellow sovereigns in the expectation that these will be reciprocated. Other early liberal thinkers placed an emphasis upon the need for institutional structures to constrain international 'outlaws'. Towards the end of the seventeenth century, William Penn advocated a 'Diet' (or Parliament) of Europe. Indeed, there are some remarkable parallels between Penn's ideas and the institutions of the European Union today. Penn envisaged that the number of delegates to the Parliament should be proportional to the power of the state, and that legislation required a kind of 'qualified majority voting', or as Penn put it, the support of 75 per cent of the delegates.

These broad sketches of ideas from some of the progenitors of liberal thinking in international relations show how, from Penn's plans for a 'Diet' in 1693 to the Treaty on European Union in 1992, there are common themes underlying Liberalism; in this instance, the theme is the importance of submitting the separate 'wills' of individual states to a general will agreed by states acting collectively (see, for example, Kant's 'third definitive article' in Box 8.2). Yet it would be wrong to suggest that the development of liberal thinking on international affairs has been linear. Indeed, it is often possible to portray current political differences in terms of contrasting liberal principles. To return to the Treaty on European Union mentioned above, the debate which raged in Britain and elsewhere, could be presented as one in which the liberal principle of integration was challenged by another liberal principle of the right of states to retain sovereignty over key aspects of social and economic policies.

How should we understand this relationship between autonomy and **integration** which is embodied in Liberalism? One way might be to apply a historical approach, providing detailed accounts of the contexts with which various philosophers, politicians and international lawyers contributed to the elaboration of key liberal values and beliefs. Although the contextual approach has merit it tends to downplay the dialogue between past and present, closing off the parallels between Immanuel Kant (an eighteenth-century philosopher-king from Konigsberg) and Francis Fukuyama (the late twentieth-century political thinker and former employee of the US State Department). An alternative method, which is favoured in this chapter, is to lay bare the variety of liberalisms thematically rather than historically.[2] To this end, the following section identifies three patterns of thought as the principal constituents of Liberalism: **liberal internationalism, idealism,** and **liberal institutionalism.**

As Box 8.2 demonstrates, many of the great liberal figures such as Immanuel Kant believed that human potentiality can only be realized through the transformation of individual attitudes as well as the binding of states together into some kind of **federation**. In this sense, Kant combines a commitment to international institutions (embodied in both idealists and liberal institutionalists) as well as the liberal internationalists' belief that democratic forms of government are inherently superior. Like Kant, the thinking of many other great liberal thinkers reaches beyond the boundaries of any single category. For this reason it is important not to use the categories as labels for particular thinkers, but as representations of a discernible strand in the history of liberal thinking on international relations.

Liberal Internationalism

Immanuel Kant and Jeremy Bentham were two of the leading **liberal internationalists** of the **Enlightenment**. Both were reacting to the barbarity of international relations, or what Kant graphically described as 'the lawless state of savagery', at a time when domestic politics was at the cusp of a new age of rights, citizenship, and constitutionalism. Their abhorrence of the lawless savagery led them individually to elaborate plans for 'perpetual peace'. Although written over two centuries ago, these manifestos contain the seeds of key liberal internationalists' ideas, in particular, the belief that reason could deliver freedom and justice in international relations. For Kant the imperative to achieve perpetual peace required the transformation of individual consciousness, republican constitutionalism and a federal contract between states to abolish war (rather than to regulate it as liberal realists such as Hugo Grotius had argued). This federation can be likened to a permanent peace treaty,

---

Box 8.2. Immanuel Kant's 'Perpetual Peace: A Philosophical Sketch'

First Definitive Article: *The Civil Constitution of Every State shall be Republican*

'If, as is inevitably the case under this constitution, the consent of the citizens is required to decide whether or not war is to be declared, it is very natural that they will have great hesitation in embarking on so dangerous an enterprise. . . . But under a constitution where the subject is not a citizen, and which is therefore not republican, it is the simplest thing in the world to go to war. For the head of state is not a fellow citizen, but the owner of the state, and a war will not force him to make the slightest sacrifice so far as his banquets, hunts, pleasure palaces and court festivals are concerned . . .' (Kant 1991: 99–102)

Second Definitive Article: *The Right of Nations shall be based on a Federation of Free States*

'Each nation, for the sake of its own security, can and ought to demand of the others that they should enter along with it into a constitution, similar to a civil one, within which the rights of each could be secured. . . . But

peace can neither be inaugurated nor secured without a general agreement between the nations; thus a particular kind of league, which we will call a *pacific federation* is required. It would be different from a *peace treaty* in that the latter terminates *one* war, whereas the former would seek to end *all* wars for good. . . . It can be shown that this idea of *federalism*, extending gradually to encompass all states and thus leading to perpetual peace, is practicable and has objective reality' (Kant 1991: 102–5).

Third Definitive Article: *Cosmopolitan Right shall be limited to Conditions of Universal Hospitality*

'The peoples of the earth have thus entered in varying degrees into a universal community, and it has developed to the point where a violation of rights in *one* part of the world is felt *everywhere*. The idea of a cosmopolitan right is therefore not fantastic and overstrained; it is a necessary complement to the unwritten code of political and international right, transforming it into a universal right of humanity (Kant 1991: 105–8).

rather than a 'superstate' actor or world government.

Jeremy Bentham tried to address the specific problem of the tendency among states to resort to war as a means of settling international disputes. 'But, establish a common tribunal', Bentham argued, and 'the necessity for war no longer follows from a difference of opinion' (Luard 1992: 416). Like many liberal thinkers after him, Bentham showed that federal states such as the German Diet, the American Confederation, and the Swiss League were able to transform their identity from one based on conflicting interests to a more peaceful federation. As Bentham famously argued, 'between the interests of nations there is nowhere any real conflict'. Note that these plans for a permanent peace imply an extension of the social contract between individuals in domestic society to states in the international system, in other words, subjecting the states to a system of legal rights and duties. But crucially, liberal internationalists—unlike the idealists of the interwar period—believed that a law-governed international society could emerge without a **world government**.

The idea of a natural order underpinning human society is the cornerstone of liberal internationalism. For the clearest statement of this position, we must turn to the Scottish political economist and moral philosopher, Adam Smith. By pursuing their own self-interest, individuals are inadvertently promoting the public good. The mechanism which intervenes between the motives of the individual and 'ends' of society as a whole, is what Smith referred to as 'an invisible hand'. Although Smith believed that the natural harmony between individual and state did not extend to a harmony between states (Wyatt-Walter 1996: 28) this is precisely what was emphasized by liberal internationalists in the nineteenth century like Richard Cobden. Like many key figures in the Liberal tradition, Cobden was a political activist as well as a writer and commentator on public affairs. He was an eloquent opponent of the exercise of arbitrary power by governments the world over. 'The progress of freedom', he compellingly argued, 'depends more upon the maintenance of peace, the spread of commerce, and the diffusion of education, than upon the labours of cabinets and foreign offices' (Hill 1996: 114). For Cobden, politics was too important to be left to politicians.

It was primarily this liberal idea of a natural '**harmony of interests**' in international political and economic relations which E. H. Carr attacked in his polemical work *The Twenty Years' Crisis*. Although Carr's book remains one of the most stimulating in the field, one 'which leaves us nowhere to hide' (Booth 1995: 123), it could be argued that Carr incorrectly targets idealists of the interwar period as the object of his attack rather than the liberal internationalists of the nineteenth century. As we will see in the following section, rather than relying a natural harmony to deliver peace, idealists fervently believed that a new international order had to be *constructed*, one which was managed by an international organization. This line of argument represents a significant shift from the nineteenth-century **liberal internationalism** to the idealist movement in the early part of the twentieth century.

Idealism

Like liberal internationalism, the era of **idealism** (from the early 1900s through to the late 1930s) was motivated by the desire to prevent war. However, many idealists were sceptical that *laissez faire* economic principles, like free trade, would deliver peace. Idealists, like J. A. Hobson, argued that imperialism—the subjugation of foreign peoples and their resources—was becoming the primary cause of conflict in international politics. For Hobson, imperialism resulted from underconsumption within developed capitalist societies. This led capitalists to search for higher profits overseas, which became a competitive dynamic between states and the catalyst for militarism, leading to war. Here we see a departure from the liberal internationalist argument that capitalism was inherently pacific. The fact that Britain and Germany had highly interdependent economies before the Great War (1914–18), seemed to confirm the fatal flaw in the liberal internationalist association of **interdependence** with peace. From the turn of the century, the contradictions within European civilization, of progress and exemplarism on the one hand and the harnessing of industrial power for military purposes on the other, could no longer be contained. Europe stumbled into a horrific war killing fifteen million people. The war not only brought an end to three empires it was also a contributing factor to the Russian Revolution of 1917.

The First World War shifted liberal thinking

towards a recognition that peace is not a natural condition but is one which must be constructed. In a powerful critique of the idea that peace and prosperity were part of a latent natural order, the publicist and author Leonard Woolf argued that peace and prosperity required 'consciously devised machinery' (Luard 1992: 465). But perhaps the most famous advocate of an international authority for the management of international relations was Woodrow Wilson. According to the US President, peace could only be secured with the creation of an international institution to regulate the international anarchy. Security could not be left to secret bilateral diplomatic deals and a blind faith in the balance of power. Like domestic society, international society must have a system of governance which has democratic procedures for coping with disputes, and an international force which could be mobilized if negotiations failed. In this sense, liberal idealism rests on a **domestic analogy** (Suganami 1989: 94–113).

In his famous 'fourteen points' speech, addressed to Congress in January 1918, Wilson argued that 'a general association of nations must be formed' to preserve the coming peace. The League of Nations, was of course, the general association which idealists willed into existence. For the League to be effective, it had to have the military power to deter aggression and, when necessary, to use a preponderance of power to enforce its will. This was the idea behind the **collective security** system which was central to the League of Nations. Collective security refers to an arrangement where 'each state in the system accepts that the security of one is the concern of all, and agrees to join in a collective response to aggression' (Roberts and Kingsbury 1993: 30). It can be contrasted with an alliance system of security, where a number of states join together usually as a response to a specific external threat (sometimes known as collective defence). In the case of the League of Nations, Article 16 noted the obligation that, in the event of war, all member states must cease normal relations with the offending state, impose sanctions, and if necessary, commit their armed forces to the disposal of the League Council should the use of force be required to restore the status quo.

The experience of the League of Nations was a disaster. Whilst the moral rhetoric at the creation of the League was decidedly idealist, in practice states remained imprisoned by self-interest. There is no better example of this than the United State's decision not to join the institution it had created. With the Soviet Union outside the system for ideological reasons, the League of Nations quickly became a talking shop for the 'satisfied' powers. Hitler's decision in March 1936 to reoccupy the Rhineland, a designated demilitarized zone according to the terms of the Treaty of Versailles, effectively pulled the plug on the League's life-support system (it had been put on the 'critical' list following the Manchurian crisis in 1931 and the Ethiopian crisis in 1935). Indeed, throughout the 1930s, the term crisis had become the most familiar one in international affairs.

Although the League of Nations was the principal organ of the idealist interwar order, it is important to note other ideas which dominated liberal thinking in the early part of the twentieth century. Education became a vital addition to the liberal agenda, hence the origins of the study of International Relations as a discipline in Aberystwyth in 1919 with the founding of the Woodrow Wilson professorship. One of the tasks of the Wilson Professor was to promote the League of Nations as well as contributing to a 'truer understanding of civilizations other than our own' (John et al. 1972: 86). It is this self-consciously **normative** approach to the discipline of International Relations, the belief that scholarship is about what *ought* to be and not just what *is*, that sets the idealists apart from the institutionalists who were to carry the torch of liberalism through the early post–1945 period.

Outside of the military-security issue area, liberal ideas made an important contribution to global politics even during the cold war. The principle of self-determination, championed by liberal internationalists for centuries, signalled the end of empire. The protection of individuals from human rights abuses was enshrined in the three key standard setting documents: the 1948 Universal Declaration, the Covenant on Economic, Social, and Cultural Rights, and the Covenant on Civil and Political Rights. Even the more radical calls in the mid–1970s for a 'New International Economic Order' emanating from poorer post-colonial states contained within it the kernel of a liberal defence of justice as fairness. The problem of the uneven distribution of wealth and power between the 'developed' and the 'developing' world is one which has been championed by a succession of liberal stateleaders, from the 1980 Brandt Report (named after the former West German Chancellor Willy Brandt) to the recently published 1995 report by the

Commission on Global Governance, chaired by Ingvar Carlson (the Swedish Prime Minister) and Shridath Ramphal (former Secretary-General of the Commonwealth).

Liberal Institutionalism

According to the history of the discipline, the collapse of the League of Nations signified the end of **idealism**. There is no doubt that the language of **liberal institutionalism** was less avowedly **normative**; how could anyone assume progress after Auschwitz? Yet certain fundamental tenets remained. Even in the early 1940s, there was a recognition of the need to replace the League with another international institution with responsibility for international peace and security. Only this time, in the case of the United Nations there was an awareness among the framers of the Charter of the need for a consensus between the Great Powers in order for enforcement action to be taken, hence the veto system (Article 27 of the UN Charter) which allowed any of the five permanent members of the Security Council the power of veto. This revision constituted an important modification to the classical model of collective security (Roberts 1996: 315). With the ideological polarity of the cold war, the UN procedures for **collective security** were still-born (as either of the superpowers and their allies would veto any action proposed by the other).[3] It was not until the end of the cold war that a **collective security** system was operationalized, following the invasion of Kuwait by Iraq on 2 August 1990 (see Case Study 1, Box 8.3, for an analysis of the Gulf War and collective security).

An important argument by liberal institutionalists in the early post-war period concerned the state's inability to cope with modernization. David Mitrany, a pioneer **integration** theorist, argued that transnational co-operation was required in order to resolve common problems (Mitrany 1943). His core concept was **ramification**, meaning the likelihood that co-operation in one sector would lead governments to extend the range of collaboration across other sectors. As states become more embedded in an **integration** process, the 'cost' of withdrawing from co-operative ventures increases.

This argument about the positive benefits from transnational co-operation is one which lies at the core of **liberal institutionalism** (and remains cen-

---

> ### Box 8.3. Case Study 1: The Gulf War and Collective Security
>
> Iraq had always argued that the sovereign state of Kuwait was an artificial creation of the imperial powers. When this political motive was allied to an economic imperative, caused primarily by the accumulated war debts following the eight-year war with Iran, the annexation of Kuwait seemed to be a solution to Iraq's problems. The Iraqi President, Saddam Hussein, also assumed that the West would not use force to defend Kuwait, a miscalculation which was fuelled by the memory of the support the West had given Iraq during the Iran–Iraq war (the so-called 'fundamentalism' of Iran was considered to be a graver threat to international order than the extreme nationalism of the Iraqi regime).
>
> The invasion of Kuwait on 2 August 1990 led to a series of UN resolutions calling for Iraq to withdraw unconditionally. Economic sanctions were applied whilst the US-led coalition of international forces gathered in Saudi Arabia. Operation 'Desert Storm' crushed the Iraqi resistance in a matter of six weeks (16 January to 28 February 1991). The Gulf War had certainly revived the UN doctrine of collective security, although a number of doubts remained about the underlying motivations for the war and the way in which it was fought (for instance, the coalition of national armies was controlled by the US rather than by a UN military command as envisaged in the Charter). President Bush declared that the war was about more than one small country, it was about a 'big idea; **a new world order**'. The content of this new world order was 'peaceful settlement of disputes, solidarity against aggression, reduced and controlled arsenals, and just treatment of all peoples'.

---

tral to neo-liberal institutionalists, as noted in the following section). For writers such as Haas, international and regional institutions were a necessary counterpart to sovereign states whose capacity to deliver welfare goals was decreasing (1968: 154–8). The work of liberal institutionalists like Mitrany and Haas, provided an important impetus to closer co-operation between European states, initially through the creation of the European Coal and Steel Community in 1952. Consistent with Mitrany's hypothesis, co-operation in the energy sector provided governments with the confidence to undertake the more ambitious plan for a European Economic Community enshrined in the Treaty of Rome in 1956.

By the late 1960s and early 1970s, a new generation of scholars (particularly in the US) influenced by the European integration literature, began to examine in greater analytical depth the impact of modernization on the states system.[4] In particular, they rejected the state-centric view of the world adopted by both traditional realists and behaviouralists. World politics, according to liberal institutionalists (or pluralists as they are often referred to) were no longer an exclusive arena for states, as it had been for the first three hundred years of the Westphalian states system. In one of the central texts of this genre, Robert Keohane and Joseph Nye argued that the centrality of other actors, such as interest groups, transnational corporations and international non-governmental organizations, had to be taken into consideration (1972). Here the overriding image of international relations is one of a cobweb of diverse actors linked through multiple channels of interaction.

Although the phenomena of **transnationalism** was an important addition to the International Relations theorists' vocabulary, it remained underdeveloped as a theoretical concept. Perhaps the most important contribution of **pluralism** was its elaboration of **interdependence**. Due to the expansion of capitalism and the emergence of a global culture, pluralists recognized a growing interconnectedness between states which brought with it a shared responsibility for the environment. The following passage sums up this position neatly:

We are all now caught up in a complex systemic web of interactions such that changes in one part of the system have direct and indirect consequences for the rest of the system. (Little 1996: 77)

Clearly absolute state autonomy, so keenly entrenched in the minds of state leaders, was being circumscribed by interdependence. Moreover, this process is irreversible (Morse 1976: 97). Unlike realists however, liberal institutionalists believe that the decline of state autonomy is not necessarily regrettable, rather, they see transnationalism and interdependence as phenomena which must be managed.

Key Points

- **Liberal internationalism**: The strand in liberal thinking which holds that the natural order has been corrupted by undemocratic state leaders

and out-dated policies such as the balance of power. Prescriptively, liberal internationalists believe that contact between the peoples of the world, through commerce or travel, will facilitate a more pacific form of international relations.

- **Idealism**: Although there are important continuities between liberal internationalism and idealism, such as the belief in the power of world public opinion to tame the interests of states, idealism is distinct in that it believes in the importance of constructing an international order. For idealists, as opposed to internationalists, the freedom of states is part of the problem of international relations and not part of the solution. Two requirements follow from their diagnosis. The first is the need for explicitly **normative** thinking: how to promote peace and build a better world. Second, states must be part of an international organization, and be bound by its rules and norms.

- Central to **idealism** was the formation of an international organization to facilitate peaceful change, disarmament, arbitration, and (where necessary) enforcement. The **League of Nations** was founded in 1920 but its collective security system failed to prevent the descent into world war in the 1930s. The victor states in the wartime alliance against Nazi Germany pushed for a new international institution to represent the society of states and resist aggression. The **United Nations** Charter was signed in June 1945 by fifty states in San Francisco. It represented a departure from the League in two important respects. Membership was near universal, and the great powers were able to prevent any enforcement action from taking place which might be contrary to their interests.

- **Liberal institutionalism**: The third figure in the pattern of Liberalism. In the 1940s, liberal institutionalists turned to international institutions to carry out a number of functions the state could not perform. This was the catalyst for integration theory in Europe and pluralism in the United States. By the early 1970s, pluralism had mounted a significant challenge to realism. It focused on new actors (transnational corporations, non-governmental organizations) and new patterns of interaction (interdependence, integration).

Three Liberal Responses to Globalization

The previous section has delineated three elements in the history of liberal thinking on International Relations. Below, the chapter will bring this conversation between contending liberalisms up to date, hence the prefix 'neo' attached to each variant. Although the underlying arguments within each element remain constant, there have been discernible shifts in the political purposes to which those arguments have been utilized.

Neo-Liberal Internationalism

One of the 'big ideas' in the theory and practice of international relations in the 1990s is known as 'the **democratic peace** thesis'. The kernel of this argument, which can be traced back to Kant's philosophical sketch on *Perpetual Peace*, is that liberal states do not go to war with other liberal states. In this sense, liberal states have created what Michael Doyle has termed, a 'separate peace'. Although liberal states are pacific in relation to other liberal states, Doyle recognizes that liberal democracies are as aggressive as any other type of state in their relations with authoritarian regimes and stateless peoples (Doyle 1995*b*: 100).

Although the empirical evidence seems to support the democratic peace thesis, it is important to bear in mind the limitations of the argument. In the first instance, for the theory to be compelling, supporters of the **democratic peace** thesis must provide an explanation as to *why* war has become unthinkable between liberal states. Over two centuries ago, Kant argued that if the decision to use force was taken by the people, rather than by the prince, then the frequency of conflicts would be drastically reduced. But logically this argument implies a lower frequency of conflicts between liberal and non-liberal states, and this has proven to be contrary to the historical evidence. An alternative explanation for the '**democratic peace** thesis' might be that liberal states tend to be wealthy, and therefore have less to gain (and more to lose) by engaging in conflicts than poorer authoritarian states. Perhaps the most convincing explanation of all is the simple fact that liberal states tend to be in relations of amity with other liberal states. War between Canada and the US is unthinkable, per-haps not because of their liberal democratic constitutions, but because they are friends. Indeed, war between states with *contrasting* political and economic systems may also be unthinkable because they have a history of friendly relations. An example here is Mexico and Cuba, who although claiming a common revolutionary tradition nevertheless embrace antithetical economic ideologies.

Irrespective of the scholarly search for an answer to the reasons why liberal democratic states are more peaceful, it is important to note the political consequences of this hypothesis. In 1989 Francis Fukuyama wrote an article entitled 'The End of History' which celebrated the triumph of liberalism over all other ideologies, contending that liberal states were more stable internally and more peaceful in their international relations (Fukuyama 1989: 3–18). Whilst restating a familiar liberal internationalist theme, albeit with a Hegelian spin, Fukuyama's article and subsequent book served the political purpose of underlining the superiority of American values, thereby providing legitimacy to those who sought to 'export' liberalism. It was no longer a case of liberalism in one country, as it had appeared to some realists during the cold war, but rather liberalism for all countries.

What instruments are available to states to spread liberal values and widen the zone of peace? There are a wide range of options open to Western states in their attempt to globalize liberalism. At one end of the spectrum, the collapse of state structures (e.g. in Somalia or Yugoslavia) prompts many liberals to call for forcible humanitarian intervention. But as any liberal realist like Hedley Bull would argue, intervention even for liberal reasons often leads to more chaos. Since the question of humanitarian intervention is dealt with in detail in Chapter 20, the paragraphs below will focus on the non-military instruments at the disposal of state-leaders and international institutions for promoting liberal values in global politics.

At the political level, the powerful states in the international system are able to use institutional leverage as a means of embedding formerly non-liberal states into the liberal world order. In other words, in order for Russia to be accepted as one of the G7 (Group of Seven most powerful industrial economies), it must demonstrate its liberal credentials first. The same process has been at work in the

Timothy Dunne

Box 8.4. Francis Fukuyama: Liberalism as the End of History?

In his 1992 book, *The End of History and the Last Man* (1993) Fukuyama celebrates the globalization of liberal capitalism. The phrase 'end of history' is not meant to be literal, but philosophical. All history hitherto has been the remorseless unfolding of the liberal idea. We are not condemned, he argues, to live for ever in the realist world of inevitable conflict. Fukuyama provides two causal explanations for progressive historical change. At the material level, the cumulative knowledge of science facilitates inexorable economic development. At the level of ideas, Fukuyama (like Hegel before him) argues that the historical struggle by individuals to be recognized by others, or what he calls *thymos*, comes to an end with the triumph of liberalism. For the first time in history, individuals can receive mutual recognition without subordinating it to the will of others (and thereby denying them recognition). Just as liberalism has achieved progress in domestic society, it has transformed relations between liberal states in international society. Like other neo-liberal internationalists (discussed below), Fukuyama believes that liberal states have established a pacific union within which war has become unthinkable.

relations between the former communist states of Central and Eastern Europe and the European Union. The goal of Western states using institutional leverage is rapid macro-economic convergence on the part of those states seeking to join the EU and the economies of the established member-states.

In relations with the Third World, where there are fewer prospects for exerting regional institutional leverage, the most effective tool has been **conditionality**: the policies developing countries must pursue in return for economic benefits (e.g. loans or investment). More recently, conditionality has expanded from the requirement to liberalize and privatize the economic sector, to include targets on 'good governance', and compliance to human rights norms. Whilst conditionality might claim some successes, its reception in Asia has been contested. The rapid economic development of the ASEAN states (Vietnam, Brunei, Singapore, Malaysia, Thailand, Indonesia, and the Philippines) has made them economically less dependent on Western aid or expertise, and at the same time they have become increasingly critical of the liberal internationalist assumption that liberal values are

universally shared. The Australian dilemma, illustrated in Case Study 2 (Box 8.5), between promoting human rights in the Asia-Pacific region without damaging its economic and security interests, might serve as a microcosm for future relations between a weaker West and a potential economic colossus like China.

The attempt by Western states to globalize liberalism has highlighted a number of endemic weaknesses in the neo-liberal internationalist position.[5] First, from an intellectual point of view, theorists like Doyle and Fukuyama are complacent about the degree to which their own society is indeed liberal and prone to overestimate the number of stable liberal democracies in the world (about two dozen, out of over 180 states according to Fred Halliday). Second, a defeat for Stalinist-style communism does not mean that liberalism has triumphed over *all* other ideologies. Social democracy remains an important ideology in Northern Europe, and a variety of forms of non-liberal consitutionalism exist, for example, in Asia and to a lesser extent in Japan. Third, Western states have done little to remove the suspicion among radicals in their own countries and public opinion in South-East Asia, that the project of spreading liberal values is a convenient fiction for promoting the commercial interests of Western firms. Finally, the neo-liberal internationalist agenda of the 1990s highlights the often conflicting principles which underpin liberalism. Promoting good governance, or economic liberalization, inevitably comes into conflict with the norms of sovereignty and self-determination. Moreover, as the West becomes more deeply involved in the organization of developing states' political and economic infrastructure, the less those states are able to be accountable to their domestic constituencies, thereby cutting through the link between the government and the people which is so central to modern liberal forms of representative democracy (Hurrell and Woods 1995: 463).

Neo-Idealism

Like the idealists of the inter-war period, neo-idealists have a good deal in common with liberal internationalism: both share a commitment to democratic forms of government, and both believe that interdependence breeds peace. That said, neo-

---

**Box 8.5. Case Study 2: Promoting Liberal Values in an Illiberal Region—
The Australian Dilemma***

Gareth Evans was Minister of the Department of Foreign Affairs and Trade between 1988 and 1996. During his tenure he attempted to shift Australian foreign policy in the direction of the Asia-Pacific region, primarily for reasons of trade and security. One barrier to closer co-operation which had to be overcome was the diverging cultures and histories: how could modern Australia, with its western liberal traditions, be accepted by northern neighbours such as Indonesia, Malaysia, Thailand, and the Philippines? This issue was compounded by the Australian Labor Government's desire to act as a 'good international citizen' by promoting values such as human rights both regionally and internationally. Evans notes that under his tutelage, Australia made more bilateral representations on human rights than any other country, 534 in 1993 in 90 countries (Evans and Grant 1995: 42–3).

The relationship between Australia and Indonesia is a good example of the dilemmas of 'comprehensive engagement' in action. Decades of diplomatic indifference were brought to an end in 1988, when the two Foreign Ministers began negotiating the Timor Gap Zone of Co-operation Treaty, outlining agreed boundaries for mineral exploitation in the Timor Sea. The security treaty with Jakarta, signed in December 1995, was the culmination of this new era of co-operation between Indonesia and Australia. Undoubtedly the normalization of bilateral relations with Indonesia is beneficial for trade and security. However, Indonesia has one of the worst human rights records in world politics: democracy is not part of its political culture (the state is run by President Soeharto in conjunction with the military), political protests are put down with excessive violence, and moreover, Indonesia has been accused of performing genocidal acts against East Timor which it annexed in 1975.

Australia's attempt to combine a realist understanding of the balance of power between the two states (Indonesia is the world's fourth most populous state with a population of 190 million as against 18 million in Australia) with liberal internationalist concerns for values such as liberty and democracy. But a synthesis between order and justice is difficult to achieve, as the reaction to Evans's policy demonstrates. From the neo-idealist 'left', critics like John Pilger have argued that Australia is complicit in the East Timorese killing fields; instead of comprehensive engagement, it should be comprehensively censuring the Indonesian regime. From the realist 'right', Evans has been criticized for endangering the national interest by keeping human rights issues on the agenda. The guiding thought here is that since Australia does not have the power to liberate East Timor any attempt to reverse the annexation would fail 'at the cost of creating antagonistic relations with Indonesia' (Hirst 1996: 10).

* In this case study the collective noun 'Australia' is used in the knowledge that there are multiple identities in Australian political culture. The referent, therefore, is the Australian government/state.

---

idealists believe that peace and justice are not natural conditions, they are the product of deliberate design. Moreover, the processes of globalization have added to the enormity of this task. Encouraging or even coercing non-liberal states to become more democratic is only part of what is required in order to bring about a truly liberal world order. Consistent with the original idealists, neo-idealists argue that reform needs to take place at the international level: like states themselves, international institutions need to be made more democratic.[6] Similarly, neo-idealists believe that global social movements must be brought into the decision-making structures, since these are often closer to ordinary people than their own governments. In addition to tackling the global 'democratic deficit', neo-idealists are more prone to point to the dark side of globalization than liberal internationalists. These arguments are discussed in greater length below.

Liberal internationalists tend to use the term globalization in positive ways, as though we lived in a global village, signifying economic and moral interconnectedness. Yet for more radical neo-idealists, the world seems more like a scene from the film *Blade Runner* with post-modern technologies coexisting with ethical anarchy and urban decay. Neo-idealists like Richard Falk recognize that globalization and community are frequently at odds with each other. 'This tension between the ethical imperatives of the global neighbourhood and the dynamics of economic globalistation', he argues, is 'an evasion that has been characteristic of all post-Wilsonian variants of liberal internationalism' (1995a: 573). In this sense, neo-liberal internationalism has fallen prey to the neo-liberal consensus which minimizes the role of the public sector in providing for welfare, and elevates the market as the appropriate mechanism for allocating resources, investment, and employment opportunities. Although the globalization of liberalism has improved the per capita income of the vast majority of the world's population, the rate of increase among the powerful states has been far greater. According to the United Nations Development Programme 'the richest billion people around the world command 60 times the income of the poorest billion'; by poor the UN means those without clean drinking water or enough food to maintain minimum standards of nutrition.[7]

Neo-idealists offer a radically different set of pre-scriptions to liberal internationalists. At the level of international institutions, writers such as David Held, Norberto Bobbio, and Danielle Archibugi (Archibugi and Held 1995) among others, believe that global politics must be democratized. Held's diagnosis begins by revealing the inadequacies of the 'Westphalian order' (or the modern states-system which is conventionally dated from the middle of the seventeenth century). During the latter stages of this period, we have witnessed rapid democratization with a number of states, but this has not been accompanied by democratization of the society of states (Held 1993). This task is increasingly urgent given the current levels of interconnectedness, since 'national' governments are no longer in control of the forces which shape their citizens' lives (e.g. the decision by one state to permit deforestation has environmental consequences for all states). After 1945, the UN Charter set limits to the sovereignty of states by recognizing the rights of individuals in a whole series of human rights conventions. But even if the UN had lived up to its Charter in the post–1945 period, it would still have left the building blocks of the Westphalian order largely intact, namely: the hierarchy between great powers and the rest (symbolized by the permanent membership of the Security Council); massive inequalities of wealth between states; and a minimal role for non-state actors to influence decision-making in international relations.

In place of the Westphalian and UN models, Held outlines a '**cosmopolitan model of democracy**'. This requires, in the first instance, the creation of regional parliaments and the extension of the authority of such regional bodies (like the European Union) which are already in existence. Second, human rights conventions must be entrenched in national parliaments and monitored by a new International Court of Human Rights. Third, reform of the UN, or the replacement of it, with a genuinely democratic and accountable global parliament. Without appearing to be too sanguine about the prospects for the realization of the **cosmopolitan model of democracy**, Held is nevertheless adamant that if democracy is to thrive, it must penetrate the institutions and regimes which manage global politics.

Neo-idealism emphasizes not just macro-institutional democratic reform, but also democratization at the 'grass-roots'. Radical liberals like Richard Falk argue that global civil society has massive emancipatory potential. The evolution of international humanitarian law, and the extent to which these laws are complied with, is largely down to the millions of individuals who are active supporters of human rights groups like Amnesty International and Human Rights Watch (Falk 1995: 164). Similarly, global protest movements have been largely responsible for the heightened global sensitivity to environmental degradation. This emphasis by neo-idealists on what Falk calls 'globalization from below' is an important antidote to mainstream liberalism's somewhat status quo oriented world view which sanctifies market forces, and seeks only piecemeal reform of international institutions such as the UN.

Neo-Liberal Institutionalism

In the 1980s, pluralism metamorphosed into **neo-liberal institutionalism**.[8] One of the problems with the former 'label' is that few of the thinkers actually identified themselves with the movement. By contrast, liberal institutionalism has attracted some of the most prolific and influential thinkers in the field, and has become the new orthodoxy in a number of key North American schools of International Relations. In addition to a high degree of self-identification on the part of contemporary liberal institutionalists, the second important revision to the earlier **pluralism** can be identified in the far more focused research agenda of liberal internationalism. The third and most substantive revision to **pluralism** concerns the shift back towards a state-centric approach to world politics (a shift signalled by Keohane and Nye in 1977).

What are the defining features of neo-liberal institutionalism? The core principles of neo-liberal institutionalism can be distilled into the following four principles.

- **Actor:** Liberal institutionalists take for granted the state as a legitimate representation of society. Although emphasizing the importance of non-state actors in his early pluralist work, Robert Keohane's understanding of neo-liberal institutionalism admits that non-state actors are subordinate to states (Keohane 1989: 8).

- **Structure:** Liberals broadly accept the structural condition of anarchy in the international system, but crucially, anarchy does not mean co-operation between states is impossible, as the existence (and proliferation) of international **regimes** demonstrates. In short, regimes and international institutions can mitigate anarchy by reducing verification costs, reinforcing reciprocity, and making defection from norms easier to punish.

- **Process:** Integration at the regional and global level is increasing. Here the future direction of the European Union is considered to be a vital test case for neo-liberal institutionalism.

- **Motivation:** States will enter into co-operative relations even if another state will gain more from the interaction, in other words, 'absolute gains' are more important for liberal institutionalists than 'relative gains' (emphasized by neo-realists).

It is vital to bear in mind the context out of which neo-liberal institutionalism developed. Leading neo-liberal institutionalists such as Axelrod, Keohane, and Oye, developed their ideas in response to Kenneth Waltz's theory of neo-realism outlined in his 1979 work *Theory of International Politics*. Moreover, this response was from *within* the mainstream as opposed to the radical critical theory challenge from the margins which also developed in the 1980s (Ashley 1984; Cox 1981). Given this context, it is not surprising that **neo-liberal institutionalism** often seems closer to contemporary realism than to the tradition of liberal thinking about international relations.

As the analysis of **neo-idealism** demonstrates, radical liberals do not take the state for granted. Legitimacy is not something that states possess by right, but something which has to be earned through humane government and democratic procedures. Moreover, early liberal institutionalists, such as Mitrany and Haas, were sceptical about whether states could deliver liberal goals of order and justice even if they had the will. Accordingly, they prescribed devolving power *down* to local government/regional assemblies or *up* to supra-state organizations or world government.

Apart from a considerable divergence between the complacent statism of neo-liberal institutionalism, and the scepticism towards the state shown by early liberal institutionalists, there is one other significant demarcation between **neo-liberal institutionalism** and the other two elements in liberal thinking. Both **liberal internationalism** and **idealism** were wider ranging, more critical, and above all, more *political* than contemporary neo-liberal institutionalism. This argument is powerfully made by David Long in a recent critique of the so-called 'Harvard School' of neo-liberal institutionalism:

Keohane's neoliberal institutionalism is an emasculated liberalism, shorn of its normative concerns with the liberty and well-being of individuals, focusing on economic variables, using the utilitarian discourses and theories of liberal economics, and making states the agents in international relations (Long 1996: 496).

In his defence, Keohane is justly critical of the naïve assumption of classical liberal internationalists that commerce breeds peace. A free trade system, according to Keohane, provides incentives for co-operation but does not guarantee it. Here he is making an important distinction between co-operation and harmony. 'Co-operation is not automatic', Keohane argues, 'but requires planning and negotiation' (1989: 11). On this point, we see an interesting overlap between the inter-war idealists and **neo-liberal institutionalism**. However, the fact that both camps see co-operation as the handiwork of individuals and institutions (as opposed to being part of a natural order) should not blind us to the point that the 'Harvard School' see the role of institutions as *regulating* interests rather than *transforming* identities, as neo-idealists believe.

Key Points

- The research agenda of **neo-liberal internationalism** is dominated by the debate about liberal states: how far the liberal zone of peace extends, why relations within it are peaceful, and what pattern is likely to evolve in relations between liberal states and authoritarian regimes? Crucially, in the post-cold war era, neo-liberal internationalists have lent their voices in support of Western (particularly American) attempts to use the levers of foreign policy to put pressure on authoritarian states to liberalize.

- Neo-idealists have responded to globalization by calling for a double democratization of both international institutions and domestic state structures. Radical **neo-idealism** is critical of mainstream liberalism's devotion to 'globalization from above' which marginalizes the possibility of change from below through the practices of global civil society.

- The most conventional of all contemporary liberalisms is **neo-liberal institutionalism**. At the centre of their research programme is how to initiate and maintain co-operation under conditions of anarchy. This task is facilitated by the creation of regimes. Notice that neo-liberal institutionalists share with realists the assumption that states are the most significant actors, and that the international environment is anarchic. Their accounts diverge, however, on the prospects for achieving sustained patterns of co-operation under anarchy

Conclusion and Postscript: The Crisis of Liberalism

There is something of a crisis in liberal thinking on international relations in the 1990s. The euphoria with which liberals greeted the end of the cold war in 1989 has to a large extent been dissipated; the great caravan of humanity, kick-started with the revolutions of 1989, is once again coming to a spluttering halt. Successive post-cold war conflicts, in Afghanistan, Liberia, Chechnya, Somalia, Burundi, and Rwanda (to name a few) remind us that in many parts of the world, the conditions which fuelled these tensions in the cold war period remain in place; for example, the geopolitical rivalry to grant massive arms transfers to states involved in 'civil' wars.

The audit of global politics in the 1990s, from a liberal point of view, begins to take on a much darker hue when the wars of the former Yugoslavia are included. Unlike the tragedies of Rwanda and Burundi, the conflict in Bosnia took place on the doorstep of the liberal zone. How could the national hatreds exhibited by all the warring parties take root once again in Western soil? Liberal internationalists like Michael Ignatieff despaired that acts of genocide had returned to haunt Europe forty years after the Holocaust. After all, it was the **Enlightenment** which provided a vocabulary for articulating liberal ideas such as human rights and humanitarian law. 'What made the Balkan wars so shocking' argued Ignatieff, 'was how little these universals were respected in their home continent' (1995).

In the remaining paragraphs, by way of a response to Ignatieff, I suggest two explanations for the growing disenchantment with Liberalism. First,

as we have seen throughout the chapter, Liberalism does not have a single voice; moreover, competing liberal arguments can often be used to defend different positions. The imperative to intervene in the wars of the former Yugoslavia, advocated by Ignatieff and other liberal internationalists, is backed up by the cosmopolitan liberal principle of the equal worth of all individuals: a sentiment captured by the words of the poet John Donne, 'any man's death diminishes me, because I am involved in Mankind'. But other liberals, of a more communitarian persuasion, argue that our obligations to all of humankind are less significant than our duties to citizens of our own state. On this line of argument, the tragedy in Bosnia may diminish us all, but this is not a sufficient reason to risk the lives of our fellow citizens in defence of abstract moral universals. How can Liberalism be our guide when, from different perspectives, it can support intervention and non-intervention? Hoffmann is surely right to argue that the case of degenerating states reveals how sovereignty, democracy, national self-determination, and human rights 'are four norms in conflict and a source of complete liberal disarray' (1995: 169).

A deeper reason for the crisis in Liberalism, and one which is prompted by Ignatieff's argument, is that is is bound up with an increasingly discredited Enlightenment view of the world. Contrary to the hopes of liberal internationalists, the application of reason and science to politics has not brought communities together. Indeed, it has arguably shown the fragmented nature of the political community, which is regularly expressed in terms of ethnic,

Box 8.6. Key Concepts of Liberalism

Collective Security
Refers to an arrangement where 'each state in the system accepts that the security of one is the concern of all, and agrees to join in a collective response to aggression' (Roberts and Kingsbury, 1993: 30).

Conditionality
The way in which states or international institutions impose conditions upon developing countries in advance of distributing economic benefits.

Cosmopolitan Model of Democracy
Associated with David Held, and other neo-idealists, a cosmopolitan model of democracy requires the following: the creation of regional parliaments and the extension of the authority of such regional bodies (like the European Union) which are already in existence; human rights conventions must be entrenched in national parliaments and monitored by a new International Court of Human Rights; the UN must be replaced with a genuinely democratic and accountable global parliament.

Democratic Peace
A central plank of liberal internationalist thought, the democratic peace thesis holds that war has become unthinkable between liberal states.

Enlightenment
Associated with rationalist thinkers of the eighteenth century. Key ideas (which some would argue remain mottoes for our age) include: secularism, progress, reason, science, knowledge, and freedom. The motto of the Enlightenment is: 'Sapere aude! Have courage to use your own understanding' (Reiss 1991: 54).

Idealism
Idealists seek to apply liberal thinking in domestic politics to international relations, in other words, institutionalize the rule of law. This reasoning is known as the **domestic analogy**. According to idealists in the early twentieth century, there were two principal requirements for a new world order. First: state leaders, intellectuals, and public opinion had to believe that progress was possible. Second: an international organization had to be created to facilitate peaceful change, disarmament, arbitration, and (where necessary) enforcement. The League of Nations was founded in 1920 but its **collective security** system failed to prevent the descent into world war in the 1930s.

Integration
A process of ever closer union between states, in a regional or international context. The process often begins by co-operation to solve technical problems, referred to by Mitrany as **ramification**.

Interdependence
A condition where states (or peoples) are affected by decisions taken by others; for example, a decision to raise interest rates in Germany automatically exerts upward pressure on interest rates in other European states. Interdependence can be symmetric, i.e. both sets of actors are affected equally, or it can be asymmetric, where the impact varies between actors.

Liberalism
An ideology whose central concern is the liberty of the individual. For most liberals, the establishment of the state is necessary to preserve individual liberty from being destroyed or harmed by other individuals or by other states. But the state must always be the servant of the collective will and not (as in the case of Realism) the master.

Liberal Institutionalism
In the 1940s, liberals turned to international institutions to carry out a number of functions the state could not perform. This was the catalyst for integration theory in Europe and pluralism in the United States. By the early 1970s, pluralism had mounted a significant challenge to realism. It focused on new actors (transnational corporations, non-governmental organizations) and new patterns of interaction (interdependence, integration).

Liberal Internationalism
The strand in liberal thinking which holds that the natural order has been corrupted by undemocratic state leaders and outdated policies such as the balance of power. Prescriptively, liberal internationalists believe that contact between the peoples of the world, through commerce or travel, will facilitate a more pacific form of international relations. Key concept of liberal internationalism: the idea of a **harmony of interests**.

Normative
The belief that theories should be concerned with what ought to be, rather than merely diagnosing what is. Norm creation refers to the setting of standards in international relations which governments (and other actors) ought to meet.

Pluralism
An umbrella term, borrowed from American political science, used to signify International Relations theorists who rejected the realist view of the primacy of the state and the coherence of the state-as-actor.

World Government
Associated in particular with those idealists who believe that peace can never be achieved in a world divided into separate sovereign states. Just as the state of nature in civil society was abolished by governments, the state of war in international society must be ended by the establishment of a world government.

linguistic, or religious differences. Critics of Liberalism such as John Gray view the very idea of 'moral universals' as dangerous. The universalizing mission of liberal values such as democracy, capitalism, and secularism, undermine the traditions and practices of non-Western cultures (Gray 1995: 146). But as a number of states in South-East Asia have demonstrated in recent years, modernization can take place without a corresponding liberalization of state and society. The key question for Liberalism as modernity draws to an end is whether it can reinvent itself as a non-universalizing, non-Westernizing political idea, which preserves the traditional liberal value of human solidarity without undermining cultural diversity.

QUESTIONS

1. Do you agree with Stanley Hoffmann that international affairs are 'inhospitable' to Liberalism? What arguments might one draw upon to support or refute this proposition?

2. Was the language of international morality, used by idealists, a way of masking over the interests of Britain and France in maintaining their dominance of the post-World War I international system?

3. Is Francis Fukuyama a complacent statist, or a visionary neo-liberal internationalist?

4. Are democracies more peaceful than authoritarian states? If so, why?

5. How much progress (if any) has there been in liberal internationalist thinking since Kant?

6. Which element of Liberalism best explains the development of the European Union, (neo)liberal institutionalism or (neo)idealism?

7. Are all forms of Liberalism premissed on an optimistic view of human nature?

8. Has Australia been 'too liberal' in its relations with states like Indonesia?

9. What do neo-liberal institutionalists have in common with idealists? At what point do their accounts of international relations diverge?

10. Given the different strands in liberal thinking, how can we meaningfully talk about a coherent liberal tradition?

GUIDE TO FURTHER READING

Excellent general discussions of liberalism include the following: S. Hoffmann, *Janus and Minerva* (Boulder, Col.: Westview, 1987), 394–436; M. J. Smith, (1992), 'Liberalism and International Reform' in T. Nardin and D. Mapel (eds.), *Traditions of International Ethics* (Cambridge: Cambridge University Press, 1992), in addition, see the essays by M. Doyle, and M. Zacher and R. A. Matthew, in C. Kegley (ed.), *Controversies in International Relations: Realism and the Neoliberal Challenge* (New York: St Martin's, 1995). The same text also contains the most up to date contributions to the 'neo-realist–neo-liberal' debate. Useful short extracts from classical liberal thinkers are contained in E. Luard, (ed.), *Basic Texts in International Relations* (London: Macmillan, 1992). For a thought-provoking critique of liberal political theory, see John Gray, *Enlightenment's Wake: Politics and Culture at the Close of the Modern Age* (London: Routledge, 1995). Critical essays on liberalism in international relations can be found in the '*Millennium* Special Issue', *The Globalization of Liberalism?* 24: 3 (1995); and Stanley Hoffmann, 'The Crisis of Liberal Internationalism', *Foreign Policy*, 98 (1995).

NOTES

1. Upper case 'Liberalism' signifies the broad Liberal tradition in international thought, whereas lower case 'liberalism' signifies a particular kind of liberal thinking, or an individual liberal thinker. As is customary, International Relations refers to the academic discipline, and international relations refers to the practices of international actors.
2. For an alternative system of classifying liberalisms, see Doyle (1995).
3. Between 1945 and 1990, there were 232 resolutions vetoed, between 1990 and 1994, there were only 4 vetoes.
4. Arguably, pluralism is an inadequate term in view of its usage in political philosophy to denote a form of liberalism which privileges difference over universalism.
5. For an excellent discussion of the 'crisis of liberal internationalism', see Hoffmann (1995).
6. The link between the inter-war idealists, and the work of writers who I have termed 'neo-idealist' is brought out well by Luigi Bonanate (1995).
7. See the United Nations Development Programme (1994).
8. Often referred to in the literature as either neo-liberal institutionalism (Keohane 1989) or simply neo-liberalism.

9 New Approaches to International Theory

Steve Smith

READER'S GUIDE

This chapter summarizes the most recent developments in international relations theory. It starts from the inter-paradigm debate represented by the three preceding chapters, and brings that story up to date. It then looks at how international relations theory maps out in the late 1990s. It offers a framework for thinking about contemporary international relations theory by looking at the differences between those theories that are explanatory and those that are constitutive, and between theories that are foundationalist and those that are non-foundationalist. In this light the chapter divides contemporary theories into three categories: first, the mainstream theories of liberalism and realism, represented by the neo-realist/neo-liberal debate, which are defined as rationalist theories; second, the chapter looks at the most influential contemporary theoretical developments which differ from the shared assumptions of rationalist theories, namely normative theory, feminist theory, critical theory, historical sociology and post-modernism. These theories are termed reflectivist theories. Third, the chapter looks at social constructivism, which is an attempt to bridge the gap between the previous two categories. The chapter provides a clear context for thinking about these new approaches, and concludes by posing the question of which of them paints the most convincing picture of world politics in a globalized era, is it the rationalist theories, the reflectivist theories or social constructivism?

Introduction

The three previous chapters have given you overviews of the three dominant theories of international relations, originally discussed in the Introduction of this book. Together these three approaches have dominated the discipline for the last fifty years, and the debate between adherents of them has defined the areas of disagreement in international theory. The resulting 'inter-paradigm debate' has been extremely influential in thinking about international relations, with generations of students told that the debate between the various elements effectively exhausts the kinds of questions that can be asked about international relations. The problem has been that the inter-paradigm debate by no means covers the range of issues that any contemporary theory of world politics needs to deal with. Instead it ends up being a rather conservative political move because it gives the impression of open-mindedness and intellectual pluralism; whereas, in fact, as Timothy Dunne has clearly pointed out in Chapter 6, of the three theories involved in the inter-paradigm debate one, realism, has tended to be dominant, with its debate with liberalism being the central theme of what debate has existed in international theory. It is important to note that one major factor supporting the dominance of realism has been that it seems to portray the world we common-sensically understand. Thus alternative views can be dismissed as **normative** or **value-laden**, to be negatively compared with the **objectivity** of realism. These two thoughts (the common-sense relevance of realism and its objectivity) lead us to what has changed in recent years to subvert the dominance of realism.

In the last decade or so this picture has changed dramatically, with a series of new approaches being developed to explain world politics. In part this reflects a changing world, as the end of the cold war system significantly reduced the credability of realism, especially in its neo-realist guise where the stability of the bipolar system was seen as a continuing feature of world politics; as that bipolarity dramatically disappeared, so too did the explanatory power of the theory that most relied on in neo-realism. But this was not by any means the only reason for the rise of new approaches. There are three other obvious reasons: **first**, there were other changes underway in world politics that made the development of new approaches important, and

mainly here I am thinking of the kinds of features discussed previously under the heading of **globalization**. Whatever the explanatory power of realism, it did not seem very good at dealing with the rise of non-state actors, social movements, radically expanding transactions, and the like. In short, new approaches were needed to explain these parts of world politics, even if realism was still good at dealing with the power politics aspects. **Second**, there were major developments underway in other academic disciplines, especially in the social sciences generally, but also in the philosophy of science and social science, that attacked the underlying methodological (i.e. how to undertake study) assumption of realism, a position known as **positivism** (we will discuss this below); in its place a whole host of alternative ways of thinking about the social sciences were being proposed, and international relations simply caught the bug. **Third**, realism's dominance was called into question by a resurgence of its historical main competitor, liberalism, in the form of **neo-liberal institutionalism**, as discussed in Chapter 8. In fact, as we will see below, the debate between neo-realism and neo-liberalism has become one of the main features of international relations theory in the 1990s. But there are others and these involve movements away from the main assumptions of the mainstream approaches.

Key Points

- Realism, liberalism, and structuralism together comprised the **inter-paradigm debate** of the 1980s, with realism dominant amongst the three theories.

- The **inter-paradigm debate**, despite promising intellectual openness, ended up naturalizing the dominance of realism by pretending that there was real debate, whereas 'common sense' and the seeming 'objectivity' of realism did the work.

- The dominance of realism has in recent years been undermined by three sets of developments: first, **globalization** has brought a host of other features of world politics to centre-stage; second, **positivism**, the underlying methodological assumption of realism, has been significantly undermined by developments in the social sciences and in philosophy; third, **neo-liberal insti-** **tutionalism** has become increasingly important in challenging realism in the mainstream literature.

Explanatory/Constitutive Theories and Foundational/Anti-Foundational Theories

In order to understand the current situation with regards to international theory I want to introduce two distinctions that might help you see the differences between the theories that we are going to look at below. The terms can be a little unsettling, but they are merely convenient words for discussing what in fact are fairly straightforward ideas. The first distinction is between **explanatory** and **constitutive** theory. An explanatory theory is one that sees the world as something external to our theories of it; in contrast a constitutive theory is one that thinks our theories actually help construct the world. Whilst this is a distinction adopted in both scientific and non-scientific disciplines, a minute's thought should make you realize why it is more appealing in the non-scientific world: the reason of course is that in a very obvious way our theories about the world in which we live make us act in certain ways, and thereby may make the theories we hold become self-confirming. If, for example, we think that individuals are naturally aggressive then we are likely to adopt a different posture towards them than if we think they are naturally peaceful. Yet you should not regard this claim as self-evidently true, since it assumes that our ability to think and reason makes us able to determine our choices, i.e. that we have free will rather than having our 'choices' determined behind our backs as it were. What if our human nature is such that we desire certain things 'naturally', and that our language and seemingly 'free choices' are simply our rationalizations for our needs? This is only the opening stage of a very complex, but fascinating, debate about what it is to be human, and you will find it dealt with in a number of texts should you wish to follow in it (see, for example, Hollis and Smith 1990). The upshot of it, whichever position you eventually adopt, is that there is a genuine debate between those theories that think of the social world as like the natural world (and that the theories we use to analyse it merely report on events rather than con-

struct that reality), and those theories that see our language and concepts as helping create that reality. Theories that think that the natural and the social worlds are the same are known as **naturalist** theories.

In International Relations the more structural realist and structuralist theories dealt with in Chapters 6 and 8 tend to be explanatory theories, which see the task of theory as being to report on a world that is external to our theories; their concern is to uncover **regularities** in human behaviour and thereby explain the social world in much the same way as a natural scientist might explain the physical world. By contrast, nearly all the approaches developed in the last decade or so tend to be constitutive theories, and interestingly the same is true of some liberal thought. For these theories, theory is not external to the things it is trying to explain, and instead may construct how we think about the world. Or, to put it another way, our theories define what we see as the external world. Thus the very concepts we use to think about the world help to make that world what it is (think about the concepts that matter in your own life, such as happiness, love, wealth, status, etc.). To make my position clear I believe our theories of the social world constitute that world; I say this not so that you should believe it but only so that you can see where my biases might lie in what follows.

The **foundational/anti-foundational** distinction refers to the simple-sounding issue of whether our beliefs about the world can be tested or evaluated against any neutral or objective procedures. This is a distinction central to the branch of the philosophy of social science known as **epistemology** (simply defined as the study of how we can claim to know something). A foundationalist position is one that thinks that all truth claims (i.e. about some feature of the world) can be judged true or false. An anti-foundationalist thinks that truth claims cannot be so judged since there are never neutral grounds for so doing; instead each theory will define what counts as the facts and so there will be no neutral position available to determine between rival claims. Think, for example, of a Marxist and a Conservative arguing about the 'true' state of the economy, or of an Islamic Fundamentalist and a Radical Feminist discussing the 'true' status of women in Muslim societies. Foundationalists look for what are termed **meta-theoretical** (above any particular theory) grounds for choosing between truth claims; anti-foundationalists think that there are no such positions available, and that believing there to be some is itself simply a reflection of an adherence to a particular view of epistemology.

In many senses most of the new approaches to international theory are much less wedded to foundationalism than were the traditional theories that comprised the inter-paradigm debate. Thus, **postmodernism**, some **feminist theory**, and much **normative theory** would tend towards anti-foundationalism, although the **neo-neo debate**, **historical sociology**, and **critical theory** would tend towards foundationalism; interestingly, **social constructivism** would be very much in the middle. On the whole, and as a rough guide, explanatory theories tend to be foundational while constitutive theories tend to be anti-foundational. The point at this stage is not to construct some check-list, nor to get you thinking about the differences as much as it is to draw your attention to the role that these assumptions about the nature of knowledge have on the theories that we are going to discuss. The central point I want to make in this section is that the two distinctions mentioned in this section were never really discussed in the literature of international relations. The last decade has seen these underlying assumptions brought more and more into the open and the most important effect of this has been to undermine realism's claim to be delivering **the** truth.

Each of the distinctions has been brought into the open because of a massively important reversal in the way in which social scientists have thought about their ways of constructing knowledge. Until the late 1980s most social scientists in International Relations tended to be **positivists**; since then positivism has been under attack. Positivism is best defined as a view of how to create knowledge that relies on four main assumptions: first a belief in the unity of science, i.e. that the same methodologies apply in both the scientific and non-scientific worlds. Second, there is a distinction between facts and values, with facts being neutral between theories. Third, that the social world, like the natural one, has regularities, and that these can be 'discovered' by our theories in much the same way as a scientist does in looking for the regularities in nature. Finally, that the way to determine the truth of statements is by appeal to these neutral facts; this is known as an **empiricist** epistemology.

It is the rejection of these assumptions that has characterized the debate in international theory in the last decade. Yosef Lapid (1989) has termed this 'a post-positivist era'. In simple terms, traditional international theory was dominated by the four kinds of positivistic assumptions noted above. Since the late 1980s, the new approaches that have emerged have tended to question these same assumptions. The resulting map of international theory in the late 1990s is one that has three main features: first the continuing dominance of the three theories that together made up the inter-paradigm debate, this can be termed the **rationalist** position, and is epitomized by the **neo-neo debate**; second, the emergence of non-positivistic theories, which together can be termed the **reflectivist** position, and epitomized by the **post-modernist, critical theory, historical sociology, normative theory**, and much **feminist** work to be discussed below; and third, the development of an approach that tries to speak to both rationalist and reflectivist positions, and this is the position, associated mainly with the work of Alexander Wendt (see especially 1992), known as **social constructivism**. Fig. 9.1 illustrates the resulting configuration of the theories in the late 1990s.

Note that this is a very rough representation of how the various theories can be categorized. It is misleading in some respects since, as the previous three chapters have shown, there are quite different versions of the three main theories and some of

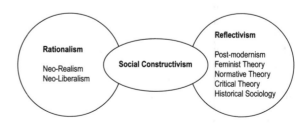

Fig. 9.1. **International theory in the late 1990s**

these are less rationalistic than others. Similarly, some of the approaches classified as 'reflectivist' are markedly less so than others; for example historical sociology tends to adopt similar theoretical methods as do rationalist approaches, although it tends to reject the central unit of rationalism, the state, hence its classification as a reflectivist approach. Having said which the classification is broadly illustrative of the theoretical landscape, and you might best think of it as a useful starting point for thinking about the differences between the theories involved. As you learn more and more about them you will see how rough and ready a picture this is, but it is as good a categorization as any other. But so as to show you some of the complexities involved, think about quite what the reflectivist approaches are reflectivist about: for feminists it is gender, for normative theories it is values, for post-modernists it is the construction of knowledge, for historical sociologists it is the state/class relationship, and for critical theorists it is the knowledge/power relationship. There are similarities but there are important differences.

Key Points

- Theories can be distinguished according to whether they are **explanatory** or **constitutive**

and whether they are **foundational** or **anti-foundational**. As a rough guide, explanatory theories are foundational and constitutive theories are anti-foundational.

- The three main theories comprising the **inter-paradigm debate** were based on a set of positivist assumptions, namely the idea that social science theories can use the same methodologies as theories of the natural sciences, that facts and values can be distinguished, that neutral facts can act as arbiters between rival truth claims, and that the social world has regularities which theories can 'discover'.

- Since the late 1980s there has been a rejection of **positivism**, with the main new approaches tending more towards **constitutive** and **anti-foundational** assumptions.

- The current theoretical situation is one in which there are three main positions: first, **rationalist** theories that are essentially the latest versions of the **realist** and **liberal** theories dealt with in previous chapters; second, **reflectivist** theories that are **post-positivist**; and thirdly **social constructivist** theories that try and bridge the gap between the first two sets.

Rationalist Theories: The Neo-Realist/Neo-Liberal Debate

Much of the ground involved in this debate has been covered in the chapters on realism and liberalism. It is also discussed in later chapters, especially the one on regimes (see Ch. 12). All I need to do here is to make some general points about this debate, so that you can see how it fits into what we have already said about the theories concerned. Essentially, the **neo-neo debate** is the 1980s and 1990s version of the long-standing confrontation between realism and liberalism. Ole Waever (1996) has spoken of this debate as the 'neo-neo synthesis', whereby the two dominant approaches effectively merge to produce a central core of the discipline. As he notes, this synthesis sees neo-realism and neo-

liberal institutionalism focusing on a common set of questions and competing with one another to see which theory can provide the best explanation. It is important to realize that this synthesis would not have been possible without the dominant strand in realism becoming neo-realism (or what Timothy Dunne calls **structural realism II**), and the dominant strand in liberalism becoming **neo-liberal institutionalism**. Indeed throughout the history of international relations theory, realism and liberalism have been portrayed as alternatives, and as incompatible. But in the 1980s, realism became more concerned with how anarchy (rather than human nature) affected the policies of states, and

Steve Smith

liberalism focused more on how international co-operation might make it possible to overcome the negative effects of anarchy. Each approach shared a specific view of how to create knowledge, and, as the 1980s went by, they began to define very similar research programmes. Essentially each looked at the same issue from different sides: that issue was the effect of international institutions on the behaviour of states in a situation of international anarchy. Neo-realists thought that institutions could not outweigh the effects of anarchy; neo-liberals thought that they could.

What resulted from this significant overlap was a common research programme, with adherents of each approach writing articles trying to show that their 'side' was right. This spawned a massive pile of articles, and for many really did seem to announce that international relations theory had finally arrived. After all, these rival arguments about the role of institutions in mitigating anarchy had the advantage that they could be expressed in quantitative terms; so, the main journals were full of very quantitative articles, each referring to both the articles of their own side, but also increasingly to the articles of the other side. In this important sense the two sides became involved in a very detailed debate about state behaviour in a condition of anarchy. What I want to stress here is not simply that the two sides debated but that they focused on the same things to explain. The result was a period of considerable unity in the discipline, with the two main theories looking at the same problems (albeit from opposite sides) and using the same methods to study them. For at least a decade from the mid-1980s this neo-neo debate dominated the mainstream of the discipline.

What was the debate about, then? Well, I have summarized the main lines of it in Box 9.1.

I think that the main features of the debate are really quite straightforward, but let me draw out the two main points. First, neo-realists stress the importance of relative gains whereas neo-liberals stress absolute gains. What does this mean? Well for neo-realists what matters to states is not so much how well they will do out of various outcomes but how well they will do **compared to their rivals**. Neo-liberals, on the other hand, think that leaders will be more interested in their absolute level of gain, preferring the outcome **that gives them most regardless what their competitors receive**. Another way of putting it is that neo-liberals worry about how to increase the size of the cake so that all

> ## Box 9.1. The Main Features of the Neo-realist/Neo-liberal Debate
>
> 1. Neo-realists see anarchy as placing more severe constraints on state behaviour than do neo-liberals.
> 2. Neo-realists see international co-operation as harder to achieve, more difficult to maintain and more dependent on state power than do neo-liberals.
> 3. Neo-liberals stress absolute gains from international co-operation, while neo-realists emphasize relative gains. Neo-realists will ask who will gain more from international co-operation, whereas neo-liberals will be concerned to maximize the total level of gain for all parties
> 4. Neo-realists assume that international anarchy requires states to be preoccupied with issues of security and survival, whereas neo-liberals focus on international political economy. Therefore, each tends to see the prospects for international co-operation differently.
> 5. Neo-realists concentrate on capabilities rather than intentions, whilst neo-liberals look more at intentions and perceptions than at capabilities.
> 6. Neo-realists do not think that international institutions and regimes can mitigate the constraining effects of international anarchy on co-operation, whereas neo-liberals believe that regimes and institutions can facilitate co-operation.
>
> *Source*: Summarized from David Baldwin (1993: 4–8).

can gain bigger slices, whereas neo-realists contend that, no matter how large the cake, each actor will look carefully at the size of their slice compared to their neighbour's. This problem may well be familiar to you if you have brothers or sisters! Quite a lot follows from this: as you will quickly see, if you think that states are going to be most concerned with how they do compared to their rivals then you think of the possibilities of international co-operation rather differently than if you think that only the absolute gains matter. Second, neo-realists think that the effects of international anarchy cannot be mitigated by institutions, whereas, of course, neo-liberals, because they think that increasing the size of the cake is the most important thing, think that institutions can make a difference, perhaps by reducing misunderstanding and by co-operation to make bigger cakes by pooling efforts. Neo-realists tend to think that physical security matters more to states than do neo-liberals, and therefore look more at national security issues, whereas neo-liberals concentrate more on political economy issues.

But note that despite these considerable overlaps, there are some obvious weaknesses in the neo-neo synthesis. Let me first note, following Baldwin (1993), that the two approaches share a lot of assumptions. He notes four: **first** that neither side seems concerned with the issue of the use of force; each seems to downplay its relevance for the modern world, whereas for decades it had tended to be one of the key differences between realism (which thought that force was a natural feature of international politics) and liberalism (which thought that it was not). **Second,** whereas liberals have tended to argue that actors are moral agents and realists have argued that they are power maximizers, neither side in the neo-neo debate seems concerned with morality and each agrees that actors are value maximizers. **Third,** and very importantly for our focus on globalization, whereas earlier rounds of the debate between realists and liberals saw the former stressing the centrality of the state as actor and the latter stressing the role of non-state actors, the neo-neo debate sees both sides agreed that the state is the primary actor in world politics. **Finally,** although historically realists have tended to see conflict as the key feature of world politics and liberals have seen co-operation as more important, in the neo-neo debate each side sees both co-operation and conflict as the focus. In short, neo-realists and neo-liberals share important assumptions which together mean that they agree on much more than liberals and realists have traditionally tended to agree on.

A further weakness is that the neo-neo debate is in fact a **very narrow one**. Although I do not want to minimize the importance of the relative gains/absolute gains debate, it clearly does not cover many of the central features of contemporary world politics. By focusing on states it automatically ignores major features, and by avoiding moral questions it locates itself in a very narrow debate. It looks very much like a debate restricted to the prosperous nations of the West, and takes for granted many of the features of this globalized world that theory should in fact call into question, such as identity, nationalism, economics, religion, and gender. All these kinds of questions are excluded from international relations theory as defined by the neo-neo debate.

Having said all of which, please note that the neo-neo debate remains the central debate in international relations theory, especially in North America; perhaps that is because it so neatly mirrors United States' foreign policy concerns. Moreover, it is very important to note that the neo-neo synthesis means that realism and liberalism are in effect variants of the same theory since they share so much. The debate between the two neo's comprises the **rationalist** side of international relations theory, opposed to those approaches known as **reflectivist** which we will discuss below. By debating with each other, note how the two theories preclude debate with other theories that do not share the same assumptions about how to create knowledge.

Key Points

- The **neo-neo synthesis** is the latest stage of the debate between realism and liberalism, made possible by the forms these theories took in the 1980s.

- By the late 1980s, the **neo-neo synthesis** had developed into a major research programme whereby both neo-realists and neo-liberals focused on the same features of world politics and used the same methods to study them. As such the **neo-neo synthesis** represents one set of theories of world politics, which we can best characterize as **rationalist**; its opponents are **reflectivist** theories.

- According to Baldwin, there are **six main features** of the neo-neo debate; most important of these is the distinction between a focus on **relative** or **absolute** gains.

- It is important to note just how many assumptions neo-realism and neo-liberalism share; critically each sees the **state** as the most important actor, and sees actors as **utility maximizers**.

- The neo-neo synthesis is **a very narrow debate**, one which ignores major features of a globalized world political system. As such is appears to fit very precisely **the foreign policy concerns of the United States**.

Steve Smith

Reflectivist Theories

In this section I want to look at a set of theories that have emerged in the last decade or so, although of course there have been versions of each of them throughout the history of international relations theory. The point to stress is that each has only gained significant attention and adherents in recent years. Many of the other chapters in this book will mention some of these theories and so all I want to do here is to offer you an idea of the main themes of each one. You will find quite a lot of material on feminist theory in Chapter 25, on some aspects of historical sociology and critical theory in Chapter 7, and on normative theory in Chapter 24. What I want to do in this section is to introduce you to the five main areas in which reflectivist work is undertaken. One word of warning: these five areas of work **do not add up to one theory of reflectivism**. That is to say that the various works I will be dealing with cannot easily be simply added together and presented as one theory to rival the **neo-neo synthesis**. This is because there are massive differences between the various reflectivist theories, so much so that they disagree with each other quite significantly over their empirical focus, and, more fundamentally, on how they see knowledge being constructed. In their own way each is **post-positivist**, but they are post-positivist in different ways! **Historical sociology** for example is far nearer to the **neo-neo synthesis** in its view of how to construct knowledge than it is to **post-modernism**. But I am classifying the five approaches as reflectivist because I think they all reject one or more of the key assumptions (either the statism or the positivism) of rationalist accounts. In short, **reflectivist accounts are united more by what they reject than by what they accept**. Since I am going to deal with five theoretical perspectives I am not going to try and summarize all the main points, I couldn't anyway in the space available; instead I am going to try and pick out some representative examples of work in the area, and refer you to the **Guide to Further Reading** for suggestions of where next to look.

Normative Theory

One of the most interesting developments in international theory in the last decade has been the re-emergence of **normative theory** as a focus of international theory. For decades this work was out of fashion as the mainstream of the discipline fell under the spell of **positivism**. Remember that the main claims of positivism included the thought that there was a clear division between 'facts' and 'values'. What this meant was that it was simply not scholarly to spend too much time on debates about what the world should look like. Instead what was preferred was a concern with the way things were. There are two basic problems with this position: first that it is a very narrow definition of what politics is about, since for thousands of years students of politics have been fascinated with the search for 'the good life', with the strengths and weaknesses of specific ways of life and of certain forms of political arrangement. Thus, defining politics as limited to the empirical domain is a very restricting move, and you may well think a political one (i.e. a move designed to support certain, that is the existing, political arrangements); after all if all we can do is to discuss **how** things operate and not **why**, then this naturalizes existing power divisions. So, when I have power the study of politics should be restricted to how it operates; if you raise the question of whether I should have power, then if I can dismiss this as 'value-laden' or 'normative' this immediately de-legitimizes your work.

A second problem with the marginalizing of normative work is the rather serious objection that **all** theories reflect values, the only question being whether or not the values are hidden or not. An example is the one given in the previous paragraph; if I can tell you that things just 'are the way they are', then this clearly represents my views of what the social world is like and which features of it are fixed and which are not. In my view, as the author of this chapter, all theories have values running throughout their analysis, from what they choose to focus on as the 'facts' to be explained, through the methods they use to study these 'facts', down to the policy-prescriptions they suggest. Thus it is not that normative theory is odd, or optional; rather all theories have normative assumptions and implications, but in most cases these are hidden.

In the last decade or so, then, there has been a major resurgence of normative theory about world politics. Probably the best survey of this literature is by Chris Brown (1992). For his view of what

---

Box 9.2. Chris Brown's View of Normative Theory

By normative international relations theory is meant that body of work which addresses the moral dimension of international relations and the wider questions of meaning and interpretation generated by the discipline. At its most basic it addresses the ethical nature of the relations between communities/states, whether in the context of the old agenda, which focused on violence and war, or the new(er) agenda, which mixes these traditional concerns with the modern demand for international distributive justice.

Source: Brown (1992: 3–4).

---

normative theory is see Box 9.2. In his book he sets up his survey by outlining two main normative positions about world politics, **cosmopolitanism** and **communitarianism**. Cosmopolitanism is the view that any normative theory of world politics should focus on either **humanity as a whole** or on **individuals**; on the other hand, communitarianism maintains that the appropriate focus is the **political community** (the state). What this distinction means is that the terms of the debate are whether there is a basis for rights and obligations between states in world politics or whether the bearers of these rights and obligations are individuals, either as individuals, or as a whole, in the sense of meaning humanity. For example do states have the right to hold large nuclear stockpiles to defend themselves if these weapons could potentially wipe out humanity? Or, is it acceptable for some cultures to perform 'female circumcision' because 'that is their way of doing things' or are there rights that the women concerned have that are more important than the rights of the state to make its own decisions? This leads us into complex questions about intervention and human rights, but you can quickly see how massive normative debates might ensue from these and related issues.

In the bulk of his book, Brown uses the distinction between cosmopolitanism and communitarianism to examine three main focal points of normative international theory: the moral value to be assigned to state autonomy, the ethics of inter-state violence (**Just War Theory**), and the issue of international justice with specific regard to the obligations that the richer states of the world have to poorer countries. As you can imagine, cosmopolitans and communitarians have rather dif-

ferent views on these issues. To take the first question, cosmopolitanism clearly rejects the notion that states have a right to autonomy if that autonomy allows the state to undertake behaviour that conflicts with the moral rights of either humanity as a whole or of individuals; communitarianism on the other hand opposes any restrictions on autonomy that do not arise out of the community itself. Similarly, cosmopolitanists and communitarians will differ over when it is right for states to intervene in the affairs of others and over how we should evaluate calls for a more just distribution of economic resources. Particularly influential theorists on the first question have been Beitz (1979), Frost (1996), and Nardin (1983); for the second question the main writer has been Walzer (1977); and for the third question the key writers have been Rawls (1971) and Barry (1989).

Key Points

- **Normative theory** was out of fashion for decades because of the dominance of **positivism**, which portrayed it as 'value-laden' and 'unscientific'.

- In the last decade or so there has been a resurgence of interest in normative theory thereby connecting international theory with the main debates that have been going on in the discipline of politics. It is now more widely accepted that **all theories have normative assumptions either explicitly or implicitly**.

- The key distinction in normative theory is between **cosmopolitanism** and **communitarianism**. The former sees the bearers of rights and obligations as individuals, the latter sees them as being the state.

- **Chris Brown** identifies three main areas of debate in contemporary normative theory: the **autonomy of the state**, the **ethics of the use of force**, and **international justice**.

Feminist Theory

Chapter 25 will deal in some detail with the main varieties of feminist theory, and I do not wish to repeat that summary here. What I want to do instead is to give you a simple overview of the four main types of feminist theory before spending most time looking at one variant of it. I want to be clear, however, that the variant I am going to spend most time on, **feminist standpoint theory,** is not necessarily my 'preferred' variant of feminism. I look at it simply because Chapter 25, on gender, does a comprehensive job of showing the great strength of one of the other variants, **liberal feminism;** the section below on **post-modernism** overlaps with what I would want to say about a third variant, **feminist post-modernism;** and the final variant, **socialist/Marxist feminism** has much in common with some of the material on **world-system theory** discussed in Chapter 7.

Feminist work on world politics has only become common since the mid-1980s. It originally developed in work on the politics of development and in peace research, but by the late 1980s a first wave of feminism, **liberal feminism**, was posing the question of 'where were the women in world politics'. They were certainly not written about in the main texts, such that they appeared invisible. Then writers such as Cynthia Enloe (1989; 1993) began to show just how involved were women in world politics. It was not that they were not there but that they in fact played central roles, either as cheap factory labour, as prostitutes around military bases, or as the wives of diplomats. The point is that the conventional picture painted by the traditional international theory deemed these activities as less important than the actions of statesmen (sic). Enloe was intent on showing just how critically important were the activities of women to the functioning of the international economic and political systems. Thus, liberal feminism, as Zalewski points out (1993*b*: 116) is the 'add women and stir' version of feminism. Accordingly, liberal feminists look at the ways in which women are excluded from power and from playing a full part in political activity, instead being restricted to roles critically important for the functioning of things but which are not usually deemed to be important for theories of world politics. Fundamentally, liberal feminists want the same rights and opportunities that are available to men, extended to women.

A second strand of feminist theory is **socialist/Marxist feminism.** As the name implies the influence here is Marxism, with its insistence on the role of material, primarily economic, forces in determining the lives of women. For Marxist feminism, the cause of women's inequality is to be found in the capitalist system; overthrowing capi-

talism is the necessary route for the achievement of the equal treatment of women. Socialist feminism, noting that the oppression of women occurred in pre-capitalist societies, and continues in socialist societies, differs from Marxist feminism in that it introduces a second central material cause in determining women's unequal treatment, namely the patriarchal system of male dominance. For Marxist feminists, then, capitalism is the primary oppressor, for socialist feminists it is capitalism plus patriarchy. For socialist/Marxist feminists, then, the focus of a theory of world politics would be on the patterns by which the world capitalist system and the patriarchal system of power lead to women being systematically disadvantaged compared to men. As you can well imagine, this approach is especially insightful when it comes to looking at the nature of the world economy and the differential advantages and disadvantages of it that apply to women.

The third variant of feminist theory I want to mention is **post-modernist** feminism. As the name implies this is a series of theoretical works that bring together post-modern work on identity with a focus on gender. Here, in distinction to other variants of feminism, the concern is with gender, and not women. Gender refers to the social construction of differences between men and women, and for post-modern feminists the key issue is what kind of social roles for men and women are constructed by the structures and processes of world politics. In other words, what kind of 'men' are required to serve in armies? Note the recent fierce debates about both women and homosexual men and women serving in the armed forces. How, to put it simply, has world politics led to certain kinds of 'men' and 'women' being produced? This is a radical question, one which we cannot go into here, but although it seems so very far removed from the main theories of world politics, and therefore you might be tempted to ignore it, please reflect on the thought that what you may be as a man or a woman may not be 'natural'; instead it may be that what it means to be a a man or woman in your society when you read this is very different to its meaning for other readers.

The final version of feminist theory I want to mention, and in fact the version I want to highlight, is **standpoint feminism** (Zalewski 1993*a*). This variant developed out of **radical** feminism. which basically claims that the world has been dominated by men and by their ideas. Accordingly, radical feminists proposed that the experiences of women had been ignored, except where they have been unfavourably compared to male experiences. The aim then is to re-describe reality according to a female view. In the work of influential feminist theorists such as Sandra Harding (1986), this approach gets developed into standpoint feminism, which is an attempt to develop a female version of reality. Since knowledge to date has been male knowledge, the result has been only a partial understanding of the world. Standpoint feminists want to improve on that understanding by incorporating female perspectives. This is a controversial move in feminism since it assumes that there is such a thing as **a** feminist view of the world (as distinct from a variety of female views according to their social/ economic/cultural/sexual locations). It also runs the risk of essentializing and fixing the views and nature of women, by saying that **this** is how women see the world. None the less despite these dangers of standpoint feminism, it has been very influential in showing just how male-dominated are the main theories of world politics. For an extremely convincing example of how standpoint feminists look at world politics, see Box 9.3, which is J. Ann Tickner's reformulation of the famous 'Six Principles of Political Realism' developed by the 'godfather' of realism, Hans Morgenthau. In each case you will see how Tickner shows how the seemingly 'objective' rules of Morgenthau in fact reflect male values and definitions of reality, rather than female ones. You will then see how she reformulates these same rules according to female rather than male characteristics.

Key Points

- There are four main variants of feminist theory, **liberal**, **Marxist/socialist**, **post-modern**, and **standpoint feminisms**.

- **Liberal** feminism looks at the roles women play in world politics and asks why they are marginalized. It wants the same opportunities afforded to women as are afforded to men.

- **Marxist/socialist** feminists focus on the **international capitalist system**. Marxist feminists see the oppression of women as a bi-product of capitalism, whereas socialist feminists see both capitalism and **patriarchy** as the structures to be

overcome if women are to have any hope of equality.

- **Post-modernist** feminists are concerned with gender as opposed to the position of women as such. They enquire into the ways in which **masculinity** and **femininity** get constructed, and are especially interested in how world politics constructs certain types of 'men' and women'.

- **Standpoint** feminists, such as **J. Ann Tickner** want to correct the male dominance of our knowledge of the world. Tickner does this by re-describing the six 'objective' principles of international politics developed by **Hans Morgenthau** according to a female version of the world.

Critical Theory

Critical theory has a long intellectual tradition, being a development of Marxist thought dating from at least the 1920s when it developed out of the work of the **Frankfurt School**. It has significant overlaps with **World System Theory**, but has become particularly influential in international theory since the early 1980s. The most influential figures have been Andrew Linklater (1990) and Robert Cox (1996).

I am going to base my comments on critical theory on a very good survey of **critical theory** by Mark Hoffman (1987). Hoffman notes that it was first articulated in detail by Max Horkheimer in a 1937 article. Horkheimer was concerned to change society and he thought that the theories to achieve this could not be developed in the way that natural science develops theories. Social scientists could not be like natural scientists in the sense of being independent from and disinterested in their subject matter; they were part of the society they were studying In a major contribution to thinking about the nature of the social sciences, Horkheimer argued that there was a close connection between knowledge and power. He thought that in the social sciences the most important forces for change were social forces, and not some 'independent' logic of the things being explained. At this point, Horkheimer differentiates between 'traditional' and 'critical' theory: traditional theory sees the world as a set of facts waiting to be discovered through the use of science. We have seen this view

---

Box 9.3. J. Ann Tickner's Reformulation of Hans Morgenthau's Principles of Political Realism

Morgenthau's Six Principles

1. Politics, like society in general, is governed by objective laws that have their roots in human nature which is unchanging: therefore it is possible to develop a rational theory that reflects these objective laws.

2. The main signpost of political realism is the concept of interest defined in terms of power which infuses rational order into the subject matter of politics, and thus makes the theoretical understanding of politics possible. Political realism stresses the rational, objective and unemotional.

3. Realism assumes that interest defined as power is an objective category which is universally valid but not with a meaning that is fixed once and for all. Power is the control of man over man.

4. Political realism is aware of the moral significance of political action. It is also aware of the tension between the moral command and the requirements of successful political action.

5. Political realism refuses to identify the moral aspirations of a particular nation with the moral laws that govern the universe. It is the concept of interest defined in terms of power that saves us from moral excess and political folly.

6. The political realist maintains the autonomy of the political sphere. He asks 'How does this policy affect the power of the nation?' Political realism is based on a pluralistic conception of human nature. A man who is nothing but 'political man' would be a beast, for he would be completely lacking in moral restraints. But, in order to develop an autonomous theory of political behaviour, 'political man' must be abstracted from other aspects of human nature.

Tickner's Six Principles

1. A feminist perspective believes that objectivity, as it is culturally defined, is associated with masculinity. Therefore supposedly 'objective' laws of human nature are based on a partial masculine view of human nature. Human nature is both masculine and feminine: it contains elements of social reproduction and development as well as political domination. Dynamic objectivity offers us a more connected view of objectivity with less potential for domination.

2. A feminist perspective believes that the national interest is multi-dimensional and contextually contingent. Therefore it cannot be defined solely in terms of power. In the contemporary world the national interest demands co-operative rather than zero-sum solutions to a set of interdependent global problems which include nuclear war, economic well-being, and environmental degradation.

3. Power cannot be infused with meaning that is universally valid. Power as domination and control privileges masculinity and ignores the possibility of collective empowerment, another aspect of power often associated with femininity.

4. A feminist perspective rejects the possibility of separating moral command from political action. All political action has moral significance. The realist agenda for maximizing order through power and control prioritizes the moral command of order over those of justice and the satisfaction of basic needs necessary to ensure social reproduction.

5. While recognizing that the moral aspirations of particular nations cannot be equated with universal moral principles, a feminist perspective seeks to find common moral elements in human aspirations which could become the basis for de-escalating international conflict and building international community.

6. A feminist perspective denies the validity of the autonomy of the political. Since autonomy is associated with masculinity in Western culture, disciplinary efforts to construct a world view which does not rest on a pluralistic conception of human nature are partial and masculine. Building boundaries around a narrowly defined political realm defines political in a way that excludes the concerns and contributions of women.

Source: Tickner (1988: 430–1, 437–8).

---

earlier when we discussed **positivism**, and Horkheimer's target is indeed the application of positivism to the social sciences. He argued that traditional theorists were wrong to argue that the 'fact' waiting to be discovered could be perceived independently of the social framework in which perception occurs. But the situation was worse than that because Horkheimer argued that traditional theory encouraged the increasing manipulation of human lives. It saw the social world as an area for control and domination, just like nature, and therefore was indifferent to the possibilities of human emancipation.

In its place Horkheimer proposed the adoption of **critical theory**. As Hoffman notes, critical theory did not see facts in the same way as did traditional theory. For critical theorists, facts are the products of specific social and historical frameworks. Realizing that theories are embedded in these frameworks allows critical theorists to reflect on the interests served by any particular theory. The explicit aim of critical theory is to advance human emancipation, and this means that theory is openly **normative**, with a role to play in political debate. This of course is the opposite of the view of theory proposed by traditional or **positivist** theory, in which theory is meant to be neutral and concerned only with uncovering pre-existing facts or regularities in an independent external world. In the postwar period the leading exponent of critical theory has been Jürgen Habermas, whose most influential claim has been his notion of the **ideal speech situation**, whereby individuals would exhibit **communicative competence** to lead to a rational consensus in political debate. Such a situation would lead to the development of an emancipatory politics. This is often known as a situation of **discourse ethics**.

In international theory the first major critical theory contribution was in 1981 by **Robert Cox** (see Cox in his 1996: Ch. 6). Cox's article was enormously influential because it was written in part as an attack on the main assumptions of **neo-realism**, which he criticizes most effectively because of its hidden **normative** commitments. Rather than being an 'objective' theory, neo-realism is exposed by Cox as having a series of views about what states should pursue in their foreign policies, namely neo-realist rationality. It is also revealed as a partial theory which defines the state in a specific (and non-economic) way, and rules out of its purview a set of other political relations. In short, Cox argues that neo-realism typifies what Horkheimer meant by traditional theory: Cox calls it **problem-solving theory**, which 'takes the world as it finds it, with the prevailing social and power relationships and the institutions into which they are organized, as the given framework for action. The general aim of problem solving is to make these relationships and institutions work smoothly by dealing effectively with particular sources of trouble . . . the general pattern of institutions and relationships is not called into question' (1996: 88). The effect then is to **reify** and **legitimize** the existing order. Problem-solving theory therefore works to make the existing distribution of power seem natural. But, Cox points out, in a famous quote, despite this, '**Theory is always *for* someone and *for* some purpose**' (1996: 87). Theories see the world from specific social and political positions and are not independent. There

is, he says, '**no such thing as theory in itself, divorced from a standpoint in time and space.** When any theory so represents itself, it is the more important to examine it as ideology, and to lay bare its **concealed** perspective' (1996: 87).

In contrast, Cox proposes that international theory should be **critical theory**. Hoffman has very clearly summarized Cox's ideas about critical theory, and they are reprinted in Box 9.4. Particularly interesting is the view of reality (ontology) adopted by critical theorists. Echoing the themes of many of the other **reflectivist** approaches, Cox notes that social structures are **intersubjective**, meaning that they are socially constructed. Thus although they do not have the same status for positivists as things like trees and buildings, the structures for a critical theorist have very similar effects. Therefore Cox focuses on how the 'givens' of traditional theory, such as 'individuals' or 'states' are produced by certain historical and social forces. Thus a state is not, *contra* neo-realism, always a state; states differ enormously throughout history and they are very differerent things at different times. For Cox, then, the state is not the given of international theory that neo-realism sees it as. Instead the state emerges out of social forces, as do other social structures. Cox is particularly interested in how these social structures can be transcended and overcome, hence his focus on the nature of **hegemony**.

Since Cox's introduction of critical theory into international theory, there have been a number of very significant contributions from other critical theorists. I am not going to summarize these, since I do not have the space, but two particularly interesting examples are the contributions of Andrew Linklater (1990) and the development of **critical security studies**, based on the work of writers such as Ken Booth (1991) and Richard Wyn Jones (1995). For a good summary of the work of these, and other, critical theorists see Devetak (1996*a*). Central to all these writers is a concern with how the present order has evolved. Thus critical theory is not limited to an examination of the inter-state system but, rather, focuses on all the main examples of power and domination. This makes it particularly suited for contemporary world politics because it does not treat the state as the 'natural' actor and instead is concerned with all the features of domination in a globalized world.

Box 9.4. Robert Cox's Critical Theory

1. It stands apart from the prevailing order of the world and asks how that order came about; it is a reflective appraisal of the framework that problem-solving takes as given.

2. It contemplates the social and political complex as a whole and seeks to understand the process of change within both the whole and its parts.

3. It entails a theory of history, understanding history as a process of continuous change and transformation.

4. It questions the origins and legitimacy of social and political institutions and how and whether they are changing; it seeks to determine what elements are universal to world order and what elements are historically contingent.

5. It contains problem-solving theory and has a concern with both technical and practical cognitive knowledge interests and constantly adjusts its concepts in light of the changing subject it seeks to understand.

6. It contains a normative, utopian element in favour of a social and political order different from the prevailing order that also recognizes the constraints placed on possible alternative world order by historical processes: the potential for transformation exists within the prevailing order but it is also constrained by the historical forces that created that order.

7. It is a guide for strategic action, for bringing about an alternative order.

Source: Hoffman (1987: 237–8).

Key Points

- **Critical theory** has its roots in Marxism, and developed out of the **Frankfurt School** in the 1920s. Its most influential proponent since 1945 has been **Jürgen Habermas**.

- In an influential 1937 article one of the founders of critical theory, **Max Horkheimer**, distinguished between **traditional** and **critical** theory.

- **Robert Cox** writes of the difference between **problem-solving** and **critical** theory. The former takes the world as given and reifies existing distributions of power. The latter enquires into how the current distribution of power came into existence.

- Cox argues that **theory is always for someone and for some purpose**, and that **there is no such thing as theory in itself**.

- Critical theory sees **social structures as real in their effects**, whereas they would not be seen as real by positivism since they can not be directly observed.

- There are many other contributions of critical theory; particularly important are the works of **Linklater** and of those working in the area of **critical security studies**.

Historical Sociology

Just as critical theory problematizes the state and refuses to see it as some kind of given in world politics, so does **historical sociology**. Indeed the main theme of historical sociology is an interest in the ways in which societies develop through history. In this sense it is concerned with the underlying structures that shape the institutions and organizations that human society is arranged into. Historical sociology has a long history. Dennis Smith, in his excellent introduction to the approach, argues that we are currently on the crest of the second wave of historical sociology, the first wave starting in the middle of the eighteenth century and running until the 1920s when interest in the approach declined. The first wave was a response to the great events of the eighteenth century, such as the American and French revolutions as well as the processes of industrialization and nation-building. The second wave has been of particular interest to international theory, because the key writers, Michael Mann, Theda Skocpol, Immanuel Wallerstein, Charles Tilly, and John Hall, have all to a greater or lesser extent focused their explanations of the development of societies on the relationship between the domestic and the international. Tilly has neatly summarized this interest with the statement that 'states made war but war made the state'. In short, the central feature of historical sociology has been an interest in how the structures that we take for granted (as 'natural') are the products of a set of complex social processes.

Thus, whereas **neo-realism** takes the state as a given, historical sociology asks how specific kinds of states have been produced by the various forces at work in domestic and international societies. I am going to look at two examples of this, one by **Charles Tilly**, the other by **Michael Mann**. The point to keep in mind is that these writers show just how complex is the state as an organization, thereby undermining the rather simple view of the state found in neo-realist writings. Also note that historical sociologists fundamentally undermine the thought that a state is a state is a state. States differ and they are not functionally similar as neo-realism portrays them as being. Furthermore, historical sociologists show that there can be no simple distinction between international and domestic societies. They are inevitably interlinked and therefore it is inaccurate to claim, as does neo-realism, that they can be separated. There is no such thing as 'an international system' that is self-contained and thereby able to exert decisive influence on the behaviour of states; but of course this is exactly what Waltz wants to argue. Finally, note that historical sociology shows that the state is created by international and domestic forces, and that the international is itself a determinant of the nature of the state; that thought looks particularly relevant to the debate on globalization, since, as we discussed in the Introduction, one of its dominant themes is that the international economic system places demands on states such that only certain kinds of states can prosper.

Charles Tilly's work is particularly interesting because it is a clear example of how complex an entity is the state. In his 1990 book, *Coercion, Capital and European States, AD 900–1990*, Tilly poses the following main question: 'What accounts for the great variation over time and space in the kinds of states that have prevailed in Europe since AD 990, and why did European states eventually converge on different variants of the national state?' (1990: 5). The answer that he gives is that the national state eventually dominated because of its role in fighting wars. Distinguishing between capital-intensive and coercion-intensive regimes (or economic power-based and military power-based systems), Tilly notes that three types of states resulted from the combinations of these forms of power, tribute-making empires, systems of fragmented sovereignty (city-states), and national states. These states were the result of the different class structures that resulted from the concentrations of capital and coercion. Broadly speaking, coercion-intensive regimes had fewer cities and more agricultural class systems than did capital-intensive systems, which led to the development of classes representing commercial and trading interests. Where capital accumulation was high relative to the ability of the state to coerce its citizens, then city-states developed; on the other hand where

there was coercion but not capital accumulation, then tribute-making empires developed. As D. Smith notes (1991: 83), each of these is a form of indirect rule, requiring the ruler to rely on the co-operation of relatively autonomous local powers. But with the rise in the scale of war, the result was that national states started to acquire a decisive advantage over the other kinds of state organizations. This was because national states could afford large armies and could respond to the demands of the classes representing both agricultural and commercial interests.

Through about a 350-year period starting around 1500, national states became the norm as they were the only states that could afford the military means to fight the kind of large-scale wars that were occurring. States, in other words, became transformed by war; Tilly notes that the three types of states noted above all converged on one version of the state, so now that is seen as the norm. Yet, in contrast to neo-realism, Tilly notes that the state has not been of one form throughout its history. His work shows how different types of states have existed throughout history, all with different combinations of class structures and modes of operating. And, crucially, **it is war that explains the convergence of these types of states into the national state form**. War plays this central role because it is through preparing for war that states gain their powers as they have to build up an infrastructure of taxation, supply, and administration. The national state thus acquires more and more power over its population by its involvement in war, and therefore can dominate other state forms because they are more efficient than either tribute-gathering empires or city-states in this process.

The second example of historical sociology is the work of Michael Mann. Mann is involved in a four-volume study of the sources of social power dealing with the whole of human history! (The first two volumes have appeared dealing with the period up to 1914, see his (1986) and (1993).) This is an enormously ambitious project, and is aimed at showing just how states have taken the forms that they have. In this sense it is similar to the work of Tilly, but the major innovation of Mann's work is that he has developed a sophisticated account of the forms of power that combine to form certain types of states. This is his IEMP model (standing for Ideological, Economic, Military, and Political forms of power). Given that the first two volumes come to nearly 1,400 pages, I am not going to summarize his work!

Box 9.5. Mann's IEMP Model of Power Organization

Mann differentiates between three aspects of power:

1. Between distributive power and collective power, where distributive power is the power of *a* over *b* (for *a* to acquire more distributive power, *b* must lose some), and collective power is the joint power of actors (where *a* and *b* can co-operate to exploit nature or another actor, *c*).

2. Power may be extensive or intensive. Extensive power can organize large numbers of people over far-flung territories. Intensive power mobilizes a high level of commitment from participants.

3. Power may be authoritative or diffused. Authoritative power comprises willed commands by an actor and conscious obedience by subordinates. It is found most typically in military and political power organizations. Diffused power is not directly commanded; it spreads in a relatively spontaneous, unconscious, and decentred way. People are constrained to act in different ways but not by command of any particular person or organization. Diffused power is found most typically in ideological and economic power organizations.

Mann argues that the most effective exercise of power combines all these three elements. He argues that there are four sources of social power which together may determine the overall structure of societies. The four are

1. Ideological power derives from the human need to find ultimate meaning in life, to share norms and values, and to participate in aesthetic and ritual practices. Control over ideology brings general social power.

2. Economic power derives from the need to extract, transform, distribute, and consume the resources of nature. It is peculiarly powerful because it combines intensive co-operation with extensive circuits of distribution, exchange, and consumption. This provides a stable blend of intensive and extensive power and normally of authoritative and diffused power.

3. Military power is the social organization of physical force. It derives from the necessity of organized defence and the utility of aggression. Military power has both intensive and extensive aspects, and it can also organize people over large areas. Those who monopolize it can wield a degree of general social power.

4. Political power derives from the usefulness of territorial and centralized regulation. Political power means state power. It is essentially authoritative, commanded, and willed from a centre.

The struggle to control ideological, economic, military, and political power organizations provides the central drama of social development. Societies are structured primarily by entwined ideological, economic, military, and political power.

Source: Mann (1993: 6–10).

Suffice it to say that his painstaking study of the ways in which the various forms of power have combined in specific historical circumstances constitutes a major contribution to our thinking of how states have come into existence and about how they have related to the international political system. What I have done is to summarize his argument in Box 9.5.

I hope that this brief summary of historical sociology gives you an idea of its potential to shed light on how the state has taken the form that it has throughout history. It should make you think that the version of the state presented by **neo-realism** is very simple, but note also that there is a surprising overlap between the focus of neo-realism on war and the focus of historical sociology on how states, classes, and war interact.

Key Points

- **Historical sociology** has a long history, having been a subject of study for several centuries. Its central focus is with **how societies develop the forms that they do.**

- Contemporary historical sociology is concerned above all with how the state has developed since the Middle Ages. It is basically a study of the **interactions between states, classes, capitalism, and war.**

- **Charles Tilly** looks at how the three main kinds of state forms that existed at the end of the Middle Ages eventually converged on one form, namely the **national state**. He argues that the decisive reason was the ability of the national state to **fight wars**.

- **Michael Mann** has developed a powerful model of the sources of state power, known as the **IEMP Model**. This helps him show how the various forms of state have taken the forms that they have.

- **Historical sociology** undercuts **neo-realism** because it shows that the state is not one functionally similar organization, but instead has altered over time. But, like neo-realism, it too is interested in war and therefore the two approaches have quite a bit in common.

Post-Modernism

Post-modernism has been a particularly influential theoretical development throughout all the social sciences in the last twenty years. It reached international theory in the mid-1980s, but could only have been said to have arrived in the last few years. It is fair to say that it is probably as popular a theoretical approach as any of the **reflectivist** theories discussed in this chapter. As Richard Devetak comments in his extremely useful summary of post-modernism, part of the difficulty is defining precisely what post-modernism is (1996b: 179). Frankly, there is far more to debate on this question of defining post-modernism than there is space for in this entire book! One useful definition is by Jean-Francois Lyotard, who writes that: 'Simplifying to the extreme, I define *postmodern* as incredulity towards metanarratives' (1984: xxiv). The key word here is 'metanarrative', by which is meant a theory that claims clear foundations for making knowledge-claims (to use the jargon, it involves a foundational epistemology). What he means by this is that post-modernism is essentially concerned with deconstructing, and distrusting any account of human life that claims to have direct access to 'the truth'. Thus, Freudian psychoanalysis, Marxism, standpoint feminism, for example, are all deemed suspect because they claim to have uncovered some truth about the world. Post-modernists are also unhappy with critical theory, since they believe that it too is just another metanarrative.

Devetak helpfully analyses the key themes of post-modernism. I will look at two of the themes he discusses, the power–knowledge relationship, and the textual strategies used by post-modernists. Post-modern work on the **power–knowledge** relationship has been most influenced by the works of **Michel Foucault**. Central to Foucault's work has been a concern with the relationship between power and knowledge; note that this is also a key concern of **critical theorists**. Foucault is opposed to the notion (dominant in **rationalist** theories) that knowledge is immune from the workings of power. As noted above, this is a key assumption of **positivism**. Instead, Foucault argues that power in fact **produces knowledge**. All power requires knowledge and all knowledge relies on and reinforces existing power relations. Thus there is no such thing as 'truth', existing outside of power. To paraphrase Foucault, how can history have a truth if truth has a history? Truth is not something external to social settings, but is instead part of them. Accordingly, post-modernists want to look at what power relations are supported by 'truths' and knowledge-practices. Post-modern international theorists have used this insight to examine the 'truths' of international relations theory to see how the concepts and knowledge-claims that dominate the discipline in fact are highly contingent on specific power relations. Two recent examples are the work of Cynthia Weber (1995) and Jens Bartelson (1995) on the concept of sovereignty. In both cases the **concept** of sovereignty is revealed to be both historically variable (despite the attempts of mainstream scholars to imbue it artificially with a fixed meaning) and to be itself caught up in the **practice** of sovereignty by producing the discourse about it.

How do post-modernists study history in the light of this relationship between power and knowledge? Foucault's answer is the approach known as **genealogy**. In Box 9.6, I summarize a very good summary of this approach by Richard Ashley (1987), which gives you the main themes of a genealogical approach.

The central message of genealogy is that there is no such thing as truth, only regimes of truth. These reflect the ways in which through history both power and truth develop together in a mutually sustaining relationship. What this means is that statements about the social world are only 'true' within specific **discourses**. Accordingly, post-modernism is concerned with how some discourses and therefore some truths dominate others. Here, of course is exactly where power comes in. It is for this reason that post-modernists are opposed to any metanarratives, since they imply that there are conditions for establishing the truth or falsity of knowledge-claims that are not the product of any discourse, and thereby not the products of power.

Devetak's second theme of post-modernism concerns the **textual strategies** it uses. This is very

Box 9.6. Foucault's Notion of Genealogy

First, adopting a genealogical attitude involves a radical shift in one's analytical focus. It involves a shift away from an interest in uncovering the structures of history and towards an interest in understanding the movement and clashes of historical practices that would impose or resist structure. . . . with this shift . . . social enquiry is increasingly disposed to find its focus in the posing of 'how' questions, not 'what' questions. How . . . are structures of history produced, differentiated, reified, and transformed? How . . . are fields of practice pried open, bounded and secured? How . . . are regions of silence established?

Second, having refused any notion of universal truth or deep identities transcending differences, a genealogical attitude is disposed to comprehend all history, including the production of order, in terms of the endless power political clash of multiple wills. Only a single drama is ever staged in this non-place, the endlessly repeated play of dominations. Practices . . . are to be understood to contain their own strategies, their own political technologies . . . for the disciplining of plural historical practices in the production of historical modes of domination.

Third, a genealogical attitude disposes one to be especially attentive to the historical emergence, bounding, conquest, and administration of social spaces . . . one might think, for example, of divisions of territory and populations among nation states . . . one might also think of the separation of spheres of politics and economics, the distinction between high and low politics, the differentiation of public and private spaces, the line of demarcation between domestic and international, the disciplinary division between science and philosophy, the boundary between the social and the natural, or the separation of the normal and legitimate from the abnor-

mal and criminal . . . a genealogical posture entails a readiness to approach a field of practice historically, as an historically emergent and always contested product of multiple practices . . . as such, a field of practice . . . is seen as a field of clashes, a battlefield . . . one is supposed to look for the strategies, techniques, and rituals of power by which multiple themes, concepts, narratives, and practices are excluded, silenced, dispersed, recombined, or given new or reverse emphases, thereby to privilege some elements over others, impose boundaries, and discipline practice in a manner producing just this normalised division of practical space.

Fourth, what goes for the production and disciplining of social space goes also for the production and disciplining of subjects. From a genealogical standpoint there are no subjects, no fully formed identical egos, having an existence prior to practice and then implicated in power political struggles. Like fields of practice, subjects emerge in history . . . as such, the subject is itself a site of political power contest and ceaselessly so.

Fifth, a genealogical posture does not sustain an interest in those noble enterprises—such as philosophy, religion, positive social science, or the utopian political crusade—that would embark on searches for the hidden essences, the universal truths, the profound insights into the secret identity that transcends difference . . . from a genealogical standpoint . . . they are instead resituated right on the surface of political life. They are seen as political practice intimately engaged in the interpretation, production, and normalisation of modes of imposed order, modes of domination. They are seen as means by which practices are disciplined and domination advances in history.

Source: Ashley (1987: 409–11).

complicated, but the main claim is that, following **Derrida**, the very way in which we construct the social world is textual. For Derrida (1976) the world is constituted like a text in the sense that interpreting the world reflects the concepts and structures of language, what he terms the textual interplay at work. Derrida has two main ways of exposing these textual interplays, **deconstruction** and **double reading**. Deconstruction is based on the idea that seemingly stable and natural concepts and relations within language are in fact artificial constructs, arranged hierarchically in that in the case of opposites in language one term is always privileged over the other. Therefore, deconstruction is a way of showing how all theories and discourses rely on artificial stabilities produced by the use of seemingly objective and natural oppositions in language

(rich/poor, good/bad, powerful/powerless, right/wrong). Double reading is Derrida's way of showing how these stabilizations operate by subjecting the text to two readings, the first is a repetition of the dominant reading to show how it achieves its coherence, the second points to the internal tensions within a text that result from the use of seemingly natural stabilizations. The aim is not to come to a 'correct' or even 'one' reading of a text, but instead to show how there is always more than one reading of any text. In international theory, **Richard Ashley** (1988) has performed exactly such a double reading of the concept of anarchy by providing first a reading of the anarchy problematique according to the traditional literature, and then a second reading that shows how the seemingly natural opposition between anarchy and sovereignty that does the work in the first reading is in fact a false opposition. By radically disrupting the first reading Ashley shows just how arbitrary is the 'truth' of the traditional assumptions made about anarchy and the kind of logic of state action that it requires. In a similar move **Rob Walker** (1993) looks at the construction of the tradition of **realism** and shows how this is only possible by ignoring the major nuances and complexities within the thoughts of the key thinkers of this tradition, such as Machiavelli and Hobbes.

As you can imagine, such a theoretical position has been very controversial in the literature. Many members of the mainstream think that post-modernism has nothing to say about the 'real' world, and that it is merely playing with words. However, it seems clear to me that post-modernism is in fact taking apart the very concepts and methods of our thinking. It helps us think about the conditions under which we are able to theorize about world politics; and to many, post-modernism is the most appropriate theory for a globalized world.

Key Points

- **Lyotard** defines **post-modernism** as **incredulity towards metanarratives**, meaning that it denies the possibility of foundations for establishing the truth of statements existing outside of a **discourse**.

- **Foucault** focuses on the **power–knowledge relationship** which sees the two as mutually constituted. It implies that there can be no truth outside of **regimes of truth**. How can history have a truth if truth has a history?

- **Foucault** proposes a **genealogical** approach to look at history, and this approach uncovers how certain regimes of truth have dominated others.

- **Derrida** argues that the world is like a text in that it cannot simply be grasped, but has to be interpreted. He looks at how texts are constructed, and proposes two main tools to enable us to see how arbitrary are the seemingly 'natural' oppositions of language. These are **deconstruction** and **double reading**.

- **Post-modern** approaches are attacked by the mainstream for being too theoretical and not enough concerned with the 'real' world; but post-modernists reply that in the social world there is no such thing as the 'real' world in the sense of a reality that is not interpreted by us.

Bridging the Gap: Social Constructivism

This development in international relations theory promises much, since its great appeal is that it sits precisely at the intersection between the two sets of approaches noted above, that is **between both rationalist and reflectivist approaches**. It does this because it deals with the same features of world politics as are central to both the **neo-realist** and the **neo-liberal** components of **rationalism**, and yet is centrally concerned with both the meanings actors give to their actions and the identity of these actors, each of which is a central theme of **reflectivist** approaches. The three main proponents of this view are Kratochwil (1989), Onuf (1989) and Wendt (1992). I am going to concentrate on Wendt simply because his work has been enormously influential in developing the **social constructivist** position. His 1992 article 'Anarchy is what states

make of it: the social construction of power politics' has probably been cited in the professional literature more than any other article in the last decade. Its title also neatly sums up exactly what is the central claim of social constructivism. Let me be absolutely clear at the outset, I do not think that social constructivism can deliver what it claims, but equally I am sure that it promises to be one of the most important theoretical developments of recent decades; the reason is that if it could deliver what it promises then it would be the dominant theory in the discipline, since it could relate to all other approaches on their own terms, whereas at the moment there is virtually no contact between **rationalist** and **reflectivist** theories since they do not share the same view of how to build knowledge. If Wendt is right then social costructivists can debate the effects of anarchy and the relative/ absolute gains issue with the **rationalists**, and at the same time discuss with post-modernists, feminists, historical sociologists, critical theorists, and normative theorists the meanings attached to action and, crucially, the processes by which the identities of the actors are formed.

Before we get into Wendt's argument, look at the contents of Box 9.7, which is a quote from the then President of the International Studies Association (ISA, which is the main, US-based, professional organization for teachers and researchers of international relations), Robert Keohane. The quote comes from his presidential address to the ISA in 1988.

Box 9.7. Robert Keohane's View of the Rationalist–Reflectivist Debate

My chief argument in this essay is that students of international institutions should direct their attention to the relative merits of two approaches, the rationalistic, and the reflective. Until we understand the strengths and weaknesses of each, we will be unable to design research strategies that are sufficiently multi-faceted to encompass our subject-matter, and our empirical work will suffer accordingly . . . indeed, the greatest weakness of the reflective school lies not in deficiencies in their critical arguments but in the lack of a clear reflective research program that could be employed by students of world politics. Waltzian neo-realism has such a research program; so does neo-liberal institutionalism . . . until the reflective scholars or others sympathetic to their arguments have delineated such a research program and shown in particular studies that it can illuminate important issues of world politics they will remain on the margins of the field, largely invisible to the preponderance of empirical researchers . . . reflective approaches are less well specified as theories: their advocates have been more adept at pointing out what is omitted in rationalistic theory than in developing theories of their own with *a priori* content. Supporters of this research program need to develop testable theories, and to be explicit about their scope . . . above all, students of world politics who are sympathetic to this position need to carry out systematic empirical investigations, guided by their ideas. Without such detailed studies, it will be impossible to evaluate their research program. Eventually, we may hope for a synthesis between the rationalistic and reflective approaches.

Source: Keohane (1989: 161, 173–4).

I hope that you can see what Keohane is saying: he is arguing that unless the reflectivists can develop 'testable hypotheses' then they will be marginalized in the study of world politics. The central thing to note is that this challenge is one made according to the rules for generating knowledge that rationalists accept **but that reflectivists do not accept**. This soon can get very complicated, but the straightforward version of it is that the challenge issued by Keohane is essentially a **positivist** one, and it is precisely positivism that the reflectivists reject. Not surprisingly, rationalists and reflectivists do not tend to talk to one another very much since they do not share a common language. Exactly the identities that rationalists take as given become the starting point for the research project of the reflectivists; accordingly, their versions of the key issues in world politics are nothing like those of the rationalists. There really is very little contact between the two positions and they resemble rival camps, publishing in different journals and going to different conferences. I say all of this simply to indicate just how much is at stake if Wendt and the constructivists can indeed bridge the gap between rationalists and reflectivists: they—the rationalists or the reflectivists—would be at the centre of the discipline. Or to put it another way, constructivists would be the acceptable face of rationalism for reflectivists and the acceptable face of reflectivism for rationalists! If Wendt can establish that his position is capable of serving as the point of contact then he will have created a theoretical synthesis of the various, previously incompatible, positions of the discipline. Wendt's central claim is shown in Box 9.8.

I want to run through his argument by summarizing it in a number of points. As I read it his argument progresses in the following way:

1. He sees the **neo-realist/neo-liberal** debate as central to international relations theory, and being concerned with the issue of whether state action is influenced more by system structure (neo-realism) or by the processes interactions and learning of institutions (neo-liberalism). (391)

2. Both **neo-realism** and **neo-liberalism** are **rationalist** theories, based on rational choice theory and taking the identities and interests of actors as given; for rationalists, processes such as those of institutions affect the behaviour but not the identities and interests of actors. For both

Box 9.8. Wendt's View of the Social Constructivist Project

My objective in this article is to build a bridge between these two traditions (rationalism and reflectivism) . . . by developing a constructivist argument . . . on behalf of the liberal claim that international institutions can transform state identities and interests . . . my strategy for building this bridge would be to argue against the neo-realist claim that self-help is given by anarchic structure exogenously to process . . . I argue that self-help and power politics do not follow logically or causally from anarchy, and if today we find ourselves in a self-help world this is due to process, not structure. There is no 'logic' of anarchy apart from the practices that create and instantiate one structure of identities and interests rather than another; structure has no existence or causal powers apart from process. Self-help and power politics are institutions, not essential features of anarchy. *Anarchy is what states make of it.*

Source: Wendt (1992: 394–5).

theories, the actors are self-interested states. (391–2)

3. There exist social theories that do not take interests and identities as given, and these are known as **reflectivist** or **constructivist** theories, and, whatever their differences, they all focus on how inter-subjective practices between actors result in identities and interests being formed in the processes of interaction rather than being formed prior to interaction. We are what we are by how we interact rather than being what we are regardless of how we interact. (393–4)

4. Whereas **neo-realists** treat the self-help nature of anarchy as **the** logic of the system, Wendt argues that collective meanings define the structures which organize our actions, and actors acquire their interests and identities by participating in such collective meanings. Identities and interests are relational and are defined as we define situations. Institutions are relatively stable sets of identities and interests. Self-help is one such institution, and is therefore not the only way of combining definitions of identities and interests in a condition of anarchy. (395–9)

5. Wendt thinks that we assume too much if we think that states have given identities and interests prior to interaction. There **is no such thing as an automatic security dilemma for states**;

such a claim, or one that says that states are in the situation of individuals in Rousseau's famous 'stag-hunt', presupposes that states have acquired selfish interests and identities prior to their interactions. Instead, self-help emerges only out of interaction between states. (400–4)

6. If states find themselves in a self-help situation then this is because their practices made it that way, and if the practices change then so will the inter-subjective knowledge that constitutes the system. This does not imply, however, that self-help, like any other social system, can be easily changed, since once constituted it becomes a social fact that reinforces certain forms of behaviour and punishes others, and it becomes part of the self-identity of actors. Inter-subjective understandings therefore may be self-perpetuating. (405–11)

7. The fact that specific formations of interests and identities may be self-perpetuating does not mean that they cannot be changed. Wendt gives three examples of alternatives to the self-help version of international relations that he has painted. These are by practices of sovereignty, by an evolution of co-operation, and by critical strategic practice. (412–22)

8. The future research agenda for international relations should be to look at the relationship between what actors **do** and what they **are**. In other words the discipline should look at how state actors define social structures such as the international system. Wendt thinks that this is where neo-liberals and reflectivists can work together to offer an account of international relations that competes with the neo-realist account by enquiring into how specific empirical practices relate to the creation and re-creation of identities and interests. (422–5)

In other words, the identities and interests that rationalists take as given and which they see as resulting in the international politics we observe are not in fact given but are things we have created. Having created them we could create them otherwise; it would be difficult because we have all internalized the 'way the world is', but we could make it otherwise.

Now, this is a very powerful argument, but I want to argue that it will not serve as the bridge between **rationalists** and **reflectivists** in the way that Wendt hopes. There are five reasons for this.

The **first** is that Wendt is in fact not really anything like as much of a constructivist as he implies, and certainly not enough to satisfy **reflectivists**. This is because he defines interests and identities very narrowly. Post-modernists, as we have seen, certainly want to say something much more radical about identity than does Wendt, who (I think) is firmly on the rationalist side of the divide, and that means he is not really a reflectivist. Thus his version of constructivism is defined from this perspective. He is in fact a very 'thin' constructivist, and not the kind of 'thick' or 'deep' constructivist that we find amongst the reflectivists.

Second, Wendt certainly accepts that the most important actors in world politics are states, and that their dominance will continue. Indeed, he is clear that his research project resembles that of neo-realism: 'to that extent, I am a statist and a realist' (424). As you will quickly see, this is much more restricted a definition of world politics than the one that the reflectivists would want to propose.

Third, although Wendt says he wants to bring together neo-liberals and reflectivists (constructivists), it is clear to me that he is not bringing together two groups that share the same view of how to construct knowledge; to put it simply, the **rationalists** are essentially **positivists** and the **reflectivists** are essentially **post-positivists**. The latter have a very different idea of how to construct knowledge from that held by the former. In plain language, they cannot be combined together because they have mutually exclusive assumptions.

Fourth, Wendt's structures (institutions) are really rather specific kinds of structures. Unlike materialist theories such as Marxism or feminism, they are composed of ideas. This means that he sees social structures as very 'light' things, comprising the ideas that actors have in their heads. Yet many other social theories would want to argue that social structures reflect strong material interests. Note that there is no place in his account for structures such as capitalism or patriarchy. In other words, many theorists think that ideational structures (Wendt's only form of structure) reflect underlying material interests; we think certain things because it is in our interests to do so. The central point here is that his structures are not material enough, being composed only of ideas.

Finally, Wendt thinks that identities are created in the process of interaction, but critics point out that we do not come to interactions without some pre-existing identity. Rather than our identities being created via interaction our identities are in part prior to that interaction. Think for example of your identity as a woman or a man; although it is clear that some aspects of this are constructed in the ways in which you relate to others via interaction, it is equally the case that some aspects of your identity exist prior to any given interaction. This means that your identity will cause you to construct the other parties to interaction in certain ways. There is never a first encounter. Again, note that this is really saying that his idea of identity is a very light or thin one.

All of these points make me think that Wendt does not quite pull it off. The main reason is that despite his genuine interest in both sets of theories he is, when pushed, revealed as a rationalist, and is actually more of a realist that he initially claims to be. Thus he is not in fact sitting between the rationalists and reflectivists, trying to bring them together, but is in fact on one side of the fence trying to talk to those on the other side; but being on the rationalist side of the fence means that although he uses many of the same terms and concepts as reflectivists, he defines them **rather more narrowly and from the opposite position in the debate about how to construct theories**. But please note that many think that he does manage to bring the two approaches together, and you will want to make up your own mind.

Key Points

- **Social constructivism** offers the prospect of bridging the gap between **rationalist** and **reflectivist** theories.

- There are many constructivists but the best example is **Alexander Wendt** and his 1992 article 'Anarchy is what states make of it'.

- Wendt's attempt is important because **Robert Keohane** pointed out that unless the reflectivists could come up with a research programme then they would remain on the margins of the discipline. Wendt offers such a research programme because he promises to bring neo-liberals and reflectivists together.

- Wendt's key claim is that international anarchy is not fixed, and does not automatically involve the self-interested state behaviour that rationalists see as built into the system. Instead he thinks that anarchy could take on several different forms because the selfish identities and interests assumed by rationalists are in fact the products of interaction and are not prior to it.

- There are several important objections to Wendt's argument. The main ones are that he is really a rationalist and a realist, so that he is not in fact bringing together rationalism and reflectivism, but is instead defining constructivism in a very narrow way, one that is acceptable to rationalists, but which would not be accepted by reflectivists who want a far deeper definition of identity and interest than he provides. Moreover, Wendt sees states as the 'givens' of world politics, but why should this be so instead of classes, or companies or ethnicities or genders? Finally, note that his view of identity is an ideational one, whereas many argue that material interests determine our ideas and therefore our ideational structures. In short, his account is really much more traditional and rationalist than at first seems to be the case.

Conclusion

In this chapter I have tried to summarize the three main areas of development in contemporary international relations theory. As you can see I have my own views as to which of these three main theoretical positions is preferable, but that is of far less importance than your own views on which perspective best explains world politics in this age of **globalization**. Each of the three positions has clear strengths, and probably the best place for you to start thinking about which is most useful is for you to cast your mind back to the Introduction and the first chapter; in each of these chapters we made a lot of points about globalization, and in the Introduction in particular we highlighted some pluses and minuses of globalization. Crucially, you now need to think about which of the contemporary theoretical perspectives discussed in this chapter gives you the best overview of the globalized world we have been discussing.

Clearly, the **rationalist** perspective, and particularly the **neo-neo synthesis** dominates the professional literature in the discipline of International Relations. That is the theoretical debate you will find in most of the journals, particularly the US-based ones. It focuses on the kinds of international political relations that concern many Western governments, particularly the debate about the future security structure of the international system. It is also very strong at looking at economic foreign policy, as the discussions on the relative gains/absolute gains issue suggests. But do you think that it is wide enough a perspective to capture what are to you the most important features of world politics? You might, on the one hand, think that we need theories that define the political realm rather more widely, so as to take in identity, economics, ethnicity, culture, and the like. On the other hand you might think that the most important features of world politics remain those that have dominated for the last two thousand years, namely the problems of war and peace, and of international stability. If you think this then you will probably prefer the rationalist theoretical agenda, and you will certainly do so if you think that these problems are 'natural', that is to say that they are features outside our control in the same way as the concerns of the natural scientist relate to a 'real' world that exists whatever we think about it.

The **reflectivist** theories obviously differ enormously with regard to what they are reflective about. As noted above they are really very different, but I put them together in one category because they are all rejecting the central concerns of rationalism. Do you think that any one of them gives you a better understanding of the main features of world politics than that provided by the rationalist mainstream? Or do you think that they are not really dealing with what are 'obviously' the most important features of world politics? The real problem with reflectivist theories is that they do not add up to one theoretical position in the way that the rationalist theories do. In some important ways, if you are a feminist then you do not necessarily agree with post-modernists or critical theorists. More fundamentally still, you cannot be **both** a critical theorist and a post-modernist! In short, the collection of theories gathered together under the reflectivist label have a set of mutually exclusive assumptions and there is no easy way to see the theories being combined. Some combinations are possible (a feminist post-modernism, or a normative critical theory) but the one thing that is clearly correct is that the whole lot cannot be added together to form one theoretical agenda in the way that the neo-neo debate serves on the rationalist side. Moreover, the reflectivists do not have the same idea of how to construct knowledge as the rationalists, and therefore they are unable to respond to Keohane's challenge for them to come up with testable hypotheses to compare with those provided by the rationalist position. This means that the prospect of a rationalist–reflectivist debate is very low. The two sides simply see world politics in very different ways. Which side (or which subdivision) do you think explains world politics most effectively?

All of this makes **social constructivism** particularly attractive since it offers the prospect of a *via media*, a middle way that represents a synthesis between rationalism and reflectivism. As discussed above, this position, most clearly associated with Wendt, looks very promising to many, and I will predict that it will become one of the main research themes in international relations in the years to come. But I also noted the problems associated with Wendt's position. Centrally, there is the difficulty that he is not really a reflectivist at all, but, rather, is a rationalist (and a statist and a realist!), and thus his attempt to bridge the gap is always going to be unsuccessful because he is actually not sitting between the two positions, but instead is on one side. This raises the question of whether you think the social constructivist project is the way forward for international theory. Do you think that the two positions can be combined? Or are their views of how to construct knowledge so different that they cannot be combined? The trouble of course is that it sounds eminently sensible to say that the two positions of rationalism and reflectivism need to be combined, and the focus of the neo-liberals on institutions and learning makes it possible to see a way of linking up with reflectivists who focus on identity and the construction of actors. But this poses the ultimate question in social theory, namely whether there are always going to be two ways of theorizing the social world: one an inside account focusing on the meanings that actors attach to their actions; the other an outsider account, which sees the beliefs of actors as the product of material interests. I cannot pretend to answer that question, and this is not because of the space available in this chapter; rather this is such a hotly disputed question in all the social sciences that the only honest thing to do is to say that there is no easy or definitive answer. What I will say is that the answer to it will depend in part on how you see the social world and on what kinds of features of world politics matter to you.

I hope that this chapter has given you a good overview of the main developments in contemporary international theory. My main hope is that you will take from what I have written the thought that there is no one theory of world politics that is right simply because it deals with the **truth**. I also hope that you will be sceptical any time any theorist tells you that s/he is dealing with 'reality' or with 'how the world really is', since I think that this is where the values of the theorist (or lecturer, or chapter writer!) can be smuggled in through the back door. I think that world politics in an era of globalization is very complex and there are a variety of theories that try and account for different parts of that complexity. You should work out which theories both explain best the things you are concerned with and also offer you the chance to reflect on their own assumptions. One thing is for sure: there are enough theories to choose between and they paint very different world politics. Which theory paints the picture that you feel best captures the most salient features of world politics?

QUESTIONS

1. Do you think that the three theories involved in the inter-paradigm debate cover all the main issues in contemporary world politics?

2. Why do the post-positivist theories reject positivism?

3. What does it mean to say that the main difference between theories is whether they are explanatory or constitutive?

4. Are the issues dealt with in the neo-neo debate the central ones in today's globalized world?

5. Do you agree with Robert Keohane when he says that the reflectivist approaches need to develop testable hypotheses, to compete with those provided by rationalism, if reflectivism is to be taken seriously as a theoretical approach?

6. Is normative theory anything more than an optional extra for the study of world politics?

7. Do you find J. Ann Tickner's reformulation of Hans Morgenthau's six principles of realism a convincing demonstration of the need to include female perspectives on world politics?

8. Do you agree with Robert Cox that theory is always for someone and for some purpose?

9. What are the main implications of historical sociology for the study of world politics?

10. What might adopting a genealogical approach, such as that proposed by Richard Ashley, do for our understanding of world politics?

11. Do you think that Alexander Wendt's social constructivism succeeds in bridging the gap between rationalism and reflectivism?

12. Which of the main alternatives discussed in this chapter do you think offers the best account of world politics? Why?

GUIDE TO FURTHER READING

There are many books dealing with contemporary international theory. A very good survey is provided by S. Burchill and A. Linklater *et al. Theories of International Relations* (Basingstoke: Macmillan, 1996). A more dated but very good coverage of the three theories of the inter-paradigm debate is P. R. Viotti and M. V. Kauppi *International Relations Theory: Realism, Pluralism, Globalism* 2nd ed. (New York: Macmillan, 1993). For two sets of essays on contemporary theory see K. Booth and S. Smith (eds.), *International Relations Theory Today* (Cambridge: Polity Press, 1995) and S. Smith, K. Booth and M. Zalewski (eds.), *International Theory: Positivism and Beyond* (Cambridge: Cambridge University Press, 1996). On the neo-neo debate see D. Baldwin (ed.), *Neorealism and Neoliberalism: The Contemporary Debate* (New York: Columbia University Press, 1993) and C. Kegley (ed.), *Controversies in International Relations Theory: Realism and the Neoliberal Challenge* (New York: St Martin's, 1995). On reflectivist approaches, see, for normative theory, C. Brown *International Relations Theory: New Normative Approaches* (Hemel Hempstead: Harvester Wheatsheaf, 1992) and M. Frost *Ethics in International Relations: A Constitutive Theory* (Cambridge: Cambridge University Press, 1996); for feminist theory see M. Zalewski 'Feminist Theory and International Relations', in M. Bowker and R. Brown (eds.), *From Cold War to Collapse* (Cambridge: Cambridge University Press, 1993), C. Enloe *Bananas, Beaches and Bases: Making Feminist Sense of International Politics* (London: Pandora, 1989) and *The Morning After: Sexual Politics at the End of the Cold War* (Berkeley: California University Press, 1993), and J. J. Pettman *Worlding Women: A Feminist International Politics* (St Leonards: Allen & Unwin, 1996); for critical theory see R. Cox with Sinclair, T., *Approaches to World Order* (Cambridge: Cambridge University Press, 1996); and A. Linklater *Beyond Realism and Marxism* (London: Macmillan, 1990); for historical sociology see M. Mann *The Sources of Social Power*, vol. i (Cambridge: Cambridge University Press, 1986) and *The Sources of Social Power*, vol. ii (Cambridge

University Press, 1993) and D. Smith *The Rise of Historical Sociology* (Cambridge: Polity Press, 1991); for post-modernism, see R. B. J. Walker *Inside/Outside: International Relations as Political Theory* (Cambridge: Cambridge University Press, 1993) and J. George *Discourses of Global Politics* (Boulder, Col.: Lynne Rienner, 1994). On social constructivism see A. Wendt 'Anarchy is What States Make of it', *International Organization*, 46: 2 (1992), F. Kratochwil *Rules, Norms, and Decisions* (Cambridge: Cambridge University Press, 1989) and N. Onuf *A World of our Making: Rules and Rule in Social Theory and International Relations* (Columbia: University of South Carolina Press, 1989).

Part Three
Structures and Processes

In this section of the book we want to introduce you to the main underlying structures and processes in contemporary world politics. There is obviously going to be some overlap between this section and the next, since the division between structures and processes, and international issues is largely one of perspective. For us, the difference is that by structure and processes we mean relatively stable features of world politics that are more enduring and constant than are the issues dealt with in the next section. Again we have two aims in this section: **first**, we want you to get a good overview of some of the most important structures and processes in world politics at the end of the twentieth century. We therefore have chosen a series of ways of thinking about world politics that draw attention to these underlying features. Again, note that we realize that what is a structure and what is a process is largely a matter of debate, but it may help to say that together these provide the setting in which the issues dealt with in the next part of the book have to be played out. All of the features examined in this section of the book will be important for the resolution of the issues we deal with in the next section, since they comprise both the main structures of world politics that these issues have to face and the main processes that will determine their fate. Our **second** aim is that these structures and processes will help you to think about globalization by forcing you to ask again whether or not it is a qualitatively different form of world politics than hitherto. Does globalization require or represent an overthrow of the structures and processes that have been central in world politics to date?

10 International Security in the Post-Cold War Era

John Baylis

READER'S GUIDE

This chapter focuses on two central arguments about the effects of the end of the cold war on international security. The first argument suggests that very little of substance has changed: international relations is likely to be as violent in the future as it has been in the past. The second argument suggests that co-operation as well as competition has been a feature of international politics in the past and the post-cold war era has opened up an opportunity for an even more benign system of international security to develop. In the context of this debate the chapter begins by looking at traditional realist and more contemporary neo-realist perspectives on international security. Refinements of the neo-realist perspective (which reflect a more optimistic view of future international security) are then considered under the headings of 'contingent realism', 'mature anarchy', 'liberal institutionalism', and 'democratic peace'. Other more radical perspectives are developed under the headings of 'collective security', 'constructivist' critical theory, 'post-modernist' approaches, and 'globalist views'. The chapter ends by considering the continuing tension between national and international security and suggests that it remains too early to make a definitive judgement about whether a fundamentally different paradigm of international politics is emerging, or whether it is possible for such a transformation to occur.

Introduction

Students of international politics deal with some of the most profound questions it is possible to consider. Amongst the most important of these is whether international security is possible to achieve in the kind of world in which we live. For much of the intellectual history of the subject a debate has raged between **realists** and **idealists**, who have been respectively pessimistic and optimistic in their response to this central question in the international politics field (see Ch. 6). In the post-World War I period idealism claimed widespread support as the League of Nations seemed to offer some hope for greater international order. In contrast, during the cold war which developed after 1945, realism became the dominant school of thought. War and violent conflict were seen as perennial features of inter-state relations stretching back through human history. With the end of the cold war, however, the debate has been renewed and intensified. For some, the end of the intense ideological confrontation between East and West was a major turning point in international history, ushering in a new paradigm in which inter-state violence would gradually become a thing of the past and new communitarian values would bring greater co-operation between individuals and human collectivities of various kinds (including states). This reflected more optimistic views about the development of a peaceful global society. For others, however, realism remained the best approach to thinking about international security. In their view, very little of substance had changed as a result of the events of 1989. The end of the cold war had brought a new, more co-operative era between the superpowers into existence, but it was likely to be temporary as states continued to compete and force remained the ultimate arbiter of international disputes.

This chapter focuses on this debate, highlighting the different strands of thinking within these two optimistic and pessimistic schools of thought. Before this can be done, however, it is necessary to consider what is meant by 'security' and to probe the relationship between national security and international security. Attention will then shift to traditional ways of thinking about national security and the influence which these ideas have had on contemporary thinking. This will be followed by a survey of alternative ideas and approaches which have emerged in the literature in recent years. The conclusion will then provide an assessment of these ideas before returning to the central question of whether or not international security is **more**, or **less**, likely in the remaining years of the twentieth century and beyond.

What is Meant by the Concept of 'Security'?

Most writers agree that security is a 'contested concept'. There is a consensus that it implies freedom from threats to core values (for both individuals and groups) but there is a major disagreement about whether the main focus of enquiry should be on 'individual', 'national', or 'international' security. For much of the cold war period most writing on the subject was dominated by the idea of *national* security, which was largely defined in militarized terms. The main area of interest for both academics and statesmen tended to be on the military capabilities that their own states should develop to deal with the threats that faced them. More recently, however, this idea of security has been criticized for being **ethnocentric** (culturally biased) and too narrowly defined. Instead a number of contemporary writers have argued for an expanded conception of security outward from the limits of parochial national security to include a range of other considerations. Barry Buzan, in his study of *People, States and Fear,* argues for a view of security which includes political, economic, societal, environmental as well as military aspects and which is also defined in broader international terms (see Box 10.1). This involves states in overcoming 'excessively self-referenced security policies' and thinking instead about the security interests of their neighbours. (Buzan 1983: 214–42). Buzan's work

---

Box 10.1. Notions of 'Security'

'A nation is secure to the extent to which it is not in danger of having to sacrifice core values if it wishes to avoid war, and is able, if challenged, to maintain them by victory in such a war.'

(Walter Lippmann)

'Security, in any objective sense, measures the absence of threats to acquired values and in a subjective sense, the absence of fear that such values will be attacked.'

(Arnold Wolfers)

'In the case of security, the discussion is about the pursuit of freedom from threat. When this discussion is in the context of the international system, security is about the ability of states and societies to maintain their independent identity and their functional integrity.'

(Barry Buzan)

'Stable security can only be achieved by people and groups if they do not deprive others of it; this can be achieved if security is conceived as a process of emancipation.'

(Booth and Wheeler)

---

raises interesting and important questions about whether national and international security considerations can be compatible and whether states, given the nature of the international system, are capable of thinking in more co-operative international and global terms.

This focus on the tension between national and international security is not accepted by all writers on security. There are those who argue that the emphasis on the state and inter-state relations ignores the fundamental changes which have been

taking place in world politics especially in the aftermath of the cold war. For some, the dual processes of integration and fragmentation which characterize the contemporary world mean that much more attention should be given to 'societal security'. According to this view, growing integration in regions like Europe is undermining the classical political order based on nation-states, leaving nations exposed within larger political frameworks (like the EU). At the same time the fragmentation of various states, like the Soviet Union and Yugoslavia, has created new problems of boundaries, minorities, and organizing ideologies which are causing increasing regional instability. (Waever *et al.* 1993: 196). This has led to the argument that ethno-national groups, rather than states, should become the centre of attention for security analysts.

At the same time, there are other commentators who argue that the stress on national and international security is less appropriate because of the emergence of an embryonic global society in the 1990s. Like the 'societal security' theorists they point to the fragmentation of the nation-state but they argue that more attention should be given, not to society at the ethno-national level, but to global society. These writers argue that one of the most important trends at the end of the twentieth century is the broad process of of *globalization* which is taking place. They accept that this process brings new risks and dangers. These include the risks associated with such things as a breakdown of the global monetary system, global warming, and the dangers of nuclear accidents. These threats to security, on a planetary level, are viewed as being largely outside the control of nation-states. Only the development of a global community, they believe, can deal with this adequately.

The Traditional Approach to National Security

As Chapter 2 has shown, from the Treaty of Westphalia in 1648 onwards states have been regarded as by far the most powerful actors in the international system. They have been 'the universal standard of political legitimacy' with no higher authority to regulate their relations with each other. This has meant that security has been seen as

the priority obligation of state governments. They have taken the view that there is no alternative but to seek their own protection in what has been described as a **self-help** world.

In the historical debate about how best to achieve national security writers, like Hobbes, Machiavelli, and Rousseau tended to paint a rather

---

Box 10.2. Different Dimensions of International Security

At the *political* level there has been a growing recognition that systems of government and ideologies have a powerful influence not only on domestic stability but also on international security. Authoritarian governments often seek to divert attention away from problems at home by pursuing foreign adventures. This appears to have been one of the major reasons for the Malvinas/Falklands war in 1982 between Argentina and Britain. The contemporary trend towards the fragmentation of states also poses wider security problems. This has been evident with the disintegration of the Soviet Union and Yugoslavia in the 1990s and could become a major problem if the Chinese Communist Party began to lose effective control in the years ahead.

Population growth and problems over access to resources and markets has also led to greater attention being given to *economic* security issues. Deprivation and poverty are not only a source of internal conflict but can also spill over into tension between states. An example of this can be seen in the late 1980s in relations between Senegal and Mauritania. Disputes over agricultural land, together with population pressures gave rise to the expulsion of minority groups and ethnic violence in the Senegal River Valley bordering on Mauritania. The dispute did not lead to war between the two states but considerable diplomatic tensions were generated,

demonstrating the growing importance of economic interdependence and the potential for conflict which can be created as a result.

Economic pressures can also encourage *social* tensions within states which can have implications for international security. In recent years large migration movements between states has produced group-identity conflicts. One of the most serious has been the migration from Bangladesh to north-east India. In the last twenty years the population of Assam has risen from 7 million to 22 million people causing major social changes which have altered the balance of political power between religious and ethnic groups in the state. This resulted in intergroup conflict which has caused difficulties between India and Bangladesh.

Many of the economic and social sources of insecurity in the contemporary world are linked to *environmental* scarcity. As Thomas Homer-Dixon has shown scarcities of cropland, water, forests and fish, together with atmospheric changes such as global warming have an important impact on international security. Control over oil was a major cause of the Gulf War in 1991 and tension over the control of water resources in the occupied West Bank has helped heighten tension between Arabs and Jews in Israel complicating the efforts to achieve a durable peace settlement in the region (Homer-Dixon 1994:18).

---

pessimistic picture of the implications of state sovereignty. The international system was viewed as a rather brutal arena in which states would seek to achieve their own security at the expense of their neighbours. Interstate relations were seen as a struggle for power as states constantly attempted to take advantage of each other. According to this view **permanent peace** was unlikely to be achieved. All that states could do was to try and balance the power of other states to prevent any one from achieving overall hegemony. This was a view which was shared by writers, like E. H. Carr and Hans Morgenthau, who developed what became known as the realist school of thought in the aftermath of World War II.

This largely pessimistic view of international relations is shared by many contemporary writers, like Kenneth Waltz and John Mearsheimer. The pessimism of these **neo-realists** rests on a number of key assumptions they make about the way the international system works.

Key Neo-Realist Assumptions

- The international system is **anarchic**. They don't mean by this that it is necessarily chaotic. Rather, anarchy implies that there is no central authority capable of controlling state behaviour.

- States claiming sovereignty will inevitably develop **offensive military capabilities** to defend themselves and extend their power. As such they are potentially dangerous to each other.

- **Uncertainty**, leading to a **lack of trust**, is inherent in the international system. States can never be sure of the intentions of their neighbours and, therefore, they must always be on their guard.

- States will want to maintain their independence and sovereignty, and, as a result, **survival** will be the most basic driving force influencing their behaviour.

- Although states are rational, there will always be **room for miscalculation**. In a world of imperfect information, potential antagonists will always have an incentive to misrepresent their own capabilities to keep their opponents guessing. This may lead to mistakes about 'real' state interests.

Taken together, neo-realists argue that these assumptions produce a tendency for states to act aggressively towards each other.

According to this view, national security, or insecurity, is largely the result of the **structure** of the international system (this is why these writers are sometimes called 'structural realists'). The structure of anarchy is seen as being highly durable. The implication of this is that international politics in the future is likely to be as violent as international politics in the past. In an important article entitled 'Back to the Future' written in 1990 John Mearsheimer argued that the end of the cold war was likely to usher in a return to the traditional multilateral **balance of power** politics of the past in which extreme nationalism and ethnic rivalries would lead to widespread instability and conflict. Mearsheimer viewed the cold war as a period of peace and stability brought about by the bipolar structure of power which prevailed. With the collapse of this system, he argued there would be a return to the kind of great power rivalries which had blighted international relations since the seventeenth century.

For neo-realist writers, like Mearsheimer, international politics may not be characterized by constant wars but there is nevertheless a relentless security competition which takes place, with war, like rain, always a possibility. It is accepted that co-operation among states can and does occur, but such co-operation has its limits. It is 'constrained by the dominating logic of security competition, which no amount of co-operation can eliminate' (Mearsheimer 1994: 9). Genuine long-lasting peace, or a world where states do not compete for power, therefore, is very unlikely to be achieved.

The 'Security Dilemma'

This view that war is a constant historical feature of international politics and is unlikely to disappear is based on the notion that states face what has been described as a **security dilemma** from which it is largely impossible to escape. The idea of a security dilemma was first clearly articulated in the 1950s by John Herz. It was, he said: 'a structural notion in which the self-help attempts of states to look after their security needs, tend regardless of intention to lead to rising insecurity for others as each interprets its own measures as defensive and the measures of others as potentially threatening' (Herz 1950: 157).

According to this view, in a self-help environment, like the international system, states are faced with an 'unresolveable uncertainty' about the military preparations made by other states. Are they designed simply for their own defence or are they part of a more aggressive design? Because the uncertainty is unresolveable, states are likely to remain mistrustful of each other. In turn, if mistrust is mutual, 'a dynamic "action–reaction" cycle may well result, which will take the fears of both to higher levels'. Insecurity will breed further insecurity, with the ever-present potential for war breaking out (Wheeler and Booth 1991: 29–31).

At the root of the security dilemma, therefore, are mistrust and fear. Even when states are believed to be benign in their intentions there is always the recognition that intentions can change. Being overly trusting opens up the prospects of being taken advantage of, with potentially disastrous consequences. This constant fear, according to Butterfield, creates an awful tragedy which afflicts international relations. 'Behind the great conflicts of mankind, he argues, there 'is a terrible predicament which lies at the heart of the story'. Writing in the 1950s Butterfield argued that there was no sign that mankind was capable of overcoming this 'irreducible dilemma'. (Butterfield 1951: 20)

The Difficulties of Co-operation between States

For most contemporary neo-realist writers there is little prospect of a significant change in the nature of security in the post-cold war world. Pointing to the Gulf War, the violent disintegration of the former Yugoslavia and parts of the former Soviet Union, it is argued that we continue to live in a world of mistrust and constant security competition. Co-operation between states occurs, but it is difficult to achieve and even more difficult to sustain. There are two main factors, it is suggested,

John Baylis

which continue to make co-operation difficult, even after the changes of 1989. The first is the prospect of **cheating**; the second is the concern which states have about what are called **relative-gains**.

The Problem of Cheating

Writers like Waltz and Mearsheimer do not deny that states often co-operate or that in the post-cold war era there are even greater opportunities than in the past for states to work together. They argue, however, that there are distinct limits to this co-operation because states have always been, and remain, fearful that others will cheat on any agreements reached and attempt to gain advantages over them. This risk is regarded as being particularly important, given the nature of modern military technology which can bring about very rapid shifts in the balance of power between states. 'Such a development', Mearsheimer has argued, 'could create a window of opportunity for the cheating side to inflict a decisive defeat on the victim state' (Mearsheimer 1994: 20). States realize that this is the case and although they join alliances and sign arms control agreements, they remain cautious and

aware of the need to provide for their own national security in the last resort. This is one of the reasons why, despite the Strategic Arms Reduction Agreements of the early 1990s and the extension of the Non-Proliferation Treaty in 1995, the nuclear powers continue to maintain some of their nuclear weapons.

The Problem of Relative-Gains

Co-operation is also inhibited, according to many neo-realist writers, because states tend to be concerned with 'relative-gains', rather than 'absolute gains'. Instead of being interested in co-operation because it will benefit both partners, states, they suggest, always have to be aware of how much they are gaining compared with the state they are co-operating with. Because all states will be attempting to maximize their gains in a competitive, mistrustful, and uncertain international environment, co-operation will **always** be very difficult to achieve and hard to maintain.

Such a view of the problems of co-operation in the post-cold war world are not, however, shared by all writers, even within the neo-realist school. There is a wide body of opinion amongst scholars (and politicians) that the traditional or 'standard' neo-realist view of international relations should be modified or even replaced. Opposition to 'standard' neo-realism takes a wide variety of different forms. To illustrate alternative ways of thinking about international security in the 1990s **eight** different approaches will be considered. Despite the differences which exist between writers in these fields they all share a common view that greater international security in the future is possible through co-operation. Indeed, many of them argue that international security in the latter years of the twentieth century is undergoing significant changes which could bring greater opportunities for peace.

The Opportunities for Co-operation between States

Contingent Realism

Contrary to the views of those neo-realists (like Waltz and Mearsheimer) who are pessimistic about co-operation between states in the post-cold war world, there are other neo-realist writers who present a rather more optimistic assessment. According to Charles Glaser, 'contrary to the conventional wisdom, the strong general propensity of adversaries to compete is not an inevitable logical consequence of structural realism's basic assumptions' (Glaser 1994/5: 51). Glaser accepts much of the analysis and assumptions of structural realism, but he argues that there are a wide range of conditions in which adversaries can best achieve their security goals through co-operative policies, rather than competitive ones. In such circumstances states will choose to co-operate rather than to compete. Security is therefore seen to be 'contingent' on the circumstances prevailing at the time.

Contingent realists argue that **standard** structural realism is flawed for **three** main reasons.

1. They reject the competition-bias inherent in the theory. Because international relations is characterized by self-help behaviour doesn't necessarily mean, they argue, that states are dammed to perpetual competition which will result in war. Faced with the uncertainties associated with being involved in an arms race, like that of the 1970s and 1980s, for example, states preferred to co-operate. There were distinct advantages in working together to reduce the risks and uncertainty in this period rather than engaging in relentless competition which characterized most of the cold war years.

2. A second, and related argument is that standard structural realism is flawed because of its emphasis on 'relative-gains'. States often pursue co-operation, it is argued, precisely because of the dangers of seeking relative advantages. As the security dilemma literature suggests, it is often best in security terms to accept rough parity rather than seek maximum gains which will spark off another round of the arms race leading to less security for all in the longer term.

3. The third flaw in the standard argument, according to contingent realists, is that the emphasis

on cheating is overdone. Cheating *is* a problem which poses risks, but so does arms racing. Schelling and Halperin have argued that 'it cannot be assumed that an agreement that leaves some possibility of cheating is unacceptable or that cheating would necessarily result in strategically important gains'. The risks involved in arms control may be preferable to the risks involved in arms racing. Contingent realists argue that this is often ignored by writers like Waltz and Mearsheimer. This was clearly the view of the superpowers in the late 1980s and early 1990s when a wide range of agreements were signed including the INF Treaty and the START I and II Treaties.

The main thrust of the argument is that there is no need to be overly pessimistic about international security in the aftermath of the cold war.

Key Points

- 'Contingent realists' regard themselves as 'structural realists' or 'neo-realists'.
- They believe standard 'neo-realism' is flawed for three main reasons: they reject the competition bias in the theory; they do not accept that states are only motivated by 'relative gains'; they believe the emphasis on cheating is exaggerated.
- 'Contingent realists' tend to be more optimistic about co-operation between states than traditional 'neo-realists'.

Mature Anarchy

The view that it is possible to ameliorate (if not necessarily to transcend) the security dilemma through greater co-operation between states is also shared by other writers who would describe themselves as 'neo-realists' or 'structural realists'. Barry Buzan has argued that one of the interesting and important features of the 1980s and 1990s is the gradual emergence of a rather more 'mature anarchy' in which states recognize the intense dangers of continuing to compete aggressively in a nuclear world. While accepting the tendency of states to focus on their own narrow parochial security interests, Buzan argues that there is a growing recognition amongst the more 'mature' states in the international system that there are good (security) reasons for taking into account the interests of their neighbours when making their own policies. States, he suggests, are increasingly internalizing 'the understanding that national securities are interdependent and that excessively self-referenced security policies, whatever their jingoistic attractions, are ultimately self-defeating' (Buzan 1983: 208). He cites the Nordic countries as providing an example of a group of states that have moved, through 'a maturing process', from fierce military rivalry to a *security community*. Buzan accepts that such an evolutionary process for international society as a whole is likely to be slow and uneven in its achievements. A change away from the preoccupation with *national* security towards a greater emphasis on *international* security, however, is, in his view, at least possible, and certainly desirable.

It could be argued that this is exactly what has happened in Western Europe over the past fifty years. After centuries of hostile relations between France and Germany, as well as between other Western European states, a new sense of 'community' was established with the Treaty of Rome which turned former enemies into close allies. Unlike the past these states no longer consider using violence or coercion to resolve their differences. Disagreements still occur but there is a consensus within the European Union that these will always be resolved peacefully by political means. Supporters of the concept of 'mature anarchy' argue that this ongoing 'civilizing' process in Europe can be extended further to achieve a wider security community by embracing other regions with whom economic and political co-operation is increasingly taking place.

Key Points

- Supporters of the concept of 'mature anarchy' also accept that **structure** is a key element in determining state behaviour.
- There is, however, it is argued, a trend towards 'mature anarchy', especially in Europe, which focuses on the growing importance of international security considerations.

Box. 10.4. Key Concepts

'A **security community** is a group of people which has become "integrated". By integration we mean the attainment, within a territory, of a "sense of community" and of institutions and practices strong enough and widespread enough to assure . . . dependable expectations of "peaceful change" among its population. By a "sense of community" we mean a belief . . . that common social problems must and can be resolved by processes of "peaceful change".'

(Karl Deutsch)

'**Security regimes** occur when a group of states co-operate to manage their disputes and avoid war by seeking to mute the security dilemma both by their own actions and by their assumptions about the behaviour of others.'

(Robert Jervis)

'A **security complex** involves a group of states whose primary security concerns link together sufficiently closely that their national securities cannot realistically be considered apart from one another.'

(Barry Buzan)

'Acceptance of **common security** as the organizing principle for efforts to reduce the risk of war, limit arms, and move towards disarmament, means, in principle, that co-operation will replace confrontation in resolving conflicts of interest. This is not to say that differences among nations should be expected to disappear . . . The task is only to ensure that these conflicts do not come to be expressed in acts of war, or in preparations for war. It means that nations must come to understand that the maintenance of world peace must be given a higher priority than the assertion of their own ideological or political positions'.

(Palme Report 1992)

- This is occurring because more states in the contemporary world are recognizing that their own security is interdependent with the security of other states.
- The more this happens the greater the chances of dampening down the security dilemma.

Liberal Institutionalism

One of the main characteristics of the standard neo-realist approach to international security is the belief that international institutions do not have a very important part to play in the prevention of war. Institutions are seen as being the product of state interests and the constraints which are imposed by the international system itself. It is these interests and constraints which shape the decisions on whether to co-operate or compete rather than the institutions to which they belong.

Such views have been challenged by both statesmen and a number of international relations specialists, particularly following the end of the cold war. The British Foreign Secretary, Douglas Hurd, for example made the case in June 1992 that institutions themselves had played, and continued to play, a crucial role in enhancing security, particularly in Europe. He argued that the West had developed 'a set of international institutions which have proved their worth for one set of problems'. He went on to argue that the great challenge of the post-cold war era was to adapt these institutions to deal with the new circumstances which prevailed. (Hurd 1992).

This view reflected a belief, widely shared among Western statesmen that a framework of complementary, mutually reinforcing institutions—the EU, NATO, WEU, and the Organization for Security and Co-operation in Europe (OSCE)—could be developed to promote a more durable and stable European security system for the post-cold war era. For many observers such an approach has considerable potential in achieving peace in other regions of the world as well. ASEAN is often cited as an institution which has an important role to play in helping to maintain stability in South-East Asia. Similarly the Organization of African States plays a part in helping to resolve differences between African states.

This is a view which is also shared by a distinctive group of academic writers which developed during the 1980s and early 1990s. These writers all share a conviction that the developing pattern of institutionalized co-operation between states opens up unprecedented opportunities to achieve greater international security in the years ahead. Although the past may have been characterized by constant wars and conflict, important changes are taking place in international relations towards the end of the twentieth century which create the opportunity to dampen down the traditional security competition between states.

This approach, known as liberal institutionalism, operates largely within the realist framework, but argues that international institutions are much more important in helping to achieve co-operation and stability than 'structural realists' realize. According to Keohane and Martin (1995: 42) 'institutions can provide information, reduce transaction costs, make commitments more credible, establish focal points for coordination and, in general, facilitate the operation of reciprocity'. Supporters of these ideas point to the importance of European economic and political institutions in overcoming the traditional hostility of European States. They also point to the developments within the European Union and NATO in the post-cold war era to demonstrate that by investing major resources states themselves clearly believe in the importance of institutions. According to this line of argument, if states were influenced only by narrow calculations of power, the EU and NATO would have withered away at the end of the cold war. In fact, the reverse has happened. Both retain their vitality in the 1990s and are engaged in a process of expansion. This is not to say that institutions can prevent wars from occurring, but they can help to mitigate the fears of cheating and alleviate fears which sometimes arise from unequal gains from co-operation. As such, it is suggested that in a world constrained by state power and divergent interests, international institutions operating on the basis of reciprocity at least will be a component of any lasting peace. In other words, international institutions themselves are unlikely to eradicate war from the international system but they can play a part in helping to achieve greater co-operation between states. This is reflected in Mrs Thatcher's call in 1990 to 'bring the new democracies of Eastern Europe into closer association with the institutions of Western Europe'. The EC, she argued had reconciled antagonisms within Western Europe and it could be used to overcome divisions between East and West in Europe.

Key Points

- Neo-realists reject the significance of international institutions in helping many to achieve peace and security.

- Contemporary politicians and academics, who write under the label of liberal institutionalism, however, see institutions as an important mechanism for achieving international security.

- Liberal institutionalists accept many of the assumptions of realism about the continuing importance of military power in international relations but argue that institutions can provide a framework for co-operation which can help to overcome the dangers of security competition between states.

Democratic Peace Theory

Another 'liberal' approach to international security has gathered momentum in the post-cold war world. This centres on the argument that democratic states tend not to fight other democratic states. Democracy, therefore, is seen as a major source of peace. As with 'liberal institutionalism', this is a notion which has received wide support in Western political and academic circles. In his state of the Union address in 1994 President Bill Clinton went out of his way to point to the absence of war between democracies as a justification for American policies of promoting a process of democratization around the world. Support for this view can be seen in the Western policy of promoting democracy in Eastern and Central Europe following the end of the cold war and opening up the possibility of these states joining the European Union.

'Democratic peace' theory has been largely associated with the writings of Michael Doyle and Bruce Russett. In the same way that contemporary realists have been influenced by the work of Hobbes, Rousseau, and Machiavelli, Doyle points to the importance of the insights contained in Immanuel Kant's 1795 essay, *Perpetual Peace*. Doyle contends that democratic representation, an ideological commitment to human rights, and transnational interdependence provide an explanation for the 'peace-prone' tendencies of democratic states. (Doyle 1995a: 180–4) Equally, the absence of these attributes, he argues, provides a reason why non-democratic states tend to be 'war-prone'. Without these domestic values and restraints the **logic of power** replaces the liberal **logic of accommodation**.

Supporters of democratic peace ideas, as a way of promoting international security in the post-cold war era, do not only argue that wars between democracies are rare or non-existent. They also contend that democracies are more likely to settle mutual conflicts of interest short of the threat or use of any military force. It is accepted that conflicts of

interest will, and do, arise between democratic states, but shared norms and institutional constraints mean that democracies rarely escalate those disputes to the point where they threaten to use military force against each other, or actually use force at all. Much more than other states, they settle their disagreement by mediation, negotiation, or other forms of peaceful diplomacy. One of the benefits of democracy, according to Doyle, is that differences will be managed long before they become violent disputes in the public arena. There is clearly a close link here with the arguments put forward by supporters of the concept of 'mature anarchy', discussed above.

These democratic peace arguments are not designed to reject realism completely but to suggest that liberal democracies do make rather more of a difference in international politics than realist writers accept. Bruce Russett has argued that there is no need to jettison the insights of realism which tell us that power and strategic considerations affect states' decisions to fight each other. But neither should one deny the limitations of those insights, and their inability to explain many of the instances when liberal states have chosen not to fight or to threaten one another. For Russett the danger resides in 'vulgar realism's' vision of war of all against all, 'in which the threat that other states pose is unaffected by their internal norms and institutions' (Russett 1995: 175).

Russett argues that democratic values are not the only influence permitting states to avoid war; power and strategic influences undoubtedly affect the calculations of all states, including democracies. And sometimes these strategic considerations can be predominant. Shared democracy, however, he believes, is important in international affairs and should not be ignored in any attempt to dampen down the security dilemma and achieve greater security. He is not saying that shared democratic values by themselves will eliminate all wars but, like liberal institutionalists, he argues that such values will contribute to a more peaceful world.

Key Points

- Democratic peace theory emerged in the 1980s. The main argument was that the spread of democracy would lead to greater international security.

- Democratic peace theory is based on a Kantian logic—emphasizing three elements—republican democratic representation; an ideological commitment to human rights; and transnational interdependence.

- Wars between democracies are seen as being rare and they are believed to settle mutual conflicts of interest without the threat or use of force more often than non-democratic states.

- Supporters of democratic peace ideas do not reject the insights of realism, but they reject 'vulgar realisms' preoccupation with the idea of war of all against all. They argue that internal norms and institutions matter.

Ideas of Collective Security

There are other approaches to contemporary international security which take realpolitik and power calculations seriously but which also argue that domestic politics, beliefs, and norms must also be included as important determinants of state behaviour. One such approach is that associated with collective security ideas. Proponents of collective security argue that although military force remains an important characteristic of international life, there are nevertheless realistic opportunities to move beyond the self-help world of realism, especially after the end of the cold war. They reject the idea that state behaviour is simply the product of the *structure* of the international system. *Ideas*, it is argued, are also important.

According to Charles and Clifford Kupchan, under collective security, states agree to abide by certain norms and rules to maintain stability, and when necessary, band together to stop aggression (C. and C. Kupchan 1995). Defined in these terms collective security involves a recognition by states that to enhance their security they must agree to three main principles in their inter-state relations.

- **First**, they must renounce the use of military force to alter the status quo and agree instead to settle all of their disputes peacefully. Changes will be possible in international relations, but ought to be achieved by negotiation rather than force.

- **Second**, they must broaden their conception of national interest to take in the interests of the international community as a whole. This means

that when a trouble-maker appears in the system, all of the responsible states automatically and collectively confront the aggressor with overwhelming military power.

- **Third**, and most importantly states must overcome the fear which dominates world politics and learn to trust each other. Such a system of security, as Inis Claude has argued, depends on states entrusting 'their destinies to collective security'.

Supporters of collective security as a way forward to achieving greater international security accept that their ideas are not a panacea for preventing war. They argue, however, that by setting up collective security institutions some of the worst excesses of the perennial competition between states can be avoided. According to this view, 'regulated, institutionalized balancing is preferable to unregulated balancing under anarchy' (C. and C. Kupchan 1995). Collective security is seen as a way of providing a more effective mechanism for balancing against an aggressor. By facing potential aggressors with preponderance, collective security arrangements are designed to provide deterrence and more effective action if deterrence breaks down.

It is also argued that collective security institutions contribute to the task of creating a more benign international system. They help create greater confidence so that states can concentrate their energies and resources on their own domestic welfare rather than on non-productive, excessive national security arrangements. Proponents argue that there are profound advantages to institutionalizing a security system that promises to deepen the accord among states rather than letting a self-help system take its course and simply hoping that great power conflict will not re-emerge. The aim, as with liberal institutionalism and democratic peace ideas, is to ameliorate security competition between states by reducing the possibility that unintended spirals of hostility will escalate into war.

Supporters of these ideas argue that although collective security arrangements, like the League of Nations, have failed in the past there is no iron law which says they must fail in the future. The post-cold war era they believe has created a more conducive international environment in which greater opportunities exist than in the past for states to share similar values and interests. This is particularly so in Europe with the spread of democratic values and the collapse of confrontation politics between East and West. These conditions provide the essential foundations for the successful functioning of a collective security system. Supporters also point to the Gulf War in 1991 as an example of effective collective security action in the post-cold war period (for a critique of collective security ideas see Box 10.6).

Key Points

- Collective security theorists take power seriously but argue that it is possible to move beyond the self-help world of realism.

- Collective security is based on three main conditions—that states must renounce the use of military force to alter the status quo; that they must broaden their view of national interest to take in the interests of the international community; and that states must overcome their fear and learn to trust each other.

- Collective security aims to create a more effective system of 'regulated institutionalized balancing' rather than relying on the unregulated balancing which takes place under anarchy.

- Collective security is believed to contribute to the creation of a more benign international system.

- Despite past failures, supporters argue that there is an opportunity to try collective security again with more success in the post-cold war world.

'Constructivist' Critical Theory

The notion that international relations are not only affected by power politics but also by *ideas* is also shared by writers who describe themselves as 'Critical Theorists'. Critical theory, however, is not a single theory, it is a family of theories, many of which differ in important ways but which share a number of things in common. One is that the fundamental structures of international politics are **social** rather than strictly **material**. Another is that changing the way we **think** about international relations can bring a fundamental shift towards greater international security.

One group of critical theorists describe themselves as 'constructivists'. At one level they share many of the major realist assumptions about international politics. They accept that international politics is anarchic; that states have offensive capabilities; that states cannot be absolutely certain of the intentions of other states; that states wish to survive; and that states attempt to behave rationally. They also see themselves as **structuralists**; that is to say they believe that the interests of individual states are in an important sense constructed by the structure of the international system.

However, 'constructivists' think about international politics in a very different way to neo-realists. The latter tend to view structure as being made only of a distribution of material capabilities. 'Constructivists', on the other hand, think that structure is the product of social relationships. Social structures, they argue, are made up of elements, such as shared knowledge, material resources and practices. This means that social structures are defined, in part, by shared understandings, expectations, or knowledge. As an example of this, Alexander Wendt argues that the security dilemma is a social structure composed of inter-subjective understandings in which states are so distrustful that they make worst-case assumptions about each other's intentions, and, as a result, define their interests in 'self-help' terms (Wendt 1992). In contrast, a security community is a rather different social structure, composed of shared knowledge in which states trust one another to resolve disputes without war.

The emphasis on the structure of shared knowledge is important in 'constructivist' thinking. Social structures include material things, like tanks and economic resources, but these only acquire **meaning** through the structure of shared knowledge in which they are embedded. The idea of power politics, or **realpolitik**, has meaning to the extent that states accept the idea as a basic rule of international politics. According to 'constructivist' writers, power politics is an *idea* which does affect the way states behave, but it doesn't describe all interstate behaviour. States are also influenced by other ideas, such as the rule of law and the importance of institutional co-operation and restraint. In his study, 'Anarchy is What States Make of it', Wendt argues that security dilemmas and wars are the result of self-fulfilling prophecies. The 'logic of reciprocity' means that states acquire a shared knowledge about the meaning of power and act accordingly. Equally, he argues, policies of reassurance can also help to bring about a structure of shared knowledge which can help to move states towards a more peaceful security community.

Although 'constructivists' argue that security dilemmas are not acts of god, they differ over whether they can be escaped. For some, the fact that structures are socially constructed does not necessarily mean that they can be changed. This is reflected in Wendt's comment that 'sometimes social structures so constrain action that transformative strategies are impossible' (Wendt 1995: 80). Many 'constructivist' writers, however, are more optimistic. They point to the changes in ideas introduced by Gorbachev during the second half of the 1980s which led to a shared knowledge about the end of the cold war. Once both sides accepted the cold war was over, it really was over. According to this view, understanding the crucial role of social structure is important in developing policies and processes of interaction which will lead towards co-operation rather than conflict. For the optimists, there is sufficient 'slack' in the international system which allows states to pursue policies of peaceful social change rather than engage in a perpetual competitive struggle for power. If there are opportunities for promoting social change most 'constructivists' believe it would be irresponsible not to pursue such policies.

Key Points

- 'Constructivist' thinkers base their ideas on two main assumptions; (1) that the fundamental structures of international politics are socially constructed and (2) that changing the way we think about international relations can help to bring about greater international security.

- 'Constructivist' thinkers accept many of the assumptions of neo-realism, but they reject the view that 'structure' consists only of material capabilities. They stress the importance of social structure defined in terms of shared knowledge and practices as well as material capabilities.

- 'Constructivists' argue that material things acquire meaning only through the structure of shared knowledge in which they are embedded.

- Power politics and realpolitik emphasized by realists is seen as being derived from shared knowledge which is self-fulfilling.

- 'Constructivists' can be pessimistic or optimistic

about changing international relations and achieving greater international security.

Post-Modernist Views on International Security

Recent years have seen the emergence of a post-modernist approach to international relations which has produced a somewhat distinctive perspective towards international security. Post-modernist writers share the view that *ideas* matter, but they also see discourse—how people talk about international politics and security—as an important driving force that shapes the way states behave. For writers, like Richard Ashley, realism is one of the central problems of international insecurity (Ashley 1984). This is because realism is a discourse of power and rule which has been dominant in international politics in the past and which has encouraged security competition by states. According to John Vasquez, power politics is an image of the world that encourages behaviour that helps bring about war. As such the attempt to balance power is itself part of the very behaviour that leads to war. According to Vasquez (1983), alliances do not produce peace, but lead to war. The aim, for many post-modernists, therefore, is to replace the discourse of realism with a 'communitarian discourse', which emphasizes peace and harmony. The idea is that once the 'software' program of realism that people carry around in their heads has been replaced by a new 'software' program based on communitarian norms, individuals, states, and regions will learn to co-operate with each other and global politics will become more peaceful.

One of the central differences between realism and post-modernism is their very different epistemologies (ideas about knowledge). John Mearsheimer has noted that, whereas realists see a fixed and knowable world, post-modernists see the possibility of 'endless interpretations of the world around them . . . there are no constants, no fixed meanings, no secure grounds, no profound secrets, no final structures or limits of history . . . there is only interpretation . . . History itself is grasped as a series of interpretations imposed upon interpretations—none primary, all arbitrary' (Mearsheimer 1994: 42–3). This emphasis on the basis of knowledge as subjective rather than objective leads post-modernists to emphasize the importance of

John Baylis

normative values. Realism is viewed not only as a statist ideology, largely out of touch with the globalizing tendencies which are occurring in world politics but also as a dangerous discourse which is the main obstacle to efforts to establish a new and more peaceful hegemonic discourse. This is because it purports to provide a universal view of how the world is organized and what states have to do if they wish to survive. Post-modernists reject what they see as the 'preposterous certainty' of realism. In their view the enormous complexity and indeterminacy of human behaviour, across all its cultural, religious, historical and linguistic variations means that there can be no single interpretation of global reality. The problem with realism according to this view, is that by reducing the complexities of world politics to a single rigidly ordered framework of understanding, alternative interpretations and approaches to international security are ruled out. If the world is thought of in terms of anarchy then 'power politics' will be seen as the solution to the problem of insecurity. On the other hand, if anarchy and power politics are not seen as being an endemic feature of global history then other more peaceful approaches

to security might be tried. This has led post-modernist writers to try and reconceptualize the debate about global security by opening up new questions which have been ignored or marginalized. Jim George has argued that in the new post-cold war strategic discourse 'attention . . . has been focused on the growing sense of insecurity concerning state involvement in military-industrial affairs and the perilous state of the global economy. Questioned, too, has been the fate of those around the world rendered insecure by lives lived at the margins of existence yet unaccounted for in the statistics on military spending and strategic calculation' (George 1994). George argues that such questions require a new communitarian discourse about security.

Post-modernist writers believe that it is not only essential to replace realism with a communitarian discourse but it is an achievable objective. Because experts, and especially academic writers, have an important role to play in influencing 'the flow of ideas about world politics' it is vital for them to play their part in the process of transforming language and discourse about international politics. The whole nature of global politics can be transformed, and the traditional security dilemma can be overcome, if post-modern 'epistemic communities' play their part in spreading communitarian ideals (see Box 10.5).

Box 10.5. **Pursuing the 'Politics of Resistance'**

As people around the planet have illustrated in recent times, given the opportunities to understand the processes by which they are constituted (as, for example, subjects in an objective world of anarchical power politics) it is possible to change power relations and overturn irreducible 'realities'. In these circumstances it becomes possible also to say no, to ask why, to understand how. A range of resistances can flow from this. People can, for example, resist the damages of extreme nationalism, the illusory certainty of nuclear deterrence theory, the transformation of global life into the construction of otherness; they can help prevent their social and environmental structures being destroyed in the name of, for example, economic rationalism; they can oppose racism and sexism and the exploitation of the marginalized and 'different'; and they can insist on participating in decisions that define and determine their life opportunities and the fate of those brutalized by dominant regimes of stability and order 'out there' in the real world. In this way, a politics of resistance is possible that 'extend(s) processes of democratization into realms where it has never been tried: into the home, into the workplace, into processes of cultural production'.

(Jim George)

Key Points

- Post-modernists emphasize the importance of ideas and discourse in thinking about international security.

- Post-modernists aim to replace the 'discourse of realism' with a 'communitarian discourse'.

- Realist and post-modernist approaches have very different epistemologies.

- Post-modernists try to reconceptualize the debate about global security by looking at new questions which have been ignored by traditional approaches.

- There is a belief amongst post-modernist writers that the nature of international politics can be changed if 'epistemic communities' help to spread communitarian ideals.

Globalist Views of International Security

The opportunity to pursue changes in the international system is shared by scholars who point to new trends which are already taking place in world politics. In the past the state has been the centre of thinking about international relations. This state-centric view, however, is now increasingly challenged. Writers from the 'global society' school of thought argue that at the end of the twentieth century the process of **globalization** (which has been developing for centuries) has accelerated to the point 'where the clear outlines of a global society' are now evident. The emergence of a global economic system, global communications, and the elements of a global culture have helped to provide a wide network of social relationships which transcend state frontiers and encompass people all over the world. At the same time, so the argument goes, new risks associated with the environment, poverty, and weapons of mass destruction are facing humanity, just at a time when the nation-state is in crisis.

Supporters of the 'global society' school accept that globalization, is an uneven and contradictory process. The end of the cold war has been characterized not only by an increasing global awareness and the creation of a range of global social movements but also by the fragmentation of nation-states. This has been most obvious amongst the former communist states, especially the Soviet Union, Yugoslavia, and Czechoslovakia. Much the same pressures, however, have been felt in Western democratic societies with key institutions like the monarchy, the churches, and the family under increasing pressure. This has created what Martin Shaw has described as 'a crisis of Western civil society'. With the end of East–West confrontation, Shaw (1994: 170) argues that 'the ideological cement of Western civil society has dissolved'. As a result, whole communities, including 'villages and towns, ethnic groupings, their ways of life, traditions and forms of social organization—are threatened, along with the lives and well-being of individuals' (Shaw 1994: 172).

The result of this 'fracture of statehood' has been a movement away from conflicts between the great powers to new forms of insecurity caused by nationalistic, ethnic, and religious rivalries within states and across state boundaries. This has been reflected in the brutal civil wars that have been fought in Bosnia, Russia, Somalia, Rwanda, Yemen, and Algeria during the 1990s. Such conflicts, involving in some instances genocide and 'ethnic cleansing' pose a critical problem for the international community of whether to intervene in the domestic affairs of sovereign states to safeguard minority rights and individual human rights. This dilemma, according to global society theorists, reflects the historic transformation of human society which is taking place at the end of the twentieth century. Although states continue to limp along, global theorists argue, it is now increasingly necessary to think of the security of individuals and of groups within the emergent global society. The traditional focus on national or state security (and sovereignty) no longer reflects the radical changes which are taking place. What is needed, according to this school of thought, is a new politics of global responsibility, designed to address issues of global inequality, poverty, and environmental stress, as well as of human rights, minority rights, democracy, and individual and group security, which cut hugely across dominant interests on a world scale as well as within just about every state. Thinking in such globalist, rather than national or international terms, supporters argue, will lead to more effective action (including intervention where necessary) to deal with the risks to security which exist in the world community at present.

The globalist approach to security is based on what Anthony Giddens (1990: 154–8) calls **utopian realism.** According to this view it is 'realistic' to envisage the radical transformation of international politics as we have known it in the past. Indeed such a transformation, it is argued, is already taking place. Given the trends towards globalization it is realistic to envisage the expansion of the regional 'security communities' which are already in existence into a broader security community. Shaw (1994) in his book *Global Society and International Relations* argues that it is possible to see emerging a gigantic northern security community. He sees this as stretching from North America and Western Europe to the major states of the former USSR and Eastern Europe and to Japan, the newly industrializing states of East Asia, and Australia. He also sees other powers, including China, India, Egypt, and South Africa, being involved in regional extensions of this community. At the root of such a vision is a process of global communications which can help to create a new consensus on norms and beliefs which, in turn, can transform the nature of global security.

John Baylis

Key Points

- Supporters of the 'global society school' argue that the end of the twentieth century is witnessing an accelerating process of globalization.

- Globalization can be seen in the fields of economic development, communications, and culture. Global social movements are also a response to new risks associated with the environment, poverty, and weapons of mass destruction.

- Globalization is encouraged by the fragmentation of the nation-state which is taking place, encouraged by the end of the cold war.

- The fracture of statehood is giving rise to new kinds of conflict within states rather than between states which the state system cannot deal with. This has helped encourage an emerging politics of global responsibility.

- Globalism is also encouraged by the spread of regional security communities and the development of a growing consensus on norms and beliefs.

The Continuing Tension between National and International Security

At the centre of the contemporary debate about global and international security dealt with above is the issue of continuity and change. This involves questions about how the past is to be interpreted and whether international politics is in fact undergoing a dramatic change at present. There are also questions about how far these changes represent a fundamental transformation of international politics and whether it is possible to create an international or global system characterized by long-term peace and security. For realists, the empirical historical record is interpreted as providing a justification for their views that international politics always has been characterized by security competition and frequent wars, and the chances are that this pattern will continue into the future. For them there was no paradigmatic shift in 1989; nothing really has changed. East–West relations may be more peaceful, at present, but the potential for a resumption of great power conflict remains and conflicts, like the one in the former Yugoslavia and the Gulf War in the early 1990s, demonstrate the continuing importance of security competition between states as well as non-state groups. This reflects the tendency by realists to reject the argument that it is possible to change the practice of power politics by achieving a universal consensus in favour of 'new thinking' or a communitarian discourse based on more peaceful norms and beliefs. The chances of ideas like collective security being

widely adopted, according to this view, are almost negligible (see Box 10.6).

Realists also reject the contention raised by some of their critics that the state is becoming less central as regional and global considerations loom larger. The continuing primacy of the state is seen as a firm reality for the foreseeable future. Even in Europe where a large group of states are steadily integrating their political economies, it is argued that this will simply result in a larger entity forced to play a state-like role in the international system. This leads many realists to argue that, whatever the attraction of trying to develop an international or global security strategy, states are still likely in the future to define their security interests largely in national terms.

There is, however, a growing awareness in the 1990s amongst realists that the twin processes of integration and fragmentation do mean that more attention has to be given to the security agenda beyond the state. This has given rise to increasing interest in the concept of 'societal security' mentioned earlier. Writers like Ole Waever, Barry Buzan, Morten Kelstrup, and Pierre Lemaitre have argued that giving more attention to 'society' (defined in ethno-national terms) does not diminish the importance of *national* security. It puts 'more of the "national" back into "national security". It also opens up that area between the state and full regional integration which is neglected by traditional analysis' (Waever *et al*. 1993: 196).

Box 10.6. The Problems with Collective Security

John Mearsheimer has argued that collective security is inescapably flawed. There are *nine main reasons*, he suggests, why it is likely to fail:

1. States often find it difficult, if not impossible, to distinguish between the 'aggressor' and the 'victim' in international conflicts.

2. Collective security assumes that all aggression is wrong, whereas there may be circumstances where conquest is warranted against a threatening neighbour.

3. Because some states are especially friendly for historical or ideological reasons they will be unlikely to join a coalition against their friends.

4. Historical enmity between states may complicate the effective working of a collective security system.

5. Because sovereign states have a tendency to pass the buck in paying the price of dealing with aggression

there is often difficulty in distributing the burden equitably.

6. Difficulties arise in securing a rapid response to aggression because of the unwillingness to engage in pre-crisis contingency planning.

7. States are often reluctant to join a coalition because collective action is likely to transform a local conflict into an international conflict.

8. Democracies are reluctant to make an automatic commitment to join collective action because of state sovereignty.

9. Collective security implies a contradiction in the way military force is viewed. It is seen as abhorrent and yet states must be willing to use it against an aggressor.

Source: J. Mearsheimer, 'The False Promise of International Institutions', *International Security*, 19: 3 (Winter 1994/5).

Conclusions

What conclusions can we come to from this analysis of different views about international security in the late 1990s? As we move towards the twenty-first century strategic calculations and power remain a vitally important ingredient of state behaviour. But just as there have been long periods of co-operation in the past, so the international anarchy of the final years of the twentieth century creates considerable opportunities for co-operation to continue and be developed further. The structure of the international system, whether defined in material or social terms, continues to be a major influence on inter-state relations particularly in the way that they regard their security interests. This does not mean, however, that states always have to define their national security interests in narrow terms. Neither does it preclude important changes in international security as ideas, discourse, and global developments which are undoubtedly taking place, modify the processes of interaction which characterize world politics.

The spread of democratic states and democratic values—together with a justifiable conviction—by Western statesmen in particular that liberal institutions have an important role to play in moderating the traditional security dilemma, is helping to develop a more mature anarchy in the 1990s. Ideas

of co-operative or **common security** (in which states take account of the security interests of their neighbours) are beginning to have a significant impact on security policies in Europe and in other parts of the world. Under the umbrella of co-operative security thinking, **security communities** and **security regimes** are being developed (see Box 10.4). This can be seen in the developments which have taken place in the European Union, the OSCE and NATO, as well as the relations between Nordic countries and between ASEAN states in South East Asia. **Security regimes** like the Non-Proliferation Treaty of 1968 (which was extended indefinitely in 1995) reflect the way that states often do accept norms and rules of behaviour that help to overcome the dangers of competition.

These developments in both the theory and practice of security involve, in some respects, something of a shift from the traditional preoccupation with national security to a growing recognition of the importance of international and global security considerations. In part, this may be the result of a shift in the discourse about security in the 1980s (as critical theorists contend) but of equal, if not greater, significance is the changing geopolitical circumstances of the period and an acceptance that many national security objectives can only be achieved through broader co-operative action. Strategic calculations (which have a symbiotic relationship with the discourse on security) in some important respects are pushing states increasingly towards greater co-operation.

It must be said, however, that despite this trend, it is not universal and there remains a continuing tension between national and international (and global) security interests which cannot be ignored. As Buzan (1983: 214–42) has argued 'the national security imperative of minimising vulnerabilities sits unhappily with the risks of international agreement, and the prospects for international agreement are weakened by the power-security dilemma effects of a national security strategy'.

An example of the practical importance of the contradiction which this tension causes can be seen from the debates which have taken place about nuclear deterrence since the end of the cold war. On one level, it has been recognized that as a 'threat-based' strategy, nuclear deterrence is a major impediment to the development of a 'co-operative security' system between East and West. This has led to a wide range of policies designed to play down the significance of nuclear weapons and to reverse the arms race. The whole process of denuclearization inherent in the START I and II Treaties, the INF Treaty, the extension of the Non-Proliferation Treaty, the Comprehensive Test Ban Agreement, ongoing negotiations on a cut-off of fissile material production, the decision by the US and Russia to stop targeting each other, and the new NATO strategic concept, all reflect a determination by national governments to try and enhance international security in the 1990s by de-emphasizing the role of nuclear weapons in their security policies.

At another level, however, the nuclear powers continue to enhance qualitatively their nuclear capabilities (through computer simulation and other techniques). Even though nuclear weapons have been pushed more into the background they continue to exist and the nuclear states (and non-declared nuclear states like Israel, India, and Pakistan) continue to maintain nuclear deterrent strategies. What this means is that states possessing nuclear weapons (both declared and undeclared) continue to pose an *implicit* threat to existing or potential adversaries simply through their continuing possession of nuclear weapons. The result is that states pursue the objective of greater co-operation which requires trust, while at the same time hedging their bets by maintaining national military capabilities which reflect a lack of trust and an uncertainty that co-operative security can ultimately succeed in overcoming the security dilemma completely. This reflects the contemporary lack of consensus generally about fully accepting co-operative security ideas as the foundation of national security.

As the twentieth century draws to a close, therefore, despite important changes which are taking place in world politics, the traditional ambiguity about international security remains. In many ways the world is a much safer place to live in as a result of the end of the cold war and the removal of nuclear confrontation as a central element in East–West relations. The spread of democratic and communitarian values, the process of globalization and the generally co-operative effects of international institutions have played an important part in dampening down some of the competitive aspects of the security dilemma between states. These significant trends, however, are offset to a certain extent by evidence of the continuing importance of military force as an arbiter of disputes both between and particularly within states. Conventional arms races continue in different regions of the world, nuclear, chemical, and biological weapons still provide a powerful influence on the security calculations of many states, crazy and ambitious politicians remain at the head of some governments, and cultural differences as well as diverse values prevent the emergence of global agreement on a wide range of important issues. Societal insecurity is also increasingly evident as the forces of fragmentation and integration destabilize traditional identities and thereby complicate relations between states.

As a result, it remains much too soon to conclude that a paradigmatic shift is taking place in international politics in the aftermath of the cold war or that such a permanent shift is possible. Undoubtedly, as many other chapters in this book indicate, new and positive developments are taking place in the world in which we live which suggest that the future of international politics does not have to be like the past. At the same time, the empirical historical evidence suggests caution. Periods of more co-operative interstate (and inter-group) relations have often led to a false dawn and an unwarranted euphoria that the 'perpetual peace' was about to break out. The structure of the international system provides an important constraint on the way that individuals, states, or international institutions behave. So does the predominance of realist attitudes towards international security amongst many of the world's political leaders. This is not to argue that there is no room for peaceful change or that new ideas and discourse about international relations are unimportant in helping to shape choices that have to be made. Opportunities to develop greater international and global security will always exist. In a world of continuing diversity, mistrust, and uncertainly, however, it is likely that the search for a more co-operative global society is likely to remain in conflict with the powerful pressures which exist for states to look after their own national security. Whether and how international security can be achieved still remains, as Herbert Butterfield once argued, 'the hardest nut of all' for students and practitioners of international politics to crack.

QUESTIONS

1. Why is security a 'contested concept'?

2. Why do traditional realist writers focus on national security?

3. What do neo-realist writers mean by 'structure'?

4. What is meant by the 'security dilemma'?

5. Why do states find it difficult to co-operate?

6. What do you understand by the terms 'contingent realism' and 'mature anarchy'?

7. Do you find 'liberal institutionalism' convincing?

8. Why might democratic states be more peaceful?

9. Why do you think collective security arrangements failed in the past?

10. How do 'constructivist' views about international security differ from those of 'neo-realists'?

11. Do you think ideas and discourse influence the way states behave?

12. Is the tension between national and international security resolvable?

GUIDE TO FURTHER READING

B. Buzan's *People's, States and Fear* (London: Harvester, 1983) provides an excellent starting point for the study of national and international security. The book is written largely from a neo-realist perspective.

Michael Joseph Smith's study of *Realist Thought from Weber to Kissinger* (Baton Rouge: Louisiana State University Press, 1986) covers the development of what has been described as classical realism and discusses some of the major thinkers in the field. Kenneth Waltz provides an overview of neo-realism in his article 'Realist Thinking and Neorealist Theory' in the *Journal of International Affairs*, 44:1 (1990).

For a very interesting alternative view see Alexander Wendt, 'Anarchy is What States Make of it : The Social Construction of Power Politics', in *International Organization*, 46:2 (1992). This article gives a very useful analysis of the 'Constructivist' perspective.

In their study *Identity, Migration and the New Security Agenda in Europe* (London: Pinter, 1993) Ole Waever, Barry Buzan, Morten Kelstrup, and Pierre Lemaitre develop the new concept of 'Societal Security'. This provides an original perspective for studying the kind of non-state aspects of security which have affected Europe in the post-cold war period.

A very useful contemporary discussion about the changing nature of security can be found in Ronnie D. Lipschutz (ed.), *On Security* (New York: Columbia University Press, 1995).

11 International Political Economy in an Age of Globalization

Roger Tooze

READER'S GUIDE

This chapter identifies 'international political economy' (IPE) as one of the most important elements of the structure of international politics and a central issue area for a globalizing International Relations. It characterizes IPE as the issues created by the blurring of the boundaries between what is considered politics and economics, and between what was considered national and international. The chapter argues that IPE is constructed through social interaction and does not represent a given external reality—therefore claims and debates about IPE in both academic debate and in formal and informal politics are an integral part of the political process.

The key problem for IPE is a structural one—a system of political units based on territory is now overlaid by a global economy that takes power away from individual states and groups of states. This structural problem acts as a context for all the other issues of IPE because it frames them—the problems of trade, finance, and investment and their political resolution are different in a globalized economy. The chapter focuses on the concepts and ideas that underpin this, and explores the consequences for our understanding of and policy for this structural problem by analysing the nature of the traditional 'international economy' and its implications for International Relations, and contrasting this with the nature and consequences of a 'global economy'. A number of developments in the world economy are identified and discussed and an assessment made of their implications for the key issue of IPE: the concentration of world economic activity in the countries of the Triad (North America, European Union, Japan/Asia); capital flows;

global firms and international production; domestic/international blurring; and the ideological basis of the global political economy.

The chapter ends by briefly reviewing the changes and bringing a number of the arguments together to conclude that the essential tension between the territorial state and the forces of globalization will dominate IPE for the foreseeable future.

Roger Tooze

Introduction: The Significance of IPE for Globalized International Relations

'International political economy' (IPE) is both an area of study—a range of issues and problems—and a way of thinking about world politics and economics. It is particularly appropriate in the context of this book that we should now consider the arena of international political economy in a globalized world as the international economy is widely regarded as the principal focus of the forces of globalization and the main way in which globalization is 'transmitted' throughout the world. In other words, what happens in the international economy (as a result of a variety of factors, influences, and forces, but crucially including what is produced and how, the nature and extent of technology, advances in the speed, reliability, and cost of transport and communications) is a *reflection* of the changes brought about by globalization. These changes are wide-ranging but include changes in the nature and extent of production and trade, the growth of very large worldwide corporations, the internationalization of finance, and the linking of people and businesses through world communication networks. However, what happens in the international economy also, and at the same time, has the potential to *cause and deepen* globalization and therefore has a significant actual and potential impact upon the nature of world politics. Hence, **if** we do now live in a globalized world, then the nature and structure of international economic relations will immediately show this because of the fact that it is these relations that first change in response to the new forms of production, investment, finance, and trade that are key elements of the condition of globalization. And any changes in these relations will have a very significant effect upon national governments (and their international relations), firms, and us as individuals,

because of the extent to which national politics and national economics are changed and influenced by what happens in the international political economy.

This chapter will concentrate on the ideas, concepts, and assumptions behind the argument on 'globalization' and builds upon the centrality of IPE in a globalizing world. We consider the nature and problems of IPE, how it is defined and interpreted, and what principal difficulties this presents for our understanding of the contemporary world. The chapter then considers 'how' we begin to understand and evaluate these problems, arguing that the way we use words and ideas to describe and argue and hence construct an understanding of the world is itself part of the political process and must be taken into consideration in trying to understand IPE. In the section on 'Thinking about IPE, IR, and Globalization' the fundamental issue for IPE is identified and discussed—the problem of an international political system based on territorial states increasingly overlaid by an economic system based on world markets and production, and the basic constituents of an 'international economy' and a 'global political economy' are laid out. On the basis of this we can identify the broad contours of 'What Kind of World have we Made?' and conclude that it is a complex one which not only includes the issues arising from challenges to state power and legitimacy, but also includes deeper analysis of the changes taking place at global levels and the links between global and local levels. The Conclusion to the chapter argues that there are no neat and easily accessible solutions to the problems of global governance and that these problems will intensify over the next ten years.

What is IPE?

Terms, Labels, and Interpretations

'International political economy' is a label for a certain way of thinking about and analysing interna-

tional relations. It has a number of distinct meanings generally linked to competing perspectives, but there is no one generally agreed definition of the term or any accepted perspective because, as we shall see, any definition will reflect certain values and preferences, and we simply do not all agree on those values and preferences. The process of resolving differences in values and preferences is the process of politics itself, and different views of IPE reflect different political positions and political judgements.

Within the study of international relations, IPE is primarily a way of thinking about the world that *asserts* two major interconnections. One interconnection is that politics and economics are inseparable—politics can only be understood if economics is taken into account and, vice versa, economics can only be understood if politics is taken into account. Politics constructs economics at the same time as economics constructs politics. This means that IPE does not accept the idea that the processes which have brought about forms of globalization have 'politicized' (made political) a previously non-political international economy organized on a purely rational 'economic' basis. For IPE the international economy has **always** been political in that it concerns the processes of 'who gets what, when and how'—and this is politics. As Paul Hirst and Grahame Thompson argue in an important new analysis, 'the term "international economy" has always been shorthand for what is actually the product of the complex interaction of economic relations and politics, shaped and reshaped by the struggles of the Great Powers' (1996: 14).

The other assertion of an interconnection comes from the observation that for international political economy the distinction between what is 'international' (i.e. outside of the state) and what is 'national' (i.e. inside the state) is no longer valid. The argument is that the extent and depth of interdependence (mutual dependence but not necessarily equal)—created through transnational economic processes that cut across state boundaries, increased trade, membership of regional economic groupings, and the processes of globalization—has effectively joined national societies and economies together to the extent that no national policy can be purely 'domestic' any more (see Case Study 1, Box 11.1).

The condition leading to the blurring of the boundaries between politics/economics and national/international is principally the creation of high levels of interdependence between national political economies. High levels of interdependence effectively connect national economies, so that each national economy becomes more sensit-

---

Box 11.1. Case Study 1: 'International' and 'National'

'ideas of national and international, of domestic and foreign, of exterior and interior, and of frontier limits that used to define the existence of an international economy, are losing their validity. The outline of nation-states is becoming blurred and the power of the state over economic activity is lessened.'

(Charles-Albert Michalet 1982)

'For developed economies, the distinction between the domestic and the international economy has ceased to be a reality, however much political, cultural or psychological strength remains in the idea.'

(Drucker 1993: 104)

---

ive, and sometimes highly vulnerable, to changes in other national economies. For example, a change in monetary interest rates in the US (a US national decision) can have far-reaching effects on other national financial conditions and policies (which are supposed to be controlled by the government of that country), and this brings changes both to 'domestic' policies and conditions in other states, by forcing a lower interest rate, and to international relations as other countries respond, either directly or through existing international institutions. Or, in the extreme, because of the extent to which the industrialized economies are linked together (interdependent) the disruption of world-traded oil supplies would have immediate and serious effects on a number of energy-dependent economies and on the world economy as a whole, and would bring about an instant and major intervention from those with the power to respond—as did the presumed threat both to world oil supplies and to global financial stability posed by the Iraqi invasion of Kuwait.

Interdependence then, acts as a transmission belt for these kinds of influences, and a key issue associated with the process of globalization is that this transmission belt between national (political) economies is transmitting more and more economic influences *into and away from* the national political economy, with greater potential effect. However, because national governments everywhere now take responsibility for managing their national economies, the changes transmitted by interdependence/globalization have significant political implications: governments find it increasingly difficult to achieve their national policies if changes generated from outside the boundaries of the state alter the conditions of economic (and hence, political) activity inside the boundaries of the state. Partly in response to this problem, states have over the past hundred years attempted to construct ways of managing industrial change within the context of the international economy that help them to achieve their national policies (Murphy 94). This has involved creating a large number of international institutions and agreements for the collective management of the international economy. In this way what could be seen previously as 'national economics' becomes rapidly translated into 'national politics', and 'national' politics and economics become the concern of 'international' actions and a major focus of international relations.

Hence, the combination of these two claimed interconnections means that IPE looks at what happens *when the boundaries between politics and economics, and between the international and the national are broken down* (see Box 11.2)—and it is one of the key claims of those who argue that globalization has had important consequences that these boundaries are now almost irrelevant to our understanding of IPE.

Different perspectives of IPE put the cells of Box 11.2 in different 'driving' positions in order to provide explanations, judgements and prescriptions. For instance, the liberal theory of IPE identifies the economic logic of the market as the proper driving force of IPE, whilst realist theory puts the state and politics in that position. Other explanations start from the international level, either politics or economics, or the national level, and argue that this

level is the starting point for explaining the IPE. However, it is clear that the dominant world view of the moment throughout the industrialized world is that of 'neo-liberalism' which asserts the values and preferences of the market above other ways of organizing society. In Box 11.2 this puts a particular kind of national economy—one in which market forces are dominant and limitations on market-based economic activity are minimal—as the driving idea and objective. It is this view which has become the basis of the changes in the world economy that we have come to call 'globalization'. Because ideas are used to bring about and justify particular distributions of economic and political power we cannot separate 'neo-liberalism' from the broad interests of those who wield economic/political power in a globalized economy.

You could usefully at this stage check back to Chapters 6 and 8 on 'Realism' and 'Liberalism' to confirm your understanding of the claims of these two theories and think about how they relate to the issues of IPE.

IPE and the Issues of IR

There are many who think and write about IPE who argue that what we know as 'international relations'—that is political and (now) economic relations between states—are ultimately part of a larger set of relations and structures, and this larger set is what is described by the term 'international political economy' (Rupert 1995; Strange 1994): i.e. traditional political relations between states can only be understood and explained as part of IPE. At the other end of the spectrum many see the term 'IPE' as indicating a subset of relations within the totality made up of international relations. This second view means that IPE considers a number of issues, such as money, finance, trade, and investment, that are not looked at by other parts of the discipline of International Relations (IR). For example, Joshua Goldstein sees IR as made up of two main subfields—international security studies and IPE, where IPE studies trade, monetary relations, and multinational corporations, the economic integration of Europe, the international politics of the global environment, the economic gap between North and South, and the issues of development (Goldstein 1994). The book this chapter is in, because it starts with the system of states as the basis

---

Box 11.2. What is Included in IPE?

national politics	national economics
international politics	international economics

IPE argues that the boundaries between politics and economics and what is national and what is international are dissolving.

for international relations, identifies IPE as a key part of the structure and process of contemporary international politics. This allows for other non-state actors to have significance and meaning, whilst retaining an initial focus on the state and the inter-state system. Hence IPE is both a core element of the structure of international politics and a set of international issues within the context of a globalizing international relations.

Key Points

- The international economy is both a reflection and a transmitter of globalization and is therefore central to the analysis of and debate on globalization and its impact on international relations.

- The international economy has always been political and hence the most appropriate label is 'the international political economy'.

- 'International political economy' as an area of study refers to the issues created when the boundaries between 'economics' and 'politics', and 'international' and 'national' are broken down and become blurred.

- Different perspectives view each of the four domains as being the principal force for change, but the dominant view of 'neo-liberalism' seeks to construct the international economy on the same basis as the 'free market' domestic economy with a minimum of political regulation.

Words and Politics

Part of the problem of thinking about and understanding politics and particularly the phenomena of globalization is that *words matter*. By this I mean that politics (or political economy) does not exist as 'something out there', ready formed and waiting for us to discover and analyse (like, perhaps, coal in the ground that we discover and mine). This is so because we, as human beings, are not separate from politics. Our actions are part of politics and because our words both frame and give meaning and purpose to those actions they are thus part of politics itself—the contest of words and ideas. The words we use both reflect and construct our reality in general and politics in particular. Moreover, we share our reality through our language and shared meanings. Our reality is also an intersubjective reality. This is an important statement, because it means that we see words and ideas not as reflecting politics or commentating on politics, but as an integral part of politics itself.

The way in which we see the world derives largely from our historical experience of the world (Cox 1992). This knowledge is codified into theory— *everyone* has a theory of the world, a 'world view', but for most people and most of the time this is hidden or not acknowledged. Often, our world view presents itself as 'common sense' and because of this we do not question the assumptions built into our 'common sense', but it is important to understand that what we take as 'common sense' is both variable through time and society and is constructed politically, that is it brings benefits to a particular group. World views are very durable and form a way of us connecting to our past, present, and future. Theory (derived from history) forms the context of what we think we can do, what we cannot do, and what we are required to do. Theory, in the form of a world view, gives us meaning and purpose. Because we act on the basis of our world views, our theories, we translate our understanding of the world into our reality—what we think (what is

---

Box 11.3. Case Study 2: Words and Reality: The State and International Economy

'What is subjective in understanding becomes objective through action. This is the only way, for instance, in which we can understand the state as an objective reality. The state has no physical existence, like a building or a lamp-post; but it is nevertheless a real entity. It is a real entity because *everyone acts as though it were*; because we know that real people with guns and batons will enforce decisions attributed to this non-physical reality.'

(emphasis added; Cox 1992: 133)

---

subjective in understanding) becomes real (objective) through our actions (see Case Study 2, Box 11.3).

This argument about the connection between words and politics has two main consequences for this chapter and for the study of IPE. The first is that the words (labels) we use to describe the world (e.g. 'international political economy', 'international politics', etc.) carry with them a specific view of what the world **is**—what are the basic units (states, companies, cities, etc.) and how they interact (war, trade, production, etc.), and what kind of order (structure) is constituted by these units and relationships. So the choice of the label is very important because it is shorthand for a whole way of describing the world—'international politics' describes a world that is very different from 'international political economy'. And the world described by 'international political economy' is different from the world described by 'global political economy'.

The second consequence, equally important, is that the words people use to describe the world are part of the political process of constructing politics. Therefore we need to look very carefully at *what is said by whom*, as this is itself part of politics and not only sets up the framework for discussion in which some ideas are accepted as legitimate and some are not, but also forms the content of our intersubjective reality (see Box 11.3). Hence, some views of the way world politics 'works' and how it is constructed become more acceptable than others—the legitimacy of different views of the world is an important part of political struggle. And what is legitimate then becomes the view that defines what the world actually is. This is particularly important when we try to reach an understanding of the impact of globalization on the issues of IPE. The process of 'globalization' (however defined—see Ch. 1) and the changes it brings about tend to serve particular interests—favouring basically those with capital or access to capital via credit above those who depend upon selling their labour, and historically those with some form of technological training or general advanced education above those that have none

(Reich 1991; Kanter 1995). This does not mean that others have not benefited and do not benefit now, but that some groups in society benefit more. As a result some favour the changes brought about by globalization and act accordingly to bring about further globalization—both in words and deeds.

If we took at face value the clamour of debate and discussion by those involved in state and inter-state politics and the descriptions and claims of those involved in the transnational political economy we could be forgiven for thinking that we and governments already live in a fully globalized society (Hirst and Thompson 1996; Hutton 1995). Most OECD member governments already seem to be basing their policy discussions and formulating their policies on the assumption of a 'globalized' political economy. On the most basic of political levels, if policy-makers believe we are existing within a global political economy they will construct political programmes appropriate to the reality of a global political economy, rather than any other version of international political economic reality, and this will favour some groups in society more than others. 'Who benefits?' is thus a key question for IPE to ask of any situation, idea, or policy proposal.

Key Points

- Words matter—the IPE is constructed through our intersubjective understanding, which is then reproduced and/or modified through our words and actions.

- 'Globalization' brings different benefits to different people, but clearly benefits some more than others.

- The argument for and about 'globalization' is itself part of politics, and is already changing the way that governments frame and implement policy.

- 'Who benefits?' is the key question that IPE asks of the world.

Thinking about IPE, IR, and Globalization

States and the International Economy

From the point of view of IPE, the relationship of states to the international economy has always been problematic because, according to realist theory, the international system is anarchic. And the anarchic is difficult to 'manage'—even with effective regimes (see Ch. 12). Hence, if the international economy is important to the wealth of states (and their populations) it immediately becomes a significant domestic political issue.

In more general terms, the 'fit' of a national economy into international structures—production, trade, resources, finance, etc.—will produce a range of political economy issues, the resolution of which will vary according to the specific circumstances of the industries and sectors of the national economy. For example, protecting domestic industries through trade restrictions, principally tariffs (trade taxes) and quotas (limits on the amount or number imported), has been a conventional way of ensuring that domestic production is not swamped by cheaper imports. But, if an industry is successful in international trade or depends itself on imports, say of semi-finished goods or key components, then that industry's interests may not necessarily be served by protection, partly because it may put up the cost of essential components and partly because of the fear of retaliation. So it is perfectly possible to have some parts of an economy (sectors) that want and support protection, e.g. steel or agriculture, and at the same time other sectors, that depend to a greater extent on an internationalized economy, to be against any policy that adds to their costs, e.g. automobile manufacturers. Hence, it is often difficult to generalize about the appropriate mix of policies that may resolve the issues resulting from national interaction with the international economy.

The Core Question

From the perspective of this book the key question and issue for IPE in a globalizing or globalized IR is not derived from the problems of international investment, production, trade, or even finance, although all these are important. And unfortunately the fundamental issue is not and has not been the alleviation of worldwide poverty and inequality either (see Ch. 23). The problem for IPE is one of the actual or potential structural mismatch between a formal state system based on territory (i.e. nation states) and an economic system that is increasingly non-territorial and globalized (see, among others, Agnew and Corbridge 1995). This is a problem at a much deeper level than, say, the political economy of trade, because it addresses the basic, underlying framework of IPE and therefore *sets the context for the consideration of all contemporary issues*. Consider the issue of trade as an important and 'live' policy issue in many national political economies and international forums. Trade generates much political controversy, for example the US–Japan trade balance has been a major feature of both US domestic politics and US–Japan international relations for some time, but its explanation and resolution as an issue for politics depends on identifying and understanding the underlying framework of the international economy (and the way in which 'national' economic activity fits into the international) within which trade takes place. Different frameworks produce different explanations and different policies according to our political objectives. Given the importance of this structural question and the fact that this whole book could be taken up with a discussion of the myriad problems and complexities of IPE, the rest of this chapter will focus principally on this core problem.

The material in Case Study 3 (Box 11.4) identifies, describes, and confirms the central problem for IPE as the tension between the national, territorial nature of the state (as the prime political unit in International Relations) and the world economy, increasingly transnational (across national boundaries) in character and global in extent and nature. This tension has been in evidence for some time, in that as a greater part of a state's economic activity has become either international or has been linked to international activities it becomes more complex to manage in order to achieve the political objectives of the government of that state. Of course, given the historical conditions of the emergence of modern states it is doubtful whether the physical boundaries of the state ever contained the total of economic activity, so managing the economy

---

Box 11.4. Case Study 3: The Core Problem for IPE in a Globalizing World

'The new reality is that the system of states is overlaid by a highly integrated, incompletely regulated, rapidly growing—but consequently somewhat unstable—world economy. There is a tension between the principle of national self-determination and the principle of openness in the world economy which is the core problematic of international political economy.'

(Strange 1994a: 212)

'The most important tension of late capitalism . . . is the national political constitution of states and the global character of accumulation.'

(Burnham 1994: 229)

'The evidence of the past four decades does show convincingly that participation in the world economy has become the controlling factor in the domestic economic performance of developed countries.'

(Drucker 1993: 105)

---

outside of the territory of the state is an old problem.

It is significant that the three quotes in Case Study 3 (Box 11.4) are also drawn from three different approaches to IPE—so there is no question of this problem simply being one derived from a particular point of view and hence allowing that point of view to set the agenda for politics. This is known as 'privileging' a perspective and the issues identified as important by the perspective, and is an important aspect of the political function of dominant ideas—what viewpoints and issues are 'privileged' and what issues are ignored or silenced?

What is 'International' and what is 'Global'

The most common starting point is with the precise nature and form of the set of relationships that is conventionally labelled 'the international economy'. Let us now look at what is meant by the term 'international economy' and what it represents 'in reality'. We have already discussed how 'international economy' is shorthand for a complex and negotiated mix of politics and economics, and therefore should be called 'the international political economy', but (as also discussed) it also signi-

fies a particular arrangement of entities and a specific set of relationships that is reproduced and modified by our actions. At its most straightforward, the 'international economy' is the sum total of economic relations between and among nation states. The basic units are national economies and the activities that are significant are initially trade (with international payments for trade) and then followed by investment.

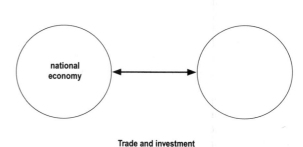

Trade and investment

Fig. 11.1. The international economy
The basic unit of the 'international economy' is the national economy, bounded by the physical limits of the state, in which national governments mediate between the 'international' and the 'national'.

This simple model of 'international economy' is the extension into international economics and political economy of the core assumptions of realism and neo-realism—the dominant world views of international relations based on the state (see Ch. 6). It is this model of the world which is the implicit basis for much international economic policy and for most media reporting on and discussion of 'international economy'. It is this model which is the basis of most sets of statistics which claim to describe and measure international economic activity, that is, they are based on flows *across* national political boundaries. And, it is this model that has become the 'common-sense' basis to our day-to-day understanding of IPE—hence, in terms of the argument above, privileging its definition of economic reality. It is, of course a gross simplification, but it clearly identifies the defining characteristics of the international economy as flows between national economies, where national economies are defined by territory (see Agnew and Corbridge 1995).

If we do live in a world where this model—of international economy—accurately describes the way that economic relationships between states are structured, then our approach to understanding and explaining the problems that are created would lead us to emphasize the competencies and authority of national governments and international governmental organizations, and the construction and operation of international regimes to regulate international economic activity. We would be concerned above all with problems of trade and investment. We would acknowledge that the continuing increase in and importance of the volume of world trade and the extent and significance of global investment produces problems for the state's ability to achieve its political goals, but, given the structure of the 'international economy', we would conclude that the state (and its international institutions) still has the fundamental capacity to control, modify, and benefit from the consequences of an **internationalized** economy. This conclusion would assert the primacy of continuity over change, and confirm that we would be working in a world that is essentially unchanged since the formalization of the modern state system over two hundred years ago.

However, there are many in business, politics, and academic life who now argue that we no longer have a simple and straightforward international economy based on trade and investment relations between separate national economies and controlled by national governments. In their view what we now have is much more complex, and as a result this simple model of 'international economy' needs to be either modified and extended or discarded in favour of a 'world' or 'global 'political economy. The essence of such a global economy is that we now have a structure that is *more than* and additional to the 'international economy', and is made up of firms and other entities that operate transnationally over the whole globe. The activities of these firms are based upon and geared towards global production and services for a global market, with much of their economic activity taking place outside of the market within their own global structures. Together these activities constitute a fundamental change in the overall structure of international political economy. The structure of global political economy contains the 'old' international economy within a new framework which is based in the territory of states, but not necessarily 'national' in terms of purpose, organization, and benefit. Perhaps the best way to demonstrate this is to use and extend the illustration for the 'international economy':

The relationships and structures of the interna-

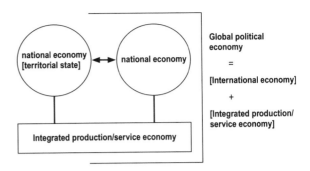

Fig. 11.2. **The basis of the global political economy**

tional economy continue to exist but they only describe a part of the total of world economic activity (around 55 per cent in 1990). So in order to describe the **total** of political economic activity we must include a consideration of what is called the 'integrated production and service' economy (Michalet 1982). Hence, a full picture of the totality of world activity—the global political economy- is a complex multi-level structure and is composed of the 'international economy' **plus** 'the integrated production and service economy'. The activities of this economy are the aggregation of the activities of a large number of transnational firms and entities (shown in Fig. 11.2 by the lines linking the national economies and the integrated economy) and they are linked organically to the national and international economy by both being located within the territory of states and within the jurisdiction of state legal/economic regimes, and having economic relations with specifically national economic entities, such as purely national suppliers of components or goods. But, and crucially, the strategies and purposes of these 'global' entities are not necessarily congruent with or supportive of the strategies and purposes of the separate national governments of the states within which they are located. This means that in analytical and political economy terms this economy is distinct from the activities that constitute the 'international economy', although clearly there are many linkages between the two.

If we now have a 'global' economy alongside and superseding the 'international economy' the ability of the state to achieve its objectives is, at the very least, challenged and, depending on the extent of 'globalization', may be severely reduced. If this is the case, then the possibility of any democratic control or accountability is also severely reduced, even from the low levels that 'executive' governments have already placed it. This situation gives rise to a number of fundamental questions and problems, to which we shall now turn.

Key Points

- The way that any national economy fits into the international economy produces distinct political problems—for the state and international relations—depending on the nature of that state's economic activity and the power it has to structure the system.
- The fundamental problem for IPE is the actual or potential mismatch between an international political system based on territorial states and an economic system increasingly non-territorial and globalized.

- The 'international economy' is the sum total of the economic relations between national economies, mediated and controlled by the national governments and their international organizations and regimes.
- A 'global economy' is the 'international economy' plus the activities of the 'integrated production and service economy' operating as a total system, with much of the dynamic provided by the latter—crucially the objectives and interests of global economic actors may not be the same as or in support of individual governments or the system as a whole.
- The greater the degree of 'globalization' the more complex the IPE becomes, the greater the problems of control for states and international governmental organizations, the more difficult it is to achieve any democratic control of national economic life and historically the greater the gap between rich and poor in the global political economy.

What Kind of World have We made?

'International' or 'Global'?

Our first task is to establish exactly what kind of world we live in—is it more like our traditional 'international economy' or is it closer to a 'global economy'? (See Figs. 11.2 and 11.3.) In either case we can safely conclude at a minimum that it is a **political economy** we are investigating, rather than a pure economy. However, the extent and implications of 'globalization' are perhaps the most hotly debated questions in IPE (see Boyer and Drache 1996; Hirst and Thompson 1996). It is probably fair to say that for most commentators and for some policy-makers the jury is still out on whether or not we have a 'globalized political economy' that has made the state increasingly redundant and will continue to do so, although some regard capitalism as necessarily 'global' in extent and clearly dominant as a form of political economy (see, in particular, Gill and Law 1988).

Of course, **any** international activity or event external to the territorial space of the 'nation state' is more of a problem in terms of governmental control than a similar activity or event within the terri-

torial space. This is one of the bases of the claim to political sovereignty and economic autonomy made by national governments. And national governments have responded to growing international linkages through trade, investment, and technology for the past 250 years and have also initiated forms of political organization designed to enable the collective 'management' of the international economy (see Murphy 1994). So even within a firmly traditional 'international economy', with the added complication for Western Europe of the EU, the level of complexity of policy and collective decision-making is very high, and the consequences of failure can be catastrophic. Hence, even if we decide that the fundamental basis of IPE remains the national/international economy, the policy problems are still immensely difficult.

Whatever our eventual judgement on the nature of our international/global world, it is relatively clear that some important aspects of the international system of political economic relations have changed and contribute centrally to the world we have made. We shall briefly consider five: the concentration of economic activity within the 'Triad' of North America, the European Union, and Japan/Asia; the vast increase in capital flows in the world economy; the growth of global firms as international 'actors' and the nature of 'international production'; the further blurring of boundaries between domestic and international realms; and the ideological basis of international economic relations.

'Uneven globalization'

More and more advanced economic activity takes place amongst the three most developed regions of the world: 'the process of technological, economic and socio-cultural integration amongst the three most developed regions of the world (Japan plus the NICs from South-East Asia, Western Europe and North America) is more diffused, intensive and significant than 'integration' between these three regions and the less-developed countries, or between the less-developed themselves' (Petrella 1996: 77). Thus, national economies outside of the Triad are increasingly marginalized from the processes of wealth creation whilst the levels of economic interdependence **within** the Triad are increasing. With this development comes an intensification of the knowledge content of advanced production and a de-linking of production to raw material resources. Both these developments further disadvantage those outside of the Triad. Moreover, with this process of economic concentration comes also the political domination of the management of the world political economy, brought into stark relief by the admission of Russia to the group of richest countries that collectively 'manage' the world economy. Of course, this begs the question as to where China fits and will fit within the global political economy, and no simple answer is possible given the unique constellation of forces and ideas that characterizes the current situation.

Hence, globalization is partial in spatial terms and selective in its impact—this conclusion is supported by a number of indicators (see Petrella 1996):

- Triad countries in 1980 accounted for 55 per cent of total world exports of manufactured goods; in 1990 the figure was 64 per cent. Imports are similarly distributed: in 1980 Triad countries accounted for 60 per cent of all imports of manufactured goods, in 1990 64 per cent.

> **Box 11.5. Global Capital Flows**
>
> Three main categories of capital flows:
>
> - money and finance—linked to trade in goods and services (e.g. imports, airline tickets)
> - foreign direct investment—financial capital transfers, also physical, human, and technological capital
> - portfolio investments (investing in a range of instruments for financial gain, rather than control over an enterprise) and various other forms of transactions (including speculation)
>
> *Source*: (after Petrella1996)

- the poorest countries' (102 countries) figures are as follows: exports of manufactured goods: 1980—7.9 per cent, 1990—1.4 per cent; imports of manufactured goods: 1980—9.0 per cent, 1990—4.9 per cent.
- capital flows—each of the three components of capital flows (see Box 11.5) has demonstrated concentration within the Triad countries. In the 1980s the Triad accounted for approximately 80 per cent of all international capital flows.
- in knowledge and technology firms—where a growing and highly significant percentage of wealth is created—co-operation between firms on 'strategic technology' is becoming the best indicator of economic success. Of the 4,000+ inter-firm agreements made in the period 1980–9 over 90 per cent were between Triad firms.

Global Capital Flows

Over the past twenty years global capital flows (see Box 11.5) have been one of the principal areas of change and growth and many argue that it is in this area that the main developments in globalization have taken place (Strange 1994). Two aspects are most pertinent: the volume and the nature of these flows and their spatial distribution. With regard to the first aspect, there has been an explosion in the volume of financial transactions—dealing in currencies and other forms of risk minimization—to the extent that the amounts now traded dwarf the value of world trade (i.e. the transactions necessary to pay for international trade in goods and services). This has brought about a fundamental shift

223

to what has been called the 'symbol' economy of capital movements, exchange rates, and credit flows (see Case Study 4, Box 11.6). The consequences of this change can sometimes be severe as national currencies are devalued and revalued by the activities and concerns of the 'market' rather than by the actions of governments—although this need not necessarily be bad, most national politicians regard it as bad in times of crisis! Much of the volume of transactions of capital flows is thus 'disembedded' from the needs of the 'real' economy, and this can cause chaos at times:

we do now live in a global economy that is thoroughly internationalised in its expanding core areas of commodity trade and production capital, and which is globalizing apace in the case of money flows and financial capital. We also live in a world in which the markets can defeat even the most concerted efforts by a government, or even groups of governments, to defend particular national exchange rates and interest rates. (Agnew and Corbridge 1995: 177–8)

The second aspect of capital flows that is important is their distribution. The 1970s saw a very large growth in foreign direct investment (see Box 11.5), partly financed by the increase in oil prices, but by the 1980s most of the capital flows were focused on the Triad economies—by 1989 more than 80 per cent of the world's Foreign Direct Investment came from and went to the Triad regions. The less-developed and poor countries together accounted for only 3 per cent of the total of world flows between 1986–91. As Petrella (1996: 70) points out, 'Less-developed countries have been abandoned as sites for investment.' This is a startling development which will surely have major political consequences in future international politics, representing as it does the triumph of private values, emphasizing short-term returns on investment over public flows of capital towards longer term infrastructural development (clean water, transport, roads, power, etc.). This development is entirely predictable given the political domination of the values of neo-liberalism, but what is surprising is how quickly it has come about.

International Production and the Transnational Corporation

Conventional IR theory recognizes the emergence of 'transnational corporations' (TNCs) as new and

---

> Box 11.6. **Case Study 4: 'The Symbol Economy'**
>
> 'The third major change that has occurred in the world economy is the emergence of the "symbol" economy—capital movements, exchange rates and credit flows—as the flywheel of the world economy, in place of the 'real' economy—the flow of goods and services . . .
>
> World trade in goods is larger, much larger, than it has ever been before. And so is the 'invisible trade', the trade in services. Together, the two amount to around $2.5 trillion to $3 trillion a year. But the London Eurodollar market, in which the world's financial institutions borrow from and lend to each other, turns over $300 billion each working day, or $75 trillion a year, a volume at least 25 times that of world trade.
>
> In addition, there are the foreign exchange transactions in the world's main money centers, in which one currency is traded against another. These run around $150 billion a day, or about $35 trillion a year—12 times the worldwide trade in goods and services.'
>
> (Drucker 1986: 781–2: figures are for 1985/6)

---

significant **actors** in international relations and international political economy. TNCs, often with turnovers as large as many states, are indeed significant actors, but what is most significant is the underlying changes that TNCs both represent and are bringing about. The importance of TNCs in the system of international production cannot be over-estimated—so much so that some observers have argued that a new form of diplomacy is necessary, that between 'state' and 'firm' (Stopford and Strange 1991). However, others argue that international production is over-emphasized (Hirst and Thompson 1996).

The problem is 'how do we know?' and the answer is 'with difficulty!' And this is because the information that we have about the international economy is just that—information about the **international** economy, based on the traditional model of trade and investment between national political economies (See Fig. 11.1). These figures do not reflect the rise of international production—production by firms outside of their home countries—because they are based on a model that takes no account of this development (see Case Study 5, Box 11.7). International production began to exceed total world trade flows in the middle of the 1980s—

Box 11.7. **Case Study 5: Taking International Production Seriously**

'A recent US Department of Commerce study sought to measure what the US position in world markets would look like if the standard balance-of-trade measure were combined with the net effects of sales by US-owned companies abroad, and by foreign-owned companies in the United States. It found that, on this more inclusive indicator of net global sales and purchases, the United States has consistently been earning a surplus, rising from $8 billion in 1981 to $24 billion in 1991, even as its trade deficit deteriorated during the same period from $16 billion to $28 billion.'

(Ruggie 1995: 518)

how does this change our understanding of the world economy?

First, and referring to Case Study 5 (Box 11.7), measures based on the model of the international economy distort the overall picture of the world economy—they only measure certain aspects and ignore the rest. And this has direct political consequences—consider the political problems generated by the conclusion based solely on conventional trade balance figures that the US has been running a massive balance of payments deficit, particularly for the US–Japan relationship.

Second, and this point is emphasized by Ruggie and others, international production has led to more and more of the world's goods being produced and marketed through firms' own organizational structures ('administrative hierarchies') rather than markets (Ruggie 1995; Stopford & Strange 1991). Rather than national firms trading internationally, with prices and quantities being set by the operation of national/international markets (as in almost all economic theory), TNCs set up production and set 'prices' within their subsidiaries and co-owned firms, across territories, on the basis of their own **internal** needs and priorities, rather than working within prices and production set by the 'market'. This has fundamentally changed both the nature of production and the possibilities of government influence on and control of production. We can see this in the growth of 'intra-firm trade': trade among the different divisions of the same TNC, or trade with other companies linked by a strategic technology agreement. We know that

this is very important, and it is growing, but we have no real way of measuring it:

Once this system of international production, *organized, managed and planned by firms*, takes over and comes to dominate the system of production for local national markets under rules laid down by national governments, there is a fundamental change in the economic base of the world of states, in the power and even possibly the legitimacy of the state (Strange 1994a: 210; emphasis added).

'Domestic' and 'International'

We have already briefly discussed the blurring of the boundaries between the 'domestic' and 'international' realms that is brought about by the processes of interdependence, but a number of recent developments take this process even further. Over the past fifty years international trade has increasingly expanded and the framework for this trade has been the subject of intense international negotiation, with the result that more trade is now nominally 'free' of tariff and quota restraint. But more trade, with the changes in production we have discussed, has led to greater openness of the trading economies. This means that 'domestic' policy is increasingly the subject of trade dispute: when is an environmental health regulation concerning automobile exhaust emissions a barrier to trade? When is a labour regulation an improper constraint on trade, or 'unfair'? It seems that almost every aspect of national economic activity is now subject to international supervision (see Case Study 6, Box 11.8). John Ruggie (1995) calls this the issue of 'contested domestic domains' and argues that this is a consequence of other far-reaching changes in political economy, and that it is a major problem of defining politically where 'external' ends and 'domestic' begins, but that there are no simple solutions. The 'global' is increasingly part of the 'local' and this often produces direct links that by-pass central government, adding to the sense that governments are either impotent or increasingly irrelevant (Horsman and Marshall 1995).

The problem is made more difficult by the growth in trade in services (one of the key areas to be considered in the last major round of trade negotiations—The Uruguay Round). Services include: transport, insurance, tourism, information services, construction, intellectual property rights, and many others, and their value is now around a

---

Box 11.8. Case Study 6: *Financial Times*, **3 April 1996: 'Labour standards "must be included in growth strategy" '**

The Group of Seven leading industrialised nations yesterday agreed that the enhancement of core labour standards was necessary in any global strategy for economic growth.

The G7 comprises the US, Japan, Germany, France, Italy, the UK and Canada.

The agreed communique ending the G7 economy and labour ministers' two-day conference in Lille in northern France was only reached after many hours of intense behind-the-scenes discussion and was seen as a setback for the views of several participants, notably Japan, Germany, the UK and Canada.

They had expressed opposition to any reference to labour standards in the document emerging from the conference.

But the UK government said last night the outcome could have been much worse from its point of view. Initially France and the US had wanted the communique to say G7 should insist the labour standards issue should be on the agenda at the December meeting in Singapore of the World Trade Organization. But this proposal was removed over yesterday's lunch after the UK and others had expressed strong opposition to it.

France, which had called the conference, put the labour standards issue at the forefront of the meeting and, along with the US, insisted on a clear commitment.

Mr Robert Reich, US labour secretary, made clear yesterday that the US intends to press hard on the issue in the WTO. He said it was 'a proper forum for a discussion' of labour standards that cover trade union freedoms, prevent the employment of children and ban forced labour.

The communique said: 'We note the importance of enhancing core labour standards around the world and examining the links between these standards and international trade in appropriate fora.'

Ministers awaited 'with interest the completion of studies currently under way at the Organization for Economic Co-operation and Development and the International Labour Organization on the social dimensions of international trade'.

However, there was also a strong commitment, backed unanimously by all the governments at the conference, to fiscal discipline in the running of their economic policies.

'The G7 countries must endeavour to control public spending more effectively in order to reduce their deficits,' said the communique. 'Reducing deficits will help to create a more favourable climate for private investment and income growth against a background of moderate interest rates.'

Other proposals which won general agreement included:

- A 'modernisation' of the 'regulatory framework' in goods and services.

- The active encouragement of small- and medium-sized enterprises with venture capital to help in new technologies.

- The need to promote policies to ensure 'the security of employability over individuals' working lives'.

- Changes in the tax and benefits system 'to make work pay particularly for the least well-off'; in addition, cuts in non-wage labour costs 'where appropriate'.

- Policies targeted on helping the long-term unemployed and to integrate young job-seekers into regular jobs.

---

quarter of total world trade, perhaps more, as we have the familiar problem of 'how we measure' things like the value-added element of design (e.g. in cars and clothes) (Ruggie 1995: 513–16). The Uruguay Round did produce a 'General Agreement on Trade in Services' (GATS), but this promises to produce many more political problems before a clear framework emerges. However, what is clear is that GATS means that more hitherto 'domestic' activities than ever before will be brought under international surveillance and attempted influence and control, particularly in the area of intellectual property (copyright, patents, licensing, etc.).

The Ideological Basis of the World Economy

The fifth aspect of change that is significant for our consideration of IPE is the ideological basis of international/global economic relations. The ending of the cold war and the internal collapse of most of the centrally planned economies has led to the 'triumph' and spread of one form of political-social-economic organization: modern capitalism. Capitalism has a number of different forms, depending on the cultural and political balance within particular national economies, but, since 1989 at least, has 'been the only game in town' as far as the arrangement of economic and political life are concerned. If we move away from the triumphalism of the immediate post-1989 phase, what we see is that the ideological basis of capitalism has been further reinforced and legitimated. This base is 'economic liberalism' (see Ch. 8) and it has been the fundamental ideology of the international economy since the reconstruction of the international economic order at Bretton Woods in 1944.

Liberalism separates 'economic' life from 'politics' and privileges 'economics', based on individual market rationality, above all other forms of social organization. 'Neo-liberalism' has now taken this to the level of the international system in the argument for unfettered global markets and a consumer-based individualist ethic which transcends national communities. It represents the triumph of the interests of capital over labour at this point of world history. This view has become the new 'common sense', the unconscious basis from which judgement is made and the basis of institutionalized power in the world economy. It forms the (often unspoken) framework for international economic policy, although the precise questions of 'who benefits' create much political dispute (see Case Study 6, Box 11.8). What is often not questioned is the neo-liberal framework itself—its assumptions, concepts, and institutions.

Neo-liberalism is not a neutral description which generates a prescription for action—it is an ideology which serves particular interests and groups of people—and should be evaluated as such. As an ideology it serves to help determine 'who gets what' in the world economy, by legitimating certain structures, processes, and behaviour, by reproduc-

ing a certain distribution of power and by laying out a framework for action based on a particular intersubjective view of the world (see Case Study 2, Box 11.3). Hence, neo-liberalism should be seen as part of the political process of globalization, rather than as an 'academic theory' purporting to offer a form of neutral, objective knowledge.

Key Points

- The processes of 'globalization' have been uneven, and most of the poor countries are now effectively left out of the global political economy, whilst in the Triad regions the process has quickened and deepened—this has created a new and different structure of international politics.

- Vast increases in global capital flows have produced a 'symbol' economy separated from the 'real' economy, and, again this has largely bypassed the poorest countries.

- International production has become the most dynamic aspect of world production and trade and has changed the structure of the IPE.

- 'Domestic' economic activity is now 'international'—almost impossible to think of a 'domestic' economic activity that is not, in some way, 'international' . . .

- 'Neo-liberalism' provides the ideological basis for globalization and has become the unquestioned 'common sense' of the world economy.

Conclusions: 'So what?'

What does all this mean? And what are we able to say about the core problem of IPE—the actual or potential structural mismatch between a formal state-system based on territory (i.e. nation states) and an economic system that is increasingly non-territorial and globalized? As we have already discovered, the meaning and implications of the developments traced in the last section are far from agreed—the interpretation of whether we are still in an essentially 'international' economy or whether we now have a 'global' economy is a highly contentious matter. What is clear is that these changes

have affected different people in different situations and in different countries in different ways. It is not sufficient to generalize on the basis of which country we live in—the gap between rich and poor has been widened not only across the world but within 'nation states' as well, and wealth has become even more concentrated in the hands of a small percentage of the population. This is world-wide and also within the countries of the Triad regions—in the US around 17 per cent of the population control over 85 per cent of the total wealth, and these figures broadly represent the global distribution of wealth also. It also matters what sector of economic activity we are in. Some sectors, like finance, have become 'global', operating in a real-time global market, but others are predominantly inter-national or sub-national. Finally, it matters what firm or organization we are in—some firms/organizations are built on the basis of a world market and international production, others not.

The net result is that it is no longer sufficient (even if it ever was) to analyse political economy at just the two 'levels' of international and national. Apart from anything else this sets up the state as the universal basis of economic life in space and time, and this ahistorical view is not only wrong, but has the important political consequence of disqualifying any other forms of political economy from legitimate consideration. We should consider at least four levels and the interactions between them (and note that within the EU this should be five levels with the addition of 'regional'). These are: global, international, national, and local. And the key to the developments we have discussed is that the global links directly to the local.

To what extent, then, has the national state 'lost' control of the economic (and political) activity within its territorial boundaries? Well, it is clear that the state is having a hard time—the very complexity of the world system means that policy is difficult to make and to implement. And the pace of technological change, particularly in the sectors of communications and computer technology, is making the policy context even more complex. Moreover, a whole new range of issues is emerging as a result of the focus on traded services and this will make the problems of managing the domestic economies of the Triad countries even more the basis of international negotiation. Amongst all this activity, the state is facing a growing threat to its legitimacy (Horsman and Marshall 1995). Citizens are realizing that national governments are not able to deliver their election promises in the face of the plethora of changes we have described. And this realization is linked into a questioning of the 'nation state' as the natural unit of political community and the given unit of international relations. It might be that a more globalized economy will allow smaller political communities to exist in terms of local-global links: that is it may make possible the economic independence of, say, Quebec. Certainly, the importance of knowledge in the global technological economy effectively de-links any territorial state from the necessity to depend on natural resources—although it is questionable as to how many 'Singapores' the world economy could support.

The key to understanding these changes is to understand the changed nature of the world political economic system as a whole. This does not mean that states are no longer important or that national governments are no longer relevant or competent. This point has been well made by one of the first researchers to identify the changes taking place in the world economy and it is more important today in the context of the current debate:

Affirming the greater importance of the world economic system over that of the nation-states should not be interpreted as showing that the latter are eclipsed: they continue to exist but their structure and their relations are determined by the whole of which they are a part. (Michalet 1982: 50).

Whatever our conclusions, it is clear that there are fundamental changes taking place which will have significant long-term implications for the nature and substance of international politics. Change in the IPE does not mean smoothly moving from one stable situation to another as conventional economics indicates—change will involve disruption and gains and losses. 'Who benefits?' remains the key question of IPE at a time when the dominance of neo-liberalism, institutionalized in the global economy of the Triad regions and the TNCs, has already begun to bring about counter-responses. The resolution of these growing tensions will be the focus of IPE for the twenty-first century.

QUESTIONS

1. What is IPE and why is it central to understanding the debate on 'globalization'?

2. What processes have led to the blurring of the distinctions between 'politics' and 'economics'?

3. What processes have led to the blurring of the distinctions between what is considered 'international' policy and what is considered 'domestic' or 'national' policy?

4. How and why do 'words matter' in the debate on a 'globalized' IPE?

5. Identify and explain the core problem for IPE in a globalized system.

6. What is the basis of an 'international economy'?

7. What is the basis of a 'global economy'?

8. What evidence is there to substantiate the claim that we now have a 'global political economy'?

9. What are the principal changes that have occurred in the world economy over the past fifteen years?

10. To what extent can nation states now achieve their economic policy objectives?

11. What is the role of the ideology of 'neo-liberalism'?

12. What forms of international co-operation are appropriate for the world economy?

GUIDE TO FURTHER READING

Agnew, J., and Corbridge, S., *Mastering Space: Hegemony, Territory and International Political Economy* (New York: Routledge, 1995)—political geography meets IPE and the result is excellent, contains the definitive chapter on IR and territory.

Axford, B., *The Global System: Economics, Politics and Culture* (Cambridge: Polity Press, 1995)—a good introduction to thinking about the global system with some thoughtful methodological material.

Boyer, R., and Drache, D., (eds.), *States against Markets: The Limits of Globalization* (New York: Routledge, 1996)—interesting and original collection of essays, mainly by Canadian writers.

Drucker, P., 'The Changed World Economy', in *Foreign Affairs*, 64: 4 (1986), 768–91—a short and significant introduction to the framework of the world economy, clearly written in non-technical language.

Hirst, P., and Thompson, G., *Globalization in Question: The International Economy and the Possibilities of Global Governance* (Cambridge: Polity Press, 1996)—perhaps the definitive examination of the 'globalization' thesis—so far. Well written, with some impressive new information.

Horsman, M., and Marshall, A., *After the Nation-State: Citizens, Tribalism and the New World Disorder* (New York: Harper Collins, 1994)—written by two journalists, provocative and excellent account of the problems facing the nation-state. A 'must read'.

Kanter, R. M., *World Class: Thriving Locally in the Global Economy* (New York: Simon and Schuster, 1995)—best-selling manual of 'how to excel' in the global economy, much analysis of global–local dynamics.

Murphy, C. N., *International Organization and Industrial Change: Global Governance since 1850*

(Cambridge Polity Press, 1994)—an analysis of international organizations as expressions of social forces, essential reading for those wishing to understand the world we live in.

Pettman, R., *Understanding International Political Economy—with Readings for the Fatigued* (St Leonards: Allen and Unwin, 1996)—a terrific book, clear and thoughtful. Unorthodox readings which really work—highly recommended.

Stopford, J., and Strange, S., *Rival States, Rival Firms: Competition for World Market Shares* (Cambridge: Cambridge University Press, 1991)—identifies the importance of international production and the 'firm' as a key actor in IPE. Sets out the basis of a new structure of IPE. Clear and accessible.

Strange, S., *States and Markets*, 2nd edn. (London: Pinter, 1994*b*)—iconoclastic analysis of IPE, eminently readable and provocative—well worth reading if only for its Prologue which is the best demonstration of the nature of political economy I have ever read.

Stubbs, R., and Underhill, G., (eds.), *Political Economy and the Changing Global Order* (Basingstoke: Macmillan, 1994)—wide ranging collection, excellent introduction to IPE and global order.

12 International Regimes

Richard Little

READER'S GUIDE

Liberal institutionalists and realists are engaged in a major debate about the role played by regimes—delineated areas of rule-governed activity—in the international system. Both schools acknowledge that although the international system is anarchic (without a ruler) in structure, it has never been anomic (without rules). Interest in regimes surfaced in the 1970s along with concern about the ability of the United States to sustain the economic regimes formed after the Second World War. What are the essential features of regimes? There is no straightforward answer to this question, and the chapter uses a definition, typology, and examples to reveal their complex character. Under what circumstances do regimes come into existence? This question forms the nub of the debate. Although liberal institutionalists and realists use very similar tools of analysis—drawing on microeconomics and game theory—they arrive at very different conclusions. Are the conclusions compatible? The question remains contested.

I am grateful to the editors for their comments and for the discussion of the chapter by the members of the International Politics Research Group at the Department of Politics, University of Bristol.

Introduction

An important dimension of globalization has been the establishment of worldwide regimes to foster rule-governed activity within the international system. Although international rule-governed activity predates the emergence of the modern state it is only during the course of the twentieth century that regimes can be regarded as a global phenomenon, with states becoming enmeshed in increasingly complex sets of rules and institutions which regulate international relations around the world. There is now no area of international intercourse devoid of regimes, where states are not circumscribed, to some extent or other, by the existence of mutually accepted sets of rules. Indeed, many regimes are so firmly embedded in the system that they are almost taken for granted. Most people do not consider it at all surprising, for example, that we can put a letter in a postbox, and be confident that it will be delivered anywhere in the world from the Antarctic to Zimbabwe, or that we can get on an aeroplane and expect to fly unmolested to our destination at any point across the globe. Only when something goes drastically wrong, as, for example, in 1983, when the Soviet Defence Forces shot down the civilian South Korean airliner, KAL 007, killing all 269 persons aboard, is our attention drawn to the fact that international relations are, in practice, extensively regulated by complex regimes negotiated and policed by states.

It may seem unremarkable, at first sight, that states have established regimes to ensure that mail gets delivered anywhere in the world and that aircraft can fly safely from one country to another. The advantages of such regimes appear so obvious that it would be more remarkable if such regimes had not been put in place. However, the existence of these regimes becomes rather more surprising when it is acknowledged how much controversy can surround the formation of regimes, how contentious established regimes can prove to be, and how frequently attempts to form regimes can fail. It is because the use of regimes to promote everything from arms control to the enhancement of global economic welfare seems to be so self-evidently beneficial, that the difficulty of securing regimes requires some explanation. Sadly, there is no agreed answer. Although few doubt that regimes are an important feature of the contemporary international system, as this chapter aims to demonstrate, theorists in the field of international relations are deeply divided about how and why regimes are formed and maintained.

The concept of a regime is relatively recent, coming into common parlance in the 1970s. But students of international relations have been interested in rules regulating the behaviour of states since the origins of the state system. The contemporary focus on regimes, therefore, needs to be seen as the current phase in a long, essentially European tradition, that can be traced back at least to the time of Hugo Grotius (1583–1645), the Dutch jurist, who is often identified as 'the father of international law'. Despite the length of this tradition, the status of international law has always been questioned within jurisprudence, that branch of legal studies investigating the theoretical or philosophical foundations of the law. It is argued by a significant school of thought that a legal system can only be established and enforced within the centralized structures provided by the state. Although this view has been contested, it is by no means obvious how law is formulated and maintained within the anarchic or decentralized structures of the international system. Indeed, the impression has sometimes been given that the international system is essentially **anomic**—devoid of agreed rules and norms. And this impression has been reinforced by the popular association of **anarchy** with a breakdown of order, rather than with a system lacking a centralized structure of government.

The problematic status of rules in the anarchic international system was largely overlooked, however, in the era after 1919, when the institutionalized study of international relations was established. In the wake of the traumatic First World War there was a widespread hope that states would now be willing to establish world order on the basis of international law, although little thought was given to whether there was any theoretical justification for such optimism. In any event, the hope was dashed when international law was so flagrantly violated during the 1930s. The approach came to be dismissed as idealistic; and after the Second World War, few accepted any longer that order in the international system could rest on international law. Moreover, theorists were preoccupied with working out the implications of moving from a multipolar system into the bipolar nuclear era.

By the 1970s, however, a series of global developments, to be discussed below, encouraged theorists in International Relations to return to the long-established theoretical concern with the role of rules in the international system. This new breed of theorists, primarily American, in the first instance, were and remain self-consciously interested in developing International Relations as a social science. They have spawned an enormous literature (Levy 1995), with research, now no longer confined to the United States (Rittberger 1993), that is becoming increasingly complex and diverse.

At the risk of over-simplification it can be suggested that regime theorists are located within the two broad schools of liberalism and realism (see Chs. 6 and 8). The debate between them complicates conventional assessments of both schools: realism, in the past, is considered to have been sceptical or uninterested, in international law, while regime theorists in the liberal camp, identified as liberal institutionalists, have accepted key assumptions made by neo-realists, and these, along with their social science credentials, are considered to have moved them beyond the established liberal tradition (see Ch. 8). But despite the shared theoretical assumptions, liberal institutionalists and realists adhere to very different assessments of regimes (see Box 12.1). Liberal institutionalists focus on the way that regimes allow states to overcome the obstacles to collaboration imposed by the anarchic structure of the international system.

Realists, by contrast, are interested in the way that states use their power capabilities in situations requiring co-ordination to influence the nature of regimes and the way that the costs and benefits derived from regime formation are divided up. Only after studying the two approaches can we assess to what extent these different approaches can be rendered compatible. Collaboration and co-ordination are see to constitute different approaches to co-operation.

Why did IR (International Relations) theorists begin to focus on regime formation in the 1970s? One factor was the growing awareness that, at least in the context of the West, the United States had played the role of **hegemon** during and after the Second World War. The term derives from the Greek, meaning leader, and it was argued that the United States had been able to play this role because of its preponderance of power in the international system. During this era, the United States, because of its hegemonic position, had been able to establish and maintain a complex array of economic regimes in the West; the regimes had played a vital role in the growing prosperity which had taken place after the Second World War. By the 1970s, however, partly because of the economic success in Europe and Japan, and partly because of the disastrous policy in Vietnam, the capacity of the United States to maintain its hegemonic status was put in doubt. It is unsurprising that an interest in regimes coincided with this development.

Liberal institutionalists and realists both reacted

Box 12.1. Liberal Institutional v. Realist Approaches to the Analysis of Regimes

Common Assuptions

1. States operate in an anarchic international system
2. States are rational and unitary actors
3. States are the units responsible for establishing regimes
4. Regimes are established on the basis of co-operation in the international system
5. Regimes promote international order

Competing Assessments

Liberal institutionalists

1. Regimes enable states to collaborate
2. Regimes promote the common good
3. Regimes flourish best when promoted and maintained by a benign hegemon
4. Regimes promote globalization and and a liberal world order

Realists

1. Regimes enable states to co-ordinate
2. Regimes generate differential benefits for states
3. Power is a central feature of regime formation and survival
4. The nature of world order depends on the underlying principles and norms of regimes

to this development, but in very different ways. Liberal institutionalists were concerned about the possibility that at a point in time when the need for regimes was becoming increasingly urgent, the loss of hegemonic status by the United States could mean that it would be increasingly difficult to establish these regimes. Realists argued, by contrast, that if the United States did lose its hegemonic status, then there would be a shift in the balance of power and the liberal principles governing the regimes established by the United States would start to be challenged more effectively by Third World states wanting a new set of regimes established on the basis of different norms and principles. Although their analysis pointed in different directions, both liberal institutionalists and realists acknowledged the need for a more sophisticated theoretical understanding of regimes.

Key Points

- Regimes represent an important feature of globalization.

- There is a growing number of global regimes being formed.

- The term, and social science approach to, regimes is recent but fits into a long-standing tradition of thought about international law.

- The loss of hegemonic status by the US sensitized social scientists to the need for a theory of regimes.

- Liberal institutionalists and realists have developed competing approaches to the analysis of regimes.

The Nature of Regimes

Before presenting the theoretical approaches to regimes developed by the liberal institutionalists and the realists, it is necessary to present their common conceptualization of an international regime in more detail and illustrate the conceptualization with an examination of some of the major areas of world politics now regulated by regimes.

Conceptualizing Regimes

Although it may be helpful in the first instance to think of regimes as rule governed behaviour, a more complex conceptualization has been developed by theorists working in the field of international relations. This conceptualization can be captured by a definition and typology of regimes.

Defining Regimes

Although there are many definitions of a regime, they all take a similar form and the one that has become most widely used was formulated in the early 1980s by Stephen Krasner. It very effectively encapsulates the complexity of the phenomenon (Box 12.2).

Krasner's definition reveals that a regime is more than a set of rules; it presupposes quite a high level of institutionalization. Indeed, regime theorists have been criticized for doing no more than introducing new terminology to characterize the familiar idea of an international organization. Regime theorists acknowledge that international organizations can be embraced by regime theory, but they insist that their approach encompasses much more. The parameters of regime theory can be demonstrated by examining a simple typology of regimes.

Classifying Regimes

One simple but useful classification, establishes a typology of regimes along two dimensions (Levy 1995). The vertical dimension highlights the formality of a regime. A regime can be associated with a highly formalized agreement or even the emergence of an international organization. But, at the other extreme, a regime can come into existence in the absence of any formal agreements. Historically, informal agreements between states have been established on the basis of precedence. The horizontal axis then focuses on the extent to which states expect or anticipate that their behaviour will

---

Box 12.2. Defining Regimes

Regimes are identified by Krasner (1983: 2) *as 'sets of implicit or explicit principles, norms, rules, and decision making procedures around which actors' expectations converge in a given area of international relations'.*

An Example of a Regime

This is a complex definition and it needs to be unpacked. Krasner has done this, by drawing on the General Agreement on Trade and Tariffs (GATT) for illustrative purposes. The GATT was initially an agreement drawn up in 1947 and reflected the belief of its signatories that it was necessary to establish an organization which would be responsible for the regulation of international trade. In fact, it proved impossible to establish such an organization at that time, and the GATT acted as a substitute. It was given a secretariat and a general director responsible for carrying out the preparatory work for a series of conferences where the signatories of the GATT met and reached agreements intended to foster international trade. In 1994, after the Uruguay Round of negotiations, it was agreed that it was now time to move beyond GATT and establish a formal World Trade Organization as originally intended. Krasner was writing before this development took place, but it does not affect the utility of the GATT as an illustration of what is meant by a regime.

The Four Defining Elements of a Regime

1. **Principles** are represented by coherent bodies of theoretical statements about how the world works. GATT operated on the basis of liberal principles which assert that global welfare will be maximized by free trade.

2. **Norms** specify general standards of behaviour, and identify the rights and obligations of states. So, in the case of the GATT, the basic norm is that tariffs and non-tariff barriers should be reduced and eventually eliminated. Together, norms and principles define the essential character of a regime and these cannot be changed without transforming the nature of the regime.

3. **Rules** operate at a lower level of generality to principles and norms, and they are often designed to reconcile conflicts which may exist between the principles and norms. Third World states, for example, wanted rules which differentiated between developed and underdeveloped countries.

4. **Decision-making procedures** identify specific prescriptions for behaviour, the system of voting, for example, which will regularly change as a regime is consolidated and extended. The rules and procedures governing the GATT, for example, underwent substantial modification during its history. Indeed, the purpose of the successive conferences was to change the rules and decision making procedures.   (Krasner 1985: 4–5)

---

be constrained by their accession to an implicit or explicit set of agreements.

If there are no formal agreements, and no convergence in the expectation that rules will be adhered to, then it is clear that there is **no regime** in existence. On the other hand, even in the absence of formal rules, there can be an expectation that informal rules will be observed, suggesting the existence of a **tacit regime**. By contrast, it is also possible to identify situations where formal rules have been brought into existence, without any expectation that they will be observed, indicating the existence of a **dead-letter regime**. Finally, there are **full-blown regimes**, where there is a high expectation that formal rules will be observed (see Box 12.3). Examples of these different types of regimes will be given in the next section.

Box 12.3. A Typology of Regimes

Convergence of expectations

Low	High	Formality
No regimes	Tacit regimes	Low
Dead-letter regimes	Full-blown regimes	High

This is not the only way that regimes can be classified. It is possible, for example, to classify them on a geographical basis: **bilateral, regional** and **global**.

Source: Adapted from Levy (1995).

Richard Little

Globalization and International Regimes

During the course of the nineteenth and twentieth centuries the advancement of technology has made it possible for more and more people to come into increasingly close contact across the globe. World-wide communication is now instantaneous in many areas of activity. Not every aspect of this globalization of world politics is beneficial however. Technology has made it possible to see and talk to people on the other side of the globe and to fill the supermarkets, at least those in the wealthy sectors of the global economy, with increasingly exotic commodities from all round the world. But it has also made it possible to build weapons with the potential to wreak global devastation and to pollute the atmosphere with chemicals that could possibly have irreversible and certainly very dangerous global consequences. Our impact on the world we inhabit is both frightening and exciting. But either way it is becoming increasingly apparent that if we are all to benefit rather than suffer from globalization, it is essential to manage the process. No one thinks that this task will be easy; pessimists doubt that it is even possible. Regime theorists, on the other hand, see grounds for optimism. They believe that survival depends upon our capacity to regulate global activity by means of regimes; and, as we demonstrate in this section, although not in any comprehensive fashion, the evidence indicates that states can establish regimes across a wide range of activities.

Security Regimes

Although security regimes are primarily a twentieth-century phenomenon, permitting states to escape from the security dilemma (see Ch. 10), it is possible to identify earlier examples. The Concert of Europe, for instance, constitutes a regime formed by the conservative states of post-Napoleonic Europe to counter future revolution and conflict. At the same time, on the other side of the Atlantic, the British and Americans established the Rush Bagot agreement in 1817 to demilitarize the Great Lakes. But whereas the tacit regime in Europe began to decay soon after it was formed, the full-blown bilateral regime in North America became steadily stronger until eventually, the long border between

Canada and the United States was permanently demilitarized.

Regular attempts to establish full-blown security regimes, however, only started to proliferate during the twentieth century, particularly after the onset of the cold war. But the effectiveness of these regimes has often been questioned. Jervis (1983), for example, argued that some of the major regimes, such as SALT 1 (1972) and SALT 2 (1979) designed to bring the arms race between the United States and the Soviet Union under control, were effectively dead-letter regimes. Despite the prolonged negotiations and detailed agreements, there was no evidence that they brought the arms race under control, because neither super power expected the other to desist from developing new weapons technology.

Nevertheless, there are arms control agreements which do seem to have established fragile security regimes. The Partial Test Ban Agreement of 1963, has undoubtedly encouraged a prohibition of atmospheric testing. And the 1968 Non-proliferation Agreement continues to act as a restraint on any increase in the number of nuclear weapons states. The agreement has been signed by over 170 states—the vast majority of states in the international system. Although fragile, the regime enjoys a very broad measure of support, so that any state breaching the agreement will confront widespread opposition.

Environmental Regimes

As scientists have become increasingly aware of the damage being done to the global environment, so the importance attached to the need to establish environmental regimes has steadily risen. Oil pollution, global warming, and damage to the ozone layer are the issues which have attracted most public attention, but regimes have been established in a wide range of areas in the attempt to protect the global environment. For example, international conventions to save endangered plant and animal species can be traced back to the 1970s, and a comprehensive Convention on Biological Diversity came into force in December 1993. There have also been attempts since the mid-1980s to regulate the international movement of hazardous waste material, with the Basle Covention establishing a complete ban in March 1993 on the shipping of hazardous waste from countries in the developed world to countries in the underdeveloped world.

Despite the wide range of agreements intended to protect the global environment, it is unlikely that many will consolidate into full-blown regimes. Instead, there is a perennial danger that they will degenerate into dead-letter regimes. Even agreements which do prove to be effective may not turn out to have solved the original problem. For example, attempts to deal with the ozone layer can be traced back to 1977 when the United Nations Environment Programme established a Co-ordinating Committee to deal with the ozone layer. With the accumulating evidence about the damage being caused by pollution, concerned states eventually agreed to implement the Montreal Protocol in 1989 which put forward a raft of measures to protect the ozone layer. Despite the rapid implementation of these measures, scientific evidence in 1996 indicated that the situation was continuing to deteriorate. The initial measures were proving to be inadequate and it was clear that the rules established in the original regime would need to be extended. Even more depressing for environmentalists was the 1995 conference on climate change which met in Berlin. Although the problem of global warming was addressed, it proved impossible to agree on measures which might deal with the issue.

Communication Regimes

Prior to the nineteenth century, the most significant areas of international communication regulated by regimes were concerned with shipping and postal services. With further developments in technology however, the need for regimes extended to the international regulation of aircraft and telecommunications. Collectively, the resulting network of regimes can be seen to provide an essential part of the infrastructure underpinning the modern international economy. Without this infrastructure, international trade, foreign investment, and the worldwide monetary system could not be sustained.

The need for a regime governing shipping can be traced back to the technological developments in ship-building in the sixteenth century that permitted in subsequent centuries an extraordinary expansion of international trade. This expansion could not have gone on, however, without the consolidation of a tacit regime ensuring, among other things, the freedom of movement for shipping on the high seas and the right of innocent passage through territorial waters under the sovereign jurisdiction of maritime states. The bulk of international trade continues to be transported by sea and these central norms remain in place. However, key rules operating under these norms have undergone change. In the third United Nations Conference on the Law of the Sea (UNCLOS) which went on from 1973 to 1982, for example, territorial waters were extended from three to twelve miles, but this new rule left the underlying norm about innocent passage undisturbed.

During the nineteenth and twentieth centuries a range of organizations have emerged to manage and strengthen the regimes which secure international communications. In 1863 the major industrial states came together to establish a standardized system for postal communication and this was formalized with the establishment of the Universal Postal Union in 1874. In 1865, the International Telegraph Union came into existence to regulate telegraphic communication and this evolved into the International Telecommunications Union in 1932 to cope with the increasingly complex technological developments in communications. Finally it is worth making reference to a range of organizations which have helped to maintain the regimes which operate in the areas of shipping and aircraft. The International Maritime Organization and the International Civil Aviation Organization, for example, are both specialized agencies of the United Nations and are responsible for the emergence of a large number of conventions which reinforce the regimes which can be observed in these crucial areas of international transport.

Economic Regimes

It is often argued that the regimes in the economic arena are more firmly entrenched than in any other. As already noted, however, the international economy could not function in the absence of the infrastructure provided by the communication regimes. The two sets of regimes are inextricably interlinked.

Indeed, over the last decade, as the regimes governing the international economy have become ever more firmly established, the underlying liberal principles governing these regimes have started to impinge on the communication regimes. This development is reflected in the growing attempts to open postal services, telecommunications, and national airlines to greater competition. This development will lead to a modification of the basic principle underlying these regimes which in the past has always favoured state control over the rules regulating these activities (Zacher and Sutton 1996).

It is not possible to provide even a brief survey of the complex economic regimes established in the era after the Second World War. But it is worth noting that they reflect the determined effort made by the United States, in particular, to consolidate a set of regimes built upon liberal principles. In particular, the United States wished to establish a trading regime established on free trade principles and, as we have seen, the GATT was established to achieve this goal. At the same time, however, the United States also recognized that trade requires stable domestic economies and a stable monetary system to flourish. A range of international organizations, such as the International Monetary Fund and the International Bank of Reconstruction and Development were established after 1945 to promote an environment where trade could flourish. Although there were fears that the economic regimes established by the United States would collapse as weaknesses in its own economy became apparent in the late 1960s, the economic regimes brought into existence after 1945 have proved to be surprisingly resilient.

Key Points

- Regime theory is an attempt initiated in the 1970s by social scientists to account for the existence of rule-governed behaviour in the anarchic international system.

- Regimes have been defined by principles, norms, rules, and decision-making procedures.

- Regimes can be classified in terms of the formality of the underlying agreements and the degree of expectation that the agreements will be observed. Full-blown, tacit, and dead-letter regimes can be identified.

- Regimes now help to regulate international relations in many spheres of activity.

Competing Theories: 1. The Liberal Institutional Approach

Both liberal institutionalists and realists acknowledge that regimes are an important feature of contemporary international relations and they also start from the same theoretical premiss that a regime represents the response of rational actors operating within the anarchic structure of the international system. But despite this common starting point, realists and liberal institutionalists go on to make very different theoretical assessments of regimes.

Liberal institutionalists work from the premiss that regimes are needed to overcome the problems generated by the anarchic structure of the international system. They have drawn on a number of theoretical ideas developed outside of international relations in an attempt to understand why anarchy inhibits collaboration and the ways in which the resulting obstacles might be overcome.

Impediments to Regime Formation

To develop a theoretical understanding of why the anarchic structure of the international system impedes regime formation, liberal institutionalists have turned to **microeconomics** and **game theory** for assistance. Microeconomists study the behaviour of economic units operating under the conditions of perfect competition found, in theory, within the market-place. An analogy is drawn by liberal institutionalists between the economic market and the international system because both are constituted by anarchic structures. But, paradoxically, whereas for liberal institutionalists the anarchic structure of the international system poses a significant problem, for microeconomists, the absence of any centralized institutions constitutes the main asset of the market-place. Unrestrained by external interference, rational economic units pursue competitive and self-interested strategies which result in goods being bought and sold at what microeconomic theory demonstrates is the optimum price, generating the best possible outcome for all the units operating within the market.

This benign image of the economic market might seem to generate very little insight for liberal institutionalists. But the microeconomic approach becomes more relevant when attention is turned to the concept of **market failure**. Although microeconomists insist that an unrestrained market provides the most effective mechanism for the production of economic goods, it is accepted that the market is not effective when it comes to the production of '**public goods**' like roads and hospitals. Indeed it is also acknowledged that there are circumstances when unrestrained competition can result in the production of what might be called '**public bads**'—the obvious example being pollution. Microeconomists argue that suboptimum outcomes, like the under-provision of public goods or the proliferation of public bads, is not the result of irrationality. Suboptimum outcomes emerge in circumstances when economic actors need to collaborate rather than compete. And under these circumstances, the market, which promotes competition, is not an appropriate mechanism for dealing with the situation.

When market failure occurs, therefore, microeconomists accept that it is necessary to find an alternative mechanism to the market—one that generates collaboration rather than competition. The principal mechanism, often only accepted with reluctance, takes the form of state intervention. The state can, when necessary, intervene into the market-place and require economic actors to collaborate rather than compete. So, for example, when rivers have become polluted as the result of industrial waste, the state can pass legislation which requires all the relevant economic actors to produce alternative outlets for the industrial waste which is polluting the rivers. Microeconomists circumvent the problem of market failure, therefore, by means of structural transformation. The anarchic structure of the market gives way to the hierarchical structure of the state.

Within the international system, of course, no global equivalent of the state exists to enact legislation compelling sovereign states to subscribe to a common policy. As a consequence, at least from the perspective of the microeconomist, it is unsurprising to find widespread evidence of global problems persisting because of the failure of sovereign states to collaborate and implement collective solutions. Global pollution, resource depletion, arms races, and trade barriers are seen by liberal institutionalists to constitute global problems arising from market failure—where states have preferred to compete rather than to collaborate. On the other hand, the existence of regimes indicates that collaboration is certainly possible within the anarchic arena. Anarchy does not preclude collaboration; it simply makes it difficult to achieve. The microeconomic approach, drawing on game theory, has helped to explain why.

The existence of collaborative as well as competitive strategies generates a much more complex situation than found in the purely competitive market setting. For instance, if a motorist fails to stop at an intersection, then whether or not an accident occurs will depend upon the behaviour of the motorists approaching the intersection on the other road. Most motorists, fortunately, adopt a cautious, co-operative strategy and so accidents at intersections are not a frequent occurrence. But in such cases of **strategic interaction**, the outcome, as the example illustrates, is determined by the interplay of decisions reached by independent actors. No single actor can dictate the outcome. **Game theory**, a branch of mathematics, has developed a very extensive study of strategic interaction, and liberal institutionalists, while generally avoiding the mathematics, have drawn on some of the conceptual apparatus developed by game theorists in order to enhance their theoretical appreciation of the factors which inhibit collaboration in an anarchic setting.

Theory-building requires an analyst to distil the essential elements of the situation under scrutiny. Game theory is particularly parsimonious. The focus is on the interaction between two actors, each with only two possible strategies—one co-operative and the other competitive—which can be followed. Strategic interaction, therefore, involves four possible outcomes. The strategies chosen are based on **rational** calculation. Rational actors, according to game theorists, (1) evaluate outcomes, (2) produce a preference ranking, and then (3) choose the best option available. These are the essential elements of rationality. What social scientists have realized is that they can use the very simple conceptual apparatus involving rational two-person games to model a wide range of social situations. The games

---

Box 12.4. The Game of Prisoners' Dilemma

The Prisoners' Dilemma Scenario

The governor of a prison once had two prisoners whom he could not hang without a voluntary confession of at least one. Accordingly, he summoned one prisoner and offered him his freedom and a sum of money if he would confess at least a day before the second prisoner did so, so that an indictment could be prepared and so that the second prisoner could be hanged. If the latter should confess at least a day before him, however, the first prisoner was told, then the prisoner would be freed and rewarded and he would be hanged. 'And what if we both should confess on the same day, your Excellency?' asked the first prisoner. 'Then you each will keep your life but will get ten years in prison'. 'And if neither of us should confess, your Excellency?' 'Then both of you will be set free—without any reward, of course. But will you bet your neck that your fellow prisoner—that crook—will not hurry to confess and pocket the reward? Now go back to your solitary cell and think about your answer until tomorrow.' The second prisoner in his interview was told the same, and each man spent the night alone considering his dilemma. (Deutsch 1968: 120).

The two actors are confronted with two possible strategies, generating a situation with four possible outcomes. Being rational, the prisoners can place these outcomes on a preference ranking. The matrix reveals the preference rankings for the two prisoners. Both prisoners will pursue the strategy which will optimize their position in the light of the strategies available to the other prisoner. To avoid being hanged, both prisoners will confess and end up in prison for ten years, thereby demonstrating how individual rationality leads to collective irra-

tionality. The suboptimal outcome could only be avoided if the two prisoners possessed a mechanism which allowed them to collaborate.

In this figure, cell numerals refer to ordinally ranked preferences: 4 = best, 1 = worst. The first number in each cell refers to A's preference and the second number refers to B's preference.

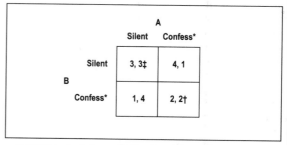

* Dominant strategy: both players have dominant rather than contingent strategies. A strategy becomes dominant if it is preferable to the alternative strategy no matter which strategy the other player adopts.
† Denotes an equilibrium outcome.
‡ A Pareto Optimal Outcome: Vilfredo Pareto (1848–1923) was an Italian sociologist and economist who developed a criterion for identifying when an exchange between two parties has reached its most efficient or optimum point. He argued, in essence, that the point is reached when one party is better off and the other party is no worse off than before the exchange took place. An implication of this optimum is discussed later.

---

are considered to distil the essential elements of situations that in reality are much more complex. By stripping away the detail, it becomes easier to understand the underlying dynamics of the situation. So, for example, it is argued that all examples of market failure can modelled by the game known as Prisoners' Dilemma (see Box 12.4).

The logic associated with the Prisoners' Dilemma is seen by liberal institutionalists to account for why a wide range of irrational outcomes in the international arena can be explained in rational terms. It explains why states have persisted in overfishing the seas, in polluting the atmosphere, in selling arms to undesirable regimes, and promoting policies which inhibit trade. All represent cases of market failure, with states choosing to pursue competitive rather than collaborative strategies. They fail to pursue collaborative strategies because they expect the other members of the anarchic system to

pursue competitive strategies. It would be irrational for one state to require its fishing industry to observe a fishing quota, for example, if it is believed that the fishing industries in other states are intending to disregard the quota and thereby become 'free-riders'. As a consequence, states avoid a Pareto optimal outcome and are driven by rational calculation to pursue a strategy which, through strategic interaction, leads to a suboptimal outcome.

If the Prisoners' Dilemma game does accurately map this situation, however, then it not only explains why anarchy inhibits collaboration, but it also indicates that states acknowledge the advantages of collaboration. They are only inhibited from moving to collaborative strategies by their expectation that other states will defect. The Prisoners' Dilemma demonstrates the importance of identifying a mechanism which will convince all the actors that there is no danger of defection. Liberal institutionalists believe that the establishment of regimes provides evidence that mechanisms of this kind must exist.

The Facilitation of Regime Formation

Two different routes have been followed by liberal institutionalists in their attempt to explain the emergence of regimes. First they have drawn on the work of microeconomists who have insisted that state intervention is not the only mechanism available to produce public goods. It is suggested that if there is a dominant or hegemonic actor operating within the market, then that actor may well be prepared to sustain the cost of producing a public good (Olson: 1965). The liberal institutionalists have had no difficulty extending this line of argument to the international arena. During the course of the nineteenth century, for example, a regime was established which outlawed the international traffic of slaves. States agreed to observe the humanitarian principle which underpinned this regime because they expected other states to do so. The expectation emerged because it was recognized that Great Britain intended to police the regime and possessed the naval capacity to do so. The regime was consolidated, therefore, because of Britain's hegemonic status within the international system.

As already indicated, it is widely accepted that the economic regimes established after the Second World War owe their existence to the presence of the United States as a hegemonic power. But when liberal institutionalist examined the consequences of hegemonic decline, they concluded that there is no reason to suppose that established regimes would cease to exist. Although the Prisoners' Dilemma indicated that market failures occur because in an anarchic system there is an expectation that states will compete rather than collaborate, once states have moved away from the suboptimum outcome resulting from mutually competitive strategies, then there is no incentive to defect from the mutually collaborative strategies

and return to the suboptimum outcome. Even in the absence of a hegemon, therefore, liberal institutionalists argue that established regimes should persist (Keohane 1984).

The second route explored by the liberal institutionalists has reinforced this conclusion. It is argued that the Prisoners' Dilemma exaggerates the difficulty of generating collaboration within the anarchic international system. The Prisoners' Dilemma presupposes that the game is only played once. But, in reality, because situations persist over time, it is more appropriate to think of the game being played over and over again. The **'shadow of the future'** looms over the players, affecting their strategic calculations. Because the game will be played on future occasions, it becomes worthwhile taking a risk and pursuing a collaborative strategy in order to produce the optimum outcome. If all states can be persuaded to do the same, then there will be little incentive to defect in the future, because if one state defects, then, 'tit for tat', all the others will follow. Accepting this line of argument, then the major mechanism for establishing and maintaining a regime is not the existence of a hegemon, but the principle of **reciprocity.** Liberal institutionalists, therefore, have increasingly come to focus on factors that will strengthen reciprocity within the system. Inspection and surveillance facilities become very important to ensure that states are operating within the parameters of a regime. The establishment of satellite surveillance, for example, was a significant factor in encouraging the United States and the Soviet Union to reach arms control agreements. Attention has also been drawn to the importance of scientific knowledge. States are unwilling to restrict their activities on the basis of speculation and respond much more effectively when scientists start to agree about the significance of their findings. As states become ever more open and the constant expansion in scientific understanding, so the international environment will become increasingly 'information rich'. It is this trend, liberal institutionalist argue, that will do most to facilitate regime-building in the future (Keohane 1984).

Richard Little

Competing Theories: 2. The Realist Approach

From a liberal institutionalist perspective, realism has little to contribute to the understanding of regimes. The traditional realist emphasis on the inherently competitive nature of the international system is seen to inhibit rather than facilitate any explanation of how and why states collaborate to achieve the mutually advantageous benefits derived from the establishment of regimes. Indeed, the growth of regimes would seem to confirm that the realist perspective is becoming increasingly anachronistic. Unsurprisingly, realists contest such an evaluation. Two problems are identified with the liberal institutional approach. First, realists attack the liberal institutional assumption that the activities of a hegemon in the international system can be compared to the role of the state when dealing with cases of market failure. Second, realists deny that regimes emerge as the result of states endeavouring to overcome the pressure to compete under conditions of anarchy. Regimes form, realists argue, in situations when unco-ordinated strategies can interact to produce suboptimum outcomes. So from the realist perspective, the influence of microeconomics has encouraged the liberal institutionalists to advance an unsound assessment of regime formation. There is an irony here, because it was the neo-realists (Waltz: 1979) who first drew the analogy between the market and the international system. The common starting point, however, can lead in very different directions.

Power and Regimes

Realists, like liberal institutionalists, were very aware in the 1970s and 1980s that the hegemonic status of the United States was being questioned. But they did not conclude that this development might lead to an anomic world. Instead, they focused on Third World demands for a new set of principles and norms to underpin the regimes associated with the world economy. Existing regimes were seen to work against the interests of Third World states, opening them up to unfair competition and malign economic forces. Realists took the case presented by the Third World seriously, but argued that the principles and norms demanded by the Third World would only come into operation if the balance of power moved against the West (Tucker 1977; Krasner 1985). This line of analysis runs directly counter to the image, presented by the liberal institutionalists, of the United States as a benign benefactor, underwriting a set of regimes which allowed the members of the anarchic international system to escape from a suboptimum outcome and into a position of Pareto optimality. In its place, it was necessary to view the United States as a hegemon using its power to sustain a regime which promoted its own long-term interests. Closer inspection of the liberal institutional position reveals a tacit support for the way that public goods have been defined by governments in the West. It may appear axiomatic to liberal institutionalists that states should wish to promote economic regimes built on liberal norms and principles. And the same argument applies to the promotion of human rights, the elimination of pollution, and all the other goals advanced by liberals in the West. But this position disregards the fact that it is by no means universally agreed that liberal norms and principles should be underpinning the regimes that are emerging in the international system.

From the realist perspective, therefore, the United States helped to ensure that regimes were underpinned by a particular set of principles and norms. But a full appreciation of the realist's position also requires the recognition that a hegemon can effectively veto the formation of a regime. For example, in 1972, when the United States launched its first remote sensing satellite, the event caused concern amongst a large range of countries. These satellites have the capacity to gather important and sensitive commercial and strategic data about countries all around the world. Not only can the satellites identify where military equipment is located, but they can also identify the size of a crop yield and the location of minerals. There were several attempts to establish a regime which would limit the right of states to acquire data without the permission of the state under surveillance (Brown et al. 1977). Many states have considered that they would benefit from such a regime. But because the balance of power was tilted in favour of the states which possessed these satellites and they were clear that such a regime would not work to their benefit they vetoed the proposed regime.

Regimes and Co-ordination

As it stands, the realist account of regimes is incomplete, because it fails to explain why states adhere to the principles and norms underlying a regime which they oppose. In accounting for this anomaly, realists, like liberal institutionalists, resort to game theory. Realists insist, however, that states wishing to form a regime confront the problem of co-ordination, as illustrated by the Battle of the Sexes (see Box 12.5), not collaboration, as illustrated by the Prisoners' Dilemma. Here the problem is not associated with the danger of defection to a competitive strategy, but the possibility of failing to co-ordinate strategies, with the consequence that a mutually desired goal is unintentionally missed.

Co-ordination problems are very familiar to strategic thinkers. Schelling (1960) illustrates the problem with the example of a couple getting separated in a department store. Both wish to get back together again, but there is a danger that they will wait for each other in different places; situations of this kind generate a co-ordination problem. In the absence of communication, solving co-ordination problems can be difficult, even impossible. But with the aid of communication, a solution can be very straightforward and uncontroversial. For example, while communication between an aircraft and an air traffic control centre can occur in any mutually agreed language, it is obviously unacceptable for the pilot and the air traffic controller not to be able to speak a common language. Under the rules of the International Civil Aviation Organization, every international pilot and some personnel in every air traffic contol centre must be able to speak English. This is a highly stable equilibrium and the rule undoubtedly contributes to air safety. But it is only one of a large body of rules which form the regime that regulates international civil aviation. It has major training implications and it is not an issue which can be constantly renegotiated. It needs to be embodied in a stable regime which all the involved parties can treat as a constant.

The decision to choose English under these circumstances may have been relatively uncontroversial, but it does not follow that a common aversion to certain outcomes (a pilot speaking only German and the air traffic controller speaking only Japanese) will necessarily generate a common interest in a particular outcome (everyone speaking English). There is little doubt that the French would have preferred their language to English; and, of course, English has no intrinsic merit over French in this context. And this is the main lesson to be learned from the Battle of the Sexes game—there can be more than one outcome reflecting a Pareto optimum. Indeed, there can be many positions that represent a Pareto optimum and they can then be located on what is referred to as the Pareto frontier (see Box 12.5). So in the context of civil aviation, every spoken language can be located on the frontier because, in principle, any language could be chosen, provided that everyone spoke it. And the use of any common language is preferable to the alternative which would arise in the event of a failure to co-ordinate and identify a common language.

Realists argue that this line of analysis helps us to understand why states might conform to a regime while wishing to change the underlying principles. The explanation is that the states are already operating on the Pareto frontier. They observe the regime because they are operating in a co-ordination situation, and a failure to co-ordinate will move them into a less advantageous situation. The French can rail against the use of English in the civil aviation context, but they have no alternative but to persist with the policy. The same argument applies to Third World states; they wish to trade with the West, while preferring to do so on more advantageous terms. The application of new trade principles would represent another point on the Pareto frontier. But, as yet, because the balance of power continues to favour the West, there are few signs that new economic principles more favourable to the Third World are likely to emerge.

The situation is somewhat different in the area of communication regimes. All forms of electronic communication use electromagnetic waves which are emitted along an electromagnetic spectrum. Co-ordination here is essential, because interference occurs if more than one user adopts the same frequency of the spectrum at the same time over the same area. It is not possible, therefore, for states to operate on a unilateral basis and the establishment of a regime was essential. Moreover, because the electromagnetic spectrum is a limited resource, principles and rules for partitioning the resource had to be determined. In the first instance, states agreed that the spectrum should be allocated on the basis of need. But by 1980 this principle had resulted in the Soviet Union and the United States claiming half of the available frequencies and 90 per cent of the spectrum was allocated to provide

---

Box 12.5. The Battle of the Sexes and Pareto's Frontier

The Battle of the Sexes

The scenario of this game envisages a couple who have just fallen in love and decide to go on holiday together. The problem is that one wants to go hiking in the mountains and the other wants to visit art galleries and museums in the city. But both much prefer to be with their partner than to go on holiday alone. When mapped onto a matrix, two stable equilibriums emerge from the scenario.

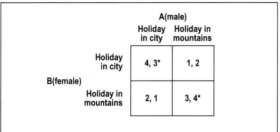

In this figure, cell numerals refer to ordinally ranked preferences: 4 = best, 1 = worst. The first number in each cell refers to A's preference and the second number refers to B's preference.

* Denotes an equilibrium outcome and a Pareto optimal strategy.

The Pareto Frontier

Wishing to reach a compromise, the couple might decide to split their week's holiday, spending time in the city and and in the mountains. Since the two extreme positions represent a Pareto optimum, so too must all the possible combinations and these can be mapped to form a Pareto frontier.

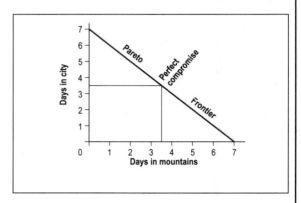

---

benefits for 10 per cent of the world's population (Krasner 1985). It is unsurprising to find this outcome being challenged by developing states which argued that part of the spectrum should be reserved for future use. More surprisingly, this new principle has been accepted. But realists argue that this is not the result of altruism on the part of the developed world. It is a consequence of the fact that developing states can interfere with the signals of neighbouring countries. This gave them access to a power lever which they otherwise would not have possessed (Krasner 1991). Through the use of power, the developing states have managed to move in a more favourable direction along the Pareto frontier. By contrast, they have had little say over the allocation of geosynchronous orbits which are the most efficient locations for broadcasting satellites. Here too co-ordination is required, but only amongst those states already in a position to launch the satellite. So a different balance of power is involved.

Key Points

- The market is used by liberal institutionalists as an analogy for the anarchic international system.

- In a market/international setting, public goods get underproduced and public bads get overproduced.

- Liberal institutionalists draw on the Prisoners' Dilemma game to account for the structural impediments to regime formation.

- A hegemon, 'the shadow of the future' and an information-rich environment promote collaboration and an escape route from Prisoners' Dilemmas.

- Realists argue that liberal institutionalists ignore the importance of power when examining regimes.

- Realists draw on the 'Battle of the Sexes' to illuminate the nature of co-ordination and its link to power in an anarchic setting.

Conclusion

Although liberal institutionalists and realists acknowledge that regimes are an important feature of the international system, and draw on similar tools of analysis, they reach very different conclusions about the circumstances in which regimes emerge. For liberal institutionalists, the need for regimes arises because there is always a danger in the anarchic international system that competitive strategies will trump co-operative strategies. Their analysis, therefore, focuses on ways of deterring competitive strategies that are otherwise seen to be the rational response within an anarchically structured system. By contrast, and paradoxically, given conventional assessments, realists link the emergence of regimes to situations where there is a mutual desire to co-operate, but where anarchy generates a problem of co-ordination. Again, in contrast to liberal institutionalists, realists assume that there is no incentive to defect once co-ordination has taken place.

The two approaches also adhere to divergent conceptions of power. For liberal institutionalists, power may be used by a hegemon to pressure other states to collaborate and conform to a regime. But it is also acknowledged that states can establish and maintain regimes in the absence of hegemonic power. Collaborative strategies are pursued and maintained because of the 'shadow of the future'—a mutual recognition that if any state defects from a regime, it will result in mass defection on a 'tit for tat' basis and states moving from an optimum to a suboptimum outcome. There seems little doubt that 'lead' states do establish regimes in the expectation that other states will follow. For example, in 1987, 22 states signed the Montreal Protocol agreeing to reduce CFC gases—which erode the ozone layer—by 50 per cent by 1998. But in 1990, the timetable was accelerated and the signatories expanded to 81, all agreeing to eliminate all CFCs by 2000.

For realists, on the other hand, power is seen to play a crucial role, not as a threat to discipline states

---

Box 12.6. Key Concepts

- **Anarchy:** a system operating in the absence of any central government.
- **Anomie:** the condition describing a system operating in the absence of norms or rules.
- **'Battle of the Sexes':** a scenario in game theory illustrating the need for a co-ordination strategy.
- **Collaboration:** a form of co-operation requiring parties not to defect from a mutually desirable strategy in favour of an individually preferable strategy.
- **Co-operation:** is required in any situation where parties must act together in order to achieve a mutually acceptable outcome.
- **Co-ordination:** a form of co-operation requiring parties to pursue a common strategy in order to avoid the mutually undesirable outcome arising from the pursuit of divergent strategies.
- **Game theory:** a branch of mathematics which explores strategic interaction.
- **Hegemony:** a system regulated by a dominant leader.
- **Microeconomics:** the branch of economics studying the behaviour of the firm in a market setting.
- **Market failure:** results from the inability of the market

to produce goods which require collaborative strategies.
- **'Prisoners' dilemma':** a scenario in game theory illustrating the need for a collaboration strategy.
- **Public goods:** goods which can only be produced by a collective decision, and cannot, therefore, be produced in the market-place.
- **Public bads:** the negative consequences which can arise when actors fail to collaborate .
- **Rationality:** reflected in the ability of individuals to rank order their preferences and choose the best available preference.
- **Reciprocity:** reflects a 'tit for tat' strategy, only co-operating if others do likewise.
- **Regimes:** sets of implicit or explicit principles, norms, rules, and decision-making procedures around which actors' expectations converge in a given area of international relations.
- **'Shadow of the future':** a metaphor indicating that decision makers are conscious of the future when making decisions.
- **Strategic interaction:** occurs when an outcome is the product of decisions arrived at independently.

caught defecting from a collaborative agreement, but in the bargaining process—to determine the shape of a regime around which all states will co-ordinate their actions. For realists, the conflict over economic regimes reveals most clearly the importance of the role played by power in the establishment of regimes. It is the rich and powerful states in the North that have primarily determined the shape of these economic regimes. Third World states have had no alternative but to accept the regimes because of the need to engage in trade. By contrast, there have been massive violations of the human rights regimes that have emerged since the end of the Second World War. These dead-letter regimes have failed to become full-blown regimes, according to realists, because there is no co-ordination involved. States can unilaterally violate human rights regimes without paying the automatic penalty incurred in co-ordination situations.

Stein (1983) who introduced the distinction between collaborative and co-ordination games into the regime literature never assumed, however, that they represented mutually incompatible approaches to regime formation. It could be argued, therefore, that the debate between the liberal institutionalists and the realists can be resolved by empirical investigation. Do decision-makers who are responsible for establishing regimes see themselves in a 'Prisoners' Dilemma' or a 'Battle of the Sexes'? Liberal institutionalists insist that the former represents the characteristic situation, whereas realists focus on the latter. Although it is not possible to foreclose on this question, it is possible that the two types of games can be viewed in sequential terms. States may escape from the Prisoners' Dilemma by agreeing to collaborate, only to find that they then enter a Battle of the Sexes when the details come to be worked out.

QUESTIONS

1. What are the defining elements of a regime?

2. Is a regime the same as an organization?

3. Why did the study of international regimes develop in the 1970s?

4. What characteristic features do the realist and liberal institutionalist approaches to regime analysis share?

5. How has microeconomics influenced the liberal institutionalist approach to regimes?

6. What is meant by rationality in the context of game theory?

7. What are the main implications of strategic interaction?

8. What are the implications of the Prisoners' Dilemma game for regime analysis?

9. What major mechanisms do liberal institutionalists advance to promote regime formation?

10. How does the realist approach to regime analysis differ from the liberal institutional approach?

11. What does the Battle of the Sexes game tell us about the role of power in regime formation?

12. What does operating at the Pareto frontier mean in the context of regime theory?

GUIDE TO FURTHER READING

Brown, S., *et al.*, *Regimes for the Ocean, Outer Space and the Weather* (Washington, DC; Brookings Institution, 1977). An early attempt to examine areas which need to be regulated by regimes.

Keohane, R. O., *After Hegemony: Co-operation and Discord in the World Political Economy* (Princeton: Princeton University Press, 1984). One of the most influential liberal institutional texts on the theory underlying regime formation.

Keohane, R. O. and Nye, J. S., *Power and Interdependence* (Boston: Little, Brown, 1977). Examines the role of regimes in an interdependent world, advancing four models to account for regime change.

Krasner, S. D. (ed)., *International Regimes* (Ithaca NY: Cornell University Press, 1983). A seminal text setting out the main theoretical issues.

Krasner, S. D., *Structural Conflict: The Third World Against Global Liberalism* (Berkeley: University of California Press, 1985). This is one of the major realist texts. It explores North–South disputes over regimes.

Oye, K. A. (ed.), *Co-operation Under Anarchy* (Princeton: Princeton University Press, 1986). An influential set of theoretical essays on how co-operation takes place under anarchic conditions.

Rittberger, V. (ed.), *Regime Theory and International Relations* (Oxford: Clarendon Press, 1993). This important book examines regime theory from European and American perspectives.

Zacher, M. W., with Sutton, B. A., *Governing Global Networks: International Regimes for Transportation and Communications* (Cambridge: Cambridge University Press, 1996). A liberal institutional account of regimes, arguing that they are based on mutual interests, and not the dictates of the most powerful states.

13 Diplomacy

Brian White

READER'S GUIDE

This chapter identifies diplomacy as a key process of communication and negotiation in world politics and as an important policy tool or instrument used by global actors. The first section focuses on problems of definition moving from general to more specific meanings of this term. The second section looks more historically at different stages in the development of modern diplomacy—from traditional to 'new'; from cold war to post-cold war. Each system of diplomacy is compared by reference to their common and divergent structures, processes, and agenda. The third section looks at the role of diplomacy as used by global actors—by states in particular—as a means of achieving their policy objectives. The chapter concludes by arguing that the context and form of diplomacy has changed over time but it remains a highly relevant process in world politics and a significant management tool for a wide range of global actors.

What is Diplomacy?

Diplomacy is one of those infuriatingly vague terms used in the study of world politics that can have a variety of meanings depending upon user and usage. It is helpful to start by trying to make sense of it in relation to two major perspectives on this study that might be labelled macro ('the big picture') and micro ('the small picture') analysis. The macro perspective tries to make sense of world politics as a whole; What are its constituent parts? How do they all fit together? The micro perspective tries to explain world politics from the different but complementary perspective of (to use a theatrical analogy—'all the world's a stage', etc.) the actors involved in world politics, a perspective that has traditionally focused on understanding the foreign policy behaviour of states and the governments that act on their behalf.

The conscientious student will be able to find uses of this term that are so general that 'diplomacy' is almost synonymous (the same thing as or can be used interchangeably) with both 'international relations' or 'world politics' and/or 'foreign policy'. You will find many references to, for example, **great power diplomacy, superpower diplomacy, summit diplomacy, crisis diplomacy** which—particularly in media reports—appear to describe and characterize a process that is much wider than a specific discussion of one facet of diplomacy might suggest. Links between international relations/world politics and international history—which is often referred to as **diplomatic history**—help to reinforce this notion of interchangeability of terms. Similarly, frequent references can be found to, for example, **'British diplomacy'**, **'Russian diplomacy'**, or **'South African diplomacy'**, both in the academic literature and in media reports, which suggest that the writer is referring not just to diplomacy as such but to British, Russian, or South African foreign policy behaviour as a whole.

If uses of the term diplomacy in such general ways are a convenient shorthand that might nevertheless mislead the reader, they do at least alert us to the fact that diplomacy is central both to an understanding of world politics as a whole and to the foreign policy behaviour of states and other international actors. To appreciate this, however, we must be much more specific in identifying what we mean by diplomacy. From the perspective of world politics as a whole, **diplomacy refers to a process**

WORLD POLITICS

Conflict	Co-operation
War	Diplomacy

Fig. 13.1. **World politics**

of communications that is central to the workings of the international system.

If world politics is simply characterized by the tension between conflict and co-operation, diplomacy together with war can be said to represent its two defining institutions. If conflict and co-operation are located at two ends of a spectrum (see Fig. 13.1), diplomacy will feature on that spectrum at the co-operation end representing forms of interaction that focus on **the resolution of conflict by negotiation and dialogue.** Negotiation in turn might involve any of the following: persuasion, compromise, conciliation, the threat of rewards or punishment. In a fundamental sense, therefore, diplomacy is related to the attempt to manage and create some sort of order within a system of world politics; **the object being to prevent conflict spilling over into war.** To be even more specific, diplomacy at the world politics level refers to a communications process that has been institutionalized and professionalized over many centuries. Some elements of this institutionalized process have remained constant over a long period of time while others have changed dramatically. This chapter will attempt to characterize the essential features of this diplomatic process in a global system of world politics.

From the 'micro' perspective of states and other international actors, the study of diplomacy provides equally revealing insights into the behaviour of the actors in a global system of world politics. From this perspective, however, **diplomacy can be identified as a method or a tool rather than a global process** and can be understood as such. All international actors have goals or objectives towards which their foreign policy behaviour is directed. In order to achieve those goals/objectives, actors clearly need means—often called instruments—to achieve their ends. **Diplomacy offers** one instrument that international actors might use to implement their foreign policy, either as a tool in its own right ('pure' diplomacy) or as a means of communicating the use or threatened use of other instruments to other parties. As with diplomacy as an international process, diplomacy as a foreign policy tool has changed over time and a second function of this chapter will be to characterize the essential features of the diplomatic instrument in the contemporary global system.

Diplomacy and World Politics

Diplomacy as a communications process between political entities has existed for literally thousands of years. The very first diplomatic document in our possession is a letter inscribed on a tablet which has been dated some time around 2500 BC. It was sent from a kingdom called Ebla near the Mediterranean coast in what we would call the Middle East to the kingdom of Hamazi in what is now Northern Iran. It was carried by a messenger who made a round trip of almost 2,000 kilometres. The tablet was discovered along with thousands of other administrative records by an Italian archaeological expedition in the 1970s.

In this one brief message, as Cohen (1995: 3) notes,

we have evidence of a fully-fledged diplomatic system: a working relationship between two distant kingdoms; the use of an emissary to convey a letter over a long distance; protocol, including the concept of equal status, an understood medium of communication, and a conventional form of address; a domestic organization for making and implementing foreign policy; an archive; a set of normative expectations about right and proper behaviour; a

sense of . . . fellowship or brotherhood; trade or reciprocal gift-giving via envoys.

Traditional Diplomacy

While the conventions and machinery of diplomacy have evolved over an extremely long historical period, with important developments at particular times—Ancient Greece, for example, saw the introduction of a diplomatic system with its immediate neighbours that had many remarkably modern features—the present global diplomatic system has its origins in fifteenth-century Italy where permanent embassies were first established (Hamilton and Langhorne 1995: chs. 1, 2). It is worth noting that this system, which we are labelling 'traditional diplomacy', is also referred to as 'old diplomacy', 'bilateral diplomacy', the 'French' or the 'Italian' system of diplomacy. However, the label is less important than the fact that traditional diplomacy had some distinctive features that need to be identified here. They can be usefully summarized under the headings of structure, process, and agenda—broadly relating to who was involved in diplomacy, how diplomatic activity was organized, and the substance of diplomacy. These headings will also help us to compare traditional diplomacy with diplomatic systems that preceded it and those that followed.

Structure

Traditional diplomacy can be distinguished from its predecessors in the ancient and medieval worlds because it constituted a communications process between recognizably modern states rather than between other forms of political organization, like the Catholic Church for example. As relations between states grew, leaders (usually monarchs)

Box 13.1. The Ebla–Hamazi Tablet

Thus says Ibubu, the director of the king's palace, to the messenger: ' You are my brother and I am your brother. As a brother I will grant whatever you desire, and you will grant whatever I desire. Give me good mercenaries (or, work-animals). Please send them. You are my brother and I am your brother. Ten beams of box-wood, two sledges of box-wood I, Ibubu have given the messenger (for you). Irkab-Damu, king of Ebla, is brother of Zizi, king of Hamazi, and Zizi, king of Hamazi, is brother of Irkab-Damu, king of Ebla.' Thus Tia-II, the scribe, has written. For the messenger of Zizi. [Reverse] Delivered.

(Cohen 1995: 3)

---

found it increasingly necessary to negotiate with other states on a variety of issues and on a regular basis. In the absence of a common international forum, state leaders had to negotiate indirectly and diplomats were sent abroad for this purpose. If diplomacy as a state-based activity is central to the structure of traditional diplomacy, the agents acting on behalf of states (or more typically their leaders) soon became institutionalized and later professionalized.

By **institutionalized**, we mean that particular institutions emerged which had diplomacy as their main function. Diplomacy ceased to be an irregular activity undertaken by *ad hoc* representatives. As already noted, the Italian city-states were the first to establish permanent, resident missions or embassies abroad and other states in Europe soon followed their lead. The obvious advantages of permanent representation in foreign countries included practicality and continuity. Embassies soon became an important expression of state interests. Permanent embassies in turn later became linked to a network of specialized foreign ministries established within home states. The institutionalization of diplomacy with a dedicated workforce of diplomats was later followed by the professionalization of diplomacy as an occupation. Though, as Berridge comments, 'the professionalization of diplomacy (with clear ranks, regular payment, and controlled entry) was a slow and fitful process and was not seriously underway . . . until well into the nineteenth century' (Berridge 1995: 8).

Processes

Traditionally, diplomacy was organized on a largely bilateral (two party) basis, usually undertaken in secrecy and characterized by distinctive rules and procedures. When two states developed a relationship of mutual importance, it became normal to exchange permanent embassies and to conduct diplomacy—or, technically, '**diplomatic relations**'—through those embassies on a state-to-state or bilateral basis. Unless one state forced the other to accept a position, mutual agreement was the only means of achieving a settlement. Limiting the relationship to two parties, of course, made it easier to keep any negotiations between them secret, although there were other good reasons in terms of the negotiating process itself for maintaining as much secrecy as possible. No good card or chess

player reveals his or her 'hand' or strategy in advance, and diplomatic negotiations are similar to these games in important respects.

If bilateralism and secrecy characterized the traditional process of diplomacy, it also drew upon **rules and procedures** for behaviour from earlier diplomatic systems. From the fifteenth century onwards, **diplomacy became not just a regular but also a regularized process.** Procedural rules known as diplomatic protocol were developed which included ceremonies which were often ostentatious and also more practical procedures relating to such things as the order in which a treaty was signed by the parties involved in a negotiation. A series of **rights, privileges, and immunities** were also attached both to diplomats and to diplomatic activities.

These derived from two principles. The first essentially practical consideration was that ambassadors should be able to conduct their business without fear and hindrance. The popular phrase, 'don't shoot the messenger !' not only suggests the idea of safeguarding the messenger who doesn't deserve to be blamed for the content of the message carried, but also indicates the importance of safeguarding the whole system of communications between political actors. The second principle was derived from the ancient idea that the ambassador is the direct representative of the sovereign monarch and, therefore, should be treated with the same consideration that a monarch would receive. This idea of representation was expanded by the controversial theory of extra-territoriality which simply means that the resident embassy is regarded as part of the territory of the home state and subject to the laws of that state and, likewise, that the ambassador is subject to the laws of the home state.

The problem with representational and 'extra-territorial' theories is that they give a misleading impression of the rights and immunities which do in fact attach to diplomats. With respect both to traditional and modern systems of diplomacy, diplomats are not in fact exempt or immune from the laws of the state in which they are located. They may, however, be exempt from methods of law enforcement which normally apply to citizens of that state. Any legal privileges diplomats can claim are justified by **functional necessity**—the need to enable the diplomatic system as a whole to work effectively. So, in practice, diplomats may get away with minor offences—non-payment of parking tickets is a good illustration from the modern period—but major misdemeanors were and are likely to result in the removal of diplomatic status and the expulsion of the person concerned.

Agenda

Traditional diplomacy can be characterized finally by the agenda of diplomacy—what issues did diplomats negotiate about? The most important point to note is that the agenda of traditional diplomacy was narrow certainly by comparison with later periods. Not only was the agenda set by the relatively underdeveloped state of bilateral relationships between states but, more importantly, **the preoccupations of diplomacy reflected the preoccupations of political leaders themselves.**

For hundreds of years, foreign policy was seen as the exclusive province of monarchs and their advisers and, not surprisingly, personal ambitions—the acquisition of territory, perhaps, or another throne—associated issues of sovereignty, together with more general issues of war and peace constituted the most important issues on the traditional diplomatic agenda. In a highly personalized structure, diplomats in essence were sent abroad by one monarch to win over other monarchs to their point of view. Not surprisingly, less desirable aspects of diplomacy occasionally surfaced as diplomats came under pressure to 'get a result' whatever the means employed. This led to at least one cynical definition of a diplomat as 'an honest man (sic) sent abroad to lie on behalf of his country!' (a remark usually credited to Henry Wotton, an Elizabethan diplomat). In general, however, it was quickly discovered that honesty rather than deceit is more likely in the longer term to be effective in achieving objectives, whatever short-term gains might be made by more duplicitous behaviour.

Traditional diplomacy reached its most highly developed form and was arguably most effective as a system for ordering international relations in nineteenth-century Europe. Though it is possible with hindsight to overstate the success of traditional diplomacy in this period, there were undoubtedly special conditions operating which contributed to that success. First, there were few states involved in this diplomatic system—five or six 'great powers' as they were called, who were able to act in harmony to an unusual extent—hence the system is often referred to as the '**Concert of Europe'**. They all, to a greater or lesser extent, had an interest in maintaining the system in operation.

There were no great ideological divisions between them; indeed they shared common interests based on elements of a common European culture which included language. The French language may not have been wholly accepted as a common language, but it was certainly the principal language of diplomatic communications. Most significantly, perhaps, diplomacy made a significant contribution to what became known, in a classic piece of overstatement, as the '**century of peace'** in Europe between 1815 and 1914.

New Diplomacy

However successful traditional diplomacy may have been in promoting stability, order and peace in nineteenth-century Europe, its failure to prevent World War I and, for some indeed, its role in actually causing this war, led to a widespread belief that a new form of diplomacy was needed. Though this was commonly referred to after World War I as the 'new' diplomacy, it is important to realize that elements of this allegedly new form of diplomacy were already in evidence in the nineteenth century if not before, and that there was a long transition period between traditional or 'old' diplomacy and the new system that evolved in the first half of the twentieth century.

To the extent, however, that there was something identifiably 'new' about the '**new' diplomacy**, it revolved around two important ideas (see Hamilton and Langhorne 1995: 137). **First**, there was a demand that diplomacy should be **more open to public scrutiny and public control.** This demand related less to a public involvement in the process than in the content of diplomacy and the provision of information about agreements reached. This focused attention on two interlinked elements of traditional diplomacy that were now seen to be problematic; excessive secrecy and the fact that diplomats were more often than not members of a social élite—the aristocracy. The **second** idea related to **the establishment of an international organization**—which became the League of Nations—that would act both as an international forum for the peaceful settlement of disputes and as a deterrent against another world war by the threat of collective action against potential aggressors.

Historically then the **new diplomacy represented the widespread hope for a new start after**

1918, but we can characterize this diplomacy more analytically and comparatively by using the structure/processes/agenda formula employed above with respect to traditional diplomacy.

Structure

The structure of the new diplomacy remained similar in form to traditional diplomacy to the extent that states/governments remained the major actors in this diplomatic system and were represented internationally by what was now a well-established network of foreign offices and permanent embassies abroad. There were two important changes to note, however, that have implications not only for the structure but also for the processes and issues that characterized the new diplomacy. First, in terms of structure, **states were no longer the only actors involved**. Increasingly, they had to share the diplomatic stage with other actors like international organizations who were also engaged in diplomacy. These organizations were of two types, intergovernmental (with governments as members) and non-governmental (with private individuals or groups as members).

The second important change to note is that states and particularly **governments** had changed in terms of the **scope of their activities** and the extent to which they sought to regulate the lives of their citizens. Where once they had simply provided for the physical security of their citizens they now had a broader concern with the social and economic well-being of their peoples. Thus, the twentieth century saw an important move from the so-called **'nightwatchman state'** to the **'welfare state'**. This has implications for the range of issues that states wish/need to negotiate about in their international diplomatic activity.

Processes

Clearly the changing interests of states/governments as international actors and the growing number of non-state actors involved changed the nature of the new diplomacy as a process of negotiation. Most obviously, it made **diplomacy a more complex activity involving more and different actors**. States continued to negotiate bilaterally with each other on a state-to-state basis, but groups of states typically negotiated **multilaterally** through the auspices of intergovernmental organizations like the League of Nations and its successor the United Nations and, increasingly, with the growing range of non-governmental organizations which sought to influence interstate behaviour to achieve their own objectives.

Again, it must be stressed that multilateral diplomacy was not new in the sense that what had been called conference diplomacy between the Great Powers had been an important feature of nineteenth-century European diplomacy. Nor did multilateral diplomacy replace bilateral diplomacy, but it did increasingly become the normal mode of international diplomacy. To the extent that it was more difficult to keep secret a process involving so many actors, it is fair to say that the new diplomacy was also a more open process than its predecessor.

Agenda

The **agenda** of the new diplomacy contained a **number of new issues as well as a distinctive emphasis on military security**. The avoidance of war became a priority as the 'new' diplomats sought to make World War I 'the war to end all wars'. But diplomatic activity focused more than ever before on **economic, social, and welfare issues** that related to material well-being. These became known as **'low politics'** issues in contrast to the **'high politics'** issues of war and peace associated with the traditional diplomatic agenda. These new issues not only reflected the wider interests of governments but also the often narrowly focused interests of non-state actors.

The other distinctive feature of the 'new' agenda is that it often featured **highly specialized issues** that raised question marks about the adequacy of the training given to diplomats. If the specialization required of 'new' diplomats challenged their competence, their distinctive role was also challenged by two other trends: the direct role political leaders themselves often played in diplomacy and the growing tendency of political leaders in the interwar period to appoint personal envoys to represent them. Clearly, professional diplomats were no longer the only 'players' involved in the new diplomatic 'game' and they enjoyed far less autonomy than traditional diplomats had enjoyed in earlier periods.

Cold War Diplomacy

Many of the characteristics of the new diplomacy continued into the period after World War II, indeed multilateralism and an increasingly specialized agenda became even more significant. In terms of changing structures and processes, however, a host of **new states** joined an already complex array of state and non-state actors as the former colonies of European powers gained their independence. The fact that these new states were unfamiliar with the customary rules and principles of diplomacy led to the first important attempts to give them the status of international law, notably in the **1961 Vienna Convention on Diplomatic Relations** (see Berridge 1995: 20–31).

The term **'cold war diplomacy'** refers to some very specific aspects of diplomacy that emerged after World War II. From the late 1940s until the late 1980s, world politics was dominated by the ideological confrontation between the United States and the Soviet Union. Each superpower supported by their allies sought to undermine and 'defeat' the other by all means short of a real or 'hot war'—hence the label 'cold war' to describe this confrontational system and set of relationships. The diplomatic activity associated with this 'East–West' confrontation had a single dramatic focus—**the absolute necessity of avoiding a global, nuclear conflict** that could destroy the international system. The most important elements of cold war diplomacy can be described under the headings of nuclear, crisis, and summit diplomacy.

Nuclear Diplomacy

Nuclear diplomacy describes the interactions between states that possess nuclear weapons where one or more states threatens to use them either to dissuade an opponent from undertaking an action or to persuade an opponent to call a halt to some action that has begun. The former is better known as **deterrence**, the latter as **compellance or coercive diplomacy.** There is nothing new about either strategy to the extent that states have always hoped that the size of their military forces would help them to persuade or dissuade potential adversaries short of actually using them in the field. The distinctiveness of nuclear diplomacy, however, is the extent to which both sides of the East–West divide relied upon their nuclear weapons to achieve their objectives but sought to avoid triggering a nuclear war. Given the nature of nuclear weapons though there were **unprecedented risks** attached to this type of diplomacy and crises frequently emerged as a result which, in turn, required a particular diplomatic response.

Crisis Diplomacy

As with deterrence, there is nothing new about the idea of a crisis in international relations—**a crisis can be simply defined as a short, intense period in which the possibility of war is perceived to increase dramatically.** In the pre-nuclear age, however, the implications of a crisis were less serious simply because the onset of war itself was a less horrendous outcome for the international system as a whole. A crisis in the nuclear age, however, involving states armed with nuclear weapons, is infinitely more serious.

The classic illustration of a nuclear crisis is the **Cuban missile crisis** of October 1962 when, almost literally, the world held its breath as the two superpowers spent thirteen days locked into an eyeball to eyeball confrontation. Eventually a settlement was negotiated between the two leaders Kennedy and Khrushchev, and Soviet missiles were removed from Cuba. But so close was disaster on that occasion that political leaders and political analysts looked for clues about behaviour in that crisis in order to handle future crises more effectively. Principles of **'crisis management'** were identified and political leaders sought to follow these guidelines in crises thereafter (these guidelines are conveniently summarized in Richardson 1994, ch. 3).

There are problems with the term 'crisis management', however,—as Richardson's extended comment explains (see Box 13.2)—and many analysts including Richardson now prefer the more traditional term **'crisis diplomacy'** to characterize the delicate communications and negotiation process involved in crises. From this perspective, the most important outcome of the Cuban missile crisis was not a checklist of guidelines for future crisis management but the agreement to set up a 'hot line'—a direct communications link between Washington and Moscow—that would maximize the chances of negotiating a direct settlement between the principal parties.

Box 13.2. Crisis Management

The term [crisis management] is often taken to mean the exercise of restraint in order to reduce the risk of war. However, this usage obscures the central problem confronting decision-makers in nuclear-age crises—that each party seeks to pursue simultaneously two potentially incompatible goals: to prevail over the adversary, while at the same time avoiding nuclear war. 'Crisis management' must address the tension between the two goals, but this brings out the questionable character of the concept itself. The dilemmas of choice are glossed over by the use of the term 'management', with its overtones of technical rationality and efficiency.

(Richardson 1994: 25)

Summit Diplomacy

If the 'hot-line' provided a direct communications link between the superpowers, summit diplomacy describes **a direct form of communication between heads of government or state** that became a regular mode of contact during the cold war. Again, we should note that 'summitry' is not new. Indeed, before the development of the resident embassy and the apparatus of the modern state, direct meetings between political leaders were quite normal.

Cold war summit meetings, however, reflected the special circumstances of that period. First, while communications of any sort were difficult because of ideological divisions, political leaders were keen to show that they were committed to peace. In the absence of regular diplomatic contact between East and West, summit meetings in the early cold war period facilitated occasional contacts even if little real negotiation took place. Summits like the four-power Geneva summit in 1955 had an important **symbolic value**. Later, when the superpowers realized that they had common interests and therefore, a basis for negotiations, summit meetings provided a **forum for negotiations** about arms control, for example, that were extremely valuable. Agreements signed at a series of summit meetings between the superpowers in the early 1970s gave substance to a relaxation of international tensions popularly known as *détente*. These were followed by a series of superpower summits from the mid-1980s onwards which played a significant role in bringing the cold war to an end.

Diplomacy after the Cold War

The end of the cold war represented a dramatic change in the international context within which diplomacy is conducted. The end of the ideological conflict between East and West and the demise of the Soviet Union raised popular expectations about what might now be achieved by diplomacy and negotiation. A **new optimism** about resolving a host of international problems was further stimulated by references in the United States to the possibility of establishing a **'new world order'**. The successful ousting of invading Iraqi forces from Kuwait in 1991 by an international coalition led by the United States and sanctioned by United Nations resolutions appeared to provide a convenient model for the future.

But optimism was soon replaced by a realization that the end of the cold war may have resolved some problems but other problems had merely been hidden from view during the cold war period. The breakdown of order in the former Yugoslavia and conflict between former parts of the Soviet Union in the first half of the 1990s provided illustrations of what might be called **post-cold war problems** on the international agenda.

As we approach the millennium, however, diplomacy can be characterized in two ways. First, diplomacy is now **genuinely global in scope** for the first time. Gone are the ideological divisions which effectively excluded a large number of states and other international actors from 'normal' diplomatic intercourse during the cold war period. Second, contemporary diplomacy can be characterized as **diverse and complex**. In terms of the analytical categories used so far in this chapter, there are multiple actors involved (a great variety of state and non-state actors), complex multilateral as well as bilateral processes at work, and the substance of diplomacy covers a wider agenda of issues than ever before, many of which would once have featured only—if at all—on a domestic political agenda.

Key Points

- Diplomacy is a key concept in world politics. It refers to a process of communication and negotiation between states and other international actors that enables them to co-operate.

- Diplomacy began in the ancient world but took

on a recognizably modern form from the fifteenth century onwards with the establishment of the permanent embassy.

- By the end of the nineteenth century all states maintained a network of permanent embassies abroad linked to foreign ministries at home. Diplomacy had become an established profession.

- World War I was a 'watershed' in the history of diplomacy. The perceived failure of traditional diplomacy to prevent this war led to a demand for a 'new' diplomacy which would be less secretive and more subject to democratic control. World War II revealed the limits of the 'new' diplomacy.

- Cold war diplomacy relates to the period after World War II when international relations were dominated by a global confrontation between the superpowers and their allies. The imperative need to avoid nuclear war while still pursuing national and allied interests produced a very delicate, dangerous form of diplomacy.

- The end of the cold war produced a mood of optimism that diplomacy could resolve all the major international problems and a 'new world order' could be established.

- Post-cold war diplomacy is now a genuinely globalized process but it remains diverse, complex and an inherently difficult process to manage.

Diplomacy and Foreign Policy

As noted in the introduction, diplomacy not only helps us to understand the nature of world politics as a whole but, from a different perspective, it also reveals much about the **behaviour of the actors** in a global system of world politics. The focus of this section is the **relationship between diplomacy and the foreign policies of states**, but it should be apparent from the discussion above that states are not the only actors in the system. The role of diplomacy in the behaviour of non-state actors will be reviewed at the end of this section.

The Making and the Implementation of Foreign Policy

We need first to locate diplomacy within what is called the **foreign policy process** of states. There are two major stages in that process—the **making** and the **implementation** (or the carrying out) of policy. A simple view suggests that the making of foreign policy is the business of government. So important is foreign policy to the achievement of the national interests of the state that the most senior members of a government will oversee the policy-making process. Having made the key decisions, they then hand them over to their foreign ministries for implementation. **Diplomacy is one of a set of instruments through which decisions**

are implemented and policy objectives (also established by the political leadership) achieved.

This is a reassuring picture in the sense that the politicians establish the objectives and make the important decisions. If they are elected, this suggests the possibility of democratic control of foreign policy—in principle at least. The **foreign policy bureaucracy**, not elected of course, plays a subordinate, non-political, essentially instrumental role. This picture is, however, an idealized one, unlikely to match the realities of the process in particular states. As we shall see, the making and the implementation of foreign policy cannot be so easily split. The two stages might be separated for the purpose of analysis but in practice they are parts of a continuous and interactive process.

Diplomacy as Policy Instrument

There is a specialized section of every government devoted to foreign policy. This usually takes the institutional form of a **foreign ministry** with a dedicated staff. In Britain, for example, the relevant department is the Foreign and Commonwealth Office and, in the United States, the Department of State performs the same functions. The specialized staff are known, respectively, as the Diplomatic Service and Foreign Service Officers. **Every foreign** ministry is linked to a network of embassies abroad. This constitutes the diplomatic machinery of government. If we identify the main functions performed by this 'machine', we can immediately note that they relate not only to the implementation but also to the making of foreign policy. Diplomacy as a governmental activity then refers not only to a policy instrument but it is also related to the whole process of policy-making and implementation.

There are five major functions performed by this diplomatic machine:

- Information gathering
- Policy advice
- Representation
- Negotiation
- Consular services

The first two of these functions are essential to the making of foreign policy. Information and data are the raw materials of foreign policy and it is part of the job of diplomats abroad to gather information and report back to the political leadership. Information relevant to policy-making can be gathered from formal and informal sources. The formal sources include the local media and government reports. Informal sources include personal contacts among the local political élite and the rest of the diplomatic corps—other states' diplomatic representatives based in that location. Some information will also be derived from covert sources but many states have dedicated intelligence units whose job is to provide restricted information to the home government.

Given the expanded agenda of modern foreign policy, noted in the first section of this chapter, the scope and range of information required by government for policy-making purposes has increased dramatically. As much of this information is specialized, it is now normal for trained representatives called attachés to be attached (as their name suggests) to the larger embassies. These may include commercial, scientific, military, agricultural, or cultural attachés, or some relevant mix depending upon the precise nature of the relationship between the parties.

It is difficult in practice to separate the function of information gathering and political reporting from the expectation that diplomats will offer policy advice to the political leadership. Part of the purpose of having permanent representatives abroad is that they develop a familiarity with the

country in which they are based and are able to use this familiarity together with other skills and experience to interpret data and to 'put a gloss' on their reports. They make assessments about likely developments and also make forecasts about the reception home government policies are likely to receive. The distinction between giving advice and actually making policy is often blurred, particularly on minor issues. Even on more significant issues, the information and advice given by diplomats will limit the perceived options available and effectively structure the choices of the political leadership.

If diplomats contribute to the policy-making process by providing information and advice, the diplomatic machinery provides an important policy instrument relevant to policy implementation through the functions of representation, negotiation, and consular services. Embassies not only represent the government abroad, they also represent the wider interests of the home state which go beyond the narrowly political realm. The ambassador and his staff will attempt to maintain good relations with the host state, to network with local élites, to be present at relevant ceremonial occasions and events where home interests need to be promoted—at trade fairs, for example. The status and size of the embassy provides a symbolic representation of the importance attached to relations with the host country. Increasing or decreasing the number of diplomats can also be used politically to signal the current state of the relationship, or to indicate problems, as the cases in Box 13.3 illustrate.

Negotiation is arguably the most important function of the diplomatic machine. This covers a variety of activities from simple consultation—known as an 'exchange of views'—to detailed negotiation on a specific issue. Professional diplomats may take the lead on negotiations or they may play a supportive role if political leaders or other envoys are involved. Whenever states require the agreement of other states for whatever purpose, diplomacy is the technique used to achieve that agreement which may or may not be in a written form. The ability to persuade other governments is central to the art of diplomacy and, on some occasions, persuasion itself may be enough. Frequently though, some pressure may be required and/or the parties involved may agree to compromise and to adjust their original positions. Pressure may take various forms including the imposition of

Box 13.3. Diplomacy by Expulsions

In May 1996, the British government both initiated and was on the receiving end of diplomatic actions designed to signal displeasure. In the first case, the Russian government required the removal of four British diplomats in the Moscow embassy who had allegedly been involved in espionage. In a 'tit for tat' response, preserving honour on both sides, the British government then required four Russian diplomats in London to be sent home. It was widely reported that had Anglo-Russian relations not been generally good at this time, a larger number of expulsions would almost certainly have resulted. In a second, unrelated case, the British government expelled three diplomats from the Sudanese embassy in London. These expulsions did not result from problems in bilateral relations, but in response to a United Nations Security Council resolution to impose diplomatic and travel sanctions on Sudan because of concern over complicity by the Sudanese military regime in acts of terrorism. In addition to the expulsions, the remaining Sudanese diplomats were required to give prior notice of trips outside London and entry visas were denied to members of the Sudanese government and military.

time limits on the negotiation, seeking to isolate the other state diplomatically or, in extreme situations, threatening to break off diplomatic relations.

The final function, the provision of **consular services**, has two elements of which the second is more directly related to diplomacy as a policy instrument. The first type of consular activity involves action to **support and protect citizens abroad**. This work, together with the processing of immigration applications from host citizens may be handled separately from embassy work. The second type of consular work is dedicated to commercial work, **supporting trade relations with the host state.** This type of work has increased dramatically in recent years and embassies are often evaluated in part at least in terms of their ability to boost home export promotion and trade activity generally.

Diplomacy and Other Policy Instruments

We have established that diplomacy is an important policy instrument in its own right. Persuasion or **'pure diplomacy'** may be sufficient to achieve a state's objectives. Typically, however, diplomacy is linked to other policy instruments to produce what is called **'mixed diplomacy'**. Here, **diplomacy becomes a communications channel through which the use or threatened use of other instruments is transmitted to other parties.** States learned long ago that persuasion is often more successful if 'sticks' and/or 'carrots' are attached. There are three other types of policy instrument that may be used in various ways either as **potential rewards or punishments** in the attempt to secure compliant behaviour in another party.

First, **military force** may be threatened or deployed to give 'muscle' to a negotiation. The diplomacy and military force combination has been used by states for so long that these instruments may be regarded as the traditional instruments of foreign policy. The growing dangers of warfare, however, led developed states at least to look for alternative instruments to strengthen their hand in negotiations. A second instrument, **economic measures**, are not new—trade diplomacy also has a long history. But trade and aid have been used increasingly since World War II to influence the outcome of negotiations. Both trade and aid can be threatened or used as a stick or as a carrot in the sense that either can be offered or withheld. The third instrument is the most recent in terms of usage and can be labelled **subversion**. Where the other instruments seek to influence target governments, subversion is rather different in that it focuses on target groups within other states with the object of undermining or overthrowing the government of that state. Subversion might include a **variety of techniques including propaganda, intelligence activities, and giving assistance to rebel groups** (See Box 13.4). Given that secrecy normally surrounds these activities—if they are to be effective—this instrument is not, strictly speaking, linked to the diplomatic process.

Clearly, the **effectiveness of mixed diplomacy** in achieving policy objectives depends on a variety of factors including the objective sought, the nature of the 'mix', the availability of particular instruments, the costs attached to the use of particular instruments, and so on. In terms of which instrument or instruments will be selected for use, it should be noted that diplomacy continues to occupy a favoured position because it has certain advantages compared to other instruments—even though it may need to be supplemented by other instruments to be effective.

Box 13.4. **Diplomacy by Subversion**

In September 1970, Salvador Allende was elected President of Chile, the first democratically elected Marxist leader. The United States government decided thereafter to use all means short of military invasion to bring down the Allende government for ideological reasons. A combination of diplomatic, economic, and subversion instruments were used to support a policy of destabilization. Chile was effectively isolated diplomatically from the international community. US influence with international banks was used to withhold economic loans from Chile and the Chilean economy was thrown into chaos. Trade in its principal export, copper, was effectively paralysed. Some $8 million dollars was made available to the US Central Intelligence Agency (CIA) for clandestine internal interference in Chile. Opposition political parties and paramilitary groups hostile to Allende were funded as were a series of crippling strikes including the famous truck-owners strike in 1972. The Allende government was finally ousted by a coup in September 1973 and Allende himself was killed (see Hersh 1983: chs. 21, 22.)

First, diplomatic resources are readily **available**. All states and other actors have some capacity to communicate with other actors. Even though less developed states are unable to afford extensive networks of diplomatic representation, this is compensated to some extent by their use of international organizations to communicate their interests. By contrast, few states beyond the most powerful have a range of other instruments available for use. Second, diplomacy has relatively **few costs** associated with it. While the use of other instruments may be regarded as politically unacceptable in certain circumstances—military force in particular—diplomacy, as Hocking and Smith suggest, is widely regarded as legitimate 'because of its association with negotiation and conciliation, which are valued as norms of international behaviour' (1990: 205).

States and Other Actors—The Management of Multilateral Diplomacy

The discussion so far in this section has focused on diplomacy as an instrument of state behaviour—on what used to be called **'statecraft'** to emphasize the traditional dominance of states as international actors. However, it was made clear in the earlier section on the historical development of a global diplomatic system that states are no longer the only significant international actors. Bilateral state-to-state diplomacy remains an important structural feature of that process but it has been increasingly supplemented by multilateral forms of diplomacy with a mixture of state and non-state actors involved. How do non-state actors (NSAs) act? How do states and NSAs manage complex multilateral systems of diplomacy?

In terms of action, as implied above, NSAs act diplomatically in very much the same way as states. NSAs may not have the extensive diplomatic apparatus performing a wide range of functions that states have developed over many years, but all have some ability and at least a rudimentary machinery—whether they are intergovernmental organizations like the United Nations or non-governmental actors like the major multinational corporations—to communicate their interests and to deploy their resources to influence the outcome of negotiations. Many of these actors, indeed, have a greater ability to influence the diplomatic process than smaller states.

It should be noted, however, that the demands of multilateral diplomacy today impose constraints on the ability of all actors to control outcomes. This is not only because, as argued earlier, it is a diverse and complex process, with multiple actors negotiating about a wider range of (often highly technical) issues than ever before. The **context** within which those negotiations takes place has also been radically transformed by **levels of interconnectedness or interdependence between societies** (part of the definition of globalization discussed in earlier chapters) and the effect of the **revolution in communications technology** which has radically transformed diplomacy both as a process and as a policy instrument in a number of different ways. The result is that multilateral diplomacy has become less of a traditional art form with a premium on negotiating skills and 'winning', and more of a management process with actors seeking to reach settlements through a process of adjustment. Gilbert Winham offers an excellent summary of these changes and is quoted at length (see Box 13.5).

Box 13.5. **Diplomacy of Interdependence**

Modern international negotiation represents a meshing of great systems. It is commonplace today to observe that the world is becoming more interdependent—and one symptom of this interdependence is the fact that complex political and economic problems are increasingly handled at the level of international negotiation rather than exclusively at the domestic level. Today, negotiators function as an extension of national policy-making processes rather than as a formal diplomatic representation between two sovereigns. The number of people involved in international negotiation has increased sharply, with consequent depersonalization of the process. It is unlikely that the 'true feelings' of leaders or diplomats are as important as they once were, but it is erroneous to assume that personalities are irrelevant—particularly as they combine in various decision-making settings. In past eras, it was fashionable to describe negotiation as an art, and art it continues to be, but it is now more akin to the art of management as practiced in large bureaucracies than to the art of guile and concealment as practiced by Cardinal Mazarin (Winham 1997, as reprinted in Sondermann *et al.* 1979: 135).

Key Points

- Diplomacy plays a key role in the foreign policy behaviour of states and other actors.

- All significant actors have a diplomatic machinery which performs important functions that contribute to the making and the implementation of foreign policy.

- Pure diplomacy involves persuading other actors to do (or not to do) what you want (don't want) them to do. To be effective, diplomacy may need to be supplemented by other instruments, but negotiating skills are central to the traditional art of diplomacy.

- Diplomacy combined with other instruments (military, economic, subversion) is called mixed diplomacy. Here, diplomacy becomes a communications channel through which the use or threatened use of other instruments is transmitted to other parties.

- Diplomacy has certain advantages compared to other instruments including high availability and low cost.

- In modern multilateral negotiations, diplomacy is less an art form and more a management process reflecting high levels of interdependence between societies.

Conclusion

This chapter has tried to demonstrate that diplomacy is neither a vague concept nor does it describe international behaviour that is of interest only to diplomatic historians. Certainly, as an international process and as a method or tool, it preceded the modern states-system. It then played a central role in the development and operation of the states-system for hundreds of years. Today, adapted to the demands of the contemporary global system, it continues to make an important contribution to order and co-operation in that system. However, diplomacy is no panacea. It cannot guarantee co-operation but it can provide the facilities and the skills to make it happen. The problem now is that diplomatic systems have become so complex and diverse that a range of skills beyond those deployed by the traditional diplomat is essential.

QUESTIONS

1. What is the difference between diplomacy as a 'process' and diplomacy as a 'method'?

2. What are the essential elements of 'traditional diplomacy'?

3. What was 'new' about the 'new diplomacy'?

4. What is the difference between the 'nightwatchman state' and the 'welfare state'? How does this difference affect the agenda of diplomacy?

5. What was distinctive about 'cold war diplomacy'?

6. What is the difference between 'crisis management' and 'crisis diplomacy'?

7. What is the foreign policy 'machine'? What functions does it perform?

8. What is the difference between 'pure' and 'mixed diplomacy'?

9. What factors determine whether or not diplomacy will be successful in achieving an actor's objectives?

10. What are the essential characteristics of multilateral diplomacy in a global system of world politics?

GUIDE TO FURTHER READING

Barston, R. P., *Modern Diplomacy* (London: Longmans, 1988). This is a useful summary of diplomacy as a policy instrument of states linked to the foreign policy process. It is a textbook aimed specifically at undergraduates with little prior knowledge.

Berridge, G. R., *Diplomacy: Theory and Practice* (Hemel Hempstead: Harvester Wheatsheaf, 1995). This is a textbook aimed at postgraduate students. It has useful material for undergraduates, nevertheless, on forms of diplomacy and the negotiating process.

Hamilton, K., and Langhorne, R., *The Practice of Diplomacy* (London: Routledge, 1995). This scholarly book looks in great detail at the evolution and development of the modern diplomatic system. It is excellent on historical detail and the changing context of diplomacy.

Richardson, J. L., *Crisis Diplomacy: The Great Powers Since the Mid-Nineteenth Century* (Cambridge: Cambridge University Press, 1994). The most comprehensive book on crisis diplomacy published to date. It has a wide range of case studies from the pre-nuclear era as well as an important critique of 'crisis management'.

Watson, A., *Diplomacy: The Dialogue Between States* (London: Methuen, 1982). An important study of diplomacy written by a former practitioner. It makes a strong case for the continuing relevance of diplomacy to solving the problems of contemporary world politics.

14 The United Nations and International Organization

Paul Taylor

READER'S GUIDE

The United Nations is made up of a group of international institutions, which includes the central system, the specialized agencies, such as the World Health Organization (WHO), and the International Labour Organization (ILO), and the so called Funds and Programmes, which include institutions like the United Nations Children's Emergency Fund (UNICEF) and the United Nations Development Programme (UNDP). This chapter argues that the work of these institutions and their role in international society have altered since the late 1980s. They have taken on an increasing range of functions, but they have also become much more involved within states, often without the immediate consent of the host governments. This development reflects changes in views about the relationship between what happens within states and what happens between them. But it also means that justice for individuals is increasingly seen as a concomitant of international order—serious deficiencies in human rights, or in economic welfare, can lead to international tension and contribute to interstate conflict. This development has led to challenges to traditional views about intervention within states, and the way in which they justify their sovereignty. The chapter concludes with a typology of the traditional functions of the United Nations, the more recent functions, and the problems that are in the way of carrying out both older and new functions more effectively. The student will need to resort to the bibliography to find detailed accounts of the items under these three headings. This chapter is concerned primarily with the relationship between the changing functions and international order, rather than the details of the functions themselves.

A Brief History of the United Nations

The United Nations was established at the the end of the Second World War as a result of initiatives taken by the governments of the states which had led the war against Germany and Japan, namely Britain, the United States, and the Soviet Union. They were determined to build upon the experience of the League of Nations from the interwar period, but to correct the problems that had been found with the earlier organization. In this they were joined by fifty-one other states at the beginning, including France and China, and over the years, since then, maintained near universal membership. By the mid-1990s there were nearly 200 member states. 'By a perverse paradox, the United Nations, identified in so many minds with internationalism, presided over the global triumph of the idea of the sovereign state.'[1]

Its main purpose was to maintain international peace and security, in the sense of dissuading states from attacking each other, and to organize countermeasures if this happened. But the founding document of the United Nations, the Charter, also referred to the needs and interests of peoples. In the Preamble it was asserted that: 'We the peoples of the United Nations [are] determined to reaffirm faith in fundamental human rights, in the dignity and worth of the human person, in the equal rights of men and women and of nations large and small.' And in Article 1, para. 2 the founders said they were determined to develop 'friendly relations among nations based on respect for the principle of equal rights and self-determination of peoples and to take other appropriate measures to strengthen universal peace'. Peoples as well as states figured in the Charter.

The arrangements of the United Nations could be understood as developments from those of the League of Nations. In the League there had been no clear division of responsibilities between the main executive committee (the League Council), and the League Assembly in which all states were represented. In contrast in the United Nations, the Security Council, made up initially of eleven states, and then, after 1965, of fifteen states, was firmly given main responsibility for maintaining international peace and security . Decisions were to be by a majority of nine out of the fifteen, and each of the five permanent members, namely the US, Britain, France, the Soviet Union (later Russia), and China,

could exercise a veto. The convention emerged that abstention by a permanent member would not be regarded as a veto. In the League there was no mechanism for co-ordinating military or economic actions against miscreant states, which was one reason for the League's weakness, as states feared that they would be vulnerable if they had to act individually and separately in response to League Council recommendations. In contrast, in the United Nations, there was to be an army set up by agreement between the Security Council and consenting states, to be commanded by the Military Staff Committeee of Chiefs of Staff of the Permanent Members of the Security Council. And the Security Council could demand member compliance under Article 25.

Security was the main concern of the United Nations proper, the so-called *central system,* based in New York, and within that the Security Council. But other institutions were set up alongside the Security Council, which were also developments from the arrangements of the League. There was to be an assembly of representatives of all members, called the General Assembly, which was now to agree its resolutions, in the main, by majority vote: the League Assembly had followed a rule of unanimity. Both institutions evolved more practical formulae, such as consensus and agreement without vote on the initiative of the Assembly President. But as the General Assembly's decisions were not necessarily unanimous, they were regarded as recommendations, rather than as binding decisions, with a small number of exceptions, such as the vote on the budget in its Fifth Committee. This was a binding decision taken by majority vote. The General Assembly was precluded from acting when a question was on the agenda of the Security Council, though in 1950, through the General Assembly's *Uniting for Peace* Resolution, a procedure was introduced by which an item could be transferred from the Council to the Assembly if the former had been unable to act. In addition to the Fifth Committee the Assembly had five other Committees of the Whole which could act on specific questions, legal, economic and social, and so on.

The central system also included the Secretariat, headed by the Secretary-General, which was given responsibility for the administration of the activities of the central system, such as servicing the meetings of the Security Council and the General Assembly. It also carried out, on the recommendation of the other bodies, a number of research functions, and some quasi-management functions, amongst which the support of peace-keeping activities had become especially important by the mid-1990s. But its role was primarily bureaucratic and it lacked the political power, and the right of initiative of, say, the Commission of the European Union (see Taylor 1996*a*). The one exception to this was the power of the Secretary-General himself, under Article 99 of the Charter, to bring situations that were likely to lead to a breakdown of international peace and security to the attention of the Security Council. This article, which at first sight appeared innocuous, was the legal basis for the remarkable expansion of the diplomatic role of the Secretary-General, compared with that of his League predecessors. Because of it he was empowered to become involved in a large range of areas, including economic and social problems, and humanitarian crises, which could be loosely interpreted as carrying a threat to peace.

The Secretariat, and the General Assembly also had functions, alongside another institution in the central system—the **Economic and Social Council** (ECOSOC)—for overseeing the activities of a large number of other international institutions which formed what came to be called the *United Nations system*. In addition to the central system the latter was made up of two main kinds of institutions, namely the **Specialized Agencies** and the **Funds and Programmes** (see Box 14.1). The former included such well-known institutions as the World Health Organization (WHO), the International Labour Organization (ILO), and the Food and Agriculture Organization (FAO), which had their own constitutions, regularly assessed budgets, executive heads, and assemblies of state representatives. They were self-contained constitutionally, financially, and politically, and not subject to direct UN control. The Funds and Programmes were much closer to the central system, in the sense that their management arrangements were subject to direct General Assembly supervision, and could be modified by Assembly resolution, and, most importantly, were largely funded on a voluntary basis. Overall, they were a response to the failure to co-ordinate social and economic activities which did not fall clearly into the sphere of responsibility of any one of the Agencies, and therefore they emerged because of changes in global economic

---

Box 14.1. **The Structure of the United Nations System**

The Central System	**The Funds and Programmes**	**The Specialized Agencies**
The Security Council of 15 members	The United Nations Development Programme (UNDP)	The World Health Organization (WHO)
The Economic and Social Council of 54 members	The United Nations Children's Emergency Fund (UNICEF)	The Food and Agriculture Organization (FAO)
The General Assembly of representatives of member states	The United Nations Fund for Population Activities (UNFPA)	The International Labour Organization (ILO)
The Secretariat of the United Nations under the Secretary General	The United Nations Conference on Trade and Development (UNCTAD)	The United Nations Industrial Development Organization (UNIDO)
	The World Food Programme (WFP)	The United Nations Educational Scientific and Cultural Organization (UNESCO)
	And many others	And many others

Note 1: The Funds and Programmes depend mainly on voluntary contributions, and are more closely supervised by the central system, especially after A/48/162 in1993 (see box 14.3)

Note 2: The Agencies are constitutionally independent of the central system—they report to the ECOSOC, but cannot be instructed by it or by the General Assembly They also have separate assessed budgets and their own Assemblies and Executives.

and social circumstances after the setting up of the Agencies. The most important were the United Nations Development Programme (UNDP), The United Nations Fund for Population Activities (UNFPA), The World Food Progamme (WFP), and the United Nations International Children's Emergency Fund (UNICEF) (see Box 14.1).

The founders of the Charter had tried to improve on the mechanisms of the League for overseeing the economic and social institutions. The League had attributed responsibility for this to its Assembly, but the founders of the UN agreed to establish a smaller body, ECOSOC (54 members), to carry out this more specialized function. This body was appointed by, and responsible to, the General Assembly. These changes in the UN, compared with the League, were a consequence of thinking in more functionalist terms, but they did not give ECOSOC the necessary powers to manage effectively.[2] It was only empowered under articles 61–66 of the Charter to issue recommendations to the Agencies, and to receive reports from them. In consequence the history of the UN's economic and social organizations was one of searching for ways of achieving effective management. The United Nations system, therefore, became multicentred and constantly concerned with the problems of co-ordination, as it was made up of a large number of constitutionally distinct institutions which had a strong urge to go their separate ways (see Taylor 1995).

The arrangements laid out in Chapter VII of the Charter for tackling an aggressor were never introduced, as in the late 1940s no agreement about the UN force on the terms of the Charter could be obtained. There followed a series of improvisations which included, **first**, an enforcement procedure under which the Security Council agreed a mandate for an agent to act on its behalf, as in Korea in the early 1950s and the Gulf War in the early 1990s, when action was undertaken principally by the United States and its allies. **Second** was classical peace-keeping, which involved the establishment, usually by the Security Council, of a UN force under UN command to be placed between the parties to a dispute after a cease-fire. Such a force would only use force to defend itself, would be established with the consent of the host state, and would not include forces from the major powers. This mechanism was first used, in the strict sense of peace-keeping, in November 1956, when a force was introduced into

Egypt to facilitate the exodus of the British and French forces from the Suez canal area, and then to stand between Egyptian and Israeli forces. (The first force was the exception in that it was established by a General Assembly resolution.) After that date there was a steady flow of such forces, and a great expansion in their number after the end of the cold war in the late 1980s. There was also a relaxation of the basic rules which led to a number of problems (see Mayall 1996).

And, **third**, after the late 1980s, the UN increasingly became involved in maintaining international *order* by helping to solve problems of *disorder* within states. Other parts of the United Nations system, the Specialized Agencies, and the Funds and Programmes, as well as a wide range of other intergovernmental and non-governmental organizations, got more involved in work which was seen as related to the maintenance of international order. The security function had been the primary function and it still was. But, whereas during the cold war it was interpreted as being concerned with the interests of states in a narrow sense, resisting aggression and defending frontiers, afterwards a wider interpretation emerged. The meaning of the interests of states was broadened so that they got mixed up with the interests of peoples. This ambiguity was, of course, in the Charter, but it had been concealed by the cold war. This is a theme that runs throughout this chapter.

Three aspects are discussed. First is the development of new ways of maintaining international order, especially those which, after the end of the cold war, involved a more direct involvement of the international organization within the state. Second is the problem of reconciling the granting of a wider range of competences to the United Nations, and other international institutions, with the sovereignty of states. And third, the chapter concludes with a typology of the traditional and evolving roles of the United Nations, and the ways of improving its contribution.

- The United Nations was set up to preserve peace between states after the Second World War.

- In a number of ways it reflected lessons learned from its predecessor, the League of Nations.

- The central system was only a part of the United Nations system.

Problems within the State and Problems between States

According to an essay by Hedley Bull, **order** among states, and **justice** within them, were often mutually exclusive: pursuing the one tended to exclude the other (see Bull 1977). But by the late 1990s there had been changes in the relationship between these two key concepts which the practice of the UN both reflected and encouraged: there were standards which the state was expected to meet which included the provision of a minimum acceptable quality of economic and social justice.

One reason for this was an increasing objection to the classical realist argument that what went on within states was no concern of any outsider. It was entirely appropriate for the international community to make the attempt to put right violations of individual rights, since the cosmopolitan moral community was indivisible: individuals throughout the world had rights in common and owed obligations to each other. Such rights were increasingly interpreted as meaning both individual political and civil rights, as well as the right to basic provisions like food, water, health care, and accommodation. Although the efforts of the United Nations, and other international organizations, were entirely inadequate in this regard, the principle of their involvement in order to promote these rights was increasingly accepted.

But it was also understood that violations of individuals' rights were a major cause of disturbances in relations between states: a lack of internal justice risked international disorder. In consequence there was increasing challenge to the traditional injunction on the behaviour of diplomats that they should ignore the internal affairs of the states with which they dealt in order to preserve international stability. There was increasing unease with a dual standard of tolerance among states at the expense of intolerance within them. There was still some mileage in the old ways but the change in the moral climate was evident. The United Nations reinforced the perception that pursuing justice for individuals was an aspect of national interest. Thus in 1996 the US Administration's view that action in support of justice in Bosnia Herzogovina was a part of US national interest, and not a betrayal of it, was attributable in part to the actions of the UN and the

expectations it generated. The organization was a constant reminder to Americans of the positive relationship between order and justice, and it was in consequence heartily disliked by American right-wing anti-internationalists.[3] If there was a clear cut conflict between perceptions of national interest and the pursuit of justice the former had priority, but more frequently the choice could not be put in such stark terms.

In an increasing number of states contributions to activities such as **peace-keeping**, or **humanitarian intervention**, were defended in terms of national interest. Indeed both the moral injunction to be involved and the link with national interest were reinforced: states like Canada accepted an obligation to develop their capacity for peace-keeping, which was the moral course, but one which could also be justified as a reflection of national interest. Canada gained status in the international community through such contributions, and because of it could punch above that country's weight in the United Nations. The Japanese also responded to moral pressure founded in hard national interest when they contributed substantially to defraying the cost of British involvement in the Gulf War. This extraordinary act could only be explained in terms of the synthesis of morality and interest. Reputation in the United Nations context had become for some states an important national good. The Japanese wanted to be a good citizen in that context because it would help their case for becoming a permanent member of the Security Council.

An analogy is suggestive: not attempting to stop your neighbour from killing his wife when you have the capacity to do so is morally repugnant. But it may also be in your interest to act if not doing so leads to a weakening of the legal order, and a fall in property values in the neighbourhood! Conversely acting morally may also improve your personal standing and help get you elected to the District Council. Moral acts and national interest became interrelated when success within a common organization became a value: the sense of what was common had moved to that point. In this the UN had achieved status well ahead of the League of Nations:

Box 14.2. **Key Concepts**

Accountability: the state of being obliged to explain and justify an act or acts to another.

Competence: the right to act in a given area. Such a right may be extended by a government to an international organization, but this does not mean that ultimate responsibility has been transferred, but only that the international organization is permitted to act on the state's behalf.

Funds and Programmes: institutions which are subject to the supervision of the General Assembly and which depend upon voluntary funding by states and other donors.

Justice: fair or morally defensible treatment for individuals, in the light of standards of human rights or economic or social well-being. In this chapter the term is interpreted broadly to include satisfactory standards with regard to human rights and economic conditions, such as adequate food, housing, and health care.

Intergovernmental and non-governmental organizations: see Box 15.12.

Intervention: when there is direct involvement within a state by an outside actor to achieve an outcome preferred by the intervening agency without the consent of the host state. In this chapter the word 'intervention' is placed in inverted commas when it is unclear whether consent has been given. Otherwise the word *involvement* is used.

Involvement: when an outsider, such as an international organization, acts within a state with or without the consent of that state .

Order: when relationships between actors, such as states, are stable, predictable, controlled, and not characterized by violence, turbulence, or chaos.

Recognition: the act, at present carried out by governments individually and separately, of acknowledging the status of another entity as a legal person, thus granting it a licence to act in international society, and to enter into contracts with its members. At present recognition is symbolized by establishing diplomatic relations, exchanging ambassadors, and accepting the other's membership in the United Nations.

Sovereignty: a condition necessary in states in that they are not subject to any higher authority. The government of a sovereign state is ultimately responsible for its citizens. In practice sovereignty has often been conditional. Internally governments have been subject to conventional standards, and externally conditions may mean that governments are more or less free to act independently. A sovereign government is free to choose within the framework of these conventions and standards.

Specialized Agencies: international institutions which have a special relationship with the central system of the United Nations but which are constitutionally independent, having their own assessed budgets, exceecutive heads and commmittees, and assemblies of the representatives of all state members.

---

it was a club within which success mattered, a development which might be attributed to the changing sense of social space in the international community. Changes in communications, and the technology for moving items and people around the world, increasingly made denying the existence of a global neighbourhood look eccentric.

Key Points

- It became more difficult for states, and diplomats, to accept that what happened within states was of no concern to anyone else.

- It became more common for governments to see active membership in the United Nations as serving their national interest as well as being right.

- The ending of the cold war had helped to promote this attitude.

The United Nations and Conditions within States

But this had not always been the case. In the past the United Nations helped to promote the traditional view of the primacy of international order over justice in two major ways. The cold war stand-off between the East and the West alerted member states to the danger of raising questions about the conditions of the sovereignty of states. Jean Kirkpatrick's notorious essay, which recommended tolerating obnoxious dictatorships in Latin America in order to fight communism, was at least a reasonable report of what the situation in fact was: unsavoury right-wing regimes in Latin America were tolerated by the US because they were anti-Soviet, and interfering in the other's sphere by East or West risked escalation of conflict.[4] Indeed interfering in one's own sphere risked creating opportunities for the other side. Ending the cold war reduced the risk that any promotion of justice could become a context of superpower rivalry. China was the chief heir to the tradition of cold war thinking, and any return to superpower bipolarity, with China replacing the Soviet Union, would revive this reason for hesitating about justice.

The UN also reflected the claims of colonies to become states, and elevated the right to statehood above any of the tests of viability, such as the existence of a nation, adequate economic performance, defensibility, or a prospect for achieving justice for citizens. This unconditional right to independence was enunciated in the December 1960 General Assembly Declaration on the Granting of Independence to Colonial Countries and Peoples, which was approved by a vote of 90 in favour, none against and 9 abstentions. In the subsequent phases of decolonization this often suited the ex-imperial powers, such as Britain, which became more anxious to be rid of them (see Drower 1992). There emerged a convention that the claims of élites in the putative states could be a sufficient indication of popular enthusiasm, even when the élites were crooks and the claims misleading. There were few attempts to test this through such devices as a pre-independence referendum.

Charles Beitz was one of the first to question such insouciance on the part of the imperial states when he concluded, in defiance of political correctness in the 1970s, that statehood should not be unconditional: attention had to be given to the situation of individuals after independence, and such considerations could mean that independence in existing circumstances was unacceptable: the majority of individuals would be worse off (see Beitz 1979). Michael Waltzer and Terry Nardin produced aguments that led to similar conclusions: states were conditional entities in that their right to exist should be dependent on a criterion of performance with regard to the interests of their citizens (Walzer 1977; Nardin 1983). Such writings surely helped to alter the moral content of diplomacy.

The clash between the principles of justice and the principles of national interest was of course never a continuous one. It appeared occasionally as a reaction to the harsh reality of international society. The skill of the diplomat who wished to pursue a moral foreign policy was to avoid situations in which the harsh choice had to be made, because it would inevitably have to be made in favour of the national interest.[5] But the United Nations in its new role provided an alternative to this stark choice. The international agency could be expected to salve the national conscience by doing something about the moral failures which national interest required the diplomat to ignore. The moment of choice increasingly became the moment of revelation: it launched the next moral crusade which states found increasingly difficult to ignore. By the late 1990s the United Nations had become the dynamic of the cosmopolitan community as envisaged by Kant. Conscience needed an agent and the United Nations was it.

The new relationship between order and justice was, therefore, very much a product of particular circumstances: the end of the cold war, the end of the period of state-building and the specific conditions attached to decolonization, and, of course, the attachment of new expectations and the placing of new demands on the United Nations. The latter was not a trivial point. The fact that the United Nations achieved a degree of success indicated that with more effort and more resources it could do better. The question of commitment to the UN was, therefore, not just a question of commitment to an ideal, but rather of making as sure as possible that something that had worked could work better. The world had never got to this point before. After the failure to achieve what had been attempted there could be no easy return to the old standards of attainment: the world would forever have higher expectations, even if these were doomed to continuing disappointment.

Key Points

- The cold war and the decolonization process discouraged more active involvement by the United Nations within states.

- Scholars involved with international theory questioned the previous orthodoxy that individuals in new states were necessarily better off after independence.

- The United Nations became a focus of the global conscience.

Paul Taylor

The United Nations and Maintaining International Order

In the mid-1990s the word **governance** was often used with reference to international organizations but there was no agreement about what was meant by this concept. In this chapter it will be seen as an indication of a step towards *legitimate* global *government* which is illuminated by reference to the distinction between order and justice. Use of the word governance in the later 1990s reflected the view that there were some international institutions, like the UN, which had acquired some but not all of the functions of *legitimate* government. One measure of the development of legitimate government was an ongoing concern with justice for individuals within the state. This meant more involvement with the performance of specific tasks, such as economic development or the promotion of higher levels of public health, but it extended beyond that to a system of international mechanisms for continuously monitoring the performance of the states with regard to their citizens, for repeating continuously the tests that were temporally abandoned in the 1960 Declaration, and for promoting action, with or without government agreement, to correct any failures. 'Governance is not just the province of the state. Rather it is a function that can be performed by a wide variety of public and private, state and non-state, national and international institutions and practices.' 'But the governing powers, international, national and regional, need to be "sutured" together into a relatively well-integrated system' (Hurst and Thompson 1996: 183–4). The state inevitably played a key part in that process, but the role of the United Nations was also of increasing importance. Whether such action was effective, and what happened if governments resisted the attempt, were different questions which are discussed later. In the final section of the chapter the improvement of the UN's role in global governance in this sense is considered.

The theme of the chapter is thus clarified. Any discussion of the United Nations and International Order has to refer to the work of the United Nations with regard to issues which impinged upon justice in a broader sense, as well as that which more directly affected relations between states. It was about human rights, refugee problems, and humanitarian crisis, as well as about Chapter Vll

activities and peace-keeping. Change in the kind of international order which the United Nations reflected and promoted might also be more clearly understood in this approach. The perception was that what happened *within* states had now to be linked with what happened *between* them.

The United Nations was concerned with the question of international order in three major ways in the mid-1990s.

First it was increasingly concerned, not just with the order of the international system, but with the promotion of internal standards within states. Increasingly it dealt with human rights infringements, administrative and economic collapse—rescuing failing states—and helped with elections and with providing humanitarian assistance. The nature of the activity was, however, secondary to the primary purpose which might be called *regime restoration*: when the state was endangered, not because of challenges to its sovereignty from without, but because its internal arrangements did not meet the standards expected in the late 1990s, the UN claimed the right to act.

Second it was concerned with what was traditionally the central principle of international order, and of the work of the United Nations and the League before it, namely the promotion of international peace and security through resisting aggression *between* states. It was in this defending the rights of states in international society. These rights, which were analagous with the primary national interests of states, were increasingly embodied in formal contracts between states. Interests had become rights and principles. The right to security was central to the United Nations, but so were the two other major rights: the right to protect the cultural life of the peoples within states, and the right to an adequate standard of economic provision. The definition of aggression had accordingly been expanded to include attempts to deny these rights. These interests/rights had become axiomatic.

The involvement of the United Nations in protection was clearly illustrated by the few actions of enforcement, such as the action in Kuwait in the early 1990s and the much earlier involvement in Korea. That such action did not strictly follow the rules of the Charter, contained in Chapter VII, was irrelevant to the principle: in both cases the sanction of the global organization was essential even though the action was carried out by an agent rather than the principal. These two cases should not be construed as the only measure of the United Nations success in this area; the organization embodied a general injunction on behaviour which could be measured by the rule as well as by the breach.

A **third** way in which the UN had become involved in the promotion of order was in its role when sovereignty was contested by rival groups of its citizens, often in civil war. The organization was then involved in the process of legitimizing states, either by recreating existing states through the reconciliation of warring internal groups, or by assisting with the dissolution of older states and creating new ones. It was useful to distinguish between the process of overcoming internal problems within existing states, where sovereignty was *not* contested—and restoring the conditions of their sovereignty—on the one hand, and helping with the resolution of disputes between internal groups which had demanded the right to set up separate states—where sovereignty *was* contested—on the other.

Key Points

- The United Nations had become involved in a multilayered system of governance sometimes working with states, sometimes alongside them, and sometimes apart from them.

- Global governance involved a stronger role for international organization in maintaining standards for individuals within states.

- By the mid-1990s the UN had become involved in maintaining international order in three main ways, listed in the text.

The United Nations and Intervention within States

A difficulty in carrying out the new tasks was that it appeared to run counter to the doctrine of non-intervention. Intervention was traditionally defined as a deliberate incursion into a state without its consent by some outside agency, in order to change the functioning, policies, and goals of its government and achieve more congenial outputs (Vincent 1974). One of the changes which was indicative of the changing role of the United Nations was that the traditional ways of justifying intervention without consent had been questioned. The point was not that this had led to the frequent use of the new justifications but rather that it indicated an anxiety about the increasing range, and changing nature, of involvements within states.[6]

Such involvements might be unopposed, or not detected, as well as positively accepted, but have the same effects as non-consensual intervention: to alter the working and output of government to suit an external actor. But very few involvements took place in defiance of the opposition of the host government. A key issue, therefore, was whether there was an increasing preparedness to intervene within states by the UN in this broader sense, as well as in the older, narrower one. A positive response would be a measure of movement towards global governance. Sovereignty was regarded as central to the system of states. It implied that they were equally members of international society, and were each equal with regard to international law. Sovereignty also implied that states recognized no higher authority than themselves, and that there was no superior jurisdiction; the governments of states had exclusive jurisdiction within their own frontiers, a principle which was enshrined in Article 2 (7) of the United Nations Charter. Intervention in the traditional sense was therefore necessarily always in opposition to the principles of international society, and it could only be tolerated as an exception to the rule.

But in earlier periods states had indeed intervened in each other's business and thought they had a right to do so in a number of situations. The American government refused to accept any curtailment of their right to intervene in the internal affairs of other states in their hemisphere until 1933, when they conceded the point at the seventh International Conference of American States, a position which was very similar to the Brezhnev doctrine of the 1970s, which held that the Soviet Union had the right to intervene in the member states of the socialist commonwealth to protect the principles of socialism.

Much earlier the British had insisted in their relations with other states on the abolition of slavery: they intervened to make sure that this had been done, in that they stopped ships on the high seas, and imposed it as a condition in treaties (see Bethell 1970). There had also been a number of occasions when states had tried to bind other states to respect certain principles in their internal affairs. A number of states in Eastern Europe were bound to respect the rights of minorities within their frontiers by the agreements made at the Berlin Conference of 1878 by the Great Powers: they included Hungary and Bulgaria. At the end of the First World War the settlements had similarly imposed conditions on the new states to guarantee the rights of minorities within their frontiers (see Claude 1955). In practice intervention was a common feature of international politics, often for good cause.

In the 1980s and 1990s the view was more frequently expressed that there should be in a sense a return to the earlier period, but this time with a greater determination, and a wider range of instruments, to protect generally accepted standards. The United Nations could be heir to the earlier aberrations but this time the principle of non-intervention would be challenged on behalf of universal, rather than particular values. To the extent that values were universal the right to intervene by the instrument of global governance would be justified. It was pointed out that the Charter had not merely asserted the rights of states, but also the rights of peoples: statehood could be interpreted as being conditional upon respect for such rights: for instance the Preamble held that the organization was 'to reaffirm faith in fundamental human rights', and Article 1(3) asserted the obligation to 'achieve international cooperation . . . in promoting and encouraging respect for human rights and fundamental freedoms for all'. There was ample evidence in the Charter to justify the view that extreme transgression of human rights could itself be a justification for intervention by the international community.

There were a few examples of this view in the early 1990s: the clearest was probably Security Council Resolution 688 which sanctioned the creation of the Safe Havens in Iraq at the end of the Gulf War, which were intended to protect the Kurds against Saddam Hussein. The allies committed themselves to defend the Kurds and to provide them with humanitarian assistance. In the major pronouncements of the United Nations General Assembly on humanitarian assistance e.g. A/43/131 and A/46/182 there was reference to the primary responsibility of the target states for dealing with complex crises within their frontiers, although A/46/182 implied some relaxation of this in its precise wording: it held that 'The sovereignty, territorial integrity and national unity of States must be fully respected in accordance with the Charter of the United Nations. In this context, humanitarian assistance *should* be provided with the consent of the affected country and *in principle* on the basis of an appeal by the affected country' (italics added). The use of the phrase 'in principle', and the normative ' should', implied that there could be occasions when government approval was not possible, but where intervention was nevertheless necessary.

There was disagreement about whether the existing procedures of the United Nations, relying in particular on the approval of the Security Council, were adequate for the authorization of such novel forms of intervention, or whether further safeguards were necessary, such as a two-thirds majority in the General Assembly, and the supervision of the International Court of Justice.[7] There was the irony here that in order to protect the interests of states a strengthening of the governance of international society might be appropriate: the erosion of the strict interpretation of Article 2(7) of the UN Charter depended upon the creation of countervailing procedures in the global organization. There could be no question of individual states, or particular groups of states, compromising the absolute prohibition on intervention. But the 'interventions' were proposed in order to strengthen rather than weaken states as the primary actors in international society.

The number of occasions was, however, very limited when there was appeal to a principle involving the rights of individuals in the target territories. Well-known interventions, such as that of India in East Pakistan in 1971, Tanzania in the Uganda of Idi Amin, or of the United States in Panama, were justified by reference to the need to protect the citizens of the *invading* states, and their right of self-defence, both of which were ancient justifications of intervention under international law.

Even Security Council Resolution 688 in 1991,

Box 14.3. Selected Documents Relevant to the Changing Role of the United Nations System

---

Development of the Economic and Social Organizations

A/32/197 The first major General Assembly Resolution on reform of the economic and social organizations, Dec. 1977.

A/48/162 A major step towards reform of the economic and social organization of the United Nations, especially the Economic and Social Council, Dec.1993.

Development of the UN's Role in Maintaining International Peace and Security

SC Res 678, Nov. 1990, sanctioned the use of force against Saddam Hussein.

SC Res. 743 Feb. 1992, established UNPROFOR in Croatia.

SC Res 770, 13 Aug. 1992, created UNPROFOR2 in Bosnia-Herzogovina.

SC 816, Apr. 1993 enforced the no-fly zone over Bosnia in that it permitted NATO war planes to intercept Bosnian Serb planes in the zones.

Development of Humanitarian Action through the UN

SC Res 688, Apr., 1991 which sanctioned intervention in Iraq at the end of the Gulf war to protect the Kurds in north Iraq, and the Shia Muslims in the south, against the regime of Saddam Hussein.

SC Res.733, 23 Jan. 1992, first sanctioned UN involvement in Somalia. A/46/182, 14 Apr. 1992, which is the major document on the development of the machinery for humanitarian assistance.

SC Res 808, July 1993, which set up an *ad hoc* war tribunal with regard to war crimes in ex- Yugoslavia.

SC Res. 794, 3 Dec. 1992, which sanctioned the American move into Somalia; by that stage the central government of Somalia had ceased to exist in the eyes of the majority of states, or at least in the eyes of the member states of the Security Council which approved the resolution unanimously.

Note: documents may now be accessed through the internet using Netscape or Spry Mosaic.

---

referred to above, was somewhat ambiguous as Saddam Hussein's consent to the operation was implied in a series of six-monthly agreements which covered its terms, known as a Memoradum(s) of Understanding (see Taylor and Groom 1992). Perhaps it was better described as near-non-consensual intervention! On other occasions, such as that of the Security Council Resolution which first sanctioned UN involvement in Somalia, Resolution 733 which was adopted on 23 January 1992, action was in response to a request by Somalia, even though the government of that country was near expiry. The basis for that intervention was in fact Chapter VII of the Charter, and not humanitarian need. In resolution 794, which authorized the United States to dispatch 30,000 troops to 'establish a secure environment for Humanitarian Relief Operations in Somalia as soon as possible', approved unanimously on 3 December 1992 the explicit consent of the Somalia authorities was not mentioned, but by that time any pretence that such existed could be abandoned.

Key Points

- New justifications for intervention in states were being considered by the early 1990s.

- But most operations of the United Nations were justified in the traditional way: there was a threat to international peace and security.

- But any relaxation of the traditional prohibition on intervention had to be treated very cautiously, and new methods of approval in the UN could be advisable if this happened.

Paul Taylor

The United Nations and Forms of Involvement within States

But there were other ways of dealing with the problem of how to act within states without the consent of the host government: the range of ways by which involvement could be contrived, to achieve the purposes usually attributed to intervention, was much wider than was usually appreciated. A small number of international organizations such as UNICEF and the ICRC were not required by their founding agreements, or the rules which governed their operations to obtain the formal consent of governments for such involvement. They naturally preferred this, but assumed that they could work on a territory unless expressly forbidden from doing so. In Cambodia UNICEF and ICRC had established a presence during the Vietnamese occupation and operated throughout the area in a low-key way. The publicity generated by reports of massive starvation there by the journalist John Pilger, who had the support of OXFAM, not only led to serious quarrels between OXFAM and the other participating organizations, but provoked the Vietnamese government to restrict aid to the area it occupied. Eventually aid had to be delivered to the Khmer Rouge area in the north-west of the country, where the people were no less deserving, from Thailand (see Black 1992: esp. 219–21).

Non-governmental organizations were more likely to succeed in 'intervening' without positive approval than intergovernmental organizations, because of their ingenuity and flexibility in devising entry strategies. They were less sensitive to political constraints; for example they were less constrained by anxiety about appearing to be partial if there was a dispute within a state; they were also less fearful of losing government funding, as they were financed to a significant degree by private voluntary contributions, and were more prepared to accept risks in the security of their staff. Non-governmental organizations had become major players both in humanitarian assistance and in development by the late 1980s. They often commanded large budgets and had very effective and skilled management (see Seaman 1996: 17–32; also Willetts 1996).

The intergovernmental organizations of the UN system were more likely to be constrained by the fear of appearing to be partial in the event of civil war within states, even at the expense of failing to provide humanitarian relief, because of their equation of sovereignty with neutrality regarding internal affairs. This was the reason for the very slow UN involvement in Somalia in 1991–2. Their preference for working through governments, even those that were feeble or in disgrace, and their preference for information provided by governments over that from non-governmental organizations, was a response to the same constraints. They were also subject to rather stricter rules about the security of their staff than were non-governmental organizations.

But once present both NGOs and IGOs were capable of pursuing strategies of greater or lesser involvement with host governments. The government's response could vary from active hostility, which would be a situation quite close to non-consensual intervention, to one of reluctant tolerance. General Assembly Resolution 46\182 stated that 'the affected state has the primary role in the initiation, organization, co-ordination and implementation of humanitarian assistance within its territory'. But there were cases where this principle did not seem to have been followed. For instance, the Kenyan authorities felt that their own Drought Recovery Programme had been dealt with in a fairly cavalier way in the SEPHA consolidated appeal in 1992. The Kenyans had drawn up an appeal in close consultation with the agencies involved, so that when the programme was launched in October 1992 they were confident that it had the full backing of the UN. But subsequently 'they felt uncertain about how far funds contributed to SEPHA would be used for the DRP'—to use the tactful words of a report written by an official (see Taylor 1996*b*).

There was a wide range of forms of relationship between the UN institutions and host state governments in the various states in which they had become involved, in Africa, Central America, and elsewhere. These are evident in the provision of humanitarian assistance and increasingly in the development process. The traditional view of sovereignty would lead to a relative indifference to the character of the regime except *in extremis*. But a government could be objectionable to the point that to work with it, even in some areas of humanitarian assistance, would be to defend the indefensible. There was the problem of how this judgement was to be made: in practice working in such circumstances, when that had the highest priority, would probably be left to non-governmental organizations, and to the few intergovernmental organizations that were willing and able to evade the regime. Simply being there had its uses: a presence would increase the chance of attracting the attention of the international community to a regime's shortcomings.

Working with acceptable regimes on what appeared to be a manageable crisis was through the UNDP system and in particular the Resident Coordinator; but if there was a collapse of such a magnitude as to constitute a complex emergency, and if the government was discredited, then a different mechanism would be indicated, brought afresh into the country. The worse the crisis, and the greater the scale of necessary humanitarian assistance, the more important it was to make a judgement about a regime's acceptibilty, and to start afresh.

The difficulty in sanctioning any relaxation in the principle of non-intervention should not, however, be underestimated. There could be occasions when states might be particularly fearful of intervention, such as if an army engaged in counter-insurrection activities was accused of gross violations of human rights. The government of India was particularly concerned about any relaxation of the principle, and it was not difficult to think of reasons for this position: the Indian army was vulnerable to accusations of infringements of human rights in various parts of the country, such as Kashmir. Conversely newly independent states were likely to be suspicious of what appeared to be the granting of a licence to Western developed states to intervene in their affairs: the unfortunate reference by British Foreign Secretary Douglas Hurd to the possible need for a new kind of imperialism, meaning the taking over by the United Nations of territories where orderly government had collapsed—in a way reminiscent of the trusteeship system—could not have dampened such fears.[8]

In summary there could be a rather fundamentalist interpretation of Article 2(7) of the United Nations Charter, that there could be no intervention within a state without the express consent of the government of that state: the implication appeared to be that no form of behaviour of a sovereign government within its own frontiers was a matter of concern to outsiders. This position was probably most frequently seen in the arguments favoured by the government of mainland China. This position might be compared with the other traditional view, namely that intervention within a country to promote human rights was only capable of justification on the basis of a threat to international peace and security. Evidence of this could be the appearance of significant numbers of refugees, or the judgement that other states might intervene militarily.

In the hands of liberal lawyers this condition appeared flexible enough to justify intervention to defend human rights whenever it seemed prudent. The gradual expansion of the interpretation of Article 99, which gave the Secretary-General the right to bring a threatening crisis situation to the attention of the Security Council, illustrates this point. By the mid-1990s developments such as humanitarian crisis, or the movement of refugees were interpreted as constituting such a threat. Hard-liners, however, had a different view of the condition in Article 2(7): though the Chinese did not dispute the general principle, and could not if they were to remain members of the United Nations, they saw it more as a way of defeating any proposal to intervene. Liberals saw it as a bridge to action, hard-liners as a way of creating barriers by denying there was a threat to international peace and security wherever posssible.

Another possibility was for intervention to take place on humanitarian grounds alone, to protect human rights. This possiblity had entered the agenda by the late 1990s, but it had been seldom used. But it should not be forgotten that the members of the United Nations system, and other international organizations, were capable of evading the formal objections of governments to intervention. They could become involved in the absence of positive opposition. They could also pursue policies and act in ways that were not directly approved by governments which had allowed them entry, but which could affect the way in which that government worked and the conditions of its survival. They could get under the skin of sovereignty in order to promote sovereignty.

Key Points

- Involvement in states did not necessarily depend on actual governmental approval.

- Organizations could act independently of governments once present, and some organizations, such as non-governmental organizations were skilful at establishing a presence without positive government consent.

The United Nations, Sovereignty and Recognition

A third issue concerning international organizations like the United Nations and the maintenance of international order should be discussed briefly. The first was the question of the new roles and their relationship with order; second was the implications of the new roles for intervention; third was the question of how the acquisition of new roles by the international organization was related to the grant of sovereignty and the related competences of the state. If the international organization was to acquire more roles it would be necessary for the state to loose some of its competences. How did this affect ways in which the state became sovereign, and the conditions of its sovereignty?

A central problem in expanding the range of justifications of intervention was how they could be reconciled with **sovereignty**. Sovereignty could be justified in a number of ways, such as the demonstration that a particular territory contained a people which wished to organize itself in the form of a state. But there was a further necessary step, which might be dubbed the conferring of a licence to practise as a sovereign state. This was its *de jure* recognition by the other state members as a fellow member of international society. It was the conferring of recognition that essentially created the barriers in the way of intervention.

Recognition remained a matter for the separate states, acting on their own account, or as individual states in co-operation with other states, as was the case with the member states of the European Union when they recognized the states emerging from the collapse of Yugoslavia. The recognition of these states was itself a fairly *ad hoc* business, driven by the interests of Germany, and imperfectly monitored by the Bartinder Commission set up under the authority of the Commission on Yugoslavia. But if the UN was to become more involved in constituting states, and more involved in rescuing failing states, and monitoring appropriate internal standards, the case was strengthened that it should also be responsible for the recognition process, and if necessary for withdrawing recognition. At its crudest the argument was that it seemed illogical to have a situation in which the recognition process was left to states individually and separately, but, as was increasingly happening, the rescuing process was left to the UN.[9]

The *ad hoc* character of the recognition of states, was matched by a corresponding ad hocery about their de-recognition. The lack of any general procedure for removing recognition was a difficulty in the way of intervention, as the states which separately continued to recognize a state were likely to argue that the sovereignty of that state could not be compromised. The logic of the situation was that both recognition and de-recognition should be a matter for the United Nations, given the changing character of its role in maintaining international order. This would fundamentally alter the principle of non-intervention as de-recognition would coincide with the call for involvement.

Several sets of circumstances involving recognition, sovereignty, and intervention may be noted:

- **First** was where a state had collapsed and there was general acceptance that its government had ceased to exist, and that 'intervention' did not compromise sovereignty in the eyes of any other states. Arguably Somalia had reached this condition by late 1991.

- **Second** was where some form of government existed, and there was a dispute about whether the state was still sovereign. In this case diplomacy would of necessity involve dispute about these questions and intervention might be delayed.

- **Third** was where there was no dispute about the continuing sovereignty of the state, but where the question of non-consensual intervention arose because threats to life and rights were such as to sustain a general consensus amongst states in its favour.

- **Fourth** was where a state was accepted as remaining sovereign but where its government accepted its responsibility for humanitarian action and worked in co-operation with the international agencies.

(In this instance there was no intervention in the sense of the traditional meaning of that term; paradoxically the Somalia case in its early stages was not one of humanitarian intervention, but rather of humanitarian assistance by international agencies and governments. Resolution 794 which sanctioned the American move into Somalia was also in a strict sense not intervention as by that stage the central government of Somalia had ceased to exist in the eyes of the majority of states, or at least in the eyes of the member states of the Security Council which approved the resolution unanimously.)

- **Fifth** were circumstances in which it proved possible to evade sovereignty, by becoming involved without government opposition, and then preserving independence with regard to action and goals from that government.

Key Points

- There was a case for taking a multilateral approach to the recognition of states.
- There were five different relationships between sovereignty and intervention.

Sovereignty and the Competence of International Organization

Sovereignty could be interpreted as being ultimately responsible—the buck stops with the sovereign. Having a role, and doing something, involved being granted a competence, and was not the same as being ultimately responsible. In recent years the analytical distinction between these two questions was more frequently reflected in the practice of states and international organizations: the question of which body was ultimately responsible, was increasingly separated from that of which body was allowed competence.[10]

New problems in the way of legitimizing states by granting them sovereignty were matched by new problems about deciding what states should be able to do in order to remain sovereign. The exercise of functions such as control of foreign policy and defence used to be regarded as being central to sovereignty, and could not be allocated to other centres. But the member states of the European Union in the late 1990s could accept that the Union should have a role in their harmonized foreign policy, and that it might increase its involvement in the common defence. There was a majority for this among the Union's citizens. This was an astonishing development which seemed to remove the dilemma, discussed *inter alia* by Rousseau, that responsibility for maintaining the peace could not be allocated to a higher, federal authority without fatally damaging the entity which it was designed to protect, namely the state itself.

The dilemma was avoided by insisting that *ultimate* responsibilty remained with the states as they retained reserve powers, including the power to recover the competences. Public opinion and governments could accept the transfer of responsibility for foreign policy and defence without necessarily thinking of this as an infringement of sovereignty: as long as the reserve power was kept!

The expectation was that the chances of the reserve powers being utilized would be progressively reduced. The hierarchy of issues, with defence and foreign policy being regarded as high politics, and questions such as trade policy as low politics, would be compressed. Outside the European Union it was unusual for issues of foreign policy or defence to involve another supranational authority. But it was common for other questions, especially in the economic, social, and other technical areas, previously regarded as essential to the exercise of national sovereignty, to be handled elsewhere in whole or in part. In all these areas questions tended to move from the category of the special to that of the routine. But paradoxically the state's survival rested on the assumption that this transfer could not be guaranteed: the competences could still be recalled in principle even if this in practice was unlikely.

The trick with regard to justice and national interest was to avoid situations where a choice had to be made, because the national interest had to come first. The trick with regard to the extension of competence in areas which were earlier regarded as essential to sovereignty was to avoid situations in which the reserve powers would have be used. The crisis points in international politics would be: when national interest and morality were in conflict; when a policy competence had to be renationalized; when a state's ability to provide for the welfare of its citizens was in doubt. The test of successful statescraft was to avoid these dilemmas. The skilled diplomat would increasingly require a sophisticated grasp of paradox. The discussion so far permits a particular arrangement of the functions of the UN in the late 1990s. A distinction could be made between those functions which were more immediately concerned with questions of justice in the larger sense and those which were primarily about the older sense of order. The latter might be called traditional UN roles, reflecting the classical principles of international society. The former reflected the new principles, and involved new forms of UN involvement within the states which occurred mainly since the end of the cold war. The possibility of a third list was implied in the discussion, and is added below: it is made up of the difficulties in the way of the more effective governance of the international system. There was an injunction to do better many of the things that had been tried. How might this be achieved?

Key Points

- Competences were increasingly granted by states to international organizations to carry out tasks previously reserved to national governments.
- This meant that the conditions of sovereignty had changed, but not that the state was under threat.
- The new arrangements were to strengthen not weaken the state.

A Typology of the Roles of the United Nations in the 1990s

In the final section of this chapter the main roles of the United Nations system will be discussed briefly. Obviously in the late 1990s a number of them were the concern of a range of international organizations in addition to the United Nations. There was a considerable literature about each of them, and the purpose of this essay is not with any one of them but with the arrangement and interpretation of the whole. There are a large number of more detailed accounts available to the reader.

A. Peace and Security *between* States

These are roles regarding the maintenance of international order in the traditional sense of promoting peace and security between states.

Traditional peace-enforcement. This was the role derived from Chapter VII of the Charter, but different in its mode of execution, as seen in operations such as that in Korea and the Gulf War. The operations were carried out through an agent, usually the US and allies, with a Security Council Mandate, rather than under UN command as stipulated in Chapter Vll.

Traditional peace-keeping. This was peace-keeping as illustrated by the UN Emergency Force sent to Egypt after the Suez crisis in November 1956. The force was made up of lightly armed forces, using weapons only if attacked, located with the consent of the host state, under UN Secretary-General control, and excluding forces from the Security Council's permaments members.

Development in co-operation with governments. In this case Specialized Agencies, and other international organizations such as the World Bank, worked with governments. After the late 1960s the ideal form of such development was working through the United Nations Development Programme (UNDP) in co-operation with the host government, but this system was plagued with problems up to the time of writing. Co-ordination through UNDP proved difficult and the Agencies and Bank tended to have their own projects.

Social and technical functions in co-operation with governments. This covered the range of social and technical functions carried out by the Agencies, Funds, and Programmes in co-operation with governments, for instance, public health improvement and disease control through the World Health Organization, agricultural development through the Food and Agriculture Organization, and promoting industrial development tnrough the United Nations Conference on Trade and Development (UNCTAD) and the United Nations Industrial Development Organization (UNIDO).

Human rights monitoring and standard setting. The wide range of conventions and machinery related to human rights, focused upon standard-setting, monitoring, and generating modest pressures to comply.

The above were all aspects of the traditional functioning of the United Nations and were compatible with the hard doctrine of exclusive domestic jurisdiction: international organizations entered states only with their consent and worked with them once admitted on terms dictated by the government. Such methods were not abandoned but new approaches emerged especially after the late 1980s.

B. Justice *within* States

(The new forms of involvement were concerned with constructing and amending the state, so that it became more successful as a state, and less likely to be a source of disruption of the international order. This was a new form of international relations!)

Humanitarian assistance. In reconstructing states which had experienced major humanitarian crises, and the collapse of administrative and political structures, the United Nations had taken on a kind of modified trusteeship role. It helped create well-founded states, and, in a sense, issued certificates of legitimacy to new regimes, which was in fact what it purported to do when it helped set up and supervise elections in Namibia, Cambodia, and Angola, and acted to ensure proper respect for human rights in El Salvador. This revealed an irony in the position of the United Nations with regard to sovereignty and Article 2(7) of the UN Charter in the late 1990s. A more flexible view of sovereignty was sought in order to facilitate more effective humanitarian assistance. At first sight, as the Secretary-General admitted (BBC Radio 4 programme, *The Thin Blue Line*, Sunday 25 April 1993) this appeared to be a licence for the richer states to act as a world policeman and to trample on the interests of the weaker and less developed states. But the underlying purpose of the UN activities was to make states stronger not weaker: to make the world safe for sovereignty. It was recognized that the Geneva Conventions, and international law regarding human rights, rested on the sovereignty of states. It was the states that sanctioned them and which were responsible for upholding them. States which were properly constituted, in respecting human rights, and in promoting human welfare effectively, were more likely to be strong and stable pillars of such a system.

A new development agenda, involving project management alongside, but not with governments, emerged. Although the World Bank and the IMF were required to work with governments, since the end of the 1980s an increasing amount of development work was being conducted through non-governmental organizations and multinational companies, as well as UN agencies, which was not necessarily under the close supervision of the host governnment. This was like the work of the Commission of the EU with regard to the regions in Mediterranean countries—frequently bypassing national goverments, and promoting development and a development agenda independently of them in direct links between the international and sub-national actors. The role of the UNDP in Palestine in the late 1990s was analagous: the organization was the recipient of large quantities of official and non-official development money which it administered in Palestine to further the rehabilitation of that territory and its people, and it worked alongside the Palestinian authorities rather than under them.

The rehabilitation of states after crisis: this involved such activities as setting up administrations, training administrators and police forces. A considerable range of resources were deployed to serve these purposes in Cambodia and in Namibia, as well as in a large number of other 'states'. This function was that of state building or rehabilitation. It was also the chief legitimizer of new regimes, in that it was regularly involved in the monitoring of elections, and in effect conferring a license of statehood.

New peace-keeping functions had developed, involving a wider range of uses for the military under UN command: such new uses included the provision of humanitarian assistance, land-mine clearance, weapon cleansing, as well as the promotion of ground rules, however feebly, in civil war. This would include the monitoring of war crimes, and the identification of the malefactors as with the Serbs in Bosnia-Herzegovina, and pronouncing on legitimate and illegitimate courses of action such as where to place various types of weapon, and which targets were non-acceptable. (UN agencies—not the Security Council—condemned an Israeli strike on a UN-protected compound in Lebanon in May 1996).

Human rights promotion and enforcement: international organization, including the United Nations, had become gradually more involved in the active defence of human rights and the charging of individuals accused of serious breaches, as with war crimes. The War Crimes Tribunal set up at the Hague in 1995 illustrated this.

Firmer standards over a wide range of issues were also promoted by international organizations with a some degree of success. These included standards for aspects of environmental protection, such as protecting endangered species, biodiversity, and pollution control, as well as more effective population control. Large-scale Special Conferences became a feature of this work (see Taylor and Groom 1989). This was not to say that by the 1990s such standards were non-contentious—far from it—but they were being more firmly enunciated, and more widely accepted. Technical imperatives were conceivable!

The arms register. The United Nations had also set up a system for registering the flow of arms around the world: who was selling what to whom? There had also been the slow development of more sophisticated techniques for monitoring the development of crises, through noting troop movements, and recording areas of possible crop failure. The frontiers of states were increasingly permiable in ways not dreamed of by John Herz in the early 1960s (see Hertz 1962) and this was one of the pillars of international accountability.

C. The Problems of Global Governance in the 1990s

The UN system had acquired many of the functions of governance but was deficient with regard to the necessary instruments, and in consequence fell short of successfully performing the new roles. What were the deficiencies?

There were continuing problems of co-ordination and planning, which were to be found in the management of the economic and social activities of the UN as well as in the performance of the expanded range of peace-keeping functions. These were extensively discussed in the literature and by 1996 had culminated in GA Resolution 48/162 of December 1994.

There were problems of coping with sovereignty and the need for neutrality, which in terms of UN activity were related problems. Sovereignty was still a problem with regard to the UN's becoming involved in grave crises within the state: the issues were discussed in the text.

The financial problem. The United Nations system with regard to the regular budget and the peace-keeping fund had a serious financial shortfall in the late 1990s, mainly because of the non-payment by the United States of assessed contributions under both headings. The sum owed was around $3 billion.

There were problems of executive competence and legitimacy. As the functions of the system expanded the problems of the executive became more apparant. First there was a problem of representation. A number of states became increasingly unhappy about the restricted membership of the Security Council, but also complained about the membership of the executive committees of other organizations in the UN system. A second problem, from the point of view of effective governance, concerned the resolutions of the Security Council. There were **three** aspects of this. First the Security Council was not obliged to seek the consistency of its resolutions with previous treaties, which remained valid and had not been abrogated. There was no instrument in the system which ensured that new resolutions were consistent with the existing body of treaty rules and agreements. For instance its recognition of the Republic of Cyprus, and non-recognition of the Turkish Republic of North Cyprus, was arguably inconsistent with the existing, valid treaties between Greece, Turkey, and Britain which guaranteed the bicommunality of Cyprus, a principle that had been unilaterally countermanded by 'Greek' Cyprus (see Ertekun 1984). **Second** there was no instrument whereby new Security Council resolutions would be required to be consistent with earlier Security Council resolutions. Frequently there were inconsistencies. Indeed in other parts of the UN system, such as the Committee on Disarmament, resolutions were approved which were inconsistent with what had been agreed previously. In instances such as these there were no procedures for ensuring that resolutions prompted the emergence of an internally consistent system of international laws. **Third** the Security Council was not subject to any requirement for technical consistency in the sense that it was not subject to a rule requiring means to be appropriate to ends. It frequently passed resolutions without providing for the means for attaining the stated goals. The classic case of this in the 1990s was the setting up of the safe areas in ex-Yugoslavia, without providing the resources for their defence, or for their demilitarization.

The UN lacked mechanisms for judicial review and supervision. The European Union was less victim of the kinds of problem discussed in the preceding paragraphs because it possessed two instruments which were designed to establish the coherent development and internal consistency of its internal mechanisms and laws: the Commission was enjoined to achieve such consistency, as was the European Court of Justice. Similary all the EU's institutions including the Council of Ministers, made up of governmental representatives, were subject to the law of the Community and the supervision of the European Court of Justice. But in the UN system the International Court of Justice (ICJ) had no superior jurisdiction. The next logical step was to make the UN's institutions subject to the jurisdiction of the ICJ, on the analogy of the EU. A parallel measure was sought by the Secretary-General in the mid-1990s: the right to seek directly the view of the ICJ about, *inter alia*, the legality of courses of action proposed by the UN institutions.

The problem of information and analysis: the capacity of the UN to collect and interpet information needed further enhancement. In the **first** phase of the development of international institutions charged with maintaining international peace and security, the security function was that of a fire brigade. The League Council, according to the Covenant, was **not** a permanent institution, but was to meet when a crisis had arisen. In a **second** phase, in the United Nations, the fire brigade was on permanent stand-by as the Security Council was a permanent institution which could be called on to act at short notice. In the **third** phase the security mechanisms of the organization were altered to facilitate an enhanced capacity to adopt an interpositional function between warring parties within states. At the same time enforcement procedures with regard to inter-state disputes developed along lines which were not foreseen by the founders, in that it became increasingly apparent that the United Nations could not take on such a role in itself. It would always need to rely on an agent of enforcement, such as an *ad hoc* coalition of states, a particular state, such as the US, or on a defence organization like NATO. In a **fourth** phase, visible by the late 1980s, the range of information and analysis had been improved, but needed further improvement, so that the best intelligence available from states would also be available to the UN; at the same time, the UN would have its own independent mechanisms as a way of validating what it had obtained from elsewhere. The fourth phase would be that of the *global watch*, taking the UN into ongoing monitoring of likely crisis situations, rather than the traditional role of responding when they occured.

Conclusion

In this chapter the nature of the changes in the role of the United Nations with regard to the maintenance of international order have been reviewed, and on the basis of the discussion under this heading a typology of traditional and new functions was constructed. This typology was revealing in that it highlighted ways of improving the governance of the society of states which could be carried out through the United Nations. These improvements carried forward alterations that had already entered the agenda; a start had been made in their direction. However badly the new functions were performed, there were now new expectations. Finding adequate means for the better governance of international society could take a long time, but a return to the *status quo ante* was unlikely. But the new world, dimly glimpsed, was not a world without states. It was one in which states were promoted and protected more effectively. But the conditions of their sovereignty had altered.

QUESTIONS

1. How does the United Nations try to maintain international order?

2. Why have more states decided to support the work of the United Nations?

3. How far have traditional restraints with regard to intervention within states been relaxed?

4. Is there a case for transferring responsibility for recognizing/de-recognizing states to the United Nations?

5. What are the major new roles taken on by international organizations like the UN since the late 1980s?

6. What problems have been in the way of the UN's carrying out its expanded roles more effectively?

7. Does allowing international organizations to do more undermine the sovereignty of states?

8. Why was there greater opposition to developing the international accountibilty of states during the cold war?

GUIDE TO FURTHER READING

Introductory Surveys

Archer, Clive, *International Organisations*, 2nd edn. (London: Routledge, 1992).
Armstrong, David, *The Rise of the International Organisation: A Short History* (London: Macmillan, 1982).
Bennett, A. LeRoy, *International Organisations: Principles and Issues*, 5th edn. (Englewood Cliffs, NJ: Prentice Hall, 1991).
Taylor, Paul, and Groom, A. J. R. (eds.), *International Institutions at Work* (London: Pinter, 1988).

More Advanced Overviews

Barston, R. P., *Modern Diplomacy* (London: Longmans, 1988).
Claude, Inis L. Jr. *Swords into Plowshares: The Progress and Problems of International Organization*, 4th edn. (New York: Random House, 1984).
Finkelstein, Lawrence S. (ed.), *Politics in the United Nations System* (Durham, NC: Duke University Press, 1988).
Roberts, Adam, and Kingsbury, Benedict, (eds.), *United Nations, Divided World: The UN's Roles in International Relations*, 2nd edn. (Oxford: Clarendon Press, 1993).

On Particular Themes

Boutros Boutros-Ghali, *An Agenda for Peace* (New York: UN, 1992).
Brundtland, Gro Harlem, *et al.* (The Brundtland Report), *Our Common Future: Report of the World Commission on Environment and Development* (Oxford: Oxford University Press, 1987).

James, Alan, *Peacekeeping in International Politics* (Basingstoke: Macmillan, 1990).

Taylor, Paul, and Groom, A. J. R. (eds.), *Global Issues in the UN Framework* (Basingstoke: Macmillan, 1989).

Williams, Douglas, *The Specialised Agencies and the United Nations: the System in Crisis* (London: Hurst, 1987).

Lyons, Gene M., and Mastanduno, Michael, *Beyond Wesphalia: State Sovereignty and International Intervention* (Baltimore: Johns Hopkins University Press, 1995).

Theoretical Work

Groom, A. J. R. and Taylor, Paul, *Frameworks for International Cooperation* (London: Pinter, 1990).

Jacobson, Harold K., *Networks of Interdependence: International Organizations and the Global Political System*, 2nd edn. (New York: Knopf, 1984).

Taylor, Paul, *International Organization in the Modern World* (London: Pinter, 1995).

Individual and National Perspectives

Jensen, Erik, and Fisher, Thomas, (eds.), *The United Kingdom—The United Nations* (London: Macmillan, 1990).

Urquhart, Sir Brian, *A Life in Peace and War* (New York: Harper and Row, 1991).

NOTES

1. See the excellent introduction to the development of the security functions of the United Nations in Roberts (1996: 283–308).
2. For an interpretation of Functionalism see Claude (1971).
3. For an account of the diplomacy leading up to the agreements at Dayton in 1996 see Spyros Economides and Paul Taylor, 'Former Yugoslavia', in James Mayall (ed.) *The New Interventionism, 1991–1994* (Cambridge University Press, 1996).
4. See discussion of this issue, and reference to the Kirkpatrick essay, in Forsythe (1988: 259–60).
5. This is one of the arguments in Vincent (1986).
6. See the excellent collection of essays on intervention in Lyons and Mastanduno (1995).
7. See Development Studies Association, evidence to the Foreign Affairs Select Committee of the House of Commons, titled *The United Nations Humanitarian Response*, Nov. 1992.
8. This issue was discussed in oral evidence to the House of Commons Foreign Affairs Select Committee by Sir John Thomson and Sir Crispin Tickell, as reported in *The Expanding Role of the United Nations and its Implications* . . . (HMSO, 17 Feb. 1993), 175–6 and *passim*.
9. See the excellent discussion of the issues raised here, including recognition by the UN, in Dugard (1987).
10. This issue is discussed by the author in *The European Union in the 1990s* (Oxford University Press, 1996).

15 Transnational Actors and International Organizations in Global Politics

Peter Willetts

READER'S GUIDE

The subject of International Relations is too often taken as covering the relations between states, for example Britain relates to India. Economic bodies and social groups, such as banks, companies, students, and environmentalists etc., are given secondary status as non-state actors. This two-tier approach can be challenged. First, ambiguities in the meaning given to 'a state', and its mismatch with the real world, result in it not being a useful concept. Greater clarity is obtained by analysing intergovernmental and inter-society relations, with no presumption that one sector is more important than the other. Second, we can recognize governments are losing sovereignty when faced with the economic activities of transnational companies and the violent threat from criminals and guerrillas. Third, non-governmental organizations (NGOs) engage in such a web of global relations, including participation in diplomacy, that governments have lost their political independence. We conclude that events in any area of global policy-making have to be understood in terms of complex systems, containing governments, companies, and NGOs interacting in a variety of international organizations.

Introduction

In diplomacy, international law, journalism, and academic analysis, it is widely assumed that international relations consists of the relations between coherent units called states. This chapter will argue that better understanding of political change is obtained by analysing the relations between governments and many other actors from each country. Global politics also includes companies and non-governmental organizations. (We will see below that this is a technical term. It does not cover all actors other than governments. In particular it excludes commercial bodies.) While there are less than 200 governments in the global system, there are approximately

- 38,500 major transnational companies (TNCs), such as Shell, Barclays Bank, Coca Cola, Ford, Microsoft, or Nestlé, with these parent companies having more than 250,000 foreign affiliates;

- 10,000 single-country non-governmental organizations (NGOs), such as Freedom House (USA), Médecins sans Frontières (France), Population Concern (UK), Sierra Club (USA), or Water Aid (UK), who have significant international activities;

- 300 intergovernmental organizations (IGOs), such as the UN, NATO, the European Union, or the International Coffee Organization; and

- 4,700 international non-governmental organizations (INGOs), such as Amnesty International, the Baptist World Alliance, the International Chamber of Shipping, or the International Red Cross.

All these actors play a regular part in global politics and interact with the governments. In addition, even though they are considered not to be legitimate participants in the system, guerrilla groups and criminal gangs have some impact. Very many more companies and NGOs only operate in a single country, but have the potential to expand into other countries.[1]

Nobody can deny the number of these organizations and the range of their activities. The controversial questions are whether the non-state world has significance in its own right and whether it makes any difference to the analysis of interstate relations. It is possible to *define* international relations as covering the relations between states. This is known as the state-centric approach, or **Realism**. Then it is only a tautology (true by definition) to say that non-state actors are of secondary importance. A more open-ended approach, known as **Pluralism**, is based on the assumption that all types of actors can affect political outcomes. It is an unacceptable analytical bias to decide, before research starts, that only states have any influence. Some state-centric writers acknowledge this point in a highly restrictive manner: 'non-state actors need to be taken into account just as and when they influence what goes on between states—and not otherwise' (James 1993: 270). This position appears to be reasonable for the study of subjects like UN peacekeeping, but it is arbitrary to make the claim for all subjects. Given that governments are important primarily because they assert the right to exercise authority over society, a suitable reply to James is 'governments need to be taken into account just as and when they influence what goes on among NGOs and not otherwise'. Until the evidence indicates otherwise, we must assume that governments and NGOs interact with each other, along with companies and international organizations. Who actually determines outcomes will vary from issue to issue.

The Importance of Words: From 'Non-State' Actors to Transnational Actors

Some preliminary comments about the vocabulary of International Relations are necessary. The very words, **non-state actors**, implies that states are dominant and other actors are secondary. It is an ambiguous word, because it is unclear whether intergovernmental organizations are regarded as interstate or non-state organizations. It also puts into a single category actors that have very different structures, different resources and different ways of influencing politics. So, from now on the word, 'non-state', will be abandoned.

An alternative word, **transnational**, has been coined by academics in order to assert forcefully that international relations are not limited to governments. Unfortunately, diplomats use the word transnational to mean a company, while other non-profit-making, non-violent groups are called

Box 15.1. Key Concepts

Realism: the theoretical approach that analyses all international relations as the relations of states engaged in the pursuit of power. Realism cannot accommodate any non-state actors within its analysis.

Pluralism: the theoretical approach that considers all organized groups as being potential political actors and analyses the processes by which actors mobilize support to achieve policy goals. Pluralism can encompass non-governmental organizations, companies, and international organizations.

State: the one word is used to refer to three distinct concepts:
1. In international law, a **state** is an entity that is recognized to exist when a government is in control of a community of people within a defined territory. It is comparable to the idea in domestic law of a company being a legal person.
2. In the study of international politics, each state is a **country**. It is a community of people who interact in the same political system and who have some common values.
3. In philosophy and sociology, the state consists of the apparatus of **government**, in its broadest sense, covering the executive, the legislature, the administration, the judiciary, the armed forces, and the police.

Sovereignty: the condition of a state being free from any higher legal authority. It is related to, but distinct from, the condition of a government being free from any external political constraints. Thus, during the cold war, many small states were sovereign, without their governments being politically independent.

Non-state actor: a term widely used to mean any actor that is not a government. Often it is not clear whether the term is being used to cover bodies such as the United Nations. Ambiguity is best avoided by referring separately to two categories, transnational actors and international organizations.

Nation: a group of people who recognize each other as sharing a common identity, with a focus on a homeland. This identity does not have to be acknowledged by other political groups for it to exist.

Nation-state: would exist if nearly all the members of a single nation were organized in a single state, without any other national communities being present. Although the term is widely used, no such entities exist.

Transnational actor: any non-governmental actor from one country that has relations with any actor from another country or with an international organization.

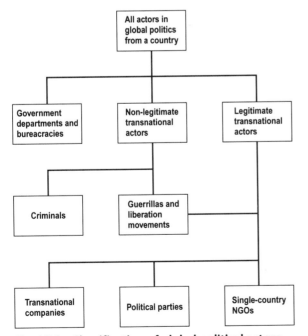

Fig. 15.1. Classification of global political actors
The bottom three categories all form international NGOs

NGOs. The differences can be handled by using 'transnational' in the academic sense, to cover any private actor, and making it plain whether a company or another type of transnational actor is being discussed. On this basis, a summary of the different categories of participants in global politics from each country is given in the chart.

It is still quite common to find analyses of international relations that concentrate primarily on the governments, give some attention to intergovernmental organizations and ignore the transnational actors. Even in fields such as environmental politics, where it is widely accepted that governments interact intensely with UN agencies, commercial companies and environmental pressure groups, it is sometimes taken for granted that governments are dominant (see for example Hurrell and Kingsbury 1992, or even Porter and Brown 1991: 35). The only way such bias towards the real world can be understood is in terms of the theoretical bias of orthodox analysis.

This chapter will first consider how assumptions made about 'states' inhibit analysis of transnational actors and international organizations. Then the nature of the different types of actors will be outlined. Finally, the case will be argued for always considering the activities of a diverse range of political actors.

Problems with the State-Centric Approach

The great advantage of the state-centric approach is that the bewildering complexity of world politics is reduced to the relative simplicity of the interactions of less than two hundred supposedly similar units. However, there are *four* major problems that suggest the benefits of simplification have been gained at the cost of the picture being distorted and blurred.

1. Ambiguity between Different Meanings of a 'State'

Writers who refer to the state often fail to use the term consistently and lack intellectual rigour by merging three concepts. The **state** as a legal person is a highly abstract fiction. This is easily confused with the concrete concept of a **country**, with a distinct political system of people sharing common values. Then there is a very dissimilar concept of a state as the apparatus of **government**. Unfortunately, no standard method exists to handle the ambiguity. From now on, this chapter will use the word, state, to indicate the abstract legal concept, while country and government will be used to analyse political behaviour. Conventional ambiguous usage will be indicated by inverted commas.

With the legal and political-community concepts, *civil society is part of the state*, whereas for philosophers and sociologists focusing on the state as government *civil society is separate from the state*. Thus, in international law or when the state means the whole country, there is very little room to acknowledge the existence of distinct transnational actors. Alternatively, when the state means the government and does not encompass society, we can investigate both intergovernmental relations and the inter-society relations of transnational actors.

2. The Lack of Similarity between Countries

The second problem is that defining all 'states' in the same way and giving them all the same legal status implies they are all essentially the same type of unit. If we consider the countries of the world, it is plain that they are not remotely similar. Orthodox analysis does acknowledge differences in size between 'the superpowers' and middle and small 'powers'. Nevertheless this does not suggest that in 1989 the United States economy was twice the size of the Soviet Union's economy, twelve times China's, 64 times Saudi Arabia's, nearly 1,000 times Ethiopia's and 58,000 times greater than the Maldives. In terms of population, the divergences are even greater. The small island countries of the Caribbean and the Pacific with populations measured in tens of thousands are not comparable entities to ordinary small countries, let alone China or India: they are truly 'micro-states'. Alternatively, comparing the governments of the world reveals a diverse range of democracies, feudal regimes, ethnic oligarchies, economic oligarchies, populist regimes, theocracies, military dictatorships, and idiosyncratic combinations. The only thing that the countries have in common is the general recognition of their right to have their own government. They are legally equal and politically very different.

The consequence of admitting the differences in size is to make it obvious that the largest transnational actors are considerably larger than many of the countries. The 50 largest transnational industrial companies have an annual sales revenue greater than the GNP of 131 members of the United Nations. Using people as the measure, many NGOs, particularly trade unions and campaigning groups in the fields of human rights, women's rights, and the environment, have their membership measured in millions, whereas 37 countries in the UN have populations of less than one million.[2] The differences also mean that there is great variation in the complexity and diversity of the economies and the societies of different countries and hence the extent to which they are each involved in transnational relations.

3. The Problem of Holism

Third, there is an underlying inconsistency in the **ontology** of supposing 'states' are located in an anarchical international system. Whether it means a legal unit, a country, or a government, the 'state' is seen as a **holistic entity**: it is considered to be a coherent unit, acting with common purpose and existing as something more than the sum of its parts (the individual people). At the same time, many advocates of the state-centric approach deny the possibility of holistic entities existing at the global level. The phrase, 'the international system', is used, but only to convey a loose assembly of 'states'. The reference to a **system** is not intended to carry its full technical meaning of a collectivity in which the component elements (the individual 'states') lose some of their independence. No philosophical argument has been put forward to explain the inconsistency in the assumptions made about the different levels of analysis. By exaggerating the coherence of 'states' and downplaying the coherence of global politics, both transnational relations and intergovernmental relations are underestimated.

4. The Difference between State and Nation

Fourth, there is a behavioural assumption that politics within 'states' is significantly different from politics between 'states'. This is based on the idea that people's loyalty to their **nation** is more intense than other loyalties. Clearly, it cannot be denied that nationalism and national identity invoke powerful emotions for most people, but various caveats must be made about their political relevance. Communal identities form a hierarchy from the local through the nation to wider groupings: a Yorkshire person may simultaneously be English and identify with the Commonwealth or with Europe. Thus, local communities and intergovernmental bodies, such as the European Community, can also make claims on a person's loyalty.

There has been a long-standing linguistic conjuring trick whereby national loyalty is made to appear as if it is focused on the '**nation-state**'. Both inter*national* relations and trans*national* relations cover relations across 'state' boundaries, although logically the words refer to relations between national groups, such as the Scots and the Welsh. In the real world, only a few countries, such as Iceland, Poland, and Japan, can make a reasonable claim that their people are from a single nation and in all such cases there are significant numbers of the national group resident in other countries, often in the USA. Most countries are multinational and many national groups are present in several countries. Thus national loyalty is actually quite different from loyalty to a country. National liberation movements, national cultural groups, and national minorities making political demands are transnational actors, which at times mount a significant challenge to governmental authority. Ironically, nationalism is one of the many sources of transnational relations.

Box 15.2. **Key Concepts**

Ontology: concerned with our view of what is *real* and the nature of the types of entities that can or cannot exist.

A holistic entity: exists when a set of elements form a system that has distinct properties at the collective level. This is often expressed as 'the whole is more than the sum of the parts'. The clearest example is the way in which the parts of your body produce the properties of a living person. Similarly, people form social groups, organizations, societies, and nations that both reflect the individuals who make up the collective entity and affect the attitudes and behaviour of the individuals.

System: term commonly used to mean any set of elements that have a complex structure. This chapter uses the technical concept from Systems Science, which is limited to a holistic entity.

Key Points

- The concept of the 'state' has three very different meanings: a legal person, a political community, and a government.

- The countries and governments around the world may be equal in law, but have few political similarities. Many governments control less resources than many transnational actors.

- It cannot be assumed that all country-based political systems are more coherent than global systems, particularly as national loyalties do not match country boundaries.

- By abandoning the language of 'states' and 'non-state' actors, we can admit the possibility of theorizing about many types of actors in global politics. By distinguishing government from society and nation from country, we can ask whether private voluntary groups, companies, and national minorities in each country engage in transnational relations.

- In summary, once 'states' are no longer described as homogeneous coherent entities, they must be

analysed as open systems, having many channels for governmental and transnational connections to international systems.

Transnational Companies as Political Actors

All companies that import or export are engaging in transnational economic activities. Often changes in health and safety standards, regulation of communication facilities or the general economic policy of foreign governments will affect their ability to trade. If this is beneficial, they will not necessarily respond, but, if they expect to lose financially, they may well decide to lobby the foreign government. This can be done by four common routes:

1. indirectly by the company asking its own government to put pressure on the foreign government;
2. indirectly by raising a general policy question in an international organization;
3. directly at home via the diplomatic embassy; or
4. directly in the other country via the government ministries.

Several other routes to apply pressure, such as trade associations and more complex indirect routes, can also be used. Thus even a company that is based in a single country may be a significant transnational political actor.

The first companies that expanded beyond their home country to become **transnational companies** (TNCs), in the fullest sense, did so in the European empires or the quasi-empire of the United States in Latin America and Asia. The classic cases were companies in agriculture, mining, or oil. After decolonization the companies often had to be split up, so that the overseas branches became separate legal entities, but still under central control of the headquarters. From the 1960s there has been a massive expansion, with many of the major industrial manufacturers establishing overseas subsidiaries. Some financial services, like banking, had

---

Box 15.3. Key Concepts

Transnational company: in the most general sense any company based in one country that has dealings with the society or government in another country. However, the term, transnational company (TNC), is normally reserved for a company that has affiliates in a foreign country. The affiliates may be branches of the parent company, separately incorporated subsidiaries or associates, with large minority shareholdings.

Intra-firm trade: international trade from one branch of a TNC to an affiliate of the same company in a different country. In the case of bauxite all the trade is intra-firm and hence there is no such thing as a world market for bauxite.

Transfer price: the price set by a TNC for intra-firm trade of goods or services. For accounting purposes, a price must be set for exports, but it need not be related to any market price. Changes in the transfer price do not necessarily have any effect on the sales or the global pre-tax profits of the company.

Triangulation: occurs when trade between two countries is routed indirectly via a third country.

Arbitrage: the process of buying a product in one market and selling it in a different market, in order to make a profit from the difference between the prices in the two markets.

Regulatory arbitrage: in the world of banking, the process of moving funds or business activity from one country to another, in order to increase profits by escaping the constraints imposed by government regulations. By analogy the term can be applied to any transfer of economic activity by any company in response to government policy.

Extraterritoriality: arises when one government attempts to exercise its legal authority in the territory of another state. It mainly arises when the US federal government deliberately tries to use domestic law to control the global activities of TNCs.

moved into the empires as the colonies began to develop, but from the 1970s onwards most of the service industries, including advertising, market research, auditing, and computing, also set up new operations around the world or formed global structures by mergers and acquisitions. Now transnational companies can be expected to operate in any major economic sector, except for products that are specific to particular cultures. The geographical spread has also widened, so industrialized countries that never had empires, such as Sweden and Canada, and also the larger developing countries have seen some of their companies expand transnationally.

Through the globalization of companies, the nature of the transnational companies has changed. Originally there was a clear demarcation with production occurring at the headquarters and secondary activities occurring in the subsidiary branches. A TNC such as IBM could be regarded as an American company with many foreign branches. Now the companies can be truly global, with the headquarters merely being a convenient site for strategic decision-making. Global communications are so efficient and sales can be so widely spread that production does not need to be located at the headquarters. There are several indicators of a company moving from being a multinational federation to a unified global company. Production can be diversified so that different stages of production are located in different countries. Marketing can promote a uniform brand image in all countries. The management personnel may develop their careers across the whole company. Full globalization has occurred when the top management includes people from several countries, with no single country predominating, and when all managers have to speak a single language, usually English.

The growth in the number of TNCs, the scale of their activities and the complexity of their transactions has had a major political impact. We will now see how TNCs have the ability to evade government attempts to control financial flows, to impose trade sanctions or to regulate production. TNCs also make intergovernmental relations more complicated. The **sovereignty** of most governments is significantly reduced.

Financial Flows and Loss of Sovereignty

The consequences of the extensive transnationalization of major companies are profound. It is no longer possible to regard each country as having its own separate economy. Two of the most fundamental attributes of sovereignty, control over the currency and control over foreign trade have been substantially diminished. The two factors combined mean governments have lost control of financial flows. In the case of the currency, the successive crises since the early 1980s for the dollar, the pound, the French franc, and the yen have established that even the governments with the greatest financial resources are helpless against the transnational banks and other speculators.

The effects of trade on domestic and international finance are less obvious. When goods move physically across frontiers, it is usually seen as being trade between the relevant countries, but it may also be **intra-firm trade**. It has been estimated that intra-firm trade accounts for around one third of all world trade in goods (UN 1995: 37), with the proportion reaching over a half in some high-technology manufacturing industries, (UN 1988: 91–2). As the logic of intra-firm trade is quite different from inter-country trade, governments cannot have clear expectations of the effects of their

---

Box 15.4. Transfer Pricing for Intra-Firm Trade

A very simple model illustrates how international intra-firm trade can be used to evade taxation. Consider a company in an industrialized country exporting semi-finished goods to a developing country, where they are finished and sold. Imagine that the government of the industrial country decides to reduce public expenditure and cut taxes, while the other government increases taxes to fund development.

The transfer price can be used by the company to determine the level of profits for each branch. By increasing the transfer price and declaring more of its profits in the low-tax industrial country, the company can avoid its global tax bill increasing. Then each government would find the effect on tax revenue is the opposite of its expectations.

TNCs may succeed in using artificial transfer prices either because the government does not know what a proper price would be or because the company fraudulently reports the volume or the quality of the goods.

financial and fiscal policies on TNCs. In Box 15.4, a hypothetical illustration is given of a company setting **transfer prices** to reduce its taxes. Several other motives might induce a company to distort transfer prices, including evasion of controls on the cross-border movements of profits or capital.

Triangulation of Trade and Loss of Sovereignty

Governments have great difficulty regulating international transactions. If one government is antagonistic to another and wishes to impose a trade boycott, it is totally impossible for the government on its own to prevent movement of information or people for business purposes. Even the so-called 'superpower', the USA, was unable to prevent its citizens visiting communist Cuba during the cold war. It may be possible to prevent the *direct* import or export of goods. However, there is no guaranteed method of preventing *indirect* trade from one country to another. A simple example of evasion by **triangulation** is given in Box 15.5. Only if a UN Security Council resolution obliges all the countries of the world to impose sanctions is there a reasonable prospect of a determined government prevent-

ing TNCs from evading sanctions. However, in such a situation sovereignty over the relevant trade then lies with the Security Council and not with the individual governments.

Regulatory Arbitrage and Loss of Sovereignty

It is difficult for governments to regulate the commercial activities of companies within their country, because companies may chose to engage in **regulatory arbitrage**. If a company objects to one government's policy, it may threaten to limit or close down its local production and increase production in another country. The government that imposes the least demanding health, safety, welfare, or environmental standards will offer competitive advantages to less socially responsible companies. It thus becomes difficult for any government to set high standards. In the case of banking the political dangers inherent in the risks of a bank collapsing through imprudent or criminal behaviour are so great that the major governments have set common capital standards. Under the Basle Committee rules all commercial banks must protect their viability by having capital to the value of 8 per cent of their outstanding loans. Similarly in the European Community the desire not to leave markets unregulated provides a political impetus towards harmonization of standards and creation of a joint social policy. While the Basle Committee and the EC are very effective, both regimes are limited by not covering all countries or all closely related activities. Nevertheless, whatever control is achieved does not represent the successful exercise of sovereignty over companies: it is the partial surrender of sovereignty to an intergovernmental body.

Box 15.5. Can Governments Control Transactions?

In April 1982 Argentina invaded the Falklands and until mid-June Argentina and Britain were at war. Both countries moved quickly to block economic transactions and the whole European Community banned imports from Argentina during the conflict.

Until February 1990, just before diplomatic relations were resumed, direct air connections were forbidden. Throughout this period it was still easy to fly between London and Buenos Aires. There was only a slight inconvenience: it was necessary to change planes in Rio de Janeiro or a European capital, such as Paris or Madrid.

The British government permitted Argentine imports from July 1985, but the Argentines did not lift restrictions until 1990. When trade was not supposed to be occurring, companies could still engage in 'triangulation', sending their exports via Brazil or Western Europe. Alternatively transnational companies could shift orders to a branch in a different country.

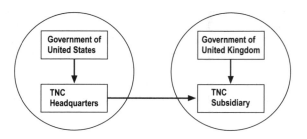

Fig. 15.2. **Who controls the United Kingdom subsidiary of a United States TNC?**

Extraterritoriality and Sovereignty

In addition transnational companies generate clashes of sovereignty between different governments. Let us consider the example of a company that has its headquarters in the United States and a subsidiary company that it owns in the United Kingdom. Three lines of authority exist. The United States government can control the main company and the United Kingdom government can control the subsidiary. Each process would be the standard exercise of a government's sovereignty over its internal affairs. In addition, both governments would accept that the TNC can, within certain limits, control its own policies on purchasing, production, and sales. Under normal circumstances these three lines of authority can be exercised simultaneously and in harmony. However, when the US government decisions cover the global operations of

the TNC, there can be a clash of sovereignty. Does the subsidiary obey the UK government or the orders of the US government issued via its headquarters? This problem of **extraterritoriality**, is inherent in the structure of all TNCs. An illustration of it producing a crisis is given in Box 15.6.

From Domestic Deregulation to Global Re-regulation

For most companies most of the time, their interests in expanding their production, increasing their market share and maximizing their profits will be in accord with the government's policy of increasing employment and promoting economic growth. Conflicts will arise over the regulation of markets to avoid the risks of market failures or externalization of social and environmental costs of production, but often these conflicts will be negotiable. The most serious conflicts occur over the desire of companies to minimize their tax burden and the desire of governments to influence the patterns of trade and investment decisions. All these questions have been features of domestic politics in modern times. Globalization of economic activity has moved the questions from the domestic agendas of each country to the global political agenda. Domestic deregulation of the economy has become a global phenomenon.

As there were many strong political pressures that led to regulation in the past, it is to be expected that reactions against deregulation will grow in strength after some years. However, the contemporary political process will be different. The examples of the International Baby Foods Action Network (IBFAN), the World Rainforest Movement and the Pesticides Action Network (PAN) indicate how the reaction against irresponsible behaviour by TNCs now is focused on the United Nations and its agencies. Re-regulation (governments again seeking to control markets) is more likely to be at the global level than within individual countries. One push towards the globalization of politics is that governments can only reassert control over transnational companies by acting collectively.

Box 15.6. **The Siberian Gas Pipeline and Extraterritoriality**

During the crisis in 1979–80 over American diplomats being held hostage in the US embassy in Teheran, the British government was startled to find that US banks in London were being ordered to freeze Iranian assets. As a result of this and earlier conflicts over shipping and uranium mining, the Protection of Trading Interests Act was passed, so that the British government could overrule the obligation of TNCs to obey any decisions taken by other governments.

The Act was applied in 1982 during the crisis over Western responses to the declaration of martial law in Poland. The US government made strenuous efforts to prevent European participation in the building of a gas pipeline from Siberia to Western Europe. In this case, the attempt was made to exercise extraterritorial control not only within unified TNCs, but also in revoking the licensing arrangement for the use of high technology by independent British companies. For ten months the US government tried to rally its NATO allies on a cold war question, yet the result was a humiliating climb-down with the lifting of the extraterritorial sanctions in November 1982.

Contrary to the common perception of the US government and US companies dominating global politics, there was total failure to break the unity of the European governments and the other companies. Although the US President and Vice-President had ranked the question as their number one international priority and made it a matter of their personal prestige, they did not even gain a face-saving compromise.

Key Points

- All major companies, because of their involvement in international trade, are potential transnational political actors, but only those operating in more than one country are regarded as transnational companies.

- The ability of TNCs to change transfer prices means that they can evade taxation or government controls on their international financial transactions.

- The ability of TNCs to use triangulation means individual governments cannot control their country's international trade.

- The ability of TNCs to engage in regulatory arbitrage, by moving production from one country to another, means individual governments are constrained against regulating companies to promote high standards of social responsibility.

- The structure of authority over TNCs generates the potential for intense conflict between governments, when the legal authority of one government has extraterritorial impact on the sovereignty of another government.

- The four problems of sovereignty, discussed above, (unpredictable financial flows, trade triangulation, regulatory arbitrage, and extraterritoriality) weaken individual governments in relation to TNCs. In some areas of economic policy, sovereignty now has to be exercised through collective action rather than independently.

Non-Legitimate Groups and Liberation Movements as Political Actors

A variety of groups engage in violent and/or criminal behaviour on a transnational basis. A distinction can be made between activity that is considered criminal around the world, such as theft, fraud, haphazard violence, or drug trafficking, and activity that is claimed by those undertaking it to have legitimate political motives. In reality, the distinction may sometimes be blurred, when criminals claim political motives or political groups are responsible for acts such as torture or killing children. For all governments neither criminal activity nor political violence can be legitimate within their own jurisdiction. From the point of view of most governments most of the time, such activities are also to be condemned when they occur in other countries.

Transnational Criminals and their Political Impact

Politically, the most important criminal industries are illicit trading in arms and in drugs. They have been estimated to be the two most valuable commodities in international trade. Trade in stolen goods generally is limited to high-value, easily transported goods, such as diamonds and computer chips. In addition, piracy of intellectual property, particularly of music, video films, and computer software, and trade in counterfeit goods is organized on a very large scale.

The same **four** sovereignty problems arise with tackling criminals as with regulating TNCs, but they take on a different significance. **First**, criminal financial flows can be massive and unpredictable. An additional problem of great complexity is that money-laundering threatens the integrity of banking and other financial institutions. **Second**, criminal trade has been so extensively diversified through triangulation that no government could confidently claim that their country is not a transit route for drug smuggling. In the arms trade, triangulation with false end-user certificates is also a common process. **Third**, using the law against criminals produces a similar effect to movement by TNCs for regulatory arbitrage. Whereas governments do not want companies to close down, forcing criminals out of business would be a political victory. Nevertheless, well-organized gangs are more likely to be displaced to another country than to be jailed and disbanded, as has been shown by the shifting patterns of drugs production in Latin America. **Fourth**, extraterritoriality does occur with respect to jurisdiction over criminal behaviour. Various special cases, such as war criminals, hijackers, and miscreant diplomats, can be prosecuted in countries not directly affected by their offence. Illicit drugs, money-laundering, and terrorism involve transnational police activities that would be unthinkable in other fields. These examples contrast with the regulation of normal economic activity. Extraterritorial jurisdiction over the criminals is supported by the overwhelming majority of governments and is endorsed in a series of international treaties and UN resolutions.

As with TNCs, the global financial system, displacement, triangulation, and extraterritoriality, limit the effective exercise of sovereignty over criminals. The difference is that in some fields, where the threat is felt to be most severe, there have been strenuous efforts to re-establish control by surrender of sovereignty through international agreement.

Transnational Guerrilla Groups and Gaining Legitimacy

Political violence has been adopted by a variety of different groups. They range from broadly based nationalist movements and other groups with a clear political programme through alienated minorities, such as the militia in the USA or religious sects in several countries, to protest groups on specific issues. These groups are often called **terrorists** to express disapproval, **guerrillas** by those who are more neutral, or **national liberation movements** by their supporters. In general, nationalists are usually able to obtain some external support, from members of the same national group in other countries, from governments hostile to their own government or from other actors who consider nationalism to be legitimate. During the cold war, both communists and anti-communists gave support to violent groups taking their side in the ideological struggle, but this tended to be most effective when the ideology was allied to nationalism. Some violent groups may obtain support, by forming alliances with similar groups based in different countries.

Governments are very reluctant to accept the use of violence by transnational groups, even when the cause meets with their approval. Hijacking, hostage-taking, and deliberate bombing of civilian

---

Box 15.7. **Key Concepts**

Terrorists: a term of abuse generally used against groups who engage in violent behaviour, by people who oppose the goals of the group. It carries the connotation that suffering has been caused to children or other non-combatants in a conflict. The term might be more appropriately applied to those, including governments, who use indiscriminate violence for the purposes of political intimidation.

Guerrillas: a neutral term to cover all groups fighting for political goals, whether or not they adopt terrorist methods.

National liberation movement: a guerrilla group that is based upon one or more nations seeking liberation from domination by the government of a foreign nation. Use of the term conveys approval for the group and for its use of violence to pursue political goals.

---

targets are so lacking in legitimacy in the intergovernmental world that governments will not seek to justify such acts, even when they have been actively involved in assisting the terrorists. Nevertheless, some groups do manage to move from the status of (bad) terrorists to (good) national liberation movements. Legitimacy in using violence is increased in *four* ways: (1) when a group appears to have widespread support within their constituency; (2) when political channels have been closed to them; (3) when the target government is exceptionally oppressive; and (4) when the violence is aimed at 'military targets' without civilian victims.

Groups such as the Provisional Irish Republican Army or the Basque separatists, *Euzkadi to Askatasuna* (ETA) that fail to match these four characteristics only obtain very limited transnational support. Some other groups are able to gain legitimacy by winning respect on all four grounds. The African National Congress (ANC) and the South West African People's Organization (SWAPO) received widespread external support for their fight against the South African apartheid regime: they gained diplomatic status, money, and weapons supplies. The position of the Palestine Liberation Organization (PLO) was less clear cut, particularly in the 1970s, because of the fear generated by their hijacking of airliners and bombing of civilians.

Although there have been many guerrilla groups fighting as oppressed national minorities, only five groups have been significant diplomatic actors in the last two decades. In the mid-1970s, the PLO and SWAPO achieved membership of the Non-Aligned Movement and the Group of 77, along with observer status in the UN General Assembly and at all UN conferences. Three other groups the ANC, the Pan-African Congress (a smaller South African group), and the Patriotic Front of Zimbabwe, did not do so well, but they did obtain the right to attend UN conferences.

The Significance of Criminals and Guerrillas

Criminals and guerrillas do not appear to present a challenge to orthodox state-centric theory. On the one hand, the drugs barons, smugglers, and thieves, along with militia, religious sects, and alienated minorities, seem to be marginal because they are not legitimate and are excluded from normal international transactions. On the other hand, the violent groups that do gain military, political, and diplomatic status on a transnational basis are generally nationalist groups, aspiring to govern a particular territory. Therefore they can be presented as endorsing the basic principles of a state-centric system.

Such an approach masks the way globalization has changed the nature of **sovereignty** and the processes of government. The operations of criminals and other non-legitimate groups have become more complex, spread over a wider geographical area and increased in scale, because the improvements in communications have made it so much

easier to transfer people, money, weapons, and ideas on a transnational basis. Government attempts to control such activities have become correspondingly more difficult. Similarly, national liberation movements cannot be seen simply as part of a static interstate system. They all start as small illegitimate groups and gain support by a process of mobilization, in which transnational legitimacy can sustain domestic legitimacy and vice versa. The legal concept of statehood may not be affected, but the practice of sovereignty has become significantly different. Now virtually every government feels it has to mobilize external support, to exercise 'domestic jurisdiction' over criminals or guerrilla groups.

Key Points

- Effective action against transnational criminals by individual governments is difficult for the same reasons as control of TNCs is difficult.

- Extraterritoriality is accepted and sovereignty is surrendered, in order to tackle the most threatening criminals.

- Groups using violence to achieve political goals generally do not achieve legitimacy, but in exceptional circumstances they may be recognized as national liberation movements and take part in diplomacy.

- The transnational activities of criminals and guerrillas shift problems of the domestic policy of countries into the realm of global politics.

Non-Governmental Organizations as Political Actors

The politics of an individual country cannot be understood without knowing what groups lobby the government and what debate there has been in the media. Similarly, international diplomacy does not operate on some separate planet, cut off from global civil society. Analysts of British politics use two terms: interest group conveys a bias towards a group, such as a company or a trade union, seeking to influence economic policy; while pressure group invokes a wider range of groups promoting their values. In the United States the terms lobby group,

public interest group, and private voluntary organization are used, with rather more normative connotations, to make similar distinctions. Because diplomats like to claim that they are pursuing 'the national interest' of a united society, they will not admit to relations with interest groups or pressure groups and they prefer the bland title, non-governmental organizations or simply NGOs. However, it must be emphasized that this established diplomatic jargon does not cover all transnational actors. Although companies, criminals, and guerril-

Box 15.8. What are NGOs?

People are often baffled by the dry, bland term, 'non-governmental organizations'. Nevertheless, some of the NGOs are better known than some of the smaller countries. They include

- Amnesty International
- Greenpeace
- Red Cross
- Save the Children
- CARE and Oxfam.

Many other NGOs are not so well known, but are of major importance, such as economic bodies, e.g. International Chamber of Shipping; technical bodies e.g. International Organization for Standardization; or professional bodies, e.g. World Medical Association.

las are literally non-governmental, they are not NGOs.

Consultative Status at the UN for NGOs

As a result of pressure, primarily from American groups, the draft United Nations Charter was amended to add an article providing for the Economic and Social Council (ECOSOC) to consult with NGOs (Article 71). In the early sessions the World Federation of Trade Unions took the lead to convert the vague general provision into a range of recognized rights of participation. After five years the Council formally codified the practice, in a resolution that effectively was a statute for NGOs. It

Box 15.9. Are You an NGO Member?

You probably do not see yourself and your family as part of the global community of NGOs, but most well-known local organizations have global links. If you attend a church, synagogue, or mosque; if you are in a trade union or a professional body; if you have joined a political party; if you attend a local family planning clinic; if you are in the Scouts, the Girl Guides, the Rotarians, or an automobile association; or if you have joined an environmental, development, human rights, or women's organization, you are very likely to be involved in the local branch of a global NGO that is represented at the United Nations.

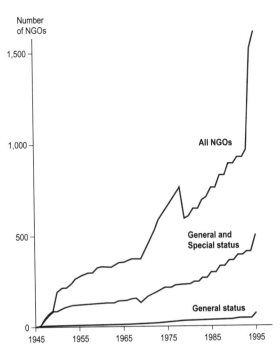

Fig. 15.3. **The Growth of NGOs at the UN**
General Status: covering all continents and most ECOSOC fields.
General and Special: global plus regional and/or specialist NGOs.
All NGOs: including also the ECOSOC Roster.

recognized *three categories* of groups: (1) a small number of high-status NGOs, concerned with most of the Council's work; (2) specialist NGOs, concerned with a few fields of activity and having a high reputation in those fields; and (3) a Roster of other NGOs that are expected to make occasional contributions to the Council.[3] Since then the term NGO has, for diplomats, been synonymous with a group that is eligible for ECOSOC consultative status.

The UN Definition of an Acceptable NGO

The ECOSOC statute and the way it has been applied embodies six principles:

1. An NGO should support the aims and the work of the UN. This has been interpreted so broadly as to place minimal restrictions on criticism of

Table 15.1. **The three levels of UN consultative status for NGOs**

1946–50	1950–68	1968–96	1996–	Type of NGO
Category A	Category A	Category I	General Status	Global, large membership and work on many issues
Category B	Category B	Category II	Special Status	Regional and general *or* specialist and high status
Category C	Register	Roster	Roster	Small or highly specialist or work with UN agencies

UN programmes. The case of Human Life International, an anti-abortion group, was a significant exception. Their campaign against American children raising money for UNICEF contributed to the ECOSOC decision to deny them consultative status.

2. An NGO should be a representative body, with identifiable headquarters, and officers, responsible to a democratic policy-making conference. In practice many highly prestigious NGOs, particularly development and environment NGOs, such as Oxfam and Greenpeace, do not have any internal democratic procedures. They are responsive to the general public rather than responsible to a membership.

3. An NGO cannot be a profit-making body. Individual companies have no possibility of gaining formal consultative status, but this does not exclude them from the UN system. International trade federations have no problem in being recognized as NGOs.

4. An NGO cannot use or advocate violence. We have seen that a few guerrilla groups have been accepted as national liberation movements, but this is distinct from and of higher status than being an NGO.

5. An NGO must respect the norm of 'non-interference in the internal affairs of states'. This means an NGO cannot be a political party. However, like companies, parties can form international federations, which do gain consultative status. The principle was extended in 1968, by adding a new clause to the statute. NGOs concerned with human rights should not restrict their activities to a particular group, nationality, or country. (Exception was made with respect to anti-apartheid groups.)

6. An international NGO is one that is not established by intergovernmental agreement. This is a technical legal expression of the property of being non-governmental. It is explicitly stated that this does not exclude governmental bodies

---

Box 15.10. International Aviation Organizations

The airlines have come together in the International Air Transport Association (IATA) forming a global NGO to manage their commercial relations.

Governments are members of the International Civil Aviation Organization (ICAO), providing an effective regime for navigation and setting safety standards. Because of the importance of weather forecasts for flight safety, close co-operation is maintained with another intergovernmental organization, the World Meteorological Organization (WMO). Both ICAO and WMO are UN specialized agencies.

The people most affected by questions of air safety are the pilots. They put forward their views at ICAO through their professional body, the International Federation of Air Line Pilots Associations (IFALPA). In September 1969

they moved from safety 'into the political field', when they took the question of hijacking to the UN Secretary-General. Eventually IFALPA achieved a significant strengthening of the international law against hijacking.

ICAO has a less formal relationship with NGOs than does the UN. IATA and IFALPA have a permanent invitation to attend meetings. Other NGOs having strong working relationships include the trade unions through the International Transport Workers' Federation; a related commercial interest, the International Union of Aviation Insurers; a research forum, the Institute of Air Transport; scientists in the International Union of Geodesy and Geophysics; a sports body, the International Aeronautical Federation; and a standards body, the International Commission on Illumination.

being members of an INGO. The significance of this blurring of the lines will be examined later.

Economic Globalization and the Expansion of NGOs

The creation of a complex global economy has had effects way beyond the international trade in goods and services. Most companies or employees, in each distinct area of activity, have formed organizations to facilitate communication, to harmonize standards and to manage adaptation to complex change. For example, air, sea, road, and rail transport, banking, telecommunications, the media, and computing could not operate transnationally without the necessary infrastructure, which includes the organizational structures of international NGOs. Co-operation is not essential to other companies, but they find agreement on common standards and procedures is more efficient and hence cheaper. Equally the employees have found they face common problems in different countries and so trade unions and professional bodies have developed their own transnational links. Any form of international regime to formulate policy for an industry, whether it is non-governmental or inter-governmental, will encourage the strengthening of the global links among the NGOs concerned with its activities. An illustration is given in Box 15.10, with eight of the major NGOs involved in the commercial and safety regimes for aviation.

The Globalization of Communications

For most of this century any individual with enough money and enough time could travel in person or communicate in writing to most parts of the world, unless communications were disrupted by war. The technical revolution of the twentieth century lies in the increased density, the increased speed and the reduced cost of communication. The political revolution lies in these changes bringing rapid global communication within the capabilities of most people. This includes even the poor, if they band together to fund a representative to articulate their case or gain access to the news media.

From the 1940s global radio broadcasting has been established, with small portable radio

---

Box 15.11. Communications and the Loss of Sovereignty

Recent events have given dramatic illustrations of the extent to which governments have lost the ability to control transnational communications.

- The Tiananmen Square killings were shown directly on Western television, as they took place.
- Kuwaitis could put through calls on radio telephones to news agencies in London and Washington during the Iraqi occupation of 1990–1.
- Saudi dissidents could circulate accusations of corruption in the Saudi government by bombardment of the country with faxes from London.
- The Zapatista leader during a rebellion in southern Mexico could transmit press releases to the United States from his portable computer, while on the run from government troops.

---

receivers appearing in the late 1950s; from the early 1960s cheap air services have linked all countries; from the early 1970s subscriber trunk dialling has provided transnational telephone connections; from the late 1980s the telephone networks have been used for facsimile transmissions; during the early 1990s satellites made possible both live television coverage of events anywhere in the world and transmission of global television services, such as CNN and the BBC; and finally in the mid-1990s the Internet has taken off as a facility for the instant exchange of massive volumes of information.

Together these changes in communications constitute a fundamental change in the structure of world politics. Governments have lost sovereignty over the transnational relations of their citizens. They can choose from *three* options:

1. keep communication facilities open and lose all ability to control transnational transactions;
2. bear the heavy costs of maintaining an elaborate security apparatus in an unsuccessful attempt to monitor and control communications; or
3. close certain facilities to prevent normal economic transactions from occurring, but fail to inhibit the determined dissident.

Borders have never been completely impermeable, but now governments can only control a limited range of communications with limited success. Normal transnational communications do not have the dramatic qualities of the examples given in Box 15.11, but they still constitute a quiet revolution.

The News Media as Agents of Globalization

The choices made by the news media in their coverage of events is at least part of the explanation of changing priorities on political agendas in most countries. Some of the similarities in political change in different countries are due to their separate responses to similar economic and social problems, but participation in the global system strengthens the similarities in the agenda for debate. Sometimes the media take the lead and sometimes they are being pushed by NGOs, TNCs, or governments, but their decisions are always important, particularly in the case of the biggest transnational press agencies and satellite television networks. The movement of ideas not only affects the agenda but also political outcomes. It is not a coincidence that individual human rights, women's rights, environmental concerns, monetarism, and privatization policies have gained increasing support in many countries around the same time. To make the illustrations more specific, the Chernobyl accident affected the politics of nuclear energy throughout the world, while the collapse of the Soviet system and of apartheid both strengthened the global process of democratization. It cannot be argued that the boundaries separating the political cultures and political systems of each country have been totally eroded, but it is the case that each country is a sub-system within the global political system.

The Movement of NGOs from the Local to the Global

One effect of the globalization of communication is to make it physically and financially feasible for small groups of people to establish and to maintain co-operation, even though they may be based thousands of miles apart from each other. Thus it is very easy for NGOs to operate transnationally, but not all NGOs make this choice. They vary from local organizations solely operating in one small town to

large global bureaucracies with a presence in most countries. The crucial factor in determining whether an NGO goes transnational is what are its goals.

- If the prime purpose is to offer a service to its own members, to pursue charitable activities locally or to campaign to change a particular law, then it may be decades before the question of establishing transnational links arises. Separate NGOs become well established in several countries before they decide to form an international NGO, as a loose federation, in order to exchange information and learn from each other's experience. Trade unions, women's organizations, charities for the elderly, and family-planning associations are examples.

- Campaigning NGOs in one country may only have the goal of affecting their own government's policy, but decide for tactical reasons to obtain support from foreign governments and NGOs. Environmental NGOs in developing countries have found support from transnational networks to be crucial.

- Sometimes campaigning NGOs decide from the start that they would be more effective as a transnational organization and they form sections simultaneously in several countries. Amnesty International and Friends of the Earth started in Britain and the United States respectively, but immediately appealed for support elsewhere.

- NGOs can be based in just one country, while defining their goals in transnational terms. For many years Oxfam in Britain and CARE in the USA raised funds to spend on disaster relief and development overseas, before they too joined international federations and then later gained sections in other countries.

- When regional or global intergovernmental organizations become the focus for policy-making, then NGOs seek to influence the proceedings. They use access to the international secretariat and the decision-making organs, as an indirect route to influence the policy of individual governments. As a result, the cities that host important IGOs also become centres for related international NGOs.

NGOs are so diverse in their goals and their tactics that the above list only indicates the main processes by which they move from local to global politics.

Key Points

- Most transnational actors can expect to gain recognition as NGOs by the UN, provided they are not individual companies, criminals, or violent groups and they do not exist solely to oppose an individual government.

- While ECOSOC consultative status does not involve all transnational NGOs, its statute does provide an authoritative statement that NGOs have a legitimate place in international diplomacy.

- The creation of a global economy leads to the globalization of unions, commercial bodies, the professions, and scientists in international NGOs, which participate in the relevant international regimes.

- The technological revolution has globalized communications, both for individuals and for the news media. This has created a political revolution. Most governments have virtually no ability to control the flow of information across the borders of their country. A few, authoritarian governments can impose some restrictions, but not without incurring very high political and economic costs.

- The improved communications make it more likely than NGOs will operate transnationally and make it very simple and cheap for them to do so.

International Organizations as Structures of Global Politics

International organizations provide the focus for global politics. The new physical infrastructure of global communications makes it easier for them to operate. In addition, when the sessions of the organizations take place, they become distinct structures for political communication. Face-to-face meetings produce different outcomes from telephone or written communications. Multilateral discussion produces different outcomes from interactions in networks of bilateral communications.

Box 15.12. Key Concepts

International organization: any institution with formal procedures and formal membership from three or more countries. The minimum number of countries is set at three rather than two, because multilateral relationships have significantly greater complexity than bilateral relationships.

Intergovernmental organization (IGO): an international organization in which full legal membership is officially solely open to states and the decision-making authority lies with representatives from governments. In practice many IGOs have also had a few colonial territories and/or national liberation movements as members.

International non-governmental organization (INGOs): an international organization in which membership is open to transnational actors. The major INGOs often mirror the world of diplomacy in being associations of 'national' NGOs that themselves group together many local NGOs from one country. For example,

Amnesty International as a global INGO is composed of country-based sections, each having a structure of local groups. INGOs can also have companies or political parties as members. Another variant is to recruit individual people. There are even a few that themselves have INGOs as members and some have mixed membership structures.

Hybrid INGO: a third type of international organization. Just as governments form IGOs, and NGOs form INGOs, the two can form joint organizations in which they are each allowed to be members. The phenomenon goes largely unrecognized, because there is no standard English word to describe these organizations. On investigation it is possible to identify many such bodies and we may call them hybrids. (Logically they should be hybrid international organizations, but in diplomatic practice they are identified among the international NGOs and so hybrid-INGOs is perhaps a more appropriate term.)

International Organizations as Systems

It was argued earlier that there is an ontological inconsistency in seeing 'states' as coherent entities, while asserting they remain independent sovereign units. We can be consistent by accepting the existence of systems at all levels of world politics. Governments, and groups making up civil society, from within countries, along with international organizations from the global level, all may have systemic properties. In the modern world, human groups are never so coherent that they are independent, closed systems (perhaps excepting monastic orders). Equally, once distinct organizational processes are established, they are never so open that the boundaries become insignificant. Thus international organizations of all types transcend country boundaries and have a major impact on the governmental actors and transnational actors composing them.

For a system to exist, there must be a sufficient density of interactions, involving each of its elements, at a sufficient intensity to result both in the emergence of properties for the system as a whole and in some consistent effect on the behaviour of the elements. In other words, systems make a difference or, as it is put in Systems Science, the whole is more than the sum of its parts. In some cases, such as the Commonwealth of Independent States and international NGO networks of people who never meet face to face, the interactions may be so weak that it could be argued the organizations are not systems. Generally, international organizations will have founding documents defining their goals, rules of procedure constraining the modes of behaviour, secretariats committed to the status and identity of the organization (or at least committed to their own careers), past decisions that provide norms for future policy, and interaction processes that socialize new participants. All these features at the systemic level will be part of the explanation of the behaviour of the members and thus the political outcomes will not be determined solely by the initial goals of the members. The statement that international organizations form systems is a statement that they are politically significant and that global politics cannot be reduced to 'interstate' relations.

The Intergovernmental versus Non-Governmental Distinction

Normally a sharp distinction is made between **intergovernmental organizations** (IGOs) and **international non-governmental organizations** (INGOs). This conveys the impression that inter-state diplomacy and transnational relations are separate from each other. In practice governments do not rigidly maintain the separation. There is an overlapping pattern of relations in another category of international organizations, **hybrid INGOs**, in which governments work with NGOs. Among the most important hybrids are the International Red Cross, the World Conservation Union (IUCN), the International Council of Scientific Unions, the International Air Transport Association and other economic bodies combining companies and governments.

In order to be regarded as a hybrid the organization must admit as full members *both* NGOs, parties, or companies *and* governments or governmental agencies. Both types of members must have full rights of participation in policy-making, including the right to vote on the final decisions. Voting may be with all members counted together, as in the International Conference of the Red Cross, or with separate majorities required in two categories of membership, as in the World Conservation Union. In the former case the principle of equality is maintained because one government's vote is equal to one Red Cross or Red Crescent society's vote. In the latter there is equality between the governments collectively and the NGOs collectively. In hybrid INGOs there is usually also a joint obligation to fund the activities of the organization. When the principle of formal equality of NGOs and governments is acknowledged by both sides in such a manner, the assumption that governments can dominate must be totally abandoned.

Relationships between International Organizations

Once it is accepted that international organizations are politically significant in producing their own distinct policy, then the relations between the organizations also become important. The mutual recognition of IGOs, by granting each other observer status, and the existence of consultative status for INGOs are not simply obscure bureaucratic procedures. They are processes that legitimize political activity by international secretariats on behalf of their organizations. The systemic outputs of the organizations are then expressed as inputs to other systems. The density of these relationships, particularly in the United Nations, means that it is not possible to separate the intergovernmental world from the transnational world. Just as the hybrid INGOs break down the distinction in a fundamental way, by producing direct relations between governments, companies and NGOs, so also IGO relations with INGOs integrate, at a higher level of aggregation.

Key Points

- International organizations are also structures for political communication. They are systems that constrain the behaviour of their members.
- Governments form intergovernmental organizations and transnational actors form international non-governmental organizations. In addition governments and transnational actors accord each other equal status by jointly creating hybrid international NGOs.

Issues and Policy Systems in Global Politics

One way state-centric writers accommodate transnational activity is by distinguishing the **high politics** of peace and security, taking place in military alliances and UN diplomacy, from the **low politics** of other policy questions, debated in specialist UN bodies, other IGOs and INGOs. Then, by asserting it is more important to analyse peace and war, actors in low politics are defined out of the analysis. In practice it is not so simple. Scientists, the Red Cross, religious groups and other NGOs are involved in arms control negotiations; economic events may be treated as crises; social policy can concern matters of life and death; and heads of government do at times make the environment a top priority. It is useful to analyse global politics in terms of a variety of dimensions describing each **policy domain** and the actors within it, but the different dimensions do not correlate. A single high/low classification does not work.

The move from a state-centric to a pluralist model, in which governments and transnational actors interact with each other bilaterally and multilaterally, depends on a shift from a static unidimensional concept of **power**. Actors enter a political process possessing resources and seeking particular goals: however, contrary to the Realist view, **capabilities** do not determine **influence**. Explaining outcomes requires examining whether the resources of actors are relevant to the goals being pursued, describing the degree of divergence

---

Box 15.13. Key Concepts

- The distinction between **high politics** and **low politics** is made by Realists but not by Pluralists. It is based on the following four dimensions.

		High Politics	Low Politics
(1)	*Policy questions*	Peace and security	Economics, social questions, human rights, environment
(2)	*Decision-makers*	Heads of government and senior ministers	Junior ministers or officials
(3)	*Involvement of non-state actors*	Minimal, unless as agents of governments	Extensive activity by NGOs, TNCs, IGOs, and INGOs
(4)	*Type of situation*	High priority or crises	Low priority, routine activity

- **An issue** consists of a set of political questions that are seen as being related, because they all invoke the same value conflicts, e.g. the issue of human rights concerns questions that invoke freedom versus order.
- **A policy domain** consists of a set of political questions that have to be decided together because they are linked by the political processes in an international organization, e.g. financial policy is resolved in the IMF. A policy domain may cover several issues: financial policy includes development, environment and gender issues.

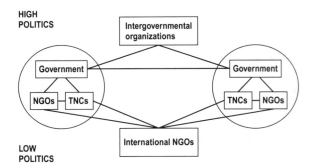

HIGH
POLITICS

LOW
POLITICS

Fig. 15.4. **The orthodox view of international relations**

between the goals of the different actors, and analysing how they are changed by the **interaction processes**.

Governments are usually characterized by having military capabilities and legal authority. They may also have high status, control economic resources, possess specialist information, and have access to communications, but all these four capabilities can also be attributes of transnational actors and international organizations. In the process of political debate something else is crucial. It is the ability to communicate in a manner that commands the attention and respect of other actors. While this is enhanced by possession of status and resources, in a particular time and place—on the news media, in a speech before a public audience, during negotiations or when lobbying in private—the ability to communicate is a personal attribute of the speaker. Some presidents and prime ministers fail to command respect, while some NGO activists are inspiring and cannot be ignored. If power is seen in military terms, governments are expected to be dominant. If power is seen in economic terms,

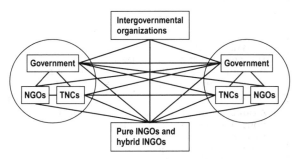

Fig. 15.5. **The full range of international connections**

Box 15.14. **Key Concepts**

Power: in the most general sense, the ability of a political actor to achieve its goals. In the study of international relations, it is common to distinguish between capabilities and influence. In the Realist approach, it is assumed that possession of capabilities will result in influence, so the single word, power, is often used ambiguously to cover both. In the Pluralist approach, it is assumed that political interactions can modify the translation of capabilities into influence and therefore it is important to distinguish between the two.

Capabilities: the resources that are under an actor's direct control. Realist theorizing concentrates primarily on military capabilities and secondarily on economic resources. Pluralists also emphasize control of communication facilities (TV, radio, and telecommunications) and possession of information. By extension two abstract attributes of actors, legal authority and high status, can also be seen as capabilities.

Interaction processes: the flows of people, materials, energy, money, and information (including political ideas and proposals for policy), between the elements of a system. War is primarily determined by flows of people as soldiers and materials as weapons; economics by the exchange of money for all the other four types of flows; and politics by the flow of information. Thus, unless and until an issue invokes armed conflict, structures of communication are the fundamental political structures.

Influence: the ability of one actor to change the values or the behaviour of another actor. Unwelcome change may be achieved as coercion by military threats, economic sanctions, or even by the possession of information, through blackmail. Acceptable change can be the result of a bargain in which the new behaviour is rewarded by military, economic, or political support. Influence may be regarded as being at its greatest when one actor uses political debate to change the political values of another actor, so that the new behaviour is adopted voluntarily.

TNCs are expected to be dominant. However, if power includes possession of status, information, and communication skills, then it is possible for NGOs and international organizations to mobilize support for their values and to exercise influence over governments.

The types of authority, status, resources, information, and skills that are relevant to political success are issue-specific. (They vary from one **issue** to another.) Thus the governments, the TNCs, the NGOs, the intergovernmental organizations, and

Table 15.2. **The variety of political actors involved in different policy domains**

	Apartheid in South Africa	Human Rights	Population Planning	Environment
Main governments involved	South Africa, UK, USA versus African governments	Democratic versus authoritarian governments	All types of governments	Those who feel threatened by problems versus those who do not
Transnational companies	Wide range, but especially mining and oil	Any working with oppressive governments	Medical, pharmaceutical, and food.	Mainly industrial, energy, and transport
Guerrillas	ANC, PAC and SWAPO	Any taking hostages	Any in control of territory	Generally not concerned
Grass-roots NGOs	Anti-Apartheid Movement	Human rights groups and the oppressed	Religious, women's, and health groups	Friends of the Earth, WWF, Greenpeace etc.
UN inter-governmental policy forum	Committee Against Apartheid and Security Council	Human Rights Commission	Population Commission	Commission on Sustainable Development
UN Secretariat	Centre Against Apartheid	Centre for Human Rights	UNICEF UN Pop. Fund	UNDP UNEP
Other IGOs	Organisation of African Unity	Council of Europe	WHO World Bank	World Bank
International NGOs	Many involved, with a secondary concern	Amnesty International and others	International Planned Parenthood Federation	Environment Liaison Centre International and other networks
Hybrid INGOs	Those concerned with trade	None	None	World Conservation Union (IUCN)

the international NGOs that have the ability to exercise influence will vary according to the issues invoked by a policy problem. Table 15.2 illustrates the point that there is not a single international system of nearly 200 'states', but a variety of **policy domains**, each involving their own distinct actors. Governments have a special role, linking the different domains, because membership of the UN obliges governments to form policy and vote on most issues. In practice, they are less central and cohesive than it appears in the UN, because different departments of government handle the different policy questions. The transnational actors and international organizations generally are more specialist and involved in a limited range of policy questions. Amnesty International rarely has significance in environmental politics and Greenpeace rarely is concerned with human rights, but each is central to their own domain. Being a specialist actor is a weakness in relation to situations where issue linkages become important, but usually it is a great

strength for NGOs and international secretariats. Being a specialist generates high status, achieves command over information, and enhances communication skills. These capabilities enable a challenge to be made to the governments that control military and economic resources.

Within both domestic and global politics, civil society is the source of change. Companies usually initiate economic change and NGOs are usually the source of new ideas for political action. At any one point in time, economics and politics may seem to be relatively stable and under governmental control. Under the exceptional circumstances of war or under exceptional leadership, governments can generate change. However, NGOs generally provide the dynamics of politics. The European empires were dismembered by nationalist movements, with support from lawyers, journalists, unions, and the churches. Democracy and human rights have been extended by women's groups, ethnic minorities, and dissident groups. The environment has moved up the agenda in response to grass-roots anger at the loss of natural beauty, protests against threats to health, and warnings from scientists about ecosystems being at risk of collapse. The start of the cold war was not simply the formation of military alliances: it was a political struggle of communism as a transnational movement against the transnational appeal of democracy, the Catholic Church, and nationalism. The arms race and the process of *détente* included conflict between arms manufacturers and peace movements, with scientists being crucial to both sides. The end of the cold war was driven by economic failure within communist countries and the political failure in response to demands from unions, human rights dissidents, the churches, and environmentalists. The response to refugee crises produced by natural and human-made disasters has been dominated by the media, the UN and NGOs. The shift from seeing development as increasing a country's GNP to meeting ordinary people's basic needs and using resources in a sustainable manner was driven by development NGOs and the environmental movement. The international relations of the twentieth century have all occurred within complex, pluralist political systems.

Key Points

- The high politics, low politics, distinction is used to marginalize transnational actors. It is invalid because politics does not reduce to these two categories. All policy domains can be described by the type of issues, the status of the governmental decision-makers, the degree of involvement of transnational actors and the priority given to the policy.

- A simple concept of power will not explain outcomes. Military and economic resources are not the only capabilities: communication facilities, information, authority, and status are also important political assets. In addition, an ability to use the interaction processes to mobilize support will contribute to influence over policy.

- Different policy domains contain different actors, depending upon the salience of the issues being debated.

- TNCs gain influence through the control of economic resources. NGOs gain influence through possessing information, gaining high status and communicating effectively. TNCs and NGOs have been the main source of economic and political change in global politics.

QUESTIONS

1. Outline three meanings of the concept of a 'state' and explain the implications of each for the study of transnational actors.

2. What are the five types of transnational actors? Give examples of each type.

3. What is a nation? What types of transnational actors can be based on national groups?

4. How do transnational companies affect the sovereignty of governments?

5. How do criminals have a significant effect upon global politics?

6. What measures could you use to compare the size of countries, TNCs, NGOs, and international organizations? Are countries always larger than transnational actors?

7. List all the NGOs that you, and your family, have joined. Assess from their newsletters how many are global organizations, how many are national, or local with global connections, and how many have no transnational relations.

8. What types of NGOs are, and what types are not, eligible to obtain consultative status with the Economic and Social Council of the United Nations?

9. Explain the expansion in the number of NGOs engaging in transnational activities.

10. What is a hybrid international NGO?

11. How is it possible for NGOs to exercise influence in global politics? (Note: this question can be answered both in theoretical terms and in practical empirical terms).

12. Explain the difference between analysing international relations as a single international system and as the global politics of many different policy domains.

GUIDE TO FURTHER READING

Case Study Materials

Keohane, R. O., and Nye, J. S. (eds.), *Transnational Relations and World Politics* (Cambridge, Mass.: Harvard University Press, 1972): the first major academic study of transnational relations, limited by the explicit decision to downplay non-economic actors.

Willetts, P. (ed.), *Pressure Groups in the Global System: The Transnational Relations of Issue-Orientated Non-Governmental Organisations* (London: Pinter, 1982): in reaction against the omission of non-economic groups by Keohane and Nye, examines how pressure groups move from single-country to global activity.

Willetts, P. (ed.), *'The Conscience of the World'. The Influence of Non-Governmental Organisations in the UN System* (London: Hurst and Co., 1996): defines what is an NGO, gives the history of the League and the UN consultative arrangements and offers seven case-studies of the influence of NGOs in the UN system.

Risse-Kappen, T. (ed.), *Bringing Transnational Relations Back In* (Cambridge: Cambridge University Press, 1995): provides a set of six case-studies around the theme that transnational influence depends upon the structures of governance for an issue-area at both the domestic level and in international institutions.

Theoretical Debate

Rosenau, J. N., T*he Study of Global Interdependence: Essays on the Transnationalisation of World Affairs* (London: Pinter, 1980): a fruitful source of theoretical ideas for a pluralist approach.

Willetts, P., 'Transactions, Networks and Systems', in A. J. R. Groom and P. Taylor, *Frameworks for International Co-operation* (London: Pinter, 1990), ch. 17: more detailed coverage of the development of International Relations theory on transnational and intergovernmental relations.

See also the editors' chapters in the case-study books.

UN Materials

Kaul, I., *et al.*, *Human Development Report 1993* (New York: Oxford University Press, 1993): an official UN annual report, which in this edition concentrates on the contribution made by NGOs to development.

UNCTAD, Division on Transnational Corporations and Investment, *World Investment Report 1995*, (New York: UN, 1995): an official UN annual report, which assesses the scale of TNC participation in global production, investment and trade.

See also documents in the appendices to Willetts, *'The Conscience of the World'*.

NOTES

1 Data on transnational corporations is given in annual reports from the United Nations. The figures quoted come from *World Investment Report 1995*, (Geneva: UN, 1995), p. 9. A parent TNC is defined as one that controls assets outside its home country and a foreign affiliate is defined as a subsidiary, a branch or an associate in which the parent has a stake of at least 10% of the equity (p. 383). The numbers of transnational and international organizations of different types are given in the statistical tables of the various editions of the UIA yearbook. The figures quoted come from *Yearbook of International Organisations 1993-1994* (Munich: K. G. Saur, for the Union of International Associations, 30th edn., 1993). In each case, the current author has rounded the figures to the nearest hundred.

2. Compare *The Times 1000, 1995* (London: Times Books, 1994), Table 1 'The world's top 50 industrial companies', p. 12, (which gives the smallest of the 50 as having sales of $32.5 bn. in 1994) with the *World Bank Atlas, 1995*, (Washington, DC: World Bank, 1994), pp. 18–9 for GNP data and pp. 8–9 for population data. (Both World Bank tables omit Monaco, Liechtenstein, and Palau, but are counted by the current author.) The data on companies, in the UN report cited above, is different, but gives broadly the same picture. The top 100 TNCs, ranked by foreign assets in 1993, included 41 with sales of more than $30 bn. and another eight with total assets of more than $30 bn. (see pp. 20–3).

3. ECOSOC Resolution 288(X)B Arrangements for Consultation with Non-Governmental Organizations was passed in February 1950. It was amended and replaced by Resolution 1296(XLIV) in May 1968. A further process of review and amendment started in February 1993 and concluded in July 1996, with the passing of Resolution 1996/31. As specified in Table 15.1, the classifications were renamed in 1950, 1968, and 1996. The basic definition of an NGO has not changed since the 1950 resolution, but the details of their participation rights have been changed.

Part Four
International Issues

In this section of the book we want to give you a wide-ranging overview of the main issues in contemporary world politics. The previous three sections have been designed to give you a comprehensive foundation for the study of contemporary international issues. As with the other sections, this one also has two aims: **first**, we want to give you an understanding of some of the more important pressing problems which appear every day in the media headlines and which, directly and indirectly, affect the lives of each of us. These issues are the stuff of globalization, and they take a number of different forms. Some, like the environment and nuclear proliferation pose dangers of global catastrophe. Others, like nationalism, cultural differences, humanitarian intervention, together with regionalism and integration, raise important questions and dilemmas about the twin processes of fragmentation and unification which characterize the world in which we live. Yet other issues such as global trade and finance, human rights, gender, poverty, development, and hunger are fundamentally intertwined with globalization. Our **second** aim, of course, is that by providing overviews of these issues we are posing questions about the nature of globalization. Is it new? Is it beneficial? Is it unavoidable? Does it serve specific interests? Does it make it more or less easy to deal with the problems dealt with in these chapters? The picture that emerges from these chapters is that the process of globalization is a highly complex one, with major disagreements existing about its significance and its impact. Some contributors see opportunities for greater co-operation because of globalization whilst others see dangers of increased levels of conflict as the end of the century beckons. What do you think?

16 Environmental Issues

Owen Greene

READER'S GUIDE

Environmental issues emerged in the late twentieth century as a major focus of international concern and activity. Understanding the causes and impacts of global environmental change is an urgent task. So too is improving knowledge of how to develop effective responses. Approaches and concepts developed within International Relations can contribute substantially to such understanding. At the same time, international environmental issues pose important challenges for International Relations theory. This chapter introduces these issues, and discusses some key characteristics of the causes and risks of global environmental change and responses to it. It outlines the historical development of international environmental politics and agreements, and then examines issues and phases in the development of environmental regimes (particularly the ozone regime), and the Earth Summit agreements and their outcomes

Introduction: International Environmental Issues

By the end of the twentieth century, environmental issues had been high on the international agenda for a whole generation of political leaders, government officials, scientists, industrialists, and concerned citizens. Since the late 1960s, awareness of the risks and implications of a wide range of international environmental problems has increased greatly, and justifiably so.

Since that time, it has become clear that most of the world's seas and oceans are over-fished. Soil is being degraded and eroded on a large scale throughout the world. Natural habitats are being destroyed: for example the area of tropical rainforest has reduced by over 50 per cent since 1950, and the process continues largely unabated. As a result, tens of thousands of species of plants and animals are probably becoming extinct each year. The dumping of waste products into the sea, air, and land means that pollution problems are ubiquitous. Huge quantities of waste, including hazardous chemicals, heavy metals, and radioactive materials, have been dumped at sea, either directly or carried by rivers. Together with sewage and oil spills, these have profoundly damaged sea environments, with lakes and semi-enclosed seas proving particularly vulnerable. Billions of people suffer daily air pollution. Acid rain, stratospheric ozone depletion, and climate change are major regional or global problems arising from atmospheric pollution.

Environmental problems are not new. Human societies have long had a major impact on their environment. Their tendency to exploit it as if it were an inexhaustible resource has repeatedly led to disaster, sometimes leading to the loss of entire human communities. Over much of human history, however, the environmental impacts of over-exploitation or pollution have typically been quite local. Communities could often escape the consequences of such activities by moving on to relatively unspoilt areas. Even if they could not, the local impoverishment did not necessarily affect the continued well-being of neighbouring societies. Widespread industrialization and rapid population growth changed this situation. Severe environmental damage and unsustainable exploitation occurred over whole regions of the world. By the late twentieth century, the impacts had become truly global.

This chapter examines the politics of **global environmental issues**. However, there are several senses in which the environment can be said to have become a global issue. First, some environmental problems are inherently global. CFCs (chorofluorocarbons) released into the atmosphere contribute to the global problem of stratospheric ozone depletion irrespective of where they are emitted, just as carbon dioxide emissions contribute to global climate change. The effects are global, and the problems can only be tackled through co-operation on a global scale.

Second, some problems relate to the exploitation of **global commons**: resources shared by all members of the international community, such as the oceans, deep-sea bed, atmosphere, and outer space. Many argue that the world's genetic resources are a global resource, which should be preserved in the common interest.

Third, many environmental problems are intrinsically **transnational**, in that by their nature they cross state boundaries, even if they are not entirely global. For example, emissions of sulphur dioxide by one state will be carried by winds and deposited as acid rain on downwind countries. Wastes dumped into an enclosed or semi-enclosed sea affect all littoral states. Such transnational or regional problems exist in many parts of the world, and pose similar technical and political challenges to those of truly global problems. Moreover, states or non-state actors from outside the region may contribute to the problems or to efforts to tackle them.

Fourth, and following on from this, many processes of over-exploitation or environmental degradation are relatively local or national in scale, and yet they are experienced in such a large number of localities around the world that they can be considered to be global problems. Examples include unsustainable agricultural practices, soil degradation and erosion, deforestation, river pollution, and the many environmental problems associated with urbanization and industrial practices.

Finally, the processes leading to over-exploitation and environmental degradation are intimately linked to broader political and socio-economic processes, which themselves are part of a global political economy. Thus it is widely recognized that the causes of most environmental problems are closely related to the generation and distribution of wealth, knowledge, and power, and to patterns of energy consumption, industrialization, population growth, affluence, and poverty. In this respect, the processes of globalization and interdependence in the economic and other spheres of life, as discussed in Chapter 1 (Globalization), increasingly give all environmental issues a global dimension.

Thus, the phrase 'global environmental issues' encompasses a wide range of types of problems and issues, posing different challenges to those who wish to develop effective responses. Although they share some common characteristics, each issue is specific and needs to be analysed in its own right. This chapter is primary concerned with intrinsically international environmental problems and particularly the development of international responses to them, and with the international politics of promoting '**sustainable development**' (i.e. environmentally sustainable patterns of economic and social development). Subsequent sections examine: the historical development of international environmental politics; some key characteristics and challenges posed; the development of environmental regimes, illustrated with brief case-studies of the ozone and climate change regimes; and the role of international institutions in promoting sustainable development.

Key Points

- International environmental issues emerged as a major focus for international politics and concern in the last three decades of the twentieth century.

- Although environmental problems are not new in themselves, industrialization and rapid population growth have greatly increased the scale and intensity of the over-exploitation of natural resources and environmental degradation, generating a wide range of urgent international and global problems.

- Environmental issues have become international and global in several senses. Many environmental problems are intrinsically transnational or global, or relate to global commons. Other local or national problems are experienced widely across the Earth. Finally, the processes generating most environmental problems are closely related to broader political or socio-economic processes, which are themselves part of an increasingly global system

- Global environmental issues come in many different types, and though they share some common characteristics, each issue needs specific examination in its own right.

Environmental Issues on the International Agenda: An Historical Outline

The Early Years

Environmental issues first emerged as a focus for international politics in the nineteenth century in the context of international agreements to manage resources. For example, the River Commissions for the Rhine and the Danube which are now deeply involved with environmental policy began life as arrangements to facilitate economic use of the rivers as waterways. The International Maritime Organization (IMO) was formed in 1948, more or less as a 'ship-owners' club' to facilitate international shipping and navigation and promote safety. But in 1954 the IMO was given responsibility for implementing a landmark treaty on marine pollution: the Convention for the Prevention of Pollution of the Sea by Oil.

The first international treaty on flora, signed in Bern in 1889, was primarily concerned with preventing the spread of a disease (Phylloxera) which threatened to destroy European vineyards. This was followed by a series of global and regional agreements on flora in the 1920s and 1950s, which were all similarly concerned with maintaining healthy stocks of cultivated plants or preventing disease. Likewise, the first agreement on fauna was the 1902 Convention for the Protection of Birds useful to Agriculture. In 1911, the USA, Canada, and Russia agreed a Convention for the Protection of Fur Seals, which were being unsustainably culled. In 1945, the UN Food and Agriculture Organization (FAO) was set up, with the conservation of natural resources included in its mandate. The 1946 International Whaling Convention essentially established a club of whaling nations to manage the 'harvesting' of whales.

Even at that time, however, there was emerging concern to protect wildlife for its own sake as well as an economic resource. Conventions were signed to protect birds, in large part due to public pressures mobilized by groups such as the Royal Society for the Protection of Birds. The first international efforts to establish wildlife parks and reserves began as early as 1900 (amongst the colonial powers in Africa), and were further advanced through a series of Conventions from the 1930s onwards.

It was in the 1960s, however, that international concern about pollution and the preservation of the natural environment began to develop rapidly, particularly in developed countries. Rachel Carson's book *Silent Spring* not only stimulated intense concern about the widespread use of DDT and other pesticides, but helped to launch the modern environmental movement (Carson, 1962). Wide awareness of the health risks posed by radioactive fall-out contributed to the pressures to conclude the ban on nuclear warhead tests in the atmosphere, agreed in 1963. Concern about sea pollution grew, stimulated by disasters such as the spill from the Torrey Canyon oil tanker in 1967, and the IMO became increasingly engaged with preventing oil pollution at sea. The problem of transboundary air pollution, and 'acid rain', attracted increasing attention, particularly in Scandinavia and Canada where damage to vulnerable forest and lake ecosystems was becoming manifest. In the mid-1960s, informal discussions began on the development of a new Law of the Sea to govern access to, and use of, the international seas and the seabed: the old regime was collapsing as unilateral claims were being made on transit rights and for economic control of waters up to 200 miles from coasts.

The Stockholm Conference

The 1972 **UN Conference on the Human Environment** was organized in response to this dramatic increase in international environmental concern in the 1960s. The aim was to establish an international framework to promote a more co-ordinated approach to pollution and other environmental problems. The conference, which was held in Stockholm, marked a turning point in the development of international environmental politics. Some of the principles that were agreed, and the institutions and programmes that were established, had an enduring effect (see Box 16.1). Just as significantly, the debates at the conference established themes and practices that would remain central to international environmental politics for the next twenty years and beyond.

The importance of international environmental issues as a focus for international concern became institutionalized, along with the principle that states have a responsibility to co-operate with efforts to manage the global commons and reduce transboundary pollution. Developing countries insisted that they had less historical responsibility for global pollution and resource depletion than industrialized countries, and that actions to protect the environment had to be linked to efforts to promote their economic and social development—arguments that developed states accepted in principle. That is, the general relationship between **environment and development** in the context of **North–South relations** was for the first time formally elaborated at an intergovernmental meeting. At the same time, **environmental non-governmental organizations (NGOs)** from many countries gathered to monitor the entire proceedings of the Conference, to exert political pressure on the participants, and to network, thus establishing a practice that has continued ever since.

From Stockholm to Rio

In the 1970s and 1980s, dozens of international environmental agreements and programmes were established. For example, a series of conventions were set up to protect the environment of the Mediterranean, North Sea, Baltic Sea, and other regional seas, with UNEP playing an important leadership role. The 1972 London Dumping Convention established a framework for restricting the dumping of toxic wastes (including nuclear wastes) at sea. In 1973, an international convention was agreed to prevent intentional oil pollution from ships (the MARPOL Convention) which was further strengthened in 1978, after further public outcries about continuing oil spills. In 1979, European and North American countries set up the Long Range Transboundary Air Pollution (LRTAP) agreement to limit emissions of sulphur dioxide and other pollutants causing air pollution and acid

Box 16.1. The Stockholm Conference and its Legacy

The UN Conference on the Human Environment, held in Stockholm in 1972, was the UN's first major conference on international environmental issues. The Stockholm Conference attracted wide publicity, and many of the participants and observers no doubt learned a lot from the discussions of a wide range of specific environmental issues. The meeting agreed upon: a Declaration containing 26 principles concerning the environment and development; an Action Plan with 109 recommendations spanning six broad areas (human settlements, natural resource management, pollution, educational and social aspects of the environment, development and the environment, and international organizations); and a Resolution on various institutional and financial arrangements.

In following years dozens of international environmental agreements were achieved. However, apart from galvanizing public concern and educating governments, the most enduring specific contributions of the Stockholm Conference are widely believed to be the following.

First, some of the agreed principles significantly strengthened the framework for future environmental co-operation, They did not immediately command universal acceptance, not least because Soviet bloc countries boycotted the Stockholm Conference for broader foreign policy reasons. But over time they gained substantial international stature, and provided a basis for much subsequent environmental diplomacy. Principle 21 had particular significance, for example. It acknowledged states' sovereignty over their natural resources but stipulated that states have 'the responsibility to ensure that activities within their jurisdiction or control do not cause damage to the environment of other states or of areas beyond the limits of national jurisdiction'. Other principles established that: the international community should determine limits on the use and abuse of 'global commons'; resources identified as the **'Common Heritage of Mankind'** (such as the deep-sea bed) should be collectively managed, preserved or used to common benefit; measures to prevent pollution and protect the natural environment should be balanced against the economic and social goals; and that international agreements should take into account the different circumstances and responsibilities of developed and developing states.

Second, the Stockholm Conference led to the establishment of global and regional environmental monitoring networks, which have improved monitoring of environmental problems, such as marine pollution and ozone depletion, and have indirectly stimulated action to tackle them.

Third, the Conference led to the creation of the UN Environment Programme (UNEP), which was tasked with co-ordinating the environment-related activities of other UN agencies and promoting the integration of environmental considerations into their work. In practice, UNEP subsequently played a key role in: raising political awareness of environmental problems; helping with the formation of scientific consensus on problems and responses to them; facilitating negotiations (particularly for the protection of regional seas and the ozone layer); and improving countries' environmental management capacities. The broader institutionalization of international environmental politics meant that the process acquired momentum to continue through periods when public and political concerns about the environment waned.

Finally, the Conference stimulated broader political and institutional changes. For example, many governments subsequently created Ministries for the Environment and national agencies for environmental monitoring or regulation. The development of international networks of environmental NGOs was stimulated. Moreover environmental NGOs, which at that time were primarily based in Europe or North America, began to engage more systematically with development issues and developing country groups.

rain. In 1985 the Vienna Convention for the Protection of the Ozone Layer was signed, followed two years later by the Montreal Protocol which imposed substantial limits on use of CFCs and other ozone depleting substances.

Largely as a result of sustained pressure by environmental NGOs, the Ramsar Convention to preserve wetland habitats of waterfowl was established in 1971, followed by the Convention on International Trade in Endangered Species (CITES) a year later. These were followed by a series of agreements to conserve habitats and animals including seals and Polar Bears. Furthermore, well-established resource-management regimes, such as the Antarctica treaty and the International Whaling Convention were transformed into environmental protection agreements. Moratoriums on whaling and on the exploitation of Antarctic resources were established—marking a considerable departure from the original aims and priorities of these regimes.

In the twenty years after the Stockholm Conference, environmental politics developed and matured. UNEP established itself as an important catalyst and broker for international environmental agreements. Governments were increasingly enmeshed in a complex of international environmental rules and institutions, serviced by international secretariats and a large, transnational community of scientists and experts. Green movements and Green parties developed throughout most of the OECD countries, and increasingly in developing countries too. In the USSR and Eastern Europe, environmental concern grew strongly in the 1980s. Environmental movements were at the forefront of broader political changes in these countries, and were particularly influential in most of the early post-communist governments.

It increasingly became the norm that non-governmental groups should have wide access to intergovernmental meetings on the environment, to an extent that would have shocked earlier generations of diplomats and is still unknown in several other spheres of international activity. Moreover, in many areas environmental NGOs came to command sufficient expertise and resources that they became substantial forces in international politics in their own right. Delegations from organizations such as Greenpeace, World Wildlife Fund, or Friends of the Earth at international meetings were frequently larger and more expert than those of all but the largest states, and through their access to the media and expertise were able to shape international agendas. Industrial associations representing interested groups in the business community likewise became directly involved in seeking to shape international environmental regimes, rather than simply working through their governments.

However, the development agendas included in the Action Plan and Declaration of Principles agreed at Stockholm were never seriously followed up. Most of the international agreements listed above focused on environmental protection or pollution, without seriously integrating development concerns. Moreover, UNEP lacked the institutional weight seriously to co-ordinate other UN agencies, which typically vigorously protect their 'turf', and thus largely failed to achieve integration of environmental and development agendas in the UN system. This caused increasing international concern, particularly amongst developing countries.

The UN established a World Commission on Environment and Development, chaired by the then Prime Minister of Norway, Gro Harlem Brundtland, to propose ways forward. The 1987 **Brundtland Report** argued for priority to be given to achieving **'sustainable development'**, and received wide international support (World

Commission on Environment and Development, 1987). Though the Report discussed a variety of issues and institutional reforms, the exact meaning of the concept of 'sustainable development' remained contested or unclear. Nevertheless, it was important because it indicated an agenda which could attract strong support from a variety of important constituencies.

As a result, the UN General Assembly decided in December 1989 to convene an 'Earth Summit' as a twenty-year follow-up to the Stockholm Meeting, so that the international community could carry the sustainable development agenda forward. A **UN Conference on Environment and Development (UNCED)** was fixed to take place in Rio de Janeiro in June 1992.

Box 16.2. **Sustainable Development**

The concept of 'sustainable development' was crystallized and popularized in the 1987 report of the UN World Commission on Environment and Development (the Brundtland Commission), which drew upon long established lines of thought which had developed substantially over the previous 20 years.

The Brundtland Commission's characterization of 'sustainable development' is development that meets the needs of the present without compromising the ability of future generations to meet their own needs. The prominence given to 'needs' reflects a concern to eradicate poverty and meet human basic needs, broadly understood.

The concept of sustainable development focused attention on finding strategies to promote economic and social development in ways that avoided environmental degradation, over-exploitation or pollution, and away from less productive debates about whether to prioritize development or the environment. The emphasis on 'development' could be widely endorsed, and was particularly welcomed by developing country representatives, development agencies, and groups primarily concerned about poverty and social deprivation. The link with 'sustainability' satisfied a variety of environmental constituencies. It addressed those who were concerned that present patterns of economic and population growth would have to change because humankind was reaching the limits of the Earth's finite natural resources and 'carrying capacity', first popularized by the Club of Rome in the early 1970s (Meadows et al. 1972, 1992). It could also be welcomed by those who doubted this, and were more concerned about problems such as pollution, climate change, and threats to habitats and biodiversity.

The Rio Conference and its outcomes are discussed below. Before proceeding further with our historical examination, however, it is useful to review some issues and challenges posed by international environmental politics, and to examine in more detail the development and implementation of international environmental regimes.

Key points

- Environmental issues first emerged on the international agenda in the late nineteenth century. By the 1950s, many international agreements had been established. These were mostly concerned with the management of the environment as an economic resource, though some flora and fauna agreements were also concerned with protecting wildlife for its own sake.

- Environmental awareness and concern developed strongly after the 1960s, particularly in relation to pollution problems. This was reflected in the transformation of several existing resource-management agreements into environmental protection regimes, and in efforts to establish additional measures for environmental protection in many new areas.

- The 1972 Stockholm Conference established a number of principles, institutions, and programmes which helped to provide a framework promoting the further development on international responses to transnational environmental problems, highlighting the need to promote both development and environmental protection, and establishing precedents.

- In the 1970s and 1980s, environmental politics developed and matured. Green movements, environmental and industrial NGOs, and international organizations established themselves as key actors in international environmental politics alongside states. NGOs and other groups from the 'South' became increasingly involved alongside actors from industrial countries. Many new environmental agreements were established.

- The Brundtland Commission's promotion of the concept of 'sustainable development' was well received, particularly by those who believed that the development dimension of the Stockholm Principles had become marginalized. It was agreed to hold a UN Conference on Environment and Development (UNCED) in 1992 in Rio de Janeiro to develop international actions to promote sustainable development.

Issues and Challenges in International Environmental Politics

Some Challenges for International Relations

As International Relations scholars came to study international environmental politics, they not surprisingly brought their established theoretical perspectives and prejudices with them. Such is the variety and complexity of the topic area that advocates of each such perspective can find plenty of evidence that seems to support their case, be it 'realist', 'neo-realist', 'pluralist', 'liberal institutionalist'; 'structuralist', 'neo-marxist', or 'feminist' (as described in earlier chapters of this book). The development and effects of international environmental regimes have, for example, provided an important focus for the debates between realists and liberal institutionalists discussed in Chapter 12 (International Regimes). Moreover, each perspective provides important insights into aspects of global environmental change or international environmental politics.

However, it is perhaps more interesting and important to note at the outset that international environmental issues pose particular challenges for some of the dominant approaches in International Relations. Theories and simplifying assumptions developed through other areas of study, such as security studies or international political economy, should not be assumed to apply equally well to this area without careful examination of the evidence. In practice, they often require significant revision to take proper account of the particular characteristics of environmental issues. Three important examples of such challenges are outlined below, with the aim of informing our approach to the examination of international environmental politics from the outset.

One example relates to the significance and role of states. The dominant tradition within International Relations is state-centric, centred around concepts of state sovereignty and the belief that states are the primary actors in international affairs and that international politics is largely driven by states pursuing their interests. However, transnational environmental problems pose real problems for established notions about the nature and limits of state sovereignty. Moreover, international environmental problems are rarely caused by deliberate acts of national policy, but are rather unintended side-effects of broader socio-economic processes. A wide range and large number of **non-state actors**—including companies, local authorities, financial institutions, social groups, and individuals—are typically at least as important as states as actors in these processes.

It is true, however, that states retain a relatively privileged position in the international politics of responding to global environmental problems. Whereas states and their central governments do not generally directly control the economic, social, and environmental activities of concern, they do have sovereign authority to legislate within their territories and thus must play a central role in developing and implementing any environmental regulations. Thus, while the rise of environmental problems has brought state power and sovereignty into question, the responses to these problems may often extend and strengthen aspects of state authority and involvement in society. Moreover, to the extent that international agreements are important for co-operative responses to environmental problems, interstate diplomacy must come to the fore and states will be the legal parties to any treaties.

But, as already illustrated, even in relation to the politics of responding to international environmental problems, non-state actors typically also play a primary role. **Supranational organizations** such as the EU play a key international role alongside states, as well as being able to regulate activities within their member states. **International organizations**, international financial institutions, transnational organizations (such as industrial associations or environmental **non-governmental**

organizations (NGOs)), social movements, consumer groups, and scientists can all play a key role. Even in relation to international environmental negotiations and agreements, there are numerous examples of non-state actors playing central roles. Moreover, as states become enmeshed in international institutions or **regimes** established to tackle environmental problems, the policy process often acquires an important transnational or international dimension which in practice can substantially limit national autonomy.

Finally, implementing international environmental commitments typically has to involve a mixture of international institutions, states, and transnational and domestic organizations. Limiting atmospheric or sea pollution, for example, can rarely be directly carried out by government decision, like dismantling a missile or withdrawing a tank division in arms control. It involves a complex process of changing a wide range of often well-established industrial or social activities, involving a wide range of non-governmental groups, local authorities, and individuals.

Just as studies of international environmental politics oblige us to take full account of a range of non-state actors, and to review the significance and role of states, they also raise questions about the relationship between the 'international' and 'domestic' spheres of political activity. Several strands of International Relations theory have been developed on the basis of there being a radical distinction between these two spheres. However, global environmental issues involve a range of connections between local, national, and international processes that raise questions about such distinctions. This is true not only for patterns of causation and impacts of environmental problems in an interdependent world, but also for responses to such problems. Transnational organizations and networks—for example, environmental NGOs, multinational companies, financial institutions, scientists—typically play a relatively important role, and these by definition cut across international/domestic boundaries. International organizations are sometimes directly involved in local projects with only nominal involvement of the national authorities. The relationship between international organizations and institutions, states, and non-state actors within countries is normally complex in this context, and particularly when it comes to implementing international programmes for environmental protection.

A third issue for International Relations raised particularly by studies of international environmental issues is the relationship between knowledge, power, and interests. Scientific or expert knowledge often plays an especially important role in environmental politics. Careful scientific monitoring and modelling of the environment is usually needed to identify and assess problems and to frame debates about possible responses. 'Knowledge' helps to set agendas, affects patterns of influence and power, and shapes assessments by key actors of their priorities and interests. Typically, there is considerable scientific uncertainty—about the problems, impacts, and effective responses. Nevertheless, communities of scientists and experts can exert substantial influence. International environmental issues therefore provide an important area for exploring the ways in which power relations, patterns of interests, knowledge and learning processes, and values interact in determining outcomes. Attempts to explain the outcomes of international policy debates on environmental issues in terms of just one or two of these factors have normally failed.

The 'Tragedy of the Commons': An Instructive Parable

Examinations of global environmental change must involve enquiries into both the causes of change and responses to it. In practice, international responses to environmental problems will be shaped by understandings of the nature of the problem and of the human activities that are causing it. These vary greatly according to the particular issue and context. However, we have already emphasized the typical importance of broader socio-economic processes and political structures in generating international environmental problems. These shape and constrain the actions of the actors involved in the over-exploitation or degradation of environmental resources, obliging us to examine the context in which they are operating before assigning responsibility or developing responses.

In 1968 Garrett Hardin proposed a particularly influential model to explain why communities may over-exploit shared environmental resources even where they know that they are doing so and are aware that it is against their long-term interests

(Hardin 1968). This is known as the 'tragedy of the commons'. It is useful to introduce and explore this notion. It illuminates a way in which environmental problems may be generated and indicates some potential responses. It also helps to introduce some of the particular challenges of tackling *international* environmental problems.

The notion of the 'tragedy of the commons' can be explained using a hypothetical example—or 'parable'—of the use of common fish resources (see Box 16.3). In brief, the notion shows how it is possible that 'rational' individual actions can lead to 'irrational' collective practices resulting in catastrophic over-exploitation of common resources. Where, for example, there is unregulated and open access to an over-fished sea, each fisher continues to have an individual interest in maximizing their catch of fish. Each fisher gains the full extra benefit of catching additional fish, while the cost of over-exploitation is shared by all of the communities that fish the sea.

Box 16.3. The 'Tragedy of the Commons': A Parable

Consider a sea or large lake on which many local fishing communities depend as a source of food and income. Each fisher has an immediate interest in making as large a catch of fish as s/he can sell or eat, in order to improve his or her standard of living. For centuries, this arrangement has worked satisfactorily. Human populations were sufficiently low, and fishing technologies were sufficiently primitive, that there was no over-fishing. Gradually, however, living conditions improved and human populations grew, increasing the number of people fishing and also the demand for fish. At the same time, fishing technologies improved. In recent years, the sea or lake has been fished at unsustainable levels, and the total fish stock is falling.

In spite of this, each individual fisher continues to have an interest in maintaining or improving their catch. Each fisher gains the full extra benefit of catching additional fish, but bears only a small part of the extra cost of fishing a depleted fish stock because this cost is shared throughout the whole community. Even concerned and environmentally aware fishers may be sorely tempted to continue to make large catches: they know that even if they desist, others are likely to continue to maximize their own catches while they can. The 'tragedy of the commons', in this parable, is that this process continues until fish stock are destroyed along with the fishing communities that depended on them.

The 'tragedy of the commons' is that this depletion of common resources can continue remorselessly to their destructive conclusion, even if each organization involved is well-intentioned, well-informed, and exercising only its traditional and legal rights. Unilateral acts of public-spirited restraint are insufficient to tackle the problem. If the rest of the community continues in its old ways, the public-spirited suffer along with the selfish without even having benefited from the 'good times' in the meantime.

Many environmental problems of industrial society appear to have a similar structure. The owners of a factory have an interest in continuing to produce goods in the cheapest way, even if that involves dispersing untreated pollutants into the rivers or atmosphere. They gain most of the benefits of cheap production, while the pollution costs are uncertain and in any case shared by the whole 'downstream' community and other species of life. That is, the costs of pollution are **externalized**, since the polluter does not have to include them in its production costs. In this way some governments have been relatively tolerant of sulphur emissions from power stations in their territory, since the resulting acid rain was dispersed over a number of downwind states. Moreover, the damage caused by acid rain to buildings and forests typically does not appear in power-generation budgets, whereas the costs of cleaning the emissions would do so.

Preventing the Over-Exploitation of the Commons

The notion of the 'tragedy of the commons' demonstrates the vulnerability of open access resources to over-exploitation. In principle, a range of types of responses to such over-exploitation are available. One traditional response is to 'exploit and move on'. This has been the approach taken by 'slash and burn' agricultural communities in the tropical forests, cattle herdsmen in regions of Africa, and many international timber companies. Increasingly, however, this is no longer an option. The environment cannot recover (or is given insufficient time and space in which to do so), and there are fewer places to move on to.

Another type of response is 'privatization'.

Hardin himself drew the conclusion that the solution to 'tragedy of the commons' was a change in property rights, arguing that the problem of the commons is that they are 'owned' by everyone and that no one in particular had the authority or interest in managing them sustainably. Thus, in relation to the over-grazing of common land, for example, if ownership of the common grazing land were divided amongst the herd-keepers, each of these would have a direct interest in maintaining the value of his or her own land by grazing it at sustainable levels. Each would bear the full costs of any unsustainable practices, and each would have the ability to control how his or her land was managed.

In principle, the 'privatization' approach could play a significant role in improving resource management of the global commons. For example, the new **International Law of the Sea**, agreed in 1982, transferred effective ownership of much of the world's ocean resources to coastal states, with a broad obligation on these states to manage sustainably their Exclusive Economic Zones (EEZ) which stretched 200 miles from their coasts. However, in general, in order for this approach to be effective the new 'owners' would have to have a clear interest in the long term conservation and management of the resources under their control, and have the capacity and knowledge necessary for effectively carrying out their management role. In practice, such conditions would often not be met. For example, without regulation, it is not clear that owners of 'privatized' forest could be relied on to manage their forests sustainably rather than sell the timber and invest the proceeds in other businesses. Moreover, the approach would be difficult to apply to tackle resources or problems which by their nature do not respect artificial 'property' boundaries, such as atmospheric or sea pollution or migratory fish.

This brings us to the third type of approach to promoting environmental conservation and sustainable management of the commons: the establishment of systems of **governance** to prevent unsustainable or damaging practices. This approach tackles the problem by restricting access to shared resources rather than by changing patterns of ownership.

This third approach is in principle applicable to the widest range of problems. But it is clear that establishing any system of norms, rules, regulations, or taxes to tackle environmental problems is bound to be controversial, particularly when traditional rules of access have to be made more restrictive. Experience with attempts to prevent over-fishing, for example, has shown that some fishers can be expected to deny that there is an over-fishing problem. Others might dispute the maximum sustainable yield. Moreover, the ways in which fishing quotas or the burdens of implementing taxes or regulations are distributed amongst the community are also sure to be controversial. The benefits or costs of any environmental policy or regulation are bound to be distributed unevenly, leading to disputes about which regulations or policies to adopt and also to possible compliance problems in the future.

Such disputes and challenges are characteristic of all attempts to tackle environmental problems or to manage common resources. Nevertheless, the prospects for overcoming them and establishing effective management could be expected to be greatly improved if there is a strong hierarchical authority capable of taking decisions and enforcing them on dissenting groups. Thus most would agree that state regulation and control is a potentially effective approach to managing local or national resources within a well-developed state.

However, there is no world government with the power or authority to impose rules on the use of global commons. Authority for legislation and enforcement is dispersed amongst over 180 sovereign states, none of which can legally be obliged to obey an international law to which they do not subscribe. In this context, Hardin and many others have been deeply sceptical about the prospects for developing effective systems for **collective governance** of the global commons.

Examination of historical experience indicates that this may be unduly pessimistic. Ostrom and others showed that many communities have developed systems to manage common resources collectively (such as shared grazing lands, fisheries, and water resources) in the absence of strong hierarchical authority, and that these worked effectively for long periods (Ostrom 1990). Statements to the contrary, for example relating to the enclosures of common lands in England, are often historical myths, perhaps promoted by landlords who expropriated the lands for their own selfish purposes.

This focuses attention on the extent to which effective collective management systems can be developed and maintained. Such systems involve the development of collective **institutions**—in the form of sets of agreed principles, norms, rules, common understandings, organizations, consultation processes and such like—governing or shaping uses of the shared environmental resources. Ostrom and others examined the conditions for the successful formation of such institutions amongst local or regional communities in the absence of a central authority. Perhaps unsurprisingly, they found them to be similar in character to the conditions conducive to the establishment of **international regimes**, particularly those identified by liberal institutionalists, as discussed in Chapter 12.

Thus, for the global commons, the third approach to preventing a tragedy of the commons amounts to developing effective international environmental regimes. While this provides another illustration of the fact that the distinction between the 'international' and 'domestic' political spheres can be overstated, the challenges of developing international regimes can be expected to be greater than more local collective management systems. For example, the political, cultural, and economic diversity of the actors involved in using the global commons will normally be much greater than amongst collections of local communities sharing local resources, making it more difficult to establish good communications, shared understandings, common interests, and trust. Similarly, whereas Ostrom found that a relatively small and stable group of concerned parties was conducive to successful collective management of natural resources, the sheer number of actors involved is typically much greater at the international level.

Regimes and Radical Agendas

Much of the international politics of responding to global environmental problems has been focused around the development and implementation of international environmental regimes. In this context, an environmental regime is understood as an international social institution with (more or less) agreed-upon principles, norms, rules, procedures, and programmes that govern the activities and shape the expectations of actors in a specific environmental issue area. Note that there is nothing in this working definition that presumes that states or treaties necessarily play a primary role. Moreover, it accommodates the possibility that regimes as social institutions may cut across the international–domestic boundary. Environmental regimes from

Owen Greene

this perspective can provide an important framework for the interactions between international and domestic actors, and between power, interests, knowledge, and values.

An environmental regime provides a focus for the formulation and implementation of policies to tackle a particular international environmental problem, including the organization of relevant resource transfers and capacity-building activities. For many, however, regimes provide too restrictive and 'reformist' a framework for examining responses to global environmental change. Insufficient attention may be devoted to the activities and struggles of local groups around the world that do not explicitly engage with the regime politics or focus on particular environmental 'issue areas'. Similarly, environmental regimes have naturally tended to develop in issue areas where influential international actors perceive international co-operation to be most useful or essential. Thus, for example, efforts to address inherently global or transnational environmental problems have been given more international political attention than the widespread but relatively local problems of land or freshwater degradation that particularly affect the poor in developing countries.

Finally, regimes are typically developed to shape and restrict the activities of relevant actors in order to tackle specific environmental problems, not to challenge or transform the socio-economic or political structures and processes that generate the global patterns of development, resource distribution and environmental degradation. Thus an emphasis on regimes can be criticized by those for whom anything other than clearly transformatory agendas are inadequate. However, the scope of such agendas soon extends far beyond specifically environmental issues.

Key Points

- Each of the main approaches within International Relations theory provide important insights into international environmental politics. At the same time, environmental issues pose major challenges, particularly relating to: the role and significance of states and the notion of sovereignty'; the relationship between international and domestic spheres of political activity; and the the relationship between knowledge, values, power, and interests.

- The notion of the 'tragedy of the commons' provides an instructive model of how common resources can become over-exploited. In relation to global commons, it indicates that 'privatization' approaches could sometimes help to prevent such over-exploitation. However, such approaches have limited application, and may sometimes be counter-productive.

- The collective management of global commons in principle is more widely applicable. Historical experience indicates that effective collective management systems can develop without hierarchical authority, at the local, regional, and international levels, though the development of international management regimes poses particular challenges.

- Much international environmental politics can be said to focus around the development and implementation of international environmental regimes. However it is important to recognize the significance of relevant activities which do not directly engage with international regimes. Moreover, regimes are essentially 'reformist' and thus may be regarded as inadequate to the task of transforming the underlying socio-economic processes generating environmental degradation.

The Development and Implementation of Environmental Regimes

By the early 1990s, there were at least 120 multilateral environmental agreements (and hundreds of bilateral ones). As indicated in Chapter 12 (International Regimes), some of these must be regarded as 'dead letters'. Others are symbolic or weak, and have probably had little or no independent effect on the behaviour of relevant actors, or on the problem which they address. Nevertheless, case studies have shown that numerous environmental regimes have really been effective, in that they have changed behaviour in line with their aims and have at least helped to tackle the problems for which they were established (Haas *et al.* 1993; Levy *et al.* 1995). The Montreal Protocol for the Protection of the Ozone Layer is a prime example. Such regimes are dynamic: they tend to develop and change over time, according to changing needs and opportunities and as the international context develops. In this section we first outline the characteristic phases in the development of environmental regimes, and then illustrate some key issues through a short case-study of the regimes to protect the ozone layer.

Phases of Environmental Regime Development

The processes of regime development can, in principle, be divided into several phases: agenda formation; negotiation and decision-making; implementation; and further development. In practice, these phases often overlap and interact— particularly as a dynamic regime becomes established. Nevertheless, it is instructive briefly to discuss each phase in turn. The basic points apply to all regimes, but this discussion focuses particularly on those addressing environmental problems.

The **agenda formation** stage includes the processes by which the problem becomes recognized, emerges onto the political stage, is framed for consideration and debate by the relevant policy communities, and rises high enough on the international political agenda to initiate negotiations and decision-making processes. For environmental issues, it can often be difficult even to secure recognition that there is a problem. Without careful scientific monitoring and assessment, problems such as pollution, depletion of fish stocks, decline in biodiversity, and climate change, may emerge slowly and not become clear until it is too late to prevent major impacts or even disaster. This is a major reason why science and 'knowledge production' processes are particularly important in environmental politics, as discussed above.

Such scientific findings are used in attempts to place the issue on the political agenda and to frame the debates about possible responses. However this process is by no means straightforward. The science

enters a political arena, and is in any case often uncertain. Typically, alongside groups that want to highlight the apparent environmental risks, there are many groups who wish to deny the existence or seriousness of a problem. Whether and how the issue is firmly placed on the international agenda normally depends on a range of factors, and is highly contingent. NGOs have typically been particularly important in agenda-setting, often in implicit coalitions with concerned scientific bodies, international secretariats, and sympathetic governments.

Vivid or dramatic events or discoveries have played an important role in mobilizing public concern and capturing political attention. Measures against oil pollution at sea were stimulated by oil tanker disasters, even though routine spillage had been posing at least as wide an environmental threat. Similarly, public concern in the UK about North Sea pollution was only mobilized sufficiently to persuade the government to support more stringent international action when it was linked to an epidemic amongst the (photogenic) seal population. In the 1970s, UNEP felt obliged to present the problem of desertification in terms of (scientifically dubious) images of desert sand-dunes advancing on farming areas in order stimulate international action.

The stage of **negotiating and agreeing commitments** takes an issue from the point where it becomes a priority item on the agenda of relevant policy-making or negotiating fora to the point where international decisions are made about which policies and rules will be adopted to address the issue. It is at this stage that choices are made about commitments, policies, and measures. In principle, there are normally a number of possible ways to respond to a given environmental problem. The ways in which the main policy response options are actually framed, considered, and assessed are a key part of environmental politics, and constitute another important dimension to the relationship between policy, science, and 'knowledge'. Some approaches may be assessed to be more effective in tackling the problem than others. In this context, transnational 'knowledge-based' communities of experts with shared understanding of the problem and preferred policy responses (i.e. **'epistemic communities'**) have proved particularly influential.

Moreover, policies also differ in the ways they distribute the costs and benefits amongst different social groups and actors, and this also has a profound effect on the policy-making process and on final decisions. The problems of achieving agreement typically multiply as the number or participants and the variety of their interests increase. Thus questions inevitably arise about which interests it is most important to try to accommodate, and which interested parties it is necessary or desirable to include.

Successfully negotiating an effective agreement typically requires leadership. When powerful states or groups of states, such as the United States or the EU, adopt a leading role, the prospects for achieving an agreement improve greatly. For example, US leadership in achieving a whaling moratorium in the IWC was critical. In any set of negotiations, it is normally possible to identify 'leaders', that want an agreement and work hard to get one through a combination of active diplomacy, promoting the production and dissemination of relevant knowledge, or (informal or formal) sanctions or 'side payments'. In this way 'laggards'—states which are reluctant to achieve agreement or agree to effective commitments—may be persuaded to sign. Further, co-ordination and persuasion can be achieved of the (often large number) of states that are willing in principle to join an agreement provided it is not too costly, but are not going to work hard to achieve one.

Naturally leader states aim to shape the commitments in line with their interests. However, for most environmental issues, they do not have the capacity to force agreement entirely on their own terms. Lasting multilateral agreements cannot typically be achieved without all or most participants perceiving them to be achieving a common interest. Moreover, in any given issue area, there are likely to be *veto* states, without whose agreement and participation an effective regime cannot be established. Malaysia, Brazil, and other developing countries in whose territories the main tropical and sub-tropical forests are located are veto states in negotiations for global forestry and biodiversity conventions, and as discussed in Section 5 they successfully exercized their veto in negotiations in the early 1990s.

The **implementation** phase includes all of the activities involved in implementing the decisions and policies adopted in response to the problem. This can include: the incorporation of international commitments into domestic law; the development and operationalization of agreed programmes; and all other measures aimed at appropriately changing government, social and economic practices.

This stage is typically no less complex than the other two. On the contrary, experience shows that it is one thing to agree to international obligations, and quite another to bring them into operation and to achieve the desired effects on the behaviour of relevant actors. Those charged with implementing the decisions may lack necessary commitment or resources, and will typically interpret the decisions in their own ways. In practice, some countries tend to take legal obligations very seriously, whereas others tend to regard them as symbols of general intentions and a stage in an ongoing negotiation process, not to be interpreted too literally. Actors whose interests are substantially affected by the changes in policy can be expected to continue to try to influence the policy and the ways it is implemented. Compliance may leave much to be desired, and in any case the actual effects of decisions can be very different to the expected ones.

Whether or not international agreements are implemented can depend greatly on the nature of the commitments themselves. Governments may not try hard to implement if they believe themselves to have been coerced into an unfair agreement, which is a reason why it is important that agreements should be regarded as legitimate and, on balance, fair or in each participant's overall interest. The will to implement may be weak if parties suspect that others may not be complying, and attempting to 'free ride', thus whether or not the implementation and compliance of commitments can be monitored may be an important factor. Similarly, international systems to review countries' progress in implementation can help, by increasing awareness of obligations and by identifying and facilitating timely responses to any emerging problems. Finally, mechanisms to provide international aid can both increase countries' capacity to implement their commitments and increase their interest in doing so.

Finally, regimes usually need to **further develop** once they have been established in order to maintain or improve their effectiveness. Institutions and commitments may be strengthened and revised to adapt to changing circumstances, such as improved understandings of the problems and policy responses, or new political or economic challenges or opportunities. As outlined above and below, 'framework' conventions are explicitly designed to facilitate further development. More broadly, at least since the 1970s, such capacity to adapt has been widely regarded as a critical characteristic of effective agreements.

The Development and Implementation of the Ozone Regime

The Montreal Protocol, signed in 1987, stands at the centre of the regime to prevent the depletion of the ozone layer. It is widely regarded as one of the success stories in international environmental regimes. Before it was signed, global consumption and production of the main **ozone depleting substances (ODS)** was increasing rapidly. By the mid-1990s, this

trend had been halted and reversed, and most developed countries had virtually phased-out consumption of CFCs and halons (the most important ODS). Natural time-lags mean that the depletion of the ozone layer will nevertheless continue to get worse until the first decade of the twenty-first century, but thereafter it is expected gradually to recover—returning to its pre-1970 levels by about 2060.

The causes and risks of the damage to the ozone layer are outlined in Box 16.4, together with a brief chronology of the development of international commitments to tackle the problem. The following paragraphs highlight some key points illustrating the phases of regime development in this case.

The agenda formation phase of the regime began in the early 1970s. In 1974, Rowland and Molina—two US-based scientists—published an analysis

---

Box 16.4. Ozone Depletion and the Montreal Protocol

Ozone is a molecule consisting of three oxygen atoms. It is relatively unstable and quite rare in the atmosphere. Most of it is found in the 'stratosphere' between 10 and 50 kilometres above the Earth's surface—the 'ozone layer'. There it absorbs nearly all of the high-energy ultraviolet radiation (UV-B) from the sun, protecting plants and animals from its damaging effects. The ozone layer is highly vulnerable to destruction by chlorine, fluorine, and bromine, which are highly reactive chemicals. However, until recently, it was relatively safe from these chemicals. Precisely because they were so reactive, their atmospheric lifetimes were too short for emissions from the Earth's surface to have time to drift up as high as the ozone layer.

Unfortunately, when humankind manufactured CFCs and halons, they created highly stable compounds containing chlorine, fluorine, or bromine. Indeed, they were so stable that they did not react in the lower atmosphere, allowing a proportion of them to drift gradually up to the ozone layer. There they were broken apart by the incoming ultraviolet radiation, releasing the chlorine and other chemicals to act as catalysts in destroying the ozone. Each atom of chlorine, for example, can destroy an average of about 100,000 ozone molecules before it is removed from the stratosphere.

For complex reasons, the losses of ozone are worst in the spring. By 1995, stratospheric ozone levels over Europe and North America, for example, were about 10% lower than in the 1970s, and in places 20–50% lower. Over the Antarctic, a particularly deep 'ozone hole' appeared annually, virtually wiping out all ozone in thick bands of the ozone layer. This led to substantial increases in the intensity of UV-B radiation at the Earth's surface. UV-B depresses immune systems, causes

cataracts and skin cancers, damages the development of crops, and reduces the productivity of phytoplankton in the sea—undermining the marine food chain.

As awareness of the risks of ozone depletion grew in the 1970s, the USA, Canada, Sweden, and Norway unilaterally banned non-essential uses of CFCs. However it was not until 1985 that an international agreement was achieved: the Vienna Convention. This was a framework convention, which did not oblige parties to reduce their consumption of CFCs or other ODS. In 1987, the Montreal Protocol was agreed by 24 mainly industrialized states and the European Community. Parties to this protocol were obliged to cut their consumption of 5 types of CFCs by 50% by 1999 and to freeze consumption of three halons.

Between 1987 and 1995, the Montreal Protocol was progressively strengthened: most importantly in London (1990), Copenhagen (1992), and Vienna (1995). The 1990 London Amendment committed developed countries to phase out an extended range of ODS (including the halons, methyl chloroform, carbon tetrachloride, and a longer list of 15 CFCs) by 2000. Developing countries were committed to phase out by 2010, with assistance from a new **Multilateral Fund (MLF)**, created for the purpose. In 1992, the phase-out dates for developed states were brought forward to 1995, and new controls were agreed to phase-out HCFCs by 2030- which had been introduced as a less destructive substitute for CFCs—and to freeze use of methyl bromide. Finally, in 1995, developing countries also accepted some controls on HCFCs and methyl bromide. By that stage, the Montreal Protocol had become truly global, with over 155 parties.

arguing that CFCs emitted into the atmosphere could lead to the destruction of stratospheric ozone (Molina and Rowland 1974). Coming at a time of intense debates in the United States about the risks that emissions from high-flying supersonic aircraft might pose to the upper atmosphere, this hypothesis immediately attracted public attention. CFCs were first invented in 1928, as a coolant for refrigeration, but since the 1960s production had increased rapidly as further uses were found in: air-conditioners; expanded foams for cushions and insulation; solvents to clean electronics; sterilants; and aerosol propellants. Halons—related chemicals including bromine—were also increasingly used as fire extinguishers and suppressants. Environmental movements and the US Environmental Protection Agency (EPA) argued that at least non-essential uses of CFCs, as in aerosols, should be banned as a precautionary measure. DuPont and the other major chemical companies producing CFCs strongly disputed this, arguing that strong scientific evidence that the problem was real and serious should be required before any restrictions were introduced. The so-called 'spray can war' raged in the USA through the mid-1970s. After a US National Academy of Science report in 1976 judged that the risks were sufficiently large that precautionary measures would be justified, the balance of influence shifted towards the environmentalists and the EPA, and domestic legislation restricting CFC uses followed in 1978. These unilateral US actions had the effect of temporarily decreasing global CFC production, since the USA accounted for some 50 per cent of world consumption in the mid-1970s.

Internationally, Canada, Sweden, and Norway adopted a similar precautionary approach, and UNEP established an international programme of research on the risks of ozone depletion in co-ordination with the WMO. However, whereas these North American and Scandinavian countries became leaders in intergovernmental efforts to establish international restrictions, the countries of the EU and Japan—the other major producers and consumers at the time—were definitely 'laggards'. Their governments generally adopted the same position as their major chemical companies: the evidence of the threat to the ozone layer did not warrant substantial restrictions. Nevertheless, the pressures were sufficient to launch negotiations in 1980 amongst the major industrial states and the EU for an international convention to protect the ozone layer, under the auspices of UNEP.

Thus began the international process of negotiating and decision-making. In the first half of the 1980s, progress was extremely slow. During the first Reagan Administration, the USA showed little enthusiasm for developing environmental agreements in general and for pressuring the EU and Japan on ozone issues in particular. Under the charismatic leadership of Mostapha Tolba, UNEP played a key brokering role. In March 1985 the Vienna Convention for the Protection of the Ozone Layer was signed. However, this was a framework convention which obliged its signatories to do little more than to: establish the principle that international action should be taken as necessary; carry out further research; exchange information; and periodically meet to review the adequacy of commitments. Within two months, however, the discovery of a deep 'ozone hole' over the Antarctic was announced by scientists from the British Antarctic Survey. The political impact of this discovery provided a key illustration of the galvanizing effect of vivid or dramatic events in regime politics. The image of being exposed to UV radiation from space was already one that resonated with the general public. However, a surprise 'ozone hole' had much greater political impact than possible average depletion of 1–2 per cent per year, particularly when reinforced by NASA satellite images. Moreover, experiments in 1987 definitively showed the link between ozone depletion and the presence of chlorine: chlorine and ozone concentrations were measured while flying an aircraft through the ozone hole.

After this, DuPont, ICI, and other major CFC producers recognized that tough international restrictions on CFCs or other ODS had become virtually inevitable. Instead of continuing to oppose them, they focused on influencing any international agreement. In particular, they realized that stringent international controls on CFCs would create a market for substitutes, which they were in a better position to produce than their less sophisticated or wealthy competitors. By this time, Green parties and environmental movements were becoming powerful in most West European countries. In this context, governments that had previously vetoed stringent international controls had every interest in reversing their position. For example, the UK Prime Minister Mrs Thatcher removed her objections and declared her government to be a world leader in efforts to ban CFCs. The 1987 Montreal Protocol committed parties to cut their CFC consumption by 50 per cent by 1999, and within two years a consensus was emerging amongst developed western countries in favour of adopting a complete ban.

However, before a phase-out of CFCs and other ODS could be agreed, it was important to extend membership of the regime beyond developed Western states to include the Soviet bloc countries (as they were then) and developing countries. By the late 1980s production and consumption of CFCs in these countries were increasing rapidly, although still much smaller than in OECD states, and it was clear that countries like Russia, India, and China would have to join the regime if it was to be successful in the long term. The Soviet Union and its allies were persuaded to join (with some transitional concessions) at the end of the 1980s. However, developing countries refused to accept any commitments to phase-out CFCs and halons unless industrialized countries paid the 'incremental' costs they incurred in implementation. After much haggling, this was agreed in 1990. A Multilateral Fund (MLF) was established for this purpose, and developing countries agreed to phase out consumption of CFCs and halons by 2010.

From that stage, the processes of implementing and further developing the Montreal Protocol proceeded in tandem. Experience with implementing the Protocol's commitments, though complex, turned out to be easier and cheaper than many had feared. The chemical producers had a strong commercial incentive to develop substitutes quickly and also to monitor compliance amongst competitors. The Technology and Economic Assessement Panel (TEAP), established to advise on the availability and effectiveness of substitutes or alternatives for controlled substances, proved very effective in identifying opportunities and persuading users to accept them. Meanwhile the international Scientific Assessment Panel and the Environmental Impacts Panel produced authoritative reports on the need for ever more stringent commitments. UNEP continued to play a key role in brokering stringent agreements, supported by sympathetic states and environmental NGOs. In 1992 and 1995, the range of ODS controlled by the Montreal Protocol was widened, and phase-out dates for CFCs and halons were brought forward to 1995 and 1994 respectively for industrialized countries.

Implementation of these phase-outs proceeded on time and reasonably effectively in Western developed states, though there were continuing problems with black-market trading of illicit CFCs in the mid-1990s. The process turned out to be much more difficult in the 'countries with economies in transition' (the former Soviet bloc countries). The profound economic, social, and economic transitions in these countries meant that several of them neglected their Montreal Protocol commitments. The regime's systems for reporting and reviewing implementation picked this up in 1995, and co-ordinated international responses aimed at bringing the 'culprits' (primarily Russia, Ukraine, Belarus, and Bulgaria) into compliance as quickly as possible. This was done through a mixture of 'carrots and sticks', including conditional offers of international aid. Thus a crisis that could have substantially weakened the regime was averted, and the institutions of the regime played a key role in achieving this. As far as developing countries are concerned, the operation of the MLF was a continuing source of friction between them and donor countries. Nevertheless, after initial problems, many projects to phase out controlled substances in developing countries were underway by the mid-1990s, and in many cases these countries were on track to phase out significantly before their legal deadline. Moreover, procedures for reviewing implementation of MLF-funded projects were developed in the mid-1990s to verify that such phase-outs actually took place.

Key points

- The development of international environmental regimes can roughly be divided into four phases: agenda formation; negotiation and decision-making; implementation; and further development. Each of these phases is complex, and has its own characteristics which are to some extent particular to environmental issues.

- The regime developed to limit and reverse ozone layer depletion is widely and justifiably regarded as an important and effective environmental regime. Its development illustrates the character and complexity of each of these phases. It also demonstrates the close interrelationship between processes of implementation and further development, and the potential significance of international institutions.

The Rio Conference and its Outcomes

As introduced above, in 1989 the UN General Assembly decided to convene an 'Earth Summit' in Rio in 1992 in order to promote and develop sustainable development.

Preparing for Rio

The agenda for the **Rio Conference** soon developed. By the end of the 1980s, there was great international concern that anthropogenic emissions of **'greenhouse gases'**, such as carbon dioxide, methane, nitrous oxides, and CFCs, could be affecting the Earth's overall energy balance and causing rapid global warming and climate change. In 1988, an international panel of scientists (the Intergovernmental Panel on Climate Change (IPCC)) was set up under the auspices of UNEP and the World Meteorological Organization (WMO) to examine the risk of such climate change. On the basis of the IPCC's 1990 report (Houghton *et al.* 1990), representatives of 137 countries at the Second World Climate Conference in Geneva in November 1990 agreed that an international convention was urgently needed to address the problem. Negotiations began three months later, with a view to completing a **Framework Convention on Climate Change (FCCC)** in time for signing at the Rio Conference.

Similarly, there was also wide concern about the loss of natural habitats and the consequent rapid extinctions of many species of life. Between 1988 and 1990 UNEP had convened an group of experts to examine the issue, and negotiations for a **Convention on Biological Diversity** started in June 1991, working to the same timetable.

In addition, there was wide support in many industrialized countries for an international forestry convention to limit deforestation, particularly of tropical rainforests. However, this proposal was strongly opposed by some developing countries possessing such forests, such as Malaysia and Brazil, on the grounds that it was their sovereign right to use their forests as they chose—just as industrialized countries had done centuries before. In an effort to win African governments' support, Western governments agreed to support negotiations to establish a **Convention to Combat Desertification**. This was a priority issue for African countries, many of which suffered from land degradation in arid areas, and also one on which UNEP had campaigned since the mid-1970s. However most developed countries were sceptical about the value of a special desertification convention, regarding the issue as a problem of developing sustainable land-use practices. In the event, efforts to negotiate a forestry convention failed, and advocates had to settle for a set of **'Forest Principles'**. Meanwhile, negotiations for the Desertification Convention went ahead.

In addition to these specific conventions, attention focused on preparing agreements to define and promote the goal of sustainable development. Negotiations centred on preparing two main documents for agreement at the Rio Conference. The first of these was a statement of agreed principles, which later emerged as the **Rio Declaration**. The second document was to be a detailed programme of action for sustainable development, which became known as **Agenda 21**.

The Rio Conference

The 1992 Rio Conference turned out to be one of the biggest summit meetings ever held. Some 150 states were presented, and at one stage 135 heads of state were present. About 45,000 people attended, including government delegations, over 10,000 press and media people, and representatives of 1,500 non-governmental organizations. Non-governmental organizations had their own parallel conference in Rio, but were also entitled to attend the intergovernmental meetings (though with so many participants, space was restricted for NGOs and national delegates alike). The meeting attracted great public attention, and received enormous media coverage. The Rio Declaration, Agenda 21, and the Declaration of Forest Principles were all agreed, and the conventions on climate change and biodiversity were respectively signed by 154 and 150 governments. The Convention on Desertification was not ready in time, and was not agreed until June 1994. Nevertheless, it is customarily included amongst the Earth Summit agreements (see Box 16.5).

Box 16.5. The UNCED Agreements

The Rio Declaration proclaims 27 general principles to guide action on environment and development. They include principles relating to: national responsibilities and international co-operation on environmental protection; the needs for development and eradication of poverty; and the roles and rights citizens, women, indigenous peoples. For example, Principle 7 affirms the 'common but differentiated responsibilities' of developed and developing states in environmental protection. Principle 10 states that environmental issues are best handled with the participation of all citizens, at the relevant level, and thus public education, participation and access to information and redress should all be promoted. Principle 15 affirms that a precautionary approach should be adopted: 'lack of full scientific certainty shall not be used as a reason for postponing cost-effective measures to prevent environmental degradation.

Agenda 21 is a 400-page document with 40 chapters aiming to provide a programme of action for sustainable development. The chapters cover a wide range of topics, such as: promoting sustainable urban development; combating deforestation; biotechnology management; managing fragile mountain ecosystems; and hazardous waste management. Several chapters are on strengthening the role of 'major groups', including local authorities, trade unions, business and industry, scientists, women, indigenous peoples, youth, and farmers. The last 8 chapters address implementation issues, including financial mechanisms and institutional arrangements. The Global Environment Facility is to provide 'agreed incremental costs' to help developing countries implement aspects of the Agenda 21 programme. The Commission for Sustainable Development is established, to promote and review progress on implementation and to help to co-ordinate activities of UN Agencies in this context.

The Framework Convention on Climate Change (FCCC) was signed by 153 states, and subsequently came into force within 18 months, on 21 March 1994. It is a 'framework convention', establishing principles, aims, institutions, and procedures which should be subsequently developed. The declared objective of the FCCC, as stated in Article 2, is to 'achieve stabilisation of greenhouse gas concentrations in the atmosphere at a level that would prevent dangerous anthropogenic interference with the climate system. Such a level should be achieved within a time frame sufficient to allow ecosystems to adapt naturally to climate change, to ensure that food production is not threatened and to enable economic development to proceed in a sustainable manner'. Recognizing that developed states should take the lead, these states should as a first step 'individually or jointly return to their 1990 levels' of greenhouse gas emissions. However, this is not a legally binding obligation. The most important obligations in the FCCC are that parties must provide regular reports on: their national greenhouse gas emissions; their emissions projections; and their policies and measures to limit such emissions. These are then carefully reviewed and assessed internationally. This review process aims not only to stimulate negotiation of further commitments as required, but also to promote the development and implementation of national targets.

The Convention on Biological Diversity was signed by 155 states, and came into force on 29 December 1993. It is a framework convention, which aims to preserve the biological diversity of the Earth, through protection of species, ecosystems, and habitats, and to establish terms for the use of genetic resources and bio-technologies. Parties must develop plans to protect biodiversity, and to submit reports which will be internationally reviewed. The principles clarifying states' sovereign rights to genetic resources on their territory were highly contentious and thus vague and highly qualified: such rights were affirmed, provided that the fruits of such resources are shared in a fair and equitable way on terms to be mutually agreed.

The Forest Principles were the residue of the failed attempts to negotiate a forestry convention. It proclaims principles for forest protection and management while emphasizing that states have a sovereign right to exploit forests on their territory.

The Convention to Combat Desertification was not open for signature until June 1994, but it is nevertheless considered to be an UNCED agreement. It aims to promote co-ordinated international actions to address problems of 'land degradation in arid, semi-arid, and dry sub-humid areas resulting from various factors, including climatic variations and human activities'. It provides a code of good practices for the management of marginal lands, for governments of affected regions, and for donors. It aims to provide a framework for co-operation between local land-users, NGOs, governments, international organizations, funding agencies, and donor countries, but includes no binding obligations.

The Implementation and Development of the Rio Conventions

The 1992 Rio Conference was widely regarded as an overall success. However, its real impact could only be judged according to how the Earth Summit agreements and conventions were subsequently developed and implemented.

It is worth noting that the conventions on climate change and biodiversity were '**framework** conventions'. That is, they established basic aims, principles, norms, institutions, and procedures for co-ordinated international actions, including procedures for regularly reviewing commitments and if necessary strengthening them. However, the initial obligations on parties in the conventions were weak. Moreover, in order to achieve agreement in time for either of these conventions to be signed at Rio, it had proved necessary for many contentious or complex issues to be side-stepped or fudged. Thus many key rules, institutions, and procedures remained to be worked out before the convention could even begin to operate. Indeed, in the case of the Biodiversity Convention, even the aims and priorities of the agreement remained unclear. Thus, the Intergovernmental Negotiating Committees (INC) that were responsible for negotiating each agreement were immediately reconvened to sort out these issues before the conventions came into force.

Before they come into force, international treaties need to be **ratified** by a minimum number of parties (with this number being defined in the treaty). In the case of the climate convention, for example, ratification by 50 states was needed. The ratification process involves the relevant national legislature of each signatory state (such as the US Senate or the UK Parliament) confirming that the state will be legally bound by the treaty. It normally takes several years for enough countries to ratify a treaty before it comes into force (the new UN Law of the Sea, signed in 1982, did not come into force until 1994). However, the three Earth summit conventions came into force remarkably quickly: all within two years of being signed. The first Conferences of the Parties (CoPs) took place within a year later, by which time the great majority of UN member states (over 125) had become parties in each case. By the standards of most international agreements, this was an impressive pace, and it took intense negotiations for most of the key institutional and procedural issues to be sorted out in time.

The first CoP of the climate convention, meeting in Berlin in March 1995, decided immediately to begin negotiations to establish more stringent commitments on industrial countries to limit their emissions of greenhouse gases. By 1995 almost all OECD countries and the EU had unilaterally pledged themselves to aim at least to stabilize their greenhouse gas emissions at 1990 levels by the year 2000. Some states, such as Germany and the Netherlands, had declared to reduce their emissions by that time. By 1996, however, progress towards achieving these goals was mixed. It was clear that most states would need to take further measures even to be sure of achieving stabilization. In this context, the prospects for negotiating further, more stringent, commitments for industrial states were not promising.

An Alliance of Small Island States (AOSIS), threatened as they were with inundation as a result of sea level rise, advocated a 20 per cent reduction in industrial country emissions by 2005. However, oil-exporting OPEC countries—their nominal allies in the G7 group of developing countries—campaigned strongly against any substantial commitments for developed countries, fearing that emission reduction measures would reduce demand for oil, and thus threaten their incomes. Similarly, the EU and some other West European states broadly supported emissions reduction targets of 5–10 per cent by 2010, but several other developed countries, including the USA, Japan, Australia, and Canada, were reluctant to support any obligations requiring emission reductions. Former communist countries in Eastern Europe and the former Soviet Union were typically suspicious of any obligations that could impede their economic recovery, and several did not think it fair that they should be classed as developed countries when relatively wealthy states such as South Korea, and Malaysia were classed as developing countries and thus under no immediate pressure to limt their emissions

These debates highlight how complex equity issues rapidly become in global negotiations. The differences in circumstances of states within the groups of developed and developing states are in many ways as great as the differences between these groups. Even within Western developed countries, Southern European governments argue that their countries are comparatively poor and should not have to stabilize their emissions yet; Japan and others have argued that they should not have to accept the same percentage cuts in emissions as the USA, for example, because they have already implemented energy efficiency measures. Moreover, élites within developing countries live 'first world' life-styles, and in countries like Brazil, India, and China their number far exceed the populations of medium or small developed countries. Surely, some say, these groups should not be entirely exempt from pressure to adopt more 'climate friendly' lifestyles. However, any attempt in the name of equity to negotiate separate targets for each country, taking into account its individual circumsntaces, is a recipe for failure. Special pleading and complexity would bog the negotiations down. For this reason, it seems likely that the first steps in strengthening commitments to limit climate change will continue to adhere to simple North–South distinctions, as much in the interests of political pragmatism as of equity.

In the meantime, reports submitted by parties on their national greenhouse gas emissions and their initial measures to limit emissions were internationally reviewed. This process got off to a relatively good start, and helped to promote the implementation of measures to limit greenhouse gas emissions while negotiations were ongoing. By increasing transparency of national performance, they helped to promote awareness of inadequacies and successes and stimulate pressures and resources to make improvements. Nevertheless, it is clear the challenges involved in developing effective co-operative actions to limit climate change are immense. There is little prospect of achieving the immediate radical actions required to prevent at least substantial anthropogenic climate change. Making the climate change convention effective is clearly a long-term challenge.

In some ways, the Biodiversity Convention also appeared to get off to a reasonably prompt start. In fact, however, fundamental disputes about aims and priorities continued. Little progress was made on what many in the developed countries regarded as the primary objective: to protect natural habitats and thus the diversity of species of wildlife that depend upon them. Many developing countries had wider agenda: securing international financial and technology transfers to help with the establishment of gene banks as well as natural conservation, and to gain a share of the economic benefits of bio-diversity in general and bio-technology in particular, by securing intellectual property rights over any genetic resources from their territory and any products made from them. The discussions on these issues became deadlocked, so in 1995 parties decided to focus on negotiating a protocol on 'biosafety' and particularly the movement of genetically engineered organisms across borders. Whether or not this exercise proved to be useful, it would clearly do little to prevent loss of species or natural habitats.

Similarly, although the Convention to Combat Desertification came into force by 1996, it was primarily designed to encourage donor countries to provide aid and assistance to developing countries in dry regions that are facing problems of land degradation. However, the multilateral funding mechanisms remained to be formally established, and it was proving difficult to attract additional donor interest.

Agenda 21: Promoting Sustainable Development

The 1992 Rio Conference established several institutions to promote the overall implementation and further development of Agenda 21. The most significant of these were the Commission for Sustainable Development (CSD) and the Global Environment Facility (GEF), working in association with UNEP, UNDP, and other UN bodies. Clearly it was not expected that these institutions could directly implement Agenda 21, or force others to do so. Rather the hope was that they could help to stimulate or shape broader international or domestic processes in a useful way.

The CSD consists of representatives of 53 states, elected for three-year tems in a way that ensures equitable geographical representation. It began its work in 1993, and has met annually since then to review progress on different aspects of Agenda 21, with numerous preparatory meetings. Ministerial participation in these meetings has been substantial, giving the process more political weight than some had feared. Morever, non-governmental groups can participate in the proceedings, making each CSD meeting a sort of mini-Earth summit. Coalitions between environmental NGOs and sympathetic states have made the CSD a forum in which environmental agendas can be set and pursued.

Broadly, the CSD process has aimed to promote sustainable development in three ways. Its role in promoting co-ordinated approaches towards sustainable development by international agencies has had some real but modest successes. However, its second role of reviewing national reports on aspects of sustainable development may be of wider significance. The significance of the CSD process in simply stimulating governments to review their practices and prepare policies for inclusion in their national reports should not be underestimated.

Moreover, the CSD has provided a forum where governments can be called to account, for the contents of their policies or for the gap between these and reality. The presence of NGOs has helped to make this process more substantial.

The third role of the CSD process has been to follow-up on unfinished business of UNCED and to promote the formation of new regimes where opportunities arise. For example, after discussions on deforestation at the CSD, an intergovernmental panel was established to review the issues. In 1996, this lead to an agreement to begin international negotiations on a forestry convention: providing a second chance after the failure in the lead-up to UNCED.

Another aspect of follow-up to UNCED has been a series of follow-up summit meetings on particular issues such as population and development (Cairo 1994), social development (Copenhagen 1995), the role and rights of women (Beijing 1995), and urban development (Istanbul 1996). The significance of such summits is controversial, but they have helped to promote political awareness and concern, and to develop international networks of con-

cerned experts, NGOs, citizens groups, and local authorities, which can then hopefully become more effective in their local activities.

Although the Global Environment Facility (GEF) was established at UNCED as the financial mechanism for funding 'agreed incremental costs' of implementing the climate change and biodiversity conventions and for contributing to the implementation of Agenda 21, this was only on condition that it was restructured to prevent the domination by developed countries. This was achieved in 1994. The new GEF was to be administered by a Council on which developing and developed countries would be equally represented. Decisions were to be taken by consensus or, failing that, by a majority of *each* of the two groups of countries. Moreover, the new GEF was made more accountable and transparent, by allowing NGO access to documents and meetings.

GEF funds only amount to a few billion dollars ($3 billion was allocated for 1994–7), which is a tiny amount compared to the massive international flows of funds that take place through normal economic transactions, and also compared to the

---

Box 16.6. Key Concepts for International Environmental Issues

agenda-formation: the processes by which an issue or problem becomes recognized, emerges onto the political stage, is framed for consideration and debate by the relevant policy communities, and rises high enough on the political agenda to initiate negotiations or decision-making processes.

collective governance: non-hierarchical (in the sense of the absence of a central coercive power) systems of management or governance.

environmental regime: an international regime addressing an environmental issue.

epistemic communities: knowledge-based transnational communities of experts with shared understandings of an issue or problem or preferred policy responses.

framework convention: an international convention establishing principles, norms, goals, organizations, and procedures for consultation, decision-making and review, with provision for flexible subsequent revision or development of rules or commitments.

global commons: resources open for use by the international community, and not under the jurisdiction of any state, such as: oceans, atmosphere, deep sea-bed, Antarctica.

international institutions: sets of internationally agreed principles, norms, rules, common understandings, organizations, and consultations and decision-making procedures that govern or shape activities in a particular area.

implementation: carrying out adopted decisions or policies.

over-exploitation: the unsustainable exploitation of a resource.

sustainable development: economic and social development that meets the needs of the present without compromising the ability of future generations to meet their own needs; programmes which maintain an appropriate balance between economic development, social development, and environmental protection. In practice, this is a contested concept, in that groups with differing political, economic, social, and environmental perspectives disagree about its exact meaning.

tragedy of the commons: the over-exploitation of open-access resources by users 'rationally' pursuing their individual interests.

transnational: cutting across national boundaries; linking the international and domestic sphere. Thus, for example, transnational processes are non-state processes that cut across national boundaries.

funds needed to implement sustainable development. However, numerous relatively small GEF grants to developing countries and to former communist states have contributed significantly to the preparation of national plans to promote sustainability. Moreover, in such countries, modest funds can contribute significantly to 'institutional capacity-building' where local expertise or resources are lacking. GEF funds for large-scale projects have been much slower to flow, and are a continual source of friction between recipients and donor countries.

Overall, therefore, the UNCED institutions to promote implementation of Agenda 21 have had some limited significance. But it is clear that they have had only a marginal impact on the broader economic and social processes that drive patterns of development.

Key Points

- Three new conventions were agreed at the Rio Conference, aimed at limiting climate change, preserving biodiversity, and combating desertification. These were all framework conventions, designed to be developed and strengthened over time. They came rapidly into force, but by 1996 the development of the biodiversity and desertification regimes seemed to have stalled.

- The negotiations to develop further the climate change convention demonstrated the immense challenges involved in achieving a sufficient response to prevent substantial anthropogenic climate change, and also the complexity of equity issues in negotiations. Nevertheless, limited progress has been made in developing and implementing the climate change regime, not least in the development of review systems to promote improved environmental performance.

- The institutions established to promote the implementation of Agenda 21 have stimulated the production of national plans for sustainable development and provided a forum where plans can be reviewed and where networks of non-governmental groups, government representa-

tives, and international secretariats can develop and influence agendas. However, their influence on overall patterns of development has been small.

Conclusions

Environmental issues emerged in the late twentieth century as a major focus of international concern and activity. Many such problems are international or global, stimulating international political activities in response. Awareness and concern about such issues grew substantially since the late 1960s. Since the 1970s, a wide range of agreements, institutions, and regimes for international environmental governance have developed. Much international political activity related to the environment has focused on the development and implementation of these regimes, involving a wide range of actors and processes. Although established perspectives within International Relations theory provide important insights into the character and outcomes of such activities, they nevertheless pose significant new challenges. They raise questions about the significance and role of states in environmental politics, about the relationship between power and knowledge, and about the distinction between the 'international' and 'domestic' spheres of activity.

Historical experience shows that, alongside many failures, some effective institutions for collective management—or regimes—have been developed to help to prevent the degradation of 'global commons'. Moreover, these systems for international governance are no longer isolated regimes dealing with narrow problems. They form a complex of interlinked institutions shaping the activities and expectations of all relevant actors across a wide range of activities. The primary challenge for the 1990s and beyond is to shape patterns of development to promote sustainability, including preserving biodiversity and preventing damaging climate change. The UNCED agreements provide a framework for international efforts to promote and co-ordinate efforts to achieve this. But the challenges are immense.

QUESTIONS

1. In what ways has 'the environment' become a global issue in the late twentieth century?

2. What was the significance of the 1972 Stockholm Conference for international environmental politics?

3. What is meant by 'sustainable development', and why has this 'contested' concept become important in international environmental politics?

4. How does the study of international environmental issues pose particular challenges for International Relations theory?

5. What is the relevance of the notion the 'tragedy of the commons' to global environmental problems, and what approaches are available for preventing the over-exploitation of global commons such as the open seas, deep sea bed, atmosphere, and Antarctica?

6. 'The nature of international society makes the prospects poor for developing collective institutions that can effectively tackle international environmental problems'. Discuss.

7. How effective has the Montreal Protocol for the Protection of the Ozone Layer been?

8. What factors can contribute to (i) the formation and (ii) the implementation of international environmental regimes? Illustrate these factors with reference to the ozone layer and climate change regimes.

9. How important was the 1992 UN Conference on Environment and Development (UNCED, or the 'Earth Summit') for environmental protection and the promotion of 'sustainable development'?

10. What are the key characteristics of a 'framework' convention. Illustrate these with reference to some existing framework conventions.

11. How have 'north–south' issues shaped international environmental politics?

12. Assess the significance of non-governmental organizations in international environmental politics. How is their role affected by international environmental institutions and regimes?

GUIDE TO FURTHER READING

There are now many good books on international environmental issues and on the environment in international relations. The following books provide good introductions, at least up to the early 1990s: A. Hurrell and B. Kingsbury (eds.), *The International Politics of the Environment* (Oxford: Clarendon Press, 1992); C. Thomas, *The Environment in International Relations* (London: Royal Institute for International Affairs, 1992); P. Smith and K. Warr (eds.), *Global Environmental Issues* (London: Hodder and Stoughton, 1991); C. Thomas (ed.), *Rio: Unravelling the Consequences* (London: Frank Cass, 1994); J. Vogler and M. Imber (eds.), *The Environment in International Relations* (London: Routledge, 1996); and L. C. Hempel, *Environmental Governance: The Global Challenge* (Washington, DC; Island Press, 1996). A. Weale, *The New Politics of Pollution* (Manchester: Manchester University Press, 1992) provides a clear and stimulating discussion of issues and themes in environmental politics in general, including some discussion of the specifically international dimension.

There are a number of journals and yearbooks of particular value in this context. For example, *Environment* (Washington DC: Heldref Publications) is a monthly journal that provides detailed but accessible discussions of contemporary global environmental issues (broadly understood, as outlined above in this chapter). Useful annual yearbooks include: the WorldWatch Institute's *State of the World* (London: Earthscan); the Fridtjof Nansen Institute's *Green Globe Yearbook* (Oxford: Oxford University Press) and VERTIC's *Verification: Arms Control and the Environment* (Oxford: Westview Press).

On the development and effectiveness of international environmental institutions, O. Young, *International Governance: Protecting the Environment in a Stateless Society* (London: Cornell University Press, 1995) and P. M. Haas, R. O. Keohane, and M. Levy (eds.), *Institutions for the Earth: Sources of Effective International Environmental Action* (London: MIT Press, 1993) provide good thematic and empirical examinations. Much of the best and most influential work on international environmental issues has focused on particular issues or regimes. For example, R. E. Benedick, *Ozone Diplomacy: New Directions in Safeguarding the Planet* (London: Harvard University Press, 1991) provides a readable 'insider's' story of the international negotiations to establish the Montreal Protocol, and I. Rowlands, *The Politics of Global Atmospheric Change* (Manchester: Manchester University Press, 1995) and E. Parson and O. Greene, 'The Complex Chemistry of Ozone Agreements', *Environment*, 37: 2 (1995), 16–20, 35–43, examine the subsequent development of the ozone regime. The UNCED agreements are clearly outlined and examined by Grubb *et al* (1993). *See also*: D. Victor, K. Raustiala, and G. Skolnikof (eds.). *The Effectiveness of International Environmental Agreements* (Cambridge, Mass.: MIT Press, 1997).

17 Nuclear Proliferation

Darryl Howlett

READER'S GUIDE

This chapter identifies those factors which have made nuclear proliferation a global phenomenon since 1945. Over this period, the nature of nuclear weapons has transformed military and political relationships, while the global diffusion of nuclear and ballistic missile technology has meant that more states are in a position both to manufacture a nuclear weapon and deliver it over considerable distances. This chapter also reveals the complexities associated with the globalization of the nuclear proliferation issue. There are difficulties in determining both the motivations which lead to the acquisition of nuclear weapons and the capabilities that might be constructed once acquisition has occurred. This complexity has been made more acute as a result of the emergence of new proliferation concerns such as the dissolution of the former Soviet Union and nuclear smuggling. To add a further dimension, there are those who argue that nuclear proliferation is no bad thing as the spread of nuclear weapons may induce stability in conflictual regional situations. This contrasts with the traditional view which argues that further nuclear proliferation is likely to increase instability between states, raising further the prospect of nuclear war. Efforts have therefore been focused primarily on measures designed to prevent the spread of nuclear weapons known, collectively, as the global nuclear non-proliferation regime.

Introduction

The issue of nuclear proliferation represents one of the more marked illustrations of the globalization of world politics. The advent of nuclear weapons and their unprecedented capacity for wreaking destruction across national borders has transformed the globe. Although only five states are acknowledged as possessing nuclear weapons and the means to deliver them over vast distances, several others have the capability to construct nuclear devices at short notice and deliver them, if necessary, by increasingly sophisticated means. These developments have changed global politics radically since 1945 and created a situation where strategic nuclear interdependence is now a fact of life.

Concern about the spread of nuclear weapons has undoubtedly increased in significance on the global agenda since the end of the cold war, yet many of the factors which have made it a global issue have been underway for several decades. Knowledge of the enormous destructive affects of nuclear weapons against human populations, for example, dates back five decades to the bombings of Hiroshima and Nagasaki at the end of the Second World War. Similarly, the explosion which ripped apart the civil nuclear power plant at Chernobyl in the former Soviet Union in 1986 revealed the devastating effects of nuclear radiation and its potential for long-term damage across national boundaries when carried on the prevailing winds.

Equally as significant, in 1945 only the United States possessed the capability to manufacture a nuclear weapon and maintain control over all nuclear technology. Today, several states have acquired a capability to construct at least crude nuclear devices, either as a direct result of a dedicated nuclear weapons programme or as a consequence of the global diffusion of nuclear technology. A similar diffusion of ballistic missile technology has also meant that the capacity to deliver nuclear weapons across national boundaries is no longer the preserve of the few.

Developments stemming from the dissolution of the former Soviet Union have also raised unprecedented problems concerning nuclear proliferation. This was the first, and so far the only, case where an acknowledged nuclear weapon state had broken up. And it was this event, perhaps more than any other, which has done most to raise the profile of nuclear proliferation as a major issue on the post-cold war agenda.

One debate which has sparked considerable controversy since the early 1980s has been a thesis which asserts that the gradual spread of nuclear weapons to additional states is to be welcomed rather than feared. This thesis is based on the proposition that just as nuclear deterrence maintained stability between East and West during the cold war, so it can induce similar stabilizing effects on other conflictual situations. This assumption has not been held widely, however, as the conventional wisdom has been that more will be worse not better and that measures to prevent nuclear proliferation represent the best way forward.

Since 1945, efforts to prevent the spread of nuclear weapons have become known as the global nuclear non-proliferation regime. This regime comprises an integrated network of arms control and disarmament treaties and other standard-setting arrangements which today provides a comprehensive framework for the behaviour of states, international organizations and other actors in the nuclear area. The prevention of nuclear proliferation in the future will therefore be dependent upon the capacity of the global nuclear non-proliferation regime to deal effectively with the range of demands for nuclear weapons that are likely to emerge.

The Nature of Nuclear Weapons and their Effects

The Technical Basis of Nuclear Weapons

In order for any state to acquire nuclear weapons it must obtain the key nuclear materials necessary for their construction. The processes involved are highly complex and involve a wide range of scientific and technical skills.

Nuclear weapons derive their energy from either the splitting of atoms (so-called **fission** weapons), or their combination (so-called thermonuclear or **fusion** weapons). Only atoms with a large mass, such as uranium or plutonium (the fissile materials), are capable of being split, while fusion can only occur in atoms with a very small mass, such as hydrogen (deuterium and tritium). A fission weapon works through the creation of an uncontrolled nuclear reaction which literally splits the atoms. A fusion weapon is basically a fission

---

Box 17.1. **Nuclear Facilities**

Nuclear Reactors

A nuclear reactor contains a core of fissile material (the fuel) within which energy is produced by sustaining a regulated chain reaction. The fissile material used varies between reactor types, but it may be natural uranium (which contains 0.7% fissile U-235) or uranium which has been enriched to increase the percentage of U-235 to around 3%. Nuclear reactors also incorporate three other features: a means for regulating the chain reaction, such as control rods for absorbing neutrons; a moderator, surrounding the fissile core, which is used for maintaining the chain reaction by slowing down faster neutrons so they can more easily hit nuclei and initiate fission; and finally, a means for removing the heat produced from the reactor core by the chain reaction, which can also provide the steam to drive turbines and generate electricity.

Nuclear reactors have been developed for four main purposes: (1) to provide electricity for civil purposes; (2) for use as propulsion units in naval vessels, especially submarines; (3) for materials testing and research or experimental uses; and (4) to produce plutonium for military explosive purposes.

Five different nuclear reactor types currently exist: (1) Light Water Reactors (LWRs)—these use ordinary water as both a moderator and a coolant and are the most widespread type of reactor in use in the world; (2) Heavy Water Reactors (HWRs)—as the name implies this type uses heavy water as both the moderator and the coolant, and it is also the type used by the United States to produce plutonium for weapons purposes; (3) Gas Cooled Reactors (GCRs or MAGNOX)—these are moderated with graphite, cooled with carbon dioxide gas, and can run on natural uranium fuel, which is contained in a cladding called MAGNOX (magnesium oxide); (4) High Temperature Gas Reactors (HTGRs)—this type is cooled by helium gas, moderated with graphite, and runs on high-enriched uranium fuel (uranium enriched to 93% U-235); (5) Fast Breeder Reactors (FBRs)—this type has a core of high-enriched uranium or plutonium and pro-duces more fissile material than it consumes (hence, a 'breeder reactor'), it operates without a moderator and has a coolant which is normally a liquid metal such as sodium.

Enrichment Technology

Uranium must be enriched if it is to be used in certain reactor types and in weapons. This means that the concentration of fissile U-235 must be increased by physical, rather than chemical, means before it can be fabricated into fuel.

There are six main technologies for increasing ('enriching') the concentration of U-235: (1) Gaseous Diffusion—in this process uranium is converted into a gas and is then diffused through a porous nickel tube (a cascade), which results in the lighter gas molecules of U-235 passing through at a quicker rate than the heavier U-238 gas molecules; (2) Gas Centrifuge—this process uses centrifugal forces whereby uranium hexafluoride gas is passed through several rapidly spinning cylinders or centrifuges; (3) Becker Nozzle or Aerodynamic Separation—this involves forcing a mixture of hexafluoride gas and either hydrogen or helium through a nozzle which creates centrifugal forces to separate the U-235 from the U-238; (4) Laser Enrichment—this uses lasers to separate U-235 from U-238 and is the most advanced technology in development; (5) Electro-Magnetic Isotope Separation (EMIS)—this technique uses a high current beam of low energy ions and allows them to pass through a magnetic field created by giant electro magnets, this causes the lighter uranium isotopes to separate from the heavier ones; and (6) Chemical Separation—this form of enrichment exploits the fact that ions of the two uranium isotopes will travel across chemical barriers at different rates due to their different masses.

Reprocessing Technology

Reprocessing facilities separate, by chemical means, plutonium from the other fissile products which are found in the spent fuel discharged by a reactor.

weapon with a second, fusion stage added, the fusion process resulting from the compression and heating of the hydrogen atoms by the primary fission device.

Box 17.2. The Technology of Nuclear Weapons

Separate processes are required to obtain the two fissile materials needed to construct a nuclear weapon. uranium is found in nature and comprises 99.3% uranium 238 (U-238) and 0.7% uranium 235 (U-235). It is the latter isotopic form (that is, the U-235 has the same chemical properties as the U-238 but has a different atomic weight), which is used in a nuclear weapon. This involves the amount of U-235 in a quantity of natural uranium being increased to weapons grade by a process called enrichment so that it becomes 90%+ of the sample. Once a sufficient quantity of weapons grade U-235 has been accumulated to achieve a critical mass, defined by the International Atomic Energy Agency (IAEA) as 25 kilograms—although the amount could be smaller, then there is enough fissile material to construct one nuclear weapon.

Plutonium does not occur naturally. Rather, it is one of the end-products of the irradiation of natural or only very slightly enriched (2–3%) uranium in a nuclear reactor. Plutonium 239 (Pu-239) is thus the result of a controlled nuclear reaction process. And because plutonium is chemically different from uranium, the two materials can be separated by a process known as reprocessing. Once separated, Pu-239 is regarded as a very efficient fissile material because it has a smaller critical mass than U-235, and only 6 to 8 kilograms is needed for one weapon.

Nuclear Weapons Effects

The effects of nuclear weapons are considerable. Because of this, the United Nations Commission for Conventional Armaments in 1948 introduced a new category of **weapons of mass destruction** to distinguish them from conventional forms. This category included 'atomic explosive weapons, radioactive material weapons, lethal chemical and biological weapons, and any weapons developed in the future which have characteristics comparable in destructive effect to those of the atomic bomb or other weapons mentioned above'.

Nuclear weapons produce their energy in three distinct forms: **blast; heat or thermal radiation; and nuclear radiation**. Each form may result in extensive damage to human populations. Awareness of these effects stems from the two weapons dropped on Hiroshima and Nagasaki in 1945, which remains the only time nuclear weapons have been used. However, what is also known is that the weapons which destroyed these Japanese cities were relatively small in comparison to the destructive forces generated by later testing of thermonuclear weapons. The largest weapon of this kind known to have been tested was estimated to be a 58 megaton (58 million tonnes of TNT) device produced by the Soviet Union during the height of the cold war.

The long-term and widespread effects of nuclear radiation were also confirmed when, at 1.23 a.m. on 26 April 1986, a large explosion ripped the roof off the number four power unit at the Chernobyl nuclear complex in the former Soviet Union. The devastation caused by this explosion of an operating nuclear power plant shook the world. And while a much more serious nuclear accident was prevented by the bravery of those who dealt with the immediate aftermath, the long-term consequences were still profound. Nuclear radiation was carried on the prevailing winds across several national borders resulting in large numbers of animals having to be destroyed and humans well outside the initial blast area suffering varying degrees of radiation-induced illnesses.

The Global Diffusion of Nuclear and Ballistic Missile Technology

The Spread of Nuclear Technology

Since 1945 nuclear technology for civil and military uses has disseminated on a global scale. In 1945 only the United States possessed the technological capability to manufacture a nuclear weapon. By 1964, four other states had crossed the nuclear weapons threshold, an event traditionally understood as the testing of a nuclear explosive device. These states were the former Soviet Union (1949), the United Kingdom (1952), France (1960), and the People's Republic of China (1964). All five states have been defined by the Treaty on the Non-Proliferation of Nuclear Weapons (NPT) as Nuclear Weapon States, this being a state which 'has manufactured and exploded a nuclear weapon or other nuclear explosive device prior to 1 January 1967'. Although no additional state has officially been acknowledged to have exploded a nuclear weapon since China's first detonation, several states have acquired the technological capability to build such a weapon and at least one has detonated a nuclear explosive device.

There has also been a structural change in the civil nuclear trading market over the same period. For several years after the Second World War, the United States remained the pre-eminent nuclear supplier. By the 1970s, this position was challenged, first by European nuclear suppliers such as France and Germany, and then by Japan. Today, there are several nuclear suppliers with many more now emerging, such as South Africa and those republics which emerged from the former Soviet Union following dissolution.

With many nuclear suppliers, and with the downturn in the global nuclear energy market seeming set to continue for the foreseeable future, there is concern that the guidelines for international nuclear trade will not be upheld and that it will become easier for nuclear proliferation to occur. Although, for the most part, these concerns are unwarranted, as explained later in certain cases disagreements about the nuclear intentions of a state can create discord among suppliers.

The Increasing Sophistication of Nuclear Delivery

During the 1950s, nuclear weapons required large bomber aircraft designed specifically for the purpose of carrying these weapons to their target. As the technology for manufacturing ballistic missiles progressed, and as the potential for constructing nuclear ordnance which was light and small enough to be deployed on these missiles also grew, then the possibility of delivering nuclear weapons by ballistic missiles became feasible.

Ballistic missiles consequently represent the most sophisticated means of nuclear delivery and were once the preserve of a few technologically advanced states. But just as the diffusion of nuclear technology has become a global phenomenon, so the technologies to construct a ballistic missile have become more commonplace. Today, several states have space-launch capabilities or ballistic missile programmes under development. Should these programmes be linked to the delivery of nuclear ordnance, then more states will have the capacity to hit targets over far greater distances and, by implication, also widen their circumference of potential strategic conflict.

Key Points

- The nature of nuclear weapons and the dissemination of the capabilities to manufacture them around the world since 1945 makes the issue of nuclear proliferation a good illustration of the globalization of world politics.

- The end of the cold war and the dissolution of the former Soviet Union has meant that new problems concerning nuclear proliferation have emerged.

- A controversial debate has emerged over the merits, for and against, of the further spread of nuclear weapons.

- The collection of measures put in place to prevent the spread of nuclear weapons are known as the global nuclear non-proliferation regime.

- A major element of the nuclear proliferation process is the acquisition of the key technologies to produce fissile materials to construct either a fission (nuclear) or fusion (thermo-nuclear) weapon.

- The effects of nuclear weapons are considerable and are manifest in the form of blast, heat, and nuclear radiation.

- Since 1945, the spread of nuclear technology for civil and military purposes has meant that several states beyond the five which have an acknowledged nuclear weapons capability now have the capacity to produce nuclear weapons at relatively short notice, if they have not already done so.

- Over the same period the structure of the civil nuclear trading market has also changed leading to concerns that nuclear proliferation could occur because there are now more nuclear suppliers around.

- The diffusion of ballistic missile and space-launch technology has also created a situation where several states have the capacity to deliver nuclear weapons over considerable distances.

The Problem of Determining Motivations and Nuclear Weapon Capability

Motivations and Acquisition Processes

For much of the post-Second World War period the pattern of nuclear weapon acquisition established by the five acknowledged Nuclear Weapon States was considered to be the one most likely to be emulated by any future proliferating state. Traditional analysis of the motivational aspect of nuclear weapons acquisition consequently tended to focus on the strategic or political rationales which led first, the United States, and then the Soviet Union, United Kingdom, France, and China to seek nuclear weapons. The **strategic motivation** focused on the role that nuclear weapons played in the context of the Second World War and its immediate aftermath when initially they were seen as war-fighting/war-winning weapons. Later, attention shifted to the role that nuclear weapons played in deterrence, leading to the assumption that one of the principal motivations for acquisition was the deterrence of other Nuclear Weapon States. In addition to these strategic motivations, the **political benefits** that nuclear weapons conferred on those states with the wherewithal to manufacture them were also deemed significant: nuclear weapons were seen as the most modern form of weaponry and their custodians, by dint of their technological prowess, were automatically to be afforded a seat at the 'top table of international affairs'.

Inherent in traditional analysis of nuclear weapons acquisition was also a form of **technological determinism**, that states seeking a nuclear weapons capability would tread the same path as the five Nuclear Weapon States. Thus, new nuclear weapon states would develop dedicated military nuclear facilities, conduct an overt nuclear test, produce a stockpile of weapons, and finally, acquire an effective means for delivering the weapons to their target. While this explanation of the acquisition process and the motivations for embarking on a nuclear weapon programme is still relevant, over time, our understanding of the dynamics of nuclear proliferation have become more complex.

It is now more difficult to explain the phenomenon of nuclear proliferation by resorting to a single variable. Increasingly, it is necessary to consider a range of variables which may have an influence on nuclear proliferation decisions. These include such variables as: technological dynamics, the idea that the very availability of nuclear technology and a cadre of trained nuclear scientists encourages acquisition; domestic imperatives, the notion that domestic political events may compel a state towards nuclear weapons; diplomatic bargaining, that acquisition of a nuclear capability can be used to influence or bargain politically with both perceived allies and enemies; non-intervention, that a nuclear capability can deter or prevent intervention by other states; and finally, economic factors, the idea that the very possession of nuclear weapons enables a state to extract economic concessions as part of a political bargaining process.

Another feature of the nuclear proliferation puzzle which needs to be explained is the motivation which leads a state to abandon the nuclear weapon option (Mitchell Reiss 1995). This refutes the technological determinist argument that once a state acquires the capability to manufacture nuclear weapons it will automatically do so. A number of factors have been identified to account for a state's decision to move away from nuclear weapons acquisition, including: a change in strategic circumstances such as the forging or renegotiation of an alliance with a Nuclear Weapon State; the encountering of technical difficulties in constructing a nuclear weapon; or a perception that the acquisition of nuclear weapons may increase rather than reduce vulnerabilities.

To add further complexity, recent developments indicate that there is now also a need to focus attention at the sub-state level as the motivations of non-state actors may be different from those associated with states. During the first three decades of nuclear development the main focus of attention was the state. States had the wherewithal to acquire nuclear capabilities, nuclear commerce was conducted on a state-to-state basis, and it was states which entered into international arms control and disarmament treaties. Today, states are no longer the sole focus of attention when considering nuclear proliferation as increasingly the part played by non-state actors has become significant.

Studies conducted during the 1970s and 1980s on nuclear terrorism indicated that there were risks associated with particular groups acquiring a nuclear device or threatening to attack civil or military nuclear installations. One study conducted by The International Task Force on Prevention of Nuclear Terrorism concluded that it was possible for a dedicated terrorist group to build a crude nuclear device provided it had sufficient quantities of chemical high-explosives and weapons-usable fissile materials. More significantly perhaps, in terms of thinking about the risks involved, it was also felt that such a group would be more interested in causing panic and social disruption by making a credible nuclear threat rather than actually detonating a nuclear device and causing mass killing and destruction (Leventhal and Alexander 1987). Recent occurrences may have served to alter this latter judgement, though the issue must still be kept in perspective as the following examples may not be indicative of any new trend.

Analysis of the 1993 bombing of the International Trade Center in New York indicated that if the bomb had been planted on the other side of the pillar one or both towers might have collapsed, thereby causing massive destruction and potentially killing many thousands of people. Similarly, the attack against the government building in Oklahoma in April 1995 revealed the extent of damage and loss of life that a dedicated individual or group can wreak. While both these instances involved traditional methods of inflicting damage and terror, the use of nerve agents (chemical weapons) in an underground train network in central Tokyo in March 1995 to cause both death and widespread panic could represent a quantum change in methods if it is proven that a non-state actor was involved. This would be the first known use by any such group of a weapon of mass destruction, but it should also be stressed that it was still not a nuclear weapon that was used and this may be the telling point.

In addition to these factors, we are only now beginning to explore issues such as nuclear smuggling and the possibility that ethnic groups involved in civil conflict might seek a nuclear option to further their political or military objectives.

Nuclear smuggling has recently been given heightened international media attention since the disconcerting discovery that materials suitable for making nuclear weapons may be being trafficked by several different groups in increasing quantities. The problem here is that it is very difficult to determine the extent of the problem, between whom it is being trafficked, and for what purpose it is being acquired. A major concern is that while it is likely that some of the smuggling is being conducted by opportunist individuals or groups, there is also the possibility that Transnational Criminal Organizations have also moved in to create an international nuclear black-market operating across traditional state boundaries in weapons-related technologies (Williams and Black 1994).

The fear that ethnic groups involved in civil conflict might resort to nuclear threats has also become a feature of the post-cold war international security debate. The concern here is that the situations in which such threats might occur would be highly unpredictable. It would be very difficult to determine whether the leaders of these groups would act responsibly or predictably in situations where the political and military conditions were unstable. Moreover, the possession of a single or small number of nuclear devices might encourage usage or pre-emptive strategies because of fear of discovery.

Nuclear Capabilities

Closely paralleling the problems of analysing the motivational aspect are those associated with determining whether a state actually possesses a nuclear capability: that is, whether nuclear proliferation has actually occurred.

In 1974 India complicated the issue by conducting an underground test of what its government termed was a peaceful nuclear explosion (PNE). The idea of using controlled nuclear explosions for civil, rather than military, purposes had gained credence during the early years of nuclear development. It has been confirmed, for example, that the former Soviet Union actively used PNEs for civil engineering projects. But it is precisely because the technologies involved in PNEs are indistinguishable from those used in military applications, as the India test made apparent, that it raises problems of definition concerning nuclear weapon possession.

The case of South Africa also indicates that determining possession of nuclear weapon capability is far from straightforward. On 24 March 1993, the then President F. W. de Klerk announced that South Africa had produced six nuclear devices up until 1989 and had then dismantled them prior to signing the NPT. While this announcement confirmed what many had previously speculated, that South Africa did possess a nuclear capability during the 1980s, what it also confirmed was that a state did not actually need to test a nuclear explosive device to be in possession of a nuclear stockpile.

During the 1970s and 1980s four other states were grouped together with India and South Africa as 'threshold' nuclear weapon states. These were Argentina, Brazil, Israel, and Pakistan.

These states were uniformly regarded as having made significant progress in nuclear technology but had not accepted nuclear inspection by the IAEA on all the nuclear facilities and materials on their respective territories. Although the situation for three states has now changed—Argentina and South Africa have signed the NPT and Brazil has become a full party to the Treaty of Tlatelolco which seeks to make Latin America and the Caribbean a **Nuclear-Weapon-Free Zone** (NWFZ)—the other

three have not made any formal commitment not to acquire nuclear weapons.

What is also known is that during the 1960s and 1970s a few other states, in addition to the 'threshold' states, did embark on a nuclear explosive research programme before abandoning them. Sweden is perhaps the most documented of these states, but other cases have become public, such as the Republic of Korea's contingency plans in the 1970s for a nuclear option if the United States' nuclear guarantee began to waver.

Both Sweden and the Republic of Korea are now parties to the NPT. In determining nuclear weapon capability, this is a significant factor. All states which sign the Treaty have to subject all their materials to IAEA safeguards. This means that their entire nuclear programme is continually being inspected and monitored. To date, there has been no known case of diversion of nuclear materials from civil nuclear programmes under IAEA safeguards to a military weapons project. What these examples do indicate, though, is that around the world there are several other advanced industrialized states with large operating nuclear power programmes which could be used to produce quantities of fissile materials for military purposes if a political decision was taken to do so. The main barrier to nuclear weapon acquisition for what have been described as the **'virtual proliferators'** is therefore not technological but political. For example, in states such as Japan and Germany which have large nuclear power programmes, there are strong domestic, as well as international, political impediments to moving in the direction of nuclear weapons acquisition.

One of the most significant developments concerning the issue of nuclear capabilities in recent years, however, has stemmed from the break-up of the former Soviet Union in 1991. Prior to its demise, the Soviet Union had deployed a vast nuclear weapon complex throughout its entire territory. This complex included a large nuclear weapons arsenal which embraced both a large number of tactical and strategic systems and a sophisticated technical support infrastructure involving around 100,000 personnel. The collapse of the Soviet Union in 1991 therefore meant that both the nuclear arsenal and the technical infrastructure were spread around many of the now separate independent republics. Ensuring that this situation does not create a further spur to the spread of nuclear weapons has thus become a major task for those dealing with it.

Following the collapse, efforts were quickly undertaken to deal with the Soviet Union's nuclear weapons complex. In December 1991, the United States introduced its **Soviet Threat Reduction Act**, otherwise known as the Nunn-Lugar Safety, Security, Dismantlement (SSD) Programme. This Programme has sought to provide financial resources for the total denuclearization of Belarus, Kazakhstan, and Ukraine, three new independent states which, in addition to the Russian Federation (formally acknowledged as the legal successor state to the Soviet Union), were left with strategic nuclear systems on their territory after the break-up.

Agreement was also reached to ensure that all the tactical nuclear weapon systems formerly spread throughout Soviet territory were transferred to the Russian Federation. However, there ensued a tense period between 1991 and 1994 during which a series of negotiations were held with the governments of Belarus, Kazakhstan, and Ukraine over the future dismantlement of the strategic systems located on their territories. This culminated in agreement by each of the three parties, the last being Ukraine, to allow these nuclear systems to be transferred to the Russian Federation for dismantling and for the three states to become non-nuclear-weapon state parties to the NPT.

Dealing with the former Soviet Union's technical nuclear infrastructure has added further complexity and raised novel questions such as, how to ensure secure employment for all the personnel involved in the weapons manufacturing process? Are the physical protection measures around the nuclear installations adequate? What should be done with any surplus nuclear materials? And are the export controls operating in the new republics adequate now that the Soviet Union's overarching system has disappeared?

In response to this situation, efforts have focused on improving the prospects of those formerly working in the nuclear weapons complex, strengthening export control procedures in Russia and the new republics, and introducing tighter security arrangements around storage sites where nuclear weapons or fissile nuclear materials are located. One particular response has been to establish two International Science and Technology Centres (ISTC) in Moscow and Kiev to try and minimize any incentives for those scientists and engineers with detailed knowledge of the former Soviet Union's nuclear weapons to seek employment in similar programmes in

other states. Finance for other schemes to enable these personnel to be gainfully employed on civilian projects in their own countries has also been provided by the European Union and Japan.

All these schemes are thus part of a so far successful, overall effort to reduce the risks of nuclear proliferation stemming from the break-up of the Soviet Union. However, until this task is complete, which will take several years and considerable resources, the risk will remain.

Intentions

While being an NPT party may be a strong indication of nuclear intention, in a very few instances, such a commitment has been shown to be misleading.

Box 17.3. Iraq's Non-Compliance with the NPT

Following the Persian Gulf War of 1991, it was discovered that Iraq had developed a large-scale clandestine nuclear weapon programme which had not been declared to the IAEA. Iraq, as an NPT party, had declared a small nuclear power programme to the IAEA and this had been subject to safeguards. No nuclear material had been diverted from the declared programme and so the IAEA had no cause to suspect any wrongdoing. But the critical factor is that Iraq's clandestine nuclear programme would have remained undetected had its existence not been revealed following the Persian Gulf War. A United Nations Special Committee (UNSCOM) operating with the IAEA was subsequently established to determine the extent of Iraq's nuclear weapon effort, destroy it, and devise a long-term monitoring programme to ensure compliance in the future. The IAEA has also subsequently undertaken a comprehensive revision of its safeguards procedures so that any state embarking on an undeclared nuclear programme would stand a good chance of detection in the future.

Another state party to the NPT which has challenged the IAEA's right to conduct inspections on its territory is the Democratic People's Republic of Korea (DPRK). The DPRK had signed the NPT in 1985 but did not sign a safeguards agreement with the IAEA until January 1992, although under the terms of the Treaty this document should have been concluded within 18 months of signature. As required by the document, the DPRK presented the IAEA with an inventory of all its nuclear facilities and materials.

Because of the problems which had arisen over Iraq's non-compliance with the NPT, the IAEA wanted to ensure that the DPRK had in fact declared the full extent of its nuclear operation and began a series of inspections to verify the DPRK inventory. By early 1993 the IAEA had identified certain discrepancies in the material inventory which would need further investigation to ensure that no material existed on DPRK territory which had not been declared. In addition, information had also been provided to the IAEA which indicated the existence of two undeclared sites which were suspected of being nuclear waste depositories. In an effort to clarify the situation, the IAEA decided to initiate a special inspection in the DPRK, but this was refused. In retaliation the DPRK announced on 12 March 1993 its intention to withdraw from the NPT. By this stage speculation was rife that the DPRK had embarked on a clandestine nuclear weapon programme and that the balking at IAEA safeguards was because it had something to hide.

In the event, the DPRK did not withdraw from the NPT. But neither was the IAEA able to clarify the anomalies which had been identified in its nuclear inventory or visit the suspected sites, which the DPRK claimed were military bases and therefore not subject to inspection. What did emerge in October 1994 was an agreement between the United States and the DPRK (the so-called '**Agreed Framework**') which sought to ensure the DPRK's full compliance with the NPT by, among other things, providing it with Light-Water Reactors (LWRs) as an alternative to the graphite-moderated ('Magnox') reactors already in operation and under construction. The argument for this switch of technology is that LWRs are considered less proliferation sensitive than Magnox reactors. This is because unlike Magnox reactors, which were used in the early British nuclear weapon programme, LWRs are not regarded as good sources of weapon-grade plutonium.

The 'Agreed Framework' has not yet been implemented and if, and until it is, the DPRK's nuclear capabilities and intentions will remain a source of contention. What this situation, and the others identified above, indicate are the difficulties associated with both determining nuclear proliferation and the nature of the nuclear capabilities which have been produced if proliferation has occurred.

Another instance where the issue of nuclear intentions has caused difficulty concerns Iran, another NPT party. In the 1970s, German companies began constructing a nuclear power complex at Bushehr on the Persian Gulf coast. This complex was subsequently bombed during the Iran–Iraq war in the 1980s before it could be completed. In recent years Iran has attempted either to have the damage to the Bushehr nuclear complex repaired or obtain alternative nuclear reactors. This attempt has met with a mixed reception from potential nuclear suppliers.

The United States has made clear its opposition to any nuclear assistance to Iran because of concerns that the technology will be used for military not civil purposes: namely, a nuclear weapons programme. By contrast both China and the Russian Federation are prepared to trade with Iran and remain unconvinced by the protestations of the United States. The dispute over a nuclear supply agreement with Iran has thus soured relations between the Russian Federation and the United States and highlighted further the problem of determining nuclear intentions.

Key Points

- Over time, the characterization of motivations for acquiring nuclear weapons has become more complex.

- There are also difficulties associated with determining whether nuclear proliferation has actually occurred due to ambiguities surrounding peaceful nuclear explosions and the fact that a nuclear capability can be constructed without the need for a nuclear test.

- Six states beyond the five declared Nuclear Weapon States have acquired the technical capability to manufacture nuclear weapons, although three of these states have recently made commitments not to do so.

- There are several other states which have the capacity to manufacture nuclear weapons if they wanted, and a few actually embarked on military nuclear programmes before abandoning them.

- New concerns about the role of non-state actors have added a further dimension to the nuclear proliferation issue in the post-cold war context.

- The dissolution of the former Soviet Union has raised unprecedented issues concerning nuclear proliferation.
- Efforts to ensure the safe custody of former Soviet nuclear forces have been implemented and new centres have been established to improve the prospects of personnel who formerly worked in the Soviet Union's nuclear weapon complex.

- Iraq was the first NPT party discovered to be in breach of its Treaty commitments by operating a clandestine nuclear weapons programme, while the DPRK, another NPT party, has also challenged the IAEA's right to conduct nuclear inspections.
- Nuclear supply arrangements with Iran, also an NPT party, have raised difficult issues of nuclear transfers under the Treaty.

Will More Nuclear Weapons be Better or Worse?

More will be Better

One of the more controversial arguments concerning nuclear proliferation is the 'more may be better' thesis advanced by Kenneth N. Waltz in the early 1980s (Waltz 1981). This thesis has been restated more recently to account for any changes brought about by the end of the cold war. Waltz adopts a theory of nuclear spread rooted in neo-realist theory. This places considerable emphasis on structural causes, which emphasizes that the units of an international political system must tend to their own security as best they can. This includes acquiring nuclear weapons to deter potential adversaries.

Waltz's initial thesis was advanced at a time when the East–West strategic relationship was still predominant and caused controversy because of his assertion that the spread of nuclear weapons should be viewed in positive rather than negative terms.

Although Waltz has restated his thesis to account for changes brought about by the end of the cold war this has done little to change his underlying argument (Sagan and Waltz 1995). Moreover, his assertion that the spread of nuclear weapons to additional states may result in greater stability has met with some support. Analysts have argued, for example, that the acquisition of the capability to manufacture nuclear weapons by India and Pakistan has introduced a new cautionary factor in their decision-making and created a kind of strategic stability between these two neighbouring states. John Mearsheimer has also adopted a positive approach to nuclear proliferation by advocating that the world would be more stable if states such as Germany and Japan became nuclear-weapon states

(Mearsheimer 1990). Yet this view is not held widely with the predominant opinion opting for a 'more may be worse' assessment.

More will be Worse

In a recent debate between Waltz and Scott D. Sagan, Sagan argues that Waltz and Mearsheimer are 'proliferation optimists', a position which he suggests 'flows easily from the logic of rational deterrence theory: the possession of nuclear

---

Box 17.4. The Main Arguments of the Waltz Thesis

1. Nuclear weapons have spread rather than proliferated because these weapons have proliferated only vertically as the Nuclear Weapon States have increased their arsenals.

2. Nuclear weapons have spread horizontally to other states only slowly. However, this slowness of pace is fortunate as rapid changes in international conditions can be unsettling.

3. The gradual spread of nuclear weapons is better than either no spread or rapid spread.

4. New nuclear states will feel the constraints that nuclear weapons impose and this will induce a sense of responsibility on the part of their possessors and a strong element of caution on their use.

5. The likelihood of war decreases as deterrent and defensive capabilities increase and that nuclear weapons, responsibly used, make wars hard to start.

---

weapons by two powers can reduce the likelihood of war precisely because it makes the costs of war so great' (Sagan and Waltz 1995: 48). Sagan offers an alternative position to the proliferation optimists, rooted in organization theory, which leads to a more pessimistic view of nuclear proliferation and the prospects for future stability.

Box 17.5. Sagan's 'Proliferation Pessimism' Argument

1. Professional military organizations, because of common biases, inflexible routines, and parochial interests, display organization behaviours that are likely to lead to deterrence failures and deliberate or accidental war.

2. Because future nuclear-armed states are likely to have military-run or weak civilian governments, they will lack the positive constraining mechanisms of civilian control while military biases may serve to encourage nuclear weapons use, especially during crisis.

Sagan concludes that it is therefore optimistic to expect a rational deterrence arrangement to operate between any future new nuclear weapon states in the way that Waltz and others postulate. By contrast, Sagan argues that the most appropriate way forward is to encourage alternative arrangements which seek to reduce the demand for nuclear weapons and for strengthening the global nuclear non-proliferation regime, especially the NPT.

Key Points

- A controversial debate has emerged concerning the consequences of the further spread of nuclear weapons.
- Kenneth N. Waltz asserts that the spread of nuclear weapons will induce greater stability since new nuclear states will use their weapons to deter other states from attacking them.
- A contrary position adopted by Scott D. Sagan argues that instability will result from the further spread of nuclear weapons because of a greater potential for preventive nuclear wars and serious nuclear weapons accidents.
- Sagan, among others, has therefore argued in favour of measures to reduce the demand for nuclear weapons and for strengthening the global nuclear non-proliferation regime.

The Evolution of the Global Nuclear Non-Proliferation Regime

Early Efforts to Control Nuclear Weapons 1945–1970

Global efforts to constrain the spread of nuclear weapons began soon after the conclusion to the Second World War. In January 1946, the United Nations General Assembly passed a resolution which established the UN Atomic Energy Commission (UNAEC). The remit of the UNAEC was to make proposals for the elimination of nuclear weapons and the use of nuclear energy for peaceful purposes under **international control**. On 14 June 1946 the United States submitted the so-called Baruch Plan as its proposal for meeting the Commissions objectives. The Soviet Union also proposed a similar scheme, but unlike the Baruch Plan which envisaged international nuclear control arrangements, theirs was based on a national scheme for ownership and control of nuclear facilities. Neither plan was implemented, however, due to the radical differences between the United States and the Soviet Union over their respective methods for controlling atomic energy. During discussion of the plans, the United States moved to introduce unilateral legislation aimed at maintaining its monopoly over 'the use of atomic energy for the national defense'. The Atomic Energy Act (also known as the McMahon Act), passed on 1 August 1946, established the United States Atomic Energy Commission (USAEC) as the sole owner of all fissionable materials and facilities in the United States and prohibited all exchanges of nuclear information with other states.

The issue of international atomic energy control was revisited following President Eisenhower's **'Atoms for Peace'** speech on 8 December 1953. It was stressed that Eisenhower's proposal was not a disarmament plan, but an initiative to open the benefits of atomic energy to the world community. There were elements of the proposal which did have arms control and security considerations, however. Negotiations to implement 'Atoms for Peace' culminated in a Conference on the Statute of the International Atomic Energy Agency (IAEA) held at UN Headquarters in New York between September-October 1956. Following agreement at this Conference on the IAEA Statute, the Agency was inaugurated on 29 July 1957. But also camouflaged in Eisenhower's 1953 proposal was the idea for a cut-off in the production of fissile nuclear materials. At the time of Eisenhower's speech, a major concern of the United States was that the Soviet Union would soon possess sufficient fissile material, and thus several nuclear weapons, to have a capability of delivering a surprise 'knock-out blow' on United States' military forces before they had time to mobilize. One obvious way of slowing down the Soviet Union's capacity for this action was to constrain the amount of fissile material it had available for military explosive purposes. A key element of Eisenhower's speech was, therefore, a proposal that both the Soviet Union and the United States should transfer significant quantities of fissile material to the proposed IAEA for use in peaceful applications of atomic energy. This would have the consequence of reducing the fissile material available to the Soviet Union for military use.

The IAEA turned out to be a different organization to the one envisaged in the Baruch Plan or by President Eisenhower. From the outset, the IAEA was unable to fulfil the role of reducing the stockpiles of fissile material in the three then existing Nuclear Weapon States (Soviet Union, United Kingdom, and United States). Due to opposition from the Soviet Union and India, it was not until after the mid-1960s that the IAEA was able to implement a comprehensive monitoring system (known as **safeguards**) to ensure peaceful nuclear energy use.

One safeguards system which did become operational at an early date was that implemented by the European Atomic Energy Community (EURATOM) which came into being on 1 January 1958 as an organization of the European Community. EURATOM has since had the task of co-ordinating nuclear energy development within the Community and implementing a regional safeguards system to ensure that nuclear materials are not diverted 'to purposes other than for those which they are intended'. The EURATOM safeguards system covers all civilian nuclear energy activities in the Member States, including those of France and the United Kingdom. The military programmes of the latter states are excluded from EURATOM safeguards coverage, however.

In the late 1950s, the United States introduced a more overt proposal for a total halt in the production of fissile materials for military purposes. This was viewed as part of a package of measures to freeze, and ultimately reverse, the 'nuclear arms race'. The idea was to start with a Comprehensive Test Ban Treaty (CTBT) and a fissile material cut-off, follow this by measures to halt the production of additional nuclear weapons, and finally, initiate a phased dismantling of national stockpiles. Given the United States' superiority in the number of weapons and in the size of its stockpile of fissile materials at this time, the proposals were greeted with little enthusiasm by the Soviet Union.

The negotiations on a CTBT occurred in the context of a Soviet Union–United Kingdom–United States moratorium on nuclear testing, from 1958 to 1961, and against a backdrop of calls for these three Nuclear Weapon States, the only ones in existence at this time, to engage in nuclear disarmament. The negotiations did not result in an agreement, largely because the three states were unable to overcome differences concerning **verification**: namely, the provisions for a system of inspections and controls that could provide adequate assurance of detection of violation, especially for underground testing. However, in 1963 the Soviet Union, United Kingdom, and United States did agree the Partial Test Ban Treaty (PTBT) which prohibited nuclear testing in the atmosphere, in outer space and underwater. This meant that future testing by those states which signed the PTBT had to be conducted underground.

Since the late 1950s, attention has also focused on measures to prevent the nuclearization of specific environments and geographical areas. The first such measure was the Antarctic Treaty of 1959 which included provisions for banning all nuclear explosions in the Antarctic and the disposal of radioactive waste. This Treaty served as a model for later measures because it seeks to limit the spread of nuclear weapons by preventing their introduction into specific areas (a 'non-armament' provision) and its explicit provisions for peaceful utilization of resources. The first NWFZ applied to a populated geographic region is the Treaty for the Prohibition of Nuclear Weapons in Latin America (the Tlatelolco Treaty), which was opened for signature in 1967.

Between 1958 and 1968 attention began to focus more specifically on the dangers posed by additional states acquiring nuclear weapons. In 1961, the UN General Assembly adopted what became known as the **'Irish Resolution'** which called for measures to limit the spread of nuclear weapons to additional countries and for all states to refrain from transfer or acquisition of such weapons. A breakthrough in the negotiation of a non-proliferation treaty came as a result of Resolution 2028 adopted by the UN General Assembly in 1965. This was followed by a period of intense negotiation to resolve differences over such issues as nuclear sharing arrangements in the NATO and Warsaw Pact alliances. Finally, on 11 March 1968 the Soviet Union and the United States tabled a joint draft NPT treaty to the ENDC. Following amendments, the draft was passed by the UN General Assembly on 12 June 1968, opened for signature on 1 July 1968, and the NPT formerly entered into force on 5 March 1970.

During negotiation of the NPT a major debate surfaced over the linkage between nuclear security assurances and nuclear proliferation. Because of the NPT's distinction between a Nuclear Weapon State and a Non-Nuclear Weapon State (referring to all other states party to the Treaty not fulfilling the nuclear test criteria of 1 January 1967), some of the latter states were concerned that by signing the NPT they would be prohibited from acquiring nuclear weapons but at the same time they might be threatened or actually attacked by a state in possession of such weapons. To allay these concerns the Soviet Union, the United Kingdom, and the United States agreed UN Security Council Resolution 255 on 19 June 1968. This Resolution contains positive security assurances whereby the Security Council and 'above all its nuclear weapon State permanent members, would have to act immediately in accordance with their obligations under the United Nations Charter' in the event of a nuclear attack against a Non-Nuclear Weapon State. However, this initiative did not go far enough for the Non-Nuclear Weapon States concerned and the matter has remained a source of contention within the context of the NPT.

Efforts to Control Nuclear Weapons 1970–

Since 1970, the global nuclear non-proliferation regime has continued to evolve, strengthened by the international legal framework the Treaty provided. In March 1971, the IAEA negotiated its so-called INFCIRC/153 safeguards document which provides a model for all safeguards negotiated with parties to the NPT. Additional arrangements have also been established for the conduct of international nuclear trade. In 1971, the **Zangger Committee** adopted guidelines pursuant to the NPT which should trigger a suppliers' request to have IAEA safeguards applied on the transfer, especially those involving the equipment or material for the processing, use or production of special fissionable materials. But following the global expansion of nuclear power programmes, the increasing trade with non-NPT parties, and India's 'peaceful' nuclear explosion of 1974, it was decided by some suppliers that further export guidelines were necessary. The **Nuclear Suppliers Group** (NSG), formed in 1975 to respond to the new developments, agreed that additional conditions should be attached to sensitive nuclear exports, such as nuclear reprocessing plants.

At the First United Nations Special Session on Disarmament (UNSSOD–1) in 1978, China, France, the Soviet Union, the United Kingdom, and the United States all issued unilateral statements on so-called **negative security assurances** on the use or threat of use of nuclear weapons against non-nuclear weapon states. These assurances embraced specific qualifications related to each state's nuclear doctrine and security arrangements, but only China's was unconditional. China stated that it would not be the first to use nuclear weapons and undertook not to threaten to use nuclear weapons against any non-nuclear weapon state.

In 1987 seven missile technology exporters agreed to establish identical export guidelines to cover the sale of nuclear-capable ballistic or cruise missiles. Known as the **Missile Technology Control Regime** (MTCR), this supply arrangement seeks 'to limit the risks of nuclear proliferation by controlling transfers of technology which could make a contribution to nuclear weapons delivery systems other than manned aircraft' (Karp 1995).

The NPT also made provision for conferences to review the implementation of the Treaty to be held every five years. Since 1970, five review conferences have been held in 1975, 1980, 1985, 1990, and 1995. The review conference of 1995 also incorporated a new element, however. Article X.2 of the NPT had stated that 'twenty-five years after the entry into force of the Treaty, a conference shall be convened to decide whether the Treaty should be extended indefinitely, or for an additional fixed period or periods'. This meant that the 1995 Conference, held at UN headquarters in New York between 17 April and 12 May, was both a meeting to review the Treaty's implementation and to decide on its future duration.

Box 17.6. The 1995 NPT Review and Extension Conference

On 11 May 1995 the 1995 NPT Review and Extension Conference decided to extend the Treaty indefinitely without a vote. This extension decision was adopted in conjunction with two other documents and a resolution which established a set of principles and objectives for nuclear non-proliferation and disarmament; outlined new procedures for strengthening the Treaty review process; and called for the establishment of a Middle East zone free of nuclear weapons and other weapons of mass destruction within the context of the Middle East peace process. However, the parties were unable to agree a consolidated text on the review of the Treaty and, as in 1980 and 1990, the Conference concluded on 12 May without a final declaration.

The outcome of the 1995 NPT Conference was largely hailed as a success. As a result of decisions taken, the Treaty became permanent for its now 183 parties, new measures were established to strengthen future NPT review conferences and a plan of action for non-proliferation and disarmament was outlined. In particular, the Conference agreed to continue holding review conferences every five years, the next in the year 2000, and for the preparatory process in advance of these conferences to be strengthened. It also called for: the conclusion of a CTBT no later than 1996; negotiations on a fissile material cut-off convention to begin

immediately; the Nuclear Weapon States to make 'systemic and progressive efforts to reduce nuclear weapons globally, with the ultimate goal of eliminating those weapons'; further efforts to prevent the proliferation of nuclear weapons; additional NWFZ and security assurances to be agreed; implementation of procedures to strengthen IAEA safeguards and Treaty compliance; and greater exchange and use of nuclear energy for peaceful purposes.

While these initiatives will strengthen the global nuclear non-proliferation, the Conference may also have highlighted some underlying tensions which could have ramifications for the future. First, for the second review conference in succession, the parties were unable to agree a Final Declaration which must cast a doubt over how effective the future strengthened Treaty review process will be. Second, the Conference also did not systematically address the issue of Treaty compliance which might have been expected given the activities of both Iraq and the DPRK which both breached their non-proliferation obligations in the period 1990–5. Third, the Conference may also have served to exacerbate the regional difficulties associated with the Middle East and South Asia as one key issue which emerged during debate concerned the universality of the NPT. Much emphasis was placed on the need to get all states, particularly those with large, unsafeguarded nuclear programmes such as India, Israel, and Pakistan, to become party to the Treaty. Concerning the Middle East, in particular, Egypt and other Arab states had indicated their dissatisfaction with Israel, both prior to and at the Conference, because it had not acceded to the NPT. And although a resolution on the Middle East was concluded at the Conference, the future of nuclear relationships in the region was still left uncertain by its outcome. Finally, concern has already been expressed that adherence to the two documents on the principles and objectives for non-proliferation and disarmament and the future review process may not be very strong because the documents are considered binding in a political form only: they are not a legal obligation (Howlett, Leigh-Phippard, and Simpson 1996).

Key Points

- The global nuclear non-proliferation regime has been evolving since the end of the Second World

War when the Baruch Plan was submitted and later rejected at the United Nations.

- The IAEA and EURATOM have established both a regional and a global safeguards system.

- Attempts to negotiate a CTBT and a fissile material cut-off have been a perennial feature since the late 1950s. However, a number of NWFZs have been negotiated, beginning with the Antarctic Treaty in 1959.

- The NPT has become the cornerstone of the global nuclear non-proliferation regime.

- Both positive and negative security assurances have been negotiated but these have proven inadequate for many non-nuclear weapon states party to the NPT.

- In 1987, seven suppliers reached an agreement (the MTCR) to restrict transfers of nuclear-capable ballistic missiles and their related technologies.

Box 17.7. Chronology

Year	Event
1945	The United States detonates its, and the world's, first nuclear weapon
1946/7	The United States and the Soviet Union submit plans for the international control of atomic energy to the newly formed United Nations Atomic Energy Commission (UNAEC)
1949	The Soviet Union tests its first nuclear weapon
1952	The United Kingdom tests its first nuclear weapon
1953	President Eisenhower of the United States introduces his 'Atoms for Peace' proposal to the United Nations General Assembly
1957	The International Atomic Energy Agency (IAEA) was inaugurated
1958	The European Atomic Energy Community (EURATOM) begins its operation within the European Community
1960	France becomes the fourth state to test a nuclear weapon
1961	The United Nations General Assembly adopts the 'Irish Resolution' calling for measures to limit the spread of nuclear weapons to additional states
1963	The Partial Test Ban Treaty (PTBT) entered into force
1964	China becomes the fifth state to test a nuclear weapon
1967	The Treaty for the Prohibition of Nuclear Weapons in Latin America ('The Tlatelolco Treaty') was opened for signature
1968	The Treaty on the Non-Proliferation of Nuclear Weapons ('The NPT') was opened for signature
1969	The Tlatelolco Treaty entered into force
1970	The NPT entered into force
1971	The IAEA concludes the INFCIRC (Information Circular)/153 Safeguards Agreement and the Zangger Committee also adopted a set of nuclear export guidelines pursuant to the NPT
1974	India detonated a nuclear explosive device declared to be for peaceful purposes and the Nuclear Suppliers Group (NSG) is formed
1975	The First Review Conference of the NPT is held in Geneva, and by the end of the year 97 states had become party to the Treaty
1978	The First United Nations Special Session on Disarmament (UNSSOD–1) provides the forum for the five Nuclear Weapon States to issue unilateral statements on negative security assurances
1980	The Second NPT Review Conference is held in Geneva
1985	The Third NPT Review Conference is held in Geneva
1987	The Missile Technology Control Regime (MTCR) is established
1990	The Fourth NPT Review Conference is held in Geneva
1991	A United Nations Special Committee (UNSCOM) was established to oversee the dismantling of Iraq's undeclared nuclear weapon programme. The United States announces its Safety, Security, Dismantlement (SSD) Programme following the dissolution of the Soviet Union
1993	South Africa announces that it had produced six nuclear devices up until 1989 and then dismantled them prior to signing the NPT. The Democratic People's Republic of Korea announced its intention to withdraw from the NPT following allegations concerning its nuclear programme
1995	The Review and Extension Conference of the NPT is held in New York and the then 179 parties to the Treaty decide to extend the NPT indefinitely and also establish a new Treaty Review Process and a set of principles and objectives for non-proliferation and disarmament

- NPT review conferences have been held every five years since 1970, however, in 1995 the Conference was tasked with both reviewing the Treaty and deciding of its further duration.

- On 11 May 1995 the NPT was extended indefinitely, and while this has undoubtedly strengthened the global nuclear non-proliferation regime a number of challenges in the area of nuclear proliferation remain.

Conclusion

Since 1945, both the nature and the context of nuclear proliferation has altered markedly. At the end of the Second World War only the United States was in a position to build a nuclear weapon, but since then knowledge of how to make nuclear weapons has diffused to a global level. This has been coupled, throughout this period, by profound changes to global politics which culminated in the momentous dislocation which occurred in the former Soviet Union following the end of the cold war.

As a result of these developments, nuclear proliferation has become a major issue on the global agenda. Yet, understanding the dimensions and complexity of this issue will represent a major challenge in the years ahead. Traditional analyses of nuclear proliferation have tended to focus on the motivations which compel states to acquire nuclear weapons, but the examples identified in this chapter indicate that determining nuclear motivations, capabilities, and intentions is not straightforward. Moreover, the outbreak of inter-communal conflict, and the collapse of some states in the post-cold war world has meant that the traditional interstate focus of nuclear proliferation may have to be revised as it is not inconceivable that non-state actors may seek a nuclear weapon capability. The consequences of an ethnic group engaged in inter-communal conflict obtaining a nuclear option is likely to be considerable—would the motivation be nuclear blackmail, deterrence, warfighting, or a strategy linked solely to political ends? Similarly, recent acts indicate that the assumptions associated with nuclear terrorism may be in need of some revision if the groups involved also consider that a nuclear capability may further their political objectives.

What might done to reduce the dangers stemming from nuclear proliferation? Some analysts advocate that the spread of nuclear weapons cannot be controlled so the most appropriate way forward is to try to manage the diffusion of nuclear capabilities to additional states so that stabilizing deterrent relationships can evolve. The difficulty with this strategy is that it places enormous faith that the process can be managed without breakdown and that the deterrent relationship will ultimately produce stability. In addition, what happens when many states have acquired nuclear weapons, will deterrence operate in a world of 20 or more states with nuclear weapons in their inventory? It may be conjectured that the problems with what used to be described as 'coming to terms with life in a nuclear-armed crowd' are likely to be more complex and more dangerous than those currently faced. For, at the very least, the numerical increase in the number of states which possess a nuclear capability raises the prospects of a nuclear conflagration, no matter whether it is started by design, by inadvertence, or by accident.

Another recent strategy for dealing with nuclear proliferation, which is currently being implemented in NATO, is that of collective defence, or **counter-proliferation** as it is known. This strategy emphasizes the use of defensive measures for dealing with potential nuclear threats, although it has not been agreed whether these arrangements should also include ballistic missile defences. Although it is prudent to consider the defensive measures that may be necessary for coping with nuclear proliferation, this strategy can only be a partial remedy. A more comprehensive strategy for dealing with nuclear proliferation would be to strengthen further the global nuclear non-proliferation regime. Today, this regime embodies measures which are aimed at the non-acquisition, the non-use, and the eventual elimination of nuclear weapons globally. While the latter objective represents the most encompassing solution for dealing with nuclear proliferation in the post-cold war era it is also likely to be the most difficult to accomplish: but, ultimately, herein lies the challenge.

QUESTIONS

1. What properties make nuclear weapons different from conventional forms?

2. What are the implications of the global spread of nuclear and long-range delivery vehicle technology?

3. How have the motivations for acquiring nuclear weapons changed since 1945?

4. In what ways has it become more difficult to determine whether nuclear proliferation has actually occurred?

5. Does the non-state actor represent a new nuclear proliferation challenge?

6. What have been the main nuclear proliferation concerns stemming from the dissolution of the Soviet Union?

7. What are the main arguments for and against the spread of nuclear weapons?

8. Were the early efforts to control nuclear weapons doomed to failure?

9. In what ways, if any, has the NPT made a contribution to preventing the spread of nuclear weapons?

10. How can the global nuclear non-proliferation regime be strengthened?

GUIDE TO FURTHER READING

Allison, Graham, Carter, Ashton B., Miller, Steven E., and Zelikow, Phillip (eds.), *Cooperative Denuclearisation*, CSIA Studies in International Security, no. 2 (Cambridge, Mass.: Harvard University Press, 1993), an excellent study of the measures undertaken by the United States and the states of the former Soviet Union towards 'cooperative denuclearisation'.

Bailey, Kathleen C., *Doomsday Weapons in the Hands of Many* (Champaign, Ill.: Illinois Press, 1991), this book was one of first post-cold war assessments to highlight the dangers of nuclear proliferation.

Bukharin, Oleg, 'Nuclear Safeguards and Security in the Former Soviet Union', *Survival*, 36: 4 (Winter 1994–5), a very useful analysis of the problems of maintaining control over nuclear facilities and materials in the former Soviet Union.

Burrows, William, and Windrem, Robert, *Critical Mass: The Dangerous Race for Superpowers in a Fragmented World* (New York: Simon and Schuster, 1994), this is a more journalistic account of the dangers stemming from nuclear proliferation.

Dunn, Lewis A., *Containing Nuclear Proliferation*, Adelphi Papers 263 (London: Brassey's for IISS, 1991), provides a concise, authoritative analysis of nuclear proliferation following the end of the cold war.

Fischer, David A. V., *Stopping the Spread of Nuclear Weapons: the Past and the Prospects* (New York and London: Routledge, 1992), a very good overview of the evolution of nuclear non-proliferation policies by a former Director-General for External Affairs of the International Atomic Energy Agency.

Frankel, Benjamin (ed.), *Opaque Nuclear Proliferation* (London: Frank Cass & Co., 1991), argues that while the NPT may have prevented the open acquisition of nuclear weapons, this situation has given rise to a new, second-generation or 'opaque' pattern of nuclear proliferation.

Ham, Peter van, *Managing Non-Proliferation Regimes in the 1990s* (London: Pinter, 1993), a thoughtful analysis of how to strengthen arms control regimes in the future, especially the nuclear non-proliferation regime.

Howlett, Darryl, and Simpson, John, 'Nuclearisation and Denuclearisation in South Africa', *Survival*, 35: 3 (Autumn 1993), provides an account of the reasons why South Africa embarked on a nuclear deterrent programme and then abandoned it.

Howlett, Darryl, Leigh-Phippard, Helen, and Simpson, John, 'After the 1995 NPT Renewal Conference: Can the Treaty Survive the Outcome?', in John B. Poole and Richard Guthrie (eds.), *Verification Report 1996: Arms Control, Peacekeeping and the Environment* (Boulder, Col.: Westview Press, 1996), analyses the debate which occurred at the Conference to decide on the extension of the NPT in 1995 and the implications of the decisions taken at that Conference for the future of the nuclear non-proliferation regime.

Karp, Aaron, *Ballistic Missile Proliferation: The Politics and Technics*, (Oxford: Oxford University Press for SIPRI, 1996), this is an authoritative analysis of the impact of the spread of ballistic missiles on international security and of the policies designed to try and stem the proliferation of these weapon systems.

Leventhal, Paul, and Alexander, Yonah, *Preventing Nuclear Terrorism* (Lexington, Mass., and Toronto: Lexington Books, 1987), although somewhat dated this volume still provides one of the few comprehensive analyses of the dangers of nuclear terrorism.

Mazarr, Micheal, 'Virtual Nuclear Arsenals', *Survival*, 37: 3 (Autumn 1995), this article explores the desirability and feasibility of the world moving to a situation of 'virtual' nuclear disarmament, not disarmament in the traditional sense but rather a situation where all assembled, ready-for-use nuclear weapons are banned and pushed into the background of global politics.

Mearsheimer, John, 'Back to the Future: Instability in Europe After the Cold War', *International Security*, 15: 1 (Summer 1990), this article has provoked a major debate about the implications of the end of the cold war for European security, particularly concerning the impact of the further spread of nuclear weapons to states in the region.

Meyer, Stephen M., *The Dynamics of Nuclear Proliferation* (Chicago: University of Chicago Press, 1984), a standard text on the motivations for acquiring nuclear weapons.

Potter, William, 'Before the Deluge? Assessing the Threat Of Nuclear Leakage From the Post-Soviet States', *Arms Control Today*, (1995), a sobre assessment of the nuclear problems and dangers stemming from the dissolution of the Soviet Union by one of the leading authorities on this issue.

Reiss, Mitchell, and Litwak, Robert (eds.), *Nuclear Proliferation After the Cold War* (Washington, DC: Woodrow Wilson Center Press, 1994), a well-informed and comprehensive appraisal of the affect of the cold war's end on the prospects for nuclear proliferation and for policies for dealing with it.

Reiss, Mitchell, *Bridled Ambition—Why Countries Constrain their Nuclear Capabilities* (Washington, DC: Woodrow Wilson Center, 1995), is an excellent account of the reasons why states decide not to acquire nuclear weapons even though they may have the capability to do so.

Sagan, Scott D., *The Limits of Safety: Organizations, Accidents and Nuclear Weapons* (Princeton: Princeton University Press, 1993), this book provides a sombre reminder that in the nuclear area things can go wrong with potentially devastating consequences.

Sagan, Scott D., and Waltz, Kenneth N., *The Spread of Nuclear Weapons. A Debate* (New York and London: Norton & Co., 1995), is the text of the 'great debate' between Waltz and Sagan on the affect of nuclear proliferation for future international security and stability.

Scheinman, Lawrence, *The International Atomic Energy Agency and World Nuclear Order* (Washington, DC: Johns Hopkins University Press, 1987), is the standard text on the history of the IAEA and the role this organization has played in nuclear non-proliferation.

Shaker, Mohamed I., *The Nuclear Non-Proliferation Treaty*, vols. 1 and 2 (London: Oceana, 1980), remains the key text on the negotiation of the NPT.

Simpson, John, and Howlett, Darryl, (eds.), *The Future of the Non-Proliferation Treaty* (New York: St Martin's Press, 1995), this book covers the debate on the extension of the NPT in 1995 by those involved in the decision-making process.

Spector, Leonard, McDonough, Mark with Medeiros, Evan, *Tracking Nuclear Proliferation: A Guide to Maps and Charts* (Washington, DC: Carnegie Endowment for International Peace, 1995), an authoritative and easy to read compendium of the regional dynamics of nuclear proliferation.

Waltz, Kenneth N., *The Spread of Nuclear Weapons: More May Be Better*, Adelphi Paper 171 (London: IISS, 1981), this Adelphi Paper provoked a heated debate when it first appeared because it challenged the conventional wisdom concerning the spread of nuclear weapons.

Williams, Phil, and Black, Stephen, 'Transnational Threats: Drug Trafficking and Weapons Proliferation', *Contemporary Security Policy*, 15: 1, (1994), this article was one of the first to highlight the transnational dimension of the nuclear proliferation problem following the end of the cold war and the dissolution of the Soviet Union.

18 Nationalism

Fred Halliday

READER'S GUIDE

Nationalism, as a system of belief, an ideology, and as a political movement has been one of the formative processes in the creation of the contemporary world. As an ideology it provides a set of ideas about the organization of humanity into communities, about the appropriate political form for organizing these, and about how relations between states representing nations should be conducted. Nationalism has occasioned many disputes in social science in general, and in international relations in particular: some of these concern the explanation of why nationalism became such a worldwide phenomenon, others concern the difficulties of reconciling nationalist claims with the requirements of international order. Often regarded as a thing of the past, nationalism has been both resistant to, and in some ways promoted by, processes of globalization. The ultimate paradox of nationalism is that while, as an ideology, it stresses the distinct character of states and peoples, it is itself a result of a global process whereby all countries are incorporated into a single political and normative system.

Nationalism and Globalization

Nationalism, as both ideology and social movement, has been one of the formative processes of the modern world. Yet until relatively recently, the topic of nationalism was not covered in most introductions to international relations. Nationalism was seen as a thing of the past, a cause of wars in Europe up to 1945, a relic of colonialism in the Third World, an irrational if necessary feature of international relations. It had been left behind as a result of the establishment of international peace between the great powers and the independence of former colonial countries. It was generally assumed that states would resort less and less to nationalism in dealings with each other and would, instead, use the new institutions of international order, be they the UN or the European Union, to promote greater cooperation. Globalization, seen as a form of closer integration of states and societies, was expected to further this process: differences mattered less between states, populations became more open to cooperation and trade, and even identities and loyalties, hitherto based on the nation state, were being affected. Indeed nothing could be seen as more contrary to the spirit of globalization than nationalism.

This approach is now no longer tenable, and there are many who would argue a contrary case. Nationalism, in both the developed and developing worlds, has been very much in evidence, be this in the demands of peoples for independence or greater autonomy within states, or in protests about migration and free trade. In relations between established states nationalism is invoked as a basis for territorial disputes, war, or for economic advantage. In contrast to the earlier period, when the emphasis in domestic and international politics was on convergence, on universalization, even the creation of a single world community, there is now much more stress on the importance of what distinguishes people—on tradition, identity, authenticity, the politics of difference.

The implications of this for globalization are many. In the first place, it is clear that globalization sets in train different, often contradictory, processes. By creating a world market and flows of goods, technology, and people between states it also provokes responses, and resistance, by those who feel their interests are threatened. This is as true in developed countries, for example in hostility to migration or free trade, as in Third World countries who feel they are being overwhelmed by the developed world. Nationalism can therefore, in the first instance, be seen as a *reaction against* globalization. But in another sense nationalism is also a *product of* globalization. On the one hand, the upsurge in nationalism of the 1980s and 1990s reflects the failure of other forms of state-building, above all in the former multi-ethnic countries of the communist world. After the collapse of Soviet communism in 1991 four states disintegrated along national lines—the USSR, Czechoslovakia, Yugoslavia, and Ethiopia. Twenty-two new states came into existence. A central reason for this process was the impact on the hitherto insulated communist world of social and economic pressures from the West. In a world of globalization, peoples began to demand not integration into larger states but **secession**, independence, and access to the world market on their own terms. On the other hand, the collapse of communism also led to another form of nationalist drive, that for **national unification**—evident in Germany, Yemen, China, Korea. The link between globalization and nationalism in the one case is **fragmentation**, through secession, while in the second case it was through **unification**, through fusion.

The argument on nationalism and globalization can, however, be taken back much further, to the very formation of the modern international system itself. Nationalism, as a doctrine, calls for the establishment of separate states. It invokes the distinct culture and history of peoples. It is, therefore, about how **unique** peoples are. But the doctrine itself has spread across the world over the past two centuries as a part of an international process: as a result of global changes, old forms of solidarity and loyalty have been broken down and a new idea has been promoted and diffused. This diffusion has itself been promoted by the transformation of the international system: the increasing integration of the world market, the establishment of European colonial empires, the rise of movements of resistance to these empires, the world wars, and the spread of democracy. The paradox is that nationalism, the doctrine that proclaims the separateness of peoples, has spread because of, and in reaction against, the international and globalizing trends of the past two hundred years.

Box 18.1. Globalization and Nationalism: Contradictory Processes

Factors opposing nationalism:
- shared prosperity
- economic integration
- migration
- travel and tourism
- employment abroad
- global threats
- world-wide communications
- end of belief in economic sovereignty

Factors promoting nationalism:
- loss of control to foreign investors
- hostility to immigration
- fears of unemployment
- resentment at supranational institutions
- dislike of alien cultures
- fears of terrorism and subversion
- hostility to global media
- attractions of secession

This link between nationalism and the modern international system is, however, more than historical. It is also **normative**, that means concerned with values, with ideas of how people **should** live, and to whom they **owe obedience**. Nationalism has, through this spreading across the world, become the main justifying or legitimizing doctrine of the international system itself. Prior to the modern period, states were justified by reference to their rulers, their dynasties, and their religion. The spread of nationalism has removed this justification and produced instead a system in which states are justified on the grounds that **they represent their peoples**. From this we get the modern term 'nation-state', which implies that all states can, and do, represent a people. We also get the principle of **national self-determination**, according to which every nation has the right to decide on its own fate, to be independent, or, if not, to choose freely to be part of a larger state. This has meant that all the principles of international order, law, legiti-

macy, derived originally from other bases, are now justified by reference to this principle. Nationalism has become the ethical, moral, basis of international relations so much so that the body grouping the states of the world is called the United Nations.

Key Points

- Nationalism only fully recognized as relevant by International Relations in the past two decades.
- Nationalism both opposed to globalization and a product of it.
- Spread of nationalism a result of the transformation of the international system over the past two centuries.
- Nationalism now the moral basis of states and of the international system.

Nationalism as Ideology

Nationalism, like many other terms in social science, such as 'democracy', 'revolution', 'liberalism', or 'socialism', is a broad one, and is used to describe two quite distinct things: **a political doctrine** or **ideology**, i.e. a set of political principles that movements and individuals espouse, and **a social and political movement**, a tendency that has, over the whole globe and for the past two centuries, affected all societies and transformed their politics. It is important, in this as in the other cases, to keep discussion of the two separate.

As an ideology nationalism has, like the other

concepts mentioned above, many variants and permits of no easy one-line definition. This is all the more so because, unlike most other political doctrines, nationalism has no clear founding theorist, no classical text which others can refer to, or argue about. It is what philosophers sometimes call a 'cluster-concept' i.e. an idea with several elements usually attached. One of the major analysts of nationalism, Anthony Smith, has provided a clear set of seven themes which comprise the core doctrine, what we can term here 'the cluster', of nationalist ideology. Another writer, Ernest Gellner, has indeed provided succinct definition: 'Nationalism is primarily a political principle, which holds that the political and the national should be congruent' (Gellner 1983: 1). This can be said to mean that nationalism is above all a moral principle, which *claims* that nations do exist, that they should coincide with, i.e. cover the same people as, political communities and that they should be self-ruling. Nationalism as an ideology is, therefore, above all a moral or normative principle, a belief about how the world is and should be.

Box 18.2. The Core Themes of Nationalist Ideology

1. Humanity is naturally divided into nations.
2. Each nation has its peculiar character.
3. The source of all political power is the nation, the whole collectivity.
4. For freedom and self-realization, men must identify with a nation.
5. Nations can only be fulfilled in their own states.
6. Loyalty to the nation-state overrides other loyalties.
7. The primary condition of global freedom and harmony is the strengthening of the nation-state.

Source: Anthony Smith, *Theories of Nationalism* 2nd edn. (London: Duckworth, 1983), 21.

One of the claims of nationalism is that individual 'nations' and indeed the very sentiment of nationalism have existed throughout time or for at least hundreds of years. The invocation of history is very central to the whole nationalist view of the world: ideas of the 'ancient', the 'primordial', the 'traditional', the 'age-old' are commonly invoked. But the doctrine itself is of more recent origin, and is a result of changes in the international system during the latter part of the eighteenth and the first part of the nineteenth centuries. The word 'nation', or equivalent words in other traditions, has existed for many centuries, variously describing what today would be called tribes, peoples, groups of subjects of a monarch, communities. Some idea of **community**, with its own history and identity, and often its own language or religion, has existed in all cultures. However, the contemporary usage of the word 'nation' and its associated doctrine 'nationalism' dates from the eighteenth century. It

can be seen as having been created in three, separate but interlinked, phases.

The **first phase** is associated with the thinking of the **Enlightenment** and in particular with the principle of the self-determination of communities, i.e. the idea that a group of people have a certain set of shared interests and should be allowed to express their wishes on how these interests should best be promoted. Derived from the ancient Greek idea of the *polis*, or political community, this idea was most influentially expressed in the thinking of Jean-Jacques Rousseau. Rousseau laid the basis for modern ideas of democracy and the legitimacy of majority rule. Later democratic thinkers, notably John Stuart Mill, added to this with their stress on representative government as being the most desirable form of political system: once the idea of representative government is accepted, as a means of realizing in a collective form the principle of individual self-determination, then it is a short step to the idea of the self-determination of nations.

The **second phase** in the evolution of the idea of nationalism came with the French revolution of 1789: the opponents of the monarch called themselves *la nation*, i.e. 'the nation', meaning by this the community of all French people irrespective of previous title or status. Here the concept 'nation' expressed above all the idea of a shared, common, equal citizenship, the unity of the people. The slogan of the French revolution 'Liberty, Equality, Fraternity' embodied this idea: perhaps the most common cry of the revolution was *'Vive la Nation'*, 'Long Live the Nation'. The concept of 'nation' was, therefore, tied to the principle of **equality** of all those living within states, to an early concept of democracy. This evolution in France was paralleled in the Americas, North and South: in the revolt against British rule in the North (1776–83), and in the later uprising against Spanish rule in the South (1820–8). Here the basis for revolt was political—i.e. rejection of rule from the imperial centres in Europe by a group of people, a settler élite, drawn from similar ethnic and linguistic backgrounds to those they were rejecting, but opposed to the denial of their political rights and of the self-determination of the community they represented.

This democratic and political conception of 'nation' was then joined by its **third**, and final, component, the German romantic idea of the *Volk* or people, a community based not so much on political identity but on history, tradition and culture. In essence, the idea of the *Volk*, promoted by such thinkers as Herder and Fichte, argued that humanity was divided up into separate peoples whose distinctiveness and identity could be discovered through investigation. Just as scientists were mapping the plants, minerals, and animals of the world, and as linguists were mapping the different languages of the world, so it would be possible to identify the different peoples of the world, each with its own character.

Out of the combination of these three trends there emerged, by the early nineteenth century, the political doctrine we recognize today as nationalism. One of those who most vigorously expressed it was the Italian Giuseppe Mazzini. For Mazzini nations were a given, with their national territory, and should have independence. The Italian case involved the unification of hitherto fragmented entities. But Mazzini also espoused two other elements of what has come to be our modern concept of nationalism. One was the *moral* conception of the nation, according to which each individual not only belongs to a nation, but also owes the nation unquestioning obedience (see Box 18.2, point 6). In this way earlier concepts of loyalty, patriotism, identification with the community became part of the modern state system. The other idea which Mazzini promoted was the idea of a *'family of nations'*: if the world was divided up into nations, then they could, through identification and self-determination, be encouraged to acquire independence. The result would, he expected, be peace between nations, on this new basis. For the French writer Ernest Renan nationalism was 'a daily plebiscite', a process by which a community, created by history, could constantly reaffirm, by its continued existence, its self-determination and its wishes.

Box 18.3. **Mazzini on Nationhood**

'. . . the divine design will infallibly be fulfilled. Natural division, the innate spontaneous tendencies of the peoples will replace the arbitrary divisions sanctioned by bad governments. The map of Europe will be remade. The Countries of the People will rise, defined by the voice of the free, upon the ruins of the Countries of Kings and privileged castes. Between these Countries there will be harmony and brotherhood. And then the work of Humanity for the general amelioration, for the discovery and application of the real law of life, carried on in association and distributed according to local capacities, will be accomplished by peaceful and progressive development; then each of you, strong in the affections and in the aid of many millions of men speaking the same language, endowed with the same tendencies, and educated by the same historic tradition, may hope by your personal effort to benefit the whole of Humanity.'

Source: J. Mazzini *The Duties of Man* (London, 1907), as quoted in Evan Luard, *Basic Texts in International Relations* (London: Macmillan, 1992) 198–9.

Key Points

- Nationalism as ideology—a normative idea; nations exist objectively and should have the right to self-determination.

- Modern idea of nationalism a combination of (1) Enlightenment and liberal concepts of self-ruling community; (2) the French revolutionary idea of the community of equal citizens; (3) German conceptions of a people formed by history, tradition and culture.

- Nationalism both an idea of a history, a tradition, and one of obligation

---

Nationalism as a Movement

From its origins in the late eighteenth century nationalism, evolving into the ideology we recognize today, has spread across the whole world. In the early nineteenth century, Europe saw the emergence of nationalism in Greece, Germany, Italy, and Ireland, and later in the multi-ethnic empires of Central and Eastern Europe—the Austro-Hungarian, Prussian, Russian, and Ottoman empires. Under pressure from within and without these empires gradually ceded to demands for independence until, in the cataclysm of World War I, all four empires foundered and a map of newly independent states was created. In Western Europe a fifth multi-national entity was forced to concede independence to one of its rebellious regions, when the British granted independence to Ireland in 1921.

World War I was the occasion on which the principle of **national self-determination**, hitherto confined to Europe and the white élites of the Americas, was now proclaimed as a universal principle, in radical *revolutionary* form by the Bolshevik Revolution in Russia (1917) and in *liberal* form by President Woodrow Wilson of the USA (1918). Prior to World War I many nationalists had argued that their rights could be realized short of secession—through the creation of federal or regional rights within states, or by forms of cultural autonomy: in some countries—Czechoslovakia, Belgium, Switzerland—this remained so. But after World War I self-determination came, increasingly, to be associated with full independence. It seemed that the era of national self-determination and of the emergence of the 'family of nations' envisioned by Mazzini was at hand. But this was not to be, for three reasons.

In the **first** place, the European colonial powers refused to allow the subject peoples of Asia and Africa to attain independence: it was only after World War II, which weakened the victors as well as destroying the vanquished, that Britain, France, Holland, and Belgium became disposed to granting independence to their Third World colonies, a process that lasted through the 1950s and 1960s. In the **second** place, nationalism, where it did achieve fulfilment, led not to peace between states but to conflict, dictatorship, and in the end world war: if there was a 'family of nations' it was a very quarrelsome and unhappy family indeed. One reason for this was the fact that peoples, in the sense of communities with one language or religion, were often mixed up with each other, or had competing historical claims: there was no simple fit between national and territorial claims. Disputes over territory and communities led in the Balkans and elsewhere to inter-ethnic quarrels that no amount of mediation or redrawing of frontiers could resolve. The independence of Ireland, conceded by Britain but excluding six of the thirty-two counties of the island, led to similar rancour. More explosively still, the nationalism that came to dominate in two European countries, Germany and Italy, was one based on an idea of power aggrandisement, military expansion and, in the case of Germany, forceful revision of frontiers and the genocidal liquidation of Jews. All of this served to underline the dangers, as much as the benefits, of nationalism.

There was, however, a **third** reason for the failure of the 1918 hopes being realized—one that became more evident after World War II. This was that, even in states that were independent and where the issue of national identity and self-determination had supposedly been recognized, new tensions began to develop. This was at first evident in the developed world, in Western Europe and in the USA, where from the 1960s onwards new demands for national self-determination, or the recognition of ethnic diversity and rights within states, began to emerge: among the Basques in Spain, among the Catholic population in Northern Ireland, in Scotland, in Belgium, in Corsica. In the USA, meanwhile, a massive upsurge of protest, associated first with the issue of civil rights for blacks, and then with growing ethnic awareness amongst a wide range of non-white ethnic communities, began to develop. In Canada the French-speaking population of Quebec began to demand greater autonomy and, in many cases, independence. This revival of national and ethnic politics in Western Europe and North America was, for all its international implications, contained: in on no case did states fragment.

The same was not so for the even more explosive development of nationalism in the communist countries of the East. Nationalism, i.e. hostility to Soviet rule and a desire to re-establish links with the pre-communist past, and linked to demands for economic improvement and for democracy, played an important part in the growing opposition to communism in Eastern Europe. It also, however, challenged the USSR itself: the Soviet Union had been created after World War I as a new multi-ethnic state. Once coercive control was relaxed, in 1991, the constituent states broke away to form fifteen independent states: in many cases this independence was carried out under the aegis of the local communist élites, who feared, as much as anything, the democratic trends emerging in Russia itself. The end result was, none the less, the greatest tide of secession and fragmentation of states—in the USSR and elsewhere—ever seen in the history of the modern international system. As we shall see later, even now the issue of nationalism's impact on the international system is far from resolved.

Key Points

- Nationalism evident first in Western Europe and in the Americas.

- After World War I, the collapse of the multi-ethnic empires in Eastern Europe, after World War II the end of the European empires in Asia and Africa.

- Decades of conflict following the proclamation of self-determination by President Wilson in 1918.

Nationalism and International Relations

The consequences of the emergence and spread of this doctrine for international relations are many, both at the level of the impact of nationalism on the international system and at the level of the problems—*analytic* and *ethical*—which nationalism poses for the study, and practice, of international relations.

In terms of **consequences**, four major ones can be identified. In the **first** place, nationalism has provided a new set of values, a new system of legitimation, for the system of states. Beyond justifications in terms of traditional understandings of sovereignty and its corollary, non-interference, represented in the **Westphalian System**, the states system can now claim to represent the interests of separate, individually legitimate, peoples. Hence the importance of the concept 'nation-state' and the implication, which many contest, that states do indeed represent nations. (The very term 'international' embodies this ambiguity: it was invented in 1780 by Jeremy Bentham, the English utilitarian political theorist, to denote the form of law existing between different Roman tribes. It has since come to mean 'inter-state', with the added implication that this is equivalent to 'inter-nation'.) Self-determination has come to be a universally accepted principle, and the supposed basis of the current international order. Both the Covenant of the League of Nations and the Charter of the United Nations rest on this assumption, and from it is derived the whole system of international law. States may or may not in practice represent their

peoples but in the international system of today, in diplomacy and law, they are deemed so to do.

Second, nationalism has served as an important, essential, component of state-building and for the formation of a **common identity and consciousness** within societies. Pre-existing forms of loyalty certainly existed. Throughout history people have asserted that it is an individual's duty to die for his or her community. But the modern state, faced with the movement of large numbers of people into the cities, and with the need to mobilize resources against external competitors and threats, has been particularly keen to promote a sense of national identity and purpose. The means of doing so include education, conscription into national armies, the promoting of national histories, the making of patriotic films. All contribute to giving a people a sense of common identity and of promoting acceptance of the state. As such nationalism serves to consolidate support for élites and the established order. Writers on nationalism often argue that this promotion of nationalism is especially strong in former colonial countries where the very boundaries and identity of the state may be of recent, externally imposed, character. Promotion of official nationalism undoubtedly has been part of this Third World, state-directed, nation-building. But it is by no means exclusive to the Third World: in developed countries—be it France, the USA, or Britain—the state has also sought to promote a sense of national identity and purpose, through education and the other means available to it. It has become part of the very formation of the link between state and society throughout the world, the indispensable domestic accompaniment of the consolidation of state power internationally. No state can survive and compete in the international arena without the promotion of a sense of national identity and purpose domestically.

Third, nationalism has provided a powerful impetus to the **drawing** and **redrawing** of the international map, i.e. to defining the territories of

---

Box 18.4. The UN Charter, Article 1, Section 2

'2. To develop friendly relations among nations based on respect for the principle of equal rights and self-determination of peoples, and to take other appropriate measures to strengthen universal peace'

---

states and the frontiers between them. In theory this means that the map of the world reflects a pre-existing reality—the distribution of peoples across the globe. The map of states we see on an atlas today is supposed to be of pre-existing peoples, a reality like that of a geological survey or of the physical features of a part of the earth: but this is far from being the case. In practice it reflects where history has, often by accident, led the lines to be drawn—in Europe where armies grew tired of fighting, elsewhere in the world where colonial administrators and soldiers chose to draw them. Even such a settled frontier as that between the USA and Canada, or between Spain and Portugal, reflects haphazard history. However, the norm that the map of states should correspond to that of peoples has continued to push against these inherited frontiers. As already noted in the context of the collapse of communism, this challenge to the map has taken the form both of **fission** and **fusion**. Thus some nationalism has involved movements that aim to break up existing states, through secession or fragmentation of various forms. Other cases have involved the drive to unite parts previously divided: Italian and German unification in the nineteenth century, Irish, Arab, Korean, Somali, and many other nationalisms in the twentieth.

A **fourth** consequence of nationalism for the international system has been that it has been a source of **conflict**, and often of **war**. In the interwar period disputes over territorial division soured the belief that, once accepted, the principle of self-determination would produce peace between peoples. In the more recent past, frontier disputes and disputes where peoples are mixed together in multi-ethnic society have occasioned many conflicts: in the Arab–Israeli context, in former Yugoslavia, Kashmir, Sri Lanka to name but some. Even more catastrophically, nationalism has become a factor, both cause and pretext, in interstate wars, most dramatically of all in the drive of Germany to dominate Europe, and of Japan to dominate East Asia, through a combination of annexation and subjugation, in World War II. From the Nazi and Japanese imperial experiences we have derived the sense of nationalism as a destructive force. This hostility to nationalism is all the greater because, as in the German and Japanese cases, ferocious nationalism abroad is often combined with dictatorial and racist policies at home: nationalism is used by dictatorial regimes to crush dissent at home, even as it is deployed to mobilize support for aggression abroad.

Key Points

- Nationalism for the past two centuries as the moral, normative, basis for the system of states.
- Nationalism both legitimates states and has been promoted by states as part of nation-building.
- Nationalism as the justification for secession and territorial claims.
- Nationalism closely related to the incidence of war.

Four Debates

The topic of nationalism is one that, at least as much as that of any other powerful ideological force, has provoked widespread controversy, in public political debate but also in the social sciences. The fact that, for many decades, only historians discussed it indicates that it presents difficulties: the lack of clear ideological definition, the apparent irrationality, the very denial of universal rational categories which it implies have all contributed to this. An important part of the difficulty has, however, been the controversy it has provoked within social science in general. Much of the debate about nationalism has taken place not in International Relations as in another social science, Sociology. But the sociological debates, and others in political theory, have important implications for International Relations and have affected or underlain much of the discussion about the subject. Here we shall look at four of these debates.

1. Justice versus Order

The international system has rested on *two* principles—the sovereignty of states and the maintenance of peace between them. It has often been assumed that national self-determination and the expression of legitimate nationalist demands are compatible with these general principles. Often they are, and when disputes occur then there are mechanisms—arbitration, plebiscites, negotiated compromises—for securing peaceful and binding agreement. But one does not have to look far in the history of the international system over the past two centuries to see that there often is a conflict, and one that has led to conflict and injustice. In the first place, the principles of **balance of power** politics often conflict with those of self-determination: the maintenance of peace between great powers may involve carving out **spheres of influence** or agreeing to each having colonies. In the 1790s, for example, Russia and Prussia partitioned Poland, before that an independent kingdom, between them as part of the maintenance of the balance of power. In the late nineteenth and early twentieth centuries European states agreed to the creation of **colonies** and **spheres of influence** in Asia and Africa. During the cold war, and after, the Western world permitted Russia to exercise domination over peoples within Eastern Europe and within the USSR or Russia itself in order not to compromise broader considerations of stability and security. (To take two obvious examples: the Hungarian uprising of 1956, the Chechen rising of 1994 onwards. In both cases there was no Western official reaction to obvious denials of the right of peoples to self-determination.) In other parts of the world undoubtedly legitimate claims to independence have been ignored for reasons of regional security: from 1961, when war there began, the African states refused, until 1991, when it was a *fait accompli*, to recognize the right of Eritrea to independence from Ethiopia: equally no state in the world is prepared to grant the right of the 15–20 million Kurds resident in Iran, Turkey, and Iraq to a separate state. When the communist system collapsed the international community was prepared to welcome the newly seceded states and recognize their independence: but this was done reluctantly, and the general consensus was that the process had to end as quickly as possible. No wonder that a meeting at the Royal Institute of International Affairs in London, in June 1993, the then British Foreign Secretary Douglas

---

Hurd declared: 'I hope we do not see the creation of any more nation-states.'

Uncertainty on this issue underlay the confusion of Western policy-making on former Yugoslavia in the early 1990s: it was not clear how much support should be given for self-determination nor where this support should stop. But this case also raised another, related, problem. If one community was entitled to secede, then the issue of secession for minorities within that community's territory also arose: this concerned the Serbs of Bosnia and Croatia, but it is also posed in Northern Ireland, for Russians living in the Ukraine, for Arabs in Israel, as it was, earlier, for Germans living outside Hitler's Reich. No one can argue that every community in the world with a legitimate claim to its own identity should have its own state. There are, for example, four thousand languages and no one envisages four thousand states. Even peoples of the same language can have separate states—as speakers of Arabic, Spanish, English, French, German, Malay, Persian do. The question is where to draw the line: for this, some **balance of justice and order** has to be found. The right to self-determination, conceived of as the right and need of peoples of one community to have an independent, single, state has always had to be set against other principles of international relations.

2. History versus Modernity

Nationalism rests upon a claim of historical continuity—this people have existed for centuries, going back to some founding moment, real or imagined, or to the mists of time. The attainment of national independence and of statehood is the culmination of this history. Hence the use of words like 'reawakening' and 'rebirth', the interest in archaeology and ancestors. Claims derived from history are also used to settle arguments within a community about what is, or is not, 'authentic' and, with great consequences for international relations, what the historic, natural, sometimes 'God-given' extent of the national territory is. When people want to deny the legitimacy of another nation's claims it is common to claim that they are 'not really' a nation, or have not existed for long, or if they have then they existed somewhere else, or were, and may still be, agents of foreign powers. History in such a context is everything.

This approach to nationalism is the one common to all nationalist movements. It has been termed the **perennialist** approach. By contrast many social scientists adopted the view that nations are (*a*) arbitrary and (*b*) recent creations. This is generally held to be the **modernist** approach. In this view today's map of nations could have been very different from what it is, and reflects arbitrary and recent processes—the drawing of colonial boundaries, accidents of war, the triumph of particular political groups claiming to represent peoples they then set about creating. Nationalism is not the working out of some historical destiny: it is a response to the breakdown of old forms of community, based on religion, dynastic rule, and rural life, and a way of giving the inhabitants of modern cities a sense of meaning and purpose. It creates a new sense of belonging—hence the term **imagined community**, coined by Benedict Anderson, to convey the idea of a group of people one knows one is part of, but all of whose members one can never meet. The past—tradition, history, language, folklore—is not what determines the present but is, rather, used to provide material, is used as a reserve, by political and intellectual leaders. Where the past is lacking, traditions are invented. There is not necessarily anything wrong with this, and, beyond its many benefits, nationalism may be unavoidable: but this **contingency** needs to be recognized. In the words of one modernist 'it is the magic of nationalism to turn chance into destiny' (Anderson 1991: 19).

In between these two positions there are other less extreme approaches. Some theorists argue that while nations and nationalism in the contemporary political sense are recent creations, they rest upon earlier cultural, linguistic, and political roots that mean they are more than just contingent creations. Thus, without accepting the perennialist case, it is possible to write a history of, say, the English, Russian, Chinese, Egyptian or Italian peoples. This is the position of the well-known writer Anthony Smith, who focuses on **symbolism** (A. Smith 1991). Smith has, in particular, argued for the use of the concept *ethnie*, based on a French term for an ethnic group, to denote the communities which, in a pre-nationalist age, still form the basis for modern nations. Some writers have taken this approach to distinguish between different kinds of nations, those with a longer history derived from an ethnic basis—obvious candidates would be the Chinese or the Germans—and those which are more recent creations, a product of the European colonial system—the USA, Australia, and many countries in Latin America and Africa would be candidates. Here a distinction can be made between **ethnic** and **political** nationalisms, or 'historic' and 'newly created' forms, i.e. between cases where the state and its associated nationalism came to represent an already existing community, and ones where it was the state itself that created the nationalism and forged a sense of solidarity amongst the people. There may be some truth in such a distinction, but it may also understate the degree to which *all* states have promoted and to a considerable degree created modern nationalism: such states as the British, the French, the German, the Japanese have devoted considerable energy to instilling a particular sense of identity, history, language into their peoples and to tidying up what had hitherto been a much less packaged sense of national tradition.

Box 18.6. **National Symbols**

(1) General
- Language
- Food and Drink
- Clothing
- Commemorative holidays
- Military heroes
- Flags, colours, and anthems
- Terms of abuse for non-nationals

(2) 'Invented' traditions in the British Isles
- Christmas
- Morris dancing
- The kilt
- The shamrock
- The leek
- The ploughman's lunch

3. Positive and Negative

In discussions of the role of nationalism in international relations it has been common to counterpoise what are the positive, desirable functions of nationalism from those that are deemed to be negative and undesirable. On the positive side *four* arguments at least can be made. **First**, nationalism does provide a **principle of legitimacy** that underpins the modern state system. It suggests that states can, and should, represent their peoples and hence that they derive legitimacy from them: the Rousseau–Mill theme of representative government finds its international fulfilment in this way. **Second**, nationalism is a **realization of democratic principles**: nationalism is the means by which the Enlightenment principles of representative government should be realized in the international arena. **Third**, nationalism serves a very important **psychological function**: it provides a sense of belonging, of where one is coming from, of a past and a future, and of what the appropriate forms of cultural expression should be. Everyone has such needs and without them there would be chaos and despair. It is nationalism which does so in modern conditions. **Fourth**, nationalism has been and remains one of the great sources of **human creativity and diversity**—the explosion of nationalism has had enormous consequences for art, literature, music, language, sport, and much else besides, not least gastronomy. It has enriched not only the individual peoples it has affected but the whole of humanity: the world would be a greyer, more boring, place without it. The explosion of multiculturalism, of cultural expression by ethnic groups living in larger communities, is the latest example of this.

There are also several powerful arguments on the negative side. The **first** is that nationalism is a cause of conflict, and war. By making unreconcilable claims to territory, and by raising the emotional temperature of national and international politics, nationalism has become the curse of the modern age, responsible for world wars, ethnic massacres, genocide, and unending low-level crises across the world. Nationalism may present itself as a reasonable, legitimate ideology but it very soon lapses into other forms of political thinking—**xenophobia**, hatred of foreigners, **chauvinism**, an aggressive approach to foreigners and foreign countries, **militarism**, the use of force to resolve problems, and **imperialism**, the desire to create empires that subject other peoples. **Second**, nationalism, even when it avoids military confrontation, may serve as an **obstacle to co-operation** on international issues—be this trade, migration, the environment, or any other issue in contemporary international politics. The world needs greater international co-operation and recognition not of separate, competing, national concerns but of common, global, interests: if this was always so it is all the more so in an era of potential nuclear proliferation or ecological challenge. **Third**, nationalism by promoting the **breakup of states** destroys viable political and economic units. Nothing is served by the fragmentation of larger states: problems of political equity and resource allocation arise in any society but can be solved in other ways than by secession. **Fourth**, nationalism is undesirable on domestic grounds: it creates a climate within states of **intolerance and dictatorship**. This may take the form of a particular ruler using nationalism and arguments of security to justify their own holding of power. It may also involve the use of nationalism by one, majority group, to oppress, expel or in extreme cases exterminate those not considered part of that majority. Such a climate makes international pressure on human rights grounds all the easier to resist: states violating the rights of their peoples resort to standard defences—that all criticism is a form of interference in the nation's life, that critics are enemies of the nation, that the values of the critics are those of another nation. On the cultural level, nationalism provokes a small-mindedness, a mean inward-looking, approach that is inimical to cultural exchange and which denies the rich interaction that has always characterized culture, religion, and language in the modern world. As long as there has been nationalism there has been criticism of it, by those who see and experience it as a tool of domination *within societies*.

4. Objects of Primary Loyalty

The moral claim underlying nationalism is one that raises issues central to political theory, but it is one that is also raised by the whole process of globalization. This is the claim that the individual, by dint of birth or subsequently acquired citizenship, owes loyalty first and foremost to the nation, and, in most circumstances, the nation as represented by the state. This is the basis upon which order within states and the legitimacy of the international states system has existed for the past two centuries or so.

The arguments for this claim are, as also noted, strong ones, but they are an answer to a question that allows, not least in an era of globalization, of other answers. In effect, an individual has *three* possible objects onto which to attach his or her primary loyalty: the nation-state, some community that is larger than or goes beyond the state (religion, the working class, humanity as a whole, Europe), or a grouping that is smaller than, contained within, the state (the family, tribe, local community, business enterprise). The choice as to which of these one owes primary loyalty is not a new one: prior to the rise of nationalism the choice was usually for some combination of the religious and the local or family unit. Many modern political or social movements—Communism, Catholicism, radical Islam, Feminism, Freemasonry, the Mafia—call on their supporters to have loyalty to something beyond the state. In some cases the decision to declare loyalty to one, minority or oppressed, nation means one rejects loyalty to a broader state-centred nation: this would be the case for a person of Scottish or Welsh nationalist orientation in Britain, or for someone belonging to any of the many ethnic groups in the USA. Many individuals have chosen to adhere primarily to one of the sub-groups. The writer Graham Greene once said he would prefer to betray his country than betray his friends. Feminist writers have criticized the way in which the nation, defined and controlled by men, and used for the advantage of men, has served to oppress women. Virginia Woolf declared: 'As a woman I have no country.'

Such choices, as between the three possible categories of objects of loyalty, need not be absolute: most individuals owe some form of loyalty to all three and seek, usually without too much problem, in combining them. But the tension is always there, and in an era of globalization, when both broader international loyalties are invoked, and when the weakening of the state in some areas of life allows of more local, small-scale, centres of legitimacy, the question is more present than is always the case: such processes as European integration, the growth of world-wide 'youth' and consumerist cultures, or employment in multinational enterprises may cre-

ate complex shifts in loyalty. As with the other issues in debate concerning nationalism, however, there is no easy or quick answer to this question.

Box 18.7. Critics of Nationalism

Communist

'The working men have no country. We cannot take from them what they have not got . . . National differences, and antagonisms between peoples, are daily more and more vanishing, owing to the development of the bourgeoisie, to freedom of commerce, to the world market, to uniformity in the mode of production and in the conditions of life corresponding thereto.'

(Karl Marx and Friedrich Engels, *Manifesto of the Communist Party* in Karl Marx, *The Revolutions of 1848* (London: Penguin Books in association with New Left Review, 1973), 84–5)

Feminist

'Therefore you insist upon fighting to gratify a sex instinct which I cannot share; to procure benefits which I have not shared and probably will not share; but not to gratify my instincts, or to protect either myself or my country. "For", the outsider will say, "in fact, as a woman I have no country. As a woman I want no country. As a woman my country is the whole world." '

(Virginia Woolf, *A Room of One's Own. Three Guineas* (Oxford: Oxford University Press, 1992) 313)

Key Points

- Nationalism as both underpinning and challenging the security of states.

- Nationalism as the fulfilment of a long historical development of peoples, or as a recent, modern, response to social change.

- Strong arguments as to the benefits of nationalism to the international system, and also as to the harm it causes relations between states.

- Nationalism—one among several answers to the question of loyalty and identity.

Towards a Post-Nationalist Age?

Since the emergence of nationalism in the early nineteenth century, there have been those who have predicted, and wished, that it would decline, and be swept away in the tide of international processes that go beyond states and separate nations. Nineteenth-century liberals and communists believed the creation of the world market would sweep away differences between states. After World War I it was hoped that international law, the spread of democracy and the very triumph of self-determination could eliminate national conflict. Since the 1970s, first in the literature on **interdependence** and then in that on **globalization**, it has been argued that we are moving towards a more unified world, where national differences, and the nation state, will be less influential and less necessary.

Nationalism remains an enduring part of international relations, yet for all the persistence of nationalism and of problems associated with it, it can, in certain respects, be argued that there is a new situation in the world. We are not simply seeing a recurrence of the pattern of national conflict that has marked the world for the past two centuries. In the **first** place, and despite all the new nationalisms that have arisen and will do so, the classical justification for nationalism and for demands for independence, namely rule by an alien, colonial, power has almost entirely gone. The collapse of the USSR and the other multi-ethnic communist states has ended that chapter of human history. So when claims for independence are made it will in the future be much harder for aspirant nationalisms to demand international recognition. There is the further constraint that following the end of European colonial rule and the fragmentation of the communist world the international system has, with close on two hundred sovereign states, decided that that is basically enough: this is not based on considerations of justice, but rather on a tired, but widespread, belief that the world now has enough states and that adding large numbers of other ones will create disorder, overload and indecision. The argument of Mazzini and Woodrow Wilson has now been turned on its head: the general belief is that the creation of more states will promote disorder, and disharmony, rather than promote it. Taking Mazzini's metaphor, we can say that more children will make the family less, not more, happy.

Second, the fate of relations between major powers depends to a considerable degree on the continuance of democracy: the argument that democratic states do not go to war with each other is a strong one, and would entail that, whatever their differences, including over economic ones, the major developed countries of the OECD will avoid war, and hence the worst consequences of nationalism (see Ch. 10). **Third**, we should not assume that the content, the political programme, of nationalism remains the same. While the 1980s and 1990s have seen a flowering of nationalisms of many kinds, not least in the former communist world, there is one respect in which the nationalist agenda has changed: as Eric Hobsbawm has argued, the old belief that national interest and greatness could be served by the promotion of a self-contained, 'national', economy has been substantially eroded to be replaced by another, also nationalist, idea, that separate statehood can provide the best means of negotiating a favourable position in the international market-place (Hobsbawm 1990).

Finally we come to the argument that is intrinsic to globalization itself, namely that the spread of links between societies—in trade, migration, tourism, communications—will erode national identities just as the growth of instruments and institutions of international and global governance, together with the globalization of markets, will erode the power of states. It is not necessary to adopt the most extreme variants of the globalization thesis, or to envisage or welcome the disappearance of the nation state, to see that there could be some truth in this argument. The counter-arguments have already been made: that integration produces a fragmenting counter-reaction, that much of what passes for globalization is the imposition of one country's values and interests on others. The process of globalization will, therefore, always be accompanied by centrifugal and separating trends as it has been throughout the history of the international system. As with nationalism, the very means and ideas of that separation may well be promoted by the international system itself. There may well, however, also be movement in the international direction, always capable of being undone, but nevertheless substantial: be this in European integration, or international co-operation to prevent and contain war, or in the growth of a cosmopolitan awareness and culture among younger generations. Nationalism in all its forms will in all probability remain part of the life of each people, and of the international system, yet as it is resisting and opposing the development of that system it is also being constrained and shaped by it. Nationalism is not an alternative to globalization, but an intrinsic part of it.

Key Points

- Nationalism remains an important part of relations between states and also of the domestic politics of many countries.

- Expectations of a disappearance of nationalism, made over the past century and a half, were mistaken.

- Nationalism is a response to the new international context: in part benefiting from resentment at globalization, in part adjusting those parts of its programme that are no longer so relevant.

QUESTIONS

1. Why should students of international relations pay attention to nationalism?

2. What accounts for the spread of nationalism across the globe in the past two centuries?

3. Can nationalism be defined?

4. What have been the consequences for the international states system of the rise of nationalism?

5. Is nationalism a 'good thing'?

6. What has been the function of nationalism in the development of the modern state?

7. 'Nations have always existed.' Discuss.

8. To what extent can the main theories of international relations provide an explanation for nationalism?

9. How has the international system dealt with demands for national self-determination?

10. Can the world do without nationalism?

11. What is the relation of nationalism to the study of international political economy?

12. What are the implications for nationalism of globalization?

A GUIDE TO FURTHER READING

J. Mayall, *Nationalism and International Society* (Cambridge: Cambridge University Press, 1990), A. Smith, *National Identity* (London: Penguin, 1991), F. H. Hinsley, *Nationalism and the International System* (London: Hodder and Stoughton, 1973), K. Deutsch, *Nationalism and Social Communication* (Cambridge, Mass.: MIT Press, 1996), and A. Heraclides, *The Self-Determination of Minorities in International Politics* (London: Cass, 1990) provide accounts of the impact of nationalism on international relations.

M. Glenny, *The Breakup of Yugoslavia* (Harmondsworth: Penguin, 1992), gives a dramatic account of one recent case.

B. Anderson, *Imagined Communities. Reflections on the Origin and Spread of Nationalism* (London: verso, 1992), E. Gellner, *Nations and Nationalism* (Oxford: Blackwell, 1983), and E. Hobsbawm, *Nations and Nationalism Since 1780: Programme, Myth, Reality* (Cambridge: Cambridge University Press, 1990) give modernist accounts of nationalism as ideology and political movement, while Smith, (1991) offers an alternative, more historical, account.

19 Cultural Conflict in International Relations: The West and Islam

Simon Murden

READER'S GUIDE

The human experience is one of cultures. Culture and cultural differences have been at the heart of human behaviour throughout the history of international politics. Indeed, at the end of the twentieth century, the significance of culture was being reaffirmed, in terms of the rethinking of the international order that took place as a result of the end of the East–West cold war and the process of 'globalization'. The 'shrinking' of the globe brought different cultures into closer contact, and represented a world-wide challenge to traditional patterns of culture and social order. Peoples across the world were having to face the dilemma of what in their cultures could be maintained and what would be lost.

The culture and political economy of the West was the dominant form in the globalization process, and whilst the West's global penetration appeared to be making the human experience more alike, it was also prompting cultural counter-reactions. When people of one culture perceive those of another not just as alien but also as threatening, serious conflict is likely. As the cold war ended, the historic cultural difference between the West and Islam re-emerged as one of the principal frontiers of cultural suspicion. Much was made of the Western–Islamic confrontation, yet the coherence of any civilizational clash remained debatable. Culture is a powerful underlying force, but in the contemporary state system it is also one that still struggles to gain a coherent voice.

Culture in Human Affairs

Wherever human beings have formed communities, cultures have come into existence. Culture is a social construction that is so multi-faceted that it may be difficult to define precisely. The literary and artistic genre of a community is a part of its culture. A political culture is also likely to develop within a community, composed of the beliefs and practices that shape social life, and imbue peoples with certain perspectives on how society should be run. Culture transcends ideology, and is about the substance of identity for individuals in a society. **An awareness of a common language, ethnicity, history, religion, customs and institutions, and reference to a landscape, represent the building blocks of culture**, and the totems of self-identification.

Cultures may be constructed on a number of levels: in village, city, and country locations, and across family, clan, and ethnic groups. Cultural identity also commonly spreads across both the nation and the state. The broadest construction of cultural identity is the civilization, where groups of peoples are able to identify with a sufficiently coherent set of aesthetic, philosophic, historic, and social traditions. **Civilizations represent transnational tendencies that imbue underlying charac-** teristics to certain peoples and areas of the world.

Civilizations are dynamic over time and place. Civilizations may have distinct elements, but most have drawn directly on ideas and examples from other cultures. For instance, medieval Christendom drew on ancient and eastern civilizations for many of its philosophical and technological advances; subsequently, Christendom was remoulded into a European civilization based around the nation-state, and, finally, was expanded and adapted in North America, and redesignated as Western civilization. The process embodied both physical and conceptual reformulation.

In the contemporary world, a number of clearly definable civilizations exist, notably the Western, Islamic, Indian, and Chinese, although some peoples of the world are not so easily pigeon-holed, either because they are not united around sufficiently distinct or powerful cultural totems, or because they are torn between different civilizations; in this respect, the civilizational location of peoples in South America, Africa, and Russia is problematic.

The Significance of Culture in the International System

A debate exists in Western international relations thinking on the significance of culture. The dominant tradition of Western thought—Realism—suggests that factors such as culture are of second order significance, and subsumed by the logic of power and of the state in the anarchy of the international system. Faced with the facts of *realpolitik*, all states essentially act in the same way (Rengger 1992: 94). Notwithstanding Realist logic, however, it is difficult to look at the international system and not see culture. The international system itself—characterized by the territorial state, and by notions of sovereignty, the balance of power, international law and diplomacy—emerged from Renaissance Europe, and was subsequently expanded to the rest of the world in the nineteenth and twentieth centuries. The state system formed an international society that was built on European-based cultural understandings and aspirations.

Culture is also meaningful in the international system to the extent that it has an impact on behaviour, and in particular in the way that it embodies and defines difference. Communities identify themselves as distinct, and by doing so, identify those outside the group. **The history of the 'Other', or of the alien, is as ancient as civilization itself**.

The History of the 'Other'

In a work on hegemony in the international system, John Agnew and Stuart Corbridge point to the importance of dominant discourses in history, and the way that 'geopolitical orders have been organized around the characterizations of space, places, and peoples' (Agnew and Corbridge 1995: 46) The dominant global discourse in the modern age was produced by European civilization, and between the late fifteenth century and the nineteenth century was characterized by Europeans defining 'a hierarchy of human societies from primitive to modern' (Agnew and Corbridge: 49). European civilization was framed in terms of its superiority, with its roots in Greek and Roman civilizations, and its modernity expressed in the form of the nation-state.

The characterization of the 'Other' by Europeans was almost always stereotyped and degrading. Identifying the 'Other' substantially shaped the forms of policy applied to particular areas and peoples of the world. Within Europe, the 'civilized' rules of international society were broadly applied; outside Europe, they were not. Europeans moved out into the world to impose modernity, in the form of enslavement within colonial empires. It was only by the mid-twentieth century that many of the deeply rooted ideas about European superiority began to change, coincidentally as the European empires were being forced to retreat, although the belief that the West still represented a model of human progress remained.

The other significant development of the mid-twentieth century was that cultural differences ostensibly took a back seat to the global political struggle that emerged between the United States and Soviet Union, which pitted models of political economy—liberal capitalism and state-centred socialism—against each other. Differences were largely defined in ideological terms, and were superimposed upon world politics regardless of local cultural characteristics. Both sides in the cold war offered their model to the Third World and non-aligned states for imitation. Alignment to one of the two great political and military blocs defined the 'Other'.

The end of the cold war not only led to a reordering of differences in the world, but highlighted a number of processes that were also taking place by this time. The triumph of Western market capitalism and liberal democracy in association with technological advances propelled an unprecedented process of 'globalization'. Agnew and Corbridge termed this new 'deterritorialized' geopolitical order, **the hegemony of 'transnational liberalism'**, and commented that 'a new ideology of the market (and of market access) [was] being embedded in and reproduced by a powerful constituency of liberal states, international institutions, and what might be called the "circuits of capital" themselves' (Agnew and Corbridge 1995: 166). Much of the world was brought into the world market economy, or at least aspired to join in. Many regimes in the developing world moved to abandon state-centred socialism as a model of economic management, and sought to engage with the West and the global economy.

Globalization and Culture

The process of globalization had major implications for cultures. **The dilemma that emerged right across the world, including in the West, was the extent to which engaging with the world market economy threatened existing patterns of culture and social order**. Whilst what Francis Fukuyama (1992: 45) termed the **'liberal idea'** did become a profound influence, and seemed to be making the world more alike, the forces of a cultural counter-reaction were gathering. In many areas of the world, the West was stereotyped, in terms of arrogance, exploitation, irresponsible individualism, and permissive sexual practices. In some parts of the developing world, liberal capitalism—based on individual autonomy and the principles of the market—was regarded as morally bankrupt.

The popular culture of the West was at the forefront of the cultural debates about globalization.

Box 19.1. Francis Fukuyama on Islam after the Cold War

For Francis Fukuyama, the end of the cold war had left the 'liberal idea'—liberal democracy and market capitalism—as mankind's universal project. To Fukuyama, it seemed that there was 'no ideology with pretensions to universality that [was] in a position to challenge liberal-democracy, and no universal principle of legitimacy other than the sovereignty of the people'. Fukuyama could only see localized resistance to the liberal idea, notably in the form of Islam. Fukuyama thought that Islam represented,

a systematic and coherent ideology . . . with its own code of morality and doctrine of political and social justice. The appeal of Islam [was] potentially universal, reaching out to all men as

men . . . And Islam has indeed defeated liberal democracy in many parts of the Islamic world, posing a grave threat to liberal practices even in countries where it has not achieved political power directly . . . Despite the power demonstrated by Islam in its current revival, however, it remains the case that this religion has virtually no appeal outside those areas that were culturally Islamic to begin with. The days of Islam's cultural conquests, it would seem, are over. It can win back lapsed adherents, but has no resonance for the young people of Berlin, Tokyo, or Moscow. And while nearly a billion are culturally Islamic—one-fifth of the world's population—they cannot challenge liberal-democracy on its own territory on the level of ideas. Indeed, the Islamic world would seem more vulnerable to liberal ideas in the long run than the reverse.

(Fukuyama 1992: 45–6)

The West's popular culture was global in its reach, but was also widely regarded with suspicion, and met with varying degrees of resistance. In the Middle East, Islamic values were reasserted as a mass phenomenon. In Saudi Arabia and Iran, Islamic regimes sought to exclude news, films, music videos, and *Baywatch* by banning satellite television. The place of women in society, and especially the issue of veiling, emerged as the key symbol for Islamists seeking to bolster the institutions of cultural resistance and social control. In Asia, a debate about the importance of 'Asian values' also got underway, with the state/business élite turning the 'liberal idea' on its head, and arguing that individualism and liberalism actually negated success in the market economy. 'Asian values' in Malaysia and Singapore meant illiberal legislation to control the aspirations and behaviour of Asian youth in the face of Western influences.

A Clash of Civilizations?

The issues raised by the end of the cold war were reflected in a debate that got underway in Western policy and academic circles, especially in the United States, which suggested that cultural differences would increasingly shape the international order of the future. The debate was led by Samuel Huntington in an article, **'The Clash of Civilizations'**, where he argued that civilizations were becoming more coherent as actors in the international system. Huntington (1993: 25) suggested that the civilizations that would shape the world were the 'Western, Confucian, Japanese, Islamic, Hindu, Slavic-Orthodox, Latin American, and possibly African'.

For Huntington, the 'clash of civilizations' was an historic development. History had been about different forms of struggle. In early modern Europe, conflicts were largely amongst monarchs seeking to expand their territories and mercantilist strength. The French Revolution fostered a new struggle between nations and nationalisms. The Russian Revolution lead to a clash of ideologies between communism, fascism, and liberal democracy. All these conflicts were struggles **within** Western civilization. The end of the cold war had inaugurated a new period, where conflict had moved out of its Western phase, and into a Western and non-Western phase. Non-Westerners would become not just the recipients of Western policy, but the new movers of history.

In the post-cold war world, conflict would also change from the ideological and economic toward the cultural. States would remain key actors, but conflict was increasingly likely to arise between civilizational groups. Huntington contended that the differences between civilizations were far deeper than between the competitive impulses within civilizations. Civilizational differences were about man and God, man and woman, the individual and the state, and notions of rights, authority, obligation and justice. Culture was not just about an artificially constructed belief system—as nationalism or communism had been—but about identity itself, and the basic perceptions of life that were the products of centuries of social construction.

According to Huntington, globalization was making civilizational conflict more likely. The world was becoming a smaller place, and this was raising consciousness about cultural differences and threats. Economic changes were also detaching peoples from local loyalties and weakening the state; the vacuum of identity and loyalty was being filled by cultural references. Finally, although the West was at the height of its powers, in many parts of the world its ideas were seen to have failed. Socialist and nationalist ideologies were giving way to a 're-Islamization, Hinduization, and Russianization'. The 'liberal idea' was universal only on a superficial level, and Western ideas of individualism, liberalism, constitutionalism, human rights, the rule of law, democracy, free markets, and the separation of the church and state often had little resonance in Islamic, Confucian, Japanese, Hindu, Buddhist, or Orthodox cultures.

International security, then, would increasingly be linked to cultural identity rather than to the sovereignty of the state or nation. Cultural conflict would manifest itself on two levels: first, in a struggle over resources across a series of territorial 'fault-lines', and second, in more general competition for capabilities and influence in the international system, and particularly over international norms and organizations. The major dynamic of the competition would be between the 'West', as the dominant civilization, and to varying degrees, the 'Rest'. Most civilizations were increasingly inclined to resist the idea that Western norms were universal; for instance, Western efforts to project a model of liberal democracy and human rights were regarded as a form of neo-imperialism in many parts of the world.

In much of the discourse on civilizational conflict, it was Islam that increasingly came into focus.

The experience of the Reagan Administration in the 1980s in relation to Iran, Libya, Syria, and Lebanon had raised the spectre of an Arab/Islamic bloc that was fiercely resistant to the United States and its values. As the cold war came to an end, the independence of this Islamic threat was emphasized in a discourse lead by Huntington and by Bernard Lewis.

Islam did seem to represent a particular source of conflict both as a homeland and as a diaspora. By the early 1990s, a case could certainly be made that Islam did represent a 'crescent of crisis', with conflicts against adjoining civilizations in the Balkans, Africa, Middle East, Central Asia, India, South-East Asia, and the Philippines. Above all, though, Islam appeared to be in an ideological and cultural battle with the West. The forms of belief that were emerging from the Muslim world did seem to be completely alien to Western values, and what was understood as modernity. The historic conflict between the West and Islam would be rearticulated by both sides.

Key Points

- Culture defines the character of social life and the identity of the individual. Culture represents the customs, heritage and genres that inform political, social and artistic life in communities.

- The Civilization represents the broadest form of identity, and may spread across both national and state borders.

- The international system has historically been characterized by the portrayal of different cultures as alien, or as the 'Other'.

- The West emerged as the dominant civilization in the modern age. The West has, and continues, to identify alien groups which are portrayed as backward or as threatening.

- As the East–West cold war came to an end, a discourse took shape in the West suggesting that a 'clash of civilizations' (of cultures) would replace the ideological struggle of the cold war. A particularly pronounced clash seemed to be developing between the West and Islam.

The Islamic 'Other'

The conflict between the West and Islam is historic. The suspicious and fearful beliefs of the two civilizations toward each other have been lodged in the 'folk memory' of both communities for many centuries.

For centuries after the seventh century AD, Christendom was challenged by Islamic power. Islamic civilization regarded itself as superior to Christendom, and, indeed, the traffic of ideas and technology was from the East to the West. By the eighth century, the Arabs/Moors had crossed North Africa, and made deep incursions into Spain and France. Centuries of war with Islam followed in Spain, the Mediterranean, and the Holy Land. Islamic power was gradually pushed back from the gates of Europe, and the sophisticated Islamic community that had developed in Spain was eliminated. A new Islamic threat, however, would

subsequently rise in the form of the Ottoman Turks. European Christendom was shaken by the fall of the historic Christian capital of Constantinople in 1453. Ottoman hegemony in the Middle East and eastern Mediterranean represented a frightening yet fascinating force to Europeans. The Ottoman empire went on to encroach violently into Europe, and it was only after the mid-seventeenth century that the Ottoman threat to Central Europe subsided.

The relationship between the West and Islam in the modern age—the period since the Industrial Revolution—has been shaped by Western superiority. The rise of the West as the world's principal industrial and military power in the eighteenth century would lead to an experience of colonial and imperial domination in much of the Islamic world. Napoleon's expedition to Egypt from 1798 was a

---

Box 19.2. The History of Islamic Expansion

610	Mohammed begins to communicate with God, recording eternal principles in the Quran, which are subsequently interpreted to become a doctrine covering all aspects of human life.
622	The Islamic era begins. Mohammed migrates (*hijra*) from Mecca to Medina.
630	Mohammed conquered Mecca.
632	Mohammed died. Abu Bakr succeeds as Caliph.
632–650s	The expansion of the Arab-Islamic empire into Iraq, Syria, Egypt, and Persia.
656	The Caliph, Uthman, was murdered, and Ali (Mohammed's son-in-law and cousin) succeeded. The province of Syria rebels, lead by its governor Muawiyya. In 661 AD, Ali's forces were defeated, and Ali later murdered. The Umayyad dynasty was founded, centred on Damascus. Islam divides into the Sunni and Shia sects.
709–11	Islamic power was extended to Spain and northern India (Sind).
750	The Umayyad dynasty was replaced by the Abbasids, centred on Baghdad.
1096	Christian Crusaders arrived in the Levant, and began a long campaign to occupy the area.

1187	Saladin defeated the Crusaders, and took Jerusalem.
1250	The emergence of the Mamluk (Turkic slave soldiers) state in Egypt leading to the final defeat of the Crusades.
1258	The Mongol irruption. Baghdad was sacked, and Arab civilization smashed. The Mamluks stopped the Mongols at the great battle of Ayn Jalut in 1260, and were left to dominate the Levant.
1453	The Ottoman Turks took Constantinople. The Byzantine empire was lost to Christendom.
1517	The Ottomans defeated the Mamluks, and conquered Syria and Egypt.
1529	The Ottomans invaded Central Europe, but failed to take Vienna.
1526	The Mughal dynasty emerged in India.
1639	The Ottomans took Iraq from Safavid Persia.
1683	The Ottomans again fail to take Vienna. The high point of Ottoman power and ambition had been reached. Ottoman territories in Europe were subsequently ceded to Austria.

Note: All dates are given their Western chronology (AD).

major turning point. The physical and political impact of the West, and how to deal with it, has pre-occupied Arab/Islamic civilization ever since. On the other hand, the West's principal interest in the Islamic world was in maintaining control.

In his landmark works, *Culture and Imperialism* and *Orientalism*, Edward Said provided a powerful account of the cultural discourse that was inherent in Western domination. Said argued that the Arab/Islamic peoples had been grossly stereotyped in Western cultural discourses over a long period, a phenomenon Said termed '**Orientalism**'. Much of the 'Orientalist' tradition was based on myth, misunderstanding, and what was left unsaid about the Orient. The belief had been shaped in the West that Oriental peoples were culturally, historically, and socially alien. The Orient became associated with references to cruelty, despotism, dishonesty, and exotic sexual practice. Ultimately, Said believed, the Orientalist discourse was about hegemony. The Orient was 'Orientalized', not because it was really 'Oriental', but because its subordinate position meant that it could be.

Said went on persuasively to argue that Orientalism remained ingrained in Western consciousness. Debates about the Orient to the present day, even within the context of the so called 'objective standard' of Western debate, continued to be informed by these cultural attitudes. Indeed, contemporary history and the spread of the mass media had reinforced the stereotypes. Said (1995: 27) noted that

it hardly needs saying that because the Middle East is now so identified with Great Power politics, oil economics, and the simple-minded dichotomy of freedom-loving, democratic Israel and evil, totalitarian, and terroristic Arabs, the chances of anything like a clear view of what one talks about in talking about the Near East are depressingly small.

The Response of Islamic Civilization to the West

European encroachment in the nineteenth century produced a number of different reactions in the Middle East, notably Islamic revivalism and nationalism. Sayyid Jamal Al-din al-Asadabadi (Al-Afghani) (d.1897) was amongst the most prominent of those who sought to use modern methods and technologies to revive an old vision of Islam. Afghani argued that the world-wide Islamic community (*al-umma al-Islamiyya*) had strayed from authentic Islam, and fallen into division and decadence. Afghani advocated the reunification of all Islamic peoples under a reinvigorated **caliphate** (a unified political–religious authority) in order to counter colonialism.

The Ottoman Caliphate itself maintained a rather loose multi-ethnic union into the nineteenth century, held together with a transnational Islamic ideology. As Ottoman power waned, however, and the Europeans continued to encroach, the Ottoman state eventually sought to revive itself not through Islam, but through Turkish nationalism and the modernization of a Turkish state. The First World War finally finished off the Ottoman empire, and, as Roger Owen (1992: 9–10) has noted, the peoples of the Middle East were forced to look toward to a new future. The future would point away from universalist Islam, and toward more narrowly based levels of identity. Turkish, Iranian, and Arab nationalisms would come to dominate the arena of political ideas in the Middle East.

When Mustafa Kemal (Ataturk) came to power in Turkey, the model adopted was that of a secular, nationalist, and authoritarian territorial state. Kemal contended that Islam itself was the cause of backwardness and decline, and that modernization required the imitation of essentially Western forms of culture and organization. The Ottoman Caliphate was abolished in 1924, and Western forms of law, script, and dress were enforced. A similar model of modernity was adopted in Iran after 1921 when Reza Pahlavi seized power, and later made himself Shah.

The Western-influenced élite that sought to transform traditional Islamic society was a dynamic that would be repeated in the Arab World. After the First World War, what was left of the Ottoman empire was replaced by British and French hegemony. A state system that was largely arbitrary in its drafting was imposed on the Levant, with the new states of Iraq, Transjordan, Palestine, Syria, and Lebanon. The imposition of a state system by Western states would encourage nationalist resistance.

Arab Nationalism became the dominant ideological force in the Middle East. Developing from a

381

cultural and literary revival in the late nineteenth century, Arab Nationalism was radicalized in the twentieth century, and eventually combined a consciousness of an Arab culture (a common language, literature, and history, as well as a dominant religion) with modernism, in the form of a secular-socialist state. The middle-ranking army officer of *petit bourgeois* origin became the driving phenomena of Arab Nationalism. Nasser's regime in Egypt, and Baath Party cadres in Syria and Iraq launched experiments in nationalist and socialist modernization. The regimes staked all on modernization, and on addressing the principal strategic and cultural challenge to the Arabs: the foundation and expansion of Israel in the midst of their world. Israel was widely regarded by the Arabs as a 'garrison state' of Western imperialism; imposed as a new means of control.

Arab Nationalism as an ideology and as a model of modernization was to be a failure. The Arab World always struggled with the paradox of transnational ideology growing up in association with the unification of power and authority, not in the Arab nation, but in territorial states that cut across the nation. Inter-Arab conflicts became endemic. The socialist state was overly bureaucratic. In Syria and Iraq, the state was captured by minorities, and used as an instrument of sectarian rule. Above all, Arab Nationalism foundered on its demonstrable inability to take on Israel. The June 1967 war was a shattering blow. Jerusalem was lost. **The June War was a turning point, and although the notion of an Arab culture retained a grip on the Arab imagination, a new force was stirring: that new force was revivalist Islam.**

Key Points

- Islam has a long history of civilizational conflict with the Christian West. Islam used to be a major power, but by the eighteenth century had been decisively overtaken by the West. The West moved to dominate the Islamic regions, and began to represent Oriental culture as backward.

- Western encroachment since the nineteenth century has been the principal issue facing Islamic civilization. In order to compete more effectively with the Western challenge, a secular state model was adopted in much of the Middle East. In the Arab world, the secular-socialist state would founder on economic and military failure.

The Emergence of Militant Islamic Discourse

The Islamic revival that took place after the June War would tap something basic in Islamic civilization. Muslim peoples saw themselves as assailed by the West, militarily through Israel, and culturally through everything from pop music to the thinking of Islamic modernists. A malaise within Islamic societies also drove the revival. According to Sohail Hashemi (1996: 17)

the Islamic revival [was] a complex mix of elements both unique to the Muslim world and shared with other postcolonial societies. The Islamic challenge is trivialised if explained as merely resentment of the power and wealth of the West. It derives its vitality and its appeal from a much more elemental factor: the widespread conviction that Islamic history has gone horribly astray, and that Muslim realities for centuries have been widely divergent from Islamic ethics. The fact today that Muslim countries are characterized by some of the most notoriously authoritarian regimes provides a powerful internal dynamic to the use of Islam as a revolutionary force. The fact that Muslim countries range in economic prosperity from the fabulously wealthy to the hopelessly impoverished provides a second powerful internal dynamic to the upsurge of religiously based calls for social justice . . . Muslim countries themselves contain ample domestic sources for the infusion of Islamic ideologies in the political arena.

A number of Islamic states sought to promote missionary (*dawa*) activities, notably the conservative states of the Gulf, but revival would really escape the control of Middle Eastern regimes. **The militant character of the Islamic revival was shaped by innovations in both Sunni and Shia theology in the 1960s and 1970s that made rebellion—historically problematic in both sects—more thinkable. What emerged was a core of militant Islamic values that struck a chord across the Islamic world.** The major figures in the ideological revision were Sayyid Qutb in Egypt (d. 1966), Abu

Box 19.3. The Sunni–Shia Divide in Islam

Sunni Islam

Establishment Islam. In the line of Mohammed and the first four 'Rightly Guided Caliphs'. Sunni interpretations of the Quran have formed into four orthodox schools of jurisprudence: the *Hanafi*, *Shafii*, *Hanbali*, and *Maliki*. In theory, the government of the Islamic community was to be conducted by the political–religious figure of the Caliph, but in practice temporal power was soon detached by monarchical dynasties (the Sultans). From the Middle Ages, Sunni Islam came down on the side of the state and of order. Insurrection against a ruler, no matter how tyrannical, was ruled out of the Sunni mainstream as long as the state enforced legitimate Islamic law (the *sharia*).

Shia Islam

Legitimacy stemmed from the line of Ali (the son-in-law and cousin of Mohammed). Shia Islam subsequently fragmented into sects—Ismailis, Zaydis, Twelvers—based on the legitimacy of different religious scholars, or *Imams*. The largest sect, the Twelvers, that dominate contemporary Iran, contend that legitimacy stems from the 12th Shia Imam, who went into Occultation in AD 873, and will return as a mahdi before the end of history. As an oppressed minority, the Shia have historically been forced into the more inaccessible parts of the Islamic world, or have adopted the doctrine of *taqiyya* (concealing their faith). The Shia clergy is more independent, hierarchical, and organized than the Sunni clergy.

al-Ala al-Mawdudi in Pakistan (d. 1979), and Ruhollah Khomeini in Iran (d. 1989).

The thinking of the Islamic revival sought to define what was *salafi*, or what was a proper Islamic order. In the Sunni world, revivalists referred to the historic works of Ahmad Ibn Hanbal (d. 851) and Ibn Taymiyya (d. 1328). 'Neo-Hanbalite' doctrine would mean a return to the basic texts of Islam—thus, the term **fundamentalists**—and an uncompromising implementation of an Islamic state and Islamic law (*sharia*); religion and politics were inseparable. A number of other themes imbued the doctrine with a militancy, notably a disillusionment with the passivity of the official Sunni clergy, the elimination of all deviations within Islam, and strong references to struggling for the faith in the language of *jihad* and martyrdom.

The Muslim Brotherhood (*Ikhwan al-Muslimin*)—an organization founded in Egypt by Hasan al-Banna in 1928, and a model spread to Syria, Palestine, Jordan, and North Africa—became the principal vehicle of the Islamic revival. **Muslim Brotherhoods were both political organizations and benevolent social foundations**. Much of the time, Muslim Brotherhoods focused on supporting Muslims in their communities, but on occasions members turned to politics and even to violence as means to the *salafi* end.

In Egypt, the Muslim Brotherhood descended into conflict with the secular socialist state led by Gamal Abdul Nasser, and was forced underground after the 1950s. Sayyid Qubt, executed by Nasser's regime in 1966, became the icon of Sunni radicalism. Qubt contended that the realm of Islam (*dar al-Islam*) was subject to a modern state of *jahiliyya*, a term referring back to the state of ignorance that existed before the Prophet Mohammed's time. Qubt refused to accept the legitimacy of the state or nation, but did engage in Egyptian politics by denouncing the Nasser regime as corrupt, and its leaders as infidels; it was a Muslim's duty to wage a *jihad* against such corruption.

In many ways, Shia theology was moving in a separate but similar direction to militant Sunni thought in the 1960s and 1970s. The seminal figure in Shia revivalism was Grand Ayatollah Ruhollah Khomeini. Khomeini insisted that the Shia doctrine of quietism, *taqiyya*, was a negation of Islam, and that Muslims were obliged to struggle for an Islamic state. In his major work, *Islamic Government* (1971), Khomeini proposed a state dominated by religious scholars, but, above all, vesting both **political and religious primacy** in a single institution, the *velayet-e faqih* (the guardianship of the jurisconsult). The senior Islamic jurisprudent would have the last say in ruling the state; it was a position that Khomeini was to fill himself. The Iranian Revolution would be about entrenching the *velayet-e faqih* in power, a process that was to take a number of years and to require the elimination of the Shia clergy's partners in the rebellion against the Shah.

The Iranian Revolution (1978–9) itself would provide an enormous impetus to the Islamic revival in the Middle East. Whilst Iran's Revolution was only of limited significance to Sunni radicals in theological terms, it was an **example** to emulate. A populist Islamic movement had overthrown a powerful secular state; what had seemed impossible had been done, and the language of *jihad* and martyrdom had been vindicated. An Islamic revolution was not about to sweep the Arab world, but Islam was to become the principal political and cultural undercurrent.

Key Points

- Islam has always been a powerful cultural force in the Middle East. When the secular socialist states

faltered, Islam began to re-establish itself at the heart of political culture.

- Innovations in Sunni and Shia theology produced an Islamic revival in the 1970s that sought to enforce an Islamic order, in the form of an Islamic state and a rigorous code of Islamic law (*sharia*).

- The Iranian Revolution after 1978–79 provided a powerful example to Islamic revivalists.

The Mass Appeal of Revivalist Islam

The Islamic revival in the 1970s owed much to a crisis of modernization. Rapid population growth and rural–urban migration had meant that urban life in much of the Middle East was characterized by poor housing, strained services, and widespread underemployment. The young urban poor was a large group with few opportunities, and the alienation and anxiety felt was not met by the authoritarian secular state. Indeed, by the 1970s, most Middle Eastern states were overloaded with obligations, and could no longer provide employment and subsidy even for the educated. Benevolent Islamic institutions moved in to fill the gap, running subsided welfare handouts, schools and clinics; thus, interest reinforced identification, and in this way Islam reinvigorated its mass appeal.

Modernization had disrupted traditional patterns of life, but the secular state had at least co-opted the population by means of nationalism and socialism. The next phase of modernization— globalization—would weaken that link, and with it the authority of the state and of secular élites. **The effort to engage with the world economy would bring new forms of belief, interest, and organization to secular élites that were essentially competitive with the state and with traditional values. The orientation of secular élites was pulled toward the West and Western cultural values.**

In Egypt, the failure of state-centred socialism under Nasser prompted President Sadat to launch the *infitah* (opening). The result was a state/business élite that was international in perspective, and whose affluent lifestyles were far removed from the lives of most Egyptians. **The élite essentially abandoned the masses**. The populist vacuum was filled by revivalist Islam. Sadat tried to cultivate Islam, but lacked credibility. **Many young Egyptians, especially those in the educated lower middle class, turned to Islam and the Muslim Brotherhood as a culture that gave the poor and the hopeless self-worth**. A few Islamists turned to secret Islamic societies, and advocated violent action against the 'corrupt' states. The pattern of a reactivated Islam in Egypt was repeated across the Islamic world.

The Cultural Struggle between Islam and the West

The idea that Islam was locked in a struggle with the West was at the root of Islamic revivalism's legitimacy, both in opposition and government. On the surface of the struggle was Islam's hostility to the corrupting popular culture of the West. The differences, however, went deeper than popular culture, and into fundamentally different visions of political and social life. **In the post-Enlightenment West, the idea of human progress and a better future has been a central one. In *salafi* Islam, Muslims look forward to a better past**. The perfect Islamic polity had been established in the first years of Islam, and the eternal principles of the 'good life' recorded in the Quran and other early scripts. For *salafi* Islamists, the Quran and a legitimate code of Islamic law represent the perfect constitution, in which sovereignty resides in God, not in human beings. In the absence of human sovereignty there can be no legitimate legislation to adapt the Islamic constitution. God is not a democrat!

Western notions of liberalism and institutionalized participation, then, are not just seen as irrelevant by *salafi* Islamists, but as un-Islamic. Many Muslims do recognize the value of consultation (*shura*) by government, but the ranking of democracy as a value is simply different to that in the West. Democratic norms and institutions cannot take precedence over Islamic injunctions. The totems of Islamic backwardness for the West—a criminal law that still conducts public executions and amputations, and the regulation of women and non-Muslims—cannot be changed within the context of the *salafi* Islam that has emerged as the dominant tendency. For Islamists, liberalism has essentially come to represent deviance, and the West's propagation of its democratic values as neo-imperial arrogance.

The March of Islamic Activism

The hostility of Islamic revivalists toward the West was not simply conducted on the level of political theory and cultural propagation. During the 1970s and 1980s, the Islamic revival would explode into violence. The crescendo of Islamic 'noise' since the late 1970s would shake the states of the Middle East, and would encouraged the belief in the West that Islam did represent a transnational threat, and a civilizational adversary.

The Islamic violence that emerged after the 1970s was clearly a symptom of some sort of raging against the West; it was certainly easy to see how Islam became associated with violence, disorder, and intolerance in the Western mind. The question was, what did this crescendo of Islamic noise really represent: localized manifestations of political conflict, or a deeper stirring across the Islamic community? In other words, was there, or would there be, a coherent civilizational conflict between Islam and the West?

Key Points

- Modernization has produced widespread social alienation in the Middle East. Globalization has further detached existing élites from the experiences of the masses. Political Islam has moved in to fill the political and social vacuum.

- Revivalist Islam has identified a cultural conflict with the West. The West's popular culture and its liberal political ideas have been stereotyped and condemned by *salafi* Islamists.

- A crescendo of revivalist Islamic violence in the 1970s and 1980s appeared to substantiate the notion that there was an active civilizational conflict between the West and Islam.

The Coherence of the Islamic Civilizational Threat to the West

The debate about whether Islam did represent a civilizational challenge to the West was important because it came just as the cold war was ending, and as Western thinkers were seeking to re-conceptualize the world; new type-casting threatened to reconstruct the Islamic 'Other'. Huntington contended, for instance, that 'civilizational rallying' would replace traditional balance of power considerations and political ideology as the principal basis for co-operation and coalition-building; thus, Islamic states and peoples would gradually gravitate toward each other.

The danger of the new type-casting was that conflict lines would unnecessarily become entrenched, and that all Islamic peoples would be unjustly stereotyped. Whilst a track record of Islamic

---

Box 19.4. The Crescendo of Revivalist Islam from the late 1970s

- The Iranian Revolution (1978–9). The Revolution talked of Western corruption, and of the United States as the 'Great Satan'. In November 1979, Iranian students took the US embassy in Tehran, and held its staff hostage. The Revolution spilled over into the Middle East, prompting the Iran–Iraq war.

- The seizure of the Grand Mosque in Mecca on the first day of *Hijra* 1400 by the 'Islam primitivist', Juhayman al-Utaiba. In the bitter fighting that followed in Nov.–Dec. 1979, hundreds were killed.

- The assassination of President Anwar Sadat at a public parade on 6 October 1981 by the Islamic radicals in the Egyptian army.

- The rise of Shia revivalism in Lebanon after the Israeli invasion of 1982. *Amal* and *Hizbullah* would wage a *jihad* against Israel and the West, notably with the bombing of the US Marine barracks in Beirut in 1983, the hijacking of a TWA airliner in 1985, and the kidnapping of Westerners in Beirut.

- The bombing of a Pan-Am airliner over Lockerbie, Scotland, in December 1988.

- The conflict over Salman Rushdie's book, *The Satanic Verses*. When the book that Muslims believed to be blasphemous lead to anti-US riots in Pakistan on 12 February 1989, Iran's Ayatollah Khomeini issued a *fatwa* condemning Rushdie to death. A S1 million bounty was also put on Rushdie's life.

- The Algerian Civil War. When the *Front Islamique du Salut* (FIS) were denied office by the army after they had won a general election in December 1991–January 1992, a bitter civil war broke out. The conflict spilled over into terrorism in France.

- The long-running campaign of Islamic terrorism in Egypt, directed not only at the government of Husni Mubarak but also at foreign tourists.

- After the outbreak of the *intifadah* in 1987, HAMAS (*Harakat al-Muqawama al-Islamiya*), or the Islamic Resistance Movement, was formed. HAMAS and Islamic Jihad re-energized the violence of the Palestinian struggle against Israel.

- Islamic fundamentalism in Afghanistan. After the *jihad* against Soviet and Soviet-backed forces, militant *salafi* Islamists descended into a civil war with conservative Islamic forces linked to tribal and *sufi* influences. Subsequently, Islamic students formed an army, the Taleban, and seized much of the country.

- In Bosnia, a travelling band of Islamic radicals (some 4,000 in 1993) assembled to fight for the mainly Muslim Bosnian government.

- After the Russian Republic of Chechenia seceded, Islamic fighters with the backing of the Muslim world engaged in a violent and prolonged struggle with Russian troops.

- The challenge presented by radicalized *salafi*-Islam to the regimes of Saudi Arabia, the Gulf States, Egypt, Jordan, Syria, Iraq, and across North Africa. Acts of terrorism against Western targets in these countries confirmed Western anxiety.

---

violence and anti-Westernism was demonstrable, to talk of a coherent Islamic civilization was another matter. In reality, Islam was thoroughly divided, and any voice that it had was diffuse. The Sunni–Shia division remained important, whilst factionalism within the sects was also evident. Above all, however, **the transnational potential of Islam has met territorial state, and the restrictions that are inherent in the state system**.

The state system that was imposed on the Middle East after the First World War was regarded with a certain ambivalence by Arabs, but this did not stop local élites from defending state sovereignty. Indeed, even in the most rigorous Islamic state, the Kingdom of Saudi Arabia, King Abdul Aziz fought a civil war in the late 1920s against some of his Islamic followers, the *Ikhwan*, that were not prepared to accept the bounds of the state system. The King himself had accepted the worldly power of the regional hegemon, the British empire, and the lim-

itations that it had imposed on the new Islamic state.

The Middle Eastern state may always have struggled with its questionable legitimacy— partly because of pan-Arabism and pan-Islamism—but the state has become the defining institution in the region. The state controls the levers of power, and almost all political groups have concentrated on politics at the state level. **Islam may be a universal idea with a tradition that transcends the state, but Islamists have almost always fought their battles within the boundaries of the state system, rather than across it.** The seizure of the territorial state and its Islamization has been the principal objective of Islamic radicals.

The confinement of Islam to the territorial state has shaped the progress of Islamic revivalism. Islamic groups have run up against the Middle Eastern state, an institution that commonly possesses formidable coercive powers. **A division has** emerged within revivalist Islam that has become a dynamic right across the Muslim world. **Whilst most revivalists broadly agree over ends—an Islamic state and a rigorous *sharia*—they tend to differ over means.** Mainstream Islamists have been reluctant to engage in an all-out war with the secular state, and have been prepared to conduct a dialogue over gradually extending Islamic principles into the political system. Mainstream Muslim Brotherhoods have also concentrated on building their role as benevolent societies, and increasing their representation within professional organizations. The language of persuasion and education adopted by most mainstreams Islamists has stood in stark contrast to that of *jihad* used by a smaller tendency of Islamic activists, which have denounced existing government as corrupt, and are prepared to take violent action against it.

For governments across the Middle East and North Africa, keeping mainstream Islamists away from the more radical tendency has become a central policy concern. In Jordan, the Muslim Brotherhood were brought into the political process quite successfully. In Egypt, the state struggled to keep the Muslim Brotherhood away from violent secret societies. In Algeria, the secular-based army took decisions that brought the mainstream and the violent Islamic tendencies together in agreement over means, and produced a savage civil war.

The inertia of the state system has also frustrated revivalist efforts to promote an Islamic voice at a state level. The case of Iran after the 1978–9 revolution is an illuminating one. The Revolution that was defined after 1979 was one that rejected the nation and the state, and instead promoted a universal Islam. The Constitution of the Islamic Republic quite explicitly embodied a mission to promote and unify all the peoples of the world under Islam. The Islamic Republic went on to establish policies and organizations that quite simply ignored the sovereignty of other states, and the traditional practices of diplomacy. The costs incurred to the Iranian state were substantial, in terms of political and economic isolation, and a major invasion by Iraq.

The demands of running a state and a war in Iran, however, almost inevitably had an impact on the ethos of the Revolution. By the mid-1980s the Revolution had produced its 'pragmatists', located in the offices of the state, and conscious of state interests. Iranian policy gradually began to adapt and become more controlled. The Islamic Republic continued to advocate a universal Islam that was hostile to the West and many other Middle Eastern states, but was increasingly less prone to act on it. The death of Grand Ayatollah Khomeini in 1989 led to a further reorganization of the state. Pragmatic elements pressed a reconstruction agenda, and the ethos of control was consolidated. **The Revolution of 1989 was not the Revolution of 1979.** When tested, notably over conflicts in Lebanon, Afghanistan, Azerbaijan, and during the Allied–Iraqi war, the foreign policy of the Islamic Republic was controlled. Practical Iranian support for international Islamic causes had become more selective and limited, although that was not to say that the Islamic Republic was disinclined to speak up for Muslim rights across the world.

The inescapable fact for Islam as a civilizational force was that it could not fully promote itself without the state, yet it has also struggled to promote itself from within the state system. No Islamic state has been able, or seems likely to be able, to seize the leadership of the Islamic community, even in the limited way that Nasser managed with pan-Arabism. The would-be leaders of the Islamic world—Saudi Arabia and the Islamic Republic of Iran—have both run into local interpretations of Islam in their missionary activities, or as Jim Piscatori notes 'over who speaks for Islam here' (Piscatori 1992: 21), and are themselves bitterly divided over a whole range of political and religious issues. Indeed, the cold war between Saudi Arabia and Iran has been one of the principal blocks to the emergence of common Islamic positions, notably in the state-based Islamic Conference Organization (ICO). Whilst common Islamic positions have been established on Muslim issues such as Kashmir, Bosnia, and Chechenia, determined action remains a distant ideal. The ICO has been paralysed by the politics and the interests of the state system. A coherent Islamic voice does not seem likely to emerge in the foreseeable future, much less challenge the power of Western hegemony in the international system.

Key Points

- Islam as a civilizational force is not as coherent as sometimes suggested in the 'clash of civilizations' thesis.

- Islamic movements have been confined to the borders of the territorial state. A division has emerged amongst revivalist Islamists over means, between the gradualist mainstream Muslim Brotherhoods and the more violent secret societies.

- The inertia of interests inherent in the state system has tended to moderate Islamic aspirations and the policies of Islamic states.

Conclusion

Political Islam has been a resurgent force in the Muslim world since the 1970s, and one that has explicitly articulated a cultural conflict with Western civilization. The underlying force of Islamic culture and the fact that Islam was so very un-Western, has lead to fears in the West that a general civilizational confrontation was taking shape. The Iranian Revolution continued to haunt the Western imagination, even though the Islamic Republic gradually ceased to be the Revolutionary force that it once was. The West was also anxious about populist Islam in Algeria, Egypt, and Saudi Arabia, since an Islamic revolution in any of these states threatened seriously to widen the cultural divide, and threaten some of the West's vital interests.

The argument that Islam represented an increasingly coherent civilizational threat to the West was more problematic. Islam was not a political–military challenge to the continued existence of the West in the way that Soviet power had been during the cold war. Islam did present local challenges to Western hegemony in the international system, but as a general threat remained too diffuse as an ideology, and too divided by the state system. Ultimately, the realm of Islam had become identified with domestic and territorial space, and not with the limitless expansion of a universal civilization. The processes of globalization might further detach secular élites from the masses, and encourage revivalist Islam, but a coherent pan-Islamic revolution looked unlikely. The search for pan-Islamic harmonization, much less integration, remained a distant one.

QUESTIONS

1. What is culture, and how useful a concept is it when thinking about international relations?

2. How are characterizations of the 'Other' in cultural discourses commonly framed?

3. Why did Samuel Huntington contend that political/ideological conflict would be replaced by civilizational conflict after the end of the cold war?

4. How did Middle Eastern peoples respond to the dominance of the West in the twentieth century?

5. What was the doctrinal basis of the Islamic revival that took shape from the 1970s?

6. How does Western culture challenge Islam?

7. What was the principal division that emerged within the Islamic revivalist movement?

8. How coherent is Islam as a civilization and as a political force?

9. What does the case of the Islamic Republic of Iran indicate about the direction of Islam in the state system?

10. How serious is the threat that Islam represents to the West, and vice versa?

GUIDE TO FURTHER READING

Agnew, John, and Corbridge, Stuart, *Mastering Space: hegemony, territory, and international political-economy* (London: Routledge, 1995). A valuable study on the world's geopolitical order since the 19th century, focusing on the practice of hegemony, in terms of the structure of the international economy, and the cultural discourses about 'spaces' and peoples. The work argues that globalization has lead to a 'deterritorialized' and diffused hegemony in a way not seen before.

Bill, James, and Springborg, Robert, *Politics in the Middle East* (London: Scott, Foresman/Little, Brown, 1990). The basic text on the recent history and current condition of the Middle East. The work runs through the historical and ideological background to Middle Eastern politics, and refers to notions of patriarchy and political development to compare the experiences of different Middle Eastern states.

Huntington, Samuel P., 'The Clash of Civilizations', *Foreign Affairs* (Summer 1993). An article that proposed a new 'big idea' about international politics after the cold war: that civilizational references were becoming the driving force of conflict in the international system. Huntington argued that a cultural reawakening was highlighting the basic differences of belief and interest between peoples of different civilizations.

Said, Edward W., *Orientalism: Western conceptions of the Orient* (London: Penguin, 1995, reprint with afterword). A landmark work that sought to explain how Oriental peoples had been negatively stereotyped in Western discourses. Much of the work is an in-depth analysis of Western literature on the Orient over the past two centuries.

20 Humanitarian Intervention and World Politics

Nicholas J. Wheeler

READER'S GUIDE

Non-intervention is the norm in international society, but should military intervention be legitimized in contravention of the sovereignty principle when governments massively violate the human rights of their citizens, or if they have collapsed into civil war and disorder? This is the guiding question addressed in this chapter. The society of states has outlawed war except for purposes of self-defence and the challenge posed by humanitarian intervention is whether it also should be exempted from the general ban on the use of force? This chapter examines the arguments for and against forcible humanitarian intervention, focusing on the tensions between considerations of power, order, and justice in world politics. This theoretical analysis is explored in relation to cold war and post-cold war cases of forcible humanitarian intervention. The final section of the chapter examines the claim that the traditional definition of humanitarian intervention should be broadened to include non-military forms of humanitarian intervention practised by states and non-state actors.

I would like to thank Rob Dixon for his incisive comments on an earlier draft of this chapter. Some of the material in this chapter develops out of collaborative work with Justin Morris at the University of Hull. I would like to take this opportunity to acknowledge my considerable debt to Justin in helping me to think about this subject.

Introduction

Humanitarian intervention poses the hardest test for an international society built on principles of sovereignty, non-intervention, and non-use of force. The society of states has committed itself in the post-holocaust world to a 'human rights culture'[1] which outlaws genocide, torture, and massive human rights abuses, but these principles of humanitarianism can and do conflict with principles of sovereignty and non-intervention. Sovereign states are expected to act as guardians of their citizens' security, but what happens if states behave as gangsters towards their own people, treating sovereignty as a licence to kill? Should **murderous**[2] states be afforded protection of the norms of sovereignty and non-intervention, and what responsibilities do other states have to act as guardians of human rights in the society of states? Humanitarian intervention was not a legitimate practice during the cold war, but there has been a significant shift of attitudes since the early 1990s. However, this shift is primarily confined to domestic publics within liberal states, and the wider legitimacy of humanitarian intervention has been challenged by many non-Western states. Thus, the normative legitimacy of humanitarian intervention is hotly disputed at the end of the millennium.

The early optimism associated with the international intervention to rescue the Kurds in northern Iraq in the immediate aftermath of the 1991 Gulf War has given way to a mood of pessimism and moral cynicism. This is the product of the UN's perceived failures in Bosnia and Somalia, and the appalling moral catastrophe of Rwanda where Western state leaders and publics watched genocide take place from the comfort of their living room chairs. Failures in Bosnia and Somalia have led to a questioning of the efficacy of military force in promoting humanitarian ends. Some have argued that what was needed in these cases was a greater willingness to employ military force in defence of humanitarian ends, but others have contended that whilst citizens have moral duties to go to the rescue of suffering humanity, these should be dis-

charged by non-violent means since the use of force is always counter-productive. If there is debate over whether the use of force can promote humanitarian values and long-term reconstruction in **murderous** and/or **failed states,** then there is also the issue of whether states can be trusted with the responsibility to act as agents of **common humanity.** The abdication of moral responsibility on the part of the society of states in the face of the genocide in Rwanda—most crucially in the capitals of Western states—suggests that we should be cautious about investing too much faith in state leaders as guardians of human rights in world politics. For both these reasons, some analysts argue for a post-statist reconceptualization of humanitarian intervention which they label **non-forcible or non-violent humanitarian intervention** (Ramsbotham and Woodhouse 1996).

This chapter is divided up into six key sections. The first part of the chapter sets up the traditional definition of humanitarian intervention. The second part identifies five key objections to the practice of forcible humanitarian advanced by realism (see Ch. 6) and **pluralist international society theory.** Conversely, the third section examines the counter-arguments advanced by **solidarist international society theory.** Next, I will look at the legitimacy of humanitarian intervention in state practice during the cold war, focusing on two case-studies of intervention which led to the ending of genocidal practices: Tanzania's intervention against Idi Amin's Uganda and Vietnam's removal of the Pol Pot regime in Cambodia. The fifth part of the chapter focuses on international interventions in Kurdistan, Somalia, and Rwanda. The analysis here is subdivided into three key areas: the role of public opinion and the media in pressurizing state leaders to intervene; the legality and legitimacy of these interventions; and an evaluation of their success in promoting humanitarian values. The final section of the chapter explores alternative conceptions of humanitarian intervention and considers the implications of globalization for practices of humanitarianism in world politics.

What is Humanitarian Intervention?

In his now classic definition in *Nonintervention and International Order*, R. J. Vincent defined intervention as set out in Box 20.1. Vincent was not writing specifically of humanitarian intervention but his definition sums up the traditional view. Humanitarian intervention is an act which seeks to intervene to stop a government murdering its own people. Traditionally, intervention has been defined in terms of a coercive breach of the walls of the castle of sovereignty. Such a breach violates the cardinal norm of sovereignty, and its logical corollary the principle of non-intervention, which is enshrined in customary international law and codified in Article 2 (7) of the UN Charter. This prohibits the UN from intervening in matters which are 'essentially within the domestic jurisdiction of any state'. Vincent's description of intervention does not offer a definitive judgement on its legality, and this is a very controversial issue in relation to humanitarian intervention. The majority of international lawyers, labelled **restrictionists**, argue that the prohibition on the use of force in Article 2 (4) of the UN Charter renders **forcible humanitarian intervention** illegal. The only legitimate exception to this general ban is the right of self-defence in Article 51 of the UN Charter. We will explore the reasoning behind this prohibition in the next section, but this position is contested by the '**counter-restrictionists**' who argue that there is a legal right of unilateral and collective humanitarian intervention in the society of states (this position is discussed in the fourth section of this chapter).

Conventionally, humanitarian intervention is defined in terms of intervention motivated by humanitarian considerations, but this raises the question as to what counts as humanitarian? The International Committee of the Red Cross defines humanitarian acts as those that 'prevent and alleviate human suffering'. This definition of humanitarianism is claimed to be non-political and impartial in the sense that all human beings are included as worthy of concern irrespective of sex, race, and

---

Box 20.1. R. J. Vincent's Definition of Intervention

Activity undertaken by a state, a group within a state, a group of states, or an international organization which interferes coercively in the domestic affairs of another state. It is a discrete event having a beginning and an end, and it is aimed at the authority structure of the target state. It is not necessarily lawful or unlawful, but it does break a conventional pattern of international relations.

(Vincent 1974: 3–19)

---

nationality. The problem with this definition is that it assumes that humanitarian acts are the same across time and space; that a capacity for humanitarianism naturally inheres in all humans by virtue of a common human nature. Critics of this position argue that what counts as human suffering changes from one historical epoch to another. There is nothing natural or inevitable about who gets defined as human/inhuman. Thus, slavery was regarded as perfectly natural in one century and identified as a scourge against humanity in the next. What this example illustrates is that '[o]ur conception of humanitarianism is culturally specific and has its own biases' (Parekh 1997).

Key Points

- Traditionally, intervention has been defined as a forcible breach of sovereignty which interferes in a state's internal affairs.

- The legality of forcible humanitarian intervention is a matter of dispute between **Restrictionists** and **Counter-Restrictionists**.

- The expression of humanitarian sentiments in world politics is a product of changing historical and social processes.

Nicholas J. Wheeler

Objections to Legitimizing Humanitarian Intervention

There are five key objections to legitimizing a practice of forcible humanitarian intervention which have been advanced, at various times, by scholars, international lawyers, and policy-makers. These objections are not mutually exclusive and they can be found in the writings of both realists and liberals. For example, liberals recognize that principles of humanitarianism are often applied selectively, but in contrast to realists, they are optimistic that state practice can be changed. This liberal aspiration is embodied in **Solidarist international society theory** but the commitment of solidarists to legitimizing a practice of humanitarian intervention is challenged by pluralist international society theorists (see below).

1. States don't Intervene for Primarily Humanitarian Reasons

Bhikhu Parekh argues that humanitarian intervention 'is an act wholly or primarily guided by the sentiment of humanity, compassion or fellow-feeling, and is in that sense disinterested' (Parekh 1997). Realism tells us that states only pursue their national interest (see Ch. 6) and that an intention of this kind is ruled out since states are motivated solely by what they judge to be their national interest.

2. States are not Allowed to Risk their Soldiers' Lives on Humanitarian Crusades

Realists not only argue that states *do* not intervene for humanitarian reasons, they are also asserting that states *should* not behave in this way. State leaders—those men and women who think and act in the name of states—do not have the moral right to shed blood on behalf of suffering humanity. Bhikhu Parekh (1997) expresses well the core postulates of the statist paradigm:[3] 'the state is only responsible for its own citizens and . . . its obligations and duties are limited to them'. Thus, if a civil authority has broken down or is behaving in an appalling way towards its citizens, this is the responsibility of that state's citizens and its political leaders. Outsiders have no moral duty to intervene even if they would be able to improve the situation and stop the killing.

3. The Problem of Abuse

This realist argument against humanitarian intervention contends that it should not be legitimized as an exception to the principle of the non-use of force because this will lead to **abuse**, a problem identified by Thomas Franck and Nigel Rodley. They contend that the prohibition on the use of force in Article 2 (4) of the UN Charter is already vulnerable to states abusing it in the name of self-defence. In the absence of an impartial mechanism for deciding when humanitarian intervention was permissible, states might espouse humanitarian motives as a pretext to cover the pursuit of national self-interest (Franck and Rodley 1973: 275–305). The problem of **abuse** leads some to argue that humanitarian intervention will always be a weapon that the strong will use against the weak.

4. Selectivity of Response

The argument here is that states will always apply principles of humanitarian intervention selectively, resulting in an inconsistency in policy. Because states will be governed by what they judge to be their national interest, they will intervene only when they deem this to be at stake. The problem of selectivity arises when an agreed moral principle is at stake in more than one situation, but national interest dictates a divergence of responses. A good recent example of the selectivity of response is the claim by Muslim states that the West was guilty of double standards in failing to respond as effectively to the plight of Bosnian Muslims as it had in the case of the Iraqi Kurds. Selectivity of response is the problem of failing to treat like cases alike.

5. Disagreement on what Principles should Govern a Right of Humanitarian Intervention

Pluralist[4] **international society theory** identifies an additional obstacle, namely, the problem of how to reach a consensus on what principles should underpin a doctrine of humanitarian intervention. Hedley Bull defined the pluralist conception as one in which states are capable of agreement only for certain minimum purposes, the most crucial being reciprocal recognition of sovereignty and the norm of non-intervention. The subject of humanitarian intervention is a difficult one for theorists of international society since it is the archetypal case where it might be expected that the society of states would agree to privilege individual justice over the norms of sovereignty and non-intervention. Bull was sensitive to considerations of individual justice, but argued that humanitarian intervention should not be permitted in the face of disagreement about what constitutes extreme human rights violations in international society. He was worried that in the absence of a legitimized consensus on what principles should govern a right of individual or collective humanitarian intervention, such a right would undermine international order. This moral defence of the non-intervention principle is based on what moral philosophers call **rule consequentialism**. International order, and hence the general well-being of all individuals, is better served by uphold-

ing the principle of non-intervention than by allowing humanitarian intervention in the absence of a consensus on what considerations are to count as humanitarian. The basic difficulty here is well summed up in the words of Chris Brown (1992: 113): 'The general problem here is that humanitarian intervention is always going to be based on the cultural predilections of those with the power to carry it out.'

Key Points

- States will not intervene for primarily humanitarian reasons.

- States should not intervene for primarily humanitarian reasons as this violates the compact between state and citizens.

- States will abuse a right of humanitarian intervention using it as a cloak to promote national interests.

- States will apply principles of humanitarian intervention selectively.

- In the absence of a legitimized consensus on what principles should govern a right of individual or collective humanitarian intervention, such a right will undermine international order.

- Humanitarian intervention will always be based on the cultural preferences of the powerful.

The Solidarist Case for Humanitarian Intervention

In contrast to **pluralist international society theory**, **solidarist international society theory** argues that there is a legal right and a moral duty of humanitarian intervention. This section is divided up into two parts. The **counter-restrictionist** case for a legal right of humanitarian intervention is explored in the first part, and in the second part I will be investigating the solidarist claim that whatever the legality of humanitarian intervention, there is a moral duty of forcible intervention in exceptional cases of human suffering. It was pointed out earlier that there is a dispute among international lawyers concerning the legality of humanitarian intervention. Anthony Clark and Robert Beck argue that the **counter-restrictionist**

case for a legal right of individual and collective humanitarian intervention rests on two key claims. **First**, that the UN Charter commits states to protecting fundamental human rights and **second**, that there is a right of humanitarian intervention in customary international law (Arend and Beck 1993: 132–7).

1. Protection of Human Rights

Counter-restrictionists challenge the view of **restrictionists** that the UN's primary purpose is to maintain international peace and security. They

Nicholas J. Wheeler

contend that the promotion of human rights should rank alongside the maintenance of international peace and security. Here, they point to the preamble to the UN Charter and Articles 1 (3), 55 and 56 of the Charter. Some **counter-restrictionists** are prepared to go even further, asserting that if the UN fails to take remedial action—as was so often the case during the cold war—individual states have a legal right to intervene with force to reduce human suffering. Michael Reisman and Mryes McDougal assert that the human rights provisions of the Charter—Articles 1 (3), 55 and 56—provide a legal basis for unilateral forcible intervention. They claim that were this not the case it 'would be suicidally destructive of the explicit purposes for which the United Nations was established' (quoted in Arend and Beck 1993: 133). As with the right to self-defence, humanitarian intervention is argued to be a legitimate exception to the non-use of force principle found in Article 2 (4) of the UN Charter.

2. A Customary Right of Humanitarian Intervention

An alternative grounding for a legal right of unilateral humanitarian intervention is found in the assertion that a customary legal right exists independently of the UN Charter. Customary international law is the law of state practice. If, over a period of time, states act in a certain way and come to regard that behaviour as required by the law, then a norm of customary international law has developed. Not only must states actually engage in the practice that is claimed to have the status of customary law, they must do so because they believe that this practice is required by the law. This is described in the language of international law as *opinio juris*. **Counter-restrictionists** contend that states were permitted to engage in humanitarian intervention under pre-Charter customary international law. However, this is a very controversial claim which is rejected by **restrictionists** like Franck and Rodley who argue that there is little or no support in state practice for a legal right of humanitarian intervention (1973: 275–305). The legitimacy of humanitarian intervention in cold war state practice is the subject of the next section, but no discussion of the solidarist case would be sufficient without an examination of the solidarist

claim that humanitarian intervention is sometimes morally required.

3. Is Humanitarian Intervention Morally Required?

How should the society of states decide when the level of human rights abuses has reached the point where forcible intervention is justified? **Solidarist**

Box 20.2. R. J. Vincent's Exceptions to the Non-Intervention Principle

[T]he attraction of the idea of basic rights . . . [is that] it seeks to put a floor under the societies of the world and a not a ceiling over them. From the floor up is the business of the several societies . . . There remains the question of whether international society itself puts in the floor or merely endorses as a good idea the suggestion that it be built. The latter, it might be said, is relatively easy. The international community has produced a number of conventions setting standards on human rights that go well beyond the proclamation of basic rights. The hard question is whether these standards legitimize action, either by international society as a whole or by states as its agents. Or, to put it another way, does a threat to life on the New York subway or in the Sahara desert trigger an international obligation to respond? Is intervention legitimate in these circumstances? The answer is plainly no in these circumstances. Humanitarian intervention is, as Walzer puts it, reserved for extraordinary oppression, not the day-to-day variety. If the threat to life on the New York subway became the systematic killing of all commuters from New Jersey, or the threat to life in the Sahara desert reached famine proportions, in which local governments were implicated by failing to meet their responsibilities, *then* there might fall to the international community a duty of humanitarian intervention

(Vincent 1986: 126–7)

Writing with Peter Wilson in a posthumous work, Vincent expressed his reservations with a 'morality of states' which requires that 'we have to act *as if* other states are legitimate, not because they *are* legitimate [in their upholding of plural conceptions of the good] but because to do otherwise would lead to chaos . . . states ought to satisfy certain basic requirements of decency before they qualify for the protection which the principle of non-intervention provides'

(Vincent and Wilson 1993: 124–5)

Box 20.3. Summary of Key Concepts in the Theory of Humanitarian Intervention

Abuse — states cloak power political interests in the guise of humanitarianism.

Common humanity — we all have human rights by virtue of our common humanity, and these rights generate correlative moral duties for individuals and state leaders.

Failed states — states that have collapsed into civil war and disorder, and where the government of the state has ceased to exist inside the territorial borders of the state. Citizens find themselves in a quasi-state of nature.

Counter-restric-tionists — international lawyers who argue that there is a legal right of humanitarian intervention in both UN Charter and customary international law.

Forcible humanitarian intervention — military intervention which breaches the principle of state sovereignty where the primary purpose is to alleviate the human suffering of some or all within a state's borders.

Murderous states — the sovereign government is massively abusing the human rights of its citizens, engaging in acts of mass murder and/or genocide.

Non-forcible/non-violent intervention — pacific intervention which can be either consensual (Red Cross) or non-consensual (Médecins Sans Frontières) and which is practised by states, international organizations and INGOs (international non-governmental organizations). It can be short-term (delivery of humanitarian aid) or long-term (conflict-resolution and reconstruction of political life within failed states).

Pluralist international society theory — states are conscious of sharing common interests and common values, but these are limited to norms of sovereignty and non-intervention. Humanitarian intervention is illegitimate in the society of states.

Restriction-ists — international lawyers who argue that humanitarian intervention violates Article 2(4) of the UN Charter and is illegal under both UN Charter law and Customary international law.

Rule-conse-quentialism — international order and hence general well-being is better served by a general prohibition against humanitarian intervention than by sanctioning humanitarian intervention in the absence of agreement on what principles should govern a right of unilateral humanitarian intervention.

Selectivity — an agreed moral principle is at stake in more than one situation, but national interest dictates a divergence of response.

Solidarist international society theory — international society is agreed or capable of agreeing on universal standards of justice and morality which would legitimize practices of humanitarian intervention.

Statism — the moral claim that states only have duties to their own citizens, and that they should not risk their soldiers' lives on humanitarian crusades.

Chapter VII — Article 39 of Chapter VII of the UN Charter authorizes the UN Security Council to 'decide what measures shall be taken in accordance with Articles 41 and 42, to maintain international peace and security'. Article 42 empowers the Security Council to 'take such action by air, sea, or land forces as may be necessary to maintain or restore international peace and security'.

---

international society theory has not provided a satisfactory response to this question, but a pioneering attempt can be found in R. J. Vincent's positing of a 'floor' of basic rights as set out in Box 20.2.

Key Points

- **Solidarist international society theory** is committed to developing consensual moral principles which would legitimize practices of humanitarian intervention in the society of states.

- **Counter-restrictionists** who argue for a collective right of forcible humanitarian intervention belong to the solidarist camp.

- **Counter-restrictionists** who argue for a unilateral right of forcible humanitarian intervention challenge the principle that normative practices should be collectively legitimized; a principle which lies at the heart of **solidarist international society theory**.

Nicholas J. Wheeler

State Practice during the Cold War

This section assesses the extent to which humanitarian intervention was a legitimate practice of states during the cold war. Here, we will focus upon two cases in the post-1945 period where interventionary action by a neighbouring state led to the ending of genocidal behaviour: Tanzania's 1978 intervention in Uganda and Vietnam's 1979 intervention in Cambodia. Two key issues will be explored in relation to these cases: (1) the place of humanitarian motives in the decisions to intervene and the justifications offered by Tanzania and Vietnam for their actions; and (2) the divergent responses of the society of states to these two cases which occurred at the same time.

1. The Motives and Official Justifications of the Tanzanian and Vietnamese Interventions

Gross human rights violations characterized Idi Amin's Uganda Government from start to finish. Amnesty International estimated that up to 300,000 people had been killed during the eight years in which he had been in power. The record is even more appalling in the case of the Khmer Rouge which seized power in Cambodia in April 1975 and immediately embarked upon a course of domestic policies which involved some of the most appalling human rights abuses in this brutally long twentieth century. While accurate figures are difficult to obtain, there is broad agreement that of a population of about 7 million some 2–3 million people lost their lives during the three and a half years in which the Khmer Rouge were in power. Despite this level of human rights abuses, there was no collective intervention to remove these murderous regimes, and it was left to Tanzania and Vietnam to take the law into their own hands. But in neither case did the intervening state claim that its motives were humanitarian. Instead, both Tanzania and Vietnam argued that they were acting in self-defence—the legitimate right of all states under Article 51 of the UN Charter. They claimed with some legitimacy that they were the victims of armed aggression since both Uganda and Cambodia had undertaken

cross-border incursions in the months prior to the invasions. At no time did the governments of Tanzania or Vietnam argue that they had a legal right to use force to stop human suffering.

What explains the reluctance on the part of Tanzania and Vietnam to claim a right of humanitarian intervention? Three explanations have been advanced. First, it is argued that neither of them acted for primarily humanitarian reasons confirming the realist view that states don't risk their soldiers' lives unless significant interests are judged to be at stake. Gary Klintworth's study of these cases led him to conclude that '[w]hile saving human beings from being killed was an inevitable consequence of intervention by Vietnam, and earlier by Tanzania and India, it was always secondary to the overriding priority imposed by concern for vital security interests' (Klintworth 1989: 59). A further reason for the unwillingness of the intervening states to claim a right of humanitarian intervention has been suggested by Adam Roberts. He writes, 'there was probably also a thought that to sanctify a doctrine of humanitarian intervention would be to store up trouble for themselves or their friends' (Roberts 1993: 434). The argument here is that some states with dubious human rights records are fearful of setting precedents for a doctrine of humanitarian intervention which might be employed against them at some future date. However, there is no available evidence to substantiate the claim in relation to Vietnam, and in the case of Tanzania, President Julius Nyerere was a rare and outspoken exponent of humanitarian values. A final explanation is offered by Hedley Bull, who suggests that the society of states was sensitive to the risks involved in taking actions which eroded the principle of non-intervention. Writing in the mid-1980s, Bull stated:

there is no present tendency for states to claim, or for the international community to recognize, any such right [of humanitarian intervention] . . . The reluctance evident in the international community even to experiment with the conception of a right of humanitarian intervention reflects not only an unwillingness to jeopardise the rules of sovereignty and non-intervention by conceding such a right to individual states, but also the lack of any agreed doctrine as to what human rights are. (Bull 1984a: 193)

2. The Response of International Society

Bull's judgement noted above reflected the fact that international society chose to condemn the Vietnamese and Tanzanian interventions as breaches of the principles of non-intervention and non-use of force. However, the international response was to a large degree conditioned by the political and strategic imperatives of the cold war. The case where armed intervention was arguably most justifiable on humanitarian grounds—Vietnam's intervention to overthrow the Pol Pot regime in Cambodia—received the greatest censure. Rather than legitimize Hanoi's overturning of the norm of non-intervention on humanitarian grounds, Vietnam was castigated by both the US-led Western bloc and China for acting as an agent of Soviet imperialism. In contrast, Tanzania's overthrow of Idi Amin received little more than ritualistic public denunciation from the cold war protagonists, with the new Ugandan government rapidly receiving widespread recognition and financial aid from a number of foreign governments. With the exception of the majority of African states which roundly condemned its actions, the rest of the international community reacted in a way which amounted to 'almost tacit approval' (Thomas 1985: 122–3). This would suggest that cold war geopolitics were not as strong a motivating influence in this case, and that Amin had almost totally alienated the Soviet Union, his superpower patron and only ally.

Key Points

- Humanitarian considerations do not seem to have been decisive in the decisions of Vietnam and Tanzania to intervene, although they were stronger in the case of the latter.

- Vietnam and Tanzania justified their interventions in terms of the traditional norms of the society of states.

- The reluctance of the society of states to legitimize humanitarian intervention reflected fears about setting precedents which could erode the non-intervention principle.

- In the polarized world of the late 1970s, reactions to the Tanzanian and Vietnemese intervention were conditioned by cold war geopolitics.

Post-Cold War Humanitarian Interventions

This section focuses on international interventions in Kurdistan, Somalia, and Rwanda. It is divided into **three** parts: (1) the place of humanitarian impulses in state decisions to intervene; (2) the legality and legitimacy of the interventions; and (3) the success of these military interventions.

1. The Role of Humanitarian Sentiments in State Decisions to Intervene

In the cases of Kurdistan and Somalia, the principal force behind intervention was not state leaders taking the lead in persuading reluctant publics to respond to human suffering. Rather, it was the media and domestic public opinion which pressurized policy-makers into taking humanitarian actions. In the face of a massive refugee crisis caused by Saddam Hussein's oppression of the Kurds, US,

British, and Dutch military forces intervened to create protected 'safe havens' for the Kurdish people. James Mayall argues that action was only taken to protect the Kurds 'because the attention devoted by the Western media to the plight of the Kurds along the Turkish border threatened the political dividends that Western governments had secured from their conduct of the war itself' (Mayall 1991: 426). Similarly, the US military intervention in Somalia in December 1992 was a response to sentiments of compassion on the part of US citizens. However, this sense of solidarity disappeared once Americans saw the blood of their fellow countrymen being spilt on the streets of Mogadishu. The fact that the US pulled the plug on its Somali intervention after the loss of eighteen US Rangers in a fire-fight in October 1993 indicates how capricious public opinion is. Television pictures of starving and dying Somalis had persuaded the outgoing Bush administration to launch a humanitarian rescue mission, but once the US public saw the consequences of this in terms of dead Americans being dragged through the streets of Mogadishu, the Clinton administration was forced to announce a timetable for the withdrawal of all US forces from Somalia. What this case demonstrates is that the 'CNN factor' is a double-edged sword: it can pressurize governments into humanitarian intervention, yet with equal rapidity, pictures of casualties arriving home can lead to public disillusionment and calls for withdrawal.

In the cases of intervention in Kurdistan and Somalia, policy-makers primarily acted to appease the humanitarian sentiments of domestic publics. But whilst sensitivity to public opinion was probably the key factor, it would be churlish to deny that moral concerns played some part in leading Western governments to embark on these interventions. What these cases suggest is that even if there are no national interests at stake, liberal states will launch humanitarian rescue missions if sufficient public pressure is mobilized. Certainly, there is no evidence in either case to support the realist claim that states will always abuse humanitarian intervention by cloaking power political motives behind the guise of humanitarianism. Nevertheless, humanitarian interventions which are motivated by the primary concern of responding to pressures from the media and public opinion clearly fail Bhikhu Parekh's definiton of humanitarian intervention as actions 'primarily guided by the sentiment of humanity, compassion or fellow-feeling'.

But if the motives driving the interventions in Somalia and Kurdistan fail Parekh's stringent criteria for a genuine humanitarian intervention, how much more so does French intervention in Rwanda in July 1994 which seems to be an example of **abuse**. The French government emphasized the strictly humanitarian character of the operation, but this interpretation lacks credibility given the evidence that they seem to have been covertly pursuing national self-interest behind the fig-leaf of humanitarianism. France had propped up the one-party Hutu state for twenty years, even providing troops when the Rwandan Patriotic Front (RPF), operating out of neighbouring Uganda, threatened to overrun the country in 1990 and 1993. The French President, Francois Mitterrand, was reportedly anxious to restore waning French credibility in Africa, and was fearful that an RPF victory in French-speaking Rwanda would result in the country coming under the influence of Anglophones. It

seems, therefore, that French behaviour accords with the realist premiss that states will only risk their soldiers in defence of the national interest. State leaders may have been partly motivated by humanitarian sentiments but this seems to be a case of a state **abusing** the concept of humanitarian intervention since the primary purpose of the intervention was to protect French national interests. This is the judgement of Bruce Jones who, on the basis of interviews with French diplomats, concludes that although humanitarian sentiment was not wholly absent, France's primary motives were non-humanitarian. The problem with this verdict, as Jones recognizes, is that for all of the criticisms made of the French intervention, it may be justified on the grounds that lives were saved (Jones 1996: 231–2).

According to Jones, the Rwandan case should lead us to broaden the traditional definition of humanitarian intervention, with its focus on the primacy of humanitarian motives, to encompass humanitarian outcomes. Figure 20.1 sets out Jones's matrix for judging the humanitarian character of interventions. For illustrative purposes, I have filled in three of the boxes with cases drawn from this chapter. Jones does not develop his understanding of humanitarian motives but it is helpful to think of the horizontal line of the matrix as a continuum with pure humanitarian motives at one end and the complete absence of humanitarian motives at the other. Humanitarian interventions launched to appease domestic publics are not examples where the humanitarian motive is primary, but they should be located nearer this end of the continuum than cases where state leaders espouse humanitarian motives to cloak the pursuit of national self-interest. Thus, in the cases of Kurdistan and Somalia, once the interventions were embarked upon, there is no evidence to suggest that the purpose of the intervention was anything other than the promotion of humanitarian values. By contrast, the securing of French national interests was the dominant factor shaping the purposes, execution, and character of French military intervention in Rwanda (Destexhe 1995: 51–5). The vertical line of the matrix indicates the success or failure of interventions in humanitarian terms, but this raises the question as to what counts as a successful humanitarian intervention. This is discussed later in the chapter.

The moral question raised by French intervention is why international society failed to intervene

HUMANITARIAN OUTCOMES

Humanitarian Motives and Outcomes: the international intervention in Northern Iraq in April 1991	**Non-Humanitarian Motives: Humanitarian Outcomes:** Vietnam's intervention in Cambodia in December 1978 and Tanzania's intervention in Uganda
Humanitarian Motives, Non-Humanitarian Outcomes: the UN intervention in Somalia from May 1993 to February 1995	**Non-Humanitarian Motives and Outcomes:** Soviet intervention in Afghanistan in 1979

HUMANITARIAN MOTIVATION (left axis)

NON-HUMANITARIAN MOTIVATION (right axis)

NON-HUMANITARIAN OUTCOMES

Fig. 20.1. Matrix of humanitarian intervention— motivation and outcomes

Source: Adapted from a matrix in Bruce Jones (1996: 239).

forcibly as soon as the genocide began in early April 1994. French intervention might have saved some lives but it came far too late to halt the genocide. The failure of international society demonstrates the limits of states to act as guardians of human rights. It is some two decades since 'Year Zero' in Cambodia—the chilling description of Pol Pot's genocide—but responses to Rwanda indicate that state leaders remain gripped by the mindset of statism. The expression of international solidarity in the face of genocide was limited to moral outrage and the provision of humanitarian aid to the victims of genocide.

2. How Legitimate Were the Interventions?

In contrast with state practice during the cold war, the interventions in Kurdistan, Somalia, and Rwanda were all legitimized in humanitarian terms by the intervening states. The norms of sovereignty and non-intervention remain the key foundations of order, but there is a growing sense—especially among Western states—that these principles should be overturned by the collectivity of states in

cases of exceptional human suffering. However, if post-cold war international interventions suggest a growing willingness on the part of international society to legitimize humanitarian intervention inside state borders, then the key point to note is that none of these interventions have been legitimized by the UN Security Council solely on humanitarian grounds. Chapter VII of the Charter enables the Security Council to authorize military enforcement action only in cases where it finds a threat to 'international peace and security'. This attempt to justify humanitarian intervention on the grounds that human suffering constitutes a threat to international security was most controversially employed in the cases of Kurdistan and Rwanda. With regard to the former, Resolution 688 passed on 5 April 1991 identified the refugee crisis caused by Saddam's repression as constituting a threat to 'international peace and security'. The Resolution was not passed under Chapter VII and there was no explicit authorization of military enforcement action to defend the Kurds in northern Iraq. The reason for this was that Resolution 688 was highly controversial in the eyes of the Soviet Union, China, and a number of other non-Western states on the Council. These states were fearful that authorizing the use of force to protect human rights would set a precedent for humanitarian intervention that might be employed against them and/or undermine the non-intervention norm in the society of states. The refusal of the UN Security Council to provide a military enforcement mandate for international intervention in Northern Iraq forced the Western powers to justify their military intervention as authorized by the language of Resolution 688. However, this attempt at securing legitimacy was not well-received among UN member-states or within the UN Secretariat because this justification was perceived as bordering on illegality.

In stark contrast to Kurdistan, the UN Security Council approved unanimously the US intervention in Somalia to create a secure environment for the delivery of humanitarian aid. Resolution 794 passed under Chapter VII in December 1992 represented a sharp break in existing practice, for as Christopher Greenwood notes, 'it was the plight of the Somali people which was given as the reason for invoking Chapter VII of the Charter and authorizing intervention' (Greenwood 1993: 37). The direct relationship between the internal governance of Sub-Saharan states and the wider security of states and peoples in that region was affirmed in Resolution 794, but this justification has to be seen in the context of a UN Security Council trying to accommodate new practices of humanitarian intervention in the society of states within the framework of the dominant **restrictionist** interpretation of UN Charter law (Roberts 1993: 440). The reason why the UN Security Council legitimized US military intervention in Somalia, in contrast to the position it had taken over intervention in Kurdistan, was because it did not conform to the classical model of intervention against a government's will. The Somali state had effectively collapsed and humanitarian intervention was legitimized because it was perceived as not undermining the principles of sovereignty and non-intervention (Roberts 1993: 440). Nevertheless, non-Western states were sufficiently sensitive to the dangers of being seen to legitimize exceptions to the non-intervention principle that they ensured that the drafting of Resolution 794 undermined its import as a case of humanitarian intervention. For example, immediately prior to noting the relationship between human suffering and threats to international peace and security, the resolution recognizes the 'unique character of the present situation in Somalia and mindful of its deteriorating, complex and extraordinary nature, requiring an immediate and exceptional response'. The use of terms such as **'unique'**, **'extraordinary'**, and **'exceptional'** have to be seen as an attempt to differentiate the humanitarian crisis in Somalia from other cases of **failed** states, hence reducing the chance of setting a precedent for future humanitarian interventions. They seem to have been inserted specifically to appease the fears of states such as China which may have otherwise blocked a Chapter VII enforcement action.

What emerges from post-cold war state practice is that any normative shift on the question of humanitarian intervention is primarily confined to the media and public opinion within liberal democratic states. Many non-western states question the West's (and especially US) motives in advocating humanitarian intervention, seeing it as a new form of 'imperialism' which will leave the weak vulnerable to the cultural preferences of the strong (Thomas 1993: 91–101). Third World state leaders may genuinely value practices of sovereignty and non-intervention as a way of pragmatically coping with cultural differences, but they may also employ this rhetoric to cover the fact that the human rights

agenda of Western governments is a threat to their own power. Whilst the reaction of some Western states to recent humanitarian crises in Kurdistan and Somalia has been substantially influenced by the need to respond to domestic electorates, public opinion is not such a powerful force in those states which are hostile to the emerging human rights agenda of the post-cold war world.

The most powerful challenger to post-cold war Western-sponsored humanitarian interventions has been China. When issues of intervention have arisen, China has proved to be the most cautious of the Security Council's permanent members, though the reason for this remains unclear. It seems unlikely that its concern over the erosion of the non-intervention principle stems from a fear that, at some future date, it may itself become the target of intervention. China is protected against such an eventuality by both its veto within the Security Council and a military capability which makes any form of coercive intervention against it wholly untenable. It seems more likely that China's experience at the hands of the colonial powers, its radically different conception of human rights, and its suspicion of Western motives in promoting humanitarian intervention, lies behind a normative position which places sovereignty and non-intervention at the pinnacle of a hierarchy of principles. If this is so, and China is genuinely concerned about the dangers of eroding Article 2 (7) of the UN Charter on grounds of both **rule-consequentialism** and fears of **abuse**, then the extent to which humanitarian intervention is likely to gain legitimate status within the UN Security Council will remain very limited.

If the practice of legitimizing humanitarian intervention through Chapter VII of the UN Charter is contested in the society of states, unilateral humanitarian intervention without UN approval remains an illegitimate practice in post-cold war international politics. Prior to French intervention in Rwanda, there were reports that Paris was considering intervention even without Security Council backing. However, French policy-makers, perhaps realizing the implications of being seen to claim a customary right of unilateral humanitarian intervention, were emphatic that their action was conditional on receiving a mandate from the UN Security Council. Nevertheless, there was suspicion on the part of many states on the Council that Paris was manipulating the legitimacy of post-cold war humanitarianism to cover actions motivated primarily by national self-interest. This fear that France was abusing humanitarian claims was reflected in the fact that five Council members abstained on the vote on Resolution 929.

Ideally, unilateral humanitarian intervention would always operate with the flag of UN Security Council legitimacy. But as we have seen with the Tanzanian and Vietnamese interventions, cases have arisen where the UN Security Council has failed as a guardian of human rights, and local states have intervened without UN Security Council approval. Humanitarian motives may not have been the principal motivation in these cases, but they still produced significant humanitarian benefits. Should Vietnam have been condemned by the international community for breaching the principles of international order, even though it ended Pol Pot's genocidal regime? Mark Hoffman argues that although undesirable, unilateral military intervention 'could be supported . . . because it may be the only effective option available to stop massive, unwarranted killings' (Hoffman 1993: 206), and Tom Farer contends that unilateral intervention might be legitimate where it 'is calculated to cause less damage to the target society than would inaction' (1993: 327). The weakness of Hoffman's and Farer's normative position is that in focusing on individual cases of human suffering, they underestimate how far legitimizing unilateral humanitarian intervention might bring about a generalized erosion of the norms of non-intervention and non-use of force, and with it a long-term reduction in general well-being. But this advocacy of **rule-consequentialism** leads to the strong claim that even if it is calculated that military intervention could prevent or halt genocide, the absence of Security Council approval renders such an action not only illegal, but also illegitimate. A tension undeniably exists between the requirements of international order and the possibility that unilateral action may be the only way of stopping gross violations of human rights.

3. Were the Interventions Successful?

The underlying assumption of those who advocate unilateral forcible humanitarian intervention is that in some cases it might be the only means of stopping massive human rights abuses. But does the record of post-cold war forcible interventions lend support to the proposition that the use of force can promote humanitarian values? We argued earlier that **humanitarian outcomes** are as significant as **humanitarian motives** in determining the humanitarian character of interventions. Humanitarian outcomes might usefully be divided into **short** and **long-term** consequences of humanitarian intervention. The former would refer to the immediate alleviation of human suffering through the termination of genocide or mass murder and/or the delivery of humanitarian aid to civilians trapped in war zones. Long-term humanitarian outcomes focus on how far intervention addresses the underlying causes of human suffering by facilitating conflict-resolution and the reconstruction of viable polities. Defining humanitarian outcomes in this manner is favoured by moral philosophers like Bhikhu Parekh and Michael Walzer. Parekh argues that the delivery of aid in complex humanitarian emergencies is not humanitarian intervention which he defines as 'a political act intended to help create a structure of civil authority acceptable to the people involved' (Parekh 1997). His contention is that humanitarian intervention differs from other forms of intervention in aiming to ensure that new structures of government are evolved in consultation with local political actors, rather than being imposed from outside. This is also the argument of Walzer who challenges the traditional **counter-restrictionist** assumption that humanitarian interveners should conduct a quick military intervention and then withdrawal having removed the source of the human rights abuses (Arend and Beck 1993: 134). This might have been realistic in the cold war period where forcible intervention could end the human rights abuses of genocidal regimes (as in Tanzania's intervention in Uganda). However, Walzer argues that this type of intervention is not appropriate to post-cold war humanitarian crises where the sources of human suffering are often deeply rooted in the political, economic, and social structures of societies. Walzer contends that if intervention does not address the underlying roots of these conflicts, the withdrawal of the intervening force will simply lead to the resumption of violent conflict. He argues that the use of force in complex humanitarian emergencies should be employed as part of a long-term project of conflict-resolution and political, economic and social reconstruction (Walzer 1995: 35–6).

Given this conceptualization of short-term and

long-term humanitarian outcomes, how should we evaluate the international interventions in Kurdistan and Somalia? 'Operation Safe Haven' enjoyed initial success in dealing with the refugee problem in Northern Iraq and clearly saved lives. However, as the media spotlight began to shift elsewhere and public interest waned, so did the commitment of Western governments to protect the Kurds. Whilst Western airforces continue to police a 'no-fly zone' over northern Iraq extending limited protection, the intervening states quickly handed over the running of the 'safe havens' to what they knew was an ill-equipped and badly supported UN relief operation. This faces enormous problems given Iraq's enduring hostility towards its Kurdish minority. Despite its success in alleviating the immediate suffering of the Kurds, five years later the intervention appears to have been little more than a short-term palliative which has failed to address their long-term plight.

The initial US intervention in Somalia in the period between December 1992 and May 1993 is adduced by some as evidence of a successful humanitarian intervention. In terms of short-term success, the US arguably saved thousands of Somalis from starvation, but the mission eventually ended in disaster and withdrawal. This can be traced to the attempt by UNOSOM II (this UN force took over from the Americans in May 1993 but it was under a US commander and its military missions were principally controlled by the US) to go beyond the initial US mission of famine relief to the demilitarization of the warring factions and the provision of law and order in Somali society. Suffering always has political causes, and the rationale behind the expanded mandate of UNOSOM II was to try and put in place a framework of political civility which would prevent a return to civil war and famine. However, this attempt to convert a short-term humanitarian outcome (famine relief) into the longer-term outcome of conflict-resolution and reconstruction proved a failure. The problem was that the UN's impartiality was more and more called into question as it tried to impose solutions upon the fragile 'clan' relations that underpin Somali society. Once the UN Security Council sanctioned the arrest of one of the clan leaders, General Aidid, after the killing of 23 UN peace-keepers in June 1993, UNOSOM II acted like an imperial power, relying on high-tech American weaponry to police the streets of Southern Mogadishu. Indeed, the shift from **famine-relief to war-making** was graphically illustrated by the television footage of US helicopter gunships firing missiles into the urban areas of southern Mogadishu.

Is **forcible intervention** in humanitarian crises always condemned to be a short-term palliative? And if so, is it the most appropriate form of intervention? The problem in the cases studied here is that the initial determination to employ force in defence of humanitarian goals was not backed up by a long-term political, economic, and social commitment to the interventionary project. States that intervene militarily as agents of common humanity need to have a clear formulation of short-term and long-term objectives, which balances immediate responses to the humanitarian crisis with a sustained commitment to conflict-resolution and social reconstruction.

Key Points

- Media images of human suffering have led Western publics to pressurize their leaders into post-cold war humanitarian interventions.

- Humanitarian intervention has only been legitimized through the Chapter VII enforcement provisions of the Security Council, confirming the dominance of the **restrictionist** view of the illegality of humanitarian intervention.

- Non-Western states, notably China, are suspicious of legitimizing humanitarian intervention through the broadening of Chapter VII.

- Fears about **rule-consequentialism** and **abuse** remain powerful barriers to legitimizing unilateral humanitarian intervention.

- The humanitarian character of interventions should be judged in terms of both **motives** and **outcomes.**

- Humanitarian outcomes should be conceptualized in terms of a continuum ranging from **short-term** (immediate relief of suffering) to **long-term** (addressing the underlying causes of suffering).

Globalization and Non-Forcible Humanitarian Intervention

As we have seen, the traditional approach to humanitarian intervention focuses on states and **forcible intervention**. Intervention is characterized by coercion, a breach of sovereignty, and is non-consensual. By contrast, **non-forcible humanitarian intervention** emphasizes the pacific activities of states, international organizations and non-governmental organizations in delivering humanitarian aid and facilitating third party conflict-resolution and reconstruction. **Non-forcible humanitarian intervention** can be consensual or non-consensual. An example of the latter is the activities of Médecins Sans Frontières which frequently operates without the consent of host governments, but which works through non-violent methods to bring humanitarian relief. Consensual acts include the diplomacy of third party mediation and the practices of the International Committee of the Red Cross which normally only operates with the consent of sovereign governments. The weakness, then, of restricting humanitarian intervention to coercive/forcible acts is that such a definition provides no framework for accommodating the non-military humanitarian activities of states and non-state actors. The humanitarian interventions in Kurdistan and Somalia have shown the problems of holding too rigidly to the narrow definition, since in both these cases, military force was deployed in an effort to create a secure 'humanitarian space' within which the non-forcible arm of humanitarianism could operate (Ramsbotham and Woodhouse 1996).

The activities of humanitarian agencies in complex humanitarian emergencies reflect the growth of a global society in which humanitarian organizations operate transnationally. Globalization has generated many of the ills of contemporary life but it has also created that growing sense of 'cosmopolitan moral awareness' (Bull 1984*b*: 12) which is beginning to make a reality of Kant's vision of a right's violation in one place being felt everywhere. The global human rights culture seeks to protect human rights and humanitarian values everywhere. This culture is a product of the post-holocaust world and it is embedded in the ideas and practices of international civil servants, media, local Non-Governmental Organizations and a global network of humanitarian International Non-Governmental Organizations which are sustained and supported by that transnational global citizenry committed to human rights and humanitarianism (Minear and Weiss 1995; Jones 1995). This community is anti-statist but not necessarily anti-state; governments often fail to act as local agents of **common humanity,** but a key challenge for those who want to deepen global moral solidarities is to harness state power to the purposes of global humanitarianism. The global human rights culture is a unique and progressive feature of the globalization of world politics at the end of the millennium. Its existence reflects the growing recognition that the causes of human rights abuses and humanitarian crises are global ones which require global solutions. **Non-forcible humanitarian intervention** is usually defined in terms of the activities of non-state actors and third party mediators in complex humanitarian emergencies, but it also needs to encompass global interventionary strategies designed to address the underlying causes of human suffering in world politics.

The question of how and why human suffering gets constructed in the way it does in late twentieth-century world politics is beyond the scope of this chapter. However, consider the following question posed by Parekh: Why, he asks, 'should suffering and death only become a matter of humanitarian intervention when they are caused by the breakdown of the state or by an outrageous abuse of its power'? (Parekh 1997). The answer to this question is that what counts as human suffering is a product of the ideological biases of global political and economic élites. It suits dominant élites to construct humanitarian intervention in terms of crisis management rather than developing the global political and economic policies to address the underlying structural causes of poverty and malnutrition. There is nothing natural or inevitable about the facts of global poverty; it is a product of the handiwork of individuals and social classes whose interactions have constructed global capitalism. These structures are deeply rooted, produce a global alienated underclass, and their transformation must be the objective of an emancipatory global politics of **non-forcible humanitarian intervention**.

Key Points

- Non-forcible humanitarian intervention is characterized by the pacific activities of states, international organizations, and INGOs in the global humanitarian community.

- Non-forcible humanitarian intervention spans the crisis management activities of humanitarian

INGOs and third party conflict-resolution by states and non-state actors.

- Dominant Western political and economic élites encourage a crisis management approach to complex humanitarian emergencies which does nothing to tackle the underlying causes of these emergencies.

- Humanitarian crises like Somalia and Rwanda are the tip of the iceberg of human suffering. The slow death of millions through poverty and malnutrition are just as pressing cases for humanitarian intervention.

Conclusion

Humanitarian intervention remains a contested issue at the end of the cold war. Realism and **pluralist international society theory** seek to interpret the cases we have discussed in this chapter as confirming their different theoretical positions. Realism purports to describe and explain the 'realities' of statecraft but the problem with this claim to objectivity is that it is the realist mindset which has constructed the very practices that realist theory seeks to explain. Realism identifies some important objections to the practice of humanitarian intervention, but this chapter has argued that **pluralist international society theory** is essential to any understanding of why the society of states has proven so reluctant to legitimize humanitarian intervention. **Pluralist international society theory** reinforces the dominant practices of the society of states which continue to subordinate human rights concerns to state sovereignty. But crucially, there is nothing natural or inevitable about this hierarchy between order and justice. Indeed, changing values and norms could lead to the growth of new solidarist sentiments which produce a just world order.

This chapter is sympathetic to **solidarist international society theory**, but solidarism is a muted voice in contemporary global politics. Solidarism relies on states acting as trustees of **common humanity**, but what emerges from a study of state practice in the 1990s, is that it is not states but an emergent global civil society which is the principal agent promoting humanitarian values in global politics. Globalization is bringing nearer Kant's

vision of moral interconnectedness, but as the Rwandan genocide so brutally demonstrates, this growth in 'cosmopolitan moral awareness' has not yet been translated into the solidarist project of **forcible humanitarian intervention**. Western publics living in the relatively secure sphere of global politics are increasingly sensitized to the human suffering of others, but this media nurtured sense of compassion is very selective in its response to human suffering. The media spotlight ensured that governments directed their humanitarian energies to the crises in Kurdistan, Somalia, and Bosnia, but during the same period millions perished in the brutal civil wars in Angola, Liberia, and Afghanistan.

A growing consciousness of **common humanity** permeates the emerging global civil society: but how can this society best promote humanitarianism? Is **forcible humanitarian intervention** sometimes the only way that global civil society can respond to massive human rights abuses? Or, is the use of violence to stop even greater violence a strategy that can only result in a spiral of bloodletting to the detriment of humanitarian goals? Each case has to be judged on its merits but as the example of Somalia demonstrates, interventions which begin with humanitarian credentials can all too easily degenerate into 'a range of policies and activities which go beyond, or even conflict with, the label 'humanitarian' (Roberts 1993: 448). A further fundamental problem with a strategy of forcible humanitarian intervention concerns the so-called 'body-bag' factor. Is domestic public opinion, especially in Western states, prepared to see their military personnel die in the cause of humanitarian intervention? The US withdrawal from Somalia after the killing of eighteen US Rangers suggests that liberal societies will not be prepared to stay the course of costly **forcible humanitarian interventions.** Indeed, a striking feature of all post-cold war humanitarian interventions is that no government has yet chosen to risk its military personnel in defence of human rights in situations where there was a high risk of casualties from the outset.

This chapter has examined the case for **non-forcible humanitarian intervention** which it has been argued is a progressive manifestation of the globalization of world politics. The actors in this drama are frequently not states and the means employed are always non-violent. This type of intervention spans a continuum ranging from humanitarian crisis management to crisis prevention, and connects the subject of humanitarian intervention to broader issues of conflict resoluton and the role of third-party mediation. The unresolved question here concerns the issue of how far

forcible intervention might have an important role to play in stimulating and supporting processes of conflict resolution in complex humanitarian emergencies. Beyond this, the **non-forcible** approach to humanitarian intervention opens up the normative question of what counts as human suffering at the end of the twentieth century? The 'loud emergencies' of genocide, ethnic cleansing, and famine receive media attention, and command the limited resources of the international donor community. This conception of humanitarianism is not rooted in objective facts; instead, it is the product of globally dominant beliefs and values which privilege the 'loud emergencies' and exclude the 'silent emergencies' of slow death through poverty and malnutrition. The question for the future is why the eradication of global poverty and malnutrition is not as urgent a subject for humanitarian intervention as the deaths of those killed by men in uniform with machine guns? If humanitarianism is what we've made of it, we don't have to make it like this in our global future.

QUESTIONS

1. How far is the use of force the defining characteristic of a humanitarian intervention?

2. Is motive or outcome the most important in deciding the humanitarian character of an intervention?

3. List the objections to humanitarian intervention.

4. How persuasive is the counter-restrictionist case for a legal right of humanitarian intervention?

5. Should considerations of international order always be privileged over concerns of individual justice in the society of states?

6. Why has the society of states failed to arrive at a collective consensus on what moral principles should underpin a right of humanitarian intervention?

7. Does the illegitimacy of humanitarian intervention in cold war state practice support the theoretical arguments of realists or pluralist international society theorists or both?

8. Have there been any genuinely humanitarian interventions since the end of the cold war?

9. Is there a new legitimate practice of humanitarian intervention at the end of the cold war?

10. How far is military force an effective instrument for the promotion of humanitarian values?

11. What are the strengths and weaknesses of a strategy of non-forcible humanitarian intervention?

12. Are late twentieth-century conceptions of humanitarianism infused with the ideological biases and cultural preferences of the dominant Western states?

GUIDE TO FURTHER READING

Ramsbotham, O., and Woodhouse, T., *Humanitarian Intervention: A Reconceptualization* (Cambridge: Polity, 1996). This is an excellent book which provides the most comprehensive analysis of the conceptual issues raised by the subject of humanitarian intervention. It presents a powerful case for broadening humanitarian intervention to include non-forcible approaches. It also contains very good case-study material on Bosnia and Somalia.

Minear, L., and Weiss, T. G., *Mercy Under Fire: War and the Global Humanitarian Community* (Boulder, Col.: Westview Press, 1995). An excellent treatment of the humanitarian principles of the contemporary global humanitarian community, and its operational effectiveness in post-cold war humanitarian conflicts.

Damrosch, L. F. (ed.), *Enforcing Restraint: Collective Intervention in Internal Conflicts* (New York: Council on Foreign Relations, 1993) This book contains some very good theoretical chapters on the legality and legitimacy of humanitarian intervention, and excellent case-study material on the former Yugoslavia, Kurdistan, Somalia, Liberia, and Haiti.

Harriss, J. (ed.), *The Politics of Humanitarian Intervention* (London: Pinter, 1995). This is very good at examining the role of the global humanitarian community in responding to complex humanitarian emergencies, and has very good case-studies of Kurdistan and Somalia.

NOTES

1. The term is Eduardo Rabossi's and was discussed by Richard Rorty in his 1993 Amnesty International lecture, 'Sentimentality and Human Rights'.
2. The term is Stanley Hoffmann's. See his 'The Politics and Ethics of Military Intervention', Survival, 37: 4 (1995–6), 31.
3. I am following Tim Dunne in conceptualizing statism as one of the common elements which make up the core of realism in world politics. Dunne identifies self-help and survival as the other two. For the purposes of this chapter, I define statism as the belief that states only have duties to their own citizens, and that they should not risk their soldiers' lives on humanitarian crusades.
4. The term pluralism here should not be confused with the idea of pluralism found in the literature on interdependence and transnationalism (see Ch. 8). Bull first used this term to refer to the debate within the international society tradition in his chapter on the 'The Grotian conception of international society' in Herbert Butterfield and Martin Wight (eds.), *Diplomatic Investigations* (London: Allen and Unwin, 1966).

21 Regionalism and Integration

Fiona Butler

READER'S GUIDE

Definition and theoretical explanation of regionalism and integration has been a consistent feature of the study of international relations. The development of relatively cohesive and integrated regional groupings has concerned some writers whose focus has been upon the maintenance of world order and stability. This chapter briefly reviews some experience of regionalism and integration within different regions of the world and concludes that whilst these examples serve different political and economic ends, in a transnational globalized economy, regional integration and co-operation may offer the only viable framework for the maintenance of 'national' polities and societies.

This chapter begins by reviewing how concepts of regionalism and integration have been defined and used in the study of international relations. We then move on to consider contemporary examples of regional co-operation and integration. A diverse range of historical, cultural, and political factors influence the type and structures of regionalism, depending on which world region we are consider-ing. Western European experience of regional integration since 1945 has dominated interna-tional relations but we should not readily transpose explanations of European integration to other world regions. The chapter concludes that in the post-cold war globalized system, regionalism and integration may constitute important world order mechanisms.

Defining Regionalism and Integration

During the 1960s and in the wake of what appeared to be widespread enthusiasm for developing regional groupings and schemes to promote eco-nomic integration, regions in international politics were described as 'a limited number of states linked by a geographical relationship and by a degree of mutual interdependence', and could be differenti-ated according to the level and scope of exchange, formal organizations, and political interdepen-dence (Nye 1968: vii). Nye suggested that processes of regionalism and integration across many areas of the globe were aided by the growing number of newly independent former colonies; by some degree of relaxation in tense superpower relations; by a growing realization that economic interdepen-dence and an open multilateral trading regime brought their own pitfalls; and by a successful rap-prochement of key West European countries through economic integration schemes.

Regionalism required not merely geographical proximity and increased economic interdepen-dence for its promotion. Other factors were also important in underpinning potential development of regional problem-solving processes. Historical experiences, power and wealth distribution within and outside the grouping, cultural social and ethnic traditions, and ideological or political preferences can be central to understanding why and how actors perceive regional solutions to be desirable.

However regionalism can be a somewhat mono-lithic concept to define. One writer suggests that we break it down into specific or concrete types (Hurrell 1995). By doing this we are more able to identify important variations of regionalism. Variations can be explained according to, for exam-ple, the level of growth in socio-economic interde-pendence; the extent to which shared values and cultural traditions persist; the extent to which for-mal institutional arrangements are sought; and the extent to which a regional grouping displays a cohesive identity and external presence. Governments and states may be key actors in some regional groupings, whilst corporate and economic interests may be more important actors in others. Regional groupings may be concerned primarily with maximizing economic welfare and gains from intra-regional trade and investment, whilst others may be more concerned with defence and security, or the protection of social and cultural traditions.

These types of regionalism include:

- Regionalism: a process involving the growth of informal linkages and transactions derived pri-marily from economic activity but involving social and political interconnectedness too.

- Regional awareness and identity: where a mix-ture of historical, cultural, and social traditions lead to a 'shared perception' of belonging to a particular community.

- Regional interstate co-operation: states or gov-ernments may sponsor agreements and co-ordi-nation amongst themselves to manage common problems and 'protect and enhance the role of the state and the power of the government'.

- State-promoted regional economic integration: often the most common form of regionalism, governments and business interests pursue eco-nomic integration (this can differ in terms of depth or sectoral scope) in order to promote trade liberalization and economic growth.

- Regional cohesion: whereby 'a combination of these first four processes might lead to the emer-gence of a cohesive and consolidated regional unit'. Such a highly politically cohesive grouping can have a decisive impact upon both its 'internal' environment and upon global politics.

(based on Hurrell 1995: 334–8)

The concept of **integration** has been rather more difficult to define. Integration can be understood as a condition or as a process; as a description of a system and its elements already in existence; or as an explanation of how a political system is sustained and developed in a particular direction. Definitions of and expectations surrounding international political economic integration have reflected problems of clarification and shared meaning (see Box 21.1 for illustration).

A useful definition sees integration as 'the creation and maintenance of intense and diversified patterns of interaction among previously autonomous units. These patterns may be partly economic in character, partly social, partly political: definitions of political integration all imply accompanying high levels of economic and social interaction' (Wallace 1990: 9). This definition is useful for understanding integration in **formal**—conscious political decisions—or **informal** terms—economic social and cultural flows. Integration within world regions can be a complex and multi-layered process involving different types of actors, operating across and between different areas of human activity, and relying on different dynamics.

Integration as a formal conscious process designed to deepen interrelatedness and exchanges between a group of countries can, of course, assume different forms. **Economic** integration often involves customs unions (removing customs duties from goods traded amongst countries), free trade arrangements (removing customs duties tariffs and other restrictions from particular goods) or common markets (liberalization of all economic activities, removal of all restrictions to economic exchange and creation of common or shared rules and regulations in place of differing national laws). **Political** integration can involve not merely the formation of institutional mechanisms and decision-making procedures but the development of shared values and expectations, peaceful resolution of disputes and socio-political cohesiveness.

The discipline of international relations has displayed a continuity for evaluating regionalism's effects upon system-wide peace, stability, and order. The study of regionalism and integration lies in the problems of how conflict can be avoided, and how co-operation and stability can be maintained. Traditional balance of power and alliance theories stressed the maintenance of order and security through establishment of (regional) defensive coalitions and by 'balancing' military capabilities relative to others. During this century's interwar period, global collective security and functional international organization were seen as desirable alternatives to bellicose 'great power concert' regionalism. Post-1945 international politics dominated by bipolar competition and rivalry inevitably led to regional alignment to one camp or the other. One significant exception concerned the Non-Aligned Movement, which emerged in the 1950s precisely to avoid relationships of dependency upon the superpowers. Successful West European co-operation and integration was heavily supported by US financial and defence committment, whilst Eastern and Central Europe was forcibly or strongly encouraged to join the Soviet bloc.

In the post-1989 period, global politics are fluid and multipolar. Mainstream international relations

---

Box 21.1. Conceptual Approaches toward Integration

The **pluralist** tradition in international relations theory emphasizes a diversity of actors, not merely nation-states, involved in political activity. Within this tradition, Karl Deutsch argued that increased patterns of communications and exchange ('transaction') between different actors could strengthen the bonds (integration) of transnational political community, leading to formation of a **'security community'** based on expectations of peaceful co-operative behaviour. Also within this tradition, Ernst Haas developed neo-functionalist analysis to predict that a federal Europe would emerge as a result of a gradual transfer of sovereignty and 'political loyalties' by political and business élites spilling over into different issue areas.

The **realist** tradition, on the other hand, emphasizes structural conditions as the explanatory factor. Intergovernmental approaches (also referred to as 'Gaullist', after the impact of France's President de Gaulle upon European politics) and neo-realist and neo-liberal perspectives see integration arising from states' interactions, interests, and bargaining or negotiation strategies. These approaches view integration processes in utilitarian terms, or in other words, how structural conditions of power and authority based upon sovereign territorial units can be employed to strengthen the position and capabilities of those units relative to each other.

theory is largely concerned with how institutionalized co-operative regional groups may, or may not, be an integral element in maintaining a peaceful multipolar international system. The development of regional co-operation and structures is often explained as a utilitarian and state-driven process enabling states to reconcile competing demands in the face of global political and economic challenges. The **neo-realist–neo-liberal** debate in international relations is divided on whether regional co-operation and groupings are effective and reliable instruments to maintain order and peace. This prominent debate in mainstream international relations theory encourages us to think about important characteristics of co-operation such as reciprocity (expectation of mutually regarding behaviour); distribution of gains from co-operation (to prevent or reduce self-seeking competitive behaviour of members of the co-operative arrangement); 'learning' processes which over time induce trust and close relations between members; and the extent to which the arrangement, supported by a high degree of institutionalization, can take autonomous or independent action over its members.

The study of international political economy sees economic and technological change as the catalyst of global political change. From this perspective, integration of 'national' economic and corporate activities can be seen as adjustment strategies in a turbulent and highly flexible global economy. Meanwhile much of the discipline of international relations remains rooted in conceptions of territorial sovereign power. This can be problematic because 'the logic and apparatus of statehood is not conducive to transnational integration, economic or political; but the outcomes of Neo-Fordism have forced many states to explore co-operative strategies of various kinds' (Knox and Agnew 1994: 380). 'Neo-Fordism' is a phrase used to capture the changed relationship between capital investment, production processes, and labour forces away from traditional reliance upon large manufacturing plants and assembly lines characterized by Henry Ford earlier in this century. These changes are associated with dominant global economic or cultural patterns are also related to regionally oriented dynamics and identities.

Key Points

- Basic conditions for the development of regionalism and integration—geographical proximity and a degree of economic interdependence—have to be supplemented by analysis of important historical, political, and cultural factors if we are to understand why and how regionalism develops.

- The interplay of these factors brings about different types of regionalism. A number of formal strategies and informal processes can successively integrate activities within a region, and therefore characterize important differences between regional groupings.

- The study of international politics is characterized by a number of different theoretical approaches, some of which are important in clarifying what we mean by and how we study the emergence of regional identities and practices. In recent years profound and rapid global changes to economic production, capital, culture, and politics have been interpreted and managed in different ways by different regional groups. International relations theory has begun to adapt to this.

Regionalism in World Politics

Development of regional blocs and groupings has become a steadily progressive feature of post-1945 world politics. International relations theories have explained such developments in terms of balancing against a hegemonic or 'great' power; protecting small or weak states against a large powerful neighbour; maintaining peaceful and co-operative political relationships; and as transformations of global power and wealth structures. In order to discuss these issues we now turn to a number of examples of regionalism in world politics, involving the Americas, South East Asia, Africa, and Europe.

Latin, Central, and North America

Factors such as a wide geographical area, different development levels and strategies of countries, and the existence of political and military conflict have been important in shaping sub-regional co-operation and integration. Region-wide economic cohesion does benefit from the lending facilities provided by the Inter-American Development Bank and the Latin American Integration Association (formerly LAFTA) since the early 1980s. Countries in Latin America have consistently pursued forms of regional economic integration, as have Central American and Caribbean states. Canada, the United States (US), and Mexico formed in 1994 the North American Free Trade Association (NAFTA).

Many Latin American countries, particularly by the 1950s, saw economic development as the key issue for their political survival and social prosperity. The post-1945 international economy dominated by free trade, free markets, and Bretton Woods institutions underpinned by US economic and political power did not augur well for Latin American countries. They feared that in an international economy driven by mass production and consumption, small import-dependent and non-industrialized countries would remain economically and politically peripheral. Regional economic integration schemes bolstered by domestic policies of import-substitution became vital to the survival and functioning of Latin America. An economic policy characterized by import substitution was designed to 'protect a nation's infant industries so that the overall industrial structure could be developed and diversified and dependence on foreign technology and capital reduced' (Dicken 1992: 177).

Population growth, social tensions resulting from an iniquitous distribution of wealth, and the limited 'import capacity' of Latin America markets were key factors in decisions by political élites to develop regional economic integration schemes.

Support for greater regionalism encouraged by the United Nations Economic Commission for Latin America built up during the 1950s and was driven largely by political fears of economic marginalization. None the less, another key factor affecting these calculations lay in the economic dominance (or hegemony) and political influence of the neighbouring US.

By 1960 the **Central American Common Market** (CACM) was set up. This arrangement, involving El Salvador, Guatemala, Honduras, Nicaragua, and Costa Rica introduced elements of regulation and policy co-ordination to foster intra-regional trade. These included a customs union, a central bank to help fund growth within the group, and a common external tariff applicable to imports entering the common market. During the 1960s the CACM proved to be a successful mechanism for stimulating trade investment and growth amongst its members. However, growing tensions and later conflict between El Salvador and Honduras resulted in Honduras' withdrawal from the CACM. During the 1970s and 1980s increasing conflict and political instability—exemplified by the Sandinista revolution, 'contra' war in Nicaragua and increasing US involvement in the region—hindered further political and economic integration. Since the late 1980s however, political initiatives undertaken by the Contadora group to end the conflict in Nicaragua have sustained a fresh approach to rebuilding the region; during 1991 the members of CACM renewed this framework and extended free trade arrangements to Mexico. The CACM members remain keen to develop close links, if not a merger, with the **Caribbean Common Market** (CARICOM).

South America is characterized by a number of regional integration schemes and co-operation between richer developing countries. For example the **Andean Group** 'was formed by LAFTA members who were dissatisfied with the course of integration but unwilling to resign from LAFTA . . . [and] aimed at accommodating the differing levels of development of their economies' (Pope Atkins 1995: 185). The Andean Group (comprising Bolivia, Columbia, Ecuador, Peru, and Venezuela) made major efforts beginning in the late 1960s to develop economic union, through liberalizing and freeing trade and creating investment and industrial development programmes. Extra help and extended timetables for the removal of trade restrictions was intended to compensate the weaker members. The members of the Andean Group were also concerned to use these arrangements in order to maintain oversight of increasing penetration by foreign corporate companies and investments. Despite the ambitious and dynamic approach of these countries actual progress has been patchy and the Group has a mixed record overall. Political difficulties associated with different government philosophies, territorial disputes, and infrastructural weaknesses combined to dilute progress already made.

None the less, the Andean Group members continued in the early 1990s to affirm their committment to regional economic integration and union.

A more recent development can be seen in the 1991 formation of **MERCOSUR (Common Market of the South**, or **Southern Cone)**. Brazilian and Argentinian political initiative has been crucial for this grouping including Paraguay and Uruguay. Given the economic, technological, and environmental significance of Brazil and Argentina it was not surprising that those states sought not merely to strengthen economic co-operation and establish a common market, but also incorporated elements of political co-operation.

All these countries in the post-cold war period have sought to revitalize earlier groupings, develop new forms of co-operation and formal integration, and in some cases underpin their economic and political security concerns by bilateral initiatives, as for example Mexican Colombian and Venezuelan co-ordination (in the Group of 3) of energy policies. Different economic strategies—from state-promoted economic development, import-substitution, debt rescheduling, regionally oriented trade liberalization and structural adjustment policies—have shaped the variegated appearance and successes of regional integration. The persistence of co-operative groupings and regional institutions to manage shared political and social problems is significant, since 'the "return to the region" and the revival of Latin American interest in hemispheric co-operation has reflected the perceived relative absence of foreign policy and foreign economic policy alternatives' (Hurrell 1994: 170).

Concern, or fear, for political and economic marginalization in a region dominated by US political power and covert strategic involvement explains much regional activity in Central and Latin America. These concerns are not new. Simon Bolivar, the nineteenth-century 'Liberator' revolutionary actively worked toward the unification of Latin America, whilst many other intellectuals and activists subsequently promoted 'pan-Americanism', a shared Latin cultural identity, nationalism, and promotion of the rights and identity of the first American peoples (Calvert 1994).

In the early post-1945 period, the US and Latin American states replaced earlier agreements with the **Inter-American Treaty of Reciprocal Assistance** (the **Rio pact)**, a collective security arrangement. By 1948, the **Organization of American States (OAS)** replaced the former Pan-

American Union and strengthened the Rio pact's security arrangements. Over time its membership expanded to include the countries of North, Central, and South America—with the exception of Cuba, technically a suspended member. The OAS and its institutional framework has faced persistent, often violent, political conflicts including border violations, disputes over the application of embargos, covert and full-scale US intervention, and narco-political disputes. Members have disagreed with each other over US involvement and initiatives. The OAS was often depicted as a moribund agency serving US foreign policy interests, and it frequently appeared unable or unwilling to manage democratization, human rights, ecological and development pressures. As one author notes, 'Latin American unity [through the OAS] was fostered partly by the attraction–repulsion syndrome between Latin American and the United States and partly by overt U.S. attempts to unify the region under its leadership' (Pope Atkins 1995: 200).

Within the OAS framework a number of significant political and diplomatic developments have taken place. One of the most visible examples is the 1967 **Tlatelolco Treaty**, vigorously promoted by Brazil and other Latin American countries culminating in the establishment of the region as a nuclear-free zone and to ensure non-proliferation of nuclear weapons in the region. This may appear a major contribution to both regional and global security but has not prevented Brazil and Argentina developing nuclear technology and potential capability. Other important political developments can be seen in the formation of the **Rio** and **Contadora** Groups during the 1980s. The Condatora Group (Mexico, Venezuela, Columbia, and Panama) undertook major initiatives to resolve the bloody and protracted conflicts in Central America. The Rio Group comprising Argentina, Brazil, Peru, and Uruguay supported these efforts, and together the groups have extended political discussion and input into regional and extra-regional matters.

Some Latin American countries, and Chile in particular, have increasingly turned their attention to the effects of the **North American Free Trade Agreement** (NAFTA), concluded in 1993 between Canada, the US, and Mexico. The NAFTA aims to remove tariffs and other forms of trade and investment impediments over a fifteen year period. NAFTA's origins lie in the earlier Canada–US Trade Agreement (1988), a development linked to burgeoning strategic trade policies and trade conflicts in the world economy. The Canada–US Agreement involved the removal of bilateral tariffs including those applicable to agricultural products, the removal of quantitative restrictions on imports (such as quotas), compatibility of technical standards applied to products, the reduction of many restrictions on trade in energy and automobiles, liberalizing federal government procurement policies, and 'most favoured nation' treatment of investment and provision of services (except banking). Prior to this Agreement's extension to Mexico, the US had pursued bilateral free trade arrangements with a number of countries in the region, first through the Caribbean Basin initiative and subsequently with Mexico and the Mercosur group.

Key Points

- The countries of Latin and Central America have persistently sought alternative economic development strategies and adjustment to their powerful US neighbour. These activities have been driven primarily by ideological, economic, and cultural expressions of difference.

- By the 1990s the region is characterized by widespread economic and political groupings which reflect economic strengths and strategies, particularly of the rapidly industrializing countries, as well as political and security concerns.

- Structural challenges facing Latin America remain vast. These countries continue to face environmental resource depletion and despoilation, social dislocation and poverty, trade in illicit narcotics, and significant debt burdens inherited from the 1980s.

- The impact and potential enlargement of NAFTA will be an important issue in Latin American regionalization. As one author indicates 'Latin American participation in world exports has declined by two-thirds since 1950. The appeal of a regional trade option lies in its potential to define and discipline a new economic strategy that can reverse that unfortunate history' (Fishlow 1994: 72).

South East Asia

Political and economic co-operation afforded by **ASEAN (Association of South East Asian Nations)** since its inception in 1967 has been invaluable. The early 1990s have witnessed further moves toward regional economic integration in the region, with agreement in 1992 to develop an ASEAN free trade area, and the development of **Asia-Pacific Economic Co-operation** (APEC) as a wider forum including Australia, New Zealand, and the US for the pursuit of common economic interests, in particular concerning the General Agreement on Tariffs and Trade (GATT).

ASEAN was formed in 1967 comprising Indonesia, Malaysia, the Philippines, Singapore, Thailand, and since 1984 Brunei. As a former participant in those negotiations has suggested, decolonization and cold war rivalry for 'client' states were instrumental in facilitating the emergence of common interests 'in order to be heard and to be effective' (Khoman 1992: xviii). Improved external cohesion and increased bargaining power was a major factor involved in ASEAN's development.

External threats—such as competition for superpower influence in the region as well as nationalist-communist revolutionary conflicts in Vietnam, Laos, and Cambodia—were not however the sole explanations. ASEAN was also an important mechanism to contain conflict between and reconcile larger powerful members, notably Indonesia and Malaysia.

Although the US extended security co-operation and guarantees to the region through the **South East Asian Treaty Organization (SEATO)**, a number of Asian nations were instrumental in forming the Non-Aligned Movement through the 1955 Bandung Conference to promote solidarity and co-operation against colonial and superpower interference. ASEAN's objectives were therefore both economic and political. Until the early 1990s the ASEAN members were politically preoccupied with avoiding internal conflict amongst themselves over war and genocide in Cambodia, as a result of differing national policies toward China and Vietnam. More recently ASEAN has made major efforts in mediating Sino-Vietnamese territorial claims upon the Spratly Islands. ASEAN's consensual voluntaristic structure therefore enabled its members to seek collective shelter in relation to their security concerns.

However, these co-operative arrangements did

not on the whole produce dramatic upswings in intra-ASEAN trade. Increased co-operation and dialogue produced some useful common decisions on tariff reductions and joint ventures/industrial programmes, but ASEAN as an example of state-promoted regional co-operation has not led to substantial integration of economic activity and growth of intra-regional trade and investment along the lines of the European Union (EU).

Intra-ASEAN trade only grew from 3.2 per cent of total trade in 1980 to 4 per cent in 1990, with much of this trade not governed by preferential trade rules (Panagariya 1994: 16–17). ASEAN is not primarily a vehicle for close economic integration but is instead a non-discriminatory political and economic sub-regional grouping.

ASEAN currently faces significant regional challenges. Growing liberalization of national tariffs and other impediments to trade, rapid industrialization leading to higher levels of trade in manufactured goods, and explosion of the 'new regionalism' since the 1980s have prompted the development of a more formalized market-oriented ASEAN free trade area (Naya and Imada 1992: 513–14).

Other countries in the region have become closely involved with the APEC grouping—China, Hong Kong, and Taiwan—whilst Australasia, India, and several Latin American countries have sought further contact with ASEAN. ASEAN also constitutes one of the major regional groupings closely connected with European trade and diplomacy.

Key Points

- The region is characterized as much by the commercial and technological strengths of several individual countries as by the development of regional cohesion. China accounts for 6 per cent of global gross domestic product (GDP) and Japan for 7.6 per cent, whilst the Chinese export-to-GDP ratio is 17 per cent, Japan's is 10 per cent, the US 7 per cent, and Germany 27 per cent (Panagariya 1994).

- ASEAN is an important sub-grouping located within this dynamic region characterized by powerful investment and innovatory capacities of individual countries. Whilst ASEAN may not provide the primary economic framework for its members, its political functions and co-

operation have been important for conflict resolution and 'learning' co-operative habits.

- Significant economic differences do characterize South East Asia despite over-generalized depictions of the region's prosperity. These differences however, are an important factor in the further development of intra-regional co-operation.

Africa

By the 1980s much academic analysis of Africa's desperate economic and political environment saw the continent as an increasingly marginalized periphery to be written off. For example, one writer suggested 'Africa is no longer very important to the major actors in the world economy . . . [and] with the end of the cold war, African countries have little politico-strategic importance for the major world powers' (Callaghy 1995: 42).

During the twentieth century most African states have continued to confront colonial legacies of arbitrary territorial boundaries, weak and inefficient state structures, profound social and cultural cleavages along with high population growth rates and protracted violent conflicts. Coherent and sustainable political management and economic development has been in short supply. Along with the fact that there are few local 'hegemons' or economic powerhouse economies around which sub-regional co-operation can flourish, utter external economic dependency of much of the continent has persisted. Africa has seen its income levels and growth rates consistently decline, its share of world exports decline from 17 per cent to 8 per cent between 1970 and 1990, whilst 'its percentage of worldwide official development assistance rose from 17 percent in 1970 to about 38 per cent in 1991' (Callaghy 1995: 42–3). It might seem surprising, therefore, to find relatively extensive regional sub-groups and integration schemes in Africa. However, many regional integration schemes involve a locally powerful 'hegemonic' state capable of dominating group activities, and/or external support and reinforcement as in the case of initially French and subsequently European Union (EU) involvement in North, West, and increasingly Southern Africa.

The **Economic Community of West African States (ECOWAS)** as well as more recent regionalization in North Africa with the **Arab Maghreb**

Union (AMU) have owed much to French post-colonial activity. The West African 'franc zone' of overseas departments and former territories and the Maghreb grouping of Algeria, Morocco, and Tunisia have long been a feature of French foreign policy.

The ECOWAS was created by the 1975 Lagos Treaty incorporating sixteen West African states, many of them former British colonies and dependencies. ECOWAS members were keen to emulate features of the European economic integration process and officially committed themselves to freeing the movement of goods, services, labour, and capital, harmonizing fiscal and agricultural policy, and eventually the removal of tariff barriers and application of a common external tariff to imports. However little practical realization of these ambitious goals has emerged, due perhaps both to internal problems—Nigerian dominance and frequent leadership or regime changes within other member countries—and the broader structural environment of 'conditional' multilateral aid programmes. None the less ECOWAS members have attempted in recent years to manage internal security problems, through for example monitoring and peacekeeping operations in Liberia.

During the 1970s the then European Community promoted greater co-operation within North Africa. The EC's 'Mediterranean' aid and trade policies aimed at the development of economic infrastructures and production capacities in both oil- and non-oil exporting North African states. Oil import requirements of West European countries, relatively important North African export markets for EC goods, and North African export dependency upon European agricultural and textile markets were important factors associated with the growth in EC development policy towards this group of countries. During the 1980s the EC became increasingly concerned for socio-economic stability and population growth in the region and has thus supported the activities of the Arab Maghreb Union and the adjoining Mashreq group in diversifying economic activity, increasing intra-region trade and attempting to reduce this region's economic dependency upon Western Europe.

The **Preferential Trade Area of Eastern and Southern Africa (PTA)** was formed in the 1980s to facilitate economic, agricultural, and industrial co-operation and aimed eventually to introduce common market provisions amongst its members. This grouping has only recently begun to move towards this goal and now includes the former Republic of South Africa. The PTA and another grouping, the **South African Development Co-ordination Committee (SADCC)** have increasingly sought close links. The SADCC was formed by the 'front-line' or neighbouring states of the former Republic of South Africa in response to the political and economic influence of the former Republic. Strongly supported by the EU and the post-apartheid South African government, this grouping has taken important steps toward coherent regional industrial development strategies to bolster the weak as well as stronger members. The SADCC members are also an important sub-grouping within the wider Lomé Conventions, which bring together the EU and 70 developing states from Africa, the Caribbean, and the Pacific.

Political cohesion amongst African countries has long been the goal of the **Organization of African Unity (OAU)**. Set up in 1963 in the context of Ghanian President Nkrumah's promotion of pan-Africanism, the OAU bolstered diplomatic resistance to colonial and superpower interference rather than actually helping to manage numerous post-1945 conflicts in the continent. In the post-cold war period the OAU and its members have had to adjust rapidly to managing long-standing conflicts, superpower withdrawal, and international reluctance to finance and support major peacekeeping and humanitarian relief activities. The OAU has begun to develop conflict management mechanisms and overcome its traditional aversion to non-interference in internal affairs of its members.

We have seen how regional initiatives can be defensive or proactive mechanisms enabling domestic élites to adapt and reinforce economic and political activities. However the effects of globalization are particularly difficult. Few developing countries enjoy high levels of technological innovation, investment and production strengths, well-educated inexpensive labour forces, comparative economic advantage, or strong trading specialization. Domestic social, political, and economic costs of **structural adjustment** (to global economic and financial structures) have been and continue to be immense. Not surprisingly, arguments supporting further '**South–South**' co-operation have been made. The development of intra-regional co-operation between developing states 'offers hope for a long-term and more balanced progression toward economic development . . . given the current international system, the alternative of inward orientation offers no superior solution' (Kotschwar 1995: 14). The 'new regionalism' appears to be the 'only card game in town' for the political and economic survival of many developing states.

Key Points

- By the 1990s, African countries have undergone profound changes to their domestic economic, political, and security environments. Media images of Africa during the 1980s reinforced perceptions of marginalization, resulting from ideological and strategic problems as well as from famine, drought, and environmental degradation.

- Trade and development aid processes have not reversed African economic decline and reliance upon raw or semi-processed materials, cash crops, and strategic minerals. Many African states committed to structural adjustment policies find themselves in direct competition for markets due to the similarity of their exports.

- Regional economic co-operation and integration schemes have begun to respond to the overwhelming scale of problems facing African countries. Regionally powerful states, such as Nigeria and the new South Africa, may help to play important roles in fostering greater political, economic, and security self-sufficiency.

Europe

During the post-1945 period Western Europe gradually constituted itself as a highly integrated and cohesive grouping of economies and peoples. By 1989, political and economic change in the European continent 'did not take place in a fragmented, balance-of-power Europe, but in a political space increasingly dominated by a single organization, so that even rivalry and competition among the members are shaped by and channelled through the common rules and institutions' (Keohane, Nye, and Hoffmann 1993: 385). Post-1989, Central and Eastern European countries as well as Russia and other members of the Commonwealth of Independent States (CIS) have reintegrated into European economic and political groupings (see Fig. 21.3 for illustration).

However, European experiences and expectations of regionalism and integration ought not to be readily transposed to the study of other regional groupings, such as NAFTA or ASEAN. The formal process of European integration, characterized by the **European Union** (**EU**), has been and continues to be shaped according to particular historical and political concerns. These concerns may not exist, or are seen as less important, in other regional groupings.

One of the most significant features of the post-1945 era was the fundamental shift in power and authority away from a European and empire-oriented balance of power to a new competitive bipolar world. As one author has indicated, the 'great powers' of Europe were no longer and 'the very effort to create a single supranational "European Community" and to invent a sense of European identity to correspond to it, replacing the old loyalties to historic nations and states, demonstrated the depth of this decline' (Hobsbawm 1994: 14).

This bipolar order demonstrated the end of Europe as a global economic, political, and cultural hub. Widespread concern for military security, devastated economic and financial infrastructures, and political instability across Europe were major factors in facilitating greater regionalization and state-sponsored integration schemes in Western Europe during the early post-1945 period. However, there was little initial consensus of views on the longer term future for Western European countries despite a gradual hardening of the cold war. British Prime Minister Winston Churchill's 1946 speech urging the formation of a 'United States of Europe' was only one example of how political élites began to adjust to the culmination of global decline.

The requirements of economic recovery, rebuilding and transformation in post-war Western Europe were initial catalysts for regional development. Severe balance of payments problems after 1945 meant that many countries faced major difficulties in earning export revenue and paying for imports. Developing the US doctrine of communist 'containment', General George Marshall's speech to the US Congress in 1947 helped convince US leaders that a strategic aid programme was crucial for Western European stability. '**Marshall Aid**' (also termed the European Recovery Programme) involved a commitment of some 2.5 per cent of US gross domestic product (GDP) in the form of loans and trade credit, notionally open to all European countries 'willing to assist in the task of recovery'.

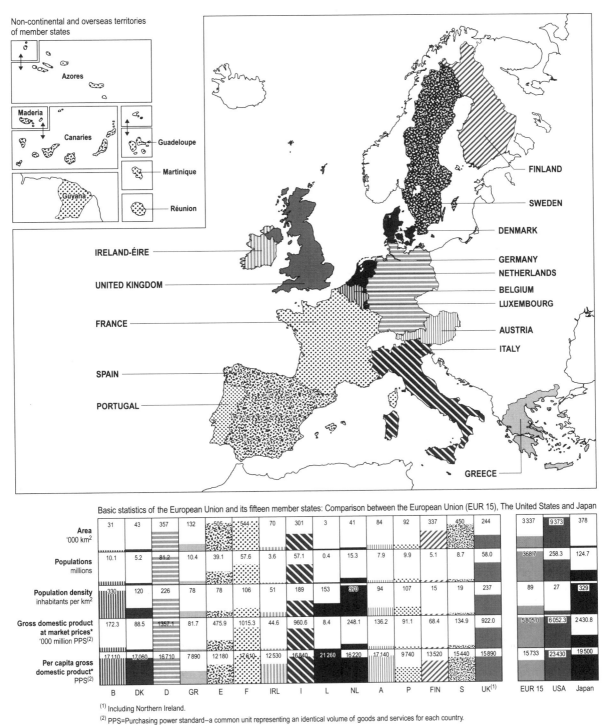

Fig. 21.1. **Map of the European Union (EU15). Reprinted with kind permission of the Office for Official Publications of the European Communities.**

Basic statistics of the European Union and its fifteen member states: Comparison between the European Union (EUR 15), The United States and Japan

	B	DK	D	GR	E	F	IRL	I	L	NL	A	P	FIN	S	UK[1]		EUR 15	USA	Japan
Area '000 km²	31	43	357	132	505	544	70	301	3	41	84	92	337	450	244		3 337	9 373	378
Populations millions	10.1	5.2	81.2	10.4	39.1	57.6	3.6	57.1	0.4	15.3	7.9	9.9	5.1	8.7	58.0		368.7	258.3	124.7
Population density inhabitants per km²	330	120	226	78	78	106	51	189	153	370	94	107	15	19	237		89	27	329
Gross domestic product at market prices* '000 million PPS[2]	172.3	88.5	1357.1	81.7	475.9	1015.3	44.6	960.6	8.4	248.1	136.2	91.1	68.4	134.9	922.0		5 805.0	6 052.3	2 430.8
Per capita gross domestic product* PPS[2]	17 110	17 060	16 710	7 890	12 180	17 610	12 530	16 840	21 260	16 220	17 140	9 740	13 520	15 440	15 890		15 733	23 430	19 500

[1] Including Northern Ireland.

[2] PPS=Purchasing power standard–a common unit representing an identical volume of goods and services for each country.

In reality receipt of Marshall Aid was heavily conditional upon collective institutional oversight through the **Organization for European Economic Co-operation** (later the **OECD**).

With Marshall Aid subsequently disbursed only to Scandinavian and West European countries, the bloc nature of superpower relations began to take shape. The USSR by 1949 responded with the creation of **Comecon** (the **Council for Mutual Economic Assistance**) and central economic planning across the Soviet bloc. US financial and economic assistance was, however, only a part of broader foreign policy goals to foster and sustain a stable like-minded regional alliance. Defence and security co-operation, stimulated by events such as the Czech coup and the Berlin blockade in 1948, soon followed with Canadian, US, and European signatures on the North Atlantic Treaty, creating a military alliance in the **North Atlantic Treaty Organization** (**NATO**). However, major domestic concerns of West European states—in particular the 'German question' and a desire for close economic co-operation—could not be sufficiently resolved within the cold war framework. The issue of German rearmament and the strengthening of European security arrangements was later pursued through the **Western European Union** (resulting from the 1948 Brussels Treaty) after the 1954 defeat of the European Defence Community project.

Changes in French political thinking proved to be a decisive factor. At the close of the Second World War, French desire to participate in control of the Ruhr, Germany's industrial heartland, along with national economic plans intending France to be a key steel producer in post-war Europe, made for the first time an explicit link between the economic recovery of France and Germany. Adequate and affordable supplies of coal were intrinsic to European economic recovery, as was Germany's continuing post-war strengths in coal and steel production.

The **Schuman Plan** of 1950 (announced by Robert Schuman, France's Foreign Minister) suggested that French and German production of coal and steel be pooled, with decision-making on production levels, prices, and investment placed with a **supranational** body (supranational meaning above the nation-state).

Prior to announcing the plan French officials had actively pursued US, German, and British support, all except the latter in favour. The Schuman Plan explicitly intended to strengthen the position of France in tandem with Germany; it appealed to the popularity of federalist and ex-Resistance groups in terms of promoting European unity and reconciliation; and it intended to make war 'materially impossible' by binding German industrial strength to others in a cohesive grouping. The plan was radical in intent and practice, and posed important political choices for those who sought to join. Political élites in Belgium, Italy, Luxembourg, and the Netherlands had their reservations and concerns but joined subsequent negotiations.

The outcome of the Schuman Plan was the **European Coal and Steel Community** (**ECSC**), operational within two years of the plan's launch. Management of decision-making on coal and steel production, prices, investment, and working conditions was the responsibility of the High Authority (the supranational politically independent central institution of the ECSC). In addition, an Assembly exercising democratic oversight, a Court of Justice ensuring compliance with ECSC laws, and a Council of Ministers representing government interests were also created. Sovereignty, or autonomy of decision-making, was thus pooled and shared amongst members. The High Authority assembled this power, undertook the responsibilities of negotiation compromise and brokering agreement amongst members, and defined and upheld the collective interest. The first president of the High Authority was Jean Monnet, a Frenchman who proved to be central to the creation of Western Europe's post-war integration.

Monnet's personal commitment to promoting durable and peaceful European unity became instrumental in furthering US support for European integration, and for reconciling differing interests and concerns of political élites within the ECSC and later the European Economic Community (EEC). Monnet, and others, shared a pragmatic as well as moral conviction that by developing this novel method of both containing and strengthening state power, a successful and expansive integration process might lead to a new political structure—perhaps federal—uniting a historically insecure, bellicose, and powerful group of countries.

The ECSC represented a key development in Western Europe's identity. By appealing to a significant set of industrial, political, and military interests, the ECSC tied France and Germany so closely together that war would be deemed too costly. Although the Franco-German relationship formed the political backbone for the integration process, important elements of political equality, reciprocity, and distribution of gains ensured that the process of integration included other members. Political equality between members also created binding obligations upon all; members were assured of mutual or reciprocal relations; and benefits or costs associated with the process of integration were distributed equally. Peaceful co-operation was based on mutual self-interest. This helped develop a greater sense of mutual political self-interest and weakened a historical tendency toward a balance of power logic and 'relative gains-seeking' behaviour of states.

The subsequent development of the **European Economic Community** (EEC) and **Euratom** (**European Atomic Energy Community**) resulted from a mix of factors; Benelux states were keen to widen sectoral economic integration into a customs union and common market, the French government sought to strengthen its civil nuclear power programme, and ambitious plans for political union failed with the non-ratification of the **European Defence Community** (EDC) Treaty.

None the less, the EEC did not emerge in 1958 as a result of uniform views on the scope and political desirability of deeper integration. The institutional and policy scope of the EEC was shaped by different demands of governments and business interests. Despite the 'political' function of integrating polities and cultures of members, moves toward overt political integration were heavily disputed.

During this period, other West European countries sought alternative mechanisms to achieve different objectives. The creation of the **European Free Trade Association** (EFTA) in 1960 as an industrial free trade area regulated by minimalist institutions was preferred by its members for its loose political structure, trade creation effects for manufactured exports, and for strict separation of economic and political issues which would not compromise the position of militarily neutral members. EFTA members sought co-operative linkages with the EEC particularly after the accession of two of its key members, Britain and Denmark, to the EEC. As a result of wider economic and political change during the 1980s, the EFTA–EC (European Communities) relationship became progressively closer. The creation of the **European Economic Area** (EEA) effectively extended much of the EC's activities to the EFTA countries, and in 1995 three EFTA members, Austria, Finland, and Sweden, joined the European Union (EU).

The **Nordic Council**, created in 1952, arose from the failure of earlier Scandinavian plans for a customs and defence union. Its activities and structure were defined by a 'bottom-up' approach. Co-operation on transport facilities, free movement of people through a passport union, and various cultural environmental and economic activities were demand-driven through the decisions of national parliamentary delegations.

The **Council of Europe**'s creation in 1949 was closely linked to the aspirations of federalist movements, and the European Movement (a non-governmental Europe-wide organization) was set up precisely to promote the cause of European unity, including a Europe-wide Assembly. The structure and purposes of the Council of Europe reflected compromise between the views of social movements and individual governments; eventually a ministerial committee and parliamentary assembly were to strengthen peaceful democratic values through common decision-making on socio-economic, cultural, and legal activities. Since that time the Council of Europe has produced a number of significant agreements. The European Convention on Human Rights, backed by an investigative Commission on Human Rights and a Court to rule on violations, is the most well-known example. The Council of Europe is an invaluable forum for bringing together a wide variety of state and non-governmental actors to create common rules, laws, and protect civil and political freedoms.

Key Points

- The regionalization and integration of Western Europe in the post-1945 period was shaped by a distinctive set of factors; the obsolescence of the European concert and empire world-system and emergence of a bipolar system underpinned by nuclear deterrence, and widespread destruction of fragile political and economic structures.

- The initial processes of regionalization were neither uniform nor linear. Differing interests and political forces led to a 'patchwork quilt' of sub-regional and issue-specific groupings.

- EFTA, NATO, WEU, and the **Council of Europe** are examples of interstate co-operation in trade, military security, and legal-administrative activities. The **ECSC** and later **EEC** are examples of state-promoted regional economic integration, although the contemporary **European Union** (EU) illustrates all aspects of Hurrell's typology. The **Nordic Council** is a good example of a largely 'bottom-up' process of informal integration with a high level of regional identity.

The European Union and the 'New' Europe

The European Union (EU), comprises the European Communities, the Common Foreign and Security Policy (CFSP) element, and the Justice and Home Affairs element, the latter two being primarily intergovernmental in character. The EU formally came into being with ratification of the (Maastricht) Treaty on European Union in 1993.

The primary position of the EU in the post-1989 'new' Europe in terms of its institutional capacity,

functional scope, and regional responsibilities illustrates the incremental progression of formal and informal integration processes since the 1950s. This has resulted from adaptation to global political and economic change, interpreted in particular political and historical terms. Although integration has not necessarily been steady nor smooth, the EU has become a cohesive and tightly knit political and economic centre both internally (for its 15 members) and externally in world politics.

What are the major characteristics and activities of the EU? We can see that the functional scope of the integration process has gradually expanded from an economic framework to encompass a significant degree of social, environmental, cultural and foreign/security policy-making. In short, political integration has grown. We can also see that the membership of the EU has been greatly extended and issues of **'widening versus deepening'** (widening membership versus deepening existing and

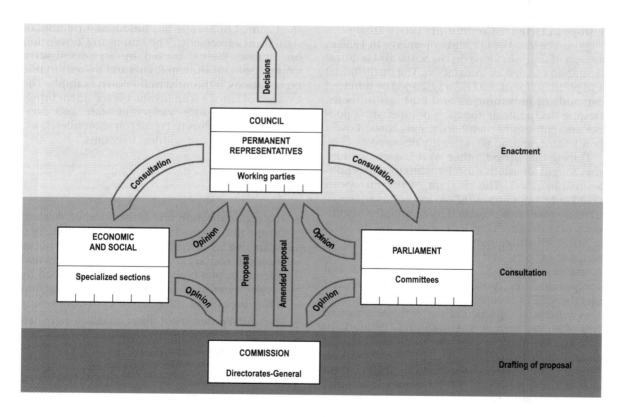

Fig. 21.2. **The EC's decision-making process (kindly reproduced from the Commission of the EU, 'Europe on the move' series 1993)**

future commitment from members) present a major challenge for the EU's future.

The institutional framework of the EU is complex though well established and authoritative in many issue areas. The Commission embodies executive and bureaucratic functions whilst also playing a key role in the politics of the integration process. The European Council with its six-monthly office of President held by each member state enables direct input from Heads of State or Government. The Council of Ministers is one of two legislative bodies in the EU, increasingly sharing power with the European Parliament and having to reform its opaque decision-taking methods. The European Parliament directly represents EU citizens, and jointly shapes and passes legislation. The European Court of Justice is the highest appellate court in Community matters, and its rulings have consistently clarified national-Community legal issues where there appears to be conflict between national and Community law.

Scope of the Integration Process

Economic integration has long provided the method underpinning the security rationale for European integration. The EEC was based upon a customs union, a common market together with freedom of movement of capital, labour, services, and goods (the 'four freedoms'), a common trade policy and external tariff, and common or co-ordinated policies on agriculture, transport, health and safety, and regional development. The turbulent international economy of the 1970s together with domestic industrial protectionism and rising unemployment led in the 1980s to major initiatives by corporate interests and Community institutions to revive the EC's regional political dynamism and global economic competitiveness. The '1992' or completing the single market programme combined deregulatory and interventionist approaches to liberalizing intra-EC trade, investment, product innovation, and employment creation and retraining. The single (or common) market is centrally linked to initiatives on unemployment and structural regeneration, and with the project for economic and monetary union (EMU). Until recently, EMU was an unrealized goal: original plans dating from 1970 were not achieved and the European Monetary System created in 1978 was an important

but limited currency stabilization device. The Maastricht Treaty contained a comprehensive and binding committment to monetary union and a single currency, by way of phased and stringent economic and fiscal convergence. EMU has fundamental implications for politics and governance inside and outside the Union. Whether monetary union will encompass all 15 present members or whether it will be embraced by a smaller grouping is an overriding issue for the EU in the medium term.

Whilst economic matters have provided the backbone for the integration process, the scope and political implications of further integration have gathered pace. Social, environmental, and local development policies are increasingly shaped, and funded, at the Community level with the involvement of a wide range of groups. Many aspects of industrial relations, equal opportunities policy, cancer and AIDS research are co-ordinated. Wide-ranging and often stringent EU environmental protection legislation complements domestic environmental standards as well as global environmental agreements; and structural policy and funding help to develop weaker areas of the EU.

Externally too, the capabilities and roles of the EU have increased. The Maastricht framework has promoted more policy co-ordination in internal security affairs (through increased policy co-operation and shared procedures on immigration, asylum-seeking, terrorism, and international criminal activities); foreign and security policy-making with a common defence force; and trade and development assistance policy. The EU has consistently sought to support peace and stability in regional groupings through use of market access initiatives, reciprocal trade relations, and development aid. Examples include the large developing-country grouping of African–Caribbean–Pacific states in the **Lomé Conventions**; the 'frontline' or neighbouring countries of the former apartheid Republic of South Africa; and North African and Middle East countries through the EU's Mediterranean policy.

However, in the post-cold war period, the EU's priority in assisting post-communist transition for Central and Eastern European countries has culminated in widespread concern expressed by Latin American and African-Caribbean states. Many developing countries closely linked to the EU have concluded that strategic trade policies, protectionist tendencies, and a harsh aid-lending environment add up to a far more competitive and uncertain future.

Fiona Butler

Key Points

- The scope and complexity of integration processes in Europe have developed considerably since the early 1950s. If we examine most domestic activities within the EU, it is clear that their management and effects have long since ceased to be purely 'national'.

- Informal integration also exerts a major impact. For example, the importance of low-level East–West contacts and co-operation in contributing to the ideological and actual collapse of communist and Soviet rule in Central and East Europe, as well as the growth in transnational coalitions such as the green and labour movements across Western Europe.

- In the early post-1989 period, the NATO and EU underwent a fundamental questioning of their roles and capabilities. The then EC's response was first to deepen existing members' commitment to political integration by way of developing the Union framework, and second to promote the reintegration of Central and Eastern Europe.

- However, economic recession and domestic political problems in the EU have led to debate on a **'multi-tier'** or **'multi-speed'** future (multi-tier meaning a breakup of the convoy approach in favour of smaller committed sub-groups proceeding with deeper integration, and multi-speed meaning widespread agreement on all EU objectives by all members achieved over different time periods).

- The EU is now a complex, extensive regional grouping. Membership involves substantial political and legal commitment; acceptance of highly integrated economic, financial and technological activities; and a substantial degree of cultural and linguistic heterogeneity. The EU is not the only framework integrating European politics, but it is increasingly perceived as the primary framework.

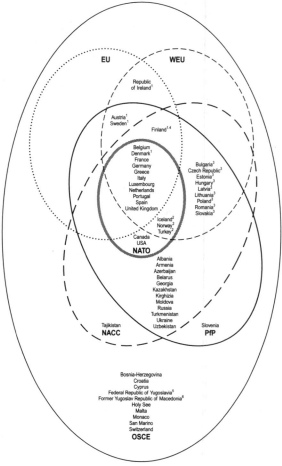

Notes:

1. Observer in the WEU.
2. Associate Member of the WEU.
3. Associate Partner in the WEU. Many of these countries also have agreements with the EU.
4. Observer at the NACC.
5. Membership suspended.
6. Observer in the OSCE.

Fig. 21.3. **European institutions (kindly reproduced from HMSO, Statement on the Defence Estimates 1995).**

Conclusion

This chapter has shown that processes of regionalism and integration are not necessarily a novel feature of contemporary global politics. Development of regional identities and formal integration mechanisms has been a widespread and persistent feature of twentieth-century politics. Theories of international politics have often been divided not merely over how to explain these developments—in terms of power-balancing defensive mechanisms or as transformations of political and economic relations between societies—but in terms of understanding how global socio-economic change poses challenges to established identities and practices.

Concern for how regionalism might affect world order is regularly expressed as concern for the Western multilateral trading regime maintained by GATT rules and procedures. The rise of regional trading blocs—invariably seen in terms of the US, EU, and Japan—may increase potential for trade conflicts or 'wars', and undermine compliance with global rules and institutions.

Regional economic groupings, by their very nature, involve some degree of preferential economic and trading relationship. In recent years global politics has witnessed strategically oriented, retaliatory, and aggressive trade policies on the part of developed countries. EU–US trade friction has increased far beyond the 'chicken wars' of the early 1960s and in 1990 Japan successfully challenged the EU within the GATT for unfair trading practices. In an increasingly globalized world economy it is a persuasive argument that regional trade blocs are the only alternative to a hegemonic 'vacuum', where one powerful state is unable or unwilling to ensure compliance with global rules (Gilpin 1987).

Our understandings of globalization processes emphasize rapid transnationalization of capital, trade, information, and technology. The world has become smaller. However, human resources and social customs are less often transnational phenomena. Globalization dominated by Western corporate identities is often perceived as a threat to local customs and communities. Regionalism and integration may be seen as mechanisms to protect and enrich 'local' identity and values. Within the EU, for example, disputes between member states have arisen over common social provisions (to create a 'level playing field' for European workers) and

corporate decisions to relocate production plants to lower-cost countries within and outside the EU. These divisive disputes concern the function of EU-level regulation to protect differing social standards and the European labour force against the effects of globalized production and investment practices. Again within the EU, concern was expressed by the French government over the penetration of the US movie industry in Europe, and the detrimental effects upon domestically produced film, music, and cultural activities. This became a significant element of US–EU conflict during the GATT's Uruguay round of trade negotiations.

This chapter has described examples of regionalism and integration in contemporary world politics. Many were initially functionally-specific subgroups of countries within a broad geographical region, although these are now more multi-purpose in terms of their scope. Comparatively, despite different organizational and political features, a number can be loosely explained according to mainstream international relations theories; power-balancing is an important characteristic (Indonesia–Malaysia in ASEAN, Argentina–Brazil–Chile–Mexico in Latin America, and France–Germany in the EU), as is the protection and enhancement of smaller or weaker neighbouring countries. Many of these groupings have found the issues of reciprocal norms and distribution of gains problematic and highly sensitive. Membership of groups may overlap considerably, and some regions—especially Europe—are characterized by widespread formal and informal cross-cutting relationships and structures. The potential for increased conflict and co-operation has not necessarily diminished with the emergence of a highly interdependent global system, but regionalism and integration have helped to redefine socio-political relations at the local level, and, in some cases, proved intrinsic to pacification and domestication of traditional inter-state relations.

Earlier debates and concerns for world order may not necessarily have been resolved, but one persuasive argument suggests that 'the very diffusion and decentralization of world politics, rather than leading to a greater instability of the system as such, will actually strengthen the stability, resilience and adaptability of the world order at the macro-level

---

Box 21.2. **Key Developments in European Integration**

1949   The North Atlantic Treaty is signed in Washington by Canada, US, Belgium, Britain, France, Luxembourg, and the Netherlands, creating the North Atlantic Treaty Organization (NATO).

1950   France's Foreign Minister, Robert Schuman, proposes a plan to pool French and German coal and steel resources, resulting in the European Coal and Steel Community (ECSC).

1951   The founding six members (Belgium, Federal Republic of Germany, France, Italy, Luxembourg, and the Netherlands) sign the ECSC treaty.

1952   The Nordic Council is formed to strengthen co-operation amongst Denmark, Finland, Iceland, Norway, and Sweden.

       The European Defence Community (EDC) treaty is signed by the ECSC members.

1954   The EDC treaty is rejected by the French Assemblée Nationale and therefore fails to be ratified.

       The Paris Treaty setting up the Western European Union (WEU) is signed by Britain, Belgium, Federal Republic of Germany, France, Italy, Luxembourg, and the Netherlands.

1955   The members of the ECSC, meeting in Messina, open negotiations on the creation of a common market and co-operation on civil uses of nuclear technology.

1958   The Treaties of Rome setting up the European Economic Community (EEC) and European Atomic Energy Community (Euratom) legally enter into force.

1960   The Stockholm Convention creating the European Free Trade Association (EFTA) is signed by Austria, Britain, Denmark, Norway, Portugal, Sweden, and Switzerland.

1963   The (first) veto of Britain's application to join the EEC is announced by French President de Gaulle.

1965–6   The 'Luxembourg compromise' enabling EEC governments to apply unanimous voting procedures (veto) to vitally important interests is agreed, after a six-month withdrawal of the French government from Council of Ministers meetings.

1969   The Hague summit of EEC Heads of State and Government makes important decisions on 'widening' and 'deepening'. The founding six EEC member states agree to open accession negotiations with Britain, Denmark, Ireland, and Norway, work towards economic and monetary union (EMU), and co-ordinate foreign policies more closely.

1973   Britain, Denmark, and Ireland join the EEC. The people of Norway in 1972 decide 54 : 47 to reject EEC membership.

1974   The informal summits of EEC Heads of State or Government are formalized in the creation of the European Council. The European Regional Development Fund (ERDF) is created.

1975   The (first) Lomé Convention is signed between the European Communities (EC) and the African–Caribbean–Pacific (ACP) Group. The European Parliament (EP) increases its co-decision-making power over the EC's budget. The Court of Auditors is set up.

1978   The European Monetary System (EMS) is proposed in order to bring about monetary co-operation and exchange-rate stability in Western Europe.

1979   The EMS begins to operate. The EP holds its first direct elections across the member countries.

1981   Greece becomes the tenth member of the EC.

1984   The British Conservative Government is granted compensation for its budgetary contributions to the EC (the 'rebate').

1985   The internal market programme (the '1992' programme) is drawn up to revitalize the European economy and make it more competitive in global markets.

1986   Spain and Portugal join the EC.

       The Single European Act (SEA) is signed and is the first major revision of the Treaty of Rome, introducing major changes to policies and decision-making in the EC.

1987   The WEU, after its revival as a security forum during the 1980s, adopts its 'Platform on European Security Interests' to strengthen defence and arms control co-operation amongst its members. Turkey formally applies to join the EC.

1988   The EC and COMECON (the Soviet bloc's economic organization) sign an important Joint Declaration on future relations and co-operation between the groups. This opens the way for subsequent EC bilateral trade agreements with Central and Eastern European members of COMECON.

1989   The Berlin Wall is brought down signalling the end of communist rule in Eastern Europe and the end of the cold war.   *cont./*

1989	Industrial nations of the world (G24) set up the PHARE aid programme (Poland and Hungary aid for reconstruction) subsequently extended to most other Central European countries. Austria applies to join the EC.
1990	The Federal Republic and the former German Democratic Republic (Eastern Germany) reunite.
	The European Bank for Reconstruction and Development (EBRD) is set up to support economic reform and transition in the former communist countries, with the EC as the major contributor of capital.
	The Schengen Agreement to remove border controls between most continental EC member states is signed. Cyprus and Malta apply to join the EC. The intergovernmental conferences begin, with the task of reforming and developing the EC's role in the 'new Europe'.
1991	The European Economic Area (EEA) agreement extending many EC activities and policies to the EFTA members is signed. Sweden applies to join the EC.
	The intergovernmental conferences conclude in the Dutch town of Maastricht, and in early 1992 the Treaty on European Union is signed by EC Heads of State or Government. The EC sends a monitoring commission to the former Yugoslavia.
1992	Finland and Switzerland apply to join the EC.
	The Petersburg Declaration extends the role of the WEU in conflict management and peacekeeping activities. The EC updates and extends former bilateral trade agreements with Central and Eastern European states through a series of 'Europe Agreements'. The EC develops its humanitarian assistance programme (ECHO). In the (first) referendum on ratifying the Maastricht Treaty, the Danish people reject the Treaty by 50.7 to 49.3. The French people narrowly accept (51.05 to 48.95 per cent). The EMS suffers a major crisis, with the British sterling and Italian lira withdrawing from the exchange-rate mechanism and other members devaluing their currencies.
1993	The single market officially comes into being, during the worst global recession ever experienced. Ratification problems continue for the Maastricht Treaty with a new Danish Government securing 'opt-out's'; subsequently the Treaty is accepted by the Danish people. By November the Treaty enters into force, establishing the European Union (EU).
	The EU members agree to prepare Central and Eastern European states for eventual membership.
	WEU membership expands to include Denmark and Ireland as observers, and EFTA and Turkey as associate members.
1994	Hungary, Poland, and the Czech Republic apply to join the EU. The Baltic states, Bulgaria, Czech Republic, Hungary, Poland, Romania, and Slovakia join the WEU as associate members.
	The NATO members propose the 'Partnership for Peace' programme and extend NATO–WEU military co-operation.
	The potential for a 'multi-speed' future development of Europe is made explicit by German and French political élites.
1995	Jacques Delors is succeeded as President of the Commission by Jacques Santer. Slovakia and Latvia apply to join the EU.
	Austria, Finland, and Sweden join the EU, bringing its membership to 15. The EU begins its intergovernmental conference to review the Maastricht Treaty and economic and monetary union.
	NATO establishes its peace-keeping force in Bosnia.
	The eventual European currency is named the 'Euro'.

. . . a major feature of the new world order, for example, will be the de-linking of local and regional conflict, on the one hand, and the stabilization of conflict in the system as a whole' (Cerny 1993: 49).

From such a perspective, regionalism and integration are not merely utilitarian devices to reconcile state interests, overcome local security dilemmas, or defend local identities and practices against global challenges but may in the post-cold war period comprise significant world-order stabilizing mechanisms.

Fiona Butler

QUESTIONS

1. Why was there such an increase in regional co-operation and groupings during the 1950s and 1960s?

2. What factors might be involved in understanding the dynamics, focus, and structure of different types of regionalism?

3. How have different international relations theories viewed the causes of conflict and co-operation?

4. What were the primary factors associated with the emergence of regional integration schemes in Latin America?

5. How significant is development of the NAFTA for the Americas region?

6. Does ASEAN constitute a 'security community' for its members?

7. Why might regional and sub-regional co-operation appear particularly significant for African countries?

8. Was Western European integration entirely driven by superpower competition for influence?

9. What might constitute the key challenges facing the EU and its member countries in the future?

10. What appear to be the likely problems, as well as benefits, associated with contemporary regionalism?

GUIDE TO FURTHER READING

For a good overview of regionalism in 1960s international relations see R. A. Falk and S. Mendlovitz (eds.) *Regional Politics and World Order* (San Francisco: W. H. Freeman, 1973), and J. S. Nye (ed.) *International Regionalism: Readings* (Boston: Little, Brown, 1968). See A. Hurrell 'Explaining the Resurgence of Regionalism in World Politics', *Review of International Studies*, 21: 4 (1995) for contemporary analysis of regionalism.

For a clear explanation of globalization and the 'new regionalism' see P. Dicken *Global Shift: The Internationalisation of Economic Activity* (London: Paul Chapman, 1992); R. Gilpin *The Political Economy of International Relations* (Princeton: Princeton University Press, 1987); and P. Knox and J. Agnew *The Geography of the World Economy* (London: Edward Arnold, 1994).

For more detailed analysis of Latin America see P. Calvert *The International Politics of Latin America* (Manchester: Manchester University Press, 1994); A. Lowenthal and G. Treverton (eds.), *Latin America in a New World* (Boulder, Col.: Westview Press, 1994); and G. Pope Atkins *Latin America and the International Political System* (Oxford: Westview Press, 1995). On ASEAN see the reader edited by K. S. Sandhu (ed.), *The ASEAN Reader* (Singapore: Institute of South Asian Studies, 1992) and on Africa see J. Harbeson and D. Rothchild (eds.), *Africa in World Politics: Post-Cold War Challenges* (Boulder, Col.: Westview Press, 1995) and B. R. Kotschwar 'South-South Economic Co-operation: Regional Trade Agreements among Developing Countries', *Co-operation South* (UN Development Programme, 1995). For in-depth historical and political analysis of European integration see chapters in E. Hobsbawm *Age of Extremes: The Short Twentieth Century, 1914–1991* (London: Michael Joseph, 1994), R. Keohane *et al.* (eds.), *After the Cold War: International Institutions and State Strategies in Europe 1989–1991* (London: Harvard University Press, 1993), and W. Wallace (ed.), *The Dynamics of European Integration* (London: Pinter, 1990).

22 Global Trade and Finance

Jan Aart Scholte

READER'S GUIDE

This chapter explores various economic aspects of contemporary globalization. It begins by distinguishing three general conceptions of economic globalization and highlights the third, geographical notion of increasing 'transborder' production, markets, and investment. This 'supraterritorial' dimension of contemporary world commerce is then described in more detail under headings of 'global trade' and 'global finance'. A fourth section of the chapter counters exaggerated claims about economic globalization by emphasizing some of its limits. Finally, globalization of commerce is linked to several major problems of inequality and insecurity in contemporary world politics.

Introduction

The globalization of world politics involves, amongst other things, a globalization of economics. As Roger Tooze has emphasized elsewhere (Ch. 11), politics and economics are inseparable within social relations. Politics (the distribution and exercise of power) is integral to economics (the production, exchange, and consumption of objects of value). At the same time, and equally, economics is integral to politics, helping to determine where power lies and how it is exercised. Economics does not explain everything, but no account of world politics (and hence no analysis of globalization as a key issue of contemporary world history) is adequate if it does not explore the economic dimension.

Countless discussions of globalization have highlighted its economic aspects. For example, Milton Friedman, the Nobel Prize-winning economist, remarks that it has become possible 'to produce a product anywhere, using resources from anywhere, by a company located anywhere, to be sold anywhere' (cited in Naisbitt 1994:19). Management consultants ceaselessly extol the virtues of global markets (e.g. Ohmae 1990). A senior researcher with American Express has described global financial integration of the late twentieth century as marking 'the end of geography' (O'Brien 1992). Global governance agencies like the Bank for International Settlements (BIS), the Group of Seven (G7), the International Monetary Fund (IMF), the Organization of Economic Co-operation and Development (OECD), the United Nations Conference on Trade and Development (UNCTAD), the World Bank Group (WBG), and the World Trade Organization (WTO) have all put the globalization of commerce high on their agendas. (On these and other institutions, see Box 22.1.) Usually these official circles have endorsed and encouraged the trend, as have most states. Meanwhile many social movements have focused their critiques of globalization on economic aspects of the process. Their analyses depict contemporary globalization of trade and finance as a major cause of high unemployment, a general decline in working standards, increased inequality, greater poverty for some, recurrent financial crises, and large-scale environmental degradation.

In their different ways, all of these assessments agree that the globalizing economy is a key development of contemporary history. True, the trend is often exaggerated. The sorts of qualifications made in Chapter 1 regarding globalization in general (pp. 18–19) also apply to its economic aspects more particularly. However, it is just as wrong to argue, as some sceptics have done, that claims about a new globalizing economy rest on nothing but hype and myth. Instead—as in the case of most historical developments—economic globalization involves an intricate interplay of continuities and changes.

A Globalizing Economy

One key reason for disagreements over the extent and significance of economic globalization relates to the contrasting definitions that different analysts apply to notions of globality. What, more precisely, is 'global' in global commerce? The following paragraphs distinguish three contrasting ways that the globalization of trade and finance has been broadly conceived, namely, in terms of: (a) the crossing of borders; (b) the opening of borders; and (c) the transcendence of borders. Although the three conceptions overlap to some extent, they involve important differences of focus. Most arguments concerning economic globalization pit sceptics who adopt the first perspective against enthusiasts who apply the second notion. However, to my mind the third conception (already introduced in Chapter 1) offers a more distinctive and revealing approach. Later sections of the present chapter will therefore develop that alternative notion in relation to trade and finance.

Cross-Border Transactions

Scepticism about the significance of contemporary economic globalization often arises when analysts

---

Box 22.1. Major Agencies of Global Economic Governance
(with membership figures as of the mid-1990s)

BIS — Bank for International Settlements. Established in 1930 with headquarters in Basle. Membership of 40 central banks. Monitors monetary policies and financial flows. The Basle Committee on Banking Supervision, formed through the BIS in 1974, has spearheaded efforts at multilateral regulation of global banking.

G7 — Group of Seven. Established in 1975 as the G5 (France, Germany, Japan, UK, and USA) and subsequently expanded to include Canada and Italy. The G7 conducts semi-formal collaboration on world economic problems. Government leaders meet in annual G7 Summits, while finance ministers and/or their leading officials periodically hold other consultations.

GATT — General Agreement on Tariffs and Trade. Established in 1947 with offices in Geneva. Membership had reached 122 states when it was absorbed into the WTO in 1995. The GATT co-ordinated eight 'rounds' of multilateral negotiations to reduce state restrictions on cross-border merchandise trade.

IMF — International Monetary Fund. Established in 1945 with headquarters in Washington DC. Membership of 182 states. The IMF oversees short-term cross-border money flows and foreign exchange questions. Since 1979 it has also formulated stabilization and systemic transformation policies for states suffering chronic difficulties with transborder debt or transitions from communist central planning.

IOSCO — International Organization of Securities Commissions. Established in 1984 with headquarters in Montreal. Membership of 115 official securities regulators and (non-voting) trade associations from 69 countries. The IOSCO develops frameworks for transborder supervision of securities firms.

OECD — Organization of Economic Co-operation and Development. Founded in 1962 with headquarters in Paris. Membership of 29 states with advanced industrial economies. Drawing on a staff of 600 professional economists, the OECD prepares advisory reports on all manner of macroeconomic questions.

UNCTAD — United Nations Conference on Trade and Development. Established in 1964 with offices in Geneva. Membership of 187 states. UNCTAD monitors the effects of cross-border trade on macroeconomic conditions, especially in the South. It provided a key forum in the 1970s for discussions of a New International Economic Order.

WBG — World Bank Group. A collection of five agencies, the first established in 1945, with head offices in Washington DC. The group provides project loans for long-term development in poor countries. Like the IMF, the World Bank has since 1979 become heavily involved in structural adjustment programmes in the South and former East.

WTO — World Trade Organization. Established in 1995 with headquarters in Geneva. The WTO is a permanent institution to replace the provisional GATT. It has a wider agenda and greater powers of enforcement.

---

conceive of the process in terms of **increased cross-border movements** between countries of people, goods, money, investments, messages, and ideas. From this perspective, globalization is seen as equivalent to internationalization. No significant distinction is drawn between global companies and international companies, between global trade and international trade, between global money and international money, between global finance and international finance.

When conceived in this way, economic globalization is nothing particularly new. Long-distance, international commerce has existed for centuries and in some cases even millennia. Ancient Babylon and the Roman empire knew forms of long-distance lending and trade finance, for example. Shipments between Arabia and China via South and South-East Asia transpired with fair regularity more than a thousand years ago. Certain coins circulated widely around maritime South-East Asia in a prototypical 'international monetary regime' of the tenth century. Long-distance monies of the pre-modern Mediterranean world included the Byzantine *solidus* from the fifth century onwards and the Muslim *dinar* from the eighth to the thirteenth century. Banks based in Italian city-states maintained (temporary) offices along long-distance trade routes as early as the twelfth century. The Hanseatic League in the fourteenth century and companies based in Amsterdam, Copenhagen,

London, and Paris in the seventeenth century operated overseas trading posts. The first brokerage houses with cross-border operations appeared in the eighteenth century with Amsterdam-based Hope & Co. and London-based Barings.

Indeed, on certain (though far from all) measures, cross-border economic activity reached similar levels in the late nineteenth century as it did a hundred years later. Relative to world population of the time, immigration flows were in fact considerably larger. When measured in relation to world output, cross-border investment in production facilities stood at roughly the same level on the eve of the First World War as it did in the early 1990s. International markets in loans and securities also flourished during the heyday of the **gold-sterling standard** between 1870 and 1914. Under this regime the British pound, fixed to a certain value in gold, served as a transworld currency and thereby greatly facilitated cross-border payments. Again citing proportional (rather than aggregate) statistics, several researchers have argued that these years witnessed larger capital flows between countries than our present day (e.g. Zevin 1992). Meanwhile the volume of international trade grew at some 3.4 per cent per annum in the period 1870–1913, until its value was equivalent to 33 per cent of world output (Barraclough 1984: 256; Hirst and Thompson 1996: 20). By this particular calculation, cross-border trade was greater at the beginning than at the end of the twentieth century.

For the sceptics, then, the contemporary globalizing economy is nothing new. In their eyes the last decades of the twentieth century have merely experienced a phase of increased cross-border trade and finance, much as occurred a hundred years before. Moreover, they note, just as growth of international interdependence in the late nineteenth century was substantially reversed with a forty-year wave of **protectionism** after 1914, so economic globalization of the present day may prove to be temporary. Governments can block cross-border flows if they wish, say the sceptics, and 'national interest' may well dictate that they once more tighten restrictions on international trade, travel, foreign exchange, and capital movements. Contemporary economic globalization gives little evidence, say these doubters, of an impending demise of the state, a weakening of national loyalties, and an end of war. Thus, for example, sceptics regularly point out that most so-called 'global' companies: (a) still conduct the majority of their business in their country of origin; (b) retain a strong national character and allegiances; and (c) remain heavily dependent on states for the success of their enterprises.

Open-Border Transactions

In contrast to the sceptics, enthusiasts for contemporary globalization of trade and finance generally define these developments as part of long-term evolution towards a global society. In this second conception, globalization entails not an extension of internationalization, but the progressive removal of border controls, and thus in a sense the end of international relations. In this world of **open borders**, global companies replace international companies, global trade replaces international trade, global money replaces international money, global finance replaces international finance. From this perspective, globalization is a function of **liberalization**, i.e. the degree to which people, articles, financial instruments, fixed assets, messages, and ideas can circulate throughout the world economy free from state-imposed restrictions. Whereas sceptics generally back up their arguments of historical repetition with proportional data, globalists usually substantiate their claims of historical change with aggregate statistics, many of which do indeed appear quite staggering. (See Table 22.1.)

Globalists regard the forty-year interlude of protectionism (c.1910–50) as a temporary detour from a longer historical trend towards the construction of a single worldwide society. In their eyes the tightening of border controls during this period was a major cause of economic depressions, authoritarian regimes, and international conflicts such as the world wars. In contrast, the emergent open world economy will (so runs the globalist promise) yield prosperity, democracy, and peace for all humanity. From this perspective—which is often termed **neoliberalism**—contemporary economic globalization continues the modern project launched several centuries ago.

The second half of the twentieth century has indeed witnessed considerable opening of borders in the world economy. For one thing, a succession of interstate accords through the **General Agreement on Tariffs and Trade (GATT)** has since 1948 brought major reductions in customs duties, quotas, and other measures that previously inhibited cross-border movements of merchandise.

Table 22.1. **The growth of global commerce: some indicators** (billions of US dollars)

Measure (Worldwide figures)	Earlier Level	1995 Level
Foreign direct investment	$66 (1960)	$2,600
Exports (1995 values)	$430 (1950)	$6,000
Official foreign exchange reserves	$100 (1970)	$650
Daily turnover on forex markets	$100 (1979)	$1,230
Bank deposits by non-residents	$20 (1964)	$7,876
Cross-border loans	$9 (1972)	$372
Cross-border bonds	$1 (1960)	$461
Euroequity issues	initiated 1984	$50
Cross-border share dealing	$10 (1980)	$120*
Daily turnover of derivatives contracts	small before 1980	$1,162

* Figure for 1994.
Sources: BIS, IMF, OECD, UNCTAD.

Average tariffs on manufactures fell from over 40 per cent in the 1930s to only 3 per cent in the mid-1990s. Following the Uruguay Round of multilateral trade negotiations (1986–94), the GATT was replaced by the **World Trade Organization**. This successor agency has greater competences both to enforce existing trade agreements and to pursue new avenues of liberalization, for example, in respect of shipping, telecommunications, and investment flows. Meanwhile, as indicated in Chapter 21, regional frameworks in most areas of the world have (to varying degrees) removed official restrictions on trade between participating countries. Encouraged by such liberalization, cross-border trade expanded between 1950 and 1994 at an annual rate of just over 6 per cent: thus almost twice as fast as in the late nineteenth century. Total international trade multiplied fourteen-fold in real terms over this period, while expansion in respect of manufactures was even greater, with a twenty-six-fold increase (WTO 1995).

Borders have also opened considerably to money flows since 1950. A **gold-dollar standard** became fully operational through the **International Monetary Fund** in 1959. Under this regime major currencies—and especially the United States dollar—could circulate worldwide (though not in communist countries) and be converted to local monies at an official fixed exchange rate. The gold–dollar standard thereby broadly recreated the situation that prevailed under the gold–sterling standard in the late nineteenth century. Contrary to many expectations, the US government's termination of dollar–gold convertibility on demand in 1971 did not trigger new restrictions on cross-border payments. Instead, a regime of **floating exchange rates** developed: *de facto* from 1973 and formalized through the IMF in 1976. Moreover, from the mid-1970s onwards most states reduced or eliminated restrictions on the import and export of national currency. In these circumstances foreign exchange trading burgeoned to historically unprecedented levels after 1980, reaching volumes of $1,230 billion per day in the mid-1990s.

Alongside liberalization of trade and money movements between countries, the second half of the twentieth century has also witnessed widespread opening of borders to international investment. These flows involve both direct investments (i.e. fixed assets like research facilities, factories, etc.) and portfolio investments (i.e. liquid assets like loans, bonds, shares, and so on).

Apart from a wave of expropriations in the South during the 1970s (many of them subsequently reversed), states have generally welcomed **foreign direct investment (FDI)** into their jurisdictions in the latter decades of the twentieth century. Indeed, many governments have actively lured externally based business by lowering corporate tax rates, reducing restrictions on the repatriation of profits, relaxing labour and environmental standards, and so on. Since 1960 there has been a proliferation of what are variously called 'international', 'multinational', 'transnational', or 'global' corporations (hence the frequently encountered abbreviations MNC and TNC). The number of such companies grew from 3,500 in 1960 to 40,000 in 1995. The aggregate stock of FDI worldwide increased in tandem from $66 billion in 1960 to $2,600 billion in 1995, as compared with only $14 billion in 1914

(UNCTAD 1996: ix, 4). In this world of more open borders, various globalists have described MNCs as 'footloose' and 'stateless'.

Substantial liberalization has also occurred since the 1970s in respect of cross-border **portfolio investments**. For example, many a state now permits non-residents to hold bank accounts within its jurisdiction. Other deregulation has removed legal restrictions on ownership and trading of stocks and bonds by non-resident investors. Further legislation has reduced controls on participation in a country's financial markets by externally based banks, brokers, and fund managers. As a result of such deregulation (e.g. London's so-called 'Big Bang' in 1986) financial institutions from all over the world have converged on **global cities** like Hong Kong, New York, Paris, and Tokyo. Levels of cross-border banking and securities business have risen markedly since the 1960s in tandem with such liberalization, as several statistics in Table 22.1 indicate. Corresponding indicators for the 1870–1914 period come nowhere close to these aggregate figures.

In sum, legal obstructions to commercial transactions between countries have greatly diminished worldwide in the late twentieth century. At the same time, cross-border flows of merchandise, services, money, and investments have reached unprecedented levels, at least in aggregate terms. To this extent enthusiasts for globalization-as-liberalization can argue, against the sceptics, that borders have opened more than ever.

That said, significant official restrictions on cross-border economic activity persist. They include countless trade restrictions and continuing foreign exchange controls in many countries. While states have on the whole welcomed investments from abroad, there is as yet no official multilateral regime comparable to the GATT/WTO in respect of trade or the IMF in respect of money which compels them to do so. In addition, although many governments have loosened visa and travel restrictions in the late twentieth century, **immigration controls** are on the whole as tight as ever. Indeed, many have recently been reinforced. To this extent sceptics may feel vindicated that international borders remain very much in place and can be opened or closed as states choose to do.

Transborder Transactions

As mentioned earlier, most debates concerning the globalization of commerce have unfolded between, on the one hand, globalists who see an inexorable trend towards an open world economy and, on the other hand, sceptics who regard the current situation as a limited and reversible expansion of cross-border transactions. However, these two most common positions do not exhaust the possible interpretations. Indeed, neither of these conventional perspectives requires a distinct concept of 'globalization'. Both views resurrect arguments that were elaborated using other vocabulary long before the word 'globalization' entered widespread circulation in the 1980s.

In a third conception, globalization refers to **processes whereby social relations acquire relatively distanceless and borderless qualities**, so that human lives are increasingly played out in **the world as a single place**. (Recall Ch. 1.) In this usage, 'globalization' refers to a fundamental transformation of geography that occurs when a host of social conditions become less tied to territoriality.

On these lines a globalizing economy is one in which patterns of production, exchange, and consumption become increasingly delinked from a geography of distances and borders. 'Global' economic activity extends across widely dispersed terrestrial locations at the same time and moves between places scattered worldwide in no time. While the patterns of 'international' economic interdependence are strongly influenced by territorial distances and national-state divisions, patterns of 'global' trade and finance often have little correspondence to distance and boundaries. With air travel, satellite links, telecommunications, worldwide organizations, global consciousness (i.e. a mindset that conceives of the world as a single place) and more, much contemporary commercial activity transcends borders. In this third sense globalization involves the growth of a **transborder** (as opposed to cross-border or open-border) economy.

This rise of **supraterritoriality** is reflected *inter alia* in increased commercial transactions between countries. However, the geographical character of these **transworld** (as opposed to long-distance) movements is different from the territorial framework that has traditionally defined international interdependence. This qualitative shift means that contemporary statistics on international trade, money, and investment can only be crudely compared with figures relating to earlier times. Hence the issue is not so much the amount of trade between countries, but the way that much of this commerce forms part of transborder production processes and global marketing networks. The problem is not only the quantity of money that moves between countries, but also the instantaneity with which most funds are transferred. The question is not simply the number of international securities deals so much as the emergence of stock and bond issues that involve participants from a number of countries at the same time. In short, if one accepts this third conception of globalization, then both the sceptics and the enthusiasts are largely missing the crucial point. The next sections elaborate further.

Key Points

- 'Globalization' of commerce can be understood in several different ways.
- Sceptical interpretations emphasize that current levels of cross-border trade, money movements, and investment flows are neither new nor as great as some claim.
- Globalist interpretations argue that relaxation of border controls has taken international economic activity to unprecedented levels in the late twentieth century.
- Geographical interpretations highlight the proliferation of commercial transactions in which territorial distance and borders present no particular constraint.

Global Trade

The distinctiveness of transborder, supraterritorial economic relations should become clearer with illustrations. Examples relating to global trade are given in the present section. Others concerning global finance follow in the next section. In each case it will be seen that, although the phenomena in question made some earlier appearances, their significance relates mainly to contemporary history.

Transborder Production

Transborder production arises when a single process is spread across widely dispersed locations both within and between countries. Supraterritorial co-ordination links research centres, design units, procurement offices, materials processing installations, fabrication plants, finishing points, assembly lines, quality control operations, advertising and marketing bureaux, data-processing offices, after-sales service, and so on. Describing a global production operation, the head of Levi Strauss explains that:

our company buys denim in North Carolina, ships it to France where it is sewn into jeans, launders these jeans in Belgium, and markets them in Germany using TV commercials developed in England   (R. D. Haas 1993: 103).

Transborder production can be contrasted with territorially centred production. In the latter instance, all stages of a given production process—from initial research to after-sales service—transpire within the same local or national unit. In globally integrated production, however, no country hosts all stages of manufacture. Each of the various links in the transborder chain specializes in one or several functions, thereby creating economies of scale and/or exploiting cost differentials between locations. Through **global sourcing**, the company draws materials, components, machinery, finance, and services from anywhere in the world. Distance and borders figure only secondarily, if at all. Indeed, a firm may relocate certain stages of production several times in short succession in search of profit maximization. In one striking example of **country-hopping**, athletic suppliers Nike during a recent five-year period opened or closed fifty-five factories in North America and East Asia in response to changes in relative costs of production (Abegglen 1994: 26).

What others have called **global factories** were virtually unknown before the 1940s. They did not gain major prominence until the 1960s and have mainly spread since the 1970s. Supraterritorial production has developed mainly in the manufacture of textiles, garments, motor vehicles, leather goods, sports articles, toys, optical products, consumer

435

electronics, semiconductors, aeroplanes, and construction equipment.

With the growth of global production, a large proportion of purportedly 'international' transfers of goods and services entails **intra-firm trade** within transborder companies. When the intermediate inputs and finished goods pass from one country to another they are officially counted as 'international' commerce; yet they primarily involve movements within a global company rather than between national economies. Conventional statistics do not measure intra-firm transfers, but estimates of the share of such exchanges in total cross-border trade range from 25 to over 40 per cent.

Much (though far from all) transborder production has taken advantage of what are variously called special economic zones (SEZs) or export processing zones (EPZs). Within such enclaves the ruling national or provincial government exempts assembly plants and other facilities for transborder production from the usual import and export duties. It may also grant other tax reductions, subsidies, and waivers of certain labour and environmental regulations. The first SEZ was established in 1954 in Ireland, but most were created after 1970, mainly in Asia, the Caribbean, and the so-called *maquiladora* areas along the Mexican frontier with the USA.

Transborder Products

Much of the output of both transborder and country-based production has acquired a **supraterritorial market** in the contemporary globalizing economy. Hence a considerable proportion of 'international' trade now involves the distribution and sale of **global goods**, often under a transworld brand name. Consumers dispersed across many corners of the planet purchase the same articles at the same time. The country location of a potential customer for, say, a Xerox photocopier, a Bob Marley single, or Kellogg's corn flakes is of limited importance. Design, packaging, and advertising determine the market far more than distance and borders.

Like other aspects of globalization, supraterritorial markets have a longer history than many contemporary observers appreciate. For example, Campbell Soup and Heinz began to become household names in the mid-1880s following the introduction of automatic canning. From the outset Henry Ford regarded his first automobile, the Model T, as a world car. Coca-Cola was bottled in 27 countries and sold in 78 by 1929 (Pendergrast 1993: 174). On the whole, however, the numbers of goods, customers, and countries involved in these earlier global markets were relatively small.

In contrast, global products pervade the contemporary world economy. They encompass a host of packaged foods, bottled beverages, cigarettes, designer clothes, household articles, music recordings, audio-visual productions, printed publications, interactive communications, office and hospital equipment, armaments, transport vehicles, and travel services. In all of these sectors and more, global products inject a touch of the familiar almost wherever on earth a person might visit. The countless examples include Nescafé (sold in 200 varieties worldwide), Heineken beer (drunk in 170 countries), Kiwi shoe polish (applied in 130 countries), Nokia mobile phones (used in 120 countries), Thomas Cook tourist bureaux (available in 140 countries), American International Group insurance policies (offered in 130 countries), television programmes by Globo of Brazil (distributed in 128 countries), and the *Financial Times* newspaper (read in 160 countries). Covering smokers in 170 lands, 'Marlboro Country' is a distinctly supraterritorial place.

Today many shops are mainly stocked with transborder articles. Moreover, since the 1970s a number of **retail chains** have gone global. Examples include Italy-based Benetton, Japan-based 7-Eleven, Sweden-based Ikea, UK-based Marks & Spencer, and US-based Toys 'R' Us (Treadgold 1993). Owing largely to the various 'megabrands' and transborder stores, shopping centres of the late twentieth century have in good part become global emporia. (See Box 22.2.)

Through transborder production and transworld products, global trade has become an integral part of everyday life for a notable proportion of the world's firms and consumers. Indeed, these developments could help to explain why the recessions of the 1970s–1990s have not, in spite of frequently expressed fears of 'trade wars', provoked a wave of protectionism. In previous prolonged periods of commercial instability and economic hardship (e.g. during the 1870s–1890s and 1920s–1930s) most states responded by imposing major protectionist restrictions on cross-border trade. Reactions

Box 22.2. Case Study: Moscow in a Globalizing Economy

The current reach and power of global markets became acutely—and indeed somewhat painfully—apparent to me on a visit to Moscow at the turn of the year 1994–5. Less than a decade after the launch of perestroika, the city was flooded with global cigarettes, to the point that it had become nearly impossible to find a Russian brand. Dove Bars and Perrier were available for anyone who could pay, but it took me five days to find a sack of potatoes. Everywhere the eye turned, Nike was competing with Reebok, Pizza Hut with Burger King, Pepsi with Coke, Martini with Asti Spumanti, Wrigley's with Hershey, Pioneer with JVC, Philips with Bosch, Gold Star with TDK, Tide with Ajax, Wella with Flex, Cosmopolitan with Burda (each in Russian-language editions), Barbie with Cindy, Konica with Kodak, Casio with Rolex, Whiskas with Pedigree Chum. Moscow travel agents were beginning to flog fun-in-the-sun package holidays and time-share vacation homes, while US Global Health offered private medical insurance for the monied few. VDNH, once the communist Exhibition to the Achievements of the People's Economy, had been turned into a consumer playground. Its pavilions were now crammed with makeshift stalls selling global products, especially consumer electronics, many of them bought duty-free in the Persian Gulf region. In the north-west corner of the park, the large Cosmos hangar had been converted into a showroom for shiny Fords and Mercedes. Lenin's statue stared blandly as hordes of buyers scuttled past now-silent fountains with televisions, portable stereos, cordless telephones, and car alarms, while public loudspeakers pumped out strains of Brian Adams: 'Baby it's hard to believe, we're in heaven'. Comrades had become customers.

to contemporary recession have been more complicated (cf. Milner 1988). While territorial interests have pressed for protectionism, global commercial interests have understandably resisted it. Thus many transborder companies actively promoted the Uruguay Round and have on the whole vigorously supported the new World Trade Organization.

Key Points

- The second half of the twentieth century has witnessed the development of transborder production and associated intra-firm trade in a number of industries.
- Many states have created special economic zones in order to attract so-called 'global factories'.
- Much contemporary commerce involves transborder marketing of global brand-name products.
- The growth of a substantial global dimension to world trade may have deterred protectionism in the late twentieth century.

Global Finance

Finance has attracted some of the greatest attention in contemporary debates on globalization, especially in business and governing circles. The rise of supraterritoriality has affected both the forms that money takes and the ways that it is deployed in banking, securities, and derivatives markets. (See Box 22.3 regarding terminology.) As international, cross-border activities, such dealings have quite a long history. However, as commerce that unfolds through telephone and computer networks that make the world a single place, global finance

has experienced its greatest growth since the 1980s.

Supraterritorial Money

The development of global production and the growth of global markets have each encouraged—and been facilitated by—the spread of global monies. It was noted earlier that the fixed and later floating exchange regimes operated through the IMF have allowed a number of 'national' currencies to enter worldwide use. As familiar 'bureau de change' signs indicate, today retail outlets in scores of countries deal in multiple currencies on demand.

No national denomination has been more global in this context than the US dollar. About as many dollars circulate outside as inside the USA. Indeed, in certain financial crises this global money has displaced the locally issued currency in the everyday life of a national economy. Such 'dollarization' has occurred in Mexico and much of Eastern Europe during the 1990s. Since the 1970s the German Mark, Japanese yen, Swiss franc, and other major currencies have also acquired a substantial global character. Hence huge stocks of notionally 'national' money are now used in countless transactions that never touch the 'home' soil.

Foreign exchange dealing has become a thoroughly supraterritorial business. This round-the-clock, round-the-world market has no central meeting place. Many of the deals have nothing directly to do with the countries where the currencies involved are initially issued or eventually spent. The trading itself also transpires without distance. Transactions are generally concluded over the telephone and confirmed by telex or e-mail between buyers and sellers across whatever distance. Meanwhile shifts in exchange rates are flashed instantaneously and simultaneously on video monitors across the main dealing rooms worldwide.

Transborder money also takes other forms besides certain national currencies. Gold has already had worldwide circulation for several centuries, although it moves cumbersomely through territorial space rather than instantly through telecommunication lines. Newer and more fully supraterritorial denominations include the **Special Drawing Right**, issued through the IMF since 1968, and the **European Currency Unit**, created through the European Community ten years later. Both the SDR and the ECU reside only in computer memories and not in pocketbooks for everyday transactions.

Meanwhile other supraterritorial money has entered daily use in plastic form. For example, certain **credit cards** (e.g. Visa and MasterCard) are

---

Box 22.3. A Glossary of Global Finance

bond: a contractual obligation of a corporation, association or governmental agency to make payments of interest and repayments of principle on borrowed funds at certain fixed times.

derivative: a financial contract that 'derives' its value from an underlying asset, exchange rate, interest level, or market index.

equity: also called stock or shares; a number of equal portions in the nominal capital of a company; the shareholder thereby owns part of the enterprise.

eurobond: a bond denominated in a currency that is alien to a substantial proportion of the underwriters through whom it is distributed and investors to whom it is sold; the borrower, the syndicate of managers, the investors, and the securities exchange on which the bond is listed are spread over a number of countries.

eurocurrency: national money in the hands of persons and institutions domiciled outside the currency area concerned: hence 'eurodollar', 'eurozloty', etc.

euroequity: a share issue that is offered simultaneously in different stock markets, usually across several time zones; also called global equity.

merchant bank: also called an investment bank or securities house; a bank specializing in securities business (as opposed to a commercial bank engaged primarily in deposit and lending business).

offshore centre: a site for financial business offering inducements such as tax reductions, regulation waivers, subsidies and rebates, secrecy guarantees, and so on; most are located in island and other mini-states, though offshore provisions also cover arrangements like International Banking Facilities in the USA and the Tokyo-based Japan Offshore Market.

petrodollars: earnings from oil exports deposited outside the USA; they provided the largest single spur to growth in the euromarkets in the 1970s.

security: a contract with a claim to future payments in which (in contrast to bank credits) there is a direct and formally identified relationship between the investor and the borrower; also unlike bank loans, securities are traded in markets.

Special Drawing Right: the supraterritorial denomination issued since 1968 through the International Monetary Fund and used as its unit of account; $21.4 billion SDRs were in circulation as of the mid-1990s

Syndicated eurocredit: a loan provided in the euromarkets by an *ad hoc* association of a number of commercial banks.

accepted at several million venues the world over to make purchases in whatever local denomination. In addition, several types of **smart cards** (e.g. Mondex and the Clip card of Europay International) can simultaneously hold several currencies as digital cash on a microchip.

In sum, then, contemporary globalization has—through the spread of transborder currencies, distinctly supraterritorial denominations, global credit cards, and digital purses—significantly altered the shape of money. No longer is money restricted to the national-state-territorial form that prevailed from the nineteenth to the middle of the twentieth century.

Supraterritorial Banking

Globalization has touched banking mainly in terms of: (*a*) the growth of transborder deposits; (*b*) the advent of transborder bank lending; (*c*) the expansion of transborder branch networks; and (*d*) the emergence of instantaneous worldwide interbank fund transfers. So-called **eurocurrency** deposits are bank assets denominated in a national money different from the official currency in the country where the funds are held. For instance, euroyen are 'Japanese' yen deposited in, say, Canada. Eurocurrency accounts first appeared in the 1950s but mainly expanded after 1970, especially with the flood of so-called **petrodollars** that followed sudden major rises of oil prices in 1973–4 and 1979–80. Eurocurrencies are supraterritorial: they do not attach neatly to any country's money supply; nor are they systematically regulated by the national central bank that issued them.

Globalization has also entered the lending side of banking. Credit creation from eurocurrency deposits first occurred in 1957, when 'American' dollars were borrowed through the 'British' office of a 'Soviet' bank. However, **euroloans** mainly proliferated after 1973 following the petrodollar deluge. In the late twentieth century it has become common for a loan to be issued in one country, denominated in the currency of a second country (or perhaps a basket of currencies of several countries), for a borrower in a third country, by a bank or syndicate of banks in fourth and more countries.

The euromarkets focus not only on age-old sites of world finance like London, New York, Tokyo, and Zurich, but also on multiple **offshore centres**.

Much like EPZs in respect of manufacturing, offshore financial arrangements offer investors low levels of taxation and regulation. Although a few including Luxembourg and Jersey predate the Second World War, most offshore centres have emerged since 1960 and are now found in over forty countries. Most of the world's major banks now have branch networks across the principal 'onshore' (i.e. normally taxed and regulated) and offshore locations. For example, less than thirty years after passing relevant legislation in 1967, the Cayman Islands hosted over 500 offshore banks, with total deposits of $442 billion, none of them in the local currency (Roberts 1994; BIS 1996: 7).

The supraterritorial character of much contemporary banking also lies in the instantaneity of interbank fund transfers. Electronic messages have largely replaced territorial transfers by cheque or draft—and cost far less. The largest conduit for such movements is the Society for Worldwide Interbank Financial Telecommunications. Launched in 1977, **SWIFT** interconnected over 5,000 financial institutions in 137 countries twenty years later.

Supraterritorial Securities

Alongside banking, globalization has also altered the shape of securities markets. First, some of the bonds and stocks themselves have become relatively detached from territorial space. Second, many investor portfolios have acquired a transborder character. Third, electronic interlinkage of trading sites has created conditions of anywhere/anytime securities dealing.

In regard to the first point, contemporary globalization has seen the emergence of several major securities instruments with a transborder character. These bonds and equities involve issuers, currencies, brokers, and/or exchanges across multiple countries at the same time. For example, a so-called **eurobond** is denominated in a currency that is alien to a substantial proportion of the parties involved: the borrower who issues it; the underwriters who distribute it; the investors who hold it; and/or the exchange(s) that list it. This transborder financial instrument is thereby different from a **foreign bond**, which is handled in one country for an external borrower. Cross-border bonds of the latter type have existed for several hundred years, but eurobonds first appeared in 1963. In that year the government highways authority in Italy issued bonds denominated in US dollars through managers in Belgium, Britain, Germany, and the Netherlands, with subsequent quotation on the London Stock Exchange. By the late 1980s eurobonds constituted the second largest bond market in the world, behind that for US domestic issues (Honeygold 1989: 19).

On a similar pattern, a **euroequity** issue involves a transborder syndicate of brokers selling a new share release for simultaneous listing on stock exchanges in several countries. This supraterritorial process contrasts with an international offer, where a company based in one country issues equity in a second country. Like foreign bonds, international share quotations have existed almost as long as stock markets themselves. However, the first transborder equity issue occurred in 1984, when 15 per cent of a privatization of British Telecommunications was offered on exchanges in Japan, North America, and Switzerland concurrently with the majority share release in the UK. Transworld placements of new shares occur less frequently than eurobond issues; however, it has become quite common for major transborder firms to list their stock on different stock exchanges across several time zones. For example, equity in Alcatel Alsthom is quoted on twelve exchanges, stock in Nestlé on eleven, and shares in Imperial Chemical Industries on nine.

Not only various securities instruments, but also many investor portfolios have become relatively de-linked from territory in the context of contemporary financial globalization. Thus, for example, an investor in one country may leave assets with a fund manager in a second country who in turn places those sums on markets in a collection of third countries. In other words, even when individual securities have a territorial character, they can be combined in a supraterritorial investment package. Indeed, a number of pension funds, insurance companies, and unit trusts have created explicitly designated 'global funds' whose component securities are drawn from many corners of the world. Many transborder institutional investors have furthermore registered offshore for tax and other cost advantages. For example, the Africa Emerging Markets Fund has its investments in Africa, its listing in Ireland, and its management base in the USA. As of 1995 Luxembourg hosted some $350 billion in offshore investment funds, largely outside the regulatory reach of the managers' home governments.

Finally, securities markets have gone global through the growing supraterritorial character of many exchanges since the 1970s. The open-outcry floors of old have largely given way to electronic trading by telephone and computer networks. These telecommunications provide the infrastructure for distanceless deals (so-called **remote trading**), in which the brokers can in principle be located anywhere. Most major investment banks (ING Barings, Daiwa Securities, Merrill Lynch, etc.) now co-ordinate offices across several time zones in round-the-clock, round-the-world trading of bonds and shares. The first computerized order-routing system became operational in 1976, connecting brokers across the USA instantly to the trading floor of the New York Stock Exchange. Similar developments have since 1996 begun to link brokers anywhere in the European Union directly to its main exchanges. For its part the National Association of Securities Dealers Automated Quotation system (Nasdaq) has since its launch in 1971 had no central meeting place at all. By the mid-1990s this transborder computer network was, with its total capitalization of $1.2 trillion, the world's second largest stock market. The London-based Seaq and Europe-wide Easdaq systems launched similar frameworks in 1985 and 1996, respectively. Meanwhile, beginning with the Toronto and American Exchanges in 1985, a number of markets have established electronic links to enable transborder dealing between them. This extensive growth of supraterritoriality in the securities markets helps to explain why, for example, the Wall Street crash of October 1987 triggered transworld reverberations within hours.

Much like global banking, transborder securities trading is mainly conducted through computerized clearing systems. The equivalents of SWIFT are the Euroclear network, established in 1968, and Cedel, launched three years later. Between them these two global electronic bookkeeping operations handled a turnover of $35 trillion in 1995.

Supraterritorial Derivatives

A fourth area of finance suffused with globalization is the **derivatives** industry. A derivative product is a contract, the value of which depends on (i.e. is 'derived' from) the price of some underlying asset (e.g. a raw material or an equity) or a particular reference rate (e.g. an interest level or stock-market index). Derivatives connected to 'tangible' assets like raw minerals and land date from the middle of the nineteenth century, while derivatives based on financial indicators have proliferated since their introduction in 1972.

Derivatives contracts take two principal forms. The first type, **futures** and **forwards**, oblige a buyer and seller to complete a transaction at a predetermined time in the future at a price agreed upon today. The second main type, **options**, give parties a right (without obligation) to buy or sell at a specified price for a stipulated period of time up to the contract's expiry date. Other derivatives include 'swaps', 'warrants', and further—seemingly ever more obscure—financial instruments (Banks 1994).

Additional technical details and the various rationales relating to derivatives need not detain us here. It suffices for present purposes to emphasize the size of this financial industry. Public derivatives exchanges have proliferated worldwide since 1982 along with even larger over-the-counter markets. By 1995 the volume of trading on world derivatives markets totalled some $1.2 trillion per day. Meanwhile the value of outstanding derivatives contracts probably ran to over $50 trillion, or more than twice the level of world GDP (Sharpe 1996; BIS 1996: 27).

Like banking and securities, much derivatives business has become relatively distanceless and borderless. For example, a number of the contracts relate to supraterritorial indicators: e.g. the world price of copper; the interest rate on euroswiss franc deposits; and so on. In addition, much derivatives trading is undertaken through global securities houses and transworld telecommunications links. A number of derivatives instruments are traded simultaneously on several exchanges in a round-the-world, round-the-clock market. For example, contracts related to three-month eurodollar inter-

est rates have been traded concurrently on the London International Financial Futures and Options Exchange (LIFFE), the New York Futures Exchange, the Sydney Futures Exchange, and the Singapore International Monetary Exchange (SIMEX). Starting with a connection between SIMEX and the Chicago Mercantile Exchange in 1984, electronic links have enabled distanceless, transborder trading between various market sites.

Owing to this tight global interconnection, major losses in the derivatives markets can have immediate world-wide repercussions. For example, deficits of $1.3 billion accumulated by the Singapore-based futures trader Nick Leeson triggered a transborder collapse of the venerable Barings investment bank in 1995. A succession of similarly huge losses in other quarters have caused some to worry that global derivatives trading could undermine the world financial system as a whole.

Key Points

- Globalization has changed forms of money with the spread of transborder currencies, distinctly supraterritorial denominations, global credit cards, and digital cash.

- Globalization has reshaped banking with the growth of supraterritorial deposits, loans, branch networks, and fund transfers.

- Securities markets have gained a global dimension through the development of transborder bonds and stocks, transworld portfolios, and electronic round-the-world trading.

- Globalization has likewise affected the instruments and modes of trading on derivatives markets.

Limits to the Globalization of Commerce

Having now reviewed the development of a supraterritorial dimension in the contemporary world economy (summarized chronologically in Box 22.4), and emphasized its significance, we must also recognize the limits of these changes. As noted in Chapter 1, and again earlier in the present chapter, many assessments of globalization are suffused

with hype and exaggeration. However, one can appreciate the importance of globalization without slipping into such 'globalism'. Four main points are highlighted in this respect below: (*a*) the unevenness with which the globalization of trade and finance has spread; (*b*) the continuing importance of territoriality in the contemporary globalizing

---

Box 22.4. Some Key Events in Global Trade and Finance

1880s	development of first global products
1929	institution of the first offshore finance arrangements (in Luxembourg)
1944	Bretton Woods Conference drafts constitutions of the IMF and World Bank
1954	establishment of the first export processing zone (in Ireland)
1954	launch of the 'Marlboro cowboy' as a global commercial icon
1955	first McDonald's restaurant opened (operating in 90 countries 40 years later)
1957	issuance of the first eurocurrency loan
1959	gold-dollar standard enters into full operation
1963	issuance of the first eurobond
1965	start of the *maquiladora* programme in Mexico
1968	introduction of a suprastate denomination, the Special Drawing Right
1968	launch of Euroclear computerized transworld settlement of securities deals
1971	establishment of the first wholly electronic stock exchange (Nasdaq)
1972	launch of markets in financial derivatives, starting with currency futures
1973	quadrupling of oil prices floods euromarkets with petrodollars
1974	formation of Basle Committee on Banking Supervision following the collapse of two banks heavily involved in foreign exchange dealing
1974	US government relaxes foreign exchange controls (other states follow in later years)
1976	IMF meeting in Jamaica formalizes the regime of floating exchange rates
1977	inauguration of SWIFT electronic interbank fund transfers worldwide
1982	Mexico's threatened default on global loans triggers Third World debt crisis
1984	formation of the International Organization of Securities Commissions
1984	first transborder equity issue (by British Telecommunications)
1985	first transborder electronic link between stock exchanges
1987	stock-market crash on Wall Street reverberates worldwide overnight
1994	conclusion of the Uruguay Round of GATT
1995	inauguration of the World Trade Organization
1995	Leeson Affair highlights the volatility of global derivatives markets

---

economy; (*c*) the continuing key place of the state amidst these changes; and (*d*) the continuing significance of national attachments, and cultural diversity more generally, in the present era of commercial globalization.

Irregular Incidence

As already stressed in Chapter 1, globalization has not been experienced everywhere and by everyone to the same extent. In general, transborder trade and finance have developed furthest: (*a*) in the so-called 'triad' of East Asia, North America, and Western Europe; (*b*) in urban areas relative to rural districts worldwide; and (*c*) in wealthy and professional circles. On the other hand, few people and places are today completely untouched by economic globalization.

Supraterritorial trade and finance have tran-

spired disproportionately in the so-called North, and then most especially amongst its cities. For example, over half of world manufacturing output and a third of merchandise exports at the end of the twentieth century are centred in just three countries: the USA, Japan, and Germany (Kidron and Segal 1995: 86–9). Usually only the labour-intensive assembly stage of a transborder production process is located in the South. The sale of most global products is also heavily concentrated in the North. For instance, although McDonald's fast food is dished up in 90 countries, the vast majority of these meals are consumed in a handful of those lands. In contrast to currencies issued in the North, the national denominations of countries in Africa have scarcely any mutual convertibility. At the time of writing, three-quarters and more of foreign direct investment, credit card transactions, stock market capitalization, derivatives trade, and transborder loans flow within the triad. In the light of such inequalities, a number of promoters as well as critics of globalization worry that the trend is largely bypassing the South.

This exclusion is far from complete, however. For instance, certain products originating in the South have figured significantly in global markets (e.g. wines from Chile and package holidays in Kenya). Electronic banking has even reached parts of rural China. A number of offshore centres and large sums of transborder bank debt are found in the South. Global portfolios have figured strongly in the development of new securities markets in major cities of Africa, Asia, Eastern Europe, and Latin America since the mid-1980s. SIMEX and the Sao Paolo-based Bolsa de Mercadorias & Futuros (BM&F) have played important parts in the burgeoning derivatives markets of the late twentieth century.

Indeed, involvement in global trade and finance is often as much a function of class as the North-South divide. The vast majority of the world's population—including many in the North—lack the means to purchase most global products. Michael Porter of the Harvard Business School puts this point more euphemistically by noting that markets 'today seem based less on country differences and more on buyer differences that transcend country boundaries' (1986: 44). Likewise, placing investments in global financial markets depends on wealth, whose distribution does not always follow a North–South pattern. For example, petrodollars have been mostly owned by élites in the oil-exporting countries of Africa, Latin America, and the Middle East. Country comparisons show that the populations of Brazil and Botswana have the world's largest income inequalities.

Space limitations do not permit full elaboration of the point here, but transborder markets and investments can be shown to have contributed significantly to growing wealth gaps within countries as well as between North and South. For example, global capital mobility, in particular to low-wage production sites and offshore financial centres, has encouraged most states to reduce upper-tax brackets and downgrade other public welfare measures. Such steps have contributed to growing inequality almost everywhere in the world of the late twentieth century (see Brecher and Costello 1994; Ghai 1994). Increasingly, poverty has become connected as much to supraterritorial class, gender, and race structures as to country of domicile (see further Chs. 23 and 25).

The Persistence of Territory

On the other hand, the transcendence of territorial space in contemporary world commerce must not be overestimated. True, evidence presented in earlier sections of this chapter suggests that distance and borders have lost the determining influence on economic geography that they once had. However, this is not to say that territoriality has lost all significance in the contemporary organization of production, exchange, and consumption. Robert Reich exaggerated when, shortly before joining the Clinton Administration, he declared that economic globalization yielded a situation of 'no *national* products or technologies, no national corporations, no national industries' (1991: 3, his emphasis).

On the contrary, after several decades of accelerated globalization a great deal of commercial activity still has only a secondary if any supraterritorial dimension. For example, although transborder manufacturing through global factories affects a significant proportion of certain industries, it involves but a small percentage of overall world production. Most processes remain self-contained within one country, and only a tiny percentage of the world's workforce is so far employed in EPZs. Even many global products (Boeing jets, Ceylon teas) are prepared within single countries although their distribution extends worldwide. Although transborder products are generally more prevalent than supraterritorial production, far from all sales items have global circulation.

Many types of money, too, are still restricted to a national or local domain. Likewise, the great bulk of retail banking remains territorial, as clients deal with their local branch offices. In spite of substantial growth since the 1980s, transborder share dealing remains a small fraction of total equity trading (T. Porter 1993: 109). Moreover, a large majority of turnover on most stock exchanges continues to involve shares of firms headquartered in the same country. The London Stock Exchange provides the only major case where externally based equity accounts for over half of business in the 1990s. Similarly, despite exponential expansion of the eurobond market, in 1995 the total value of outstanding transborder bonds ($2.8 trillion) was still dwarfed by the aggregate value of outstanding domestic issues ($23.9 trillion) (BIS 1996: 20).

Nor is most global commercial activity wholly divorced from territorial geography. For example, local circumstances strongly influence corporate decisions regarding the location of transborder production facilities. In the foreign exchange markets dealers are mainly clustered in half a dozen cities, even if their transactions are largely cyberspatial and can have immediate consequences anywhere in the world. It remains rare for a transborder company to issue a large proportion of its stock outside its country of origin. In the light of such qualifications Richard O'Brien has readily conceded the hyperbole in his depiction of global finance as 'the end of geography' (1992: 2).

Hence the importance of globalization is that it has ended the monopoly of territoriality in defining social space in the world political economy. This is not to say that the trend has eliminated territoriality altogether. The global dimension of contemporary world commerce has grown alongside and in complex relations with its territorial aspects. Globalization is reconfiguring geography rather than obliterating territory.

The Survival of the State

Similarly, as already seen in Chapter 1, globalization has repositioned the (territorial) state rather than signalled its demise. The expansion of transborder trade and finance has made claims of **sovereign statehood** obsolete, but the significance of states themselves remains. Through both unilateral decisions and multilaterally co-ordinated policies, states have done much to facilitate economic globalization and influence its course.

As already mentioned, states have encouraged the globalization of commerce *inter alia* through various policies of liberalization and the creation of special economic zones and offshore financial centres. At the same time, some governments have also slowed globalization within their jurisdiction by retaining certain restrictions on transborder activity. However, most states—including those still nominally 'communist'—have sooner or later responded to strong pressures to liberalize. Those retaining strict regulations have generally suffered capital flight abroad, especially offshore. In any case, governments have often lacked effective means to enforce their territorially bound controls on globally mobile capital. Only in respect of immigration restrictions have states largely sustained their borders against economic globalization.

However, states are by no means powerless in the face of economic globalization. Even the common claim that global finance lies beyond the state requires some qualification. After all, governments and central banks continue to exert major influence on money supplies and interest rates, even if they no longer monopolize money creation and lack direct control over the euromarkets. Likewise, particularly through co-operative action, states can significantly shift exchange rates, even if they have lost the capacity to fix the conversion ratios and are sometimes overridden by currency dealers. Governments have also pursued collective regulation of transborder banking to some effect through the Basle Committee on Banking Supervision, set up through the BIS in 1974. The survival of offshore financial centres, too, depends to a considerable extent on the goodwill of governments, both the host regime and external authorities. Similarly, national regulators of securities markets have collaborated since 1984 through the International Organization of Securities Commissions (IOSCO). State oversight of derivatives trading may also intensify as those transactions become better understood.

In short, there is little sign that global commerce and the state are inherently antithetical. On the contrary, the two have shown considerable mutual dependence. States have provided much of the regulatory framework for global trade and finance, albeit that they have (as indicated in Ch. 1) shared these competences with substate and suprastate agencies.

The Continuance of Cultural Diversity

Much evidence also confounds the common presumption that economic globalization is effecting cultural homogenization and a rise of cosmopolitan orientations over national identities. The growth of transborder production, the proliferation of global products, the multiplication of supraterritorial monies and the expansion of transworld financial flows show little sign of heralding an end of difference in the world economy.

True, global trade and finance are moved by much more than national loyalties. Consumers repeatedly ignore exhortations to 'buy British' and the like in favour of global products. Shareholders and managers rarely put national sentiments ahead of the profit margin. For example, the global media magnate Rupert Murdoch happily traded Australian for US citizenship when it suited his commercial purposes. Foreign exchange dealers readily desert their national currency in order to reap financial gain.

However, in other respects national identities and solidarities survive—and sometimes positively thrive—in the contemporary globalizing economy. Most transborder companies retain a readily recognized national affiliation, even if the situation is in practice not always so clearcut. Most firms involved in global trade and finance retain a mononational board of directors, and the operations of many of these enterprises continue to reflect a national style of business practice connected with the country of origin. Different national conventions persist in global finance as well. For instance, since equities have traditionally held a smaller place in German finance, globalization in that country has mainly involved banks and the bond markets.

Cultural diversity also persists in transborder marketing. Local peculiarities often affect the way that a global product is sold and used in different places. Advertising must often be adjusted to local tastes to be effective. New technologies like computer-aided design have moreover allowed companies to tailor some global products to local proclivities. In this vein Michael Porter has argued that 'national differences in character and culture, far from being threatened by global competition, prove integral to success in it' (1990: 30).

In sum, then, like globalization in general, its economic dimension does not have universal scope. Nor has the rise of global trade and finance

marked the end of territorial space, the demise of the state, or full-scale cultural homogenization. However, recognition of these limitations does not entail a rejection of notions of globalization altogether, on the lines of the sceptics noted earlier. After discounting for exaggeration and *non sequiturs*, the growth of supraterritoriality remains a highly significant development in the contemporary world economy. The challenge for analysis is to tease out the interplay in economic globalization between territoriality and supraterritoriality, between territorial states and other governance arrangements, and between territorial identities and transborder affiliations.

Key Points

- Global trade and finance have spread unevenly between different regions and different circles of people.
- Transborder commerce has to date often widened material inequalities within and between countries.
- Territorial geography continues to be important in the contemporary globalizing economy.
- Although lacking sovereign powers, states exercise significant influence in global trade and finance.
- While economic globalization has weakened cultural diversity and national attachments in some respects, it has reproduced them in others.

Conclusion

The present chapter has shown that, amongst other things, the globalization of world politics is a deeply economic affair. The growth of global trade and finance has deeply shaped—and been shaped by—the developments in governance described in Chapter 1. Commercial globalization has affected different places and people to different extents, and it has far from eliminated older core structures of world politics: territory, state, and nation. However, these developments have already shifted many contours of geography, governance, and community, and economic globalization seems likely unfold further still in the future.

The preceding pages have only touched on the wide-ranging and deeply significant questions of global trade and finance. In particular, this discussion has but hinted at the substantial problems of equity and distributive justice that contemporary globalization has raised. The following chapter by Caroline Thomas will address a number of these matters at greater length. For its part the present chapter will, I hope, have established the far-reaching importance of economic globalization when it is understood as the growth of a supraterritorial dimension in world commerce.

QUESTIONS

1. Distinguish different conceptions of economic globalization.

2. To what extent is economic globalization new to contemporary history?

3. How is a transborder production process different from territorial production?

4. How has globalization been manifested in changed forms of money?

5. What makes financial dealings in the euromarkets 'supraterritorial'?

6. What is an offshore financial centre?

7. To what extent does economic globalization mark 'the end of geography'?

8. How has globalization of trade and finance affected state sovereignty?

9. Discuss the impact of global products on cultural diversity.

10. To what extent can it be said that global capital carries no flag?

11. Assess the relationship between globalization and income inequality.

12. In what ways might global commerce be reshaped to promote greater distributive justice?

GUIDE TO FURTHER READING

Barnet, R. J., and Cavanagh, J., *Global Dreams: Imperial Corporations and the New World Order* (New York: Simon and Schuster, 1994). A highly readable critical examination of transborder companies and global consumerism.

Brecher, J., and Costello, T., *Global Village or Global Pillage: Economic Reconstruction from the Bottom up* (Boston: South End, 1994). A denunciation of the globalization of trade as a worldwide 'race to the bottom' of labour and environmental standards.

Grunwald, J., and Flamm, K., *The Global Factory: Foreign Assembly in International Trade* (Washington, DC: Brookings Institution, 1985). A detailed study of transborder production.

Helleiner, E., *States and the Reemergence of Global Finance: From Bretton Woods to the 1990s* (Ithaca, NY: Cornell University Press, 1994). A history that emphasizes the importance of state policies in promoting financial globalization.

Hirst, P., and Thompson, G., *Globalization in Question: The International Economy and the Possibilities of Governance* (Cambridge: Polity Press, 1996). A critique of 'globalist' presumptions that economic globalization is new, irreversible, and wholly beyond state control.

Mittelman, J. H. (ed.), *Globalization: Critical Reflections* (Boulder, Col.: Lynne Rienner, 1996). A collection of essays by leading researchers in the subfield of International Political Economy.

O'Brien, R., *Global Financial Integration: The End of Geography* (London: Pinter, 1992). A concise survey of financial globalization in the 1980s.

Ohmae, K., *The Borderless World: Power and Strategy in the Interlinked Economy* (London: Fontana, 1990). A management consultant's celebration of global business.

Peterson, V. S., and Runyan, A. S., *Global Gender Issues* (Boulder, Col.: Westview Press, 1993). A critical examination of the impacts of globalization on, *inter alia*, women's employment and the feminization of poverty.

Porter, M. E. (ed.), *Competition in Global Industries* (Boston: Harvard Business School Press, 1986). A general discussion of global trade supplemented with numerous case studies from the Harvard Business School.

Stubbs, R., and Underhill, G. R. D. (eds.), *Political Economy and the Changing Global Order* (Basingstoke: Macmillan, 1994). A textbook in International Political Economy with much concerning global trade and finance.

UNDP *Human Development Report* (New York: Oxford University Press, 1990). This annual publication of the United Nations Development Programme since 1990 includes much on the welfare consequences of economic globalization.

23 Poverty, Development, and Hunger

Caroline Thomas

READER'S GUIDE

This chapter explores and illustrates the contested nature of a number of important concepts in International Relations. It examines the orthodox mainstream understanding of poverty, development, and hunger, and contrasts this with a critical alternative approach. Consideration is given to how successful the development orthodoxy has been in incorporating and thereby neutralizing the concerns of the critical alternative. The chapter then closes with an assessment of the likelihood of a reduction in inequality and hunger in a context marked by increased globalization.

Introduction

Since 1945 we have witnessed fifty years of unprecedented official development policies and impressive global economic growth. Yet the economic gap between the richest and poorest 20 per cent of global population has grown from 30 : 1 in 1960, to 61 : 1 in 1991. Poverty, hunger, and disease are still widespread throughout the world. Moreover, this situation is not confined to that part of the world that we term the 'South' or the 'Third World', and poor living conditions and rising social inequalities are also evident in the Western world as a result of economic liberalization policies. Traditionally, the discipline of International Relations has focused on issues relating to interstate conflict, and has neglected the less dramatic challenges presented to human well-being by the existence of global underdevelopment. Some measure of the relative importance of these matters can perhaps be gained from the observation that in the first two years of the 1980s more people died from hunger than were killed as a result of the First and Second World Wars, and that during this period the number of people who died every two days of hunger was equivalent to the number of deaths caused by the dropping of the atom bomb on Hiroshima in 1945 (The Hunger Project 1985: 7). In the mid-1990s, the number of people who die annually from hunger is thought to be even higher.

The appalling statistics of global hunger and poverty, and the even more appalling reality that they represent in the daily lives of much of the world's population, clearly point to the need for further investigation by those who are concerned with human welfare. This necessity should not be obviated by the fact that the global media tend to direct attention away from the ever-present unvoiced crisis that hunger represents and towards crises of a more 'newsworthy' and sensational nature.

Behind the blaring headlines of the world's many conflicts and emergencies, there lies a silent crisis—a crisis of underdevelopment, of global poverty, of ever-mounting population pressures, of thoughtless degradation of the environment. This is not a crisis that will respond to emergency relief. Or to fitful policy interventions. It requires a long, quiet process of sustainable human development. (UNDP 1994: iii)

The attempts of governments, intergovernmental organizations and non-governmental organizations (NGOs) since 1945 to address the global hunger and poverty can be categorized into two very broad types, depending on the explanations they provide for the existence of these problems and the respective solutions that they prescribe. This can be illustrated by reference to the recent UN World Summit for Social Development in Copenhagen, March 1995, which was convened primarily to address the related matters of increasing global inequality and the continuation of widespread poverty and under- and unemployment. Various views were expressed at the formal Summit, and at the parallel Non-Governmental (NGO) Forum, as to why an estimated 500–1,000 million people still have no access to clean water, sanitation, or adequate nutrition, and why 30 per cent of the global labour force are classified as under- or unemployed. Likewise, a variety of solutions were advocated. The different approaches evident in these various solutions could, broadly speaking, be said to mirror two fundamentally different interpretations of how and why the various development-related problems came into existence. These can be identified as the dominant **mainstream** or **orthodox approach**, which provides and values a particular body of developmental knowledge, and a **critical alternative approach**, which incorporates other more marginalized understandings of the developmental process. Most of this chapter will be devoted to an examination of the differences between these two approaches in relationship to the three related topics of poverty, development, and hunger, with particular emphasis being placed upon the topic of development. At the end of the chapter, we then conclude with an assessment of whether the desperate conditions in which so many of the world's citizens find themselves today are likely to improve given current trends and policies.

Poverty

Different conceptions of poverty underpin the mainstream and alternative views of development. There is basic agreement on the material aspect of poverty, such as lack of food, clean water, and sanitation. However, key differences emerge in regard to how such needs should be met, and hence about the goal of development: cash transactions in the market, or subsistence via community-regulated common resources such as land, water, and fodder.

Most governments, international organizations, citizens in the West and many elsewhere adhere to the orthodox conception of poverty. This refers to a situation where people do not have the **money** to buy adequate food or satisfy other basic needs, and are often classified as un- or underemployed. For example, the Report of the South Commission—an important statement on development in the 'South' drawn up by eminent persons of Southern origins—reflects an orthodox conception of poverty when it claims that a billion people in the developing countries 'are too poor to buy enough food to sustain their energy' (South Commission: 84).

This mainstream understanding of poverty based on money has arisen as a result of the globalization of western culture and the attendant expansion of the market. Thus a community which provides for itself outside of monetized cash transactions and wage labour, such as a hunter-gatherer pygmy group, is regarded as poor. Consequently it is increasingly common for people around the world to regard as poor those 'who provide for themselves rather than sell their crops and buy commercially produced food . . . wear handmade clothes rather than factory-made garments . . . build their own houses with the help of their neighbours rather than employing labourers . . . [and] whose children are educated by family and friends rather than by paid teachers' (*The Ecologist* 1993: 96).

In traditional subsistence methods, a common strategy for survival is provision for oneself and one's family via community-regulated access to common water, land, and fodder. However, mainstream development classifies this method of provision as outmoded and representative of poverty. Yet the autonomy characteristic of such methods may be highly valued by those who have traditionally practised them. Indeed some such methods have been sustained over thousands of years. For many people in the developing world the ability to provide for oneself and one's family may be preferable to dependence on an unpredictable market and/or an unreliable government.

Critical, alternative views of poverty exist in other cultures where the emphasis is not simply on money, but on spiritual values, community ties, and availability of common resources. Some would regard us in the West as deprived of the most basic human need of spiritual fulfilment. Similarly, others would consider us impoverished for our loss of the extended family and sense of community belonging. Critical views have emanated from within Western society also. For example, it has been asserted that our emphasis on monetary values has led to the creation of 'a system of production that ravishes nature and a society that mutilates man' (Schumacher 1973).

Since 1945, the meaning of poverty has been homogenized and almost universalized. Poverty is seen as an economic condition dependent on cash transactions in the market-place for its eradication. These transactions in turn are dependent on development defined as economic growth. An economic yardstick is used to measure and to judge all societies. Poverty has widely been regarded as characterizing the Third World, and an approach has developed whereby it is seen as incumbent upon the developed countries to 'help' the Third World eradicate 'poverty'. The solution advocated is the further integration of these countries into the market economy. Increasingly however, poverty, defined in such economic terms is also coming to characterize significant sectors of population in advanced developed countries such as the USA (See Bello 1994).

Key Points

- The monetary-based conception of poverty has been almost universalized among governments and international organizations since 1945.

- Poverty is interpreted as a condition suffered by people who do not earn enough money to satisfy their basic material requirements in the market place.

- Developed countries have regarded poverty as being something external to them and a defining feature of the Third World. This view has provided justification for the former to help 'develop' the latter by promoting their further integration into the global market.

- However, such poverty is increasingly endured by significant sectors of the population in the North, as well as the Third World, hence rendering traditional categories less useful.

- A critical alternative view of poverty places more emphasis on lack of access to community-regulated common resources, the erosion of community ties and spiritual values.

Having considered the orthodox and critical alternative views of poverty, we will now turn to an examination of the important topic of development. This examination will be conducted in three main parts. The first part will start by examining the orthodox view of development and will then proceed to an assessment of its effect on post-war development in the Third World. The second part will examine the critical alternative view of development and its application to subjects such as land ownership and democracy. In the third part consideration will be given to the ways in which the orthodox approach to development has responded to some of the criticisms made of it by the critical alternative approach.

Development

When we consider the topic of development it is important to realize that all conceptions of development necessarily reflect a particular set of social and political values. Indeed, it is true to say that, 'Development can be conceived only within an ideological framework' (Roberts 1984: 7).

Since the Second World War the dominant understanding, favoured by the majority of governments and multilateral agencies, has seen development as synonymous with economic growth within the context of a free market international economy. Economic growth is identified as necessary for combating poverty, defined as the inability of people to meet their basic material needs through cash transactions. This is seen in the influential reports of the World Bank, where countries are categorized according to whether they are low-income, lower middle-income, upper middle-income, or high-income countries. Those countries that have the lower national incomes per head of population are regarded as being less developed than those with higher incomes, and they are perceived as being in need of increased integration into the global market-place.

An alternative view of development has, however, emerged from the occasional government, grassroots movements, NGOs, and some academics. Their concerns have centred broadly on entitlement and distribution. Poverty is identified as the inability to provide for the material needs of oneself and one's family by subsistence or cash transactions, and by the absence of an environment conducive to human well-being broadly conceived in spiritual and community terms. These voices of opposition are growing significantly louder, as ideas polarize following the apparent universal triumph of economic liberalism. The language of opposition is changing to incorporate matters of democracy such as political empowerment, participation, meaningful self-determination for the majority and protection of the commons. The differences between the orthodox and the alternative views of development are summarized in Box 23.1. In the following two sections we will examine how the orthodox view of development has been applied at a global level and assess what measure of success it has achieved.

The Development Orthodoxy

Economic Liberalism and the Post-1945 International Economic Order

During the Second World War there was a strong belief amongst the allied powers that the protectionist trade policies of the 1930s had contributed significantly to the outbreak of the War. Plans were drawn up by the US and the UK for the creation of a stable post-war international order with the United Nations (UN), its affiliates the International

---

Box 23.1. The Orthodox versus the Alternative View of Development

The Orthodox View

Poverty: A situation suffered by people who do not have the *money to buy food* and satisfy other basic *material needs*.

Purpose: Transformation of traditional subsistence economies defined as 'backward' into industrial, commodified economies defined as 'modern'. Production of surplus. Individuals sell their labour for money, rather than producing to meet their family's needs.

Core Ideas and Assumptions: The possibility of unlimited economic growth in a free-market system. Economies would reach a 'take-off' point and thereafter wealth would trickle down to those at the bottom. Superiority of the 'Western' model and knowledge. Belief that the process would ultimately benefit everyone. Domination, exploitation of nature.

Measurement: Economic growth; Gross Domestic Product (GDP) per capita; industrialization, including of agriculture.

Process: Top-down; reliance on 'expert knowledge', usually Western and definitely external; large capital investments in large projects; advanced technology; expansion of the private sphere.

The Alternative View

Poverty: A situation suffered by people who are not able to meet their *material and non-material needs* through their own effort.

Purpose: Creation of human well-being through sustainable societies in social, cultural, political, and economic terms.

Core Ideas and Assumptions: Self-sufficiency. The inherent value of nature, cultural diversity and the community-controlled commons (water, land, air, forest). Human activity in balance with nature. Self-reliance. Voice for marginalized groups e.g. women, indigenous groups. Local control.

Measurement: Fulfilment of basic material and non-material human needs of everyone; condition of the natural environment. Political empowerment of marginalized.

Process: Bottom-up; participatory; reliance on appropriate (often local) knowledge and technology; small investments in small-scale projects; protection of the commons.

Monetary Fund (IMF) and the World Bank, plus the General Agreement on Tariffs and Trade (GATT) providing the institutional bases. The latter three provided the foundations of a liberal international economic order based on the pursuit of free trade. Their decision-making procedures favoured a small group of developed Western states. Their relationship with the UN, which in the General Assembly has more democratic procedures, has not always been an easy one.

By championing liberal economic values, the post-war international order has played an important role in accelerating globalization, particularly in the 1980s and 1990s. Prior to then, the system established was one of **'embedded liberalism'**. This meant that whilst the system aimed at reducing barriers to trade, in reality significant levels of state intervention in the market continued. Governments were highly responsive to domestic pressures, and were unwilling to leave everything up to the market for reasons of domestic political stability and national interest.

In the early post-war years, reconstruction of previously developed states took priority over assisting developing states. This reconstruction process really took off in the context of the cold war, with the transfer of huge sums of money from the United States to Europe in the form of bilateral aid from the Marshall Plan of 1947. In the 1950s and 1960s as decolonization progressed, the focus of the World Bank and the UN system generally shifted to the needs of developing countries. The US was heavily involved as the most important funder of the World Bank and UN, and also in a bilateral capacity.

There was a widespread belief in the developed Western countries, amongst the managers of the major multilateral institutions, and throughout the UN system, that Third World states were economically backward and needed to be 'developed'. This attitude was widely shared by Western-educated élites in those countries. In the context of independence movements the development imperative came to be shared by many citizens in the Third World. The underlying assumption was that the Western lifestyle and mode of economic organization were superior and should be universally aspired to.

The cold war provided a context in which there

was a competition between the West and the Eastern Bloc to win allies in the 'Third World'. The US believed that the path of liberal economic growth would result in development, and that development would result in hostility to socialist ideals. The USSR, by contrast, attempted to sell its economic system as the most rapid means for the newly independent states to achieve industrialization and development. The process of industrialization underpinned conceptions of development in both East and West, but whereas in the capitalist sphere the market was to be the engine of growth, in the socialist sphere central planning by the state was the preferred method. The majority of Third World states were born into and accepted a place within the Western, capitalist orbit, while a few either by choice or lack of options ended up in the socialist camp.

The Achievements of the Post-1945 International Economic Order

There have been major gains for developing countries since 1945 as measured by the orthodox criteria of economic growth, Gross Domestic Product (GDP) per capita and industrialization. With respect to economic growth, from 1950 to the end of the 1980s, the economies of developing countries grew on average at 4.9 per cent per year, compared with a growth of 3.5 per cent for developed economies (Adams 1993: 8). The rates of growth for developing countries in the periods 1960–70, 1970–80 and 1980–7 are shown in Fig. 1.

The situation with regard to changes in GDP per capita is revealed in Table 23.1. This shows that in countries with over 90 per cent of the population of the developing world, the annual average growth-rate of the GDP per capita remained positive. The other most striking feature about the economic growth of developing countries revealed in Table 23.1 is its marked diversity, with some countries (largely in Asia and the Americas) achieving substantial growth rates, and others (largely in Africa) not doing so well.

Lastly with respect to industrialization, Fig. 23.2 shows that over the period 1960–80, the contribution of industry to GDP in the South (excluding China), rose from 21 to 34 per cent.

Having looked at the achievements of the post-war international economic order, we will now proceed to an assessment of these achievements from, first of all, the perspective of the mainstream ortho-

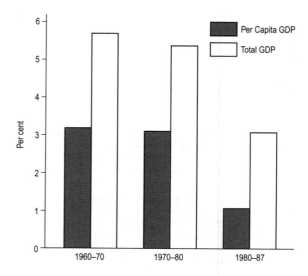

Fig. 23.1. Per capita and total GDP growth rates in the South between 1960 and 1987

Source: South Commission, 1990, p. 33 (based on UNCTAD data)

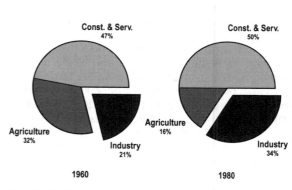

Fig. 23.2. Economic transformation of the South: sectoral distribution of GDP, 1960–1980*

* Excluding China
Source: South Commission, 1990, p. 34 (based on UNCTAD data)

dox view of development, and then from the critical alternative view of development.

The Orthodox Assessment of the Post-War International Economic Order

Prior to the late 1970s, the rate of industrial growth was higher in the developing world as a whole than

Table 23.1. **Annual average rates of growth of per capita GDP of individual developing countries, 1960–1989**

	<0%	0–2%	2–4%	>4%	Totals
No. of countries with growth rates falling within designed ranges	26	43	26	11	106
Breakdown of countries by major geographical regions:					
Americas	4	13	11	0	28
Africa	19	20	6	3	48
Asia	3	10	9	8	30
Share of total population* accounted for by countries in each growth range (%)	7.0	56.4	30.7	5.0	100

Source: Adams (1993: 12; based on UNCTAD data for 1989).
* Total population of those countries covered in the table.

in the developed capitalist countries taken as a group. Many developing countries exhibited an impressive economic performance, and average per capita incomes in many developing states were rising. Following the first oil price shock of 1973, developing countries undertook large-scale borrowing of recycled petrodollars from Western commercial banks in an attempt to sustain their rates of economic growth. However, during the 1980s there was a serious regression in much of the developing world as a result of the rich countries' strategy for dealing with the second oil price hike in 1979, which resulted in massive rises in interest rates and steep falls in commodity prices in the early 1980s.

These changes precipitated the debt crisis. Once the debt crisis had come to a head in 1982, following Mexico's threat to default, the Group of Seven leading developed Western countries decided to deal with the debt problem on a country-by-country basis, with the goal of avoiding the collapse of the international banking system by ensuring continued repayment of debt. In this regard, the IMF and the World Bank pursued a vigorous policy of **structural adjustment lending** throughout the developing world.

In applying the policy of structural adjustment lending, the Fund and Bank worked together in an unprecedented fashion to encourage developing countries to pursue market-oriented strategies based on rolling back the power of the state and opening Third World economies to foreign investment. Exports were promoted so that these coun-

tries would earn the foreign exchange necessary to keep up with their debt repayments. The strategy worked, in that debt repayments have largely been met, the exposure of Western banks has been significantly reduced and any threat to the international financial system has been removed. However, the anticipated influx of foreign investment into developing countries has not occurred.

Despite the negative effects of the debt crisis upon many countries within the South, some of them have enjoyed significant and sustained economic growth over the decade. China's economy grew at 9.4 per cent per annum, while India and South East Asia averaged 5.5 per cent per annum. China and India benefited in this respect from their large size, the fact that they had negligible foreign debts at the beginning of the decade, and they were self-sufficient in food and capital goods.

With the collapse of Communism in the late 1980s, economic liberalism appears to have triumphed throughout the world. The Western countries continue to advocate free market policies throughout the rest of the world. This strategy is pursued not just through the IMF and the World Bank, but very importantly, through the Uruguay Round, which is the latest round of trade discussions carried out under the auspices of the GATT. Importantly this has expanded the private realm of the market into areas previously considered part of the public domain or subject to national regulation: for example, intellectual property rights, such as patents on seeds.

Caroline Thomas

A Critical Alternative Assessment of the Post-War International Economic Order

Critics of the development orthodoxy do not believe that, on their own, statistical measurements of economic growth and per capita GDP give us an adequate picture of what is happening in developing countries. For example, Glyn Roberts points out that, 'GNP growth statistics might mean a good deal to an economist or to a maharajah, but they do not tell us a thing about the quality of life in a Third World fishing village' (Roberts 1984: 6). Those who advocate an alternative approach therefore place more emphasis on the **pattern of distribution** of gains within global society and within individual states. They believe that the economic liberalism which forms a crucial part of the process of globalization has resulted, and continues to result, in increasing economic differentiation between and within countries.

Overall, there has been an explosive widening of the gap between the rich and the poor since 1945 compared with previous history (Adams 1993: vii). This has been occurring over the very period when key global actors have been committed to promoting development worldwide, and indeed when there has been fairly continuous world economic growth and positive rates of GDP growth per capita, at least until 1990 (Brown and Kane 1995). The widening economic gap between the rich and the poor at a global level is shown in Table 23.2.

This increasing gap between rich and poor was regarded as inevitable by **dependency theorists** such as André Gunder Frank (Frank 1967). Writing in the 1960s and 70s, they stressed how the periphery, or Third World, was actively underdeveloped by activities which promoted the growth in wealth of the core Western countries, and of élites in the periphery. The periphery produced cheap primary products which were exported to the core. There,

they were processed or converted into manufactured goods, then re-exported to the periphery with value added. For the periphery the terms of trade, by which we mean the selling-price of primary commodities relative to the buying-price of manufactured goods, have tended to decline over the long-term, and as a result conditions have generally worsened in the periphery.

Informed by such concerns in the 1970s the developing countries campaigned unsuccessfully for a **New International Economic Order**. In fact they were calling for reforms of the existing order, and were especially concerned about declining terms of trade. They wanted the prevailing order to be made more user-friendly for the producers of primary commodities through such mechanisms as index-linking the prices of primary products to the prices of manufactured goods. They were also concerned to defend their right to exercise sovereignty over their natural resources and to form producer cartels.

By the end of the 1970s it was clear that the orthodox conception of 'trickle-down' (the idea that overall economic growth as measured by increases in the GDP would automatically bring benefits for the poorer classes) had not worked. Despite impressive rates of growth in GDP per capita enjoyed by developing countries, this success was not reflected in their societies at large, and whilst a minority became substantially wealthier, the mass of the population saw no significant change. The South Commission concluded of this period that,

Inequalities tended to widen as the economy grew and became more industrialized . . . Increasingly, the rich and powerful in the countries of the South were able to enjoy the life-style and consumption patterns of developed countries of the North. But large segments of the population experienced no significant improvement in their

Table 23.2. **Global income distribution, 1960–1990**

Year	Percentage of global income going to richest 20 per cent	Percentage of global income going to poorest 20 per cent	Ratio of richest to poorest
1960	70.2	2.3	30 : 1
1970	73.9	2.3	32 : 1
1980	76.3	1.7	45 : 1
1990	82.8	1.3	64 : 1

Source: Brown and Kane (1995: 46).

standard of living, while being able to see the growing affluence of the few.   (South Commission 1990: 38).

There was consequently a dawning recognition in some quarters that growth reduces poverty only if accompanied by specific economic and social policies directed to that end (Ibid.: 36).

The 1980s have been described as the 'lost decade' for the majority of Southern states, with sub-Saharan Africa suffering the most. In the first half of the 1980s, over half of developing countries experienced a declining per capita GDP, whilst over the whole decade, developing countries as a group faced a 10 per cent decline in per capita GDP. As well as the stringent structural adjustment policies, they were faced with rising floating interest rates which increased their debt burden; commodity price fluctuations; declining terms of trade; uncertain markets for their goods as developed countries pursued protectionist policies whilst advocating free market policies for the rest of the world; and insufficient financial and technological transfers from the developed world. Not surprisingly therefore the international economic structure was perceived by developing states as being inherently unfair and disadvantageous to their interests.

In 1987, UNICEF published a report entitled *Adjustment with A Human Face* (Cornia *et al.* 1987). This study highlighted the social cost of structural adjustment policies (SAPs) and argued for a redesign of structural adjustment to take these costs into account. For the majority of debtor states and their populations the pursuit of SAPs in the context of an unsupportive external economic environment has resulted in increased debt, social hardship, political tension, and environmental degradation. As a group, debtor states entered the 1990s 61 per cent more indebted than in 1982, whilst sub-Saharan Africa's debt increased by 113 per cent over the same period (George 1992: xvi). Those paying the price are not the people who borrowed the money in the first place, nor the wealthy élites, but the poor.

In 1990 the United Nations Development Programme (UNDP) developed the **Human Development Index** (HDI) to measure the development achievements of individual countries. Giving equal weight to life expectancy, adult literacy, and average local purchasing power, HDI results in a very different assessment of countries'

achievements than does the traditional measurement of development based on per capita GDP (Thomas *et al.* 1994: 22). For example, China, Sri Lanka, Poland, and Cuba fare much better under HDI assessments, than they do under more orthodox assessments, whilst Saudi Arabia and Kuwait fare much worse. The promotion of the HDI reveals the contrasting approaches to development of the UN on the one hand, and the IMF and World Bank on the other.

Key Points

- In 1945 the USA had *carte blanche* to set up a liberal international economic order, the institutional pillars of which were the IMF, the World Bank, and the GATT.

- The cold war stimulated competition between the West and the East to win allies in the developing world. Most of the latter were born into the Western international economy and saw their development within the context of that system i.e. based on growth within a free market.

- Progress was achieved under the orthodox development criteria of GDP per capita, economic growth and industrialization. Yet despite apparent success in conventional terms, there has been an explosive widening of the gap between the richest and poorest 20 per cent of the world's population, and the developing countries as a group have entered the 1990s more indebted than the 1980s.

- Dependency theorists see this as predictable, arguing that export-oriented, free-market development promoted in the Third World has increased the wealth of the West and of Southern élites.

- Trickle-down has been discredited, and it has been recognized that economic growth only reduces poverty if accompanied by specific economic and social policies. In recognition of the failure of economic growth-based indices of development, the UNDP Human Development Index was designed in 1990 to measure development in terms of longevity, education, and average purchasing power.

Caroline Thomas

A Critical Alternative View of Development

Over the last two decades there have been numerous efforts to stimulate debate about development and to highlight its contested nature. Noteworthy was the publication in 1975 by the Dag Hammarskjold Foundation of *What Now? Another Development?*. This alternative conception of development (see Ekins 1992: 99) argued that the process of development should be:

1. need-oriented (material and non-material);
2. endogenous (coming from within a society);
3. self-reliant, (in terms of human, natural and cultural resources);
4. ecologically sound; and
5. based on structural transformations (of economy, society, power relations).

Since then various NGOs, such as the World Development Movement, have campaigned for a form of development which takes aspects of this alternative approach on board. Grassroots movements have often grown up around specific issues, such as dams (e.g. Narmada in India) or access to common resources (the rubber tappers of the Brazilian Amazon; the Chipko movement to secure trees in the Himalayas). Such campaigns received a

great impetus in the 1980s with the growth of the green movement worldwide. The two-year preparatory process before the UN Conference on Environment and Development (UNCED) in Rio, June 1992, gave indigenous groups, women, children, and other previously voiceless groups a chance to express their views. This momentum was continued with the holding of an alternative NGO forum in Copenhagen, parallel to the UN Social Summit there in 1995.

The alternative vision of development is based on the **transformation of power structures** (such as race, class, patriarchy) which are seen as upholding current inequalities. We have already examined above the international economic structure. Here we look briefly at a more locally determined structure, that of land tenure.

Land Ownership

Within states the structure of land ownership is an important determinant of the economic condition of large sectors of the population. Land ownership is related to the ability of peasants to provide for themselves via subsistence. Transformation of the structure of land ownership is thus vital if access to resources is to be significantly altered. Many developing countries, as Table 23.3 demonstrates, are characterized by highly unequal patterns of land

Table 23.3. **Landless and near-landless agricultural households, selected countries and Africa, mid-1970s to mid-1980s**

Country or Region	Percentage of rural households that are near-landless	Percentage of rural households that are landless	Combined percentage
Dominican Republic*	48	44	92
Guatemala	47	38	85
Ecuador	52	23	75
Peru	46	29	75
Brazil	10	60	70
Philippines	34	35	69
Colombia	24	42	66
El Salvador*	—	65	65
Honduras	46	18	64
Bangladesh*	33	29	62
Costa Rica	11	44	55
India	13	40	53
Mexico	33	18	51
Malaysia	35	12	47
Africa	30	10	40

* Data from late 1970s to mid-1980s.
Source: Brown *et al.* (1990: 142).

ownership that prevent many rural-dwellers from providing for their own needs.

Unfortunately, when it comes to changing the pattern of land ownership, 'Third World leaders often proclaim a commitment to land reform but as often fail to implement it' (Kohli 1985: 95). The failure of Third World governments of various political hues to carry out promises of land reform are due partly to lack of inclination, and partly due to lack of capacity. Kohli (ibid.) has identified two particular hurdles that confront any attempt to carry out land reform: firstly, the requirement of isolating the landed classes from the political process, and secondly the organizational capacity to link centralized decisions with decentralized implementation procedures. Land reform has been implemented vigorously in China and Taiwan, and less successfully in India. In Central and Latin America, very little progress has been made.

Democracy, Empowerment, and Development

Democracy is at the heart of the alternative conception of development. The worldwide democratic transition over the last decade has been characterized more by the establishment of the formal institutions of Western democracy, such as regular multiparty elections, than by substantive changes in the power structure of societies and the associated entitlements of their members to resources (Gills *et al.* 1993). Thus the government may have changed from military to civilian, but its membership is often drawn from the same élite and shares similar values. The quality of life for the majority will have changed very little.

Grassroots movements are playing an important role in challenging entrenched structures of power in formal democratic societies. In the face of increasing globalization, with the further erosion of local community control over daily life and the further extension of the power of the market and transnational corporations, people are standing up for their rights as they define them. They are making a case for local control and local empowerment as the heart of development. They are protecting what they identify as the immediate source of their survival—water, forest, and land. They are rejecting the dominant agenda of private and public (government-controlled) spheres and setting an alternative one. Examples include the Chipkos in India, the Rubber Tappers in the Amazon, the Chiapas uprising in Mexico and Indian peasant protests

against foreign-owned seed factories. Such protests symbolize the struggle for substantive democracy which communities across the world are working for. In this context development is about facilitating a community's participation and lead role in deciding what sort of development is appropriate for it; it is not about assuming the desirability of the Western model and its associated values. This alternative conception of development therefore values diversity above universality, and is based on a different conception of rights.

The *Alternative Declaration* produced by the NGO Forum at the Copenhagen Summit enshrined principles of community participation and empowerment. It laid stress on equity, participation, self-reliance, and sustainability. The role of women and youth was singled out. After all, by the year 2000, half of the population of the world will be under 15 years old. The *Alternative Declaration* represents an alternative vision of past, present, and future which rejects the importance of the private sphere. It rejects the economic liberalism accepted by governments of North and South, seeing it as a path to aggravation rather than alleviation of the global social crisis. Moreover it identified trade liberalization and privatization as the cause of the growing concentration of wealth globally. It called for immediate cancellation of all debt, improved terms of trade, transparency and accountability of the IMF and World Bank, and the regulation of multinationals. An alternative view of democracy was central to its conception of development.

Key Points

- The last two decades have seen increasing debate about what constitutes development, with NGOs and grassroots activists playing a significant role.

- An alternative view of development has emerged, based on the transformation of existing power structures which uphold the status quo. Such structures vary in scope from the global to the local; for example, at a global level the international economy severely disadvantages the poorest 20 per cent of the global population, whilst at a local level land tenure patterns affect the ability of people to provide for themselves.

- Grassroots organizations challenge entrenched power structures as people defend their rights, as they define them, seeking local control and empowerment. Development in this alternative view can be seen as facilitating a community's progress on its own terms. The *Alternative Declaration* of NGOs at the Copenhagen Summit stressed community participation, empowerment, equity, self-reliance, and sustainability.

Now that we have looked at the critical alternative view of development, we will look at the way in which the orthodox view has attempted to respond to the criticisms of the alternative view.

The Orthodoxy Incorporates Criticisms

In the mainstream debate the focus has shifted from growth to **sustainable development**. The concept was championed in the late 1980s by the influential **Brundtland Commission** (officially titled the World Commission on Environment and Development—see WCED, 1987). Central to the concept of sustainable development is the idea that the pursuit of development by the present generation should not be at the expense of future generations. In other words, it stressed **inter-generational equity** as well as **intra-generational equity**. The importance of maintaining the environmental resource base was highlighted, and with this comes the idea that there are natural limits to growth. The **Brundtland Report** made clear, however, that further growth was essential; but it needed to be made environment-friendly. The Report did not address the belief, widespread amongst a sector of the NGO community, that the emphasis on growth had caused the environmental crisis in the first place. The concerns of the Report were taken on board to some degree by the World Bank. When faced with an NGO spotlight on the adverse environmental implications of its projects, it moved to introduce more rigorous environmental assessments of its funding activities.

With the **United Nations Conference on the Environment and Development** (UNCED—sometimes referred to as the Rio Summit) in June 1992, the idea that the environment and development were inextricably interlinked was taken further. However, what came out of the official interstate process was legitimation of market-based development policies to further sustainable development. Official output from Rio, such as *Agenda 21*, however, recognized the huge importance of the sub-state level for addressing sustainability

issues, and supported the involvement of marginalized groups. But while the groups had a role in the preparatory process, they have not been given an official role in the follow-up to UNCED. At the alternative summit where the largest selection of non-governmental views ever expressed were aired, the viability of this strategy was challenged. For example, the possibility of structural adjustment policies being made environment-friendly was seriously questioned.

The process of incorporation continued with the **UN World Summit for Social Development** held at Copenhagen in March, 1995. Three main issues were addressed: poverty reduction, social disintegration, and employment. The wide divergence of views between Northern and Southern governments in the run up to the Summit on matters such as debt, structural adjustment, multinational regulation, and reform of the Bretton Woods institutions dissipated at the Summit proper.

Governments of developing countries accepted economic growth and the free-market strategy as the preferred route to development, but in many cases argued that this was insufficient to ensure social progress. Implicitly, countries like Malaysia were arguing for **embedded liberalism** such as that enjoyed by the developed countries since 1945. This would allow national needs to be taken into account.

Nevertheless, the intergovernmental *Summit Declaration and Programme of Action* contained only very watered down references to debt, structural adjustment, and IMF/World Bank—UN dialogue, and no reference to the social responsibility of transnational corporations. Also whereas the UNCED had resulted in the creation of an organ (the Commission on Sustainable Development) to monitor progress on implementation of what had been agreed, no such monitoring machinery was put in place at Copenhagen. In line with the UK and US governments' position, the overall outcome of the Summit was to lend greater legitimacy to the pursuit of economic growth, free-market policies, and individual initiative as the best road to development. The traditional approach to development held sway, and the contribution of that method to the increasing global inequality was not on the agenda.

Interestingly, there was no discussion of, or commitment to, new transfers of finance from developed to developing countries. The North/South agenda had changed in the three years since the Rio Summit.

An Appraisal of the Responses of the Orthodox Approach to its Critics

The orthodox view of development remains largely unaltered in the mid-1990s. Voices of criticism are few. They are not heard in the corridors of power of the rich states or international institutions, and not as loud as one might expect in the governments of poorer countries. The terminology of alternative conceptions of development has however been incorporated to a limited degree into the mainstream: 'sustainable development' or 'growth with a greener face' are the buzz words.

Small but nevertheless important changes are taking place. For example, the World Bank has guidelines on the treatment of indigenous peoples, on resettlement and on the environmental impact of its projects. What is important however, is whether these guidelines inform practical policy outcomes. The Bank has admitted that such changes have been incorporated largely due to the efforts of NGOs which have monitored its work closely and undertaken vigorous international campaigns to change the way the Bank funds projects. These campaigns continue, with calls for open, transparent, and accountable decision-making, and local involvement in project planning.

There is a tremendously long way to go in terms of gaining credence for the core values of the alternative model of development in the corridors of power nationally, and internationally. Nevertheless, the alternative view, marginal though it is, has had some noteworthy successes in modifying orthodox development. These may not be insignificant for those whose destinies have up till now been largely determined by the universal application of a localized, Western set of values.

Key Points

- The development orthodoxy remains essentially unchanged. However, the mainstream debate has shifted from growth to sustainable development—the view that current development should not be at the expense of future generations or the natural environment.

- The orthodox view asserts that sustainable development is to be achieved by further growth through a universal free-market. It is believed that this will free up resources to care for the environment and to ensure social progress.

- This approach has been approved by UNCED and the Copenhagen Summit, both of which legitimated further global integration via the free market. However, at Copenhagen many developing countries advocated embedded liberalism rather than pure free market economics, as necessary to help meet the basic needs of their people and ensure political stability.

- Critical alternative views of development have been effectively neutralized by the formal incorporation of their language and concerns into the orthodox view. Nevertheless, the process of incorporation has resulted in some small positive changes in the implementation of the orthodox view, for example by the World Bank.

- Nevertheless, despite semantic changes, fundamental questions remain about the sustainability of the dominant model of development.

We have now concluded our examination of the topic of development from the orthodox and alternative approaches and will turn our attention to the topic of hunger.

Hunger

In addressing the topic of global hunger, it is necessary to face the paradox that whilst 'the production of food to meet the needs of a burgeoning population has been one of the outstanding global achievements of the post-war period', there are nevertheless around 800 million people in 46 countries who are malnourished, and 40,000 die every day from hunger-related causes (ICPF 1994: 104; 106). While famines may be exceptional phenomena, hunger is ongoing. Why is this so?

Broadly speaking there are two schools of thought with regard to hunger: the orthodox, **nature-focused approach** which identifies the problem largely as one of over-population, and the entitlement, **society-focused approach**, which sees the problem more in terms of distribution. Let us consider each of these two approaches in turn.

461

Caroline Thomas

The Orthodox, Nature-Focused Explanation of Hunger

The orthodox explanation of hunger, first mapped out in its essentials by Thomas Robert Malthus in his *Essay on the Principle of Population* in 1798, focuses on the relationship between human population growth and the food supply. It asserts that population growth naturally outstrips the growth in food production, so that a decrease in the per capita availability of food is inevitable, until eventually a point is reached at which starvation, or some other disaster, drastically reduces the human population to a level which can be sustained by the available food supply. This approach therefore places great stress on human over-population as being the cause of the problem, and seeks for ways to reduce the fertility of the human race, or rather, that part of the human race which seems to breed faster than the rest—the poor of the 'Third World'. Recent supporters of this approach, such as Paul Ehrlich and Denis and Donella Meadows, argue that there are natural limits to population growth— principally that of the carrying capacity of the land—and that when these limits are exceeded disaster is inevitable.

The available data on the growth of the global human population indicates that it has quintupled since the early 1800s, and is expected to grow from 5.4 billion in 1991 to 10 billion in 2050. Over 50 per cent of this increase is expected to occur in seven countries: Bangladesh, Brazil, China, India, Indonesia, Nigeria, and Pakistan. Lately, population projections have had to be revised upwards because of a slowing down in the decline of fertility rates in some countries such as China, India, the Philippines, and Colombia. Unless this slow-down is arrested, population could increase to 23 billion by the end of the twenty-first century, as opposed to the current estimate of 11.3 billion. Tables 23.4 and 23.5 provide further data on population growth between the years 1950 and 1990, with projections to the year 2030. Table 23.4 focuses on the world population, whilst Table 23.5 focuses on the world's most populous countries. Table 23.4 shows that the world's population is likely to have tripled between 1950 and 2030, and that the rate of growth of the world's population is set to increase over the coming decades. Table 23.5 demonstrates that the world's most populous countries are located in the Third World and that only eleven of them account for over half of the world's population. Furthermore it shows that these eleven countries are also likely to account for an increasing proportion of the world's population growth in the future. It is figures such as these that have convinced many adherents of the orthodox approach to hunger that it is essential that Third World countries adhere to strict family-planning policies which one way or another limit their population growth rates.

The Entitlement, Society-Focused Explanation of Hunger

Critics of the orthodox approach to hunger and its associated implications argue that it is too simplistic in its analysis of the situation and ignores the vital factor of food distribution. They point out that it fails to account for the paradox we observed at the beginning of this discussion on hunger: that despite the enormous increase in food production per capita that has occurred over the post-war period (largely due to the development of high-yielding seeds and industrial agricultural techniques), little impact has been made on the huge numbers of people in the world who experience chronic hunger. For example, the UN Food and Agriculture Organization estimates that although

Table 23.4. **World population growth, 1950–1990, with projections to 2030**

Year	Population (in billions)	Population growth (in billions)	Population growth per year (in millions)
1950	2.5		
1990	5.3	2.8	70
2030	8.9	3.6	90

Source: Brown and Kane (1995: 58).

462

Table 23.5. **Population growth, 1950–1990, with projections to 2030, for the most populous countries**

Country	Population (in millions)			Population increase (in millions)	
	1950	1990	2030	1950–1990	1990–2030
Bangladesh	46	114	243	68	129
Brazil	53	153	252	100	99
China	563	1,134	1,624	571	490
Egypt	21	54	111	33	57
Ethiopia and Eritea	21	51	157	30	106
India	369	853	1,443	484	590
Indonesia	83	189	307	106	118
Iran	16	57	183	41	126
Mexico	28	85	150	57	65
Nigeria	32	87	278	55	191
Pakistan	39	115	312	76	197
Total	1,271	2,892	5,060	1,621	2,168
Total as Percentage of World Figure	50.8	54.6	56.8	57.9	60.2

Source: adapted from Brown and Kane (1995: 59).

there is enough grain alone to provide everyone in the world with 3,600 calories a day (i.e. 1,200 more than the UN's recommended minimum daily intake), there are still over 800 million hungry people.

Furthermore critics note that the Third World, where the majority of starving people are found, produces much of the world's food, whilst those who consume most of it are located in the Western world. This latter point is supported by evidence such as that shown in Table 7 below, which demonstrates that the Third World countries of China and India, despite their enormous agricultural outputs, consume far less grain and livestock products per capita than do the two Western countries of Italy and the United States. Such evidence leads opponents of the orthodox approach to argue that we need to look much more closely at the social, polit-ical, and economic factors that determine how food is distributed and why access to food is achieved by some and denied to others.

A convincing alternative to the orthodox explanation of hunger was set forward in Amartya Sen's pioneering book, *Poverty and Famines: An Essay on Entitlement and Deprivation*, which was first published in 1981. From the results of his empirical research work on the causes of famines, Sen concluded that hunger is due to people not **having** enough to eat, rather than there not **being** enough to eat. He discovered that famines have frequently occurred when there has been no significant reduction in the level of per capita food availability and, furthermore, that some famines have occurred during years of peak food availability. For example, the Bangladesh Famine of 1974 occurred in a year of peak food availability, yet because floods wiped out

Table 23.6. **Annual per capita grain use and consumption of livestock products in selected countries, 1990**

Country	Consumption (in kilograms)						
	Grain	Beef	Pork	Poultry	Lamb	Milk	Eggs
US	800	42	28	44	1	271	16
Italy	400	16	20	19	1	182	12
China	300	1	21	3	1	4	7
India	200	—	0.4	0.4	0.2	31	13

Source: Brown and Kane (1995: 64).

the normal employment opportunities of rural labourers, the latter were left with no money to purchase the food which was readily available, and many of them starved.

Therefore, what determines whether a person starves or eats is not so much the amount of food **available** to them, but whether or not they can establish an **entitlement** to that food. For example, if there is plenty of food available in the shops, but a family does not have the money to purchase that food, and does not have the means of growing their own food, then they are likely to starve. The key issue is not therefore **per capita food availability**, but the **distribution of food** as determined by the ability of people to establish entitlements to food. With the globalization of the market, and the associated curtailing of subsistence agriculture, the predominant method of establishing an entitlement to food has become that of the exercise of purchasing power, and consequently it is those without purchasing power who will go hungry amidst a world of plenty (Sen 1981; 1983).

Sen's focus on entitlement enables him to identify two groups who at the moment are particularly at risk of losing their access to food: landless rural labourers—such as in South Asia and Latin America—and pastoralists—such as in sub-Saharan Africa. The landless rural labourers are especially at risk because no arrangements are in place to protect their access to food. In the traditional peasant economy there is some security of land ownership, and therefore rural labourers have the possibility of growing their own food. However, this possibility is lost in the early stages of the transition to capitalist agriculture, when the labourers are obliged to sell their land and join the wage-based economy. Unlike in the developed countries of the West, no social security arrangements are in place to ensure that their access to food is maintained. In this context it is important to note that the IMF/World Bank austerity policies of the 1980s ensured that any little welfare arrangements that were previously enjoyed by vulnerable groups in developing countries were largely removed, and therefore these policies directly contributed to a higher risk of hunger in the Third World.

Building upon the work of Sen, the researcher Susan George in *The Hunger Machine* (Bennett and George 1987: 1–10) details how different groups of people experience unequal levels of access to food. She identifies six factors which are important in determining who goes hungry: the North/South divide between developed and developing countries; national policies on how wealth is shared; the rural–urban bias; social class; gender; and age. In addition, one could add to the list two other very important, and often neglected, factors determining hunger—that of race and disability. Consequently a person is more likely to experience hunger if they are disabled rather than able-bodied, black rather than white, a child rather than an adult, poor rather than wealthy, a rural-dweller rather than a town-dweller, a citizen of a non-welfare state rather than a welfare state, and an inhabitant a developing country rather than a developed country.

Globalization and Hunger

It is possible to explain the occurrence of hunger by reference to the process of **globalization**. Globalization means that events occurring in one part of the globe can affect, and be affected by, events occurring in other, distant parts of the globe. Often as individuals we remain unaware of our role in this process and its ramifications. When we drink a cup of tea or smoke a cigarette in the developed countries, we tend not to reflect on the changes experienced at the site of production of these cash crops in the developing world. However, it is possible to look at the effect of the establishment of a global, as opposed to a local, national or regional system of food production. This has been done by David Goodman and Michael Redclift in their book, *Refashioning Nature: Food, Ecology and Culture* (1991), and the closing part of this discussion on hunger is largely based on their findings.

Since 1945 a global food regime has been established. This has been based on the incorporation of local systems of food production into a global system of food production. In other words, local subsistence producers who traditionally have produced to meet the needs of their family and community may now be involved in cash-crop production for a distant market. Alternatively they may have left the land and become involved in the process of industrialization. The most important actor in the development and expansion of this global food regime has been the US, which, at the end of the Second World War, was producing large food surpluses. These surpluses became cheap food exports and initially were welcomed by the war-ravaged countries of Europe. They were also welcomed by many developing countries, for the model of development prevalent then depended on the creation of a pool of cheap wage labour to serve the industrialization process. Hence in order to encourage people off the land and away from subsistence production, the incentive to produce for oneself and one's family had to be removed. Cheap imported food provided this incentive, whilst the resulting low prices paid for domestic subsistence crops made them unattractive to grow; indeed, for those who continued to produce for the local market, such as in Sudan, the consequence has been the production of food at a loss (Bennett and George 1987: 78). Not surprisingly therefore the production of subsistence crops in the developing world for local consumption has drastically declined in the post-war period.

The post-war, US-dominated, global food regime has therefore had a number of unforeseen consequences. First, the domestic production of food staples in developing countries was disrupted. Secondly, consumer preferences in the importing countries changed in line with the cheap imports, and export markets for US-produced food were created. Effectively, a dependence on food aid was created (Goodman and Redclift 1991: 123). Third, there has been a stress on cash-crop production. The result has been the drive toward export-oriented, large-scale, intensively mechanized agriculture in the South. Technical progress resulted in the 'Green Revolution', with massively increased yields being produced from high-yield seeds and industrialized agricultural practices. This has in some respects been an important achievement, however the cost has been millions of peasants thrown off the land because their labour was no longer required, greater concentration of land in a smaller number of hands, and environmental damage from pesticides, fertilizers and inappropriate irrigation techniques.

By the late 1980s the South produced well over 40 per cent of the world's food, but most of this was cash-crops for export. Production and marketing of these crops is controlled largely by transnational corporations such as Unilever. These large companies control food production and marketing from the seed to the supermarket shelf, and for them food is just another tradable commodity like diamonds or tin. As a result agribusiness has become a powerful force in global politics. Moreover, as a result of the encouragement given to the globalization of food markets by the Uruguay Round of trade talks, the power of such companies is set to increase. The effects of their policies are also likely to provide the focus for the formation of protest movements in the Third World; for example, in India disputes over intellectual property rights in regard to high-yielding crop-seeds has resulted in violent protest by peasant farmers at foreign-owned seed factories.

Key Points

- In recent decades global food production has burgeoned, but paradoxically hunger and malnourishment remain widespread.

- The orthodox explanation for the continued existence of hunger is that population growth outstrips food production.

- An alternative explanation for the continuance of hunger focuses on lack of access or entitlement to available food. Access and entitlement are affected by factors such as the North/South global divide; particular national policies; rural/urban divides; class; gender; and race.

- Globalization can simultaneously contribute to increased food production and increased hunger: the South produces over 40 per cent of the world's food, but the majority of hungry people live in the South. Hunger in the South is not being reduced, because self-sufficiency is being replaced by cash-crop production for agribusinesses, which are now a powerful force in global politics.

We have now concluded our discussion of the three topics of poverty, development, and hunger, and in the last part of this chapter we will assess the likelihood of inequality and hunger being decreased in the context of an increasingly globalized world.

Caroline Thomas

Looking to the Future: Globalization, Inequality, Hunger, and Resistance

There is a tendency within the discipline of International Relations and within the field of practical diplomacy to define crises in military terms. Concentration on this approach alone, rooted in the state-centric perspective of realism, risks a failure to identify important sources of change in global politics. Such information may be vital to furthering our understanding of where the globalization of world politics is taking us as we approach the twenty-first century. We must look beyond the state to appreciate how the power of the market influences the daily lives of the global population. Similarly, to understand challenges to the globalization process we need to look to non-state actors such as NGOs and grassroots organizations. Such actors are resisting the inequalities, and the accompanying poverty, hunger, and disease, which they see globalization or the universalization of Western values as bringing in its wake. These rising levels of inequalities, which cut across state boundaries, lend support to the view that globalization is primarily the process by which capitalism, private power, the power of the market, are being extended across the globe.

The orthodox view argues that development as economic growth via the classical free market has been successful to date and that what is required now is an intensification of the dominant model worldwide. The critical alternative argues that the dominant model has clearly failed, and what is needed is a radical new approach to defining development and a new development strategy. However, it seems likely that the policies of economic liberalization preferred by the IMF, World Bank, Group of Seven, and indeed most Third World governments and élites, and legitimated at the Rio and Copenhagen Summits, are likely to continue the trend towards increasing the gap between the rich and the poor. For the foreseeable future, political power rests with those who support this approach. However, the continued application of this approach will lead to further resistance from those who see themselves as failing to benefit from the process. Increasingly voices from both the South and the North are questioning the ability of this approach to meet the needs of the majority of the world's citizens today and tomorrow.

QUESTIONS

1. What does poverty mean?

2. Explain the orthodox approach to development and outline the criteria by which it measures development.

3. Assess the critical alternative model of development.

4. How effectively has the orthodox model of development neutralized the critical, alternative view?

5. What is the significance of recent attempts at empowerment by grassroots movements?

6. What is the orthodox explanation of hunger?

7. Explain Sen's ideas about entitlement to food.

8. What are the pros and cons of the global food regime established since World War Two.

9. Account for the increasing gap between rich and poor after forty years of official development policies.

GUIDE TO FURTHER READING

General

Adams, N .B., *Worlds Apart: The North–South Divide and the International System* (London: Zed, 1993) presents an economic and political history of the North/South divide, and focuses on the role of the international economic system.

Cavanagh, J., Wysham, D., and Arruda, M. (eds.), *Beyond Bretton Woods: Alternatives to the Global Economic Order* (London: Pluto, 1994) looks back over 50 years of World Bank and IMF activities to reflect on the impact of these institutions on the peoples of the world. It offers some provocative ideas for change.

The Ecologist, 'Whose Common Future? Reclaiming the Commons' (London: Earthscan, 1993) interprets accelerating environmental/developmental problems within the framework of the enclosure of the commons and the domination and dispossession of local communities over several centuries.

Ekins, P., *A New World Order: Grassroots Movements for Global Change* (London: Routledge, 1992) examines alternative approaches to development that are being advocated by diverse grassroots movements around the world.

Hunger

Dreze, J., Hussain, A., Sen, A. (eds.), *The Political Economy of Hunger* (Oxford: Clarendon Press, 1995) is an excellent, up-to-date volume on the political economy of hunger.

Sen, A., *Poverty and Families* (Oxford: Clarendon Press, 1981) provides a ground-breaking analysis of the causes of hunger which incorporates detailed studies of a number of famines and convincingly challenges the orthodox view of the causes of hunger.

24 Human Rights

Chris Brown

READER'S GUIDE

Over the last fifty years the idea that human rights—political, social, and economic, and the rights of peoples—should be internationally protected has taken hold and seems a prime example of globalization. However, the record of compliance with human rights law is patchy, and states seem unwilling to give international action in support of human rights a high priority. Moreover there are serious conceptual problems involved in widening the notion of 'rights' to incorporate economic and collective rights. The Western origins of the doctrine of rights has also come to be seen as problematic in the post-colonial era, and with the apparently widespread unwillingness to accept the naturalness of human rights. It may be that in the next century only a limited notion of human rights will be defensible—or perhaps human rights will have to be defended in explicitly cultural terms.

Introduction

On the face of it, human rights is an ideal focus for a consideration of processes of globalization. Whereas it was once the case that rights were almost always associated with domestic legal and political systems, in the last half century a complex network of international law and practice has grown up around the idea that individuals possess rights not solely as citizens of particular countries, but also by virtue of being human, of sharing in a common humanity. The purpose of this chapter is to explain how this came about, but also, and in particular, to examine the many problems associated with the idea of universal human rights. This introduction will set the scene; the next section will examine some basic issues raised by rights language; the liberal position on human rights will then be examined, followed by discussion of the politics of international human rights protection as this has developed since 1945.

The origins of the idea of 'rights' can be found in the theory and practice of politics in medieval Europe, that is, on the one hand, as an implication of the doctrine of 'Natural Law', and, on the other, as symbolized by documents such as **Magna Carta**, the 'Great Charter' extracted by the Barons from King John in 1215. This notion came to be broadened into an account of the rights of citizens and embodied in the positive law of a few countries in the early modern era: here the US **'Bill of Rights'** of 1791 is the best example. Even before this latter date, in 1789, the French Revolution widened the scope with the Declaration of the Rights of Man and of the Citizen. Politics and thought in the revolutionary era of the 1790s also began tentatively to broaden the definition of Man by recognizing the rights of women, and, via campaigns against the slave trade, those of non-Europeans, positions built upon in the nineteenth century. These preliminary moves set the scene for the globalization processes of the twentieth century and especially of the post-1945 era. Here we have seen a number of global, regional, and specific statements.

All of this amounts to an impressive body of international law, and within these declarations, covenants, and conventions can be found further broadening and deepening of the idea of rights (see Box 24.2). Early statements concentrated on *First Generation* rights such as freedom of speech and assembly and 'the right to take part in the govern-

---

Box 24.1. The International Protection of Human Rights

The **Universal Declaration of Human Rights** adopted by the United Nations General Assembly in 1948

The **International Covenant on Civil and Political Rights** and the **International Covenant on Economic, Social and Cultural Rights** of 1966

The **European Convention for the Protection of Human Rights and Fundamental Freedoms** of 1950

The **American Convention on Human Rights** of 1969

The **African Charter on Human and Peoples' Rights** of 1981, usually referred to as the **Banjul Charter**

The **Convention on the Prevention and Punishment of the Crime of Genocide** of 1948

The **International Convention on the Elimination of All Forms of Racial Discrimination** of 1965

The **International Convention on the Elimination of Discrimination Against Women** of 1979

---

ment of his (*sic*) country, directly or through freely chosen representatives' (**UN Declaration, Article 21**). But the same declaration also recognized *Second Generation* rights to the 'economic, social

---

Box 24.2. Key Concepts: First, Second, and Third Generation Rights

It is common nowadays to distinguish these three notions of rights. **First Generation** Rights are the classic political rights associated in the past with liberal Western regimes, such as the rights to freedom of speech, of assembly, of religion. **Second Generation** Rights concern economic and social issues, and involve notions such as the right to an adequate standard of living or the right to education. **Third Generation** rights are the rights of peoples, such as the right to preserve one's culture, or the right of a community to protect its environment. The designation **First, Second** and **Third** refers to the order in which these rights have been pressed; as will become apparent in this chapter, there are potential contradictions between these different kinds of rights, and some, particularly liberal thinkers, would deny that **Second** or **Third** generation rights are really 'rights' at all.

and cultural rights indispensable for his dignity and the free development of his personality' (**Article 22**) such as the right to an adequate standard of living (**Article 25**) or to education (**Article 26**) and these economic and social rights feature very largely in later UN documents, especially, of course, the **International Covenant on Economic, Social, and Cultural Rights**. Both first and second generation rights are, in essence, possessed by individuals. *Third Generation* rights build on this collective dimension and concern the rights of 'peoples'; for example, under the **Banjul Charter** (see Box 24.1) peoples have the right to 'freely dispose of their wealth and natural resources' (**Article 21 (1)**), while the individual has a duty 'to serve his natural community by placing his physical and intellectual abilities at its service' and to 'preserve and strengthen positive African cultural values in his relations with other members of the society' (**Article 29 (2) and (7)**)

This body of international legislation provides a mixed and varied menu of items for discussion. There are *legal* issues concerning the ratification of these treaties, the interpretation of particular clauses and so on. These legal issues lead into *politico-legal* questions such as the vexed issue of 'compliance'. As with much of the rest of international law there are serious difficulties involved in making states live up to their legal obligations. This in turn raises *foreign policy* issues such as whether it is either practicable or prudent to make compliance with human rights law a touchstone of one's foreign relations. Clearly, there are straightforward *political* and *moral* issues here concerning the trade-off between particular values—is it worth risking a trading contract in order to make a point about a violation of human rights, or, putting the matter the other way round, should one overlook an obvious wrong in the interests of profit? Finally, there are *conceptual*—perhaps *philosophical*—issues that cannot be avoided even by an account of human rights that tries to keep both feet firmly planted on the ground. For example, are first, second, and third generation rights compatible with each other?

Each of these dimensions of human rights is worthy of discussion—although the early items on this menu have been discussed so often that it is difficult to think that anything new (at least anything new and sensible) is likely to be said about them—but nowadays the latter, philosophical, issues are increasingly coming to the fore. This is because of a general change of atmosphere in the late twentieth century, and especially after the end of the cold war. Until comparatively recently, few objected to the notion that human rights are universal; the *content* of human rights Declarations and Conventions was regarded by practical people as being rather less problematic than the issue of *compliance*. The key human rights problem was seen as one of forcing states to adhere to reasonably uncontroversial standards of behaviour.

This problem has not gone away, but nowadays is increasingly accompanied by another set of issues which put in question the universality of human rights. The rights of peoples—third generation rights—already puts this universality in question, because clearly one of the rights of a *'people'* must be to be different from other people and could such difference be achieved other than at the expense of universal standards? In any event, does not the universality of human rights hide the privileging of an essentially Western notion of politics? Moreover, the 'masculinist' assumptions of human rights language have already been noted, and are reinforced by articles in the Declaration and Covenants which assume traditional gender roles.

These issues challenge, indeed reverse, the assumption of a process of globalization. The sequence from local and national to global and universal is usually seen as the great, albeit incomplete, achievement of the human rights movement—but from these perspectives this achievement is hollow.

Key Points

- **Human Rights** are an established part of contemporary international law, and a good example of the processes of **globalization**.

- Modern thinking distinguishes between three **generations** of rights; **first generation** are broadly political, **second generation** economic and social, **third generation** the rights of peoples.

- One major set of contemporary problems concerns **compliance** and **enforcement**.

- More recently, the **universal** status of human rights has come to be challenged by critics who stress the **western**, **masculine**, **intolerant** nature of this universalism.

Back to Basics: Rights in General

As we can no longer take the idea of rights for granted, we must now ask some fundamental questions—What **kinds** of rights might there be? Do rights necessarily imply **duties**? On what **foundations** do rights rest?

Box 24.3. **Kinds of Rights**

A standard analysis here, deriving from the American jurist Welsey Hofeld (P. Jones 1994 for a modern version) distinguishes four kinds of rights. **Claim-rights** are the most basic rights—the only true rights, Hofeld believed; the classic example of a claim-right is a right generated by a contract and accompanied by correlative duties. **Liberty-rights** occur when I have the right to do something in the sense that I have no obligation *not* to do it—for example, to dress as I please. Here there is no correlative duty, except perhaps the duty to let me do as I choose. Sometimes a right involves the exercise of a **power**. For example, to have the *right* to vote means to be *empowered* to vote, to be enfranchised. Finally, a right sometimes means an **immunity**, the essence of which is that others are disbarred from making claims under certain circumstances, for example, to be legally insane, or under age, is to be *immune* from criminal prosecution.

The standard answer to the first two questions is to distinguish four kinds of legal 'rights': claim-rights, liberty rights, powers, and immunities. This analysis covers legal rights, but the same categories can be used to classify moral rights. For the time being we will continue to analyse in legal terms in order to approach the third question, which was 'On what foundations do rights rest'? The answer in legal terms must be that they rest within a legal system, but what kind of legal system? Here we must return and re-examine the starting point of this chapter—the identification of the origin of rights in the theory and practice of medieval politics.

The theory of rights in the Middle Ages rested on the idea of **Natural Law**. Natural law theorists differed on many issues, but the central proposition is clear. Universal moral standards exist and the rights that individuals have—whether claims, liberties, powers, or immunities—are based on these moral standards and accompanied by the general duty to adhere to these standards.

More will be said about this later, but for the

Box 24.4. **Key Concepts: Natural Law**

The origin of natural law thinking can be traced to the classical Greeks and early Christians, but in its modern form it is based on medieval Catholic theology. The central idea is that human beings have an essential nature which dictates that certain kinds of human goods are always and everywhere desired; because of this there are common moral standards that govern all human relations and these common standards can be discerned by the application of reason to human affairs. For a modern defender of the traditional Catholic doctrine, see Finnis, 1980.

---

moment it should be noted that the most important feature of this position is that it is not limited in application to any particular legal system, community, state, race, creed, or civilization. Some natural law theorists believed that Christians were under slightly different obligations from non-Christians by virtue of the acceptance of Revelation by the former, but, in principle, everyone was subject to natural law and everyone was capable of discerning its contents and standards. Here is to be found the origin of much of the rhetoric of universal human rights.

Natural law provided the basis for a theory of rights in the Middle Ages; however, in the rougher world of medieval political practice, rights had rather different connotations. Here a right was a concession one extracted from a nominal superior, probably by main force. The **Magna Carta** is a case in point. The Barons of England obliged King John to grant to them and their heirs in perpetuity a series of *liberties* which are, for the most part, very specific and related to particular grievances. Thus: for example,

Heirs may be given in marriage but not to someone of lower social standing. Before a marriage takes place it shall be made known to the heir's next-of-kin. (**Article 6**)

Neither We nor any royal official will take wood for our castle or for any other purpose without the consent of the owner. (**Article 31**)

From these clauses we can construct a list of practices by the King which were deplored by his subjects and which he is being forced to abjure. His subjects obtain thereby a series of rights, liberties, powers, and immunities, while the Great Charter as a whole is based on the principle that the subjects of the King owe him duty only if he meets their claims. This is clearly a political bargain or contract. There is no necessary incompatibility between the rights established by political bargaining between monarch and subjects and the rights entailed by natural law—for the most part, the articles of the **Magna Carta** would pass the test of reasonableness and human flourishing, although, as Sellar and Yeatman notice, the liberties granted by the King do seem to have limited general applicability (see Box 24.5).

Because of this general compatibility it is easy to forget that these two sources of the notion of rights

are actually based not simply on different, but on opposed principles. Whereas rights based on **natural law** are derived from reason and the notion of human flourishing, 'Charter Rights' simply describe in legal terms the result of a political bargain or contract. On the other hand, natural rights are universal in time and space, while contractual rights are by definition limited to the parties to the bargain, and thus restricted in time and space.

All the while the results of practice remain compatible with the demands of theory—human rights being much the same as the rights of particular peoples and communities—there is no reason for these oppositions to become apparent; however, as later sections will demonstrate, there is an untapped potential for conflict here.

Box. 24.5. A Jaundiced View of the Magna Carta

'the Barons compelled John to sign the Magna Charter which said:

1. That no one was to be put to death, save for some reason—(except the common people).
2. That everyone should be free—(except the common people).
3. That everything should be of the same weight and measure throughout the realm—(except the common people).
4. That the Courts should be stationary, instead of following a very tiresome medieval official known as the *King's Person* all over the country.
5. That 'no person should be fined to his utter ruin' (except the King's Person).
6. That the Barons should not be tried except by a jury of other Barons who would understand.

Magna Charter was therefore the chief cause of Democracy in England, and thus a *Good Thing* for everyone (except the Common People).'

Walter Carruthers Sellar (*Aegrotat: Oxon*) and Robert Julian Yeatman (*Failed M.A. etc. Oxon*) 1066 and All That: A Memorable History of England (London: Methuen, 1930)

Key Points

- We need to establish the *status* of rights—what a right **is**, what **kind** of rights people have, whether rights imply **duties**, and **why**?

- The distinction between rights as **claims**, **liberties**, **powers**, and **immunities** helps to clarify these questions.

- The origin of thinking about rights can be traced to two features of medieval political and intellectual life, the doctrine of **natural law** and the political practice of extracting **charters of liberties**.

- Natural law generates **universal** rights and duties, while a Charter confers **local** and **particular** liberties. The **actual** rights and liberties conveyed by Charters may be **compatible** with natural law, but this compatibility cannot **necessarily** be relied upon.

The Liberal Position on Human Rights

The complex language of medieval thinking on rights carried over into the modern period. Political philosophers such as **Hugo Grotius**, **Thomas Hobbes**, and **John Locke** continued to use notions of natural law, albeit in radically different ways from their predecessors. Political activists such as the Parliamentarians in the English Civil War drew

on the rights and privileges they believed to have been granted to their forebears to sustain their notion of themselves as '*free-born Englishmen*'. Gradually, a synthesis emerged which can be termed the **Liberal Position on Rights**. This position is made up of two basic components;

1. Human beings possess rights to life, liberty, the secure possession of property, the exercise of freedom of speech and so on which are inalienable—cannot be traded away—and unconditional—the only acceptable reason for constraining any one individual being to protect the rights of another.

2. The primary function of government is to protect these rights, political institutions are to be judged on their performance of this function, and political obligation rests on their success in this—in short, political life is based on a kind of implicit or explicit contract between people and government.

From a philosophical and conceptual point of view this position is easy to denigrate as a mish-mash of half-digested medieval ideas. As **Hegel** and many subsequent **communitarian** thinkers have pointed out, it assumes that individual rights, indeed individuals, predate society—and yet it is difficult to see how one could exist as an individual without being part of a society. For **Bentham** the function of government was to promote the general good (which he called utility) and the idea that individuals might have the right to undermine this seemed to him madness, especially since no one could tell him where these rights came from—the whole idea was 'nonsense upon stilts'. **Marx**, on the other hand, and many subsequent radicals, pointed to the way in which the liberal position stresses property rights to the advantage of the rich and powerful.

All these points are very well and good, and some will re-emerge later in this chapter, but what they underestimate is the powerful rhetorical appeal of the liberal position. Perhaps fortunately, most people are not political philosophers, and are less likely to be worried about the conceptual inadequacies associated with the liberal position on human rights than they are to be attracted by the obvious benefits of living in a political system based on or influenced by it. The plain fact is that the relatively few liberal democratic polities that have attempted to order their life in accordance with the liberal position have been the freest, safest, most congenial and civilized societies known to history—which, of course, is not to deny that these societies have also seen great and continuing injustices, injustices perhaps psychologically more difficult to bear because they exist in broadly just regimes.

The liberal position is a synthesis of the medieval universalism of natural law and the particularism of a contract between rulers and ruled, and one of its uncertain features is the extent to which the rights it generates are considered to be universal. The **US Bill of Rights**, for example, is cast in quite general terms, but at crucial moments refers to the people in ways which make it clear that the people in question are the American people; the French Revolutionary **Declaration of the Rights of Man and of the Citizen** clearly by its very title is intended to be of universal scope, but even here the universalism of **Article 1** *Men are born and remain free and equal in respect of rights* is soon followed by **Article 3** *The nation is essentially the source of all sovereignty* . . . and when Revolutionary and Napoleonic France moved to bring the Rights of Man to the rest of Europe the end result looked to most contemporaries remarkably similar to a French empire. The liberal position while universal in principle, is particularistic in application and state boundaries are more or less taken for granted—to use some modern terminology, the liberal position is cosmopolitan in moral but not in institutional terms.

Where both the international dimension of the liberal position on rights and its uncertain universalism emerges in the nineteenth and twentieth centuries is in the context of humanitarianism and international standard-setting. The **Congress of Vienna** of 1815 saw the Great powers accept an obligation to end the slave trade, which was finally abolished by the **Brussels Convention** of 1890, while slavery itself was formally outlawed by the **Slavery Convention** of 1926. The **Hague Conventions** of 1907 and the **Geneva Conventions** of 1926 were designed to introduce humanitarian considerations into the conduct of war. The **International Labour Office** formed in 1901, and its successor the **International Labour Organisation** attempted to set standards in the workplace via measures such as the **Convention Concerning Forced or Compulsory Labour** of 1930.

However, although these and other measures taken together do provide a quite elaborate structure for 'global governance', they exist within a context in which notions of sovereignty and non-intervention are taken for granted and are only to be overridden with great reluctance—thus, abolishing the slave trade, which involves international transactions, was much easier than abolishing slavery, which concerns what states do to their own people—indeed, pockets of slavery survive to this day in parts of West Africa and the Middle East. Although the norms of international society condemned gross violations of human dignity, they did not support intervention under any less extreme circumstances.

All the while sovereignty remains the norm of the system, humanitarian impulses can only take the form of exhortation and standard-setting, and, for much of the nineteenth century, liberal supporters of human rights tended also to be supporters of this norm. In England, Manchester School radical liberals such as John Bright and Richard Cobden were bitterly critical of traditional diplomacy, but supported the norm of non-intervention on the grounds that opponents such as Britain's long-standing Foreign Secretary and Prime Minister Lord Palmerston used moral arguments in support of interventions which were really engaged in for reasons of power-politics and general mischief-making—a familiar enough criticism most likely in the late twentieth century to be directed at the American heirs of Britain's position in the world.

Cobden was a consistent anti-interventionist and anti-imperialist—other liberals were more selective; Gladstone's 1870s campaign to throw the Ottoman empire out of Europe bag and baggage was based on the commoner view that different standards applied as between civilized and uncivilized peoples. In Gladstone's view the Ottoman empire could not claim the rights of a sovereign state—although, since 1856, a full member of international society—because its institutions did not come up to the requisite standards. Indeed this latter position was briefly established in international law in the notion of **Standards of Civilization** whereby non-European peoples such as the Chinese and Japanese could only achieve full sovereignty by adapting their ways to standards of good practice set in Europe. In the late twentieth century, this notion—and certainly talk of *civilization*—disturbs and unsettles, yet, as we shall see, current conventional wisdom on human rights is based on quite similar ideas.

The willingness of liberals to extend their thinking on human rights in a more interventionist direction has been characteristic of the second half of the twentieth century. The horrors of the **1914–18 War** stimulated attempts to create a peace-system based on a form of international government, and although the **League of Nations** of 1919—which was the inspiration of British and

Box 24.6. **Key Concepts: Sovereignty and the Standards of Civilization**

When nineteenth-century Europeans travelled to China, Japan, and other non-European countries in pursuit of trade, they were reluctant to put themselves under the jurisdiction of local legal systems, which often violated what Europeans regarded as basic principles of justice, for example, by allowing the aristocracy and military élite to dispense summary justice. However, a basic principle of international society is the sovereignty of states, which required respect towards and non-interference with the institutions of the states which were its members. Where they had the power to do so, Europeans solved this problem by requiring that the countries concerned respected European legal conventions (the 'standards of civilization') before they were allowed full membership of international society. In the meantime, special courts would be established by and for Europeans and those who dealt with them. These restrictions were bitterly resented as implying inferior status, and removing the regime of 'Capitulations'—as it was called—was a key nationalist demand everywhere in which they were set in place.

American liberal internationalists—had no explicit human rights provision, the underlying assumption was that its members would be states governed by the rule of law and respecting individual rights. The **Charter of the United Nations** of 1945 in the wake of the **Second World War** does have some explicit reference to human rights—a tribute to the impact on the general climate of thought of the horrors of that war, and, in particular of the murder of millions of Jews, Gypsies, and Slavs in the extermination camps of National Socialist Germany. In this context the need to assert a universal position was deeply felt, and the scene was set for the burst of international human rights legislation of the post-war era.

Key Points

- From out of medieval theory and practice a synthesis emerged, the **Liberal Position on Human Rights**, which combines universal and particularist thinking—**universal rights** established by a **contract** between rulers and ruled.

- This position is **conceptually** suspect, but **politically** and **rhetorically** powerful.

- Nineteenth-century liberalism supported **international humanitarian reform** but within the limits of the **norms of sovereignty and non-intervention**.

- For some liberals these norms did not apply when the **Standards of Civilization** were in question. Twentieth-century thinking on human rights has been less restrictive, largely because of the horrors of the **World Wars** and the **Holocaust**.

1948 and the Agenda of the Politics of Human Rights

The post-1945 humanitarian impulse identified above led to the burst of law-making and standard-setting described in the introduction to this chapter. Although the 1966 **Covenants** have, since entering into force in 1976, the status of international law, and although the **European Convention** of 1950 has the most effective enforcement machinery via the **European Commission on Human Rights** and the **European Court of Human Rights**, none the less, for all its declamatory status and lack of teeth, the **Universal Declaration of Human Rights** by the UN General assembly in 1948 is, symbolically, central. This was the first time in history that the international community had attempted to define a comprehensive code for the internal government of its members. During the late 1940s the United Nations was dominated by the West, and the contents of the **Declaration** represented this fact, with its emphasis on political freedom. The voting was forty-eight for and none against. Eight states abstained:

South Africa abstained, to no one's surprise. The white-dominated regime in South Africa denied political rights to the majority of its people and clearly could not accept that *all are born free and equal in dignity and rights* (Article 1) or that everyone was *entitled to the rights and freedoms set forth in this Declaration, without distinction of any kind such as race, colour . . .* (Article 2). The South African government objected to the Declaration on the grounds that it violated the protection of the *domestic jurisdiction* of states guaranteed by Article 2 (7) of the **United Nations Charter**. This is about as clear and uncomplicated a case of a first generation rights issue as one could imagine (see Box 24.2).

The **Soviet Union** and five Soviet Bloc countries abstained. Although Stalin's Russia was clearly a tyranny, the Soviet government did not officially

object to the political freedoms set forth in the **Declaration**. After all, did not the **Soviet Constitution** of 1936 guarantee (on paper) exactly such freedoms? Instead the Soviet objection was to the absence of sufficient attention to social and economic rights by comparison to the detailed elaboration of 'bourgeois' freedoms and property rights. The Soviets saw the **Declaration** as a cold war document, designed to stigmatize socialist regimes—a not wholly inaccurate description of the motives of its promulgators. Here we see the first expression of second generation rights issues, which would later be taken up by more worthy proponents.

Saudi Arabia abstained. Saudi Arabia was one of the few non-Western members of the United Nations in 1948 and just about the only UN member whose system of government was **not**, in principle, based on some Western model. Saudi Arabia objected to the **Declaration** on religious grounds, specifically objecting to Article 18 which specifies the freedom to change and practice the religion of one's choice. These provisions did not simply contravene Saudi laws which, for example, forbade (and still forbids) the practice of the Christian religion in Saudi Arabia, they contravened the requirements of Islam which does not recognize a right of apostasy. Here, to complete the picture, we have an assertion of third generation rights; the Saudi position denied the very *universalism* of the **Declaration**—different rules should apply to Saudi Arabia because Saudi Arabia **is** different from other countries—specifically, the Saudi Ruler is the Custodian of the Holy Places of the One True Religion.

Thus, the opening moment of the **Universal Human Rights Regime** sees the emergence of the themes which will make up the politics of human rights over the subsequent fifty years.

Key Points

- The politics of the **Universal Declaration** of 1948 allow us to identify the three major human rights issues of the post 1945 era.
- First, there is the contest between the old norm of **sovereignty** and the new norm of **universal domestic standards**.

- Second, there is the contest between **political and liberal** and **social and economic** formulations of human rights.
- Finally, there is the assertion of the **rights of peoples** to be **different**.

First and Second Generation Rights and Duties

It is generally agreed that 'No one shall be subjected to torture or to cruel, inhuman or degrading treatment or punishment' (**UN Declaration Article 5, Covenant on Civil and Political Rights Article 7, European Convention Article 3, American Convention Article 5 (2)**, etc.). This is an *immunity* that is now so well established as to be part of customary international law. How might I (or anyone else) claim this immunity in circumstances where I am facing ill-treatment?

If I am fortunate enough to live in a country governed by the rule of law, its **domestic courts** may well uphold my immunity. The international side of things will come into play on the margins. Thus, if I am a Western European I may be able to continue a legal dispute over a particular practice beyond my national courts to the **European Commission** and **European Court**. US citizens do not have this recourse, but, for example, if I were unfortunate enough to be facing the death penalty in Georgia it would be open to my lawyers to try to argue on my behalf that the international consensus was that the electric chair, and delays on death row, constituted a form of torture—although the **US Supreme Court** has, in the past, refused such pleas. In any event, the international, universal, side of human rights, at best, merely reinforces rights which are established elsewhere, in the domestic political order.

The more interesting case emerges if I do not live in such a law-governed society, if, that is, 'my' government and courts are the problem and not a possible solution. What assistance have I the right to expect from the international community in such circumstances? What consequences will flow from my government's failure to live up to its obligations? Here, in circumstances where universal human rights are my first line of defence rather

than a back-up system problems can clearly be identified. Even in cases where violations are quite blatant it may be difficult to see what other states are able actually to **do** and, in any event, states rarely if ever act **simply** in terms of human rights considerations—instead the whole range of relations between particular states will come into play.

Thus, during the cold war, the West regularly issued **verbal condemnations** of human rights violations by the Soviet Union and its associates, but rarely **acted** on these condemnations—the power of the Soviet Union made direct intervention imprudent, while even relatively minor sanctions would only be adopted if the general state of East–West relations suggested this would be appropriate. Conversely, violations by countries associated with the West were routinely overlooked or, in some cases, even justified—as with Ambassador Kirkpatrick's dubious distinction between totalitarian and authoritarian regimes (Kirkpatrick 1979). Even outside of the context of the cold war, commercial considerations may be determinant— hence, for example, the unwillingness of the international community to penalize Indonesia for its behaviour in East Timor.

All told it seems unlikely that individuals ill-treated by non-constitutional regimes will find any real support from the international community unless their persecutors are weak, of no strategic significance, and commercially unimportant—and even then it is unlikely that effective action will be taken unless one further factor is present, namely the force of public opinion. This is the one positive factor that may goad states into action—the post-war growth of humanitarian non-governmental organizations has produced a context in which sometimes the force of public opinion can make itself felt, not necessarily in the oppressing regime,

Box 24.7. The Ending of Apartheid in South Africa

White-dominated South Africa was commercially important to many Western businesses, and of some strategic importance in the cold war; initial attempts to boycott South African goods and stem the flow of investment to the country were unsuccessful. However, the impact of public opinion—reinforced in the United States by the power of the Black Congressional lobby, and African-American pressure groups—gradually made it commercially unwise to be associated with South Africa, while pressure in the United Nations and elsewhere produced a reasonably effective arms embargo. This international pressure certainly contributed to the decision of the South African regime to end apartheid and enter into negotiation with the African National Congress. However, this comparatively rare success story for the international human rights community may be a product of some of the peculiarities of the South African system. Although blatantly unjust, the old South Africa claimed to be preserving Western 'civilization', and did indeed have a freer judiciary and press than might have been expected. This made it more vulnerable to Western pressure than is the case with those repressive regimes who do not make this claim, or possess those institutions.

but in the policy-formation processes of the potential providers of succour.

The situation with respect to *second generation* rights is more complicated, although equally depressing. Consider, for example, 'the right of everyone to an adequate standard of living for himself and his family, including adequate food, clothing and housing, and to the continuous improvement of living conditions' (**Covenant on Economic, Social and Cultural Rights, Article 11.1**), or the 'right of everyone to be free from hunger' (**Article 11.2**).

The **Covenant** makes the realization of these rights an obligation on its signatories, but this is a different kind of obligation to the obligation to refrain from, for example, 'cruel or degrading' punishments. In the latter case, as with other basically political rights, the remedy is clearly in the hands of national governments. The way to end torture is for states to stop torturing. The right not to be tortured is associated with a duty not to torture. The right to be free from hunger, on the other hand, is not simply a matter of a duty on the part of one's own and other states not to pursue policies that lead to star-

vation—it also involves a positive duty to 'ensure an equitable distribution of world food supplies in relation to need' (**Covenant on Economic, Social and Cultural Rights, Article 11.2 (b)**).

There are problems here: **first**, it is by no means clear that, even assuming goodwill, these social and economic goals could always be met, and to think in terms of having a right to something that could not be achieved is to misuse language. In such circumstances a right simply means 'a generally desirable state of affairs'—and this weakening of the concept may have the effect of undermining more precise claims to rights which can be achieved, such as the right not to be tortured. **Second**, some states may seek to use economic and social rights more directly to undermine political rights. Thus, dictatorial regimes in poor countries quite frequently justify the curtailment of political rights in the alleged name of promoting economic growth, or economic equality. In fact, there is no reason to accept the general validity of this argument—Sen's work, for example, makes it clear that political 'entitlements' are crucial in preventing famines (Sen 1981)—but it will still be made, and not always in bad faith. **Finally**, if it is accepted that all states have a positive duty to promote economic well-being and freedom from hunger everywhere, then the consequences go beyond the requirement of the rich to share with the poor, revolutionary though such a requirement would be. They also make virtually all national social and economic policies a matter for international regulation. Clearly rich states would have a duty to make economic and social policy with a view to its consequences on the poor, but so would poor states. The poor's right to assistance creates a duty on the rich to assist, but this in turn creates a right of the rich to insist that the poor have a duty not to worsen their plight—for example, by failing to restrict population growth or by inappropriate economic policies. In turn, the problem with this is that it contradicts another widely supported economic and social right that: 'All peoples have the right of self-determination. By virtue of that right they freely determine their political status and freely pursue their economic, social and cultural development' (**Covenant on Economic, Social and Cultural Rights, Article 1.1**).

All notions of human rights necessarily involve restrictions in the exercise of state sovereignty, but whereas political conceptions of human rights may still be just about compatible with the underlying norms of the existing international order, economic and social rights *if taken seriously as* rights are not. Perhaps the answer is to change these norms, but this leads into a different set of problems.

Key Points

- The politics of rights varies according to whether **constitutional** or **non-constitutional** regimes are involved.

- In any event, the international community rarely acts on human rights cases unless **public opinion** is engaged.

- **Economic and social rights** are conceptually different from **political rights**, and present a more basic challenge to existing norms of **sovereignty** and **non-intervention**.

The End of Universalism?

The very idea of human rights implies limits to the range of variation in domestic regimes that is acceptable internationally. The **standards of civilization** of the last century implied such limits also, but post-1945 human rights law, if taken seriously and at face value, would create a situation where all states would be obliged to conform to a quite rigid template which dictated most aspects of their political, social, and economic structures and policies.

Conventional defenders of human rights argue that this would be a 'Good Thing'—the universal spread of best practice in human rights matters is in the interest of all people. Others disagree. First, does post-1945 law actually constitute best practice? The feminist critique of universal human rights is particularly apposite here. The universal documents all, in varying degrees, privilege a **patriarchal** view of the family as the basic unit of society, and, implicitly or explicitly, of the subordination of women within the family. Even such documents as the UN's **Declaration on Elimination of Discrimination against Women** of 1967, and the various **International Labour Organization** Conventions concerning women at work do no more than extend to women the standard liberal package of rights, and modern feminists wish to go beyond this (Peterson 1990).

More fundamentally, is the idea of best practice sound? We have already met one objection to the idea in the Saudi abstention of 1948. The argument is simple: universalism is destructive not just of undesirable differences between societies but of desirable and desired differences. The human rights movement stresses the common humanity of the peoples of the world, but for many, the things that distinguish us from one another are as important as the things that unify us.

The movement towards establishing the **Rights of Peoples** partially reflects this perspective. For example, the **Banjul Charter**'s reference to the *duty* to strengthen '*African cultural values*' conveys clearly the idea that Africans have rights and duties different from non-Africans. The **Declaration of Principles of Indigenous Rights** adopted in Panama in 1984 by a non-governmental group, the **World Council of Indigenous Peoples** lays out positions which are designed to preserve the traditions, customs, institutions, and practices of indigenous peoples. More generally, the argument is connected to the communitarian critique of liberal individualism, and to the notion of multiculturalism.

Returning to the history of rights, it is here that the distinction between rights grounded in natural law and rights grounded in a contract becomes crucial. If rights are based on a contract or charter then whether or not rights exist is an empirical matter—clearly in many societies no rights-creating contract exists. It is only if rights are grounded in the universalism of natural law that they are truly human in scope. But is natural law truly, as its adherents insist, free of cultural bias, a set of ideas that all rational beings must accept? It seems not, at least in so far as many apparently rational Muslims, Hindus, Buddhists, Atheists, Utilitarians, and so on clearly do not accept its doctrines! There is a serious point here which potentially undermines any doctrine which purports to derive rights from human

Chris Brown

Box 24.8. Key Concepts: Communitarianism and Multiculturalism

Communitarianism and Multiculturalism are political and intellectual movements which have implications in both domestic and international politics. **Communitarians** argue that the liberal view of the individual as a bearer of rights disregards or underestimates the formative role of the community in constituting individuality. The problem with the liberal position on human rights is that it assumes that rights-bearing individuals exist prior to societies whereas in reality it is societies that confer rights on individuals—and different kinds of societies will produce different kinds of individuals, sometimes conferring rights, sometimes finding other ways of giving meaning to people's lives. In any event, the rights of individuals do not necessarily override the rights of the community. The cardinal tenet of **multiculturalism** follows on from this; there are many different ways in which human beings may lead dignified and fulfilling lives—the idea that dignity *only* comes with the possession of rights is peculiarly Western, with no claim to universal status. Political orders, domestic and international, should be established in such a way that no one particular way of life is privileged.

say, Saudi Arabia prefer not to live in a democratic system with Western liberal rights? There is an obvious dilemma here: if we insist that we will only accept democratically validated regimes we will be imposing an alien test of legitimacy on this society—yet what other form of validation is not open to the charge that it simply reflects the interests and values of the privileged?

In any event, does not the body of legal acts for the protection of universal human rights outlined in earlier sections of this chapter override local considerations? Should not the international community be given the last word? Again, defenders of difference will argue that international law is itself a Western, universalist, notion and that to pose the issue in these terms is to beg the question—in any event the Western record of adherence to universal norms is not such as to justify any claim to moral superiority.

The general point is that there is no neutral language with which to discuss human rights—whatever way the question is posed reflects a particular viewpoint, and this is no accident, it is built into the nature of the discourse.

nature; *either* the standards derived from natural law are cast in such general terms that virtually any continuing social system will exemplify them—in which case the cutting edge of the doctrine is lost; *or,* if cast more specifically, the standards described are not in fact universal—in which case the claim that they are based on general features of human nature or the human condition falls.

Of course, we are under no obligation to accept all critiques of universalism at face value: it may be that an apparently principled rejection of universalism is, in fact, no more than a rationalization of tyranny. How do we know that the inhabitants of,

Key Points

- The **human rights template** severely limits the degree of acceptable variation in social practices.
- This universalism can be challenged on **feminist** grounds as privileging **patriarchy**.
- More generally, the **liberal position on rights** privileges a particular account of **human dignity**.
- **Cultural** critics of universal rights can be seen as **self-serving**, but, by definition, no neutral criteria for assessing this criticism can exist.

Conclusion

It seems the future for universal human rights is bleak. Not only is it difficult to enforce compliance with universal standards, the very idea that there should be universal standards in the first place is under threat. On the other hand, many will be reluctant to give up on the idea—it is not only

old-fashioned cultural imperialists who believe that it is good to live in a world where the rights of the individual—political, economic and social—are taken seriously.

Is there any way in which the notion of universal rights can be saved from its critics? Two modern approaches seem fruitful. Even if we find it difficult to specify human rights, it may still be possible to talk of human wrongs—similarly, some have argued it is easier to specify what is unjust than what is just; to use Walzer's terminology (1994) there may be no thick moral code that is universally acceptable, to which all local codes conform, but there may be a thin code which at least can be used to de-legitimize some actions. Thus, to give two different kinds of example:

1. The **Genocide Convention** of 1948 seems a plausible example of a piece of international legislation that outlaws an obvious wrong—obvious in the sense that any moral code that did **not** condemn genocide would not be worthy of respect.

2. Whereas some local variations in the rights associated with gender may be unavoidable, it is still possible to say that practices such as **female genital mutilation** are simply **wrong**—again in the sense that any code which did not condemn such suffering would be unworthy of respect.

This may not take us as far as some would wish—essential to this approach is the notion that there are going to be some practices which many would condemn but which will have to be tolerated because the condemnation stems from a thick rather than a thin account of right and wrong—but it may be the most appropriate response to contemporary pluralism.

An alternative approach is more supportive of universal ideas but on a non-foundationalist basis. This involves recognizing that human rights are based on a particular culture—Richard Rorty (1993) actually calls this the human rights culture—and defending them in these terms rather than by reference to some universal cross-cultural code. This approach would involve abandoning the idea that it is possible to demonstrate that human rights exist; instead, it involves proselytizing on behalf of the sort of culture in which rights exist. The basic point is that human life is safer, pleasanter, and more dignified when rights are acknowledged than when they are not.

This final point highlights a central truth—it may not be possible to produce a philosophically watertight defence of rights, but most people are not philosophers, and it is on the strength of the popular support for universal human rights that the idea will flourish or die in the next century.

QUESTIONS

1. Is there a clear difference between first, second, and third generation rights?

2. Does a right always involve a duty?

3. Are there such things as natural rights?

4. Should the promotion of human rights be a foreign policy goal of states? Are there moral as well as practical objections to such a policy?

5. Does it make sense to talk of a right to an adequate standard of living?

6. Should peoples as well as individuals have rights?

7. What sort of rights ought groups to possess?

8. Are advocates of human rights necessarily cultural imperialists?

9. Is there a distinctively feminist approach to human rights?

10. What role can International Organizations play in promoting human rights?

11. How important is public opinion in mobilizing support for victims of human rights violations?

12. Is a democratic form of government a necessary pre-condition for the existence of human rights?

GUIDE TO FURTHER READING

Brownlie, I. (ed.), *Basic Documents on Human Rights*, edn. (Oxford: Clarendon Press, 1992) is the best source for the texts of international human rights legislation. A more up-to date source of information is the Internet: a useful home page is Human Rights on the WEB at http://www.traveller.com/~hrweb/hrweb.html

Jones, P., *Rights* (Basingstoke: Macmillan, 1994) is the best single source for the philosophical problems posed by the idea of rights.

Finnis, J., *Natural Law and Natural Rights* (Oxford: Clarendon Press, 1980) is more difficult, but a very good introduction to modern natural law thinking.

Vincent R. J., *Human Rights and International Relations* (Cambridge: Cambridge University Press, 1986), which links human rights protection to the theory of International Society, is a very fine study on international human rights, as is:

Donnelly, J., *International Human Rights* (Boulder, Col.: Westview, 1993), a good summary of the standard liberal account of international human rights.

Rodley, N. S. (ed.), *To Loose the Bands of Wickedness: International Intervention in Defence of Human Rights* (London: Brasseys 1992) is a good collection by a human rights activist.

Kirkpatrick, J., 'Dictatorships and Double Standards', *Commentary*, 68 (Nov. 1979), is a famous (perhaps infamous) attempt to draw a distinction between totalitarian and authoritarian regimes.

Shue, H., *Basic Rights* (Princeton: Princeton University Press, 1980) is a very influential defence of second generation rights, and critique of the United States government for privileging first generation rights at the expense of second generation rights.

Sen, A., *Poverty and Famines* (Oxford: Clarendon Press, 1981) provides the evidence that first generation rights may be crucial for securing second generation rights.

Walzer, M., *Thick and Thin: Moral Argument at Home and Abroad* (Notre Dame: University of Notre Dame Press, 1994) makes the case for a 'thin' moral code that can operate cross culturally.

Shute, S., and Hurley, S. (eds.), *On Human Rights* (New York: Basic Books, 1993) is an excellent recent collection of papers including essays by John Rawls, Richard Rorty, and Catherine Mackinnon. The latter offers one feminist view; for another see Peterson, V. S., 'Whose Rights? A Critique of the "Givens" in Human Rights discourse', *Alternatives*, 15 (1990).

Crawford, J. (ed.), *The Rights of Peoples* (Oxford: Clarendon Press, 1988), is the best collection on Third Generation Rights.

25 Gender Issues

Jan Jindy Pettman

READER'S GUIDE

This chapter asks why feminist scholarship and gender issues have come so late to the study of international politics, and suggests the difference asking feminist questions might make. It then identifies different kinds of feminism, and traces the shifting debates about gender relations and sexual difference. The rest of the chapter explores a gender analysis of several aspects of globalization: deregulation and structural adjustment politics, the changing international division of labour and the 'export' of women workers; rising identity politics, and in particular the uses nationalisms make of women, and women's different responses to nationalism; and the ways women's transnational alliances and international conferences have globalized gender issues, too.

Introduction

International Relations has long been taught and theorized as if women were invisible: as if either there were no women in world politics, which was only men's business; or as if women and men were active in and affected by world politics in the same ways, in which case there would be no need to 'gen-der' the analysis. Now feminist scholarship is visible, if still marginal, and women's and gender issues are the focus of transnational politics too. Both feminist understandings and women's organizing provide us with perspectives that contribute a more **inclusive** view of globalization.

Gendering International Politics

Feminist International Politics

Feminist scholarship is often strongly resisted by academic gatekeepers, for it reveals the partial and gendered nature of intellectual work which is built on (élite?) men's experiences. But feminism has come even later to International Relations, one of the most masculinist of the social sciences. Suggested explanations include that the discipline is male-dominated, and so more likely to reflect men's interests and fears; and that the way the discipline constructs its subject matter makes most people, including almost all women, disappear. Its focus on the 'high politics' of diplomacy, war, and statecraft called up a world of statesmen and soldiers, who were assumed to be male. Even when international political economy became a concern, this often took the form of analysis of relations between states and markets, or of structures of domination and exploitation. In either case, **gender relations** were rarely considered a necessary part of the analysis.

The intellectual field, or territory, further disguised women and gender relations through its distinction between the domestic or the inside of states, and the international or the in-between of states. In the process differences within states, including gender differences, were relegated away from its interest, and left to other disciplines like Political Science and Sociology to attend to. At the same time, world politics was often characterized in terms of conflict, competition, security (defined as military security), and power (demonstrated through the threat or use of force), drawing on a particular notion of human nature that was **gendered,** and perhaps class and culture specific, too.

But many women too have written on and thought about war and peace. The discipline of International Relations was established in 1919 in the wake of World War I, in the hope that there should never again be such a war. However, it ignored the critiques of women organizing for peace, including those who had held the Hague peace conference in 1915, in the midst of that war, and who opposed the punishing conditions imposed on Germany at its conclusion on the grounds that it would spread poverty, disease, and enmity through Europe, and generate further conflict (which it did). This is why feminists are concerned to ask **whose** experiences are being taken seriously? Whose understandings of politics, including international politics, become the material for theorizing about, and acting in, 'the world'?

Where are Women in Global Politics?

Feminist questions unsettle assumptions which reflect only (some) men's experiences. In an early feminist intervention in the discipline, Cynthia Enloe asked the question: **'Where are the women?'** (1989). She found that women often were there, even where we might not expect them: keeping a military base going, for example, or as the majority of workers in export-processing zones.

Asking the question 'Where are the women?' can suggest different kinds of answers. For some, it leads to **'the famous few'**—to name Indira Gandhi, Margaret Thatcher, or Golda Meir for example. These particular women were strong leaders who showed no hesitation to use force in international conflicts. This led some to say that the only difference between men and women is that women are so rarely in power; if they are, they behave like men. Others argue that in national and world politics, only those who play the main game well will succeed. It may show more about contemporary politics as **masculinist**, than about whether women and men are 'different'. So, too, men who appear compassionate or seek to negotiate away from conflict may be accused of being wimps, 'women', or girls.

Others use the question 'Where are the women?' to identify places where women are not, because they are women. Until very recently, and still in many states, women were prohibited from combat roles, which in turn made it impossible for them to rise to commanding levels in their state's armed forces. But not just any man is seen as a soldier. The fierce debates over whether gay men should be allowed to serve are similar to those used against women soldiers, too: that they may break down under fire, or threaten group cohesion for example. Here military service is associated with men, and with certain kinds of **masculinity**, too.

Asking 'Where are the women?' reveals women in places where, otherwise, we mightn't look for them. Feminists take women seriously as knowledge-makers about the world. This means seeking to learn from their experiences of politics and global processes. This extends our understandings of politics, too. Women are often under-represented in formal politics, as heads of state or parliamentary representatives or executive bureaucrats for example, though in the Scandinavian states, they are now close to equal (see Fig. 25.1). Women are more likely to organize in other politics, in social movements, and in non-governmental organizations (NGOs) for example. Through these politics, women were **actors** in global politics long before they were noticed in the study of these politics.

Discovering Gender

Asking 'Where are the women?' usually reveals women in different roles, in different relations to the military for example, or the market, compared with men. There are rarely simply more, or fewer, or no women. When we find women, we find **gender relations**, too. So war stories from very different states tell of brave soldier men, the protectors, and the women they protect, who wait, and weep, and have more sons for the killing (Elshtain 1987). These stories construct men as the agents of the state or nation, and women as passive, regardless of what actual men and women are doing. These constructions in turn place pressure on peaceful or unwilling men to fight, to protect 'women and children'. They disguise women's active support of or participation in wars, including as warriors. And they force conditions of dependence on women, who are expected to be grateful for this protection, even when they do not wish it.

The gendered war script is not an exception. The citizen is often presumed to be male, with public responsibilities, while women are relegated into the family, the domestic world. In foundation stories in political theory, women were also relegated away from the world of reason to one of emotions and passions, making them unreliable citizens, and dangerous to men, too. The **public/private** split coincides with other splits, like reason/emotion, mind/body, and male/female. These are gendered divisions: they associate certain kinds of character or behaviour with a particular gender. The 'male' side of the dichotomy is usually given more value, and privileged, while the female side is devalued. In the process, 'gender' becomes both relational, and a power relationship.

Feminism makes several very important strategic claims here. The first is that women's experiences are **systematically** different from men's, even from men of their own family or group. Another is that all social relations are gendered; so we experience our class, or race, for example, in gendered forms. We don't experience our gender alone, or in isolation from other social identities, including for example whether we are citizens, or where we live, or our age. Nor do we experience any of our other identities without gender. Gender is constitutive of other social relations too. This reveals as partial those representations of social relations including global politics that appear gender-neutral, but on closer examination turn out to be universalizing (élite) men's experiences and knowledge.

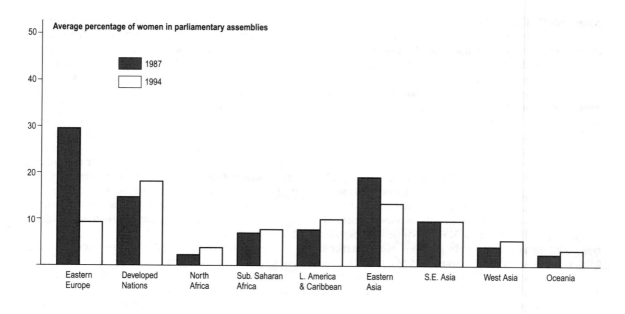

Average percentage of women in parliamentary assemblies

- 1987
- 1994

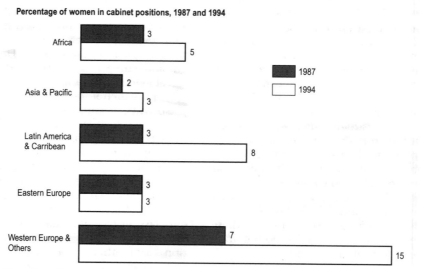

Percentage of women in cabinet positions, 1987 and 1994

- 1987
- 1994

Fig. 25.1. Women's political participation

Sources: New Internationalist, April 1995 and *World Government Directory,* 1994

Key Points

- Gender analysis and feminism came late to International Relations.
- Women's experiences of and ideas about world politics were rarely admitted to the discipline.

- Asking the question 'Where are the women?' makes women visible in world politics.
- Making women visible also reveals gender relations, as power relations.
- Feminism claims that women's experiences are systematically different from men's, and that all social relations are gendered.

Feminisms

woman who are in a [?] have the luxury of examining [?] as other basic rights & equalities have been fought for & established allowing them to take it to a further level

Feminism is often identified as Western. There is a very complicated politics here about who names feminism, and whether other women's struggles for equal rights can be called feminist, even if they themselves don't use that name. But it is not true that either feminism or women's rights movements were only or largely of western origins. So in a number of Asian and Middle Eastern colonies, 'the woman question' arose in the late nineteenth and early twentieth centuries, alongside or in connection with early anti-colonial nationalism. These early feminists were familiar with suffrage struggles in other places, and some travelled to participate in international conferences, too.

The Politics of Feminism

Second-wave feminism came to prominence in a number of Western states in the 1970s, alongside or in uneasy relations with other social movements for a more inclusive citizenship and social rights. Feminism had a rather different relation to socialist states, whose treatment of women as workers and their support for women working outside the home allowed state leaders to declare that they had solved the woman question. That has made post-cold war feminist organizing in these states very difficult, both because of the association of women's rights language with state socialism, and because the rush to marketization and deregulation of their economies swept away many of the gains that had led socialist state women to see Western feminists as 'coming from behind'. This helps explain the declining numbers of women in parliamentary politics in East European states. Generalizing to 'Third World states' is even more difficult, given the variety of pre-colonial, colonial, and post-colonial experiences included within this big category.

We might describe feminism as a **political project** to understand so as to change women's inequality, or exploitation, or oppression. But any generalizations about feminist politics globally is made even more difficult by the **differences** within feminism, within and between states. First-wave feminism was concerned with suffrage, with women's legal and civil rights, including their rights to education. Many of these early feminists were active in other politics—as socialists, or anti-colonial nationalists, or pacifists for example. So too second-wave feminists had very different politics, that affected their understanding of sexual difference, and their views on the possibility of alliances with progressive men, for example. In the 1970s and 1980s, these differences were often summed up under labels of liberal, radical, and socialist feminist. While many feminists are not easily put under one label, and the lines of difference and alliance shift over time and place, the differences between them are important for thinking about gender, and about strategies necessary to overcome gender inequality or oppression.

Very broadly, **liberal feminists** are equality feminists, seeking an end to women's exclusion from or under representation in office, power and employment. They seek women's equal rights in the military, including in combat, for they see women's 'protection' as a way of keeping them from power, and their dependence on men as compromising their claims to full citizenship, which is usually understood to include fighting for one's country.

Other feminists are critical of liberal feminists as seeking equality in masculinist institutions, on men's terms. In different ways, they seek to change institutions themselves, to be women-friendly. They disagree however, on what lies at the heart of the problem. So **radical feminists** see women's subordination as universal, though taking different forms at different times. Some argue women are a sex-class, systematically and everywhere subject to men's sex-right, or their claims for access to their bodies, children, and labour. Violence against women is seen as key keeping women resourceless, and 'in their place'. They draw attention to sexuality as politics too.

must look @ all [?] before [?] issues [?]

Cultural feminists include those who see women as different from men, more nurturing and peaceable for example. They do not reject 'women's values', as liberal feminists do, but rather they argue that these values are just what world politics, and ecology, need now. Some cultural feminists are accused of essentialism, of representing these values as naturally women's, and so reinforcing the gendered stereotypes that underpin women's oppression. Others see women's values more as learned skills, as women are almost always those responsible for the care of children, for health and

WHY Such divisions
→ like w/ many movements
→ throw out don't want but
once eliminated loose
cohesion

community care. They argue that men, too, can learn to nurture.

Socialist feminists put together class and gender, finding that a class analysis alone leaves out much that women experience. It cannot explain why women are those responsible for reproductive and family labour, why women are so over-represented among the poor, or why gender inequities, often reinforced by violence against women, continue even where women are integrated into the workforce, too.

These classic lines of difference in feminism are less clear these days, and are now supplemented by naming other feminisms. So in the 1980s **black** and **Third World feminists** accused white feminists of ignoring race, culture, and colonial relations as affecting women, too. These locate white women in ambiguous ways, as oppressed in relation to gender and perhaps class, but privileged by their membership of the dominant race and/or culture, and by citizenship rights in rich countries. However, geographic location or social identity cannot predict a person's politics. Some Third World feminists are liberal feminists, seeking admission to their state or profession on equal terms with men, while others are socialist or left feminists who are concerned to build alliances across class lines between élite and poorer women, for example. And some white feminists pursue anti-racist theories and politics, too.

Developments within feminism in recent years have shifted both theory and practical politics. **Post-modern feminists** have added to growing recognition of differences between women, too. These shifts have unsettled the category 'woman'. They raise issues about who speaks for 'women'? Whose experiences as women are not reflected in feminist knowledge-making and politicking? There is an ongoing tension in much feminism between equality and difference claims; and between trying to build up the category woman for the purposes of claim; while trying to tear it down in the face of its use against women (Snitow 1989). This is made even more difficult in these times of growing right-wing and fundamentalist movements, which seek to discredit feminism and attack women's rights.

Sex and Gender

Different feminisms, then, have different views on gender relations, and how to change them so they do not routinely count against women. The conversations and sometimes conflicts between these feminisms have taken us further in understanding gender relations and sexual difference. Jane Flax asks 'how do we think, or do not think or avoid thinking about gender' (1987). Just because gender is not made visible in many accounts of the world or our lives in it does not mean that it is absent. What then does a gender analysis contribute to our understanding of international and increasingly globalized politics?

Gender is often used as a code word for **women**. This does draw our attention to the ways in which dominant groups can normalize or naturalize their own identities—they name others while remaining themselves unnamed. But of course men have gender too, just as white people are also 'raced', and dominant culture members have culture too.

An important early second-wave feminist intervention made a distinction between **sex** and **gender.** Sex was seen as biology: we are born male or female. Gender was seen as a social construction: what it means to be male or female in any particular place or time. This distinction was politically very important, for women have been very badly done by biology, in explanations of their inequality or extra burdens as natural, an inevitable extension of their child-bearing difference. It built on the fact that while **women's work** appeared to be universal, just what that work involved, and how sexual difference was understood, varied from society to society, group to group, and over time (see Box 25.1). More recently, Men's Studies have explored the social construction of masculinities, too.

The distinction between sex and gender made room for a feminist project—for if gender is a social construction, it can be changed. It has also enabled us to explore different meanings of gender. Gender is a **personal** identity—how do I experience being a woman? a **social** identity—what do others expect of me, as a woman? and a **power relation**—why are women as a social category almost always under-represented in relations of power for example? Gender is political—it is contested, by men and women who regularly subvert, challenge, or bolster gender difference, at home or in other places, by feminists who seek women's liberation, and by anti-feminists, who seek to take back what women have won through struggle. Gender may be the basis for a **mobilized political identity**—of which 'feminist' is one. So too is the Australian anti-feminist women's group called Women Who Want to be Women.

it seems that ⓐ has allowed women to pursue ⓑ moments.

conc,

Box 25.1. Accounting for Unpaid Work

Much work in society goes unrecognized and unvalued—work in the household and in the community. And most of it is done by women.

Human Development Report 1995 estimated that, in addition to the $23 trillion in recorded world output in 1993, household and community work accounts for another $16 trillion. And women contribute $11 trillion of this invisible output.

In most countries women do more work than men. In Japan women's work burden is about 7% higher than men's, in Austria 11% higher and in Italy 28% higher. Women in developing countries tend to carry an even larger share of the workload than those in industrial countries—on average about 13% higher than men's share, and in rural areas 20% higher. In rural Kenya women do 35% more work than men.

In some countries women's work burden is extreme. Indian women work 69 hours a week, while men work 59. Nepalese women work about 77 hours, men 56. Moldova women work about 74 hours a week, and in Kyrgystan more than 76 hours.

Source: Human Development Report, 1996.

Lately, some feminists have developed more fluid representations of gender. 'Doing gender', or gender as performance, suggests ways that we select and negotiate our ways through social possibilities and expectations. Gender as process reminds us that gender never just is, but rather that much work goes into its reproduction. Some feminists fault gender constructionists who continue to use the sex–gender distinction, for reinforcing yet another dichotomy nature and nurture—and for treating the body as a neutral 'thing' on which gender difference is written. They find it more productive to think about sexual difference, and stress **embodiment**—that our first place of location is our body. By drawing attention to *bodies*, they say, attention is inevitably drawn to sexual difference.

Women's politics and contests around gender, though still anchored often in local and particular sexual politics, are now increasingly globalized. These politics are a response to the gendered impact of **globalization**, and also take advantage of the opportunities for communication and organization transnationally that globalization offers. The rest of this chapter will pursue the changing international sexual division of labour, crises of the state in the face of globalization and restructuring, and rising identity conflicts. It will conclude by looking at women's politics, which are being globalized, too.

Key Points

- Feminism is not restricted to Western states.
- Contemporary feminisms are diverse in their understandings of the difference gender makes, and how to stop this difference from counting against women.
- Since the early 1980s, the issue of differences between women has become visible in feminist politics.
- Women's rights are not being progressively achieved. Today there is a global-wide backlash against women's rights.

Gender in the Global Political Economy

Until recently, women and gender relations rarely appeared in studies of the international political economy. An exception was development studies (though these often remained separate from IPE, too). From 1970, feminist critiques and women's NGOs made visible the ways in which development planners overlooked women, including in their roles as workers, owners, and entrepreneurs, as well as in subsistence and family production. They pointed out both that women were differently affected by development, often losing access to land and resources, and expected to take on additional work; and that the outcomes of development policies were affected by already existing gender relations, including local notions of what was women's work.

Women in Development

The international **Decade for Women** (1976–85) generated a huge amount of material on women's lives, and the discriminations they faced. It documented, too, the gendered effects of development, and provided a base for the themes peace, justice, development—coming out of the third women's conference, in Nairobi in 1985. In the process, it supported a new field, known as **Women in Development** (WID).

There are very different approaches to WID, including between those liberal feminists who seek to integrate women more, and more equally, into development, and other feminists who see development as currently defined as damaging to women. They seek the empowerment of women, including through participation in development decisions that affect their own lives and choices.

Not all women are poor, in the 'Third World' or elsewhere. But no state treats its women as well as its men. Some years ago, it was said that women did one third of the paid work, two thirds of the productive work, for one tenth of the income and less than one hundredth of the property. Now it is likely that the figures are even more against women.

The Human Development Index (HDI) is based on three measures: life expectancy at birth, educational attainment, and standard of living. The Gender Development Index (GDI) measures these too, but adjusts for the disparity between women and men in each case. The Gender Empowerment Index (GEM) measures relative empowerment between men and women in political and economic spheres, and in terms of political representation.

A series of **global crises**, in terms of trade dependence, debt, and restructuring, have hit women especially hard. The conditions imposed on states in return for loans include structural adjustment policies, deregulating finance, liberalizing trade, favouring export industries and reducing social services and public support, including food subsidies.

These policies are not restricted to poorer 'Third World' states. They are evident in former and some existing communist states, where marketization has similar effects, including removing state provision of many services that supported working women. They are reshaping Western states, too, as their governments give up on much economic regulation and cut back on social security and public enterprise.

These dramatic changes are part of globalization of production and of 'the market'. Within states, they represent a dramatic shift from public to private expenditure, and from state to family, especially women's, responsibilities. We live in times of high unemployment, polarizing wealth within and between states, reducing state provision and growing impoverishment. These are gendered in their effects. **First**, cut-backs in state services like health, education, and social security especially affect women's employment opportunities. **Second**, women are everywhere overwhelmingly responsible for family and household maintenance, and must compensate through their own time and labour when (often inadequate) state support is

Table 25.1. **Gender disparity—GEM, GDI, and HDI rankings**

	GEM rank	GDI rank	HDI rank
Norway	1	3	5
Sweden	2	1	8
Denmark	3	6	16
Finland	4	5	6
New Zealand	5	9	13
Canada	6	2	1
Germany	7	16	7
Netherlands	8	10	4
USA	9	4	2
Austria	10	12	12
Nigeria	98	78	87
Togo	100	80	89
Pakistan	101	77	84
Mauritania	102	83	95
Comoros	103	76	88
Niger	104	93	104

Source: Human Development Report, 1996.

reduced or removed. **Third**, the cost of globalization is not evenly spread: the 'feminization of poverty' refers to the growing proportion, as well as numbers, of women and their children living in poverty. This is in part a reflection of the worldwide trend, so that now between a third and a half of all families do not have a male breadwinner. The gendered effects of restructuring, then, amount to a massive crisis in reproduction. This has led UNICEF to identify an invisible adjustment, which is women's responsibility, largely unaided by those who allocate resources and wealth elsewhere.

The Changing International Division of Labour

Fourth, the changing international division of labour is gendered, too. Transnational corporations go on the global prowl for cheap labour, which often means women's labour (Enloe 1992). Especially since the 1980s, increasingly competitive trading and labour deregulation in many states has accompanied the rise of a largely female marginalized workforce, with a core of skilled and professional workers who are mainly male.

Women are concentrated in poorly paid work, including in part-time and outwork. This partly reflects many women's juggling between their domestic and their paid work. But it also reflects the construction of women workers as cheap labour— or, more accurately, as **'labour made cheap'**. In many different cultures and states, women's labour is seen to be temporary, filling **in** before marriage, or supplementing husbands' income. At the same time, they are seen as 'naturally' good with their hands, patient and docile, and so particularly fitted to do work which men would not tolerate. Assumptions about women's work means that it is often classified as unskilled, even where, like sewing, it is seen as skilled if men do it. In these ways, particular constructions of **femininity** enter into the organization of work, and shape its status and rewards. So women are now the vast majority of workers on the global assembly line, in factories and in export processing zones, where their gender and often their youth help keep wages down.

The Export of Women

Women or girls come from rural areas into the towns or cities, into export processing zones or to military base servicing areas, or cross state borders in search of work. They may be their family's only income earner. This in turn unsettles gender relations, and gives those women experiences which range from liberating to extremely exploitative or downright dangerous.

Where once the labour migrant was presumed to be male (and often was), now about half of all those outside their country of birth are women. In some particular migrant labour flows, women are in the overwhelming majority. In Italy 95 per cent of Filipinos are women. Most are domestic workers and child carers. They are part of a **global flow** of women from poorer states to wealthier ones, from Sri Lanka and the Philippines to Japan, Hong Kong, and oil-rich Middle East states, and from Central and South American states into the United States, for example.

This labour migration was largely unnoticed until the Gulf War revealed some 400,000 Asian women workers in Kuwait and a further 100,000 in Iraq. There are between 1 and 1.7 million women in the domestic worker trade from South and South-East Asia alone. This trade reinforces the assumption that it is women who are responsible for domestic labour, even where that labour is paid for and releases other women to go into paid work.

This **traffic in women** is big business. Recruitment agencies, banks, and airlines profit from it. So do the exporting states, in the form of remittances, an estimated $3 billion per year to the Philippines for example. This trade contributes to those states' search for hard currency in the face of growing debt pressures, and relieves unemployment at home, too. It is therefore unlikely that the home state will act strongly in support of their citizens' rights when women are subject to abuse in other states; though their own poor record in labour and women's rights is also a factor here.

This trade in women reflects power and wealth relations globally. Those South-East Asian states exporting domestic workers had an average annual income in 1992 of $680, while those importing women had an average income of $10,376. It also has implications for states' standing, as some states become associated with servant status. In a further complication, the gendered representations of national difference reinforce earlier colonial and racist images of South-East Asian women as exotic and sexually available. In this way, the export of domestic workers is not so different from the international purchase of 'mail-order brides', and the international sex tourist industry. Women's organizations work transnationally to publicize the dangers in all these forms of trafficking in women, and to support the women caught up in these traffics.

Other forms of labour migration are not so obviously sexualized, though they may also involve exploitative working conditions and insecure rights in relation to both work and residence or citizenship. Many migrants move to and take up work in older industrial cities in Western states, and do work in clothing, textiles, electronics, and information services for example not so different from that which women do in some 'Third World' states. In conditions of urban decay, high unemployment, and cut-backs in public expenditure and services, migrants can easily become scapegoats for other people's troubles. In this way, globalization and **migration** become targets in politics against 'outsiders'. **Racism** marks the boundaries of national belonging, and immigration and citizenship become major political issues. In these circum-

stances, those who are seen as different often organize in defence of their own rights, and may use their perceived difference as a basis for organizing. Instead of reducing differences between people, these aspects of globalization appear to heighten difference, and intolerance.

Key Points

- Feminist critiques, women's NGOs and the Decade for Women helped genderate 'Women in Development' (WID).

- WID includes very different approaches to gender and development.

- Recent crises associated with intensifying globalization and restructuring impact on women in particular, generating a crisis in reproduction.

- The 'export of women' is big business, and also contributes significantly through remittances to poorer states' economies.

- Migrants and foreign workers are often scapegoated for rising unemployment and social distress.

Gender and Nationalism

While we do now live in 'the world as a whole' for some purposes, we also live in a world where difference and particular political identities are as important as ever—perhaps more so. This can be seen in the resurgence of nationalisms and ethno-nationalisms and the rise of revivalist or fundamentalist religious politics globally. These **identity politics** usually call for a return to an imagined past. Women's roles and gender relations are a key element in the construction of the past and in the political mobilization of these identities.

Gendered Nationalism

Since the end of the cold war, there has been an upsurge in identity conflicts. **Nationalism** is unsettling the presumed coincidence of nation and state. While in the past nationalism was more associated

with progressive politics, for example in anti-colonial nationalism, nowadays it is often cast in exclusivist terms, against 'the other'. In the process, women get caught up in nationalist politics in different ways, and identity politics impact on gender relations, too.

The language of nationalism is **familial** language—home, blood, kin. The state is often imagined as male, and the nation as female. The nation **is** often represented as a woman under threat of violation or domination, so that her citizen-sons must fight for her honour. The 'rape of Kuwait' told a typical story—of a feminized victim, with male villain and male hero fighting for her possession. These stories associate boundary transgression with sexual danger, and also associate proving manhood with nationalism and war. In these ways, men become the agents of nationalism, and women the passive ones or national possessions, whatever actual men and women are doing.

Where the nation is feminized, men are the responsible protectors. But women have obligations to the nation, too. Here we can trace a move from **nation-as-woman** to women as **mothers-of-the-nation**. This symbolic use of women, and their confinement within roles as mothers can mean the policing of their bodies and behaviour, especially in wartime or in times of heightened identity conflicts.

Women and Nationalism

Women are seen as the physical **reproducers** of the nation: they are 'nationalist wombs' (Enloe 1989).This makes it important that women have the right children, with the right men. They are also seen as social reproducers and cultural transmitters, bringing up their children as Palestinian for example, even—or especially—if they do not have a state of their own. Women are also seen as **signifiers of difference**, marking the boundaries of belonging. For this reason, much importance is attached to women's clothing and movements, especially their relations with those outside the nation. Beyond the symbolic uses made of them, women are also **agents** in or against nationalist politics in their own right.

It is easier for women to mobilize in support of nationalist causes, if this cause is in power in their state or region. Some women do organize in movements that are dangerous for others, including other women. So there are many women supporters and some leaders of the Indian right-wing Hindu movement, and some of these women participated in violence against Muslim women and children. Many Serbian women supported the Serbian nationalist project, which involved systematic violence against women, too, as part of 'ethnic cleansing'.

However, in some states women from dominant nationalist groups or states have organized in support for other women. Israeli Women in Black demonstrated in support of Palestinian women, and Belgrade feminists also demonstrated as Women in Black against Serbian nationalist aggression. These women have been subjected to much threat and sometimes violence, for their loyalty is supposed to be to their community, and not to women, or to people more generally. At the same time, the idea of Women in Black has been taken up in many states experiencing nationalist violence, in expressions of solidarity with women across the nationalist lines.

The high **symbolic** value attached to women in community conflicts makes them susceptible to attack from their own men, if they are seen as disloyal or rebellious. It also makes them especially vulnerable to attack from other-side men, as a way of getting at their men. So mass rape in war and identity conflicts is not only war spoils. It is also a war strategy, aimed at humiliating the enemy men by showing they are unable to protect their women.

War rape has a long history, though it is not usually regarded as political. So despite evidence of mass rape and of military sexual slavery in World War II, these were not prosecuted as war crimes. The recent visibility of sexual violence as part of war work, especially in terms of the former Yugoslavia and the Korean and other South-East Asian women forcibly recruited in to Japanese military brothels in World War II, is partly due to feminist work within states, to name rape and other violence against women as crimes against the women, not against the honour of men. It is also a sign of globalizing gender issues, especially in the form of women's rights' claims.

Key Points

- Nationalism is usually called up in gendered language.
- Women get caught up in nationalist politics in their construction as mothers of the nation and as markers of difference.
- Women also participate in or oppose nationalist politics.
- Women's symbolic significance in nationalism makes them vulnerable to violence, including war rape.

Globalizing Gender Issues

Women organizing in the face of global processes and documenting their impact on women become players in new global politics.

Naming **gender-specific violence** against women has been part of women's transnational politics. Violence against women in their homes is the most common crime in the world. It knows no boundaries, in terms of class, culture, or nationality. Other kinds of violence against women vary by region for example, or take culture-specific forms. So there has been an increase in dowry-burnings in India; in many states there are still 'honour' crimes which see husbands, fathers, and brothers exempt from punishment after killing women whose behaviour the family opposes; female genital mutilation maims and often kills girl children and women in some North African states.

Transnational Women's Movements

In some states, women are subjected to bodily violence through forced contraception or abortion, as in the China one-child policy. Many poor, racialized and minority women in Western states face discrimination and lack of care in terms of health and social choices. There is now an **international women's health movement**, which struggles with different state policies and practices, and different views within women's NGOs and outside them, over how to secure women's sexuality and reproductive rights. 'Third World' women point out that these must go beyond individual rights, to ensure enabling conditions to access choice, including maternal and child health more generally. The 1994 international conference on population and development in Cairo was crucial in mobilizing women and building regional and global linkages. But even rhetorical gains are at risk in these backlash days. And there is no easy unity or single political position on these issues among women, either.

International Women's Conferences

International conferences and preparations for them have been especially important in globalizing women's issues, networks, and alliances. The first two women's conferences in 1975 and 1980 (see Box 25.2) witnessed conflicting priorities between First World and Third World women. By the **Nairobi conference** in 1985 there were alliances across these divides, and more evident splits among women from the same state or region, especially between state-sponsored women's organizations and more radical dissident or exiled women. But Nairobi did place women's issues on the international agenda, and generated webs of connection between women's NGOs across state borders.

Box 25.2. Globalizing Gender Issues through the UN System

1946	The Commission on the Status of Women
1975	International Women's Year
1975	Mexico Women's Conference
1976–85	UN Decade for Women
1979	UN Convention on the Elimination of All Forms of Discrimination Against Women
1980	Copenhagen Women's Conference
1985	Nairobi Women's Conference
1993	Vienna Human Rights' Conference
1993	UN General Assembly Declaration on the Elimination of Violence Against Women
1994	Cairo International Conference on Population and Development
1995	Beijing Women's Conference

In recent years, women's activism has impacted on other kinds of international conferences. At the 1992 Earth Summit for example women named gender as shaping relations with the **environment**, including for example women's primary responsibilities for fuel and water in much of the world. They also identified militarism as the cause of much environmental degradation. The 1993 Human Rights conference was even more significant in highlighting **women's rights** claims internationally. In the lead-up to the conference, a series of preparatory committees and regional women's NGO meetings made their concerns visible. The Bangkok (Asia-Pacific) regional forum identified five **priority issues** to take to Vienna. These were violence against women, the international traffic in women, rising fundamentalisms (which usually target women's rights), military rape as a crime, and women's reproductive rights.

Women's global political campaigns helped win the adoption of the UN General Assembly Declaration against Violence against Women in 1993. This represents a significant advance in global gender issues. It recognizes violence as gender-based, supported by structural conditions which include women's subordination, and calls on states to punish perpetrators of violence whether in public or private places. It rejects religion or culture as excuses to abuse or discriminate against women. There are still huge problems with implementation, but this declaration does politicize violence against women, and give states formal responsibility for the security of women, too.

Over 30,000 women attended the NGO forum at Huairoou, which ran parallel to the official fourth international women's conference in Beijing in 1995. In many states and in regional meetings, there was a process of consultation which culminated in the Platform for Action, which identified 12 crucial areas and strategies for pursuing them (see Fig. 25.2). The conference recognized the disproportionate costs to women of restructuring. It also witnessed reactions against women's rights which meant that much effort went into defending earlier gains. Of the themes of equality, development, and peace, the first took priority, though the NGO forum especially recognized the interconnections here.

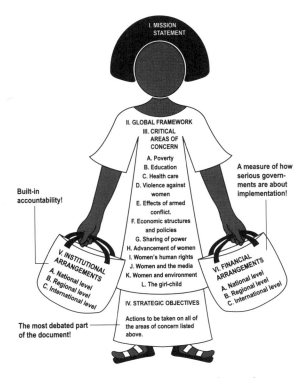

Fig. 25.2. Anatomy of the Platform for Action
Source: The Tribune no. 54, August 1995

- International conferences, especially women's conferences, have been very important in building transnational women's networks, and in putting women's issues on the global agenda.
- There is a new visibility of women's rights claims lately.
- The Beijing conference is seen by some as an example of global feminism in action, while for others it illustrated the difficulties facing women's rights struggles globally.

Key Points

- There are now different transnational women's movements, for women's health and reproductive rights for example.

Conclusion

Gender is a relevant category for analysis in global politics. Globalization affects women somewhat differently from men, though how it does so also depends on women's other identities and interests. In times of intensifying globalization which affects everyone, the state is no longer either willing or able to act in support of global response. At the same time, both global restructuring and rising right-wing identity politics threaten hard-won gains, and in turn generate more women's activism. Now women are organizing transnationally, and gender issues are globalized in the process.

QUESTIONS

1. Why did feminism come so late to International Relations?

2. What difference does it make to ask the question 'Where are the women?' about global politics?

3. What difference does it make being female, or male, in your experience?

4. What do you understand by gender?

5. What is feminism? What might different kinds of feminism contribute to our study of globalization?

6. What are the different approaches that are summed up under the label Women in Development?

7. What effects has globalization had on women, and on gender relations?

8. Why is there an increasing feminization of migrant labour, and of the global assembly line?

9. Are notions like the export of women, the global trade in women, or international traffic in women useful for tracking some global flows?

10. Discuss women's contradictory relations with nationalism.

11. Discuss the role of international conferences in putting women's rights on the global agenda.

12. Can we talk about global feminism, or transnational sisterhood?

GUIDE TO FURTHER READING

Beckman, P., and D'Amico, F. (eds.), *Women, Gender and World Politics: Perspectives, Policies and Prospects* (Westport, Conn.: Bergin & Gervey, 1994). This text pursues the question 'Does gender matter in world politics?' through the study of world politics and policies.

Enloe, C. *Bananas, Bases and Beaches: Making Feminist Sense of International Politics* (London, Pinter, 1989). This book asks 'Where are the women?' and reveals them in many different roles in international politics, in militaries, in export production, in prostitution and the sex trade, and in diplomacy.

Nelson, B., and Chowdhury, N. (eds.), *Women and Politics Worldwide* (Newhaven: Yale University Press, 1994). This useful resource book begins with overview chapters about women's different experiences of politics, and then has a number of chapters about women's participation in politics in different countries.

Peterson, V. S., and Runyan, A. S., *Global Gender Issues,* (Boulder, Col.: Westview Press, 1993). This text analyses gender in global politics, the gendered divisions of power, violence, and labour; and the politics of resistance, including women's politics.

Pettman, J. J., *Worlding Women: A Feminist International Politics* (London: Routledge, 1996). In this book, I explore aspects of global politics only briefly touched on in this chapter. It is organized in three sections: the gendered politics of identities, of war and peace, and of the international political economy.

Sen, G., and Grown, C., *Development, Crises and Alternative Visions: Third World Women's Perspectives* (New York: Monthly Review Press, 1987). This is a brief but broad-ranging review of the gendered impact of debt, dependence, and exploitation in Third World countries, and women's responses to these challenges.

Tickner, A., *Gender in International Relations* (New York: Columbia University Press, 1992). A careful feminist critique of mainstream IR approaches to security, international political economy, and ecology.

References

ABEGGLEN, J. C. (1994), *Sea Change: Pacific Asia as the New World Industrial Center* (New York: Free Press).

ADAMS, N. B. (1993), *Worlds Apart: The North–South Divide and the International System* (London: Zed).

AGNEW, J. and CORBRIDGE, S. (1995), *Mastering Space: Hegemony, Territory, and International Political-Economy* (London: Routledge).

AHMED, A. S. (1992), *Post-Modernism and Islam: Predicament and Promise* (London: Routledge).

ALBROW, M. (1990), 'Introduction', in M. Albrow and Elizabeth King (eds.), *Globalization, Knowledge and Society* (London: Sage).

ALLISON, G., CARTER, A. B., MILLER, S. E., and ZELIKOW, P. (eds.) (1993), *Cooperative Denuclearisation*, CSIA Studies in International Security, 2, (Cambridge, Mass.: Harvard University Press).

ALPEROVITZ, G. (1965), *Atomic Diplomacy : Hiroshima and Potsdam: The Use of the Atomic Bomb and the American Confrontation with Soviet Power* (New York: Simon and Schuster).

ANDERSON, B. (1991), *Imagined Communities: Reflections on the Origin and Spread of Nationalism* (London: Verso).

ANGELO, S. (1969), *Machiavelli: A Dissection.* (New York: Harcourt Brace).

ARCHIBUGI, D., and HELD, D. (eds.) (1995), *Cosmopolitan Democracy: An Agenda for a New World Order* (Cambridge: Polity Press).

AREND, A. C., and BECK, R. J. (1993), *International Law and the use of Force* (London: Routledge).

ASHLEY, R. K. (1984), 'The Poverty of Neorealism', *International Organisation,* 38 (2).

—— (1987), 'The Geopolitics of Geopolitical Space: Toward a Critical Social Theory of International Politics', *Alternatives,* 12 (4) .

—— (1988), 'Untying the Sovereign State: A Double Reading of the Anarchy Problematique', *Millennium,* 17 (2).

BAILEY, K. C. (1991), *Doomsday Weapons in the Hands of Many,* (Champaign, Ill.: Illinois Press).

BALDWIN, D. (ed.) (1993), *Neorealism and Neoliberalism: The Contemporary Debate* (New York: Columbia University Press).

BANKS, E. (1994), *Complex Derivatives: Understanding and Managing the Risks of Exotic Options, Complex Swaps, Warrants and Other Synthetic Derivatives* (Chicago: Probus).

BARAN, P. (1957), *The Political Economy of Growth,* (New York: Monthly Review Press).

BARBER, P. (1979), *Diplomacy: The World of the Honest Spy* (London: The British Library).

BARRACLOUGH, G. (ed.) (1984), *The Times Atlas of World History* (London: Times Books).

BARRY, B. (1989), *Theories of Justice* (Hemel Hempstead: Harvester Wheatsheaf).

BARTELSON, J. (1995), *A Genealogy of Sovereignty* (Cambridge: Cambridge University Press).

BEITZ, C. (1979), *Political Theory and International Relations* (Princeton: Princeton University Press).

BELLO, W. (1994), *Dark Victory: The United States, Structural Adjustment and Global Poverty* (London: Pluto Press).

BENNETT, J., and George, S. (1987), *The Hunger Machine* (Cambridge: Polity Press).

BERRIDGE, G. R. (1995), *Diplomacy: Theory and Practice* (Hemel Hempstead: Harvester Wheatsheaf).

BETHELL, L. (1970), *The Abolition of the Brazilian Slave Trade: Britain, Brazil and the Slave Trade Question 1807–1869* (Cambridge: Cambridge University Press).

BIALER, S. (1986), *The Soviet Paradox: External Expansion, Internal Decline* (New York: Knopf).

BILL, J., and SPRINGBORG, R. (1990), *Politics in the Middle East* (London: Scott, Foresman/Little, Brown Higher Education).

BIS (1996), *International Banking and Financial Market Developments* (Basle: Bank for International Settlements).

BLACK, M. (1992), *A Cause for our Times: Oxfam, the First 50 Years* (Oxford: Oxford University Press).

BONANATE, L. (1995), 'Peace or Democracy', in D. Archibugi and D. Held (eds.), *Cosmopolitan Democracy* (Cambridge: Polity Press).

BOOTH, J., and WALKER, T. (1993), *Understanding Central America* (Boulder, Col.: Westview Press).

BOOTH, K. (1991), 'Security Emancipation', *Review of International Studies,* 17 (4).

—— (1995a), 'Dare not to Know: International Relations Theory versus the Future', in K. Booth and S. Smith, *International Relations Theory Today* (Cambridge: Polity Press).

—— (1995b), 'Human Wrongs and International Relations', *International Affairs,* 71 (1): 103–26.

—— and SMITH, S. (eds.) (1995), *International Relations Theory Today* (Cambridge: Polity Press).

BOYER, R., and DRACHE, D. (1996) (eds.), *States against Markets: The Limits of Globalization* (New York: Routledge).

BRAUDEL, F. (1975), *The Mediterranean and the Mediterranean World in the Age of Philip II,* 2 vols. (London: Fontana).

BRECHER, J., and COSTELLO, T. (1994), *Global Village or Global Pillage: Economic Reconstruction from the Bottom up* (Boston, Mass.: South End).

BRECHER, M., and WILKENFELD, J. (1991), 'International Crises and Global Instability: The Myth of the "Long Peace" ', in C. Kegley (ed.), *The Long Postwar Peace: Contending Explanations and Projections* (New York: Harper Collins).

BRENNER, R. (1977), 'The Origins of Capitalist Development: A Critique of Neo-Smithian Marxism', *New Left Review,* 104.

BREWER, A. (1990), *Marxist Theories of Imperialism: A Critical Survey,* 2nd edn. (London: Routledge).

BROWN, C. (1992), *International Relations Theory: New Normative Approaches* (Hemel Hempstead: Harvester Wheatsheaf).

BROWN, L. R. *et al.* (1990), *State of the World 1990* (London: Unwin).

—— and KANE, H. (1995), *Full House: Reassessing the Earth's Population Carrying Capacity* (London: Earthscan).

BROWN, S. *et al.* (1977), *Regimes for the Ocean, Outer Space and the Weather* (Washington: Brookings Institution).

BROWNLIE, I. (ed.) (1971), *Basic Documents on African Affairs* (Oxford: Clarendon).

—— (1979), *Principles of Public International Law* (Oxford: Clarendon).

BRUCE, D. (1995), 'Intervention without Borders: Humanitarian Intervention in Rwanda, 1990–4', *Millennium,* 24 (2).

BUCHBINDER, D. (1994), *Masculinities and Identities* (Melbourne: Melbourne University Press).

BUKHARIN, O. (1994/5), 'Nuclear Safeguards and Security in the Former Soviet Union', *Survival,* 36 (4).

BULL, H. (1977), *The Anarchical Society. A Study of Order in World Politics,* (London: Macmillan).

—— (ed.) (1984a), *Intervention in World Politics* (Oxford: Clarendon Press).

—— (1984b), *Justice in International Relations* (Ontario: Hagey Lectures, University of Waterloo).

—— and WATSON, A. (1984), *The Expansion of International Society* (Oxford: Clarendon Press).

BURCHILL, S., and LINKLATER, A., *et al.* (1996), *Theories of International Relations* (Basingstoke: Macmillan).

BURCKHARDT, J. (1958), *The Civilization of the Renaissance in Italy,* 1 (New York: Harper).

BURNHAM, P. (1994), 'Open Marxism and Vulgar International Political Economy', *Review of International Political Economy* 1 (2).

BURROWS, W., and WINDREM, R. (1994), *Critical Mass: The Dangerous Race for Superpowers in a Fragmented World,* (New York: Simon and Schuster).

References

Burton, J. (1972), *World Society* (Cambridge: Cambridge University Press).

—— (1990), 'International Relations or World Society', in J. A. Vasquez (ed.), *Classics of International Relations* (New Jersey: Prentice Hall).

Butterfield, H. (1951), *History and Human Relations* (London: Collins).

Buzan, B. (1983), *People, States and Fear* (London: Harvester Wheatsheaf).

Callaghy, T. M. (1995), 'Africa and the World Political Economy: Still Caught between a Rock and a Hard Place', in J. W. Harbeson and D. Rothchild (eds.), *Africa in World Politics: Post-Cold War Challenges* (Oxford: Westview Press).

Calvert, P. (1994), *The International Politics of Latin America* (Manchester: Manchester University Press).

Camilleri, J. A., and Falk, J. (1992), *The End of Sovereignty* (Aldershot: Edward Elgar).

Cardoso, F. H., and Faletto, E. (1979), *Dependency and Development in Latin America* (Berkeley: University of California Press).

Carr, E. H. (1939; 2nd edn. 1946), *The Twenty Years' Crisis 1919–1939: An Introduction to the Study of International Relations* (London: Macmillan).

Carson, R. (1962), *Silent Spring* (Harmondsworth: Penguin).

Cavanagh, J., Wysham, D., and Arruda, M. (eds.) (1994), *Beyond Bretton Woods: Alternatives to the Global Economic Order* (London: Pluto Press).

Cerny, P. (1993), 'Plurilateralism: Structural Differentiation and Functional Conflict in the Post-Cold War World Order', *Millenium*, 22 (1).

Chase-Dunn, C. (1989), *Global Formation: Structures of the World-Economy* (Oxford: Blackwell).

—— (1994), 'Technology and the Logic of World-Systems' in R. Palan and B. Gills (eds.), *Transcending the State-global Divide: A Neostructuralist Agenda in International Relations* (Boulder, Col.: Lynne Rienner).

Chirot, D. (1982), Review of Wallerstein's 'The Modern World-System Vol. 2', *Journal of Social History*, 15 (3).

Clark, I. (1989), *The Hierarchy of States: Reform and Resistance in the International Order* (Cambridge: Cambridge University Press).

Claude, I. Jr. (1955), *National Minorities: An International Problem* (Cambridge, Mass.: Harvard University Press).

—— (1984), *Swords into Plowshares* (New York: Random House).

Cooper, R. (1968), *The Economics of Interdependence* (New York: McGraw Hill).

Cornia, G. A. *et al.* (1987), *Adjustment with a Human Face* (Oxford: UNICEF/Clarendon Press).

Cox, M. (1995), *United States Foreign Policy Since the End of the Cold War* (London: Pinter and the Royal Institute of International Affairs).

Cox, R. (1981), 'Social Forces, States and World Orders: Beyond International Relations Theory', *Millennium* 10 (2).

—— (1986), 'Social Forces, States and World Orders: Beyond International Relations Theory', in R. Keohane (ed.), *Neorealism and its Critics* (New York: Columbia University Press).

—— (1992), 'Towards a Post-Hegemonic Conceptualization of World Order: Reflections on the Relevancy of Ibn Khaldun', in J. Rosenau, and E.-O. Czempiel, *Governance without Government: Order and Change in World Politics* (Cambridge: Cambridge University Press).

—— with Sinclair, T. (1996), *Approaches to World Order* (Cambridge: Cambridge University Press).

Cox, R. W. (1994), 'Multilateralism and the Democratization of World Order', Paper for International Symposium on Sources of Innovation in Multilateralism, 26–28 May, Lausanne.

Crawford, J. (ed.) (1988), *The Rights of Peoples* (Oxford: Clarendon Press).

Crockatt, R. (1995), *The Fifty Years War: The United States and the Soviet Union in World Politics, 1941–1991* (London: Routledge).

D'Amico, F., and Beckman, P. (eds.) (1995), *Women in World Politics* (Westport, Conn.: Bergin & Garvey).

DAWISHA, K. (1990), *Eastern Europe, Gorbachev and Reform: The Great Challenge* (Cambridge: Cambridge University Press).

DERRIDA, J. (1976), *Of Grammatology* (Baltimore: Johns Hopkins University Press).

DESTEXHE, A. (1995), *Rwanda and Genocide in the Twentieth Century* (London: Pluto Press).

DEUTSCH, K. (1996), *Nationalism and Social Communication* (Cambridge, Mass.: MIT Press).

DEUTSCH, K. W. (1968), *The Analysis of International Relations* (Englewood Cliffs, NJ: Prentice Hall).

DEVETAK, R. (1996a), 'Critical Theory', in Burchill, Linklater, *et al.*, 145–78.

—— (1996b), 'Postmodernism', in Burchill, Linklater, *et al.*, 179–209.

DIBB, P. (1988), *The Soviet Union: The Incomplete Superpower* (London: International Institute for Strategic Studies/ Macmillan).

DICKEN, P. (1992), *Global Shift: The Internationalisation of Economic Activity* (London: Paul Chapman).

DONELAN, M. (1990), *Elements of International Political Theory* (Oxford: Clarendon Press).

DONNELLY, J. (1993), *International Human Rights* (Boulder, Col.: Westview).

DOYLE, M. W. (1983a), 'Kant, Liberal Legacies, and Foreign Affairs, part 1' *Philosophy and Public Affairs*, 12 (3).

—— (1983b), 'Kant, Liberal Legacies, and Foreign Affairs, part 2', *Philosophy and Public Affairs*, 12 (4).

—— (1995a), 'On the Democratic Peace', *International Security*, 19 (4).

—— 'Liberalism and World Politics Revisited', in Charles W. Kegley (ed.), *Controversies in International Relations Theory: Realism and the Neoliberal challenge* (New York: St Martin's Press).

DREZE, J., HUSSAIN A., SEN A., (eds.) (1995), *The Political Economy of Hunger* (Oxford: Clarendon Press).

DROWER, G. (1992), *Britain's Dependent Territories* (Aldershot: Dartmouth).

DRUCKER, P. (1993), *Managing in Turbulent Times* (Oxford: Butterworth & Heinemann).

DUGARD, J. (1987), *Recognition and the United Nations* (Cambridge: Groitius Publications Ltd).

DUNN, L. A. (1991), *Containing Nuclear Proliferation*, Adelphi Papers 263 (London: Brassey's for IISS).

DUNNE, T. (1995), 'The Social Construction of International Society', *European Journal of International Relations* 1 (3).

The Ecologist (1993), 'Whose Common Future? Reclaiming the Commons' (London: Earthscan).

ECONOMIDES, S., and TAYLOR, P. (1996), 'Former Yugoslavia', in James Mayall (ed.), *The New Interventionism, 1991–1994* (Cambridge: Cambridge University Press).

EKINS, P. (1992), *A New World Order: Grassroots Movements for Global Change* (London: Routledge).

ELSHTAIN, J. B. (1987), *Women and* War (New York: Basic Books).

ENLOE, C. (1989), *Bananas, Beaches and Bases: Making Feminist Sense of International Politics* (London: Pandora Books).

—— (1992), 'Silicon Tricks and the Two Dollar Woman', *New Internationalist* July 1994.

—— (1993), *The Morning After: Sexual Politics at the End of the Cold War* (Berkeley: University of California Press).

ERTEKUN, N. M. (1984), *The Cyprus Dispute and the Birth of the Turkish Republic of Northern Cyprus* (Rustem and Brother).

ESPOSITO, J. (ed.) (1983), *Voices of Resurgent Islam* (Oxford: Oxford University Press).

—— (1991), *The Straight Path* (Oxford: Oxford University Press).

ESPOSITO, J., and PISCATORI, J. (1991), 'Democratization and Islam', *Middle East Journal*, Washington, 45 (3).

EVANS, G., and GRANT, B. (1995), *Australia's Foreign Relations: In the World of the 1990s* (Melbourne: Melbourne University Press).

References

FALK, R. (1975), *A Study of Future Worlds* (New York: Free Press).

—— (1993), 'Global Apartheid: The Structure of the World Economy', *Third World Resurgence*, 37 (Nov.).

—— (1995*a*), 'Liberalism at the Global Level: The Last of the Independent Commissions', *Millennium* Special Issue: *The Globalization of Liberalism?* 24 (3).

—— (1995*b*), *On Humane Governance: Toward a New Global Politics* (Cambridge: Polity Press).

FALK, R. A., and MENDLOVITZ, S. (eds.) (1973), *Regional Politics and World Order,* (San Francisco: W. H. Freeman).

FINNIS, J. (1980), *Natural Law and Natural Rights* (Oxford: Clarendon Press).

FISCHER, D. A. V. (1992), *Stopping the Spread of Nuclear Weapons: the Past and the Prospects* (New York and London: Routledge).

FISCHER, F. (1961), *Griff Nach der Weltmacht (*Dusseldorf: Drosle Verlag).

FISHLOW, A. (1994), 'Latin America and the United States in a Changing World Economy', in A. F. Lowenthal and G. F. Treverton (eds.), *Latin America in a New World* (Boulder, Col.: Westview Press).

FLAX, J. (1987), 'Postmodernism and Gender Relations in Feminist Theory', *Signs.*

FORDE, S. (1992), 'Classical Realism' in T. Nardin and D. Mapel (eds*.), Traditions of International Ethics* (Cambridge: Cambridge University Press).

FORSYTHE, D. P. (1988), 'The United Nations and Human Rights', in Lawrence S. Finkelstein (ed.), *Politics in the United Nations System* (Durham and London: Duyke University Press).

FRANCK, T., and RODLEY, N. (1973), 'After Bangladesh: The Law of Humanitarian Intervention by Force', *American Journal of International Law*, 67.

FRANK, A. G. (1979), *Dependent Accumulation and Underdevelopment* (New York: Monthly Review Press).

FRANK, A. J. (1967), *Capitalism and Underdevelopment in Latin America* (New York: Monthly Review Press).

FRANKEL, B. (ed.) (1991), *Opaque Nuclear Proliferation,* (London: Frank Cass and Company).

FROST, M. (1996), *Ethics in International Relations: A Constitutive Theory* (Cambridge: Cambridge University Press).

FUKUYAMA, F. (1989), 'The End of History', *The National Interest*, 16.

—— (1992), *The End of History and the Last Man* (London: Hamish Hamilton).

GADDIS, J. (1986), 'The Long Peace: Elements of Stability in the Postwar International System', *International Security* 10 (4).

GALTUNG, J. (1971), 'A Structural Theory of Imperialism', *Journal of Peace Research*, 8 (1).

GAMBLE, C. (1994), *Timewalkers: The Prehistory of Global Colonization* (London: Sutton).

GARTHOFF, R. (1994), *The Great Transition: American-Soviet Relations and the End of the Cold War* (Washington, DC: Brookings Institution).

GATI, C. (1990), *The Bloc that Failed: Soviet–East European Relations in Transition* (Bloomington: Indiana University Press).

GELLNER, E. (1983), *Nations and Nationalism* (Oxford: Blackwell).

GEORGE, J. (1994), *Discourses of Global Politics:A Critical (Re)Introduction to International Relations* (Boulder, Col.: Lynne Rienner).

GEORGE, S. (1992), *The Debt Boomerang* (Boulder, Colorado: Westview Press).

GHAI, D. (1994), 'Structural Adjustment, Global Integration and Social Democracy', in R. Prendergast and F. Stewart (eds.), *Market Forces and World Development* (New York: St Martin's).

GIDDENS, A. (1990), *The Consequences of Modernity: Self and Society in the Late Modern Age* (Cambridge: Polity Press, and Stanford: Stanford University Press).

GIERKE, O. (1987), *Political Theories of the Middle Ages* (tr. by F. W. Maitland), (Cambridge: Cambridge University Press).

GILL, S., and LAW, D. (1988), *The Global Political Economy: Perspectives, Problems and Policies* (Hemel Hempstead: Harvester Wheatsheaf).

GILLS, B. K. *et al.* (eds.) (1993), *Low Intensity Democracy: Political Power in the New World Order* (London: Pluto Press).

GILPIN, R. (1981), *War and Change in World Politics* (New York: Cambridge University Press).

—— (1986), 'The Richness of the Tradition of Political Realism' in R. Keohane (ed.), *Neorealism and its Critics* (New York: Columbia University Press).

—— (1987), *The Political Economy of International Relations* (Princeton: Princeton University Press).

GLASER, C. (1994/5), 'Realists as Optimists: Cooperation as Self-Help', *International Security*, 19 (3).

GOLDMAN, M. (1992), *What Went Wrong With Perestroika* (New York: Norton).

GOLDSTEIN, J. S. (1994), *International Relations* (New York: Harper Collins).

GOODMAN, D., and REDCLIFT, M. (1991), *Refashioning Nature: Food, Ecology and Culture* (London: Routledge).

GORBACHEV, M. (1988), *Perestroika: New Thinking for Our Country And the World* (London: Fontana).

GRANT, R., and NEWLAND, K. (eds.) (1989), *Gender and International Relations* (Milton Keynes: Open University Press).

GRAY, J. (1995), *Enlightenment's Wake: Politics and Culture at the Close of the Modern Age* (London: Routledge).

GREENWOOD, C. (1993), 'Is there a right of humanitarian intervention?', *The World Today*, 49.

GRUBB, M., KOCH, M., MUNSON, A., SULLIVAN, F., and THOMPSON, K. (1993) *The Earth Summit Agreements: A Guide and Assessment* (London: Royal Institute for International Affairs).

HAAS, E. B. (1968), 'Technology, Pluralism, and the New Europe', in J. S. Nye (ed.), *International Regionalism* (Boston: Little, Brown).

HAAS, R. D. (1993), 'The Corporation without Boundaries', in M. Ray and A. Rinzler (eds.), *The New Paradigm in Business: Emerging Strategies for Leadership and Organizational Change* (New York: Tarcher/Perigee).

HAAS, P. M., KEOHANE, R. O., and LEVY, M. (1993) (eds.), *Institutions for the Earth: Sources of Effective International Environmental Action* (London: MIT Press).

HALLIDAY, F. (1983), *The Making of the Second Cold War* (London: Verso; 2nd edn. 1986).

—— (1994), *Rethinking International Relations* (London: Macmillan).

HAM, P. VAN (1993), *Managing Non-Proliferation Regimes in the 1990s* (London: Royal Institute of International Affairs, Pinter Publishers).

HARDIN, G. (1968), 'The Tragedy of the Commons', *Science*, 162: 1243–8.

HARDING, S. (1986), *The Science Question in Feminism* (Milton Keynes: Open University Press).

HARVEY, D. (1987), 'The World Systems Theory Trap', *Studies in Comparative International Development*, 22 (1).

—— (1989), *The Condition of Postmodernity: An Enquiry into the Conditions of Cultural Change* (Oxford: Blackwell).

HASHEMI, S. (1996), 'International society and its Islamic malcontents', *The Fletcher Forum of World Affairs*, 20 (2).

HELD, D. (1993), 'Democracy: From City-states to a Cosmopolitan Order?', in Held (ed.), *Prospects for Democracy: North, South, East, West* (Cambridge: Polity Press).

—— (1995), *Democracy and the Global Order: From the Modern State to Cosmopolitan Governance* (Cambridge: Polity Press).

HEMPEL, L. C. (1996), *Environmental Governance: The Global Challenge* (Washington, DC: Island Press).

HERACLIDES, A. (1990), *The Self-Determination of Minorities in International Politics* (London: Cass).

HERSH, S. M. (1983), *The Price of Power: Kissinger in the Nixon White House* (New York: Summit Books).

References

HERTZ, J. H. (1962), *International Politics in the Atomic Age* (New York: Columbia University Press).

HERZ, J. (1950), 'Idealist Internationalism and the Security Dilemma', *World Politics*, 2 (2).

HILL, C. (1996), 'World Opinion and the Empire of Circumstance', *International Affairs*, 72 (1).

HINSLEY, F. H. (1967), *Power and the Pursuit of Peace* (Cambridge: Cambridge University Press).

—— (1973), *Nationalism and the International System* (London: Hodder and Stoughton).

HIRST, J. (1996), 'In Defence of Appeasement: Indonesia and Australian Foreign Policy', *Quadrant*, 40 (4).

HIRST, P., and Thompson, G. (1996), *Globalization in Question: The International Economy and the Possibilities of Governance* (Cambridge: Polity Press).

HOBBES, T. (1991), *Leviathan*, ed. R.Tuck (Cambridge: Cambridge University Press).

HOBSBAWM, E. (1990), *Nations and Nationalism Since 1780: Programme, Myth, Reality* (Cambridge: Cambridge University Press).

—— (1994), *Age of Extremes: The Short Twentieth Century, 1914–1991* (London: Michael Joseph).

—— (1995), 'Pax Americana: Bosnia is its First Success', *Independent,* 22 Nov.

HOCKING, B., and SMITH, M. (1990), *World Politics: An Introduction to International Relations* (London: Harvester Wheatsheaf).

HOFFMAN, M. (1987), 'Critical Theory and the Inter-Paradigm Debate', *Millennium*, 16 (2).

—— (1993), 'Agency, Identity and Intervention', in I. Forbes and M. Hoffman (eds.), *Political Theory, International Relations and the Ethics of Intervention* (Houndmills, Basingstoke: St Martin's Press).

HOFFMANN, S. (1987), *Janus and Minerva: Essays on the Theory and Practice of International Politics* (Boulder, Col.: Westview).

—— (1995), 'The Politics and Ethics of Military Intervention', *Survival*, 37 (4).

HOGAN, M. (ed.) (1992), *The End of the Cold War: Its Meaning and Implications* (Cambridge: Cambridge University Press).

HOLLIS, M., and SMITH, S. (1990), *Explaining and Understanding International Relations* (Oxford: Clarendon).

HOLSTI, K. J. (1996), *War, the State, and the State of War* (Cambridge: Cambridge University Press).

HOLT, P. M., LAMBTON, A., and LEWIS, B. (1970), *The Cambridge History of Islam*, vols. 1 and 2 (Cambridge: Cambridge University Press).

HOMER-DIXON, T. F. (1994), 'Environmental Scarcities and Violent Conflict: Evidence from Cases', *International Security* 19 (1).

HONEYGOLD, D. (1989), *International Financial Markets* (Cambridge: Woodhead-Faulkner).

HORSMAN, M., and MARSHALL, A. (1994), *After the Nation-State: Citizens, Tribalism and the New World Disorder* (New York: Harper Collins).

HOUGH, J. (1988), *Opening up the Soviet Economy* (Washington, DC: Brookings Institution).

HOUGHTON, J., JENKINS, G., and EPHRAUMS, J. (1990) (eds.), *Climate Change: The Ipcc Assessment* (Cambridge: Cambridge University Press).

HOWLETT, D., and SIMPSON, J. (1993), 'Nuclearisation and Denuclearisation in South Africa', *Survival*, 35 (3).

—— LEIGH-PHIPPARD, H., and SIMPSON, J. (1996), 'After the 1995 NPT Renewal Conference: Can the Treaty Survive the Outcome?', in John B. Poole and Richard Guthrie (eds.), *Verification Report 1996. Arms Control, Peacekeeping and the Environment*, (Boulder, San Francisco, and Oxford: Westview Press).

HUMM, M. (1992), *Feminisms: A Reader* (New York: Harvester Wheatsheaf).

Hunger Project (1985), *Ending Hunger: An Idea whose Time has Come* (New York: Praeger).

HUNTER, S. (ed.) (1988), *The Politics of Islamic Revivalism: Diversity and Unit* (Bloomington, Ind.: Indiana University Press).

HUNTINGTON, S. (1993), 'The Clash of Civilizations'', *Foreign Affairs*, 72 (3).

HURD, D., quoted in J. Mearsheimer (1994/5), 'The False Promise of Institutions', *International Security* 19 (3).

Hurrell, A. (1994), 'Regionalism in the Americas', in A. Lowenthal and G. Treverton (eds.), *Latin America in a New World Order* (Boulder, Col.: Westview Press).

—— (1995), 'Explaining the Resurgence of Regionalism in World Politics', *Review of International Studies* 21 (4).

—— and Kingsbury B. (eds.) (1992), *The International Politics of the Environment: Actors, Interests and Institutions* (Oxford: Clarendon Press).

——and Woods, N. (1996), 'Globalization and Inequality', *Millennium*, 24 (3): 447–70.

Hutton, W. (1995), *The State We're In* (London: Jonathan Cape).

ICPF (1994), *Uncommon Opportunities: An Agenda for Peace and Equitable Development* (London: Zed).

Ignatieff, M. 'The Show that Europe Missed' *Independent*, 22 Nov.

Jackson, B. (1990), *Poverty and the Planet* (London: Penguin).

Jackson, R. H. (1990), *Quasi-States: Sovereignty, International Relations and the Third World* (Cambridge: Cambridge University Press).

James, A. (1986), *Sovereign Statehood: The Basis of International Society* (London: Allen & Unwin).

—— (1993), 'System or Society?', *Review of International Studies*, 19 (3).

Jayawardena, K. (1986), *Feminism and Nationalism in the Third World,* (London: Zed Books).

Jervis, R. (1983), *The Illogic of American Nuclear Strategy* (Ithaca, NY: Cornell University Press).

John, I. M. W., and Garnett, J. (1972), 'International Politics at Aberystwyth 1919–1969', in B. Porter, *The Aberystwyth Papers: International Politics 1919–1969* (London: Oxford University Press).

Jones, B. D. (1995), ' "Intervention Without Borders": Humanitarian Intervention in Rwanda, 1990–94', *Millennium: Journal of International Studies*, 24.

Jones, P. (1994), *Rights* (Basingstoke: Macmillan).

Jones, R. W. (1995), ' "Message in a Bottle"? Theory and Praxis in Critical Security Studies', *Contemporary Security Policy*, 16 (3).

Kaldor, M. (1995), 'Who Killed the Cold War?', *The Bulletin of The Atomic Scientists*, July/Aug.

Kant, I. (1991), *Political Writings*, ed. Hans Reiss (Cambridge: Cambridge University Press).

Kanter, R. M. (1995), *World Class: Thriving Locally in the Global Economy* (New York: Simon and Schuster).

Karp, A. (1995), *Ballistic Missile Proliferation: The Politics and Technics* (Oxford: Oxford University Press for SIPRI).

Kegley, C. (ed.) (1995), *Controversies in International Relations Theory: Realism and the Neoliberal Challenge* (New York: St Martin's).

Kennan, G. (1992), 'The GOP Won the Cold War? Ridiculous', *New York Times*, 28 Oct.

Keohane, R. (1984), *After Hegemony: Cooperation and Discord in the World Political Economy* (Princeton: Princeton University Press).

—— (ed.) (1989*a*), *International Institutions and State Power: Essays in International Relations Theory* (Boulder, Col.: Westview).

—— (1989*b*), 'Theory of World Politics: Structural Realism and Beyond' in Keohane (ed.), *International Institutions and State Power* (Boulder, Col.: Westview).

—— and Martin, (1995), 'The Promise of Institutionalist Theory', *International Security*, 20 (1).

—— and Nye, J. (eds.) (1972), *Transnational Relations and World Politics* (Cambridge, Mass.: Harvard University Press).

—— and—— (1977), *Power and Interdependence: World Politics in Transition* (Boston: Little, Brown).

—— , —— and Hoffmann, S. (eds.) (1993), *After the Cold War: International Institutions and State Strategies in Europe 1989–1991* (London: Harvard University Press).

Keylor, W. (1992), *The Twentieth Century World: An International History* (New York: Oxford University Press).

Keynes, J. M. (1919), *The Economic Consequences of the Peace* (London: Macmillan).

Khoman, T. (1992), 'ASEAN: Conception and Evolution', in Sandhu *et al.* (eds.).

References

KIDRON, M., and Segal, R. (1995), *The State of the World Atlas* (London: Penguin).

KIRKPATRICK, J. (1979), 'Dictatorships and double Standards', *Commentary*, 68.

KISSINGER, H. A. (1977), *American Foreign Policy*, 3rd edn. (New York: W. W. Norton).

KLINTWORTH, G. (1989), *Vietnam's Intervention in Cambodia in International Law* (Canberra: AGPS Press).

KNOX, P., and AGNEW, J. (1994), *The Geography of the World Economy* (London: Edward Arnold).

KOHLI, A. (1985), 'The Politics of Land Reform', in A. Gauhar (ed.), *Third World Affairs* (London: Third World Foundation).

KOTSCHWAR, B. R. (1995), 'South–South Economic Cooperation: Regional Trade Agreements among Developing Countries', *Cooperation South* (UN Development Programme).

KRASNER, S. D. (ed.). (1983), *International Regimes* (Ithaca, NY: Cornell University Press).

—— (1985), *Structural Conflict: The Third World Against Global Liberalism* (Berkeley: University of California Press).

—— (1991), 'Global Communications and National Power: Life on the Pareto Frontier', *World Politics*, 43.

KRATOCHWIL, F. (1989), *Rules, Norms, and Decisions* (Cambridge: Cambridge University Press).

KRAUTHAMMER, C. (1990–1), 'The Unipolar Moment', *Foreign Affairs*, 70: 23–33.

—— (1992), 'In Bosnia, Partition Might Do', *International Herald Tribune*, 9 Sept.

KUPCHAN, C., and KUPCHAN, C. (1991), 'Concerts, Collective Security and the Future of Europe', *International Security*, 16 (1).

LAPID, Y. (1989), 'The Third Debate: On the Prospects of International Theory in a Post-Positivist Era', *International Studies Quarterly*, 33 (3).

LEBOW, R., and STEIN, J. (1994), 'Reagan and the Russians', *Atlantic Monthly*, 273 (2), Feb.

LENIN, V. I. (1966), *Imperialism, the Highest Stage of Capitalism: A Popular Outline*, 13th edn., (Moscow: Progress Publishers).

LEVENTHAL, P., and Alexander, Y. (eds.) (1987), *Preventing Nuclear Terrorism*, (Lexington, Mass., and Toronto: Lexington Books).

LEVY, M. A., YOUNG, O. R., and ZURN, M. (1995), 'The Study of International Regimes', *European Journal of International Relations*, 1 (3): 267–330.

LINKLATER, A. (1990), *Beyond Realism and Marxism: Critical Theory and International Relations* (London: Macmillan).

LITTLE, R. (1996), 'The Growing Relevance of Pluralism?', in S. Smith, K. Booth, and M. Zalewski (eds.), *International Theory: Positivism and Beyond* (Cambridge: Cambridge University Press).

LONG, D. (1996), 'The Harvard School of International Theory: A Case for Closure', *Millennium*, 24 (3): 489–506.

LUARD, E. (1992) (ed.), *Basic Texts in International Relations* (London: Macmillan).

LYONS, G. M., and MASTANDUNO, M. (eds.) (1995), *Beyond Westphalia? State Sovereignty and International Intervention* (Baltimore and London: John Hopkins University Press).

LYOTARD, J.-F. (1984), *The Postmodern Condition: A Report on Knowledge* (Manchester: Manchester University Press).

McGREW, A., LEWIS, P., *et al.* (1992), *Global Politics* (Cambridge: Polity Press).

MACHIAVELLI, N. (1965), *The Art of War*, ed. Neal Wood (New York: Da Capo Press).

—— (1988), *The Prince*, ed. Q. Skinner (Cambridge: Cambridge University Press).

McLUHAN, M. (1964), *Understanding Media* (London: Routledge).

MANN, M. (1986), *The Sources of Social Power, I: A History of Power from the Beginning to A.D. 1760* (Cambridge: Cambridge University Press).

—— (1993) *The Sources of Social Power II: The Rise of Classes and Nation States, 1760–1914* (Cambridge: Cambridge University Press).

MANSBACH, R., FERGUSON, Y., and LAMPERT, D. (1976), *The Web of World Politics* (Englewood Cliffs, NJ: Prentice-Hall).

MARSHALL, J. (1996) (ed.), *The New Interventionism 1991–1994* (Cambridge: Cambridge University Press).

MARTEL, G. (1986) (ed.), *The Origins of the Second World War Reconsidered* (London: Allen & Unwin).

MAYALL, J. (1990), *Nationalism and International Society* (Cambridge: Cambridge University Press).

—— (1991), 'Non-Intervention, Self-Determination and the "New World Order"'. *International Affairs*, 67.

MAYNARD, M. (1995), 'Beyond the 'Big Three': The Development of Feminist Theory in the 1990s', *Women's History Review*, 4 (3).

MEADOWS, D. H., MEADOWS, D. L., and RANDERS, J. (1972), *The Limits to Growth* (London: Earth Island).

—— (1992), *Beyond the Limits: Global Collapse or a Sustainable Future* (London: Earthscan).

MAZARR, M. (1995), 'Virtual Nuclear Arsenals', *Survival*, 37 (3).

MEARSHEIMER, J. (1990), 'Back to the Future: Instability After the Cold War', *International Security*, 15 (1).

MENDLOVITZ, S. (1975), *On the Creation of a Just World Order* (New York: Free Press).

MEYER, S. M. (1984), *The Dynamics of Nuclear Proliferation* (Chicago: University of Chicago Press)

MICHALET, C.-A. (1982), 'From International Trade to World Economy: A New Paradigm', in H. Makler *et al.*, *The New International Economy* (London: Sage), 37–58.

MILLER, J. (1993), 'The Challenge of Radical Islam', *Foreign Affairs*, 72.

MILNER, H. V. (1988), *Resisting Protectionism: Global Industries and the Politics of International Trade* (Princeton: Princeton University Press).

MINEAR, L., and WEISS, T. G. (1995), *Mercy Under Fire: War and the Global Humanitarian Community* (Boulder, Col.: Westview Press).

MITCHELL, R. (1995), *Bridled Ambition—Why Countries Constrain their Nuclear Capabilities* (Washington, DC: Woodrow Wilson Center).

MITRANY, D. (1943), *A Working Peace System* (London: RIIA).

MODELSKI, G. (1972), *Principles of World Politics* (New York: Free Press).

—— (1988), *Sea Power in Global Politics 1494–1943* (Seattle: University of Washington Press).

MOHANTY, C. *et al.* (eds.) (1991), *Third World Women and the Politics of Feminism* (Bloomington: Indiana University Press).

MOLINA, M. J., and ROWLAND, F. S. (1974), 'Stratospheric Sink for Chlorofluoromethanes: Chlorine Atom Catalysed Destruction of Ozone', *Nature*, 249: 810–14.

MORGENTHAU, H. J. (1978), *Politics Among Nations: The Struggle for Power and Peace* (New York: Knopf).

MORSE, E. (1976), *Modernization and the Transformation of International Relations* (New York: Free Press).

MUNTING, R. (1982), *The Economic Development of the USSR* (London: Macmillan).

MURPHY, C. N. (1994), *International Organization and Industrial Change* (Cambridge: Polity Press).

NAISBITT, J. (1994), *Global Paradox: The Bigger the World Economy, The More Powerful Its Smallest Players* (London: Brealey).

NARDIN, T. (1983), *Law, Morality and the Relations of States* (Princeton: Princeton University Press).

NAYA, S., and Imada, P. (1992), 'Implementing AFTA, 1992–2007', in K. S. Sandhu (ed.).

NICOLSON, H. (1954), *The Evolution of Diplomatic Method* (London: Constable).

NYE, J. S. (ed.) (1968), *International Regionalism: Readings* (Boston: Little, Brown).

OBERDORFER, D. (1992), *The Turn: From the Cold War to a New Era* (New York: Touchstone Books).

O'BRIEN, P. (1984), 'Europe in the World Economy', in H. Bull and A. Watson (eds.), *The Expansion of International Society* (Oxford: Clarendon Press).

O'BRIEN, R. (1992), *Global Financial Integration: The End of Geography* (London: Pinter).

OHMAE, K. (1990), *The Borderless World: Power and Strategy in the Interlinked Economy* (London: Fontana).

References

Olson, M. (1965)*The Logic of Collective Action* (Cambridge: Harvard University Press).

Onuf, N. (1989), *A World of our Making: Rules and Rule in Social Theory and International Relations* (Columbia: University of South Carolina Press).

Ostrom, E. (1990), *Governing the Commons: Evolution of Institutions for Collective Action* (Cambridge: Cambridge University Press).

Owen, R. (1992), *State, power and politics in the making of the modern Middle East* (London: Routledge).

Oye, K. A. (ed.) (1986), *Cooperation Under Anarchy* (Princeton: Princeton University Press).

Panagariya, A. (1994), 'East Asia; A New Trading Bloc?' *Finance and Development*, March.

Parekh, B. (1996), 'Beyond Humanitarian Intervention', in O. Ramsbotham and T. Woodhouse, *Humanitarian Intervention: A Reconceptualisation* (Cambridge: Polity Press).

—— (1997), 'Rethinking Humanitarian Intervention', *International Political Science Review*, 18 (1): 49–70.

Pendergrast, M. (1993), *For God, Country and Coca-Cola: The Unauthorized History of the Great American Soft Drink and the Company that Makes It* (London: Weidenfeld and Nicolson).

Peterson, V. S. (1990), 'Whose Rights? A Critique of the "Givens" in Human Rights Discourse', *Alternatives*, 15.

—— (1992) 'Security and Sovereign States: What is at Stake in Taking Feminism Seriously', in Peterson (ed.), *Gendered States: Feminist (Re)Visions of International Relations Theory* (London: Lynne Reinner).

—— (1994), 'Gendered Nationalism', *Peace Review*, 6.

Petrella, R. (1996), 'Globalization and Internationalization: The Dynamics of the Emerging World Order', in Boyer and Drache.

Pettman, J. J. (1996), *Worlding Women: A Feminist International Politics* (St Leonards: Allen and Unwin).

Pipes, R. (1992), Letter to the Editor, *New York Times*, 6 Nov.

Piscatori, J. (1992), 'Islam and World Politics', in John Baylis and N. J. Rengger (eds.), *Dilemmas of World Politics; International Issues in a Changing World* (Oxford: Oxford University Press).

Pope Atkins, G. (1995), *Latin America in the International Political System* (Oxford, Westview Press).

Porter, G., and Brown, J. W. (1991), *Global Environmental Politics* (Boulder, Col.: Westview Press).

Porter, M. E. (ed.), (1986), *Competition in Global Industries* (Boston: Harvard Business School Press).

—— (1990), *The Competitive Advantage of Nations* (London: Macmillan).

Porter, T. (1993), *States, Markets, and Regimes in Global Finance* (London: Macmillan).

Potter, W. (1995), 'Before the Deluge? Assessing the Threat Of Nuclear Leakage From the Post-Soviet States', *Arms Control Today*, Oct.

Prebisch, R. (1964), *Towards a New Trade Policy for Development* (New York: United Nations).

Raffety, F. W. (1928), *The Works of the Right Honourable Edmund Burke*, vi (Oxford: Oxford University Press).

Ramsbotham, O., and Woodhouse, T. (1996), *Humanitarian Intervention: A Reconceptualisation* (London: Pinter).

Rawls, J. (1971), *A Theory of Justice* (Oxford: Oxford University Press).

Reich, R. B. (1991), *The Work of Nations: Preparing Ourselves for 21st-Century Capitalism* (New York: Simon & Schuster).

Reiser, O. L., and Davies, B. (1944), *Planetary Democracy: An Introduction to Scientific Humanism and Applied Semantics* (New York: Creative Age Press).

Reiss, M. (1995), *Bridled Ambition—Why Countries Constrain Their Nuclear Capabilities* (published by the Wilson Center Press, Washington, DC: and distributed by the Johns Hopkins University Press, Baltimore).

Reiss, M., and Lutwak, R. (eds.) (1994), *Nuclear Proliferation After the Cold War*, (Washington, DC: Woodrow Wilson Center Press).

RENGGER, N. (1992), 'Culture, Society and Order in World Politics', in John Baylis and N. J. Rengger (eds.), *Dilemmas of World Politics: International Issues in a Changing World* (Oxford: Oxford University Press).

RICHARDSON, J. L. (1994), *Crisis Diplomacy: The Great Powers since the Mid-Nineteenth Century* (Cambridge: Cambridge University Press).

RITTBERGER, V. (ed.) (1993), *Regime Theory and International Relations* (Oxford: Clarendon Press).

ROBERTS, A. (1993), 'Humanitarian War: Military Intervention and Human Rights', *International Affairs, 69.*

—— (1996), 'The United Nations: Variants of Collective Security', in Ngaire Woods, *Explaining International Relations Since 1945* (Oxford: Oxford University Press).

—— and KINGSBURY, B. (1993), 'Introduction: The UN's Roles in International Society since 1945', in Roberts and Kingsbury (eds.), *United Nations, Divided World* (Oxford: Clarendon Press).

ROBERTS, G. (1984), *Questioning Development* (London: Returned Volunteer Action).

ROBERTS, S. (1994), 'Fictitious Capital, Fictitious Spaces: The Geography of Offshore Financial Flows', in S. Corbridge *et al.* (eds.), *Money, Power and Space* (Oxford: Blackwell).

ROBERTSON, E. M. (1971) (ed.), *The Origins of the Second World War: Historical Interpretations* (London: Macmillan).

ROBERTSON, R. (1992), *Globalization: Social Theory and Global Culture* (London: Sage).

RODLEY, N. S. (ed.) (1992), *To Loose the Bands of Wickedness: International Intervention in Defence of Human Rights* (London: Brasseys).

RODNEY, W. (1972), *How Europe Underdeveloped Africa* (London: Bogle-L'Ouverture).

RORTY, R. (1993), 'Sentimentality and Human Rights', in S. Shute and S. Hurley (eds.), *On Human Rights* (New York: Basic Books).

ROSENAU, J. N. (1990), *Turbulence in World Politics* (Princeton: Princeton University Press).

—— and CZEMPIEL, E.-O. (1992), *Governance without Government: Order and Change in World Politics* (Cambridge: Cambridge University Press).

ROSTOW, W. (1960), *The Stages of Economic Growth: A Non-Communist Manifesto* (London: Cambridge University Press).

ROUSSEAU, J.-J. (1991), 'The State of War', in S. Hoffmann and D. P. Fidler (eds.), *Rousseau on International Relations* (Oxford: Clarendon Press).

ROXBURGH, A. (1991), *The Second Russian Revolution* (London: BBC Publications).

RUGGIE, J. G. (1995), 'At Home Abroad, Abroad at Home: International Liberalisation and Domestic Stability in the New World Economy', *Millennium; Journal of International Studies,* 24 (3).

RUPERT, M. (1995), *Producing Hegemony: The Politics of Mass Production and American Global Power* (Cambridge: Cambridge University Press).

RUSSETT, B. (1993), *Grasping the Democratic Peace: Principles for a Post-Cold War World* (Princeton: Princeton University Press).

—— (1995), 'The Democratic Peace', *International Security* 19 (4).

SAGAN, S. D. (1993), *The Limits of Safety: Organisations, Accidents and Nuclear Weapons* (Princeton: Princeton University Press).

—— and WALTZ, K. N. (1995), *The Spread of Nuclear Weapons: A Debate* (New York and London: W. W. Norton and Co.).

SAID, E. W. (1993), *Culture and Imperialism* (London: Chatto and Windus).

—— (1995), *Orientalism: Western Conceptions of the Orient* (London: Penguin Books).

SANDHU, K. S. (ed.) (1992), *The ASEAN Reader* (Singapore: Institute of South East Asian Studies).

SCHEINMAN, L. (1987), *The International Atomic Energy Agency and World Nuclear Order* (Washington, DC: Johns Hopkins University Press).

SCHELLING, T. C. (1960), *The Strategy of Conflict* (Oxford: Oxford University Press).

References

SCHOLTE, J. A. (1993), *International Relations of Social Change* (Buckingham: Open University Press).

—— (1996), 'Globalisation and Collective Identities', in J. Krause and N. Renwick (eds.), *Identities in International Relations* (London: Macmillan).

—— (1997), *Globalisation: A Critical Introduction* (London: Macmillan).

SCHUMACHER, E. F. (1973), *Small is Beautiful: Economics as if People Mattered* (New York: Harper and Row).

SEAMAN, J. (1996), 'The International System of Humanitarian Relief in the "New World Order" ', in John Harriss (ed.), *The Politics of Humanitarian Intervention* (London: Pinter).

SEN, A. (1981), *Poverty and Famines* (Oxford: Clarendon Press).

—— (1983), 'The Food Problem: Theory and Policy', in A. Gauhar (ed.), *South-South Strategy* (London: Zed).

SHAKER, M. I. (1980), *The Nuclear Non-Proliferation Treaty*, i–ii (London: Oceana).

SHANNON, T. R. (1989), *An Introduction to the World-System Perspective* (Boulder, Col.: Westview Press).

SHARPE, A. (1996), 'Exotic Derivatives "Less Favoured" ', *Financial Times*, 12 Feb., 8.

SHAW, M. (1994), *Global Society and International Relations* (Cambridge: Polity Press).

SHUE, H. (1980), *Basic Rights* (Princeton: Princeton University Press).

SHUTE, S., and Hurley, S. (eds.) (1993), *On Human Rights* (New York: Basic Books).

SIMPSON, J., and HOWLETT, D. (eds.) (1995), *The Future of the Non-Proliferation Treaty* (New York: St Martin's Press)

SINCLAIR, T. J. (1994), 'Passing Judgement: Credit Rating Processes as Regulatory Mechanisms of Governance in the Emerging World Order', *Review of International Political Economy*, 1 (Spring).

SINGER, H., and ROY, S. (1993), *Economic Progress and Prospects in the Third World* (Aldershot: Edward Elgar).

SIVAN, E. (1989), 'Sunni Radicalism in the Middle East and the Iranian Revolution', *International Journal of Middle Eastern Studies*, 21 (1).

SKINNER, Q. (1988), 'Meaning and Understanding in the History of Ideas', in J. Tully (ed.), *Meaning and Context: Quentin Skinner and his Critics* (Cambridge: Polity Press).

SKOCPOL, T. (1977), 'Wallerstein's *World Capitalist System*: A Theoretical and Historical Critique', *American Journal of Sociology*, 82 (5).

SMITH, A. (1991), *National Identity* (London: Penguin).

SMITH, D. (1991), *The Rise of Historical Sociology* (Cambridge: Polity Press).

SMITH, M. (1986), *Realist Thought from Weber to Kissinger* (Baton Rouge: Louisiana State University Press).

SMITH, S., BOOTH, K., and ZALEWSKI, M. (eds.) (1996), *International Theory: Positivism and Beyond* (Cambridge: Cambridge University Press).

SNITOW, A. (1989), 'Pages from a Gender Diary: Basic Divisions in Feminism', *Dissent*, 36: 205–24.

South Commission (1990), *The Challenge to the South* (Oxford: Oxford University Press).

SPECTOR, L., McDONOUGH, M., with MEDEIROS, E. (1995), *Tracking Nuclear Proliferation: A Guide to Maps and Charts*, (Washington, DC: Carnegie Endowment for International Peace).

STEIN, A. (1982), 'Coordination and Collaboration in an Anarchic World', *International Organization*, 36 (2): 299–324.

STOPFORD, J., and STRANGE, S. (1991), *Rival States, Rival Firms: Competition for World Market Shares* (Cambridge: Cambridge University Press).

STRANGE, S. (1994*a*), 'Wake up, Krasner! The world HAS changed', *Review of International Political Economy*, 1 (2).

—— (1994*b*), *States and Markets*, 2nd edn. (London: Pinter).

SUGANAMI, H. (1989), *The Domestic Analogy and World Order Proposals* (Cambridge: Cambridge University Press).

SYLVESTER, C. (1994), *Feminist Theory and International Relations in a Postmodern Era* (Cambridge: Cambridge University Press).

TAYLOR, A. J. P. (1983), *A Personal History* (London: Hamish Hamilton).

TAYLOR, P. (1995), *International Organization in the Modern World* (London: Pinter).

—— (1996*a*), *The European Union since the 1990s* (Oxford: Oxford University Press).

—— (1996*b*), 'Options for the Reform of the International System for Humanitarian Assistance', in J. Harriss (ed.) *The Politics of Humanitarian Intervention* (London: Pinter).

—— and GROOM, A. J. R. (1989) (eds.), *Global Issues in the United Nations Framework* (Basingstoke: Macmillan).

—— and —— (1992), *The United Nations and the Gulf War, 1990–91*, RIIS discussion paper no. 38.

THOMAS, A. *et al.* (1994), *Third World Atlas*, 2nd edn. (Milton Keynes: Open University Press).

THOMAS, C. (1985), *New States, Sovereignty and Intervention* (Aldershot: Gower).

—— (1993), 'The Pragmatic Case Against Intervention', in I. Forbes and M. Hoffmann (eds.), *Political Theory, International Relations and the Ethics of Intervention* (Basingstoke: St Martin's Press).

THOMPSON, E. (1990), 'The Ends of Cold War', *New Left Review*, 182, July/Aug.

THOMAS, SIR J., and TICKELL, SIR C. (1993), *The Expanding Role of the United Nations and its Implications . . .* (London: HMSO).

THUCYDIDES (1954), *History of the Peloponnesian War*, trans. R. Warner (London: Penguin).

TICKNER, J. A. (1988), 'Hans Morgenthau's Principles of Political Realism: A Feminist Reformulation', *Millennium*, 17 (3).

TILLY, C. (1990), *Coercion, Capital, and European States, AD 990–1990* (Oxford: Blackwell).

TREADGOLD, A. (1993), 'Cross-Border Retailing in Europe: Present Status and Future Prospects', in H. Cox *et al.* (eds.), *The Growth of Global Business* (London: Routledge).

TUCKER, R. W. (1977) *The Inequality of Nations* (New York: Basic Books).

UN Centre on Transnational Corporations (1988), *Transnational Corporations in World Development. Trends and Prospects* (New York: United Nations).

UN Conference on Environment and Development (1992) *Nations of the Earth* (New York: United Nations).

UN Conference on Trade and Development, Division on Transnational Corporations and Investment (1995), *World Investment Report 1995* (New York: United Nations).

UNCTAD (1996), *Transnational Corporations and World Development* (London: International Thomson Business Press).

UNDP (1994), *Human Development Report, 1994* (New York: Oxford University Press).

UNFPA/MYERS, N. (1991), *Population, Resources and the Environment* (New York: UNFPA).

VAN DER WEE, H. (1987), *Prosperity and Upheaval: The World Economy 1945–1980* (Harmondsworth: Penguin).

VASQUEZ, J. A. (1993), *The War Puzzle* (Cambridge: Cambridge University Press).

VINCENT, R. J. (1974), *Nonintervention and International Order* (Princeton: Princeton University Press).

—— (1981), 'The Hobbesian Tradition in Twentieth Century International Thought', *Millennium*, 10 (2).

—— (1982), 'Realpolitik', in James Mayall (ed.), *The Community of States* (London: George Allen & Unwin).

—— (1986), *Human Rights and International Relations* (Cambrdige: Cambridge University Press).

VIOTTI, P. R., and KAUPPI, M. V. (1993), *International Relations Theory: Realism, Pluralism, Globalism* (New York: Macmillan).

WAEVER, O. (1996), 'The Rise and Fall of the Inter-Paradigm Debate', in Smith *et al.*, 149–85.

WAEVER, O., BUZAN, B., KELSTRUP, M., and LEMAITRE, P. (1993*)*, *Identity, Migration and the New Security Agenda in Europe* (London: Pinter).

WALKER, R. B. J. (1993), *Inside/Outside: International Relations as Political Theory* (Cambridge: Cambridge University Press).

WALLACE, W. (ed.) (1990), *The Dynamics of European Integration* (London: Pinter).

References

WALLERSTEIN, I. (1974), *The Modern World-System, i, Capitalist Agriculture and the Origins of the European World-Economy in the Sixteenth Century* (San Diego: Academic Press).

—— (1979), *The Capitalist World-Economy* (Cambridge: Cambridge University Press).

—— (1980), *The Modern World-System, ii, Mercantilism and the Consolidation of the European World-Economy, 1600–1750* (San Diego: Academic Press).

—— (1984), *The Politics of the World Economy: The States, the Movements, and the Civilisations* (Cambridge: Cambridge University Press).

—— (1989), *The Modern World-System, iii, The Second Era of Great Expansion of the Capitalist World-Economy* (San Diego: Academic Press).

—— (1991a), *Unthinking Social Science: The Limits of Nineteenth-Century Paradigms* (Cambridge: Polity Press).

—— (1991b), *Geopolitics and Geoculture: Essays on the Changing World-System* (Cambridge: Cambridge University Press).

—— (1994), 'The Agonies of Liberalism—What Hope Progress?', *New Left Review*, 204.

—— (1995), *After Liberalism* (New York: New Press).

—— (1996), 'The Inter-State Structure of the Modern World-System', in S. Smith, K. Booth, and M. Zalewski (eds.).

WALTZ, K. (1959), *Man, the State and War* (New York: Columbia University Press).

—— (1979), *Theory of International Politics* (Reading, Mass: Addison-Wesley).

—— (1981), *The Spread of Nuclear Weapons: More May Be Better*, Adelphi Paper 171 (London: International Institute for Strategic Studies).

WALZER, M. (1977), *Just And Unjust Wars: A Moral Argument with Historical Illustration* (Harmondsworth: Penguin, and New York: Basic Books).

—— (1994), *Thick and Thin: Moral Argument at Home and Abroad* (Notre Dame: University of Notre Dame Press).

—— (1995), 'The Politics of Rescue', *Dissent* (Winter).

WASHBROOK, D. (1990), 'South Asia, The World System and World Capitalism', *Journal of Asian Studies*, 49 (3).

WATERS, M. (1995), *Globalization* (London: Routledge).

WATSON, A. (1992), *The Evolution of International Society* (London: Routledge).

WEBER, C. (1995), *Simulating Sovereignty: Intervention, the State and Symbolic Exchange* (Cambridge: Cambridge University Press).

WEBSTER (1961), *Webster's Third New International Dictionary of the English Language Unabridged* (Springfield, Mass.: Merriam).

WEDGWOOD, C. V. (1992), *The Thirty Years War* (London: Pimlico).

WEISS, T. G. *et al.* (1994), *The United Nations and Changing World Politics.* (Boulder, Col.: Westview).

WENDT, A. (1992), 'Anarchy is What States Make of It: The Social Construction of Power Politics,' *International Organisation*, 46 (2).

WENDT, A. (1994), 'Collective Identity Formation and the International State', *American Political Science Review*, 88 (2).

WHEELER, N. J. (1996), 'Guardian Angel or Global Gangster? A Review of the Ethical Claims of the Society of States', *Political Studies*, 44 (2).

WHEELER, N. J., and BOOTH, K. (1992), 'The Security Dilemma', in J. Baylis and N. J. Rengger (eds.), *Dilemmas of World Politics: International Issues in a Changing World* (Oxford: Oxford University Press).

WHITE, S. (1990), *Gorbachev in Power* (Cambridge: Cambridge University Press).

WHITWORTH, S. (1989), 'Gender and the Inter Paradigm Debate', *Millennium*.

WIGHT, M. (1977), *Systems of States* (Leicester: Leicester University Press).

—— (1986), *Power Politics* (2nd edn.) (London: Penguin).

WILLETTS, P. (ed.) (1996), '*The Conscience of the World*' (London: Hurst and Co.).

WILLIAMS, P., and BLACK, S. (1994), 'Transnational Threats: Drug Trafficking and Weapons Proliferation', *Contemporary Security Policy*, 15 (1).

WINHAM, G. (1977), 'Negotiation as a Management Process' *World Politics*, 30 (1) (Oct.) as reprinted in F. S. Sondermann, D. S. McClellan, and W. C. Olsen, *The Theory and Practice of International Relations* (Englewood Cliffs, NY: Prentice-Hall)

WOLIN, S. (1960), *Politics and Vision* (Boston: Little, Brown).

World Commission on Environment and Development (1987), *Our Common Future* (The Brundtland Report) (Oxford: Oxford University Press).

WORSLEY, P. (1980), 'One World or Three? A Critique of the World-System Theory of Immanuel Wallerstein', *Socialist Register* (London: Merlin Press).

WYATT-WALTER, A. (1996). 'Adam Smith and the Liberal Tradition in International Relations', *Review of International Studies*, 22 (1).

YUVAL-DAVIS, N., and ANTHIAS, F. (eds.) (1989), *Woman Nation State* (London: Macmillan).

ZACHER, M. W., with SUTTON, B. A. (1996), *Governing Global Networks: International Regimes for Transportation and Communications* (Cambridge: Cambridge University Press).

ZALEWSKI, M. (1993a), 'Feminist Standpoint Theory Meets International Relations Theory: A Feminist Version of David and Goliath', *The Fletcher Forum of World Affairs*, 17 (2).

—— (1993b), 'Feminist Theory and International Relations', in M. Bowker and R. Brown (eds.), *From Cold War to Collapse: Theory and World Politics in the 1980s* (Cambridge: Cambridge University Press).

—— and ENLOE, C. (1995), 'Questions of Identity in International Relations', in K. Booth and S. Smith (eds.), *International Relations Theory Today* (Cambridge: Polity Press).

ZARTMAN, I. W. (1995), *Collapsed States* (Boulder and London: Lynne Reinner).

ZEVIN, R. (1992), 'Are World Financial Markets More Open? If So, Why and With What Effects?', in T. Banuri and J. B. Schor (eds.), *Financial Openness and National Autonomy: Opportunities and Constraints* (Oxford: Clarendon Press).

Index

N.B. Page references to boxes and figures are *italicized*.